THE

MID-ATLANTIC STATES

OF AMERICA

By Neal R. Peirce

THE MEGASTATES OF AMERICA

THE PACIFIC STATES OF AMERICA

THE MOUNTAIN STATES OF AMERICA

THE GREAT PLAINS STATES OF AMERICA

THE DEEP SOUTH STATES OF AMERICA

THE BORDER SOUTH STATES

THE NEW ENGLAND STATES

THE MID-ATLANTIC STATES OF AMERICA

THE PEOPLE'S PRESIDENT

By Michael Barone

THE ALMANAC OF AMERICAN POLITICS
1972, 1974, 1976

THE MID-ATLANTIC STATES

A

N

Lake Superior

Duluth

Sault Ste. Marie

L. Huron

L. Michigan

WIS.

MICH.

NN.

polis

St. Paul

IOWA Madison

Lansing

Detroit

MAINE

VT. Montpelier Augusta

Burlington

N.Y.

Portland

Concord

N.H.

Boston

MASS.

S.

P.

Ho

R.I.

N.H. CONN.

New York

L. Ontario

Rochester

Buffalo

Albany

Milwaukee

Chicago

ILL.

Gary

IND.

L. Erie

Cleve-

land

PA. Scranton

N.

T. N.J.

Philadelphia

Atlantic City

Des Moines

Indianapolis

OHIO

Columbus

Pittsburgh

Harrisburg

W.

MD. B.

A.

Washington

Dover

DEL.

lux

ls

lux

y

coln MO. Springfield

Kansas City

a

St. Louis

E. St. Louis

Cairo

Louisville

Frankfort

KY.

Cincinnati

W. VA.

Charleston

VA.

Richmond

N.C.

Norfolk

A - Annapolis

B - Baltimore

W - Wilmington

T - Trenton

N - Newark

NH - New Haven

H - Hartford

S - Springfield

P - Providence

sa

ARK.

Memphis

Nashville

Chattanooga

TENN. Knoxville

Charlotte

Raleigh

Little

Rock

MISS.

Birmingham

Huntsville

ALA.

Montgomery

GA.

Atlanta

S.C.

Columbia

Charleston

Atlantic

Jackson

Selma

LA.

llas

New Orleans

Houston

Gulf of

Mexico

Tallahassee

FLA.

Jacksonville

Cape

Kennedy

Ocean

Tampa

Miami

KAUAI

NIIHAU

OAHU

Honolulu

MOLOKAI

MAUI

Pacific

Ocean

HAWAII

HAWAII

Hilo

MILES

0   50   100   200

THE

MID-ATLANTIC

STATES

OF AMERICA

People, Politics, and Power in the Five

Mid-Atlantic States and the Nation's Capital

NEAL R. PEIRCE

AND MICHAEL BARONE

W · W · NORTON & COMPANY · INC ·
NEW YORK

Library of Congress Cataloging in Publication Data
Peirce, Neal R
    The Mid-Atlantic States.
    Bibliography: p.
    Includes index.
    1. Middle Atlantic States—Politics and government.
2. Washington, D. C.—Politics and government.
I. Barone, Michael, joint author. II. Title.
F106.P38   320.9'74   76-54713

ISBN 0-393-5541-8

2 3 4 5 6 7 8 9 0

285934

CONTENTS

FOREWORD

THIS IS A BOOK ABOUT the Mid-Atlantic states, part of a series covering the story of each major geographic region and all of the 50 states of America in our time. The objective is simply to let Americans (and foreigners too) know something of the profound diversity of peoples and life styles and geographic habitat and political behavior that make this the most fascinating nation on earth.

The previous books in this series, written by Neal Peirce alone, began in 1972 with *The Megastates of America*, treating America's 10 most heavily populated states. (Three chapters from that book—New York, New Jersey, and Pennsylvania—are included in this volume, substantially updated, revised, and expanded.) The series of eight regional volumes began, also in 1972, with publication of *The Mountain States of America* and *The Pacific States of America*, followed by *The Great Plains States of America* (1973), *The Deep South States of America* (1974), *The Border South States* (1975), and *The New England States* (1976). A separate volume will follow on the Great Lakes states.

In this book, Michael Barone, co-author of *The Almanac of American Politics* and vice-president of the survey research firm of Peter D. Hart Research Associates, joins Neal Peirce as a co-author. In addition, acknowledgment is made to Jerry Hagstrom and James Humphreys for substantial editorial assistance. Others to whom the authors are particularly indebted are Evan Thomas, senior editor, and Calvin Towle, copy editor, of W. W. Norton & Company, as well as Frederick H. Sontag, Barbara Hurlbutt, Jean Allaway, Geneva Torrey, Otis D. Wilson, Jr., David B. H. Martin, Mabel R. Allen, and Richard G. Bradford. Credit goes to Russell Lenz, former chief cartographer of the *Christian Science Monitor*, for the state and city maps.

The authors wish to express their thanks to the several persons in each state who consented to read and comment on the draft manuscript about their state. The names of these persons appear in the interviewee list at the back of the book; we choose not to list them here lest someone hold them responsible for something said or unsaid in one of the chapters, and of course the full responsibility lies with the authors.

THE

MID-ATLANTIC STATES

OF AMERICA

THE MID-ATLANTIC STATES

SUPREMACY IN DECLINE

THERE ARE no songs written about the Middle Atlantic States. There is no regional history, no Middle Atlantic history which is taught to schoolchildren. No one, when asked where he is from, replies, "The Middle Atlantic States"; people will firmly state they are from New York, Philadelphia, or Washington. This is a region without a joint identity, with no clear image, but it is also a collection of metropolitan areas and rural counties with very distinct and very strong individual images.

It does, however, make sense to treat the Middle Atlantic States—the District of Columbia, Maryland, Delaware, Pennsylvania, New Jersey, and New York—as a single region. They do share common characteristics which distinguish them from the rest of the nation. If there is not a conscious sense of unity among them as there is in New England or the Deep South, then there are certainly common characteristics and an interdependence, symbolized by the casualness with which hundreds of thousands of commuters cross the boundaries of New Jersey, Pennsylvania, and Maryland every working day.

What ties the Middle Atlantic States together is that they are, indisputably, the capital of the nation. Within these bounds lie America's political capital, in Washington; its financial capital, in the square mile at the southern tip of Manhattan known as Wall Street; the cultural and artistic and entertainment capitals, also in Manhattan; and, spread throughout the region, the manufacturing capital of the nation. The Middle Atlantic States produce more books and more steel, they produce more political and investment decisions than any other part of the nation. The population of the United States is decentralized to a greater extent than that of any other major industrial nation; yet the power so far has developed and remains here, in the relatively confined geographic space between the Potomac and Long Island Sound. As recently as 1971, California writer Paul Jacobs could write:

Those who live in the West and want to participate in the conduct of national political power or communicate through national media or seek recognition in the arts must either commute or move to the headquarters of the American empire, located in that Eastern area which encompasses Boston, New York, and Washington. If Horace Greeley were alive, he might advise the ambitious and the restless to "go east."

It is possible to make plenty of money in San Francisco or Chicago or Atlanta, Jacobs went on, but to really affect the national destiny one must head to the Middle Atlantic States.

The gnawing question as these lines were written in the mid-1970s was how long these states would continue to dominate national decision-making. The position of the Washington, D.C. orbit as the fountainhead of political power seemed assured into the far future—but will New York remain financially mighty, will the region continue to dominate manufacturing?

People, jobs, and wealth are fleeing to the newly fabled American "sunbelt" of the South and West. The latest Census estimates, for 1975, show only one half of one percent population increase in the Middle Atlantic States in the 1970s. New Jersey's increased by only 2 percent. New York declined by more than 120,000 in the 1970s. The real shocker, though, was the absolute decline of 313,600 or 1.8 percent in New York City and its suburbs—the first such recorded decline since the Census began in 1790. Employment, moreover, grew only 1.7 percent in the Mid-Atlantic states between 1970 and 1973.

A sharp differentiation was appearing between the northern and southern parts of the region. Maryland and Delaware were growing in population at approximately the national level during the first half of the '70s, in sharp contrast to the decline of the states to the north. And suspicion was growing that the spending and tax policies of the federal government—so beneficial in the area around Washington, D.C.—were particularly deleterious to New York, New Jersey, and Pennsylvania, as well as most of New England and all of the Great Lakes states—the nation's aging industrial heartland. Reporting on each state's and region's "balance of payments" with the federal government—total taxes paid by individuals and businesses, compared with total federal government outlays in fiscal year 1975—the *National Journal* in 1976 reported that Maryland benefited royally, by $1.3 billion. The entire Southern U.S., as defined by the Census Bureau, from Delaware and Maryland to Texas—had a balance of payments *surplus* with Washington of $11.5 billion. But for the three states of New York, New Jersey, and Pennsylvania, there was a combined *deficit* of $10.0 billion.

The *National Journal* figures helped fuel a nascent regional protest movement—indeed, one of the most quickly-organized protests by a region in the nation's history. A Coalition of Northeast Governors—including New York, Pennsylvania, New Jersey, Connecticut, Massachusetts, and Rhode Island—was officially organized in June 1976. That September, Representatives of 16 states—from Iowa to Maine, formed a Northeast-Midwest Economic Advancement Coalition in the U.S. House, seeking to assure a better break for the Northeast and Midwest on a broad front of congressional action. In November 1976, the Northeast governors met at Saratoga Springs with more than 100 industrialists, bankers, academicians, and labor leaders from the area to focus regional demands. A potentially historic action agenda was drawn up, mostly focused on federal action—steps to equalize energy costs between regions, to set up a multi-billion dollar Northeast energy and development corporation with federal guarantees for its bonds, to reverse the rapid flow of military bases and contracts to the sunbelt, to enact tax inducements which would encourage industries to expand or locate in the Northeast, and to revise federal manpower, transportation, and welfare policies to benefit the region.

Only time would tell whether the Saratoga Springs manifesto, which the governors quickly carried to Jimmy Carter, then the President-elect, would prove a blueprint for major change or just another blip on the radar screen of periodic regional gripes about federal policy. But it was clear that the region had begun to "get its act together" as never before in American history.

Beyond any regional decline due to federal policies, it was possible to detect a number of broader trends contributing to population and economic decline in the Northeast region. The Census figures were showing a precipitous drop in birth rates in the major metropolitan areas of the East, especially in New York since that state substantially liberalized its abortion law in 1970. Secondly, the great northward migrations from the rural South seem to have slowed down or even stopped—a development that, in the long run, is probably a beneficial one for the northern cities (and the South as well). But there is a third reason, which does not bode so well for the Middle Atlantic states, a lessening of the migration of the young, talented, and affluent (or likely to be affluent) to Megalopolis and its countryside. In the 1930s, a period of comparably low population growth, New York as well as Washington grew faster than the nation as a whole; today New York has clearly lost that attractiveness. Fourth, the migration of working class white people and retirees away from these states, out to the West or in some cases down to the South, is continuing as it has for many years and is apparently accelerating. This is a major factor in the life of Pennsylvania, as we shall see in the chapter on that state; it has also become one for upstate New York, and not just its rural fringes, but its industrial heartland along the Mohawk River Valley and the Lake Ontario Plain and Buffalo. The great exception to regional population decline is, of course, Megalopolis's southernmost urban area—that of Washington, D.C. Government has been the great growth industry of the recent past, and Washington stands for government.

Residents of the Middle Atlantic States also lost in the race to keep the same standard of living as previous generations. In 1929, per capita income in the area from the District of Columbia to New York was 141 percent of the national average; in 1975, only 113 percent—and the cost of living and tax burden had grown enormously.

Yet it will be many decades before the Middle Atlantic States lose their immense numbers of people, more than any other region of the nation. In 1975, there were still 42.6 million people in this territory—20 percent of the national total.

Politically, the Middle Atlantic States continue to bulk large. They elect, in the 1970s, 88 members of the House of Representatives (plus the nonvoting delegate from D.C.); they have 101 electoral votes in presidential elections. John F. Kennedy's sweep in the Middle Atlantic States was absolutely essential to his victory in the 1960 presidential election. For decades to come, it will be exceedingly difficult for any Democratic candidate to win without carrying New York and Pennsylvania—as Jimmy Carter was able to do in his narrow win of 1976. The Middle Atlantic States have also been the traditional home of the progressive wing of the Republican party, producing such presidential candidates as Thomas Dewey of New York, William Scranton of Pennsylvania, and New York's Nelson Rockefeller.

Megalopolis

As has been the case throughout this series, we have discussed each state separately. But if we were basing our divisions on economic rather than political facts we would describe only two sections in the Middle Atlantic region. The division would be the Appalachian Trail, the hikers' path that strides along one of the first Appalachian chains. It enters the Middle Atlantic States just across the Potomac from Harper's Ferry, West Virginia; passes northwest of Frederick, Maryland; just to the north of Harrisburg, Reading, and Allentown, Pennsylvania; crosses the Delaware River at the Delaware Water Gap and the Hudson at the Bear Mountain Bridge, at the northern extremity of Westchester County. North and west of the Trail are upstate New York, northeastern, central, and western Pennsylvania, and western Maryland. This is a land of farms and mines and—most important economically—heavy industry.

South and east of the Appalachian Trail, facing the Atlantic, is the geographically much smaller but much more populous section of the Middle Atlantic States which we may call Megalopolis. That is the title of the 1961 book by the French geographer Jean Gottmann, which treated the area from Rockingham County, New Hampshire to Fauquier County, Virginia (and stretching inland as far as Wilkes-Barre, Pennsylvania and Cumberland, Maryland) as a single entity, economically and socially. Our Middle Atlantic States do not include the New England and Virginia edges of Gottmann's Megalopolis, but they cover its heart and three-quarters of its population, clustered as it is in the New York-to-Washington corridor.

We tend to take the Middle Atlantic Megalopolis almost for granted, but from his international perspective Gottmann found it remarkable:

No other section of the United States has such a large concentration of population, with such a high average density, spread over such a large area. And no other section has a comparable role within the nation or a comparable importance in the world. Here has been developed a kind of supremacy, in politics, in economics, and possibly even in cultural activities, seldom before attained by an area of this size.

Indeed, Megalopolis, whether one counts Gottmann's 42.3 million-person area, or the 31.3 million within our six states, vastly overshadows its conceivable counterparts in the industrial world—greater London, Paris, or Tokyo, or the Ruhr complex in West Germany; there are just about as many people in Megalopolis as in the rest of these put together.

In the years since Gottmann wrote, we have become rather accustomed to the idea of a continuous city, and it no longer seems so remarkable. It is a little more so when we consider that none of the other strip cities magazine writers were predicting would grow have yet come to exist. There is no urban-suburban belt connecting Cleveland, Detroit, and Chicago or Los Angeles and San Francisco or Houston and Dallas—nothing like the belt of continuous settlement from Washington to New York. This has not been the standard form of urban development in the United States —or, indeed, anywhere else.

Just about everyone is familiar with the litany of the problems afflicting Megalopolis. With factories, power plants, and automobiles spewing noxious vapors constantly, its air is badly and often dangerously polluted. The water of several major rivers and even some areas of the Atlantic are hopelessly fouled.

And now there is the question of whether there will be money to try to solve these problems—or even continue the services that residents of Megalopolis have come to expect. As the capital of the nation, cities in the Middle Atlantic States have often pioneered in offering services to their residents. New York led with the most extensive array of services, and it has come to the brink of bankruptcy. Other Megalopolis cities, notably Philadelphia, are suffering severe financial problems. As affluent and middle class people move out to the suburbs, the central cities of Megalopolis are increasingly the province of the poor and those unable to cope; the demand for increased suburban services grows too rapidly to satisfy, while the central cities' tax bases inexorably decline. Crime has reached epidemic proportions in some central city areas (although no one is sure just how much crime is being committed, and where). This leads people to desert the streets—which, in turn, encourages more crime. Ethnic minorities—blacks and Puerto Ricans—continue to suffer many of the pains of discrimination, and still seem to enjoy less than their fair share of ———.

Yet by the same token it can be argued that the problems of pollution are just as grave in California or the Great Lakes cities, of crime as serious, or even more so, in cities of the South and West. The most distinctive problem of the Middle Atlantic States may be cities hemmed in by nineteenth-century boundaries that prevent annexation to take in the wealth on the suburban periphery. But that is a problem of the Midwest, too, and of a few Southern and Western cities, such as Atlanta, New Orleans, San Francisco, and Seattle. The problems may have come earlier, and in more vivid form, to the East—but they may bespeak fundamental failings of American society, which will eventually afflict every region, and will demand solutions from all levels of government—local, state, regional, and federal.

From the early days, the Middle Atlantic cities have played the roles of port of entry, banker, corporate boss, and bureaucrat to the rest of the nation—and have become the wealthiest and most thickly settled part of the country. Natural resources have played a secondary role; indeed Megalopolis has often imported commodities from other states that even today feel raped by the mighty East that usually sets the prices.

But today Megalopolis' commercial primacy is in eclipse. The region has failed to look after its fundamental problems, and obsolescence has reared its head. Major cities of Megalopolis never recovered from the 1970–71 recession and suffered grievously in the economic downturn of the mid-1970s, in large part because they contain the oldest, least efficient manufacturing facilities, which are the first to be closed down as production is reduced. Between 1967 and 1972, the Census Bureau reports, employment in manufacturing declined by 12 percent in the Middle Atlantic States. The slippage goes beyond manufacturing: major oil companies, for instance, had moved their headquarters from New York and Philadelphia and Pittsburgh to Houston by the mid-1970s; the downtown office space market in New York was virtually paralyzed.

The story of the Penn Central Railroad is illustrative of the region's problems. The line was formed as recently as February 1968, by the merger of what were then the nation's two largest railroads—the New York Central and Pennsylvania. With more than 90,000 employees and more than 20,000 miles of track—centered in the heart of industrial America, from Megalopolis through western Pennsylvania and New York to Ohio, Indiana, Michigan, and Illinois—the Penn Central should have been prosperous. Even though passenger travel was clearly declining, thousands of industrial plants still depended on its service. Yet on June 21, 1970, little more than two years after the merger, the Penn Central went into bankruptcy. Finally it had to be reorganized as ConRail, with a massive, latter-day infusion of federal dollars.*

---

* Ironically, it was public funds which in large part gave the Pennsylvania Railroad, one of the Penn Central partners, its start; of the first $12 million in stock sold, in 1846, more than $5 million came from the city of Philadelphia, and another $1 million from Allegheny County (Pittsburgh). Their motive was to promote the commercial primacy of Philadelphia, against its rivals New York and Baltimore, as the point of entry from the East Coast to the great interior.

One reason writers have seldom concentrated on the Middle Atlantic States Megalopolis is its proliferation of political entities. This is the legacy, primarily, of colonial days, when colonies were established along a river's mouth (New York, Pennsylvania, Delaware), astride a bay (Maryland), or just in between (New Jersey). In the colonial period and the 19th century, the Middle Atlantic States were further divided into counties on the basis of the usual American criterion that the county seat should be no more than a day's carriage ride from any farm in the county. As a result, the present-day traveler on the Metroliner train from Washington to New York passes through 17 different counties or county equivalents—which does not seem so many until one remembers that each has its own governmental powers, and that the decisions of each inevitably affect the others. And counties are by no means the end of it: altogether, the Middle Atlantic States in 1970 contained no fewer than 2,743 incorporated cities, towns, villages, and boroughs, and 4,483 county subdivisions. Not all of these are in the Megalopolitan belt, but enough are—for example, there are 53 incorporated cities and 257 boroughs in little New Jersey alone—to hopelessly snarl the process of rationally providing governmental services and planning for the future of the region.

There have been a number of efforts at regional government, but their accomplishments have been, by any measure, limited. The Delaware River Basin Commission made a small bit of history by becoming the first governmental body set up by interstate compact; but it has not had great impact on the river or the people who surround it. The Port of New York Authority has done a competent job of building container terminals in New Jersey and running Kennedy, LaGuardia, and Newark Airports, and it has erected—apparently simply as a revenue-earning device—two of the world's tallest structures in Manhattan's International Trade Center (twin 110-story buildings). But until very recently indeed, the Port Authority has avoided like the plague any responsibility for the mode of transportation which makes more difference to the quality of life in the New York area than any other: the subways. It does operate the PATH tubes from New Jersey to Manhattan, but for years steadfastly declined any further obligation—despite its bulging coffers.

There have been some cases in which voluntary regional associations have made some difference—the Metropolitan Washington Council of Governments, for example. But such instances are few, and cover pathetically small ground. The basic decisions remain in too many—or too few—hands. Land use, in practically the entire region, is left to the often too numerous local governments, each of which naturally is more eager to protect parochial interests than to further broader programs. It takes a major effort, such as that by which the state of New Jersey created the Meadowlands commission, to overturn this usual pattern. When it comes to basic transportation decisions, the problem now is that, too often, such decisions are simply not made at all. Megalopolis now has just about all the federally-financed expressways it is going to get through the Interstate highway program; the dotted lines which you still may see on maps of Brooklyn and Washington, purportedly showing the routes of future Interstates, are going to remain just dotted lines.

As for mass transit, there are in the 1970s some signs of activity—after 40 years of neglect. Greater Washington has opened its Metro subway system, after the kind of delays subway watchers are becoming used to and with such large cost overruns that it may be one of the last underground transit systems in the country. In the Philadelphia area, the Southwest Pennsylvania Transportation Authority has taken control of the bus and subway lines both in and outside Philadelphia. To the north, around New York, the Metropolitan Transit Authority has accumulated the New York subways and the financially (and physically) ramshackle commuter lines under its sole control. For many years improvement of transportation in Megalopolis, as elsewhere through the nation, meant building roads, and nothing more; in contrast, often even routine maintenance of subways was discontinued.

West of the Appalachian Trail

Discussions of depressed areas naturally have the tendency of shifting the geographical focus from Megalopolis west, across the Appalachian Trail, to what one might call the outback of the Middle Atlantic States. Upstate New York, central and western Pennsylvania, the western tip of Maryland —this is anything but an insignificant region, even in a national perspective. It is not, like the Megalopolitan belt, a cluster of corporate or governmental headquarters, although Pittsburgh. does have more than its share of national companies (U.S. Steel, Westinghouse, Alcoa, Heinz, and various other steel companies).

What this larger geographic hunk of the Middle Atlantic States is is an industrial empire. The steel factories that line the Monongahela and Ohio Rivers near Pittsburgh are known around the world, so much so that to speak of a Pittsburgh has long since been to talk of a major industrial center. But there are also huge steel plants in Buffalo and huge electrical machine plants in Schenectady and Syracuse (General Electric) and Pittsburgh (Westinghouse). This western half of the Middle Atlantic States also sits astride the northern end of the largest concentration of bituminous coal in the world, the veins that reach south from western Pennsylvania into West Virginia and Kentucky. The first oil well in the United States was drilled at Titusville, Pennsylvania, in 1859.

So if Megalopolis owes its prosperity and its importance to its geographical position and historical primacy, the western part of the Middle Atlantic States owes its prominence to its natural resources. Indeed, one can see what this hilly, often hauntingly beautiful, yet not particularly fertile land might have remained when we look at some of the remote counties in New York and Pennsylvania where coal was never mined and few migrants ever reached. Here the land is green and cool, with a vacant look to it; the towns have a remote air one seldom finds in Iowa or Wisconsin. It is a part of America quite literally off the beaten path, and probably always will be.

Not so the industrial parts of the western Middle Atlantic States. Here the land has been scarred, the air serrated with noxious emissions, the water empurpled with free-flowing waste. Sometime in the 1950s, or perhaps before, heavy industry lost its status as the leading edge of the American economy, and even before, the signs of stagnation were visible in this great industrial region. Coal, despite a revival in the 1970s, is not the centrally important fuel it was 30 years before (compare the national reactions to the 1974 and 1946 coal miners' strikes). Steel, too, found itself far more vulnerable to competition in the '60s and '70s than its complacent management class had anticipated; and steel production, to the extent it increased, was being decentralized from its historic home in and around Pittsburgh.

The result has been literally hundreds of thousands of young people leaving upstate New York and western Pennsylvania, usually heading to other parts of the nation where jobs were more easily available and opportunities greater. This outmigration—and, in many cases, absolute population loss—has in turn stunted the growth of all the accoutrements of economic life one finds in a community—the small businesses, the local institutions. These were once boom towns, first when the over-the-mountains transportation modes were perfected, then with the development of the steel industry. Now, like so many boom towns, they have found themselves faced with something that looks uncomfortably like a bust. And they have been there a long time; for much of central and western Pennsylvania, the depression of the '30s never seemed to end.

The Regional Future

The primacy—and the problems—of the Middle Atlantic States are something beyond politics. The government could decree the capital in Washington, but it could not create New York or Philadelphia, Pittsburgh or Buffalo as they are. Nor, it appears, can government at any level have all that much effect on what they become. The decade since the mid-'60s was a time of lessening belief in the efficacy of government at all levels, a time of growing cynicism and distrust of politicians. The Middle Atlantic States provide as good examples as any of government actually accomplishing what it sets out to do—the many achievements of Nelson Rockefeller in New York State; the physical rebirth of Philadelphia; the cleaning up of the skies around Pittsburgh. But not one of these, interestingly enough, is remembered with much affection by the people most closely concerned. Rockefeller is viewed, in light of later fiscal crises, with sour skepticism in the state he ruled for 15 years; Edmund Bacon is forgotten in a Philadelphia whose chief focus of political attention is on the brawls of Mayor Frank L. Rizzo; the current mayor of Pittsburgh has virtually no communication with either the business leaders or the Democratic pols who made his city's "rebirth" possible.

Yet while these "accomplishments" were taking place, federal government programs intentionally or unintentionally were helping other parts of the country develop at the expense of the Middle Atlantic States. For three decades, the sunbelt has been first in line at the pork barrel, amassing vast sums for defense installations, space exploration, and technological development. The net result was the grave imbalance in federal outlays reviewed earlier in this chapter.

Congressional seniority and control of important committees played a role in those allocations, but other factors complete a picture of the Middle Atlantic States as what the economists call a mature economy. In a mature economy, the transition from agriculture to industry is long since accomplished, a major manufacturing base is in place, and wages have worked themselves up to a high level, at least in comparision to other regions. The capital stock tends to be aged, costs of operation high, and new job opportunities scarce. Such an economy is likely to be an exporter of capital, dependent on the interest and dividends it receives from it; this leads in turn to a more cautious approach to investment, aversion to risk taking, and a drying up of the entrepreneurial juices. The region with a mature economy is seriously disadvantaged in competing with areas that are still moving to an industrial base where plants are newer, wages lower, the average age of the population lower, and there is less of a public burden to be carried on in terms of retirees, the unemployed, and the welfare population.

And so the industrialists are finding lower tax burdens, relatively low energy costs, and cheap land available in the South, and the jobs are leaving. But the people seem to be following willingly. New Yorkers used to explain breathlessly that their city "has everything," but today that statement is more likely to conjure up views of bankruptcy, filth, and social tension than sophisticated theaters, nightclubs, and beautiful skyscrapers—even though those shining attractions of the metropolis are still there. Thirty percent of New York's retiree checks are mailed outside the city—an annual contribution of $180 million to the economy of communities often thousands of miles away. In the 1970s, lower living costs and a more relaxed life style appear to be the greatest draw. Widespread air conditioning has done for the hot lands what central heating once did for the cold North.

This is not to say that future rejuvenation is not possible. In the words of Jon Nordheimer of the New York *Times*:

> It has been the American experience that new frontiers, once they are open for settlement, are overrun and the environment battered. Then they are abandoned when greener pastures beckon. But this time, the continent is being exhausted by

the movement; it is the last migration into relatively unused open space. The next cycle of mass movement will be one of reclamation: to rehabilitate the great metropolitan centers that were allowed to succumb to the same social malaise now being hailed as the inescapable byproduct of progress in the Sunbelt.

Nordheimer's optimism, however, should not suggest that short-term solutions will be found to the problems of the Mid-Atlantic States. The best they may be able to do is to age gracefully, to let the South and West have their fling at growth and its problems. The East's old supremacy may never be regained in full measure. But the future will be immeasurably brighter if a regional consciousness, a sense of common fate and common purpose, followed by common regional planning for the first time in the region's history, begins to take form in the closing quarter of the 20th century.

WASHINGTON, D.C.

WORLD CAPITAL, DIVIDED CITY

WASHINGTON, D.C.,* world capital, city of monuments, symbol of nation-hood, seat of power brokers, workplace of bureaucrats, loved and reviled by its countrymen, is a metropolis of profound contradictions. The most obvious may be the many ways in which it is the polar opposite of the nation of which it is the capital. More than 87 percent of the nation's citizens are whites, but, in 1974, 77 percent of Washington's residents were black. The United States as a whole gave Richard Nixon and Spiro Agnew 61 percent of its votes in 1972, while Washington went 78 percent for George Mc-Govern—a Democratic percentage exceeded that year in only one *county* in the U.S. (Duval County, Texas). Yet Washington's blackness and Demo-cratic voting habits do not mean that it is a place of pervasive poverty or economic backwardness. Though the city ranks fourth nationally in the per-centage of its people on welfare, per capita income is higher than in any state (with a high cost of living to match). The city has a higher per-centage of college graduates among its adult population (17.7 percent) than any state. Then there is the crowning paradox: for 100 years, from 1874 to 1974, the citizens of a nation dedicated to representative government were

---

* Few people who have been in Washington more than a week ever utter the cumbersome sylla-bles "District of Columbia." The capital is referred to as "Washington," or, to distinguish it from the suburbs, "the District," or even "D.C." Since there is little chance here of confusion with the state of Washington, we will eschew the "Washington, D.C." form, of which our greatest authority on place names, George R. Stewart, has written: "The two initials have become attached to the name of the capital like an ugly parasitic growth."

not allowed to elect their own local officials. Until 1964, Washingtonians could not even vote for President.

All of these facts and paradoxes are the result of Washington's unique history. Unlike other great capitals—London, Paris, Moscow, Tokyo—Washington is not the economic or cultural capital of the nation it rules. Accordingly, it lacks the diversity and mammoth size of those other capitals. Indeed, it has been called the world's largest company town, and the company is of course the federal government. And that is the ultimate root of most of its peculiarities.

The continuing increase in government spending and government-dependent business, even during Republican administrations, has made Washington a continual boom town since the early 1930s.

As the government and the city have grown, Washington has become an increasingly sophisticated place to live. What the city lacks in ethnic concentrations, it makes up for in the truly cosmopolitan nature of the people it draws from the 50 states and from almost every country in the world.

Much publicity has been given to the growth of the bureaucracy with its high pay for dull, secure jobs, but Washington also serves as a magnet for some of the nation's most talented people hoping for work that will deal with the fate of the nation and the world, yearning to be part of the "Washington" that writer Elizabeth Drew described in her book on the Watergate period, *Washington Journal:*

> . . . There is the quality of a nervous system about Washington, or, at least, about that part of Washington which professionally concerns itself with official events. Obviously, there are people here who sell shoes and insurance and fix teeth and automobiles and live as people do anywhere else. But there is a constantly growing, bipartisan collection of people here—journalists, politicians, politicians' aides, lawyers, lobbyists, government workers, hangers-on, and the geological strata of several Administrations' worth of former officials—who make up what is usually referred to as "Washington," as in "What does Washington think?" or "What is the mood in Washington?" These people concern themselves with what is going on, whether or not what is going on concerns them. They talk about it over their meals and on their telephones. "Washington" not only does a great deal of talking about what's happening but also does a great deal of speculating about what might happen.

For these Washingtonians, work is the main attraction. Status in the capital depends on the job and the employer, not on family background or even wealth. Washington society does have a permanent hard core of "blue-bloods," which can trace its ancestry back through an impressive number of administrations, but attention is paid only to those who keep up with "the issues." Hard work is important, and the workaholic (the man, and increasingly the woman, who finds the greatest pleasure or escape in the job) is a common phenomenon and local social problem. Yet the excitement of the capital compels people to stay. Each year politicians who leave office—and their staffs—come down with Potomac Fever: they find they can't tear themselves away. Often they never go home.

Beyond the attraction of exciting employment, Washington is becoming recognized more and more as a pleasant place to live. What the city lacks in diversity and creativity, it makes up for in accessibility. Only 10 minutes from the White House, it is possible to live in the city or the suburbs in a house with a yard and no trouble parking. In the words of *Newsweek* bureau chief Mel Elfin, "Unlike New York, from whence I have sprung—and fled—Washington today has fewer creature discomforts and more civilized assets than it did when I arrived a decade ago."

Washington has long been on the corridor for people planning to move. Blacks fleeing repression in the South and job hunters in the depression came to Washington. Now that people are leaving the North, Washington again is a first stop.

Even for people who don't experience exciting employment and/or the security of government work, the area has attractions: many beautiful parks, close proximity to fishing and hunting, boating on the Chesapeake, and more rural atmosphere than most cities. The hot humid summer is no bargain, but air conditioning has made it tolerable. And it's always nice to be able to drive over to the Smithsonian at a moment's notice.

It is misleading to speak of Washington alone, without considering the giant metropolitan area that spreads far beyond the District line. In this chapter we will, of necessity, be talking both about the District and the Washington metropolitan area. But the metropolitan area, taken as a whole, is scarcely less distinctive than the central city. Of all the nation's major metropolitan areas, Washington has by far the largest proportion of government employees and—these facts are not unrelated—the highest income and education levels.* Metropolitan Washington also has an unusually high percentage of black residents, 24.6 percent. Interestingly, that last figure has not changed significantly since the 1920s; what has changed, of course, has been the proportion of blacks in the central city.

The District itself, like most central cities, has been losing population since 1950; but most of its downtown is vital, and new construction is constant. The real growth becomes apparent when one looks at the 1960s growth rates of the nation's urban agglomerations with populations over one million. Metro Washington's growth rate (37.8 percent) ranked second behind Houston's (40.0 percent), and Washington actually grew faster than such sunbelt metropolises as Dallas-Fort Worth (36.9 percent), Atlanta (36.7 percent), Miami (35.6 percent), and Los Angeles and environs (27.1 percent.) The heady growth was halted in the first years of the 1970s, with a slight net outmigration of population from the metropolitan region—the re-

---

* The figures are as follows: fully 42 percent of the workers in the Washington metropolitan area are employed by government. Some 58 percent of the workers, public and private, hold white collar jobs. By 1974, the median family income for the city was $10,800 while income for a suburban family was $16,900. Over 16,000 employees earned the highest regular government salary of $37,800, and government employees making over $18,000 constituted 35 percent of the work force, compared to less than one percent in 1960. The fact that many of these salaries are vastly inflated in contrast to positions of similar responsibility in private industry does not detract from the enormous economic advantage they represent for the Washington area.

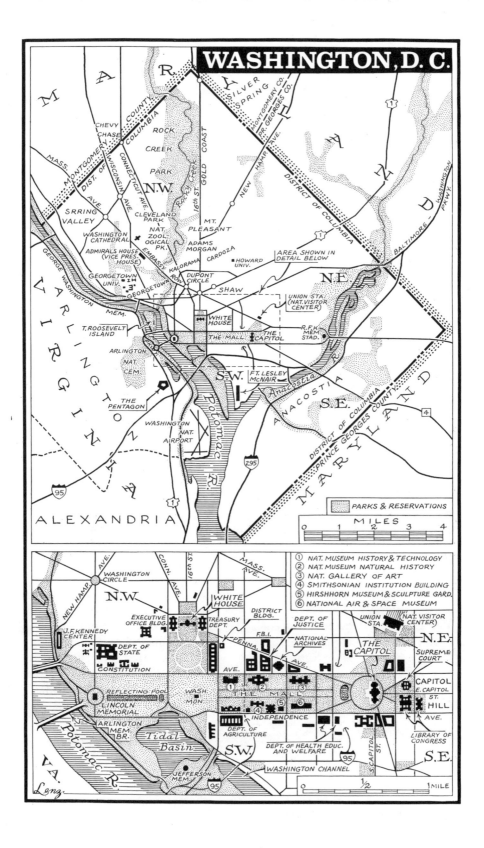

sult of less ebullient growth of the federal government and the sundry institutions that live on it. Yet even as the region slowed down to absorb the vast influx of people that had been underway since the 1930s, Washington and its suburbs bore all the marks of a resilient, vital economy.*

It was not always so. In its early days, Washington was a disappointment to its boosters, who imagined that it would become another London or Paris. Foreign visitors were often appalled at the empty fields directly adjacent to the major government structures and at the sight of pigs running freely through the streets. Charles Dickens, who visited the capital in 1842, had a typical reaction: he found "spacious avenues that begin in nothing and lead nowhere; streets a mile long that only want houses, roads, and inhabitants; public buildings that need but a public to be complete; and ornaments of great thoroughfares which need only great thoroughfares to ornament."

Washington's reputation as a hick town lingers on for many Americans, especially some of those in the more northern reaches of Megalopolis. They like to recall the remark John F. Kennedy made while a Senator, that Washington was "a city of Southern efficiency and Northern charm." But a lot has changed since the 1950s, when Washingtonians in search of fine food sometimes made the 40-mile trek to Baltimore.

Today Washington has its share of topflight restaurants, and it buys more books per person than New York. It has one of the nation's better and more solvent repertory theater companies in the Arena Stage; a newly revived Ford's Theater (where Lincoln was shot); the National Theater, and since 1971, the success of the John F. Kennedy Center for the Performing Arts has created something of a cultural craze in the capital. Washington still relies mostly on touring artists and companies (the greatest creativity in town may be the preparation of Broadway-bound shows), but far more attractions play in the capital than in just about any other city in America except New York.† The National Symphony, under its new director, Antal Dorati, has improved greatly in recent years, and the Smithsonian Institution, which used to have the reputation of a musty old attic overrun by tourists, is now a vital and exciting complex of national museums. Washington also offers the visitor a number of excellent art galleries, ranging from the National Gallery, Renwick, National Portrait, and new Hirshhorn galleries in the Smithsonian galaxy to surprise-filled treasures like the small Phillips Gallery in an old mansion off Massachusetts Avenue.

Washington has a very adequate evening newspaper, the Washington *Star*, control of which was acquired in 1974 from the families who owned it for more than 100 years by Texas millionaire Joe Albritton. The *Star*'s

* The 1975 estimated population for the District was 716,000, a decrease from the 1970 census figure of 756,510. The estimated population of the metropolitan area was 3,015,300 in 1974.
† A cavil must be entered, however, about the location of the Kennedy Center. Sadly, it was placed alongside the Potomac in Foggy Bottom, where it is accessible by foot only for those who live in the Watergate complex next door. It could have been a major factor in revitalizing some of the drabber parts of downtown, but its backers and architect (Edward Durrell Stone) were fascinated with the idea of creating a striking monument on the banks of the Potomac.

continued life has been endangered by severe financial problems, even though its quality and liveliness have improved dramatically in the 1970s. Even more important, of course, is the Washington *Post*, known nationally as the paper whose aggressive reporting led to the forced resignation of a President. The paper has improved in just about every respect in the last dozen years, rivaling the New York *Times* as the nation's best. The *Post* itself is the centerpiece of the Post-Newsweek media empire, which includes *Newsweek* magazine and television and radio stations in Washington and around the country. This is one of the major businesses in the country run by a woman, Katharine Graham, who took over the reins after her husband's death in 1963.

What non-Washingtonians do not know is how firmly the *Post* dominates the Washington market, with the lion's share of ad revenue and circulation in both the District and the suburbs. The *Post* takes seriously its obligations as a local newspaper, and it is somehow fitting that Bob Woodward and Carl Bernstein, the reporters who broke the story of the Watergate cover-up, were part of its metropolitan staff.

Determined to bolster its profits and win back operating control of its own pressroom from the powerful and well-paid pressmen's union, the *Post* endured and "won" in a four-month strike in 1975–76. The pressmen made a grievous tactical error when some members vandalized the presses at the opening of the strike; as a result the Newspaper Guild (reporters and commercial employees) voted to continue working, and the paper was able to print every day but one during the strike. No settlement was ever reached with the pressmen's union; the *Post* finally resolved its problems by hiring nonunion personnel.

A Brief History of the Federal City

Washington had its beginnings on a summer night in 1790 when Secretary of State Thomas Jefferson invited Secretary of the Treasury Alexander Hamilton over to supper at Jefferson's quarters in New York, the nation's temporary capital. Both men had suffered defeats in the Congress at the hands of the other's supporters, and both were ready to compromise. Hamilton wanted the federal government to assume the debts of the states; Jefferson wanted the new capital located somewhere in the South, in or near his native Virginia. Over Madeira they made a deal. Jefferson would deliver crucial Virginia votes for assumption, and Hamilton would deliver Northern votes for a Southern capital. Thus Washington, which would be the scene of so many political compromises, had its genesis in one.

The new bill allowed the President to designate a 10-mile-square site along the Potomac River, and George Washington made the actual decision. The land selected was at the head of navigation of the Potomac River, conveniently near Washington's own landholdings at Mount Vernon. Maryland

and Virginia obliged by ceding the territory to the federal government, including the then-thriving small ports of Alexandria on the Virginia side and Georgetown on the Maryland side. (Congress, however, gave the portion of the District south of the Potomac back to Virginia in 1846.) *

The site was often criticized later. Much of the land was low and marshy; the land where tourists today swarm over the Lincoln and Jefferson Memorials was under water well into the 19th century. The climate was hot and exceedingly humid and, in those days, conducive to disease. But a site farther up the Potomac would have precluded the possibility of navigation, and the founders, who traveled mainly by water, had hopes that the federal city would become a great emporium of trade and the dominant urban center in the nation.

But New York and Philadelphia and Boston and even Baltimore had too much of a head start. George Washington himself had planned a canal that would connect the capital with the Ohio River Valley, but amid tussling in Congress work proceeded only slowly. President John Quincy Adams turned the first spadeful of dirt on the Chesapeake and Ohio Canal in 1828, but it did not reach Cumberland, Maryland, until 1850—eight years after the Baltimore & Ohio Railroad. Today the canal is a spot of tranquil beauty that underscores its commercial failure. It was badly damaged by the waters churned up by tropical storm Agnes in 1971, but subsequently restored for the pleasure of hikers, bicyclists, and those who enjoy leisurely barge trips as much as their 19th-century ancestors.

Washington has never been a great port or a great manufacturing center; the main industry here, as it always has been, is the federal government—and in modern times, the satellite industries that gather around it. Metropolitan Washington has a huge percentage of the nation's scientists; it probably has more consulting firms, lawyer-lobbyists, and journalists than any other place on earth. In recent years national trade associations have moved almost by the dozen to Washington from Chicago and New York and the capital is even becoming something of a financial center. The World Bank and the International Monetary Fund are in the city, and international financiers can be found today in such considerable numbers on Washington's 15th Street that *Washingtonian* magazine suggested, not entirely tongue-in-cheek, that Wall Street was in eclipse.

If the founders' dreams of another London were never realized, the physical layout for the capital still resembles what they planned. In 1791 Major Pierre Charles L'Enfant was commissioned to draw a plan for the

* Alexandria was then a major slave-trading center for Virginia and the eastern seaboard of the United States; the inland portion of the D.C. enclave, however, was scarcely populated. The residents of Alexandria believed themselves ignored by the D.C. government, which sat across the Potomac and sought to rejoin their brethren in Virginia. Richmond favored the re-annexation of the territory because it would give the slave-holding planter section of the state additional support in the state legislature against the small farm regions of the piedmont and mountains. Congress approved the return of nearly one-third of the District to Virginia with the single provision that a vote be taken within the area and that the citizens there approve of their proposed new status. By a margin of 763 yeas to 222 nays, the residents of Alexandria voted to return their allegiance to Virginia. Radical Republicans in the mid-19th century and city planners in the mid- and later-20th century found themselves regretting the generosity of the Congress of 1846.

federal city. The result was the series of grid streets (with letter and num-ber names) and diagonal avenues, squares, and circles which are familiar to anyone who has been in downtown Washington. L'Enfant thought big: he designed streets 200 and 250 and even 400 feet wide; he examined the topography carefully and planned for long vistas down the avenues; he chose the site for the Capitol and the White House. But though much of his vi-sion was adopted, he was not appreciated much at the time, especially by some of the big land speculators whose plans he tried to thwart. After less than a year on the job, he was fired; he refused the $2,500 proffered by Congress and asked for what he thought his efforts were worth, $100,000. Years later he died penniless. His initial sketches were reconstructed by a surveyor named Benjamin Banneker, a free Negro—the first of many black Americans who would play a major role in Washington's history.

Situated below the Mason-Dixon line, Washington was slave territory before the Civil War; abolition of the slave trade (but not of slavery) in the District was one of the planks of the Compromise of 1850. Nevertheless, even in antebellum days, Washington was a city of special significance for black Americans. Near enough to the Deep South to have a large black population, but at the same time under the control of legislators mainly from free states, Washington became a haven for free blacks. By 1860 there were nearly four times as many free Negroes as slaves in the District. Dur-ing the war, thousands of blacks thronged to Washington, and a special 1867 census showed that fully 30 percent of the District's residents were black. That fact gave Washington a very special place in Reconstruction; with pro-Negro Republicans in control of Congress, and hence the District, Washington became a kind of laboratory for civil rights measures. The radi-cal Republicans set up the Freedmen's Bureau in 1865 to aid newly free blacks, and among its lasting accomplishments were Freedmen's Hospital and Howard University. There were black policemen in Washington in the 1860s, black firemen in the 1870s, and blacks were elected to the territorial council set up in 1871. During the late 19th century, it was said that Wash-ington had the largest Negro population of any city in the world.

Up through the Civil War, Washington had had an elective city gov-ernment (as had Georgetown, then still a separate city within the District). But the Republican Congress had suspected Washington's white majority of Confederate sympathies during the War, and in 1871 a new territorial government, encompassing the entire District, was set up. Its dominant figure was Alexander Shepherd, a 37-year-old Washington native. As a mem-ber of the board of public works and later governor, Shepherd started a massive program of building sewers, paving streets (unfortunately, with wood), and planting trees. He saw himself, perhaps, as the American Baron Haussmann; Congress saw him as an irresponsible spendthrift. Congress had authorized the District to go $10 million into debt for public improve-ments; Shepherd's ambitious programs ran the debt up to $22 million. In 1874, Congress abolished the territorial government, and the Senate later refused to confirm Shepherd as one of the District's three commissioners. Under the territorial arrangement, Washington's voters had been able to elect a 22-member house of delegates. The new system, formalized in the Organic Act of 1878, provided for governance by three commissioners appointed by the President and confirmed by the Senate. Shepherd's profligacy was to lead directly to 100 years of nonelective government.

The termination of territorial rule coincided with the end of Reconstruction—and the end of any hope for equal treatment of Washington's black minority. As in most of the South, Jim Crow laws did not follow immediately. Certain patronage positions were reserved for blacks, and Washington had as prominent a black middle class as any city in the country, led by men like Blanche K. Bruce, onetime Senator from Mississippi; Frederick Douglass, longtime federal Marshal of the District; and James Wormley, owner of a large hotel who left an estate of more than $100,000. For years, the District's public accommodations laws remained on the books, though they were generally ignored. It was not until the Wilson Administration that blacks working at the Treasury were segregated—a practice Wilson himself personally endorsed. As Washington grew larger, an increasingly smaller percentage of its residents were black, until the figure reached a low of 25 percent in 1920. Nevertheless, that was still a much larger figure than in any other city outside the Deep South.

Physically, of course, the city was growing, and what visitors saw was far different from the empty vistas reported by Dickens. But in the gilded age of the late 19th century, its growth was far eclipsed by that of industrial cities like Chicago and Pittsburgh or immigrant entrepots like New York and Philadelphia. Washington had few factories, and the federal city attracted few immigrants. As a voteless city, it never developed old-style political machines, although it did have a healthy culture of civic associations (for the guidance of which Robert's Rules of Order were drafted in the 1870s). A major force in the District from its establishment in 1889 was the Washington Board of Trade. In its later years, the Board of Trade was a major supporter of segregation and opponent of home rule in the District, but around the turn of the century it included in its membership prominent Jews and blacks, and was a major force for public health, charities, and parks.

The basic park system of the District was established as a result of the McMillan Commission of 1902, headed by Sen. James McMillan of Michigan. The Commission recommended a design for the Mall which has mostly been followed (there was still a railroad station there at the time), spearheaded the building of Union Station, picked the site for the Lincoln Memorial, and provided for the roadways through Potomac and Rock Creek Parks. That lush green parkland which is thronged by tourists during the Cherry Blossom Festival in early April and then through late fall, is largely the legacy of the commission.

How Washington Became a Majority-Black
and Self-Governing City

The highwater mark of segregation in Washington came during and after the Wilson Administration. When the Lincoln Memorial was dedicated in 1922, a separate stand was set up, aside from all the others, for Negro dignitaries. Blacks were not allowed in white restaurants and theaters; the only integration in Washington in the 1920s was on trolleys and buses, at Griffiths Stadium (but not on the baseball field itself, of course), and in libraries. When contralto Marian Anderson was denied permission to sing at the Daughters of the American Revolution's Constitution Hall in 1939, it was considered a daring act for Eleanor Roosevelt and others in her husband's administration to arrange for her appearance at the Lincoln Memorial instead.

It was at about this time that the specter of large numbers of blacks began to interfere with the accomplishment of a goal shared by Washingtonians of all races: home rule. In the 1930s, agitation for self-government grew, after a quietus of 60 years, and a straw vote conducted by the District Suffrage League showed Washington residents in favor by a seven to one margin. In 1948, a home rule measure even managed to get to the floor of the then Republican House, only to be talked down by a Southern Congressman. At that time, few people thought Washington likely to become mostly black; even the 1940 census showed the District to be 72 percent white. But the facts of demography—and massive growth—were working in that direction.

In the decade of the 1940s, there was still plenty of residential construction in the District, particularly in the far northwest and in Anacostia, the area to the east of the river of that name. But by 1950, the District had reached its maximum population of 802,178 and there was very little room for new dwellings; one could say it had reached capacity. But the Washington *metropolitan* area was increasing its population by near record proportions. Its growth in the New Deal '30s was 42.5 percent (at a time when the national population grew scarcely at all); in the '40s, it was 49.9 percent; in the '50s, 37.7 percent, and the '60s, 37.8 percent. Most of this growth represented in-migration from rural and other metropolitan areas, and the racial composition of the in-migrants was about the same as that of the metro area itself, three-to-one white over black. That meant that in 1950, there were 344,000 blacks in the Washington metro area, with 280,000 of them in the District—enough to boost the District's black percentage to 35 percent.

In the next decade, when blacks were unable to buy houses or rent in most of Washington's suburbs, nearly all the black population growth occurred within the District lines. By 1960 Washington had become the first officially black-majority major city in the United States. There were 495,-000 blacks in the metro area that year, and 411,000 lived in the District—enough to outnumber the whites in the city 54 to 46 percent. Although, as we shall see, most of Washington's suburbs became open to blacks in the '60s, and a handful even became solidly black, still the city proper was almost 71 percent black by 1970.

Henry Fairlie, a British journalist who has lived in several American cities, has written that "in no other great city in America are the blacks so evidently and so vividly a part of its whole life." He continues: "How many blacks do you see on Fifth Avenue in midtown Manhattan? But walk along Connecticut Avenue any day, between Farragut Square and Dupont Circle, and they make the sidewalks bloom: employed and young, alert and confident, well-dressed and colorful, with a swing in their stride, they are alive in themselves, but also as American as one could imagine: an American sight in America's capital."

Some observers have pointed to the desegregation of the D.C. schools in 1954 as the turning point, an event which in effect forced whites out of the city into the suburbs. It is true that Washington moved from a totally segregated system in 1954 to one which, for a few years at least, had substantial integration—and whose quality declined sharply. But too much can be made of this explanation. As early as 1948, before anyone thought the schools would be desegregated, 48 percent of Washington's public school pupils were black, and the number of white students in the D.C. public schools had been declining since 1935—an indication that younger white families were settling increasingly in the suburbs, long before integration. While school desegregation doubtless spurred many whites to flee the District, and may have led others to enroll their children in private schools, the patterns had already been set.

As Washington's future as a black-majority city became more and more certain, opposition to home rule hardened in Congress. After 1948, except for one interval of Republican control, the House District of Columbia Committee was chaired by John McMillan of South Carolina, until he was defeated for reelection in 1972. McMillan led a bloc of Southern votes implacably opposed to home rule, because it would mean black control of the city government.* They were often joined by conservative Republicans, perhaps unaware of the fact that earlier Republicans—Senator Arthur Capper of Kansas, for one—had been leading proponents of votes for the District. Strong opposition came from Joel T. Broyhill, a conservative Republican then representing the northern Virginia suburbs. During

---

* Home rule, McMillan said, was backed by "Communist sympathizers" who hoped to take over the city. He may also have had selfish reasons for opposing home rule. In 1970 columnist Jack Anderson summarized the suspicions of many Washingtonians when he wrote that McMillan "accepts favors from used-car dealers, parking-lot barons and liquor lobbies" in return for "obstructing public parking, welfare payments, and home rule." Reporters were never able to prove that McMillan took a crooked dollar, but his patronizing attitudes toward black people and his conduct of District Committee business, which ranged from dilatory to dictatorial, were a matter of public record. The factors which led to "Johnny Mac's" ultimate defeat in his own South Carolina lowlands district were related in the previous volume in this series, *The Deep South States of America*, p. 408.

the 1950s and early 1960s, polls showed most suburban Washingtonians against home rule, as was the Board of Trade, representing the city's leading retail and banking interests. Opponents talked, of course, about the need to maintain federal (i.e., congressional) control of the federal capital, but few believed that race was not an underlying motivation of opposition to home rule.

The District consequently was ruled by men hostile to the majority of its residents and their views: McMillan, House D.C. Appropriations Subcommittee Chairman William Natcher of Kentucky, and, for a while, Senate Appropriations Subcommittee Chairman Robert Byrd of West Virginia. In the 1960s, the Senate regularly passed home rule bills, and they were just as regularly killed—ignored, really—in McMillan's committee. An attempt in 1965 to sidestep McMillan failed when the House Rules Committee failed to act favorably. Finally, in 1973, with McMillan defeated and Charles Diggs, a black from Detroit, in command of a large pro-home rule majority on the House District Committee, home rule reached the floor of the House—and passed. For District self-government advocates, it was less than a full victory. In order to win Congressman Natcher's support, Diggs had agreed to allow Congress to retain full veto review power over the D.C. budget. And there would be a substantial amount of federal property over which the new city government would not have jurisdiction. But the bill did provide for an elected mayor and city council, with authority to pass laws and draw up a budget. And the retention of budget powers by the Congress did not appear so ominous when one considered that most large central cities have been obliged, in recent years, to go hat in hand to their state legislatures for funds, often giving the legislatures the upper hand: Washington in this regard may not be so much worse off than New York or Newark or Philadelphia. Efforts in the Congress to place a commuter tax on suburbanites who work in D.C. have met with strong opposition from Maryland and Virginia congressmen. The hard line emerges, not so much from the commuters, who could deduct the taxes, dollar for dollar, from their state income taxes, but from state politicians in Maryland and Virginia whose treasuries would lose tens of millions of dollars annually. The District does, however, tax a portion of the net profits earned by professionals with offices in the city.

The District did gain some rights in the 1960s. The Twenty-Third Amendment, ratified in 1961, gave District voters the right to cast their ballots for President; turnout, however, has declined from an already abysmal 39.4 percent of voting age population in 1964 to 29.6 percent in 1976. One reason is that the District's three electoral votes inevitably go to the Democratic candidate. In 1969, the District was finally able to elect a nonvoting Delegate to Congress. This is not quite as empty a gesture as it appears, since Delegate Walter Fauntroy, elected that year and returned easily since, obtained a voting seat on the House District Committee and was able to affect the content of the home rule act. But in 1976, the House of Representatives rejected a proposed constitutional amendment to give the District at least one vote in Congress. It was the first vote on the issue in 150 years.

Amazingly, the District's gun control law, one of the toughest in the nation, was enacted without effective opposition in the Congress—which has failed for so long to pass national gun control legislation. (Even with home rule, Congress had 30 days in which to veto the district's law.) The measure froze forever the number of legal handguns in the city to those registered in 1976 and prohibited sales of new guns or transfers of registered guns.

How the District Is Governed: The Story of Walter Washington

The leading figure in moving Washington from colonial status to self-government, from the mid 1960s to this writing, was Walter Washington. WW, as he is sometimes referred to, was not the best known candidate when Lyndon Johnson was looking around for a mayor to appoint in 1967, even in Washington's black community. He had grown up in the small upstate New York city of Jamestown—scarcely the place to learn ghetto politics. He had gone to Howard and married a member of a prominent black Washington family. (Bennetta Washington became a high-ranking official in the U.S. Labor Department.) He had gone into public administration and had risen to head the National Capital Housing Authority, then Washington's public housing agency, in the 1960s. He was generally considered the District's ablest black official, but when Lyndon Johnson declined to offer him the top commissioner post in the old D.C. government, he left the city to head John Lindsay's housing department in New York.

Then, in 1967, Johnson decided to abolish the old three-commissioner system of government by executive reorganization, and WW received the call to return to Washington as mayor. Within six months he faced his most serious crisis. Martin Luther King, Jr., was murdered in Memphis, and Washington, like so many cities around the country, erupted. The looting began at 14th and U Streets, N.W., long a gathering place for unemployed young men and gaudily dressed prostitutes. Soon the main shopping streets in the old ghetto—14th, 7th Street, and H Street, N.W.—were in flames. Walter Washington was on television urging calm; the man he would soon appoint as police commissioner, Jerry Wilson, was on 14th Street. The nation was treated to the shame of seeing smoke rise within sight of the White House. But somehow Washington and his police managed to contain the riot with less bloodshed than had occurred in Newark and Detroit the year before. There were many arrests (more than 7,000), but, in line with Washington's orders, scarcely any casualties. For all the horror of the event, Walter Washington's performance was reassuring—for both black and white Washingtonians. And there was rather universal agreement that the weak commissioners, who had been reorganized out of office less than a year before, would have been far less able to cope with the situation.

It is sad to report that WW did less, in the years that followed, to rebuild the riot corridors. Even in 1976, a drive up 14th or 7th Streets revealed more boarded-up than operating stores. As a housing expert, Washington knew how HUD worked, and at least during the first years of the Nixon administration, the White House was very much interested in helping. (Richard Nixon himself appeared outside a gutted record shop called Waxey Maxie's on 14th Street, and his White House liaison to D.C. was an earnest, helpful young man named Egil Krogh, Jr., who would have been better off if he had continued to concentrate on District matters.) But it was not until 1976—eight full years after the conflagration of '68—that the first federally-sponsored housing began with a number of units on 14th Street. Richard Nixon, some cynics remembered, had promised that the rebuilding would be complete for the Bicentennial year. It was also possible to be deeply cynical about the long-term success of the project, since the years since the riots had seen large numbers of midde-class whites, like the whites who preceded them, move to other parts of the city or to the suburbs.

Another area where Walter Washington failed to make much progress was in the running of the city's basic institutions. The D.C. Jail and Lorton Reformatory, out in Fairfax County, were no better run under his administration and perhaps worse run than most of the nation's prisons. St. Elizabeth's Hospital, the District's institution for the mentally ill, lost its national accreditation. Another problem spot was Junior Village, where juvenile delinquents and homeless children were kept in the same cramped cottages in unspeakable conditions. Washington did nothing about this until after Aaron Latham wrote a series of exposés in the *Post*; then Junior Village, at least, was phased out of existence in favor of a foster home system.

Washington's greatest achievement was the reform of the police department. The man he had inherited as police commissioner had, in the mid-'60s, refused to order patrolmen to stop calling black men "boy." Washington bypassed him by appointing Patrick Murphy, later police commissioner in Detroit and New York, as public safety director. Soon after Murphy left, Jerry Wilson became police chief, and the public safety post was left vacant. Wilson seemed an unlikely choice for modernizing an old-fashioned police department. His voice was still rich with the accent of his native rural North Carolina; periodically he threatened to quit (once to play the saxophone). But by many measures Wilson did an excellent job. By the time he finally left in 1974, blacks had moved from 20 percent to nearly 50 percent of the positions in the department.* Wilson inaugurated scooter patrols to keep cops on the beat closer to citizens; he insisted on training policemen in the mores of the black majority community. He even

---

* Upward mobility for blacks in the police force was not as rapid. A Howard University study, released in 1976, showed that 84 percent of the blacks on the force were in the lower ranks. The study also revealed that two-thirds of black police believed they could trust few white officers.

ordered that women police be treated just like men, and sent out on male-female patrol teams. (The result, from early surveys: women make fewer arrests and draw their guns less often than men; they apparently find it easier to smooth over the domestic fights and street arguments that are so much of a police officer's work.) The overall result seemed to be—though it is impossible to quantify this—that Washington's relationships between policemen and the black community were superior to those in many other major cities. As long ago as 1970, Washington *Post* columnist William Raspberry was reporting that most District blacks had shifted the focus of their complaints from police brutality to the young thugs who terrorized their streets; they had come to see the police as allies rather than enemies.

But the bottom line for any police department is how well it prevents crime—or at least how well citizens perceive it is preventing crime. By this latter criterion, at least, Washington has made great strides since Richard Nixon became President in 1969. Nixon had run, of course, as a "law and order" candidate, and crime in Washington during the '60s had become a national rallying cry for conservatives; Nixon himself, not anticipating perhaps how he would contribute to it, had called Washington "the crime capital of the nation." The most famous part of the Nixon crime program, the D.C. crime bill, was aimed directly at the city; passed in 1971, it provided for no-knock searches and preventive detention. But these measures were at best only minor reasons for the reduction in Washington's crime rate. No-knock was at first seldom, then never used by Washington police (in 1974, Jerry Wilson said he wouldn't mind if Congress repealed it, and it soon did so); preventive detention was utilized quite rarely.

Nonetheless, crime fell in those years; Jerry Wilson claimed a decline in the crime rate of 50 percent in the first four Nixon years. Two reasons were generally cited. First, the police force was vastly increased in size. This allowed Wilson to recruit many more blacks, and it also allowed heavy patrolling of the streets. Second, through methadone maintenance and other programs, heroin addiction was apparently considerably reduced in the District—thus reducing the crimes committed by addicts needing a fix. By the mid-1970s the Washington area crime rate began to creep upward again, though most of the increase was in the suburbs, not the District. Maurice Cullinane, the chief appointed by Walter Washington in 1974, stated that the rise was abetted by a glut of illegal handguns and the growth of hard-core drug addiction. Others pointed to the bail and sentencing procedures of the local courts, mandated by Congress, which permitted many violent criminals (as well as some innocent defendants) to return to the streets shortly after their arrest. However serious Washington area crime may have remained—and every resident had some reason to fear it—the fact was that the District had the greatest number of policemen per capita in the nation (and probably the world) and that many other U.S. cities, to the extent that official crime figures can be given credence, were worse off.

Perhaps impressionistic evidence is as good as statistics here. In the late 1960s, cocktail party chatter seemed always to come around to the crime problem; by the 1970s, though there were horror stories here as in any other large city, talk seemed to turn to other things, like real estate prices. There were still many suburbanites who huddled in their subdivisions and would not go to downtown Washington, no matter how glittering the inducement. But the downtown streets, or at least many of them, were no longer deserted by the midevening hours. More important to the majority of District residents, streets in the black residential neighborhoods seemed safer than they had five or ten years before.

But at least one blot must be entered on the record of the District's misnamed Metropolitan Police. Wilson worked as closely with the Nixon White House on dealing with antiwar demonstrations as he did on the District crime problem; and during the May Day 1971 demonstrations District police arrested literally thousands of people on the streets—many of them not demonstrators at all, and most of the demonstrators utterly peaceful. The department's actions were nothing more than an attempt to suppress the expression of views contrary to current government policy. Suit was brought, and in 1975 U.S. District Judge Joseph C. Waddy ruled that the police illegally used truncheons, tear gas, and stampede techniques, and that they had violated the civil rights of participants in every major demonstration in the city since 1969, when Nixon took office. Altogether, Waddy ordered the government to pay $12 million to 1,200 persons arrested in the May Day demonstrations.

What else did Walter Washington accomplish? That was a little hard to say. John Nevius, the last appointed city council chairman, said: "You never see Walter out there hoeing, but the town is full of flowers." Others would stop after the first clause. Certainly back in the days when the District depended utterly on a conservative White House and a conservative Congress, Walter Washington's low key style of operating was an advantage. It made considerable sense for this appointed mayor to eschew militant rhetoric and to deal in soothing tones with the likes of John McMillan or Bud Krogh or the head of the Board of Trade. And so he never attacked the police force or fired the police chief directly; he just quietly put other people in charge. In similar ways, Washington eased aside some of the District's longtime bureaucrats, many of whom got their jobs as patronage from Southern Congressmen and were anything but sympathetic to the needs of the city's black majority. The result was a somewhat messy organization chart, and a government that no one claimed was efficient.*

But if Washington was busy soothing the conservative power sources,

---

* Washington was also burdened with a tax structure mandated by Congress. Liquor taxes in the District were for many years the lowest in the nation, and cigarette taxes among the lowest (after North Carolina and Kentucky). This might be explained by the fact that longtime House District Committee chairman John McMillan was from a tobacco-growing district, and that some of his colleagues were known to be fond of a drink. D.C. cab fares, by act of Congress, were also extremely low; and Washington remained the only city which had zone fares rather than meters. Many cab drivers found it difficult to make a living, but even in 1976 a Congressman could ride from Capitol Hill to downtown, a distance of as much as three miles, and pay a one-zone fare of $1.10.

he was also in those early years busy talking—and listening—to people in the black community. District residents began to get the feeling that they finally had a responsive government. Unfortunately, after several years in office, Washington grew less accessible. He was available to the White House, of course, and to the heads of District committees on the Hill, and he conferred regularly and frequently with leading appointees like Julian Dugas, his chief of staff, and Joseph Yeldell, human resources director. Fears that Washington made appointments on friendship rather than ability were confirmed in late 1976 when he had to remove Yeldell, who had been charged by both Washington newspapers with putting his friends and relatives and political allies of the mayor on the payroll, abusing his department's leasing authority and generally mismanaging his agency.

More important, the mayor who had almost furtively reformed much of the District government, back in a time when one could make a good case for furtiveness, seemed to be interested in changing little and in covering up what was bad. Washington appointees, by the mid-1970s, had taken to charging racism when criticized for administrative shortcomings; the irony, of course, was that it is largely helpless black constituents who were harmed by their incompetence.

Indeed, there was every sign by the mid-1970s that the District had become one of the nation's most poorly managed, personnel-heavy, and high-spending cities. Comparisons are somewhat clouded by the fact that Washington has a dual role as a city and a state, but even for basic municipal services (police, fire, and the like), studies have shown an inordinately high ratio of city workers to population. During the first six years of Walter Washington's rule, the District budget rose 127 percent—in large part because teachers' salaries rose 162 percent, policemen's 149 percent, sanitation workers' 134 percent. The District was saddled with exorbitantly high pension obligations—all unfunded, and most a fault of congressional action in earlier years. But Congress could no longer be blamed for all the problems. U.S. Comptroller General Elmer B. Staats testified that the District's records were in such disarray that they could not be audited. The maladministration was so grievous that Senate District Committee chairman Thomas F. Eagleton, who had been a staunch friend of home rule, ordered an independent accounting agency to survey the city's books and recommend an accounting system. The study found that the District government was losing millions in revenues annually because the city did not keep track of its money, its debts, or its accounts receivable. The city's water and sewer billing was so badly snarled, the study said, that receipts went down in 1975 even though rates went up. The District's computerized hospital system contained more than $100 million in unpaid bills, much of it eligible for repayment from the federal government. No funds had been set aside for almost $1.8 billion in long-term pension obligations. Washington's response: "I'm not going to bicker about the report, and I'm not going to let my office heads nitpick about it."

In other words, the days were gone when all shortcomings of the District government could be blamed on John McMillan and his ilk. The buck stopped, whether he liked it or not, on Walter Washington's desk. The mayor who indubitably accomplished much for the District began to appear more often than not as an apologist for its faults and a roadblock to improvements. Election returns suggested that judgment was shared by many of his constituents. In 1974, Washington was opposed in the city's first Democratic mayoral primary under home rule, by attorney Clifford Alexander, a former head of the federal Equal Employment Opportunity Commission. Alexander's involvement in District affairs had been slight, but he was able to hammer at figures that showed that a high percentage of Washington's top officials and police and fire officers lived outside the District line. Alexander was also able to (1) attack Washington for refusing to divulge names of campaign contributors and (2) attack Washington when he finally did so on the ground that he was taking the money of many of the city's biggest businessmen and others who had long opposed home rule.

Washington also unwisely, but characteristically, defended the city's assessor, whose seemingly random assessments were widely unpopular and were ruled illegal in a court suit brought by former council chairman Gilbert Hahn. Apparently Washington's strategy was to count on support from middle class blacks who recognized his achievements; instead, the support won by the inexperienced Alexander showed that there was an undercurrent of deep discontent with the District government. Washington won, but only by a 49,600 to 41,600 margin—just 53 percent of the vote.

Washington announced immediately that he wanted to run for mayor again in 1978, but the figures announced more eloquently that another term would be extremely difficult to achieve. "The Yeldell Affair," as it came to be known, damaged his reputation further. So the question turned to succession. Among the competitors were Sterling Tucker, former head of the local Urban League, who maneuvered himself into effectively unopposed election as city council president in 1974, and Marion Barry, the former head of PRIDE, Inc., a militant turned mainstream politician, once head of the school board and elected in 1974 to the comparative placidity of the city council from an at-large seat. Another conceivable competitor, but a much longer shot, was councilman Julius Hobson, Sr. He was the man who brought the court case that overturned control of the D.C. schools; for years he was the most headlined black militant in the city. His star seemed on the wane when he ran for Delegate in 1971 as a candidate of the Statehood Party, and won only 13 percent of the vote; and he contracted a serious illness not long thereafter. But Hobson recovered his health and his confidence, and in 1974, again on the Statehood ticket, was elected to the council; his son Julius, Jr., served on the school board.

The city's other leading politician of the 1970s was Delegate Walter Fauntroy, a minister who beat Hobson in 1971 and subsequently held the city's nonvoting seat in the House (he did have a vote, though, on the District Committee). Fauntroy had once been an aide to Martin Luther King, and he assembled a core of backers—enough to be called a machine, and to control the District delegation to the 1972 Democratic National Convention. But Fauntroy seemed not especially interested in executive office, though he was an outspoken adversary of Walter Washington.

The School Dilemma

Back in the days of segregation, whites in the suburbs used to pay tuition to send their children to D.C. schools. The District's Dunbar High School, the first black high school in the United States, was noted throughout the segregation period as an outstanding academic institution; its graduates included Benjamin O. Davis, the first black general in the Army, Charles Drew, the discoverer of blood plasma, and Edward Brooke, the first black U.S. Senator since Reconstruction. But by the 1960s the distinction that both black and white District schools once boasted was gone.

How did the schools get to be, as almost everyone admits, so bad? Part of the answer is simply socioeconomic. At the time of the *Brown* decision, the D.C. schools had their share of the metropolitan area's middle and upper income pupils of both races, children who came from homes where learning was prized and literacy instilled early. But even then, an increasing number of D.C. pupils were from poorly educated and often culturally deprived families recently migrated from the South. Because of the white flight that followed integration, a larger and larger proportion of D.C. pupils were of this "problem" group. Naturally, such schools did not attract, or hold, children from either race whose parents placed a high value on education. As a result, white parents and, since the mid-1960s, middle class blacks with children of school age are locating more and more often in the suburbs, or placing their children in private schools. One of the tragedies of the school situation is the rarity of outcry from the parents of the poor children who now populate District of Columbia schools. In the Washington Urban League's 1976 survey of the city's poor, 55 percent of those interviewed said they do not think that the D.C. public schools are providing their children with a "quality education." But 53 percent called their children's school "good," and only 9 percent listed educational opportunities for their children as their most important concern.

The situation was not helped over the years by a hostile, penny-pinching Congress. The school board, until 1967, was picked in about the most undemocratic way possible, by the United States District Court judges. Various reforms were tried. Carl Hansen, the white superintendent who implemented integration, set up a track system, supposedly grouping together students of equal ability. That was overturned in 1967 by the ruling of Judge J. Skelly Wright in a suit brought by Julius Hobson. Hobson charged, with some justification, that Hansen was putting more money into white middle class schools, and that the tracking system was an inherently unfair device that was designed to keep whites in the system. After Judge Wright's decision, tracking was abandoned and Hansen quit. More white students did leave the system, and by the 1970s the few nonblack D.C. schoolchildren—less than 5 percent of the total—were concentrated in elementary schools west of Rock Creek Park, a largely well-to-do area.

It was not clear, however, that Judge Wright's ruling improved the education received by most black children in the public schools. In 1970 Dr. Kenneth Clark, a black psychologist who had done much of the research on segregation which was cited in the original *Brown* decision, put forth a plan for a "reading year"—an all-out attempt to raise D.C. pupils' reading and arithmetic skills to national norms. Clark's plan would have graded teachers on how well their pupils did on standardized tests; after initial support from the then superintendent, Hugh Scott, it was dropped. The Washington Teachers Union, for one, vehemently opposed it. Reading scores are believed to still be well below national levels, although under the Scott regime all systematic testing was abandoned. Scott was finally let go in 1973. His successor, Barbara Sizemore, promised innovations, but succeeded more in generating conflict and crisis. Under her administration the quality of the education received by the children of the District continued to fall in almost every category tested; budgets, however, continued to rise. Sizemore was able to unite most of the greatly divided Washington community which dealt with education in one cause—getting rid of her. The school board, acknowledging the protests of parents, both black and white, at the failure of the school system to turn around its falling quality, and the teachers' organizations protests over the chaos and drift in administration, relieved her of her job in October 1975.

The schools are not, technically, Walter Washington's problem. Since the Hobson decision, they have been under the control of an elected school board. Unfortunately, much of the board's time has been devoted to internecine feuds, and it seems unable—like most school boards in the nation's central cities—to do much about the decline in quality of the schools. In the early 1970s, the school board found it had spent nearly $180 million to build 22 schools, more space than it needed for its declining enrollment. What makes the situation all the more poignant is that the District's suburbs, notably Montgomery County, have some of the best school systems in the nation—and most do not spend much more per pupil than does the District.

A Tour of the District

The proper place to begin is the Mall. This greensward, planned by L'Enfant and laid out in much its current form by the McMillan Commission, runs west from the Capitol, past the Smithsonian and to the Washington Monument, between the Jefferson Memorial and the White House, and across the Reflecting Pool to the Lincoln Memorial. Along the Potomac's Tidal Basin are the famous cherry trees, and from the Cherry Blossom Festival in early April to the late fall the entire Mall area is thronged with tourists. (Washington's tourist trade was in the doldrums following the 1968 riots, but it has now rebounded, and nearly 20 million people visit the capital every year.)

But the Mall is more than a tourist attraction; it has also been the stage for many of our great national dramas. It was here in the shadow of the Lincoln Memorial that Martin Luther King proclaimed his noble dream before 200,000 civil rights marchers in 1963, and here that the mule wagons of the Poor People's march came after his death in 1968. It was here that thousands of antiwar marchers gathered to petition their President, even as one chief executive—Richard Nixon—ringed the White House with buses and let it be known he was watching a football game. Our tripartite system of government has no natural physical focus, and so the Mall has become, as it were, the town square of the nation.

But it is also, simply, a place of great beauty, and home to much of the nation's highest culture. The National Gallery, donated by Andrew Mellon and recently expanded with a new annex, is on the north side of the Mall, along with the Museum of Natural History and the highly popular newer Museum of History and Technology. Across the Mall rise the brick turrets of the magnificent old original Smithsonian Institution Building— "the castle," as it is affectionately known, along with the 19th-century Arts and Industries Building and two sparkling new additions—the Hirshhorn Gallery and the Air and Space Museum completed in the Bicentennial year. Yet despite the new construction and a subway stop, the center of the Mall remains undefiled open green space. With the throngs of tourists, the scene is often a bustling one yet, with the Capitol looming above, also a serene one.

After seeing the Mall, many tourists venture into Washington's old downtown, north of Pennsylvania Avenue, perhaps to browse in the National Portrait Gallery or to visit Ford's Theater. The façade of Pennsylvania Avenue north of the Federal Triangle and the business section north of it must surely be a disappointment to most visitors: many of the buildings are shabby, a few even gutted, the merchandise in the stores generally undistinguished. What most tourists do not realize is that this is only one of Washington's two major downtowns; the other, north and northwest of the White House, is gleaming with new buildings and expensive shops. The old downtown has seen little office building in recent years, and its major department stores are patronized mainly by lower-income black Washingtonians.

There has been talk for years about rebuilding Pennsylvania Avenue, which L'Enfant intended to be the great parade ground for the nation. Indeed, it is the site of the inaugural parade, but the backdrop scarcely matches the majesty of the occasion. At one end of the street, as L'Enfant intended, the Capitol rises thrillingly, but any view of the White House has been blocked off since Andrew Jackson built the Treasury where it is in the 1830s. Across from the Treasury, on a key corner, is the Willard Hotel, once Washington's finest, now literally empty. President Kennedy set up a Pennsylvania Avenue redevelopment commission, with eminent members and strong backing, but nothing much has happened. One reason, in our unprofessional view, is the nature of the buildings on the Avenue itself. From the Treasury to the Capitol grounds, its south side is dominated by the Federal Triangle, those huge office buildings where government employees work or read the *Post* funnies, where they eat in government-subsidized cafeterias and shop for necessities in government-maintained stands. Few of them find much reason to leave the confines of their monumental buildings until 4:30, when they get back into their cars or take buses home. The new FBI building on the north side of the Avenue (it dwarfs the Justice Department, technically its parent, across the street) only adds to the problem; J. Edgar Hoover vetoed street-level shops, which would have added some life, as a threat to FBI security.

Private development money is scarcely available now for the north side of Pennsylvania and the nearby, aging shopping district. Rather, it is flowing—and in significant amounts—to the "new downtown" west of 16th Street. Even government agencies seem to prefer this location. The Federal Home Loan Bank Board, for example, insisted on office space west of the White House, allegedly to be near the financial community; actually most of the bank headquarters are east of the White House, around 15th Street near the Treasury. But if you walk on 15th Street, you might almost think that you are in one of those downtowns that have seen little construction since the 1920s, like Buffalo's. West of 16th is quite another matter. One after another there are dozens of glass and marble buildings (many of them look like glass and plastic), marching in tandem up Connecticut Avenue or along K and L and M and 17th Streets.

This new downtown is architecturally monotonous, because of the District's height limit. Back in 1910, when it was imposed, the 130-foot height limit was not distinctive to Washington; most cities so restricted the size of buildings, for safety reasons. Over the years, one after another dropped their height limits—but not Washington. A prime argument, albeit one not developed until after the limit was imposed, is that no building should be higher than the Capitol or the Washington Monument. But since the city is so hilly, some outlying buildings are higher; the National Cathedral, for example, can clearly be seen on the skyline, with a substantially greater elevation than anything downtown. In the 1920s, when other cities' height limits were abolished, there was not much commercial incentive for building more than 13 stories in the then sleepy capital. Today, of course, there is, and many developers would like to put in as many stories as they could. But it appears that the height limit will stay on. "Development" is a bad word in many quarters today, and the height limit—even if it produces boring buildings—also keeps the city at a reasonably human scale, avoiding the dwarfing of historic old structures that has occurred in other world capitals, including London and Paris. It also prevents downtown Washingtonians from being pummeled by the fierce winds which are created by the 50-story canyons of New York and Chicago.

Downtown Washington is spreading, as it has for years, into some of Washington's most desirable neighborhoods. DuPont Circle (named for an admiral, not the chemical family), just eight blocks northwest of the White House, was once the focus of Washington's grandest mansions. More recently it has become the center of a hip neighborhood of young, sometimes affluent, sometimes poor people, living in the 19th-century townhouses all around. Beyond the Circle, Massachusetts Avenue becomes "embassy row," where Arab and African ambassadors now work and live in Victorian mansions built by the railroad or silver millionaires who had bought themselves seats in the Senate. Embassies abound in the streets off Kalorama, just north of Massachusetts (the Chinese, for example, have moved in there); this posh neighborhood a few years ago seemed in trouble because of crime. Now, with heavy police protection, it is thriving again.

But the most famous of Washington's plush neighborhoods is Georgetown. Just west of Rock Creek, set on high ground north of the Potomac, it is a not difficult walk (or bike ride) from downtown office buildings; its mostly tiny lots comprise some of the most expensive residential real estate in the world. On the edge of Georgetown is the university of the same name, founded as a seminary in 1789 by Roman Catholic Bishop John Carroll. Today it is most famous for its Graduate School of Foreign Service. Georgetown, as we have seen, began as a river port; it was once part of Maryland and antedates Washington. In the 19th century it suffered from various depressions, and by the 1920s was one of Washington's better known slums. But its location and the native beauty of its townhouses inspired many young New Dealers. They bought houses for a song, renovated the interiors, and restored the exteriors. By no means all of Georgetown's row houses are Georgian; many more are Victorian. But today the area is an historic preservation district, and no exterior can be altered without permission. Most of the poor blacks who lived there in the '20s have long since been forced out by economics, and the narrowest 14-foot townhouse now commands an easy $80,000. Georgetown is also one of the major shopping areas of the city, and its small specialty stores attract both wealthy matrons and bearded, barefoot kids. There are disadvantages to Georgetown—parking is scarce, and it is right under the main flightpath to National Airport— but some Washingtonians would live nowhere else.

Less well known to outsiders are the other neighborhoods of northwest Washington, fanning out from Wisconsin and Connecticut Avenues west of Rock Creek Park. Cleveland Park, just a mile north of Georgetown, received its name because President Cleveland used to summer there; it is notably cooler on these hilly streets than it is on the once-swampy grounds near the White House. Cleveland Park is more spacious than Georgetown, and its rambling clapboard Victorian houses became particularly fashionable during the Kennedy Administration. Prices rose at astronomical rates, to levels that compare with Georgetown. Before he moved to New York, NBC newsman John Chancellor lived in Cleveland Park and once remarked, "You know why I like this neighborhood? It's because if I stood on my back porch and shot an arrow in the air, any rooftop it landed on would be a house containing somebody vaguely interesting to talk to." Other swank addresses include the carefully manicured colonial houses of Spring Valley, the almost rustic homes in the Palisades neighborhood just above the Potomac, the sprawling mansions of Foxhall Road where Nelson Rockefeller kept a huge mansion from 1945 until he relinquished the Vice Presidency in 1977. Although Rockefeller and his wife helped furnish the new Vice President's house on the secure grounds of the Naval Observatory, they continued to occupy their own home when in Washington. North of Cleveland Park there are neighborhoods just as pleasant, though less distinguished, built by real estate speculators in the '20s and '30s and '40s, quiet tree-lined streets and comfortable houses.

This whole area west of Rock Creek Park is heavily (97 percent) white. But it is not a typical cross-section of the white population of the metropolitan area. It contains more old people (especially retirees in the apartment houses that line Connecticut and Wisconsin Avenues), young single people (doubling up often in Georgetown or Cleveland Park houses), and more political liberals (the area west of the park went for McGovern over Nixon in 1972). There are fewer families with children and, apart from retirees, very few low-income whites. Some families do send their children to public schools, but almost always only through the elementary grades. The neighborhood schools of the Northwest have been integrated through voluntary busing of black students from east of the Park, but even so classrooms are underutilized and many of the schools here may be closed. As for junior highs and high schools, Northwest parents, black as well as white, tend either to ante up for private schools or to move to the suburbs.

Washingtonians west of the park have quite a different view of the city from those who live to the east. From the upper Northwest, it appears that almost half the city is west of Rock Creek, but in fact only 13 percent of Washington's residents live in these not particularly densely populated precincts. East of the park is mostly—but not all—black Washington, and that is the focus of our attention now. To make the transition easier, we start at the Gold Coast and Shepherd Park, the extreme northern tip of the District just before it moves into Silver Spring, Maryland. These tranquil streets—visually indistinguishable from neighborhoods west of the Park—were once a predominantly Jewish neighborhood. Now most of the pepole who live here are black and affluent; the elite of black Washington is concentrated here. But it is also an integrated neighborhood. When racial change started to accelerate, an association called Neighbors, Inc., was formed. It maintains its own real estate listings, and tries to see that whites as well as blacks continue to move in. It managed to stop the blockbusting of the '50s and early '60s, and after some troubles following the 1968 riots, housing prices in the Gold Coast and Shepherd Park began to rise almost as fast as in any of the virtually all-white parts of the District.

Just below Shepherd Park, both in social class and geographically along 16th Street, is Brightwood, a solidly middle-class, predominantly black neighborhood; this is one of those areas that changed racial composition rapidly in the 1950s. So is the Brookland neighborhood in the Northeast, along South Dakota Avenue and beyond the Catholic University, founded in 1889 and noted for its drama school, whose supporters include Helen Hayes. Both these areas are anything but slums; middle-income blacks here live on pleasant streets in comfortable houses, and property values are rising. That is not the case when one gets closer to downtown, in the Shaw and Cardozo neighborhoods west and south of Howard University, founded in 1867 and long the preeminent black college in the country. These are the places where social disintegration has moved farthest. They have the highest crime rates in the city, and elderly residents who cannot afford to move out are terrorized by teenage criminals. These are the neighborhoods where destruction was greatest in the 1968 riot, and where little has been rebuilt—partly through the inertia of the bureaucracy, partly because it probably would not pay commercially. That is true also of parts of the close-in Northeast and Southeast, where supermarkets are constantly being closed and houses sometimes abandoned. What can be done about these neighborhoods? No one in Washington has a ready answer. There is an urban homestead program now, but there is little, if any, federal money for rehabilitation or rebuilding. Despite a trickle of hardy middle-class white pioneers who see such neighborhoods eventually reviving, most residents with the means to do so have voted with their feet and moved out.

To white Washingtonians, Anacostia is almost a complete mystery, an area that they encounter only if they drive across it on one of the expressways to Prince Georges County. Yet it is a major part of the city, with 165,000 residents—nearly twice as many as the area west of Rock Creek. Almost at the banks of the Anacostia River, the land rises rapidly in large hills; this could be a pleasant residential area. Indeed, part of it is —or was; Frederick Douglass moved here from Capitol Hill in the 19th century, and there are still pleasant streets and apartments in the Hillcrest Area along Pennsylvania Avenue, S.E. But most of Anacostia is in bad shape. This is not because it is old and decaying; northern and southern Anacostia were among the last areas developed in the District, in the 1940s and even in the 1950s. Much of that development, particularly in the northern end, was intended exclusively for blacks, and virtually no whites live— or have ever lived—there. Southern Anacostia, near St. Elizabeth's, was the scene of very rapid white flight in the '50s; it, too, is now more than 95 percent black. But though Anacostia has some potential, it has also inherited many of the people—and problems—of the close-in Southeast and Northeast, and has not coped very well. Crime rates are high, and there are only three supermarkets to serve so many people. (Most Anacostians, if they can get there, shop in the suburbs.) For years, Anacostia has been neglected by the District government, and even now it seems to get less attention than the gutted slums of Shaw and Cardozo. Schools there are the most overcrowded in the District; with 22 percent of the total D.C. population, Anacostia has 35 percent of its children under 18.

Finally, we come to the areas on the margins between black and white Washington. First, there is the Southwest. Once this was Washington's worst slum, and those pictures from the 1940s which show filthy alley dwellings with the Capitol dome clearly visible behind were taken there. That juxtaposition was one of the goads that pushed Congress to pass urban renewal legislation in 1949, and Southwest was one of the first urban renewal projects. In the fashion of the time, it was a massive project, with some 500 acres subjected to the bulldozer. The assumption was that bad buildings were the cause of other social problems, and if one simply tore down the slums people would be regenerated. As it happened, the poor people of the Southwest were not so much regenerated as relocated—perhaps to their detriment and often to the detriment of the neighborhoods where they moved. In defense of the planners of the time, however, it must be noted that Southwest had such a notorious reputation that piecemeal redevelopment might have proven highly impracticable; in fact, the developers of the first renewal housing thought they were engaged in a highly risky venture.

Southwest is now a community of attractive townhouses and high-rise apartments (rising only as high, of course, as the D.C. height limit allows). The waterfront has been cleaned up with new restaurants and marinas, and the sight of sailboats and yachts gives a little color to the scene. The offices of the Environmental Protection Agency are in the area's principal shopping center. Probably Southwest's greatest attractions are its location—within easy bicycling distance of downtown or the Hill—and its integration (although there is little contact between residents of the high-priced new buildings and the low-income public housing projects almost directly adjacent).* A principal disadvantage of Southwest is something that plagues all similar projects: the number and quality of stores are totally inadequate to the area's population. The major shopping area has turned out to be a disaster, through poor management and problems of vandalism.

Quite a different kind of area—though with much the same population mix—is Capitol Hill. In the 1950s, young whites—Congressmen's aides,

---

* One of the authors of this book was a founder and the first chairman of Southwest Neighborhood Assembly, formed in the early post-renewal era as the first integrated citizens group in the history of Southwest Washington. That organization provides a forum for discussion of community issues between the high- and low-income populations, but has been relatively helpless to prevent the occasional conflicts, on the streets and in the stores, between disadvantaged black youngsters and the more affluent citizens of both races.

lawyers, journalists—began buying up old rooming houses and Victorian row houses on the Hill, with the intent and expectation that this would be another Georgetown. The area is moving, slowly but certainly, in that direction. Each year the "frontier" between the ghetto and the redeveloped area moves another block or so to the east, and real estate prices inexorably rise.

Washington thinks of itself, with some justification, as the restored row house capital of the United States. Now Georgetown and Capitol Hill seem to have other followers: the neighborhood north and east of DuPont Circle, referred to as Adams-Morgan (the names of two local schools and a community organization), north of that and just east of Rock Creek Park, Mount Pleasant, and even Shaw, one of the roughest neighborhoods in Northwest Washington. What is happening in these areas is something like what happened to Georgetown in the 1930s and Capitol Hill in the '50s and early '60s: young people buying old houses, renovating them, and slowly becoming the majority in their new communities. A side effect is the displacement, first, of the elderly rooming house population of the District and, gradually, of the poorer people, most of them black or, in Adams-Morgan, Spanish-speaking, who have lived there for some time. The liberal newcomers like to talk about their integrated neighborhoods, but while a sort of side-by-side economic integration persists during the restoration period, when the neighborhoods become fully developed only affluent, and mostly white, people can afford to live there. The success of the restorers is, ironically, inversely proportionate to their realization of their social goals.

This same conflict—between young affluent liberal people who want to live near the center of the city and the poorer people they must inevitably replace—is also apparent when one looks at the decisions currently facing the city in housing. In the spring of 1974, the District sold most of the choice, centrally located urban renewal land it still owns to investors who plan to put up mostly high-income housing. These people are surely right in their commercial calculation that there is sufficient demand to justify such projects; one need only look at real estate prices in "desirable" areas near downtown to know that. But this plan collides with the goal that governments build housing for their poor. The problem is that it is impossible, at current construction costs, to build housing which poor people can afford, and subsidies large enough to put new housing within their price range are simply not available. Washington has, rather silently, resolved this problem by deciding not to let potentially high-value land stand vacant. What is happening here, and elsewhere in the country, is an abandonment of the dream of building new, subsidized low-income housing (which never worked well anyway) and a reversion to letting the private market set prices and determine the allocation of land. The result for Washington will not be too unhappy; even for those who are displaced, it is probably easier if that happens as the result of many private decisions, spaced over a long period of time, rather than when it happens in one large transaction (as the Southwest was cleared) with the government setting the price and handling—or not handling—the problems of relocation. Washington, at least, has what many central cities do not have and desperately want: a large affluent population willing to pay premium prices to live close in town.

Metropolitan Boom Town

A chapter written on Washington 30 years ago would need to take only a cursory look at the suburbs, mentioning, perhaps, the wealthy enclaves of Chevy Chase, the faded charm of the "old town" section of Alexandria, and the residential growth in Arlington. At that time, more than two-thirds of the people in metropolitan Washington lived in the District, and an even larger percentage of them worked there. Indeed, John Gunther's *Inside U.S.A.*, which does not touch on the capital itself, mentions Alexandria only in passing and the Maryland suburbs not at all.

Today the picture is quite different. In 1974, 76 percent of the people of metropolitan Washington lived outside the District line, and more than half the working population was employed in the suburbs. These shifts, of course, are the result of booming growth; metropolitan Washington has simply—and long since—burst outside the lines set up by the First Congress.

So any portrait of the Washington metropolitan area should take into account the suburbs as well as the city. Moreover, it should view the suburbs and city as a single sociological unit. There is a temptation to do otherwise, a temptation that is especially strong in Washington because 71 percent of the people living in the central city are black and 92 percent of the people living in the suburbs are white. But the District line is not some kind of Berlin wall, and many parts of the District have more in common with the suburbs nearby than they do with other parts of the District.

This is particularly true when one considers the facts of racial residential patterns. The major movement of blacks out from the central ghettos in Washington—along the 7th, 14th, and H Street corridors—has not been westward in the District across Rock Creek Park, but northward and eastward into Prince Georges County, Maryland. Thus, only 2.5 percent of the people west of the park in 1970 were black, while at the same time only 23 percent of the residents of Seat Pleasant, Maryland, right at the easternmost extremity of the District-Maryland line, were white. Essentially, this represents the extension of the ghetto area outside the city limits—a fact with important repercussions for the Prince Georges County school system. But if neighborhoods in Washington are still basically segregated, there is also some progress toward free choice. The 1970 census showed that at least some blacks lived in all but a handful of metropolitan Washington's census tracts. This was definitely not the case in 1960 or 1950 and is still not in many metropolitan areas (like nearby Baltimore), and it is

solid evidence that at least some blacks are able to move where they choose
—if they are able to afford the prices of suburban Washington's real estate
market.

Those who say that this has not made much difference for the majority
of blacks are probably right. But it is getting harder, in an era of black pride,
to know how many blacks move to an all-black neighborhood because they
have to and how many do because they want to. It should have become
clear by now that we are not going to see salt-and-pepper residential patterns throughout any metropolitan area, including Washington.

What becomes apparent when one looks at the patterns of growth
and residential change in metropolitan Washington is that the continuing
racial segregation is in large part just a specific example of a broader and
more voluntary system: self-segregation by lifestyle. This pattern is visible
in many of our metropolitan areas—one thinks of greater Los Angeles—
but it is as marked here as anywhere, for the simple reason that Washington, by virtue of the fact that it has doubled its metropolitan population
in the last 20 years or so, is one of our newest metropolitan areas. As this
growth has taken place, people have tended to sort themselves out, not only
by their racial background, but according to whether they are single or
married, whether they are rich or middle-income or poor, whether they
have children or not, and even according to their tastes in food and entertainment and shopping.

The Washington metropolitan area can really be described as having
three basic economic zones, within which neighborhoods are increasingly
becoming segregated on a lifestyle basis. There is, first, the superaffluent zone,
which hugs both sides of the Potomac River. In the District, it includes
Georgetown and most of the area west of Rock Creek Park; in Maryland
it takes in Bethesda, Chevy Chase, some of Rockville, and the hunt-
country area of Potomac; in Virginia it includes north Arlington and the Fairfax communities of McLean and the "new town" of Reston. This is not to
say there are not superaffluent enclaves elsewhere, especially in northern
Virginia; they just tend to be concentrated in this zone. Most Senators and
Congressmen, for example, live in the areas indicated. (The number of
members of Congress who maintain only fictional or vacation residences
in their home states has been rising every year; we have almost gotten to
the point long since reached by the British, who do not require members
of Parliament to live in the district they represent.)

There is also a middle-class belt, more or less surrounding the superaffluent zone; with the rise in government salaries since 1960, this might
as well be called the affluent zone. It includes such predominantly black
neighborhoods in the District as Brookland and Brightwood and Shepherd
Park, virtually all the remaining suburbs in Montgomery County, and most
of Prince Georges County out to the edge of suburban sprawl; it also takes
in most of Arlington and Alexandria and virtually all of Fairfax County in
Virginia.

Finally, there are the poor areas, although, thanks to government salaries, incomes here tend to be higher than in poor areas in most cities. These include, naturally, the central black ghettos of Shaw and Cardozo, immediately north of Pennsylvania Avenue and the old downtown; much of close-in Northeast and Southeast Washington; the southern and northern ends of Anacostia, and the part of Prince Georges County immediately adjacent. There are also isolated black ghettos in Alexandria, Arlington, Rockville, and Fairfax Counties.

All these patterns shift when one gets far enough away from the city. Well-to-do Washingtonians still cherish the idea of living reasonably close to where they work (which may be in an office building in the suburbs as well as downtown), and they have priced close-in real estate up to phenomenal heights. That means that the white $10,000 to $15,000-a-year government employee with a wife and two children must move farther and farther out to find housing he can afford. Much housing of this type was built in Prince Georges County in the boom years of the 1960s (before sewer moratoria there clamped a lid on growth), and it is being built now in the greatest numbers in Virginia's Prince William County, south of Fairfax. So the lower-paid workers are having to commute 20 miles from new townhouses in historic Manassas or tract homes in Dale City (where each street name ends in "-dale").

High suburban growth has been accompanied, sometimes preceded, by dispersion of job sites throughout the metropolitan area. Until the Pentagon was built in the 1940s, a federal law prohibited the construction of any government buildings on the Virginia side of the Potomac. Today, of course, there are huge numbers of federal employees who work in the suburbs, in the Pentagon in Arlington, at the Census Bureau in Suitland, Maryland, the National Institutes of Health in Bethesda, or the CIA in McLean. This has come about not through some deliberate federal plan, but rather as one or another bureaucracy has decided to make the move. Which is not to say that the government does not expand in downtown, too; but the biggest growth has been in the suburbs.

This governmental trend has been reflected, as these things usually are in Washington, by the private sector. Today there are mini-downtowns in Bethesda and Silver Spring, Maryland, and in the historic old section of Alexandria, and there are two brand new high-rise cluster-downtowns within the limits of Arlington County: Crystal City, between the Pentagon and National Airport, and Rosslyn, just across the Key Bridge from Georgetown. (The main developers of Rosslyn, the Pomponio brothers, overextended themselves and went bankrupt in 1973. Nevertheless new construction continued.) These mini-downtowns are in addition to the all-American shopping centers that dot the suburban landscape, around one of which at least, Tyson's Corner in McLean, Virginia, there is considerable office development.

What ties all this metropolitan melange together is the Capital Beltway. Completed in 1965, this highway encircles the District without ever quite touching it; as is often the case, it was built with too few lanes (only four in part of northern Virginia) on the wooden-headed assumption seemingly shared by all highway engineers that a new limited-access highway will attract only as much traffic as the narrow streets it parallels. The Beltway has become a suburb-to-suburb commuting road, with attendant traffic jams; indeed, it is the main limited-access highway in the Washington area, since anti-expressway activists have effectively prevented the building of designed interstate routes through the District.

What is the future for metropolitan growth in the Washington area? A clue is provided by Royce Hanson, chairman of the Montgomery County Planning Board, who told us: "Civilization follows the sewers." Today the sewers really are the key to where growth will occur. In low-lying Prince Georges County, sewer capacity is limited, and a state-imposed moratorium on building permits was imposed before the building of giant new sewer systems. Montgomery County, on higher land above the fall line, still has some sewer capacity left. In Virginia, the Fairfax County Board of Supervisors, controlled by Democrats who campaigned on an antigrowth platform, tried to stop or at least modulate growth by allocating sewer permits slowly; later their actions were declared invalid in state courts, and the more growth-minded Republicans won control in the 1975 election. Planned communities like Reston, Virginia, and Columbia, Maryland, continued to grow toward their large population projections, but in general subdivision expansion, there was considerably less than in the frantic '60s.

Royce Hanson believes that a metropolitan area "no-growth policy is stupid"; the question as he sees it is how will growth be managed. The children of the postwar baby boom are forming families, the trend is for a larger number of smaller households (single people living alone, for instance, instead of with relatives). These trends, national in scope, are accentuated in Washington.

One factor that may alter that future is Metro—the Washington Metropolitan Area Transit subway. First suggested by a study in 1959, begun ten years later, the first section of the Metro, connecting Rhode Island Avenue N.E. and Connecticut and L, N.W. in downtown Washington, finally went into service March 27 of the Bicentennial year of 1976. Washingtonians and tourists poured into the subway at triple advance estimates. All this was far behind schedule however; indeed, the first section was originally supposed to open in 1972, and in the meantime the cost of the project—ballyhooed as the biggest public works project in the history of man—had ballooned far past the original estimate of $2.5 billion to the $5 billion level. When completed, which was not expected to happen until 1981 at the earliest, the Metro was to consist of 87 well designed stations on 10 fixed-rail lines radiating out from downtown Washington. Like San Francisco's BART, it would not entirely be a subway; out in the suburbs, most of the lines would be at ground level.

Land prices around Metro station sites have increased vastly, and already some development at these locations has taken place: the Van Ness Centre office-and-apartment complex in northwest Washington and the Friendship Heights area just two stops beyond on the District-Montgomery County line. But on the whole, there has been surprisingly little planning for Metro, and no one is sure just what its effect will be. Even mass transit optimists do not see it replacing the automobile as the basic means of transportation in metropolitan Washington. The Metro is designed to transport people in and out of downtown Washington, but its radial lines will not serve particularly well the needs of the majority of suburban Washingtonians who work in other suburbs. There are only seven Metro stations planned, for example, for the 500,000-plus people who live in Fairfax County, and it does not take much imagination to see that most of them are still going to be cruising the Beltway even when those stations are in service. The Metro may enable some people to live far out in the country —driving in to the stations and then riding to their jobs—but most of its benefits will likely be conferred on the District itself and close-in suburbs like Arlington. There it will probably relieve some traffic congestion, increase most property values, and keep downtown Washington thoroughly vital.

A Note on Metro Government

One would think that the Washington metropolitan area, situated as it is in two states and a state-equivalent governed ultimately by Congress, would be a nightmare for those who seek regional cooperation. Yet Washington has the largest council of governments in the country, with a budget of $5.5 million and 150 employees—and some significant achievements to its credit. The Washington Metropolitan Council of Governments was able, for instance, to secure the approval of the several local governments for a "fair share" housing plan—that is, an allocation, metro-area wide, of low-income federally assisted housing. Some jurisdictions—the District, Prince Georges County, Alexandria—felt that they were bearing too much of the public housing burden. Other, wealthier areas—Montgomery and Fairfax Counties—found that local housing costs were rising above what the counties' own employees could afford. After two years of conferences and computer programs, all the member governments reached agreement. The timing was fortunate; when HUD stopped all subsidized housing programs in January 1973, it decided that the adoption of the fair share formula by Washington communities was a preexisting commitment which would still be honored.

Of course such an agreement could not have been reached if the area governments did not want it. In the words of Walter Scheiber, WMCOG's executive director, what was finally adopted "happened by coincidence to accord with positions they were ready to take." But COG was able to swing some clout in another area. The Virginia Highway Department dearly wanted to build I-66 in from the Beltway to the Potomac. But WMCOG, after impassioned debate, voted in 1974 not to put it on the official plan. That might not seem important, except that WMCOG is the designated planning agency for transportation for the Washington metropolitan area. (In the closing days of the Ford administration, however, tentative approval was given to a drastically scaled-down version of I-66.)

One reason Scheiber and others give for the fact that Washington area jurisdictions have been able to work amicably together, despite their great racial and economic differences, is that the suburban governments are comparatively large and bureaucratically sophisticated. In many metropolitan areas, there are literally hundreds of local governments and special districts; in the Washington metropolitan area, as defined by the Census, there are only the seven counties, five incorporated cities, and the District. This makes things comprehensible, not just for the officials but for the public as well. When Montgomery citizens were discontented with a development-happy county council in the 1960s, they were able to throw them out in the next election; the same thing happened in Fairfax not long after, with the new group itself losing control in 1975. The metropolitan newspapers, both the *Post* and the *Star-News*, are able to assign reporters full time to each suburban jurisdiction, and readers can keep up on affairs in their home area in ways that a reader of The New York *Times* living in White Plains or Massapequa cannot.

So despite the slums of Shaw and Cardozo, despite the visual pollution of strip highways like Rockville Pike in Maryland and Jefferson Davis Highway in Virginia, despite the often unplanned growth and the remaining crime and the prolonged Metro construction, Washington, as a city and a metropolitan area, was working tolerably well by the mid-1970s. In the District, home rule—despite its gross inefficiencies—was at least providing representative government. In the suburbs, people were showing a willingness to curb the excesses of growth, even as they continued to enjoy its benefits. Overall, Washington, richer, better educated, and blacker than the nation as a whole, remained a boom town—with no letup in sight. And in the process of growth, Washington, like the federal government which is responsible for its existence, had become more diversified, more sophisticated, more tolerant—beginning, for the first time really, to live up to the Founding Fathers' dreams.

MARYLAND

THE SUPERIMPOSED CIVILIZATIONS

IT'S DIFFICULT to put all of Maryland into one portrait. What does the crowded port city of Baltimore, 46 percent of whose residents are black, have in common with the Washington, D. C., suburbs of Montgomery County, which have the highest family incomes in the nation? What do the fishermen of the somnolent Eastern Shore have in common with the residents of mountain-locked Cumberland? What do the people who live in the almost continuous string of middle class suburbs from Washington to Baltimore, in Prince Georges and Anne Arundel and Baltimore Counties, have in common with the others?

Not very much, except that they all live within the convoluted boundaries of the state of Maryland. The lines were drawn in the days when water was the main mode of transportation, and so the state spans Chesapeake Bay and includes much of the Potomac River valley. (Its northern boundary is the famous Mason-Dixon line, the traditional boundary between slave and free territory.) It is a state with Southern ancestry—just about the northernmost slave state before the Civil War—inhabited today mainly by Yankees. It was founded, as a colony, as a refuge for Catholics; it has become mainly Protestant; yet it has one of the largest Jewish percentages of any state (4.8 percent). Some of its residents live in extreme poverty, in the Baltimore ghetto or rural backwaters. But there is great wealth in Maryland; in 1970, for instance, it ranked fifth among the 50 in median family income. Economically, the state is booming—perhaps too much, as we will see, for its own good.

Politically, this is a state with profound conservative instincts, yet it regularly elects distinguished liberals to high office. There is insularity here, isolation from what is current; yet Maryland has profited from the growth of the federal government more than any other state. It is one of the smallest states in area (ranking 42nd in this department), yet the drive from its easternmost point, Ocean City on the Atlantic, to its westernmost, in Garrett County high in the Appalachians, is at least 350 miles.

One of Maryland's most distinguished citizens, H. L. Mencken, once called Maryland the most average of states—average in the sense that certain vital statistics were close to the national average. Mencken's list included the percentage of native-born whites, the rate of illiteracy, the salaries of high school teachers, the rate of murder, the date of the first killing frost, the number of people converted annually at religious revivals, and, presciently, "the percentage of its lawyers sent to prison yearly for felony." The list could easily be updated, and items added. In the last three presidential elections, for example, Maryland's percentage for each major candidate came within two percent of the national average—closer than any other state's. Yet Maryland, as even our brief survey indicates, is not simply the United States writ small. It is too distinctive in its diversity, too unusual in its recent growth and development.

The best way to understand Maryland as it is today is to focus on that process of growth. For what has been happening in the last 35 years is that a new Maryland has sprouted up in what once was countryside, right next to the old one which Mencken alternately loathed and loved. The magnitude of the process is most easily demonstrated by looking at the growth in population between 1940 and 1970. In those 30 years, Maryland more than doubled in size, but the older, earlier populated parts of the state, the city of Baltimore* and the rural counties of the Eastern shore and the mountains, grew scarcely at all.

Thus in 1940, almost half the people in Maryland lived in Baltimore, with another third in rural counties; only 22 percent of the state's population was in the suburbs. By 1970, Maryland had become a predominantly suburban state, with 54 percent of its population in four suburban counties. The suburbanites had come to outnumber Baltimore City and the rural counties put together:

Area	1940 population	1970 population	Change
Maryland	1,281,244	3,922,399	+2,101,155 (+115%)
Baltimore City	859,100	905,759	+ 46,659 (+ 5%)
Baltimore suburbs	224,200	918,616	+ 694,416 (+310%)
Washington suburbs	173,402	1,183,376	+1,009,974 (+582%)
Rural remainder	564,542	914,648	+ 350,106 (+ 62%)

* The city of Baltimore is not part of any county, and is often referred to as Baltimore City, to distinguish it from entirely suburban Baltimore County. It was Baltimore County, of course, that Spiro Agnew once served as County Executive.

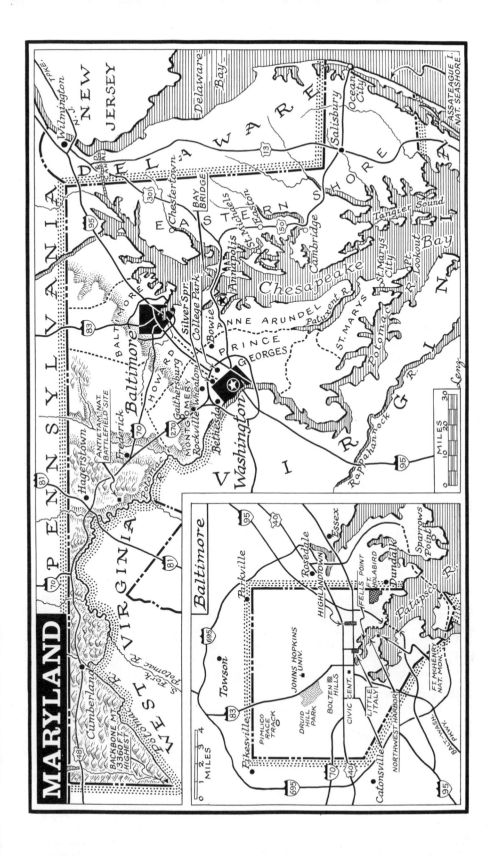

For the first half of the 1970s, population growth in the state slowed to 4.4 percent. The growth in the Washington suburbs dropped to 4.9 percent. The big suburbs had become "saturated and expensive," Census officials said; Prince Georges County, under court-ordered desegregation and plagued by sewer problems, actually lost population. From 1970 to 1975 the rural areas of the state grew rapidly. New industry was spreading around the state, and city workers were willing to travel farther to their jobs. Southern Maryland—Calvert, Charles, and St. Marys counties—grew by 16.8 percent and Western Maryland by 5.2 percent.

But in those 30 years of heavy growth up to 1970, a new suburban Maryland, almost precisely the size of the old Maryland, was superimposed on the hilly, rolling country between the Potomac and Chesapeake Bay.

Take, for a moment, a broader perspective. In the East Coast megalopolis, in the last 35 years, the fastest-growing metropolitan areas have been Washington and Baltimore. More than half of Washington's suburban growth and all of Baltimore's have taken place within the boundaries of Maryland. Back in the days before World War II this was a sleepy, content state that did not realize it was in the path of the biggest population shifts in the megalopolitan seaboard.

One result for this rapid growth is that many of the residents of the New Maryland have no ties to the Old. They have moved here from other states, and in many cases they have done so only because most of the Washington suburbs happen to be in Maryland. In 1970 fully 20 percent of Maryland's suburbanites had moved into the state within the preceding five years —an in-migration as heavy as in boom states like Florida and Arizona. By way of comparision, only 5 percent of Baltimore residents and 11 percent of those in the rest of the state had migrated to Maryland within the last five years.

And this is not the only contrast between the New and the Old Maryland. Money is another. In 1970 again (and the percentage obviously has risen sharply since), 38 percent of the suburban families had incomes over $15,000—a level reached then by only 17 percent of those in Baltimore and 19 percent in the rest of the state. And while 13 percent of the families in Baltimore and 9 percent of those in the nonsuburban counties had incomes under $3,000 in that year, only 4 percent of the suburban families were so poor.

Few states have such a contrast between the new and the old, between affluence and comparative poverty. So when one seeks to know how Maryland came to be what it is, one must really pursue two lines of inquiry: the traditional history of Maryland, from its colonial founding to the growth of Baltimore as a major port and manufacturing center; and the post-World War II explosive growth of the New Maryland.

A Thumbnail Sketch of Maryland History

Before looking at the gleaming New Maryland, let us turn back to the history of this strangely shaped state. The traditional histories tell the story basically in three episodes—the initial settlement, the struggle against the British, and the Civil War—and of these the most singular story is the one of settlement. It began in 1619, when George Calvert became the principal secretary of state to King James I. Five years later Calvert converted to Catholicism, a religion which disqualified him from public office; the King made him an Irish peer (Baron Baltimore) to keep him on the Privy Council. King James died the next year, but his son Charles I remembered his affection for Calvert, and in 1632 he granted Cecil, the second Lord Baltimore, a charter to what is now called the Delmarva peninsula and the land west of the Chesapeake Bay from the Potomac River north to the 40th parallel.* Baltimore tactfully left the name of the colony blank on the document, and King Charles wrote in "Maryland," in honor of his queen.

The next year Baltimore's brother, Leonard Calvert, led an expedition to Maryland and established St. Marys as its first capital. Maryland patriots like to remember that this was the first colony to allow freedom of religion. But that fact seems to have been a result more of prudence than of any affection for the principle of toleration: the Catholic Calverts, after all, held the land at the sufferance of a Protestant King and Parliament, and in other respects the Calverts ran the colony as autocratically as they could. Curiously, Catholics were apparently never a majority among the settlers, and the Lord Baltimore after whom Maryland's chief city is named, never crossed the Atlantic.

Tobacco was the great crop of colonial Maryland, but by the time of the Revolution much of the Tidewater soil had been exhausted, some of the rivers were silting up, and Maryland was not producing enough to pay for its imports. Though the state had many rich landholders—notably Charles Carroll of Carrollton, much of whose lands are today part of Washington —it seems also to have supported the Revolution enthusiastically, and as early as 1810 it abolished property qualifications for voting. (But not until 1826 did the state, which by 1969 had a Jewish governor, enfranchise Jews.) Maryland was the only one of the original states invaded by the British in the War of 1812; and of course every schoolboy knows that Francis Scott Key wrote *The Star-Spangled Banner* when the British were repulsed from Baltimore by the guns of Fort McHenry in 1814.

Maryland was a slave state, and although it was never dominated by big plantations—there were almost as many free Negroes counted in the 1860 census as slaves—there was a division of sympathies during the Civil War. If Maryland had seceded, of course Washington would have been cut off

---

* Maryland's boundaries were later whittled back several times in disputes with its neighbors.

from the rest of the Union; Abraham Lincoln accordingly placed the state under military control. It was the scene of much bloody fighting, including the Battle of Antietam in 1862; and it was across Maryland's fertile uplands that Lee's troops marched the next year to their great defeat at Gettysburg. It was on one of these marches through the town of Frederick that the Confederate troops were supposed to have encountered Barbara Fritchie, still flying the Stars and Stripes from her window. "'Shoot if you must this old gray head,'" Whittier's poem ran, "'but spare your country's flag,' she said." The story is probably apocryphal (even Whittier would not attest its authenticity), but it is an illustration of the strong feelings which ran through Maryland during the war.

But the real story of Maryland in the 19th century is an economic one. With Chesapeake Bay and Baltimore far closer to the expanding west than other northeastern ports, Maryland was a natural avenue for commerce. The first federally financed highway, the National Road, was completed from Baltimore to Wheeling and the Ohio River in 1818. Maryland, however, lagged behind in canals; New York state's Erie Canal was completed before the Chesapeake and Ohio Canal was even begun in Washington. It was in railroads that the state excelled. In 1830, the first stretch of the Baltimore & Ohio was built—the first railroad in the country. By 1842 the B&O reached Cumberland, by 1852 Wheeling, and before the Civil War Baltimore was connected by rail to Cincinnati and St. Louis.

The B&O did not provide Baltimore with enough of a head start to enable it to overtake New York or Philadelphia commercially; but the rails did insure that the city would be one of the nation's major ports and commercial centers, a status it retains today. Indeed, during the later 1800s, Baltimore accounted for most of the growth in what was otherwise a fairly moribund state; by 1890, half of all Marylanders lived in Baltimore or just outside its boundaries. Fertilizer, refined sugar, and spices are just three of the commodities on which Baltimore's 19th-century growth was based. Like the other northeastern port cities, it never was dependent on a single industry.

This growth of a large metropolis in an otherwise rural state made for an unusually heterogeneous mix. The rural areas themselves were always divided, as Senator Charles Mathias, one of the state's leading amateur historians, explained to us, by the fall line, which passes through Washington and up past Baltimore. East of the fall line, on the Chesapeake Bay, one found an English corn culture, generally Southern in its sympathies and Democratic in its politics. West of the fall line, almost as an extension of the Pennsylvania Dutch region, was a German wheat culture, sympathetic to the North in the Civil War and for years after Republican. Add to that the watermen of the eastern shore and the immigrants of Baltimore, where the Irish and Polish tended to vote Democratic and the Italians and blacks Republican, and one had—long before anyone dreamed of the suburban New Maryland—as heterogeneous a state as any.

Politically, this produced strange consequences. Maryland voted in a "white supremacy" ticket in 1903, but less than 10 years later a man named Isaac Lobe Straus controlled the House of Delegates and pushed through a public service commission and a child labor law. Maryland segregated its schoolchildren by race, but unlike its Southern neighbors it opposed Prohibition, it licensed race tracks, and even—until the 1960s—allowed slot machines in a few of its counties. Traditionally in Maryland, politics has not had much of an ideological cast; it was too obviously necessary to compromise constantly to accommodate all the different types of people who found themselves within the boundaries of the same state. Such a climate of accommodation can produce civilized, sensible government. But it can also lead to an easygoing tolerance of political shenanigans, given the right set of circumstances. By all accounts, the pre-World War II Old Maryland had a basically honest, if cautious, political system—in vivid contrast to some of its Middle Atlantic neighbors. But with the explosive growth of the New Maryland, the old system was placed under strains it could not withstand, and the state's traditional tolerance became almost a blindness to corruption, as we shall shortly see.

The New Maryland and Its Political Morals

A good place to look for the New Maryland is on the boundary of the District of Columbia, at the corner of Western Avenue and Wisconsin Avenue in Montgomery County. Below the 25-story high-rise apartments, next to shops like Saks and Lord & Taylor, directly across the street from a new Neiman-Marcus, is a complex of office buildings. Those steel and glass, modernistic buildings set in from the road are the headquarters of GEICO, the Government Employees Insurance Company. This firm was set up several decades ago to provide auto and fire insurance to government employees, in the days when a civil servant was expected to live on a modest salary, indeed sometimes in a Washington boarding house, in return for the security his or her job offered. GEICO started on an appropriately modest level. But today it is a major insurer, and though it no longer limits its business to government employees, its size is a reflection of theirs.* Likewise, Maryland's population and wealth are related to the federal government.

One can see why by examining some basic facts. The number of federal employees in the Washington metropolitan area has increased by more than 40 percent since the Kennedy administration took office; interestingly enough, despite Richard Nixon's conservative policies, federal employment rose at the fastest rate during his administration. And federal salaries have been rising even faster. Even if an employee has stayed at the same level in

---

* Like the federal government, GEICO has found that growth has its problems. After operating at a profit for 32 years, GEICO lost $75 million in 1975; its management has since tried to tighten its policy requirements and reduce the number of customers.

the federal service, his salary has more than doubled since 1961. That is more than enough to keep up with inflation, and it is a rate which exceeds that in many private industries.

What this has meant for Maryland is that its rapid growth has consisted almost entirely of affluent people. There were more federal employees in the state than in any other save California and New York in 1970, and almost twice as many as live in the District of Columbia. Most, of course, are concentrated in Montgomery and Prince Georges Counties, adjacent to Washington—and their salaries have helped to make Montgomery the nation's richest county. But there is plenty of federal employment in the Baltimore area, too; for one thing, the Social Security Administration's huge headquarters is just outside the city limits in Baltimore County. Even Maryland's smaller counties have been the beneficiary of federal largesse: the Army's Aberdeen Proving Ground is the largest employer in Harford County, east of Baltimore, and in long-isolated St. Marys County, south of Annapolis, the largest civilian employer by far is the Patuxent Naval Air Station. More and more federal agencies—the National Institutes of Health, the Census Bureau, NASA—have major facilities in Maryland, and of course Maryland benefits indirectly from increased federal employment in the District.

These infusions of federal dollars over the last three decades have made old Maryland one of our richest states. In per capita income, it ranked 17th in the country in 1950 but 12th in 1973. Correspondingly, education levels and just about every social indicator have been rising here. For most megalopolitan states, in-migration has meant the creation of new problems as undereducated, unskilled blacks from the lowlands of the Carolinas and whites from the hills of the Appalachians poured into their cities. There has been similar migration into Baltimore. But, to a large extent, Maryland has been getting as in-migrants the cream of the crop: highly educated, well-to-do, upwardly mobile people from all over the country who come to work for the government or for some private enterprise which depends on the government.

One might expect that the immigrants with that high socioeconomic profile would have propelled Maryland toward an era of good government and clean politics. Before the postwar boom began, Maryland was ruled by courthouse cliques in the counties and urban bosses in Baltimore—and ruled, if you can believe present day witnesses' memories, reasonably well, if not in the style some civics books would lead one to desire. But the existence of the New Maryland seems, if anything, to have lowered the political tone of the state. As in New Jersey, that other predominantly suburban state farther north in the megalopolitan chain, Maryland has not seen a group of crusading good government advocates take over its parties or its politics. Quite the contrary. Its former governor (and later our Vice President) pleaded guilty to not paying income taxes on payoffs; one of its leading county executives was sentenced to jail on similar charges; and in

1976 its governor and his close political and personal associates were tried on bribery indictments. Maryland is fast winning the distinction of being, next to New Jersey, the most corrupt state in the nation.

To the extent the reputation is deserved, the stench has arisen, not from Baltimore City or the small counties, but from the New Maryland of the suburbs. Lincoln Steffens said that corruption will be found where local government has the power to confer lucrative benefits on certain people. In Steffens' time, just after the turn of the century, this kind of corrupt money was most plentiful in the big cities, where a streetcar franchise, sewer or paving contracts, or the construction of a public building could make someone a multimillionaire. In Maryland, since World War II, practically all of that kind of money has been in the suburbs. Baltimore has long since been built up; the rural counties are small potatoes by comparison. As the rolling farmland and swamps of Montgomery and Prince Georges and Anne Arundel and Baltimore Counties have been transformed into shopping centers and subdivisions and office buildings, some people have become very rich—and not all of them by means which are honest or ethical. "I'm a farmer," said Senator Charles "Mac" Mathias, whose roots are deep in Frederick County, "and I know that when you turn up the soil, you're bound to get weeds."

It is not entirely unfitting, then, that Maryland's best known felon, Spiro T. Agnew, got his political start, after a stint in the Loch Raven Kiwanis, as a member of the Baltimore County Board of Zoning Appeals. Zoning decisions can mean big money to developers—a fact which Agnew must have soon learned. From that time on, his rise in politics was a series of happy accidents: a feud among the Democrats helped him win the post of county executive in 1962; a disastrous Democratic primary produced an anti-civil rights candidate so that Agnew won liberal and black support for governor in 1966; a falling out with Nelson Rockefeller and Agnew's stern denunciation of black rioters made him acceptable to Strom Thurmond and thus to Richard Nixon as a vice presidential nominee in 1968. Through all this rapid rise, Agnew never had time to make much money, and as he rose politically he kept complaining to friends that he could not afford the life style to which he thought he was entitled. As it happened, some of these friends were contractors who did much of their business with Baltimore County and the state of Maryland. Some were architects and engineers, who are chosen for public contracts without competitive bidding, because evaluation of their ability is supposed to involve unquantifiable factors. So some of these men began giving kickbacks—percentages of their public contracts—back to the county executive-governor-Vice President. Even as he was making speeches sternly denouncing supposedly lawless peace demonstrators, Spiro Agnew was on the take.

It would take a battery of psychiatrists to give us clues to how Agnew justified these arrangements in his mind, although his farewell speech to the nation after he pleaded guilty—when he referred to the "post-Watergate morality"—left little doubt that he felt he had not done much, if anything, wrong. What is easier to speculate about is the reactions Agnew inspired in his constituents. His smooth, crisp manner (his suit pants always had perfect creases) led people to think he was efficient and knowledgeable; his mouthing of at first liberal and then conservative watchwords convinced people as diverse as Montgomery County liberals and East Baltimore hardhats and Eastern Shore farmers that he was on their side. To the extent that Agnew had an ideology, it seems to have been a firm belief in the rectitude of the suburban way of life, a credo that affluence came to those who deserved it and that others (the black, the young) should be allowed to do nothing to challenge the authority of their betters or to disturb their suburban tranquillity.

After his forced resignation as Vice President, Agnew moved into one of the newest Maryland suburbs, Crofton, about equidistant from Baltimore, Washington, and Annapolis. Apparently he saw little of his old Maryland friends, and his trips to old haunts seemed limited to the Italian restaurants he favors in Baltimore. Crofton is an appropriate place to come to rest for this rootless man, who moved from Italian to Jewish to Waspy neighborhoods in his youth and young manhood, and never seemed to keep close ties in any of them. (Most of his vice presidential years he lived in a Washington hotel.) Crofton is a place without tradition, an almost entirely new town with colonial single-family houses, modernistic low-rise apartment complexes, and small office buildings. About the only thing people here seem to have in common is a fair amount of money and a desire to live in a bland, quiet environment.

It would be unfair to argue that Spiro Agnew is typical of Maryland suburbanites or of Maryland suburban politicians. Yet he is not the only politician who has gotten into trouble. His successor as Baltimore County executive, Democrat Dale Anderson, was convicted in 1974 on kickback charges and expelled from office; it was Anderson that the federal prosecutors were going after when they found evidence that Agnew was a crook. Another suburban Baltimore figure, Anne Arundel County Executive (and former sheriff) Joseph Alton served part of an 18-month prison sentence after pleading guilty to federal charges of obstructing interstate commerce in connection with an alleged scheme to extract kickback payments from consultants doing business with the county while he was executive. In the 1960s, several Prince Georges County officeholders went to jail, and scandal has even touched wealthy Montgomery County.

Eventually a sitting governor came under the prosecutors' scrutiny, and late in 1975 Governor Marvin Mandel and five businessmen were indicted by a federal grand jury on charges that they had participated in a "corrupt relationship" designed to defraud the citizens of the state, its government agencies, and the Maryland General Assembly.

When the trial commenced in autumn 1976, the prosecution was able to produce witnesses who described a long chain of gifts—jewelry, free vacations, insurance premiums, and business interests—which Mandel received from his business friends, allegedly in return for help in manipulating the state legislature and state agencies to increase the value of the Marlboro Race Track, which Mandel's friends secretly owned. The defense argument was that the gifts were simply those between friends, and had not influenced Mandel in his official actions.

Shortly after the defense had begun to present its witnesses in rebuttal of the prosecution charges, two incidents of attempted tampering with the jury were reported. News of the tampering effort reached the belatedly sequestered jury, and the judge felt compelled to declare a mistrial, 13 weeks after the trial had begun. The prosecutors immediately announced they would seek a new trial, but when—and if—that would occur was difficult to discern. What was clear was that the personal reputation and political standing of Marvin Mandel had been seriously damaged.

Is Maryland, for some reason, peculiarly corrupt? Maryland politicians bridle at the suggestion. Senator Mathias, looking back on hundreds of years of history, told us there was nothing typically Maryland in what corruption had been unearthed. Even the most cynical observers are inclined to say that the only difference between Maryland and most other states is that more of the rascals have been caught here lately.

There is something to this. Maryland has had a fine tradition of United States Attorneys, going back to Joseph Tydings, who served from 1961 to 1964. Tydings successfully prosecuted a Congressman who was also a fellow Democrat, and his successor, Stephen Sachs, continued the tradition by making out a bribery case against former Democratic Senator Daniel Brewster. (Brewster's conviction was reversed on appeal in 1974.) Sachs stayed in office two years during the Nixon Administration, only to be replaced by George Beall, who prosecuted the Agnew case. And Beall did not get his job solely through political pull, although his brother was the state's junior Senator; Mathias, himself Maryland's shining example of political rectitude, was his chief sponsor. Beall handled the Vice President's case with tact and determination. His office, like those of his predecessors, went after corruption in a systematic way, subpoenaing hundreds of records of firms that do business with the government, combing through them, and finding telltale cash, an almost sure sign that someone is on the take.

If every state had federal prosecutors like Beall or Sachs or Herbert Stern and Frederick Lacey in New Jersey, we might be hearing more about corruption elsewhere. But granting that, we still believe that the political climate in Maryland is unusually hospitable to corruption. This is not the only state to experience vast suburban expansion in the last quarter century. California has grown more rapidly for many of those years, yet one finds virtually no evidence of a prevailing practice of paying off public officials there as there has been in Maryland. The same might be said of Delaware or Minnesota or Colorado or Michigan. Bribes, payoffs, and kickbacks are not peculialr to Maryland, but they have become accepted as a way of life by many government officials and businessmen.

How is such a climate created? To answer that question would require a book in itself. But one answer suggests itself: this is a state where the public does not demand clean government. Voter participation is low, and the new Marylanders, the suburbanites who have moved in often from other states or regions, show relatively little interest in state or local government. (The same phenomenon is apparent in New Jersey.) There is an assumption that a few political leaders (bosses to their enemies) will make most major political and governmental decisions, and because just about everyone believes this, it happens. In the old rural Maryland, officeholders were known to everyone in the community and were—and still are—held to fairly high standards. In Baltimore, there are still networks of ward politicians who keep closely in touch with their constituents, and relatively little corruption (and virtually no major organized crime) in this old Maryland city. But in the new suburban Maryland, and in the state as a whole which it now dominates, officeholders are distant folk, of whom most constituents know nothing or only what they see on television. For all their education and brains and money, the New Marylanders have not done a very good job of creating a civic environment. For the most part, they have just defaulted, and watched, with mild disapproval, as one after another of their leaders is exposed as a crook.

No easy solution is in sight. The Republican Party, despite the easy 1974 reelection victory of Senator Mathias, is in disarray. The fallout of the Mandel indictment threatened the Democratic party's regular faction, and influence could shift to the political machine dominated by State Senator Steny H. Hoyer and Peter F. O'Malley, a Prince Georges County lawyer. In their affluent, comfortable subdivisions, the new Marylanders are willing to throw out proven crooks, as they voted out Dale Anderson's Baltimore County Machine in 1974; but there is little zeal here or viligance against it happening again.

State Politics and Marvin Mandel

Where the old Maryland and the new Maryland come together is the old State House in Annapolis. In this oldest of state capitols still in use, with its mellowed brick walls, its marble columns and paintings of Revolutionary heroes, gather legislators, most of them now from the new suburbs, and statewide officials, who depend for their votes primarily on suburban voters. Running the show in the mid-1970s—"the name of the game is control," his press secretary said—was Governor Marvin Mandel. He was from the old Maryland, specifically the Jewish northwest side of Baltimore. He was first elected to the legislature in 1952, and became speaker in 1963. When Spiro Agnew resigned the governorship to become Vice President, the Maryland constitution provided that the legislature elect the new governor. (Now there is a lieutenant governor, elected on a slate with the governor.) Marvin Mandel had the votes, as he usually did, and so became the state's chief executive.

Surely Mandel never expected to reach that office. Though he speaks well, with a thick Baltimore accent, he is diminutive in stature and scarcely a charismatic person; from his years as a legislator, and a very successful one, he had something of an image as a wheeler-dealer. But even if he never could have been elected on his own, once in office Mandel proved to be unbeatable. Sargent Shriver, before his 1972 vice presidential nomination, was thinking about running for governor in 1970. Before Shriver could get organized, Mandel had put on a fundraiser, netting $600,000. (Maryland law provides that no one can contribute more than a total of $250 to candidates for governor; Mandel rounded up the obvious contributors and got them to donate their $250 to him.) Then Mandel put on a media blitz, long before the campaign. The Shriver campaign quietly folded.

Equally striking to his political skill was Marvin Mandel's success at the business of government. In his first year, he submitted more than 50 bills to the legislature; all but two passed. In 1970, as Shriver was pondering the race, Mandel submitted another 50-plus bills; again, all but two passed. And they were not minor housekeeping items. Among the reforms was a long-overdue reorganization of the state government, which had previously consisted of a hopeless hodgepodge of 247 agencies. They were consolidated into 11 cabinet-level departments, each with a secretary appointed by the governor.*

Mandel boasted that Maryland was the first state to have a unified department of transportation, with authority over highways, mass transit, Baltimore-Washington Airport, and the port of Baltimore. The state also took on the responsibility for all public school construction in the state—a substantial job in fast-growing Maryland, but one which allowed county property taxes to be lowered. (It helps that Maryland has one of the best bond ratings in the country, and consequently can undertake massive financing of such improvements.)

After beating Agnew protegé C. Stanley Blair in 1970, Mandel slowed down—but only a little. In 1972 he persuaded the legislature to pass a handgun control law, an act of no little political courage in a state whose senior Senator, Joseph Tydings had been defeated in large part because of the gun issue less than two years before. In 1973, Mandel successfully pushed through an auto insurance reform bill, which set up the first state-owned insurance company, to provide policies to those who could not obtain them from private companies. In 1974, he got at least a modified state land use law through the legislature.

In all these cases, there was strong opposition from powerful lobbies: the gun enthusiasts, the insurance companies, the land developers. But in all three cases Mandel and his lobbyists were at least in large part the winners. Indeed, Mandel's command over the legislature was such as to eclipse the power of the traditional lobbies—the insurance companies and

* Excluded from the reorganization, however, were education, the two elective offices of attorney general and comptroller, and the state treasurer, who is elected by the legislature.

savings and loans, the highway lobby, the various liquor lobbies. He did not always win, but he was always the major force to be reckoned with.

Moreover, as Agnew never did, Mandel mastered the executive branch of the state government. When Agnew was first elected, he went on television to announce the appointment of a Baltimore banker as state treasurer; Mandel had to call him up and tell him that the legislature made that appointment and that Agnew's man would not get it. Mandel would never make such a mistake. He appointed well known liberals to some posts, conservatives with friends in the legislature to others; but no one doubted who was in control.

And that, it often seemed, was Marvin Mandel's paramount goal, to be in control. Baltimore *Sun* political writer Bentley Orrick called him "a man totally without ideology," and he certainly did not fit conveniently into one of the slots into which we are accustomed to place politicians. On gun control, he managed to offend both gun nuts and blacks who disliked his bill's stop-and-frisk provision—but his bill became law. On transportation, he provided much needed support to mass transit efforts, particularly the Metro in the Washington suburbs; but he also strongly backed Baltimore Mayor Donald Schaefer's desire to build an expressway across the middle of the city. State assumption of school construction certainly helped the public schools, but teachers' organizations were unhappy that Mandel backed aid to private and parochial schools. (Such laws have been routinely struck down by the courts.) Mandel displeased programmatic conservatives when, as one of his first acts in office, he restored 26,000 people to Medicaid rolls; on the other hand, he displeased many programmatic liberals by vetoing liberalized abortion legislation. Rather quietly, he increased the state budget for prisons and mental health; but he incurred the wrath of labor unions in 1974 by backing the Baltimore police chief's threat to fire policemen who had gone out on strike.

In fact, the state AFL-CIO was so angry at Mandel's stand that it pointedly refused to endorse him for reelection in 1974. But in Maryland organized labor is anything but a major political force, either in the antechambers of Annapolis or at the polls. This is a state, after all, where the largest employer—the federal government—has discouraged unionization and prohibited strikes. Only 23 percent of Maryland's workers are union members, the lowest such figure in the Middle Atlantic States. Moreover, most of Maryland's union leaders are not much involved in politics. In other states, Democrats became heavily dependent on union donations because they had no other sure sources of campaign funds; in Maryland, where Democrats have controlled state and local governments more often than not, they have always been able to depend on the contributions of those who in the nature of things favor the "ins."

If there was anything that tied Mandel's record together, it was a taste for innovation—that is, quiet, soundly managed innovation. Frank de Filippo, his press secretary and top aide, became fairly rhapsodic when describing things like the state's emergency health care program, which, with helicopters as well as ambulances, put anyone in Maryland within 18 minutes of a fully staffed emergency medical facility. That, and many other programs like it, will be Mandel's greatest legacy. Washington *Post* reporter Richard Cohen cornered Mandel several years ago and asked him what, really, his greatest goal was as governor. Mandel, Cohen reported, looked puzzled, paused, then finally replied: "I want the state to buy Friendship (now Baltimore-Washington) Airport."

The airport now belongs to the state, but there remain some gaps in Mandel's record. The state's basic tax structure is not tremendously progressive, with an income tax ranging from 2 to 5 percent, and a 4 percent sales tax. Moreover, the tax base of the state's counties varies widely; Baltimore City is hard-pressed to keep up current levels of service, while Montgomery County, for one, has relatively few problems of this nature. Then there is higher education. Twenty years ago the University of Maryland at College Park, just outside Washington, had fewer than 10,000 students and a nationally top-ranked football team. By 1976, the football team, after years of mediocrity, was reaching toward a national ranking again, and the University had more than 35,000 students. But the increase in quantity has not been matched sufficiently by an increase in quality. Some departments, notably physics, are outstanding, but overall Maryland is not among the top-ranking state universities. In vivid contrast is the state's leading private university, Johns Hopkins, which has explicitly chosen quality over quantity. A century ago Hopkins was the first American institution to adopt the German universities' system of graduate education; before that, the few Americans who wanted Ph.D.'s got them abroad. For years, Hopkins has been most renowned for its medical school, and justly so, but it is also strong in the sciences and humanities. Enrollment is sternly limited to fewer than 10,000 students, graduate and undergraduate. That seems to make sense for Hopkins, but taking the state's higher education institutions as a whole, it means that prosperous Maryland is exporting college students to other states and not really taking up its share of the national burden.

The 1975 federal grand jury indictments against Marvin Mandel came as something of a surprise to many Maryland residents. The general opinion throughout most of his political career was that he was at the very least too smart to do anything crooked. There had been no signs that he had grown wealthy in public office or that he had the kind of passion for money that Agnew did.*

But the pattern of lucrative connections for the state's chief executive, according to Bentley Orrick, was actually inherited by Mandel from former

---

* In July 1973 Mandel stunned Marylanders by announcing he was leaving his wife of 33 years to "marry the woman I love," Jeanne B. Dorsey. The marriage took place in August 1974, less than an hour after his divorce was finalized. Later the Washington *Post* disclosed that the Pallotine Fathers, a Catholic mission whose questionable charitable activities have come under Vatican scrutiny, loaned Mandel $54,000 to finance his divorce settlement.

Governor J. Millard Tawes (1959–67). A canny, conservative Democrat from the Eastern Shore, Tawes apparently recognized the growing political power and potential of the suburbs and acted accordingly. It was members of his family who set up the Tidewater Insurance Company, a firm providing coverage to government employees and corporations that do business with the state or are concerned with state regulatory activities. Tidewater's President, Harry W. Rodgers III, was one of Mandel's chief fundraisers and was indicted with him. Tawes continued to play an important role in the firm; the appointed state treasurer in the mid-1970s, he was one of three members of the board of public works which approves all state contracts. Agnew, in Orrick's opinion, was "an amateur," and Tawes and Mandel "the professionals."

Politics in the New / Old Maryland

Keeping up with Maryland politics is like keeping track of the feuds and wars of the Italian city states in the 15th century. There are so many Medicis and Sforzas and Cesare Borgias that it is hard to make sense of them all. No one should think that the party organizations have much to do either with the outcomes of elections or the governmental process. To the extent parties fill any of these functions in Maryland, it is at the county level, and even there the usually dominant Democrats are often split into so many factions that there is no cohesion. There are some exceptions. Until 1974, Dale Anderson's Democratic machine in Baltimore County, which took over after Agnew left for the governorship, was in firm control. But after Anderson was convicted of taking bribes and forced to resign, his chosen successor was heavily rejected in the Democratic primary. (Even as the Baltimore County machine was going under, a Democratic organization slate was winning virtually every office in Prince Georges.)

On the whole, Maryland county politics is characterized by a kind of Brownian movement: constantly shifting alliances and allegiances, with occasional upheavals brought about by disgruntled voters. Only when their very power base is threatened do the local politicos across the stage get together. This is what happened when a new state constitution was submitted to the voters in 1968. The proposed document, written by a group of constitutional convention delegates who reflected the civic and educational aristocracy of the state, was a model of progressive reform. Among other things, it would have reorganized the state government into a cabinet system,* put constitutional weight behind an exemplary bill of rights, reduced the size of the legislature and made decennial reapportionment obligatory, completely reformed the state's court system and the method of appointment of judges, and required counties to adopt home rule. Practically all the state's best known leaders endorsed the new constitution, along with

---

* The cabinet system was later put into effect by act of the legislature.

major newspapers, labor unions, chambers of commerce, bar associations, and the League of Women Voters.

Yet when the new charter was submitted to the people, it lost by a final vote of only 284,033 votes in favor compared to 367,101 against. Maryland's reformers had forgotten to organize an effective political campaign for ratification; the educational job with the voters was incomplete. And the constitution had proposed eliminating many patronage-heavy county offices, thus triggering a strong campaign in opposition by the state organizations of registers of wills, sheriffs, and clerks of courts, and the courthouse cliques in general. In the vote, only Montgomery and Prince Georges Counties were in favor; from there support dropped off to a mere 15 to 32 percent in the rural counties of the Eastern Shore and southern and western Maryland.

Because of ancestral Southern background and national trends since the 1930s, Maryland Democrats have an overwhelming 3–1 edge in registration over Republicans, but this is meaningless when it comes to statewide, and often countywide elections. Senator Mathias has said, "You find Democrats losing statewide elections when Democratic candidates· are alienated from Democratic voters," and technically this is true, as we have seen in the rise of Spiro Agnew. But there is really no cement, no common bond that logically can hold together all the Marylanders who call themselves Democrats—the conservative fishermen and farmers on the Eastern Shore, blacks in West Baltimore and Polish-Americans in East Baltimore, cocktail party liberals in Montgomery County and antibusing demonstrators in Prince Georges. What is surprising, then, is not so much that Maryland Democrats fail to stick together in many elections, but that they ever stick together at all.

A case in point: this overwhelmingly Democratic state went through most of the 1970s with two Republican U.S. Senators. "Mac" Mathias was elected in 1968 with less than a majority, by beating his old law school roommate, Democratic Senator Daniel Brewster, and George P. Mahoney, who was running as an Independent.* Mathias had represented a congressional district including both Montgomery County and western Maryland since 1960; he had strong support in the Washington suburbs, in part because he was something of a Vietnam "dove" and Brewster an unrepentant "hawk." Once elected Senator, Mathias proved his liberal Republicanism

---

* Mahoney is a Maryland original. He made his money as a paving contractor in Baltimore—a business where, to say the least, political contacts are helpful. Since the early 1950s he has run for governor or Senator eight times, and although he has never won, he often helped shape the outcome. He was the Democratic nominee for Senator in 1952 and 1956 (which helped Republicans win those close elections) and for governor in 1966—when his anti-open housing, "your home is your castle" campaign outraged so many blacks and liberals that Spiro Agnew won. Mahoney's 1968 independent candidacy helped beat Brewster and elect Mathias. In 1970, his strong showing in the Democratic Senate primary helped soften up incumbent Joseph Tydings for the Republicans in the fall. In 1972, to everyone's surprise, Mahoney didn't run for anything, and shortly thereafter he was named by Governor Mandel to run the state's new lottery—a move presumably intended to keep him out of electoral politics. Nevertheless, he ran for Baltimore County Executive in 1974, and lost disastrously. Mahoney is now in his mid 70s, and despite his money he still has the seedy look of a man who cannot get rid of his dandruff. But no one is sure that he has entered his last election.

and independence by voting against the Nixon position on so many issues—including the ABM, Haynesworth and Carswell appointments, and others—that he qualified for the White House "enemies" list. He also worked hard on legislation to restore integrity in government, including a 1969 bill (well before Watergate) to require all high-level government officials to make regular public disclosures of their financial holdings. In his 1974 re-election race, despite the strong Democratic trend of the year, Mathias swept to a second Senate term with a plurality of 125,333 votes (57 percent). In 1976, Mathias conducted a brief but not very serious "third force" presidential campaign aimed at uniting liberal Republicans, "disaffected Democrats," and independents in a "coalition of the center," which he said is larger than either the Republican or the Democratic majority.

In 1970, Democratic Senator Joseph Tydings was beaten. J. Glenn Beall, Jr., who had succeeded Mathias in the western congressional district, was the Republican candidate, and he had aid from gun enthusiasts who targeted Tydings. Also, it did not hurt Beall's campaign that in October *Life* magazine printed an exposé charging Tydings with conflict of interest on an investment. The story had been planted by then White House aide Charles Colson, and Tydings was not cleared by John Mitchell's Justice Department until after he had lost the election by 24,000 votes out of nearly a million cast. Tydings had other problems, too, including his aloof manner which alienated some Democratic leaders and voters. And he was never regarded with great favor by Marvin Mandel, who must have seen him as a competitor for control of the Democratic Party.

There was another sidelight to the Tydings-Beall contest that deserves mention. As in Renaissance Italy, pedigree counts in Maryland politics. Tydings had won his Senate seat in the first place by beating Beall's father in 1964. Before that, the Democrat's father, Millard Tydings, had served as Senator from 1927 to 1951.* Beall's successor in the House, Goodloe Byron, had a similar background: both his parents had served in the Congress in the 1940s. Senators Brewster and Mathias, though their fathers had not served before them, were both from well-to-do, locally prominent families. Mathias's great-grandfather had served on the Maryland legislature and ran on Abraham Lincoln's ticket in 1860; his grandfather was a state senator who supported Theodore Roosevelt and the Bull Moose ticket. Young "Mac's" father took him when he was only six to visit President Calvin Coolidge in the White House. So one sees that, oddly enough, a distinguished background and a familiar name seem to be major political assets in this state where nearly half the voters are not natives and where corruption has become such a problem.

---

* Franklin D. Roosevelt tried to purge the conservative elder Tydings in the 1938 primary, unsuccessfully. But later the old man incurred the wrath of Wisconsin's Senator Joseph McCarthy and was the target of a vicious smear campaign in 1950. Some Maryland Republicans circulated a photograph which purported to show Tydings talking amiably with Communist Party leader Earl Browder. It was a clumsy mock-up, obviously a fake, and perhaps even in those emotion-charged days it did not influence many voters—but then Tydings lost by only 43,000 votes.

This is not to say that politicians of non-pedigreed background cannot win. Paul Sarbanes, whose roots went back to a Greek immigrant family that settled in Salisbury, Maryland, overwhelmingly defeated Beall in his bid for re-election in 1976. (It would be the first time since the Great Depression that a J. Glenn Beall would not be holding public office in Maryland.) Sarbanes, a Princeton graduate and Rhodes Scholar who rose through the hurly-burly of Baltimore politics, had served three terms in the House with a low profile and without a smudge on his character. He had become nationally known as a cautious, erudite member of the House Judiciary Committee who sponsored the first article of impeachment against Richard Nixon in 1974.

A prominent non-pedigree Republican was Theodore Roosevelt McKeldin, one of the 11 children of a Baltimore stonemason and later policeman. As a boy, McKeldin was obliged to go to work as a gravedigger, but he worked his way through night courses to win his law degree from the University of Maryland and later was elected twice as mayor of Baltimore (once in the 1940s, again in the early 1960s) and twice as governor of the state, in 1950 and 1954.

In his own rough-hewn way, McKeldin established himself as one of the most appealing political figures of his time. He was a bombastic speaker, a buoyant campaigner, and a man of deep integrity and belief in human rights. He befriended minority groups, including Jews, speaking frequently at synagogues (though he was an Episcopalian himself). He was a fervent believer in the Republican party as the party of Lincoln and refused to support Barry Goldwater for President in 1964, saying that "Barry Goldwater left the Republican party when he voted against civil rights." During McKeldin's governorship, Maryland repealed its last "Jim Crow" law, which had segregated the races on ferries and other intrastate carriers. At the 1952 Republican National Convention, he placed Dwight Eisenhower's name in nomination for the presidency, and might have been nominated for Vice President if a more regular Republican from California, Richard Nixon, had not been chosen. In the late 1960s, after his elective service was ended, McKeldin tried to do something about poverty conditions in Baltimore by serving as chairman of the city's Urban Coalition.

McKeldin was a fervent anticommunist, but in 1952 he repudiated Joe McCarthy's witch-hunt and smear tactics. A measure of McKeldin the man was his statement on capital punishment before a state legislative committee in 1968. Though he had commuted 15 death sentences while governor, he had allowed four men to be executed. "I am ashamed to say I hanged four men," McKeldin said. "The public clamor was such that I yielded to it. May God forgive me."

If one were writing about Maryland's U.S. House delegation before 1970, one would begin—and probably end—by mentioning Baltimore's three committee chairmen: George Fallon of Public Works, Samuel Friedel of House Administration, and Edward Garmatz of Merchant Marine and Fisheries. All three were products of the machine politics of old Baltimore, and it is fair to say that none had a particularly distinguished career on Capitol Hill. In 1970, two were defeated: Fallon by Sarbanes, and Friedel by Parren Mitchell, nephew of longtime Washington NAACP lobbyist Clarence Mitchell (another dynasty: Clarence Mitchell III was a Baltimore state senator until he lost his seat after revelations that he had not paid his income tax). The third chairman, Garmatz, retired in 1972 rather than face Sarbanes in a primary when their districts were joined together.

Besides these three Baltimore Congressmen, one should mention former Representative (1966–77) Gilbert Gude, a thoughtful liberal Republican in the Mathias mold from Montgomery County, and Clarence Long, a former economics professor from Baltimore County, who was one of the leaders of the successful move to cut off bombing in Cambodia in 1973. The delegation had two women in the mid-1970s—Majorie Holt, a conservative Republican from a district encompassing Anne Arundel and southern Prince Georges Counties, and Gladys N. Spellman, a liberal-to-moderate Democrat from the Washington suburban portion of Prince Georges. Mrs. Spellman was formerly a county councilwoman and achieved national stature as president of the National Association of Counties. A third, Barbara Mikulski, on whom more later, was elected in 1976.

If the Maryland delegation has tended to be rather quiet, the legislature is quite another matter. Here is where the knack for understanding Renaissance politics comes in handy. It is as if delegates and senators were sent to Annapolis by rival and antagonistic duchies, to make—and dissolve—entangling alliances in accordance with their county's interest or perhaps just for the byzantine pleasure of it. An outstanding practitioner of the art is Baltimore City's Harry J. "Soft Shoes" McGuirk. The story, related by Richard Cohen, is that one day McGuirk, then a delegate, wanted a piece of legislation to go through. He approached the podium and whispered something to then speaker Marvin Mandel. Mandel nodded yes. Then McGuirk whispered another question. Mandel nodded yes again—and when the vote came minutes later, McGuirk won. Someone asked him later what he had said to Mandel. Well, McGuirk replied, I just asked him if he wanted a cup of coffee; then I asked him whether he wanted cream and sugar.

Another Baltimore luminary was William L. (Bip) Hodges, a cigar-chomping veteran of the political wars and father of nine who died in the midst of his 1974 reelection race. According to his obituary: "While not associated with any particular cause as a legislator, Mr. Hodges had a deep interest in horse racing and gambling legislation. 'I play the numbers every day, and I make no bones about it,' he said during a debate in 1971. 'I play my grave plot number and I have a better chance of going to heaven than hitting that number.' "

The moral tone of the legislature, despite some advances in recent years, is still not particularly high. Consider the reaction of Baltimore City state Senator Joseph Staszak when he was asked whether it was a conflict of interest for him to vote on a liquor bill when he made much of his living off a liquor license. Not at all, said Staszak; there was no conflict because his interests and what the bill would do coincided exactly.

One might suppose that the suburbs, with all their power in a one-man-one-vote legislature, would dominate the show. But that is far from being the case. For one thing, the Montgomery County delegation is looked upon, according to longtime Montgomery Democrat Royce Hanson, as an odd duck, a bunch of idealistic people one can't do business with. Even when, as on Washington Metro subway funding, Montgomery is able to get together with Prince Georges, they are likely to find that Baltimore County legislators, long dominated by Dale Anderson's machine, are not interested in cooperating. Then there are deals cut by the Baltimore City delegation, including the blacks, and legislators from the small counties. In 1974, for example, the small county men were generally against Mandel's land use legislation. Baltimore City legislators were exercised by a Mandel proposal to eliminate the college scholarships which each legislator can designate—one of the last bits of straight patronage in Maryland. So a deal was made. The small county men came out against scholarship reform. The Baltimore City delegation, whose direct interest in the question was minimal, came out against land use. The result was that Mandel had to compromise away part of his land use program, and lost the scholarship issue altogether.

Having said that, one must add that the Maryland legislature is a more sophisticated, and probably more responsible, body than it was a decade or two ago. The legislative department of fiscal services consults with executive branch budgeteers even before the basic state budget is drawn up, and committee staffing is generally good. Unfortunately, individual legislators do not have their own staffs, or even their own secretaries. And the usually hectic pace of the session (the standard length is 90 days, with an option for 30 more) sometimes makes informed decisions impossible—except for those in the know. The minority party, which of course is always the Republicans, does not have particularly good access to information, but then decisions are seldom made along straight party lines, for the Democrats are too diverse.

Baltimore: Maryland's Spiritual Capital

The spiritual capital of the Old Maryland is not Annapolis, where suburban legislators make deals in the 1772 State House and bureaucrats run the state government in 1960s replicas of Georgian homes. Rather, it is in Baltimore, the old but still lively port at the head of the Chesapeake Bay.

Always one of America's largest urban centers, and yet never one of America's premier cities, Baltimore seems left behind by the suburban rush of the '50s and '60s. This is a city which is 46 percent black, yet readily elects a white mayor of the neighborhoods who backs a crosstown expressway, a city where the distribution of "walking around money" is an essential ingredient of electioneering and where local ward bosses can still control the votes of sizable numbers of their constituents. It is a city which, despite some attractive modern architecture, has the look and feel of the immediate postwar years. In those days, big cities tended to *work* and, to an unappreciated extent, Baltimore still does. It is still a city whose tax rate is not entirely out of control like Boston's or Newark's, and whose government provides services with some efficiency. It is not a city, like Detroit or Cleveland, which people are leaving in droves; there is still even a little residential growth within the city limits. An amazing percentage of the old Baltimore row houses, with their polished white steps, are still in good condition, and if one block is run down and abandoned, the next may well be spotlessly clean and genteel.

It is hard, however, to capture the Baltimore spirit. This was done best, surely, by the late H. L. Mencken who caressed his town with polysyllabic scorn and adoration. Another longtime Baltimore observer, Russell Baker of the New York *Times*, was moved to write about the city after the resignation of Spiro Agnew:

> Now, of course, now that it is all out in the open—all that business about the money passing back and forth between fat cats and big shots—it seems so obvious. Baltimore *is* permissiveness. "The Land of Pleasant Living," according to an old advertising jingle for a local beer. The pleasures of the flesh, the table, the bottle and the purse are tolerated with a civilized understanding of the subtleties of moral questions that would have been perfectly comprehensible to Edwardian Londoners.
>
> Gross and overt indulgence, however, is frowned upon. The gunned corpses that litter New Jersey are not part of Baltimore life. That sort of thing is a vice. Baltimore does not like vice. Vice leads to cruelty and suffering and, what's more, is in bad taste. Sin is something else. Baltimore tolerates sin. Sin is the human condition, and though it may be deplorable, Baltimore has the intuitive European knowledge that however deplorable sin may be, yet society must live with it.

One manifestation of Baltimore's pleasure-loving ways is, or was, The Block—actually a three-block stretch of East Baltimore Street near the docks which, we have been assured by aficionados, used to boast the finest live burlesque in the country. Blaze Starr, for one, got her start here and still appears from time to time. Never, one of the authors recalls from off-duty evenings while serving at Baltimore's Fort Holabird some 20 years ago, was a very fine line observed between the onstage and offstage diversions offered by the girls in The Block's nightclubs. But rumors of graft and gambling have long plagued The Block, and in recent years it has visibly declined. Some city fathers have been eager to efface this blot from Baltimore and, sadly, some buildings here were torn down a few years ago and replaced by a police station. The line between pleasure and sin, even in Baltimore, is hard for some to discern.

But sin, however pleasurable, is not enough to keep a city going on as comfortably as Baltimore is; it also takes money. And here, despite its seeming indifference, despite its secondary status among major American metropolises, Baltimore does well enough. The primary basis of its economy, of course, is the port; that is why the city grew here in the first place. In tonnage Baltimore is the nation's sixth largest port, a rank it achieves without reliance on the single commodities—coal at Norfolk and oil at Houston—that characterizes two of those which are larger. (The others are New York, New Orleans, and Philadelphia.) The port of Baltimore—the authority is run by the state's department of transportation—has installed modern containerization facilities, and the port is probably the most up-to-date and efficient on the East Coast. It is also relatively free of graft and payoffs, a fact that has enabled Baltimore to win the East Coast distribution facilities for Volkswagen and Volvo away from other ports.

If a port city is inclined to develop a sophisticated appreciation of sin, it is also apt to build a diversified economy. And Baltimore has. It is a major producer of such diverse commodities as steel (Bethlehem's Sparrows Point plant is just across the line in Baltimore County) and spices (McCormick, the leading firm in the field, is headquartered here). Baltimore is the home of big insurance companies like USF&G, of Fairchild-Hiller (the big defense contractor which is now diversifying), and of the Black and Decker power tool firm. It has a major copper refinery and imports large amounts of bauxite, used in aluminum processing, from South America. Baltimore also has more than its share of federal installations, most notably the Social Security Administration headquarters; but it is by no means as dependent on the federal dollar as Washington or even places like Seattle or Fort Worth.

Yet somehow, despite its diversity and size, Baltimore has never really broken into the economic big leagues—and perhaps has never really wanted to. One of Baltimore's most astute and veteran observers, Gerald W. Johnson, has opined that the city's banks lost their financial supremacy together with their Southern accounts at the outbreak of the Civil War. Baltimore has the nation's oldest investment banking house, Alex. Brown & Sons, but it has nowhere near the resources and clout of its New York counterparts, and Baltimore has become known, and justifiably so, as a branch office town.

There is, of course, a local power structure, whose lineaments have been sketched out with probably the greatest accuracy by Mandel's press secretary Frank de Filippo, when he was a reporter for the Baltimore *News-American*. Its members are dominated by the big bankers who make major capital decisions, who sit on the Greater Baltimore Committee (a driving force behind Charles Center and other renewal projects), and who dominate the local charities. But few Baltimoreans know the names of these people, and for the most part they seem to exercise their power with little vigor. Overall, the city's financial community is conservative; Baltimore *Sun* financial editor Jesse Glasgow told us that one of the banks in the '30s "never got the word and never closed," and another continued to operate during the bank holiday out the back door. This conservatism made for stability in the '30s, of course, but in the booming '50s and '60s the old money tied in Baltimore bank accounts and trust funds was not put to much use in the city. As Glasgow put it, "I'll go to a luncheon for some civic milestone and there'll be a Washington or Philadelphia banker there who put up all the capital." The city's biggest employers—Bethlehem, the insurance companies, Westinghouse, Fairchild, the federal government, even the big retailers—are all run by people from somewhere else, and Baltimore can lose an uncomfortable number of jobs as a result of decisions made in New York or Washington. But it is unlikely that everything will close down here at once (unless it does everywhere in the nation), and in the meantime Baltimore's diversification gives it a certain security; a big steel strike will just about devastate Pittsburgh's economy, but despite the size of Sparrows Point it would not greatly harm Baltimore's.

With this economic base, Baltimore is anything but a twin of its sister metropolis 40 miles away on the Potomac. (Indeed, it is hard to think of any two major metropolitan areas so close together that have so little to do with each other.) Baltimore's economy is dominated by the private sector, Washington's by the public: Baltimore's work force is still largely blue collar, while the vast bulk of Washington's sits at desks. These basic economic facts have shaped the growth of the two cities—the kind of people who have moved there as well as the work they do. Like Philadelphia, New York, and Boston, and unlike Washington, Baltimore attracted thousands of immigrants from Ireland, Italy, Poland, and Greece, to work in its factories and on its docks, and today it still has the kind of close-knit ethnic communities that have never existed in Washington. There is Highlandtown, for example, (the pronunciation is HAH-Luhn-t'n) in east Baltimore, a predominately Polish-American enclave north of the port and east of downtown. Along Eastern Avenue beyond Patterson Park on a Saturday afternoon, the street is thronged with shoppers, much as it must have been 30 or 40 years ago. Some of the older women wear babushkas, though the younger ones, with children in tow, are more likely to be in pants; and the signs on the stores as often as not feature Polish names. There are few if any blacks in Highlandtown, for they would probably be no more welcome than the Polish-Americans would be in the west Baltimore ghetto. But if there is prejudice here, there is also vitality, and though many of the young who grew up in Highlandtown have moved on to the suburbs, the neighborhood shows few signs of dying.

Or consider the scene at the Lexington market on the western edge of downtown. The crowd is thoroughly integrated (the neighborhood just to the west is predominantly black), but the stalls overflowing with soft shell crabs and oysters from the Bay and fresh corn and green vegetables from the farmland to the west must not be so very dissimilar from what one would have seen here when Mencken was still alive. The seafood of Baltimore is justifiably renowned, and it is particularly satisfying in one of the city's old restaurants like Macroni's, where elderly waiters dressed in business suits serve sauteed soft shell crabs.

This is not to suggest that all is always well in Baltimore. Its crime rate, if the FBI's figures are to be believed, is one of the nation's highest.* In the

* Baltimore has tried various ways to cope with its crime. In 1974, going the tough state handgun statute one better, it offered a $50 bounty for every handgun turned in to the police. The program produced more than 11,000 guns, and one cannot help wondering how many of them, if they had remained in private hands, would have ended up being instruments of death during some heated argument.

summer of 1974, the city's sanitation workers went on strike, followed by large numbers of the police in the first official strike by police in a major American city since Boston in 1919. Trash was piled high and began to stink and smolder in the summer heat; manure at the zoo accumulated at the rate of a ton a day; a health officer warned of an outbreak of bubonic plague; hundreds of stores were vandalized or looted; and state police had to be called in to quell an outbreak of racial violence.

Less than two months later, the Inner Harbor came alive with the multi-splendored Baltimore City Fair. Hundreds of thousands of Baltimoreans—an excellent racial and ethnic cross-section of the city—were on hand to see the exhibits of 93 participating city institutions, to visit a big midway, an island of art, and the original U.S.F. *Constellation,* to hear Cab Callaway and the Baltimore Symphony, to buy the offerings of local potters, quilters, and weavers, to view the exhibits of 62 neighborhoods (from the Waverly Block-builders to the Bentalou Improvement Association), and to sample a wild variety of ethnic foods and, of course, Chesapeake Bay crabs and oysters. Walking through the crowds those warm September days, it was hard to believe this was the same city that had experienced such civic discord such a short time before. And the fair is not the only occasion where the races of Baltimore get together; it happens each summertime in the jazz concerts at Charles Center or the Orioles baseball games, where the rednecks and blacks have great fun joshing each other.

In fact, the entire pace of Baltimore somehow seems less hurried and more polite than in the other great cities of Megalopolis. If Baltimore has not become the commercial powerhouse it might have been, it is because people there are more willing, as Russell Baker suggested, to pause and appreciate the pleasant things in life—and who can say that they have not chosen the better alternative? Or to put it another way: a city where a politician can remember what time of year a certain dinner table conversation took place because it was soft shell crab season is doing something right.

Politics in Baltimore

People like to talk as if Baltimore is run by a big city machine, with unchallenged power over elections and contracts and all the things big city machines are supposed to care about. And that may have been true 20 years ago, when a man named Jack Pollack had a fairly firm control of the local Democratic party. But no one has ever held power in this city as Frank Hague once did in New Jersey, and if there is a machine in Baltimore today it has so many cogs and components whirring and buzzing in so many different directions that no one can be sure just what it is trying to do. The things that characterized big city machines of yore are just not present in Baltimore today: there are relatively few patronage jobs in the city government; the big money in public contracts, as we have already seen, has long since moved out to the suburbs; there is, from all accounts, very little graft and corruption within the city limits.

Nevertheless, Baltimore politics still look like machine politics. One Baltimore institution redolent of the bad old days is "walking around money"—cash given to local worthies who are supposed to scour the streets in the poorer parts of town for votes on election day. With some qualms, both the Nixon and McGovern campaigns anted up $50,000 of walking around money in 1972 and distributed it to various local bosses; Marvin Mandel reportedly provided $90,000 in 1974. It is an article of faith among many Baltimoreans that this practice is necessary to win votes in the ghetto, but the election returns in recent years show that turnout in black precincts—indeed, even in the long-settled white ethnic neighborhoods—lags considerably behind that in real machine cities like Chicago and Philadelphia. One suspects that a lot of this money is simply pocketed and never does any walking around at all.

Despite the lack of a single organization that can really produce votes, Baltimore politicians are still labeled as machine men or insurgents. The mayor at this writing, for example, is William Donald Schaefer, generally regarded as a Democratic machine product. He is an amiable man who, even his adversaries admit, is devoted to his city and has no ambitions for higher office. A bachelor, he lives with his mother in a typical Baltimore row house in a neighborhood now predominantly black; he served on the council for many years, finally as council president (a citywide post), and when Mayor Thomas d'Alessandro Jr. retired in 1971, Schaefer won easily.

In many ways, Schaefer has been the kind of mayor one saw in many cities in the late '50s or early '60s, before the era of the John Lindsays and Carl Stokeses. One of his favorite projects—"the cornerstone of his political career for 20 years," one reporter told us—is building the much-disputed crosstown expressway, and despite a determined fight, the highway's opponents were only able to force a few modifications, like putting a tunnel under the Fort McHenry area.

Schaefer also supported, but pushed less, for a rapid rail transit system. The city formally broke ground for the system in the midst of the 1974 political campaigns, but it took until 1976 for the legislature to pass its share of the funding for the project. (The federal government will provide most of the money.) Scheduled to open in 1982, the system could technically one day be extended to join with Washington, D.C.'s Metro.

In other respects, Schaefer does not act like an old-fashioned machine pol. His personal staff, for example, is young and includes blacks and women—none with a ward-heeling background. And when he took office, Schaefer retained as commissioner of housing and urban development Robert Embry, who had a few years ago won a council seat against the wishes of some of the old-time bosses. A scion of an old blueblood family, Embry has proven to be one of the more effective and imaginative people in his field (even winning kudos from conservative columnist James Jackson Kilpatrick). He has hired top architects like Moshe Safdie, who is designing the Cold Spring new town project on a piece of land long considered too hilly for development; and he has put together an impressive Inner Harbor project, just south of downtown, which will include commercial, governmental and educational institutions—and which at the same time will preserve many of the present buildings there. Baltimore's modern-day pride is the Charles Center, an attractive office-and-hotel complex planned in the late '50s and early '60s and a model of its kind. The physical redevelopment of the '70s, however, promises to be even more tasteful and successful.

How does a mayor like Schaefer win election in a city where almost half the eligible voters are black? One is tempted to ascribe his 1971 victory to machine politics; but his main opponent, George Russell, a black, was also counted as a machine man. The basic reasons were (1) the usual low voter turnout in black areas and (2) a bitter, continuing split in the black community. The division is sometimes described as between east side and west side blacks, sometimes as between the Mitchell family and their adversaries. In any case, state Senator Clarence Mitchell III entered the 1971 mayor's race with the almost explicit purpose of siphoning votes away from Russell (who, as it turns out, would have lost anyway). A year later, Russell nearly beat Congressman Parren Mitchell, Clarence III's uncle, in the Democratic primary. With such divisions, it seems unlikely that any black candidate could beat Schaefer; the only black figure who has had united black support and has been able to win white votes is Judge Joseph Howard, who declined to leave the bench to run for mayor in 1971. In 1975, Schaefer won, virtually unopposed; one might have been in the '50s again.

Most members of the Baltimore city council are elected by districts, and here, for the most part, the type of politicians who thrive look like machine products. But they are not selected by some central panjandrum; they seem to survive by that oldest of political techniques, taking good care of their constituents—smoothing out their problems with the city and state bureaucracies, making sure they get the services they are entitled to, looking after the interests of their neighborhoods.

For several years the best known Baltimore council member nationally was another "insurgent," Barbara Mikulski, the chairman of the Democratic Party's delegate selection committee, her party's candidate for U.S. Senate in 1974, and successful candidate for the U.S. House in 1976. Mikulski's roots are deep in the Polish-American community of east Baltimore. Unlike most of her contemporaries, she got a master's degree in social work and never married; unhappy with the way her neighborhood was represented, she ran for council and won in 1971. As a Polish-American woman who had an ethnic constituency and who supported George McGovern, she found her way to the national Democratic post. Despite occasional naiveté (she was amazed to hear that Vermont elected only one Congressman) and several spirited tussles, she presided over some artful compromises without giving in on most of her basic principles. As a Senate candidate in 1974 Mikulski made no concessions to the usual image-making; she wore little make-up and still dressed in pant-suits that did anything but disguise the fact she was somewhat overweight. But her peppery assaults on Mac Mathias's record on economic issues gained her a respectful hearing—and more votes than had been expected from Marylanders in 1974. In her 1976 race for the House, she inadvertently invented a new campaign gimmick: the diet. After she shed 40 pounds, Mikulski found people asked her more about how to lose weight than about issues.

The existence and political survival of people like Mikulski and Paul Sarbanes and Parren Mitchell is conclusive evidence that there is no longer a monolithic, all-powerful Baltimore machine. One might have expected Governor Marvin Mandel, as an old Baltimore politico himself, to play a strong role here, but usually he deferred to local decision-makers. One example was the proposal to build a huge sports complex; although it technically did not need council approval, Mandel required it before the state would move ahead, and eventually the proposal was killed when the Baltimore *Sun* ran a series on cost overruns in similar projects in cities like New Orleans.

Our review of Baltimore life would be incomplete without reference to the *Sun*, once renowned as the "newspaperman's newspaper" among American dailies.* As recently as the 1950s and early 1960s, the paper was a kind of mini-New York *Times*, often out-reporting the Washington papers, for instance, on news in the nation's capital. The paper seems to have less ambitious goals now, but it is still very adequate. In addition to an excellent Washington bureau (now apparently kept mainly for purposes of prestige), it has overseas bureaus in Moscow, Bonn, Beirut, Rio de Janeiro, London, Tokyo, and Hong Kong. It sent its own reporters to cover the Vietnam war and did a good job of it. In the last several years the paper has probed in depth into many of Maryland's major scandals; local reporting in general has been excellent. The *Sun* has also been constructive on racial problems. Its lack of flashiness, one could say, reflects the unspectacularity of Baltimore in our time. But the public life of many a major American city could be improved by a newspaper that showed a comparable commitment to serious news coverage.

A Brief Tour of the New Maryland

The New Maryland, where the vital growth since World War II has taken place, lacks the culture, the historic roots, the ambiance of Baltimore City or the still-rural counties. But it is where the mass of the people now live, and their story must be ours.

Let us start in the Washington orbit. We have already mentioned those Maryland suburbs in our District of Columbia chapter, but they need to be viewed more clearly in their Maryland context. We begin, again, in the Bethesda-Chevy Chase area of Montgomery County, in some of the most well-

---

* The Sunpapers publish separate morning and evening editions that combine into a Sunday edition with almost 350,000 circulation. They completely outclass the Hearst-owned *News-American* in quality, but do not lead by much in circulation.

to-do precincts in the nation. These suburbs, proceeding out River Road and Wisconsin and Connecticut Avenues, are really extensions of the wealthy part of the District of Columbia west of Rock Creek Park; to the extent they differ sociologically, it is because more of the people here have children (many having left the District because of the poor quality of the public schools).

Much of Bethesda (1970 population 71,621) and Chevy Chase (20,955) is not particularly prepossessing, especially if one stays on the major arteries; to see how the rich really live, one has to go down one of the winding side streets and cul-de-sacs. An example is Shadow Lane in the WASPish Kenwood subdivision, where Spiro Agnew lived during his last days as Vice President; Agnew bought the house for $185,000—the going rate then in Kenwood— and sold it for $300,000.

Prices tend to run about that high beyond Bethesda, in the village of Potomac. Here houses sit on multi-acre lots or even huge pastures; the local Safeway sells horse feed. But not all of Montgomery County is for the very wealthy. As one proceeds clockwise around the Capital Beltway (Interstate 495), one goes through the county seat of Rockville (41,564), which has its own small black ghetto and a downtown shopping mall which has proved strikingly unsuccessful. Above Rockville is Wheaton, a solidly middle class, 1950s suburb if there ever was one, and below it Silver Spring (77,496), which has the Washington area's largest Jewish community. East of Silver Spring is the old suburb of Takoma Park (18,455), laid out in 1890; in the last 10 years, considerable numbers of blacks have been moving there from the District.

Takoma Park straddles the Montgomery-Prince Georges county line, and is a good place to pause to examine the differences between these two suburban jurisdictions. One is tempted to say that Montgomery has the white collar suburbs and Prince Georges the blue collar, but for the fact that by national standards Prince Georges is very white collar indeed. Nonetheless, it is true that residents of Prince Georges, as it is often called, tend to have lower incomes and less education than their Montgomery neighbors; more Prince Georges residents are from the South (including blacks* as well as whites), and fewer from the East. And even more than Montgomery, Prince Georges lacks a central focus. The county seat is Upper Marlboro, still a sleepy town of around 600 souls surrounded by farms in the eastern end of the county, far from where most of its residents live. Prince Georges of course has its share of shopping centers, but no really significant mini-downtowns have developed here, as they have in Montgomery and northern Virginia. Middle class suburbs like Langley Park (11,564), College Park (population 25,156),

* Following the 1968 riots in Washington, blacks began to move out from the District into adjacent areas of Prince Georges in large numbers: by 1973, most of the population increase in fast-growing Prince Georges consisted of blacks. This migration had its greatest impact on the county's school system, which is the 10th largest in the nation. A federal judge required substantial busing to eliminate segregation in 1973, and in white areas there was great discontent. There was some racial fighting in the high schools, and the elected school board seemed to be doing what it could to make sure the busing plan wouldn't work. One saw little evidence of political leadership, either in Prince Georges or in the State House, to calm down local feelings or make the system work better; however, as in busing situations around the country, much of the furor abated once the plan was set into motion and was actually working.

the home of the University of Maryland, Suitland (30,355) and Oxon Hill (11,974), are well connected to the District by radial highways, but, except for the Capital Beltway, they are not very well connected with each other. Far removed from the rest of the county are the towns of Laurel (10,525) and Bowie (35,028) each long known as the site of a racetrack, and each the scene of major development in the 1960s. Laurel is separated from the rest of the county by the National Agricultural Research Center, Bowie by several miles of fields.

Bowie and Laurel are at the edge of the border land where the Baltimore television stations start coming in better than the Washington ones. Just a few miles away is another town but with a difference. This is Columbia, the oft-written about "new town" which is usually discussed in tandem with Reston, Virginia.* Columbia is the creation of an unusual mortgage banker named James Rouse, who in the middle '60s rather clandestinely assembled a block of 14,000 acres in rural Howard County, about 20 miles from downtown Baltimore and 25 miles from downtown Washington. In 1967 Rouse was ready to announce his plans for a new city which would have a population of 110,000 by 1980—not just another suburb, but a city with its own employment base, racially and economically integrated.

It sounded visionary, but Rouse's dream was backed up by $18 million in financing from the Connecticut General Life Insurance Company and Rouse's own considerable acumen. To date, most of Columbia's goals have been achieved. By 1974, Columbia had a population of 35,500 and 17,000 jobs, 580 businesses, and 92 industries—including a $250 million General Electric appliance part complex. New clusters ("villages") were continually going up, and although some of them were standard subdivision-colonials, there was also scattered subsidized housing, where eligible people could move in for as little as $92 a month. About 15 percent of Columbia's residents were black—a vivid contrast from the almost entirely segregated Baltimore suburbs—and Antioch College built a branch campus there.

There are, of course, problems. The Rouse company did not incorporate the new town, instead retaining control over physical planning through an entity it controls, and will control till 1980, when Columbia reaches its full size. Far less than half of all Columbians actually work there; and though the Rouse people project 21,000 jobs for Columbia by 1980, even then there will be massive commuting in and out of the town. Finally, Columbia perhaps promised too much. Rouse called it "an America" and breathlessly proclaimed that "Columbia wants a style of living distinctly its own." To be sure, Columbia is not just another suburb, but there are many resemblances. Its population, however integrated, is still predominantly upper-income; the architecture is closer to the conventional than is Reston's; the shopping mall is, after all, not so different from what one can find in suburbs from Massachusetts to California, though it is a lively meeting place.

---

* For a discussion of Reston, see the Virginia chapter of *The Border South States*, pages 106–107.

Unfortunately, Columbia has found few imitators. A major financial commitment is required for such a large, long-range project, and although Rouse, who is as much a hard-headed businessman as a visionary, can argue that Columbia is getting a better return than smaller, more conventional developments, in these days of inflation and high interest rates few investors seem willing to make a similar outlay. It is nonetheless at the very least an innovative way to develop and market suburban acreage, and the nation could use many more Columbias and a few more Rouses.

Certainly there is nothing quite so unusual or interesting about the closer-in Baltimore suburbs, which have grown up along the city's radial avenues in the '50s and '60s and '70s. Starting at the Chesapeake Bay, south of the city, there are towns like Severna Park (1970 population 16,358) and Glen Burnie (38,608)in Anne Arundel County, which are basically where the sons and daughters of the blue collar workers in south Baltimore have moved; the march of unplanned development has moved south almost all the way to historic Annapolis and the Bay Bridge (near the approaches to which a chunk of real estate was bought and sold, at a nice profit, some years ago by Spiro T. Agnew).

Baltimore City is surrounded on the east and west, and then northerly all the way to the Pennsylvania border by overwhelmingly suburban Baltimore County. On the city's western flank lies Catonsville (54,812) a town which actually antedates Baltimore and is famous these days primarily as the place where the Berrigan brothers poured blood on the local draft board's files. Catonsville seems a most unlikely hotbed for such radicalism: it is a comfortable, middle-class, heavily Catholic town, where Baltimore's typical row houses suddenly are transformed into cozy Cape Cods. To the north, past the Social Security Administration's headquarters just west of the Baltimore city limit, are the predominantly Jewish suburbs, Pikesville (25,395) and Randallstown (33,683). These are an almost linear extension of the northwest Baltimore Jewish community, once centered on the Pimlico Race Track, now moving rapidly outward one step ahead of the blacks.

There is not really much in common—except for high income levels—between Pikesville and the main suburb to the east, Towson, which happens to be the Baltimore County seat. Its population grew by a spectacular 308 percent—from 19,090 to 77,809—during the 1960s. If Catonsville is Catholic and Pikesville Jewish, Towson is decidedly Protestant, an extension of the WASPy neighborhoods near Johns Hopkins University in the City. This is where the never-very-ethnic Spiro Agnew moved from the city, trying to eke out a law practice until he found that politics made him a better living. Towson and the suburbs to the north—Lutherville, Timonium, Cockeysville—are almost desperately proud that they are not part of the city of Baltimore, and any political reporter who ventures there hears over and over again the fact that Baltimore County does not include, and has nothing to do with, Baltimore City.

The northeast and east suburbs seem somehow less separate from the city, and have more to do with the Baltimore neighborhoods that adjoin them; one reason is that those neighborhoods remain all white. Parkville (33,897), northeast of the city, has many Italian-Americans; Dundalk (85,377), directly east of downtown Baltimore, has a distinct Polish tone. These are the blue collar suburbs, where the paychecks are more likely to come from Bethlehem Steel or Martin-Marietta than from one of the insurance companies or the federal government; they are also the areas which provided the majorities for Dale Anderson's corrupt Democratic machine until its demise in 1974. Finally, one comes to the Bay again. There are a few yacht clubs here, but the emphasis is on the industrial, particularly at the sprawling Bethlehem Steel Sparrows Point plant. Situated right on the water, this is one of the nation's largest steel mills, dominating the landscape for miles around. It draws much of its work force from Dundalk and Baltimore City, of course, but there has also long been a little community right across from the mill gates, including a couple of blocks reserved for blacks. It was not so long ago that the work force at Sparrows Point was rigidly segregated (blacks tended to work in maintenance and in the foundry, the dirtiest part of any steel mill). Now that has changed, and in addition Bethlehem has been buying up the old houses nearby, including the tiny ghetto—leaving its aging residents to find housing somewhere else in the still-segregated suburbs.

The Old Maryland: the Rural Counties

If one wants a good glimpse of what the old Maryland outside Baltimore was—and is—like, a good place to start is the town square in Bel Air. Just 25 miles east of downtown Baltimore, this is the county seat of Harford County, which has more than doubled in population (to 115,378 in 1970) over the past two decades. A few blocks away, there stands one of the fast hamburger outlets which seem to be the signs of modern civilization, but the square itself is still pristine. It is encircled with two-story buildings which are the offices of lawyers and real estate agencies; there is the inevitable barbershop. Tucked away in a tiny street, just across from the courthouse, is the law office of William S. James. The floor is linoleum, and what looks to be a corridor is also the law library. Off to the side is the tiny office where Mr. James works, with barely enough room for chairs for two visitors.

At the time we talked with him in 1974, Mr. James was completing his 28th year in the Maryland senate and his 12th year as senate president. He did not seek reelection in 1974, and the General Assembly elected him State Treasurer. From what one had read and heard of Maryland politicians in the months after the downfall of Spiro Agnew, we had almost expected that a political figure of that eminence would command a thick-carpeted, mammoth office in some chrome-and-steel suburban high-rise. What we saw was a long way from Agnew playing golf with Frank Sinatra in Palm Springs. It was hard to believe that Agnew and James had practiced politics in the same state, indeed just a few miles away from each other.

When Bill James was first elected to the legislature, Harford was basically a rural county, and he was probably classified as a rural conservative Democrat. But during the intervening years, he also proved to be one of Maryland's—and perhaps the nation's—more innovative and thoughtful state legislators. He was one of the major forces behind the creation of Maryland's community college system, and he drafted the state's wetlands preservation bill. He helped to set up the department of fiscal services, which provides the legislature with information to act intelligently in passing the state budget, and the department of legislative reference. And in his last two terms, he was the major proponent in Annapolis of land use reform legislation.

"I live on a farm," James told us, "and the thoughtless destruction of land, the ruthless destruction of farms have made a deep impression on me. How far can we go destroying fertile soil? We're the greatest land butchers in the world. That's where I've changed since I've been in the legislature." But despite his fervor, James was still willing to accept a compromise on his land use bill in the 1974 legislative session, a compromise which required local subdivisions to identify problem areas and make recommendations to the state planning department and gave the state the authority to appear as a party in local zoning cases. It was the best bill James and Governor Mandel could extract from the legislature, and it did promise some modulation of the planned growth that has been taking place in many of the state's smaller counties, which have lacked the planning expertise and sophistication to deal with big developers.

James, like all the Maryland politicians we interviewed, was quick to reject the suggestion that there is anything peculiarly corrupt about the state's public life. "I assume people are honest until shown otherwise," he said, "and I've only had one small offer in 28 years."

It is interesting, though, that the Maryland politicians whom everyone agrees are absolutely beyond reproach—Democrats like James and Republicans like Mathias—tend to have deep roots in the smaller and at least formerly rural counties of the state. The problem is, as James's push for land use reform indicates, that honesty is not enough to preserve the quality of life in his part of the old Maryland. Howard County, southwest of Baltimore, has been lucky in that the development it has attracted has been almost entirely in the new town of Columbia. But in counties like James's Harford and St. Marys, the inexorable outward pressures of metropolitan growth are creating a sort of McDonald's culture in what was hilly countryside. Demand by developers, which after all ultimately reflects demand by the buying public, is pushing the price of farmland so high that property taxes are forcing farmers to sell. County governments, eager for additional tax money, have been only too glad to encourage unplanned development—until it becomes apparent that it has generated more demand for services than additional revenue. One can say that these, after all, are the problems of prosperity, and that they are preferable to the kind of squeeze people in these counties faced in the depression years. But they are problems nonetheless.

Before we move on to the Eastern Shore and Western Maryland, a word should be said about the three small counties—Charles, Calvert, and St. Marys—south of Annapolis and Washington on the western shore of Chesapeake Bay.* This is where the first of the Calverts settled, in what is now the small town of St. Marys, just above the point where the Potomac empties into the Bay. There is still much of the insularity here one finds on the Eastern Shore, and in some of the town watermen still make their livings catching oysters and crabs. But the suburbs are also creeping in. Charles County, just below Prince Georges, was added to the Washington standard metropolitan statistical area in 1973, and when one sees the shopping centers and subdivisions sprouting up in Waldorf, a town whose population rose 603 percent in the 1960s, one can see why. There is also considerable development around the Patuxent Naval Air Test Center, in Lexington Park in St. Marys County, not far from where some of the Catholic descendants of Maryland's first settlers still live. But perhaps the most noteworthy thing about these three counties is that, under Maryland law, slot machines were legal here until as late as 1968. The actual machines, we were told by House of Delegates Speaker John Hanson Briscoe, a St. Marys native, are now in warehouses, presumably ready to be put back in service should the state ever legalize them again.

The Bay and the Shore

The Chesapeake Bay separates Maryland into two quite unequal parts: the major portion of the state and the Eastern Shore. The Bay itself is really the submerged valley of the Susquehanna River; it is as if the Gulf of Mexico rose 200 feet and submerged the Mississippi Valley, converting small creeks which had fed into the river into wide tidal estuaries. The result is an incredibly erose 3,600-mile shoreline, with hundreds of wide bays, which, as one goes up them, suddenly become tiny rivers. An example is the Patapsco, wide and deep enough at its mouth to lead into Baltimore harbor, which can handle all but the largest supertankers; but just a few miles upstream, the Patapsco becomes a rather narrow stream. One of the authors had a college classmate, a native Marylander, who could draw the 200-mile length of the Bay, with virtually every estuary, bay, river, and island, *from memory*. These waterways, of course, have become one of the great boating centers of America, filled on summer days with every kind of craft from rowboats to graceful sailing craft to the yachts of the affluent—not to mention the great freighters plying their way to or from Baltimore.

Maryland was first settled by white men who sailed up the Bay and into its streams and established little villages. Many of their descendants—especially on the Eastern Shore—have made their livings off the richness of the Bay's marine life ever since. The crabs here, especially the soft-shelled crabs which are caught in late spring and early summer, may well be the finest in the country, and the oysters over the years have been more plentiful than

* The three counties' combined population was 115,749 in the 1970 Census—up from 42,722 in 1940.

anywhere but the waters around New Orleans. The Bay is also the habitat—
or was—of the diamondback terrapin, the shellfish delicacy whose name is
still commemorated by the University of Maryland's sports teams (the
"Terps"). In 1940, the Maryland WPA Guide informs us, terrapin could
still be had in the "old conservative clubs in large Eastern cities, noted old
hotels, and households able and willing to pay from $20 to $50 a dozen for
them." Today, alas, they are exceedingly rare.

That pollution, however, is not as serious for the Bay as a whole as one
might expect in a body of water that is used as a main ship channel and faces
all the dangers of sewage waste from a population of eight million people
along its shores or tributary rivers. But the danger signs are there: domestic
waste increasing in the rivers, growth of suffocating algae, siltation from
shore developments, degradation of tidal land. Federally supported sewage
disposal facilities, one hopes, will finally be completed along the Potomac and
Susquehanna Rivers, together with effective state land use planning and shoreline controls, before worse damage is done to the Bay.

The pollution of the last several years has been a continuing problem for
Maryland's watermen, a hardy breed who live mostly in the tiny villages of the
Eastern and Western Shores. The industry is regulated closely by the state:
oystermen are allowed 25 bushels per day, with a 75 bushel limit per boat; all
oysters less than three inches long must be thrown back. In good years, a
single oysterman can gross as much as $625 per week; altogether, Maryland
oystering is a $13 million a year industry. But that is in good years; in 1974,
oystermen were catching only 10 to 13 bushels a day. One reason for the low
catch was 1972's hurricane Agnes, which inundated the Bay with fresh water
and killed the set (the baby oysters). But the chief culprit is man-made pollution, even though the state has managed to open some beds to the oystermen
which had been placed off limits a few years ago. Despite all this regulation,
oystering remains a solitary business and, as one Washington *Post* reporter
put it, "whether it is long stretches of hard cold work in the gloomy winter
mornings or a general distrust of lurking tax agents, oystermen are not generally disposed to paint their industry in financially generous terms." For no
one really doubts that these hardy men—and, in many cases, their wives—will
continue to ply their trade unless the Bay becomes another Lake Erie.

Like the oystermen who give it so much of its flavor, the Eastern Shore
is a profoundly conservative land—not just in political terms (though it is
that), but in its whole way of life. For many years, the Shore was isolated
from the rest of Maryland, and much of it hardly changed from the days of
the Revolutionary War. In 1790, there were 94,000 people living there; by
1950, the number had less than doubled, to 177,000. Over the years, the
Methodists of the Shore have sent the more venturesome of their young west
to populate the rest of the country, and even today the old families still dominate the phone book. What other part of the United States can boast a full
column of Dashiells (the writer Dashiell Hammett grew up on the Shore) or
Tilghmans?

But if one looks for little Williamsburgs or miniature Monticellos on the

Eastern Shore, he will not find them. Even the terrain is a little disappointing to the visitor, for the land is mostly flat and sometimes swampy; it is more pleasing viewed from a boat on one of the many inlets and coves than from ashore. Nor was the Eastern Shore ever a land of great plantations like those that lined the James River in Tidewater Virginia. This was fishing, farming, and hunting country at the time of the Revolution, and for the most part it still is.

Yet in many ways, the Eastern Shore was, and is, part—really the northernmost extension—of the Deep South. Maryland was, after all, a slave state, and more than 20 percent of the people who live on the Shore today are black. Back in the days when civil rights demonstrators were sitting in at lunch counters in Georgia and Alabama, there was a similar civil rights movement in the town of Cambridge (1970 population 11,595), in Dorchester County on the Choptank River. (H.L. Mencken used to refer to what he considered the benighted areas of the Eastern Shore as "Transchoptankiana.") In 1962 and 1963, local leader Gloria Richardson and others who would become more famous, like Stokely Carmichael, John Lewis, and H. Rap Brown, led sit-ins in Cambridge. It seems that the state of Maryland had a law banning racial discrimination in public accommodations—but until 1964 it explicitly excluded the Eastern Shore counties from coverage.

Later, in 1967, demonstrations in Cambridge took an uglier turn, when buildings were burned and Rap Brown was arrested for incitement to riot and arson. But not all the Eastern Shore has been the scene of such turbulence. Talbot County, just north of Dorchester, has at least partially and more quietly changed its ways, in large part because of the leadership of wealthy residents. While Cambridge was suffering in the early '60s from the loss of a fork lift plant, Talbot was attracting, as it had for years, wealthy residents from all over the East. The courthouse square in Easton and the docks in the quaint little town of St. Michaels bear the unmistakable imprint of big money, and the long fingerlike peninsulas jutting out into the Bay have dozens of comfortable country estates. The rich do have their eccentricities, however, which can grate on local sensibilities, as a story told by former Washington *Post* reporter Peter Jay indicates:

The late William duPont Jr. ringed his 1,000-acre waterfront estate with over three miles of chain link fence to keep in the foxes he imported for his hounds to chase.* Local farmers, more used to shooting foxes than galloping after them, thought the procedure a bit odd but paid little attention—until the winter that the rivers froze and duPont's foxes crossed the ice and spread out into the countryside, pillaging chicken coops for miles around.

But it is not only the very rich who are changing the life of the Shore. Probably the major historical event here since the Revolution was the opening of the Bay Bridge in 1952.† Suddenly the Atlantic beach resorts of Ocean

---

* Perhaps this is an appropriate place to mention that until quite recently, the Episcopal Bishop of Maryland used to bless the hounds at the start of each season.

† Recently, a second, parallel span has been completed; it was built to relieve the monstrous traffic jams of the summer weekends.

City, Maryland, and Rehoboth Beach, Delaware, were easily accessible by car from Baltimore and Washington, and residents of those fast-growing metropolitan areas who did not own boats that could get them across the Bay began to discover little towns like St. Michaels and Oxford. Predictably, real estate prices rose (estates in Talbot County have changed hands for more than $1 million), and so did property taxes. Farmers began to wonder whether it might be more profitable to tear down their chicken coops and subdivide their acreage. In the '50s and '60s the Shore's population grew as much as it had in the previous 75 years, and the summertime population grew even more. Still, the Eastern Shore counties retain, along with the almost unintelligible local accent, their placid air—with one conspicuous exception: Ocean City.

This is a narrow strip of land not much more than a mile wide and a dozen miles long with a year-round population of 1,493 and a summer weekend population that reaches 200,000. The southern end of the town, with its rundown rooming houses, amusement park, and soft ice cream stands seems to attract half the high school populations of greater Baltimore and Washington. But the real action, economically anyway, is to the north, where one 30-story high rise condominium after another has been rising over the muddy sands. "We're going to turn Ocean City into another Miami Beach," boasted Worcester County Commissioner (and local realtor) Louis Hickman. "The more people, the more development, the better." Some local residents demurred and organized a group to preserve the wetlands, but the Miamiization of Ocean City continued anyway. The splendid, unspoiled stretch of beach to the south was preserved by the creation in 1965 of the Assateague National Seashore, and to the north the state of Delaware has kept much of its beach frontage undeveloped; but in Ocean City people seem to be caught up in a speculative fever. The bubble seemed in danger of bursting in the spring of 1974, when the gasoline shortage threatened to make Ocean City less accessible and new condominium apartments went unsold. But the developers rallied with the claim—and it was not a great exaggeration—that the round trip to Ocean City from Baltimore or Washington could be negotiated on a single tank of gas. If some real estate speculators got burned, Ocean City still seemed on its way to Miami Beach-dom.

The Mountains

Looking west as the sun sets over the green hills of central Maryland, one can almost imagine how the early settlers here must have felt. The hills beckon, hiding the mysteries of a continent beyond. What must the 22-year-old George Washington have thought when, fresh from his family's lands on the lower Potomac, he blazed a trail for General Braddock and his ill-fated redcoats west toward French and Indian country in 1760? Braddock's army was the first large body of English-speaking white men to cross the Appalachian ridges, and in the years that followed the route they took through Maryland became a familiar one. The National Road, now U.S. 40 and in places Interstate 70, started at Baltimore and passed through Frederick, Hagerstown, and Cumberland; the Baltimore and Ohio Railroad, the nation's first, followed much the same path.

It is not much more than 50 miles across the fertile Piedmont from Baltimore Harbor to the first major mountain ridge, the Catoctins, just beyond Frederick: they are the northern extension of Virginia's Blue Ridge and nestled among them, although you will not find it on the map, is the presidential retreat, Camp David. Beyond the Catoctins is the valley in which Hagerstown sits, and beyond that the mountains become almost continuous, extending far west of the Maryland border. This is the forgotten part of Maryland, where the accent is closer to West Virginia than Baltimore.

The largest city is Cumberland, situated on the upper Potomac on land as hilly as Pittsburgh's. George Washington built a military outpost here on his way to Braddock's defeat, and the National Road and the B&O pass through. Cumberland's strategic position on these major arteries made it, from almost the beginning, and its 19th-century town fathers may well have seen it as a fit rival to Pittsburgh itself. That dream was never realized. By the early years of World War II, it had reached its peak population of 40,000, and ever since has been in decline. (The 1970 figure was 29,724). Celanese employed 13,000 people here in 1942; the corresponding figure in 1972 was 2,000. Railroad passenger service has almost vanished, and would be gone entirely but for the fact that House Commerce Committee Chairman Harley Staggers' home is in nearby Keyser, West Virginia.

Still, Cumberland has the look of a larger city; there are 10-story office buildings crowding narrow downtown streets, and there is still some smoke coming out of its smokestacks. Probably the biggest blow to the city came in the late '50s, when the Interstate highway builders decided to route Interstate 70 north from Hagerstown up to the Pennsylvania Turnpike. Cumberland seemed to have lost any chance at a lucrative tourist trade, and its industrial base continued to decline; the onetime gateway to the west had become an isolated backwater.

Today the Cumberland area seems to be reviving somewhat, and the catalyst is a new highway, the National Freeway, for which western Maryland lobbied long and hard. But interestingly, the city fathers of Cumberland and the town of Frostburg just to the west have been studying the example of the rest of Maryland and have at least a few qualms about the growth they have longed for and finally expect. The Freeway already bypasses downtown Cumberland and will also bypass Frostburg's business section, and local merchants are not sure that that will help their business. And neither community is eager for the kind of strip-highway-and-interchange development that is so common in the rest of Maryland. Once places like Cumberland would have sacrificed just about everything for growth, but today even this remote part of the Old Maryland seems to be learning some lessons from the New.

DELAWARE

DIMINUTIVE STATE OF THE DIVERSE DU PONTS

WHY, ONE IS tempted to ask, is Delaware a state at all? Surely no modern planner would create such a unit. Even as a vestige of the disorder of colonial rule, it is singular: a tiny strip of land 110 miles long and no more than 35 miles wide, the 47th state in population (ahead of only Vermont, Wyoming and Alaska) and the 49th in area (ahead of only Rhode Island). With 2,056 square miles, it is half the size of Los Angeles County; with 573,080 people (1974 Census estimate), it has a smaller population than Delaware County, Pennsylvania, just to the north—and less than a third as many people as nearby Philadelphia.

Yet there it is, a state with sovereign powers, with its own set of laws, with two United States Senators and three electoral votes. There is even a Delaware accent, which sounds like a cross between the Philadelphia dialect (not the Main Liner's but the ordinary Philadelphian's) and the unintelligible patois of Maryland's Eastern Shore. And there is the E.I. du Pont de Nemours & Company (1974 assets $6 billion, sales $7 billion, the nation's 17th largest corporation), with its headquarters in Wilmington, and the du Pont family, whose influence is evident throughout the state.

How Delaware Came to Be

Most of the 13 colonies were founded and settled by relatively cohesive groups, as part of a planned, purposive enterprise. The Puritans of Massachusetts, the planters of Virginia, Roger Williams and his fellows in Rhode Island, and James Oglethorpe and his band in Georgia—all of them had a pretty clear idea of what kind of society they wanted to foster. Not so Delaware. The first white man to set eyes on what now is the state gave his name to quite another place (this was Henry Hudson); the man whose name the state bears never set eyes on it. He was Sir Thomas West, Lord de la Warre, who happened to be governor of Virginia in 1610, when Captain Samuel Argall (or Argoll) sailed past and named Cape Delaware what now is known as Cape Henlopen, the point where the Delaware River empties into the ocean. The name was attached to the bay and later the river; it was used to describe the territory only when the British took it over after the conquest of Nieuw Amsterdam in 1664. In the meantime, what is now Delaware had had a polyglot history: the first white settlers were Dutch, at Zwanendael, in 1631; later it was the site of New Sweden (most of whose settlers were rebellious Dutchmen); for a while it was owned by the city of Amsterdam. Even when the English had won secure control, Delaware was still only a collection of tiny settlements, with not much more than 1,000 English, Dutch, and Swedish inhabitants.

Thus stood matters when William Penn, the Quaker son of a wealthy English admiral, proceeded to collect a 16,000-pound debt King Charles II owed his late father. The King, relieved that Penn wanted land in North America rather than cash, granted him title to Pennsylvania—and, almost as an afterthought, the deed to what Penn called the "territories" along the Delaware River.* There were no white settlers yet in the larger of the territories, where Penn and his followers set about creating the Quaker paradise that became Pennsylvania. But Penn's title to Delaware was clouded (it seems that the King had failed to execute certain papers, and Lord Baltimore was claiming it as part of Maryland), and the fractious residents were not at all sure they wanted to be part of Penn's commonwealth. They were also unhappy that Penn was not protecting them from the depredations of pirates like Blackbeard and Captain Kidd or from the exactions of Lord Baltimore's tax collectors. Finally, in 1704, Penn gave up, and Delaware became a colony of the crown, separate from both Pennsylvania and Maryland.

One of the reasons Delaware retained this separate political identity is that no one coveted it. It produced no tobacco or rice, it had no thriving port, indeed it had very few settlers (37,000 at the time of the Revolution). London generally let the Delawareans run things as they wished; given this benign neglect, Delaware was naturally one of the first colonies to protest George III's stamp tax. This was the first colony to call itself a "state," and it even had its own "presidents" during the Revolutionary War (the first of whom, unfortunately, was captured by the British). After the war, tiny, well-to-do Rhode Island resisted joining the Union; tiny, poor Delaware hastened to sign up. It was the first state—as its license plates testify today—

---

* The latter deed granted Penn the territory within a 12-mile circular arc around the town of New Castle (just below Wilmington), plus all the land south of that to Cape Henlopen. After a little sharp dealing with Lord Baltimore's agents, the southern boundary was extended further, but the circular northern boundary remains to this day—indeed the only circular state boundary in the United States.

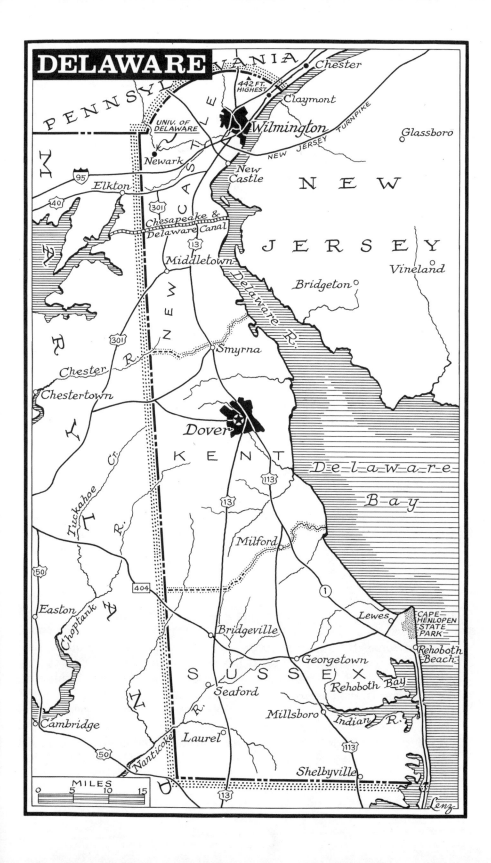

to ratify the Constitution, on December 7, 1787. One cannot help thinking that one of the reasons Delawareans were so eager to go along was to preserve their separate identity.

Most of the later history of Delaware, to be frank, is a little dull. Its chief interest derives from the fact that it was very much a border state. It allowed slavery but prohibited the importation of slaves as early as 1787; it stayed with the Union during the Civil War but supported white supremacy by voting Democratic for several decades thereafter. The liveliest time in the state's political history was around the turn of the century when a Massachusetts gas company promoter, one J. Edward Addicks, moved in with the avowed intention of buying himself a U.S. Senate seat. He never succeeded, but he helped corrupt the state's politics and created so much acrimony that during one two-year period the state legislature was unable to elect anyone at all to the Senate.

For most of its history, Delaware was an economic backwater, a state of small and not particularly prosperous farms which sent its children west in search of more fertile lands. Yet it became the headquarters of what was to be one of the nation's largest corporations and perhaps its wealthiest family, both named du Pont. Finally, this is the state which perfected the so-called liberal incorporation law, making it the legal home not only of du Pont but of hundreds of other corporate entities in America.

We will look at the du Ponts, company and family, in a moment, but first consider incorporation. Back in the days when Daniel Webster was arguing cases before the Supreme Court, states chartered business corporations one by one, with the legislatures passing acts setting up each company and setting strict limits on its powers. Needless to say, this slow process did not exactly encourage entrepreneurism. As a result, states began enacting laws allowing incorporation generally, but still with some pretty sharp limits. New Jersey and then Delaware got the idea—or were persuaded of its wisdom by corporate lobbyists—of liberal incorporation laws, which would allow management to pretty much run things as it liked, without much interference from stockholders, directors, or the state. Delaware also had the idea that by imposing lower corporate franchise taxes than states like New York or Illinois it could persuade major corporations to incorporate in Delaware—and that the taxes they paid, at however low a rate, would bulk large in the tiny state's revenues.

That is exactly how it has worked out. Delaware by 1974 was the home of 76,000 corporations—one for every seven residents—including about one-third of the companies listed on the New York and American Stock Exchanges. Most of these corporations, of course, do not have their headquarters in Delaware; there is just a paper office, usually on the premises of firms set up for just that purpose, while the real business is done elsewhere. But the franchise taxes still are Delaware's second biggest source of revenue, and there is a steady business among lawyers and incorporating firms, set up to help non-Delawareans establish their own corporations. One of the authors of this book once had occasion to incorporate a company in Delaware, with the aid of one such firm. The place where the deed is actually done, where the corporation springs into legal existence, is the second story of a Georgian building in the tiny state capital of Dover. One is escorted up a steep flight of stairs by a pleasant lady to a room full of green metal files. In those drawers are the sheets of paper which created and continue to embody, legally, the existence of General Motors and General Electric and IBM and ITT and all the hundreds of others, the major corporations which control so much of the productive assets of the American economy.

A smaller proportion of new incorporations are taking place in Delaware in the mid-'70s, as other states lower their taxes or liberalize their restrictions on management's corporate power. Nevertheless, Delaware is still a leader in the field, and incorporation in Delaware retains several basic advantages, at least from management's point of view: (1) well-established corporate law precedents, so that management knows what it can and can't do; (2) prompt (and usually pro-management) court decisions, preventing shakedown suits by minority shareholders; and (3) good service in the secretary of state's office.

Du Pont

We have come so far in this account with only passing mention of the name of the company and family which have dominated Delaware longer than any single company or single family have dominated any state: du Pont. The association with the state began almost accidentally. In the late 18th century, Pierre Samuel du Pont was a minor French nobleman nimble enough to survive the Revolution with much of his money and his head. One son was the French Ambassador to the United States during the first Adams administration; another, Éleuthère Irénée du Pont, had learned the mundane gunpowder business in Europe. In 1799, Pierre decided to move his family to America, and they arrived—having eaten boiled rats during the slow sea voyage—on New Year's Day, 1800. Pierre had grand dreams: he wanted to create an inland empire called Pontiana, with houses, schools, roads and waterways, somewhere in the vastness of Ohio. He employed considerable sophistication in trying to realize his elaborate schemes, nurturing his friendship with Thomas Jefferson and at the same time hiring as his lawyer one Alexander Hamilton. But none of Pierre's enterprises made much money, and in 1802 he acquiesced to Éleuthère Irénée's prosaic plan to set up a gunpowder mill.

The younger du Pont, after scouting the East Coast from New York to Washington, had chanced on a likely site on the Brandywine Creek in Delaware, 12 miles above the then tiny village of Wilmington. Irénée lacked his father's imperial vision, but instead had a certain hard-headed practicality, as shown by du Pont biographer William H.A. Carr's description of the first of the Eleutherian mills (as they are now called):

Instead of one big building, he put up several small ones. He allowed for a generous space between each, so that a fire or explosion in one would be less likely to spread in a chain reaction to the others. Three sides of each building were constructed of stone walls three times as thick as those of an ordinary structure. The fourth side, facing the creek, was not as high as the wall opposite and it was not as strong. The roof, which slanted down toward the stream, was only a flimsy cover of wood. The reason for this design was simple: when an explosion occurred, the force of the blast was directly upward and toward the creek, thus minimizing the damage and the number of casualties.

Even with all these precautions there was always the possibility that the entire enterprise would, literally, go up in smoke; instead, it became an empire with far greater resources than papa Pierre could have dreamed. One reason for that growth, inevitably in the powder business, was war; as Irénée wrote his father in 1803, "The condition of war that exists in Europe is very promising for my enterprise. I will do all I can to profit by it." And that is just what the du Pont company did—in the War of 1812, the Civil War, the Spanish-American War, various European conflicts, and World War I. At the time of the Civil War the company was already producing half the nation's gunpowder. By the 1890s, du Pont had an effective monopoly over the manufacture of explosives in the United States. That monopoly was broken by a federal antitrust suit launched in 1907, but only technically—since the two new companies created to compete with du Pont, Atlas and Hercules, were owned largely by members of the du Pont family.

At about the same time, the du Pont family and firm were rent by a feud with a personal origin. Alfred I. du Pont, one of three younger members of the family who had taken over the company in 1902, had divorced his wife and married a cousin, also divorced; and most of the rest of the du Ponts snubbed them. The family feud resulted in a battle for control of the company, with Alfred outmaneuvered by his younger cousin, Pierre. Having lost the company, Alfred continued the contest in the political arena, as a progressive Republican against his more conservative Republican relatives. As the state's Progressive boss, Alfred helped to defeat Senator Henry A. du Pont in 1916. Six years later, Alfred supported Democrat Thomas F. Bayard, Jr., against T. Coleman du Pont; Bayard, a du Pont in-law and a member of a family that has produced several Senators, barely won. (Coleman later won in 1924.) During much of this time Alfred owned the Wilmington *News* and Senator Henry A. the Wilmington *Journal*—with predictable results. So bitter was Alfred against his relatives that he influenced the legislature to pass a graduated inheritance tax (since repealed).*

The real founder of the du Pont empire as we know it today was Alfred's rival Pierre. Pierre won control of the company as World War I was raging in Europe—a conflict which made du Pont very wealthy indeed. Insisting on 50 percent cash up front from the Allies, du Pont's gross income during the war was $1 billion, and profits were $237 million. With huge amounts of cash in the till, du Pont diversified widely, into chemicals, paints, plastics—and General Motors, of which du Pont gained control in 1920. The story of how Pierre du Pont placed Alfred P. Sloan, Jr., at the head of GM properly belongs

---

* The eccentric Alfred du Pont left Delaware in the late 1920s for Florida, where he acquired much property; his estate, under the control of his late brother-in-law, Edward Ball, has been a financial and political power in the sunshine state for years. Ironically, the rather progressive Alfred's money has been devoted there to the most conservative of causes. See *The Deep South States of America*, pp. 481–82.

to Michigan, not Delaware, but GM was not the only major corporation the du Ponts sired; Francis I., an ally of Alfred's, founded Francis I. du Pont and Company, the nation's second largest brokerage firm until its collapse in the early 1970s, and Henry B. played a key role in the development of what became Trans World Airlines.

The du Pont corporation that emerged from these years was one of the more innovative of the major American companies. Besides introducing into the United States foreign-developed products like rubber, cellophane (which was considerably improved by du Pont), lucite, and polyethylene, du Pont developed by itself artificial rubber (originally "DuPrene"), nylon, teflon, orlon, dacron, and mylar polyester film. Or, as du Pont's longtime slogan put it, "better things for better living—through chemistry." * But the things which had made du Pont such an industrial colossus also came back to haunt it. In the 1930s, Pierre du Pont and his brothers Irénée and Lammot were dubbed the "merchants of death" as they appeared before Senator Gerald P. Nye's committee investigating World War I munition-makers' profits. (Pierre and his brothers were also in trouble with a majority of the American public at the time as the best known opponents of Franklin D. Roosevelt. In 1936 they poured $1 million into the Landon campaign and largely bank-rolled the anti-New Deal Liberty League—which James Farley called the Cellophane League because, he said, it was made by du Pont and you could see through it.)

Years later, in 1949, du Pont was challenged in a government antitrust suit for its continuing ownership of 23 percent of the shares in General Motors. Eight years later, the Supreme Court declared the arrangement illegal. Suddenly, it appeared that the du Ponts would have to pay huge taxes on the divestiture of the GM shares—a calamity which was averted through special legislation passed by the Congress of the United States (the du Ponts hired, among others, Clark Clifford to help them in this fight) and the Delaware legislature.

Amidst all this tumult, du Pont remained the largest family-run firm in the world except the Ford Motor Company. Young du Ponts were encouraged to enter the business, in chemistry or engineering if they had such inclinations, or as sales or finance executives. And the top spots, or so it seemed for many years, were reserved for du Ponts or du Pont in-laws; Lammot and Irénée du Pont were succeeded as chief operating officers by Walter S. Carpenter, Crawford H. Greenewalt, Lammot du Pont Copeland, and Charles B. McCoy—all sons, husbands, or in-laws of du Ponts.

But as the 1960s turned into the 1970s, the tradition of family control was on the wane. To be sure, pedigreed du Ponts retained the lion's share of seats on the company's board of directors. But the younger du Ponts did not seem to be climbing so fast—and in at least one case, they seemed to fall. That was the instance of Lammot du Pont Copeland, Jr., who in 1970—while his father was still du Pont's chairman of the board—went into personal

---

* In 1971, du Pont broadened its image with a new slogan: "There's a world of things we're doing something about."

bankruptcy. It wasn't that he didn't have assets—he listed $25 million worth —but rather that he had become involved in business deals which left him with former partners who had absconded to countries without extradition treaties and with personal debts of $59 million. Happily for "Motsey" Copeland, Delaware law prevented his creditors from touching his $500,000 house or certain trusts which yielded him income of $300,000 a year; embarrassingly for his family, the Wilmington Trust, wholly du Pont-owned, had somehow managed to grab off some of Motsey's assets before bankruptcy. Less fortunate was the Chemical Bank of New York, on whose board Motsey's father sat. It had loaned young Copeland $3 million.

No one is willing to say that Copeland senior's retirement shortly after his son's bankruptcy happened as a direct result; indeed, the case could be made that du Pont had not been doing quite as well as it should have been under the stewardship of these latter day du Ponts, and that it was time for new blood. In any event, the new head of the company, Charles B. McCoy, though not technically a du Pont himself, did have two sons who married into the family, and it was only in 1974 that a truly major departure from tradition occurred. This was the selection as chairman of Irving S. Shapiro, a lawyer, a Democrat, and a Jew. And in the same year, the Securities and Exchange Commission approved the merger into the du Pont Company of Christiana Securities, a holding company set up by the du Ponts in 1915 as a vehicle for maintaining their control of the corporation their ancestors founded. (Christiana owned 28 percent of du Pont's outstanding common stock.) The SEC said that "those who control Christiana think that Christiana has outlived its usefulness. Du Pont, they say, is no longer a family firm. Hence, the family no longer needs Christiana."

Another milestone was reached in 1974 when du Pont finally quit making dynamite, the traditional base of the company's business, and substituted a du Pont-invented synthetic. The company's major business now is not in explosives but in mundane products like textile fibers and fabrics.

We should add that du Pont, for all its weight, is not the only big corporate employer in Delaware. It is true that the du Pont headquarters office in Wilmington, together with a du Pont laboratory in the city and a du Pont nylon fiber plant in Seaford employ almost 14,000 workers between them. But (at least in good times) Chrysler has 5,000 workers in an auto assembly plant in Newark, General Motors 3,600 in Wilmington, Rollins International 4,200 in Wilmington, American Finance Systems 3,570 in Wilmington, and Phoenix Steel 2,300 in Claymont, just to mention a few of the largest non-du Pont firms.

The du Ponts and Delaware

No one is quite sure just how many du Ponts there are; estimates range up to 2,000, and there are perhaps 400 living in Delaware. In other words, this is a much more numerous, and inevitably much more various, family than, say, the Rockefellers or the (Henry) Fords. Concentrated as they are in this tiny state, these extremely wealthy men and women make up a discernible one-tenth of one percent of the state's population—surely the only state where the rich bulk so large even in votes.

Naturally, by virtue of their numbers as well as their wealth, the du Ponts have been heavily involved in the state's affairs over the years, not simply in politics but in the very exercise of governmental functions. Back in the 1920s, for example, Pierre du Pont had commissioned a study of the state's educational system and, while the legislature dawdled over his recommendations, personally paid for more than 100 new school buildings (including many for blacks) ultimately costing $4 million. Pierre was then appointed state tax commissioner and, at his own expense, assembled a list of delinquent taxpayers and pursued them in court. (At the same time, Pierre was running du Pont and GM and building his huge estate, Longwood, across the Delaware line in Pennsylvania.) Pierre's rival, Alfred du Pont, started up his own old-age pension system, paying out $350,000 until he persuaded the legislature to adopt the program. And earlier, T. Coleman du Pont had begun building and paid for the first paved highway to run up and down the state, at a cost of $4 million.

Then there is the University of Delaware—a school which "comes close to being a du Pont-directed enterprise," according to *Science* magazine. Over the years, the du Ponts have poured an estimated $100 million into the school, establishing a particularly strong chemistry department, which of course was of some help to the company. A major benefactor of the university for many years until his death in 1970 was Henry B. du Pont, the unofficial patriarch of the clan, a man as formidable physically as financially. Yet Richard Sanger, then editor of the Wilmington *News-Journal*, told us, "appearance deceived. Henry B. was actually quite shy and introverted and, like many du Ponts, hard of hearing." Shy and introverted as he may have been, Henry B. was not above remonstrating with the newspaper editors or others if the university or some other favorite du Pont institution were, in the family's opinion, slandered. To a du Pont, used to hearing pleasant things, mild criticism could sound like slander. And at the university, faculty members reportedly felt constrained to keep to themselves their antiwar or other unorthodox opinions, lest one of the crankier du Ponts on the board made a fuss.*

The problems of du Pont control received a greater public airing in the case of Wilmington's two daily newspapers, *The Morning News* and *Evening*

---

* The *Science* magazine article already quoted gives another instance of du Pont influence on the university. "One research project sponsored by Robert R.M. Carpenter, Jr., a member of the du Pont family who serves as a university trustee, has particularly provoked charges that the family is 'using' the university for its own purposes. The project, which is somewhat outside the usual line of university research, involves analyzing baseball swings with electronic sensors. Carpenter, who owns the Philadelphia Phillies professional baseball team, hopes that electronic gadgetry produced by researchers at the university will ultimately help him pick the most promising prospects for major league baseball careers on his team."

Journal, which had long been a du Pont property through the family's holding company, Christiana Securities. There had been past instances of suspicious subservience of the editors to du Pont whims and interests, but in the early 1970s editorial direction of the papers passed to young editors who occasionally published articles critical of both the du Pont Company and family interests. There followed a heavy confrontation between the 66-year-old chairman of the *News-Journal* board of directors, David H. Dawson, a du Pont senior vice president, and John G. Craig Jr., the 41-year-old executive editor of the two papers. Dawson was determined to cut down on perceived editorial department extravagances and increase low profits because Christiana had announced its intention to sell the papers ("It's possible to make too good a newspaper," Dawson was quoted as saying at one point). Craig, on the other hand, wanted lively, high-grade papers with full editorial independence. Finally the board removed so much of Craig's authority that he resigned; there followed mass protests from the newsroom and a public brouhaha about imperiled editorial independence and du Pont heavyhandedness. Out of the mess came a happy solution: appointment of Norman Isaacs, the prestigious former executive editor of the Louisville *Courier-Journal,* as president and publisher of the papers, vested with complete editorial control. (Isaacs served from winter 1975 to August 1976, when he was replaced by Andrew Fisher, former executive vice president of the New York *Times.*) The du Pont interests still planned to sell the *News-Journal* when the court action surrounding the breakup of Christiana Securities is completed.

The newspaper incident was preceded by considerable fuss in Delaware over the 1973 publication of *The Company State,* written by a group of Ralph Nader's raiders. The book helped to quantify the degree of du Pont control, calculating that the du Pont company generated 21 percent of the gross state product. Also tabulated were the number of du Pont relatives, spouses, and employees in the legislature. Besides that, as Nader authors James Phelan and Robert Pozen pointed out, the du Ponts owned the Wilmington newspapers, the du Pont and Nemours and Brandywine Buildings in downtown Wilmington, and much of Delaware's most valuable commercial real estate, and had a major share of control in the state's leading banks. The conclusion was inevitable: there is simply no equivalent to this one-family, one-company dominance in any state in the nation. (The last parallel may have been Anaconda Copper's domination of economic life—and ownership of most newspapers—in Montana in past years. But that has faded, and in any event it was just a corporate, not a family affair.)

But having said all this, what of it? *The Company State* reaches a ponderously negative conclusion: "In short, du Pont in Delaware is the prototype of the large corporation in the American community. . . . In Delaware, the mother state has virtually been replaced by the mother company; corporate power is no longer private, but has nearly preempted public power." And all that is surely so; here is a massive concentration of power in a few hands. To what ends? Well, we have already seen how mixed the actions of the du

Ponts have been—open-handed generosity and creative philanthropy have been alternated with tight-fisted crabbiness and reactionary attempts at thought control. The Nader writers admit there is a problem here for the very wealthy: "If du Pont runs social action programs, then it is accused of usurping public functions; if du Pont does nothing, it is chastised for corporate apathy." Then *The Company State* bores right ahead and condemns du Pont for both meddling and inaction, and provides a simplistic solution: "a large corporation should act so as to provide the community with a maximum of benefits and a minimum of domination." Of course, this just ducks all the difficult questions—who decides what is a benefit? How does one avoid domination? What it is really saying is that the people, presumably through the government, should control this vast wealth; and it is too bad that the Nader people shy away from making what is, after all, the intellectually respectable, if hardly politically salable, case for socialism.

Indeed, one can see why du Pont executives must have been exasperated with *The Company State*. The book criticizes the company on the one hand for not obeying antipollution laws and on the other attacks du Pont executives for supporting the state's pioneer coastal preservation act (on which more later). Its most interesting charges are that the company has deliberately kept most of its manufacturing plants out of Delware to hold down the state's blue collar (and Democratic) population and, for that same reason, and to prevent competitive wages, has discouraged other industries from locating in Delaware. (Du Pont is a largely non-union firm, with only 5 percent of its employees in ALF-CIO unions.) We are skeptical that du Pont has made its plant location decisions with partisan political effects in mind, but it is true that—for whatever reason—the policy of concentrating the bulk of du Pont's white collar employment in Delaware and spreading its blue collar work force across the nation has had the effect of making Delaware an increasingly white collar, affluent state; its work force was 49 percent white collar in 1970, as against 43 percent in 1960.

There are other criticisms worth noting too, for example the laboriously documented charges that various du Pont properties are grossly underassessed by the local taxing authorities. Du Pont has a very liberal policy of allowing executives time off for public services, and dozens have served in the legislature, on county boards, and even, in recent years, in the United States Senate (William V. Roth) and the governor's chair (Russell Peterson). But that same policy, the Nader researchers found, does not apply to blue collar employees. Certainly there are abuses of du Pont's power which should be corrected. But the central problem remains: a family and a company which are so hugely wealthy and which are located primarily in a single, tiny state are inevitably going to dominate financial and governmental affairs there. For that one might as well blame William Penn for allowing Delaware to split away from Pennsylvania, or the man who interested Éleuthère du Pont in building his powder mill on Brandywine Creek.

Governing Delaware

What is surprising about Delaware's state government is that it is as progressive as it is, given the inevitable du Pont influence and the deep-seated conservatism of so many members of the family. We have already seen how Alfred du Pont's feud with Pierre led to progressive state tax laws, and even today Delaware has one of the most steeply progressive state income taxes, with rates ranging up to 19.8 percent on income over $100,000. *The Company State* charges that exemptions and loopholes left the highest effective rate at 6.8 percent in 1967 despite a nominal 11 percent levy then. Even so, that represents a bigger tax bite on the wealthy than in the large majority of the states. Moreover, in 1974 Delaware's effective income tax rates for a family of four with a $25,000 income was 5 percent—more than in all but two other states, Wisconsin and Minnesota. The state has also enacted a gift tax, ranging up to as much as 16 percent on gifts over $200,000—which even *The Company State* admits will produce substantial revenue, since people as wealthy as the du Ponts transfer much of their property to their heirs during their lifetimes. Interestingly, despite a number of recent fiscal crises, Delaware is one of five states without a general sales tax—a tax essentially regressive in character. If we were conservative-minded, wealthy oligarchs in absolute control of a small state, this is certainly not the tax system we would design.

Delaware can afford such an odd tax structure because the corporate franchise tax, which we have already mentioned, is the second-largest revenue producer in the state. But in this case, that does not mean very much; even though combined state and local taxes rose faster in Delaware than in any other state between 1953 and 1975 (from 4.21 to 11.4 percent of personal income), the overall tax burden is still the lightest of any state in the Union (and a spectacular 35 percent below the average for the Mid-Atlantic states). The state budget is smaller than those of all but four other states, smaller than the amount of salaries paid to employees in Delaware by du Pont, indeed only one-tenth the size of total du Pont Company revenues. Only Alaska, Vermont, and Wyoming have fewer state employees. In other words, state government in Delaware is pretty small potatoes, bulking far less large in the Middle Atlantic States picture than the municipal budgets of places like Baltimore or Philadelphia or even some of the larger suburban counties.

But Delaware still has something those cities and counties can never enjoy, the power as a sovereign state to regulate its own affairs. And lest that look like bombastic Fourth of July rhetoric, consider what Delaware has done with its coastline. To many, the 115-mile Delaware shoreline, most of it on Delaware Bay but the southern portion directly on the Atlantic, is not particularly exciting. Around Wilmington, the shore is heavily industrialized, as is the Delaware River above it well beyond Philadelphia. But below New

Castle, little industry had reached the Delaware shore as the 1970s began. Much of the land was swampy, some was farmland, some—particularly the southernmost stands, near Maryland's gaudy Ocean City—had been set aside for parkland.

But the prospect was that all this would change shortly. Shell Oil wanted to build a refinery in Delaware, and a Texas firm was planning a coal and ore loading station. Into that situation stepped Governor Russell Peterson, a Republican, a chemist at du Pont for 28 years, and, in his spare time, a bird-watcher. Peterson conceived and in 1971 pushed through the legislature Delaware's Coastal Zone Act. The first such measure in the nation, it flatly banned new oil refineries, superports, petrochemical plants, steel mills, and paper mills within two miles of the coast. Shell was stymied (it decided to build in New Jersey), environmentalists around the nation saluted little Delaware, and in 1972 California voters passed a somewhat similar act.

But by 1974, there was a strong movement for repeal. Many Delawareans began worrying less about the effects of growth than about whether there would be any growth at all. Peterson had been defeated for re-election in 1972 and had moved on to Washington to become chairman of the Council on Environmental Quality. The new Governor, Democrat Sherman Tribbett, was equivocal. And of course the oil shortage of 1974 had made new refineries seem in many people's eyes a blessing rather than a curse.

The various alliances that arose over this issue tell us a lot about Delaware politics and power. Among the leaders of the fight for repeal were the head of the state AFL-CIO, who was especially worried about high unemployment among construction workers, and Irving Shapiro, the new chairman of du Pont (the company had been quite neutral on the 1971 act, and Shapiro insisted that it was not putting any pressure on employee-legislators in 1974). Arrayed against repeal were Mrs. Henry B. du Pont and Congressman Pierre S. du Pont IV. The state legislators leading the fight for and against repeal were both Republicans and both chemists at du Pont.

So much for the theory that du Pont is some kind of monolith imposing its will on the state. The coastal zone act was not repealed, despite its formidable opponents. The writers of *The Company State* attempted to spin a theory that du Pont supported the coastal zone act in order to keep other industry out of Delaware and out of competition in the local labor market, but three years later the head of du Pont took just the opposite position. At the same time, the du Pont employees in the legislature—and they make up about one-quarter of its members—were obviously not acting in subservience to the corporation; they showed no more cohesion than members of, say, the national Democratic Party. As for the family, any group of several hundred extremely wealthy people is going to be in disagreement on many matters, and so with the du Ponts.

It was convenient for anyone trying to prove that Delaware was run entirely by the du Pont interests to point out that Governor Peterson was a former du Pont employee; what was not convenient for someone with such a theory was Peterson's record in office and the fact that he was defeated. Indeed, the cumulative record of Peterson's four years in office (1969–73) outshone anything Delaware had seen in generations, and can be compared favorably with the accomplishments of practically any other American governor in recent times. Besides the coastal zone act, Peterson was responsible for many reforms in the criminal justice system (including work release programs for prisoners and abolition of the state's archaic debtor prison and whipping post), a crackdown on drunken drivers, improved highway safety, the first state aid to equalize funding between affluent and poorer school districts, expanded kindergartens, the first blacks on the state police, a state council for the arts, and important management economies. On taking office in 1969, Peterson immediately removed National Guard troops from Wilmington. Following racial disturbances, they had been stationed there for nine months by his ultraconservative Democratic predecessor, much to the dismay of the city's mayor.

A lasting monument to the Peterson administration is the thoroughgoing reorganization of state government accomplished during his tenure. Traditionally, Delaware had been ruled by a commission form of government, with some 140 separate entities. The commissioners all had other regular employment, and met only once a month. To get action on a problem, a citizen might have to cultivate all the members of a particular commission. Logrolling was prevalent; to get a particular road blacktopped, for instance, there might have to be agreement to get a bridge built in the home area of a recalcitrant highway commissioner. "It took a whole term of a governor," Peterson told us, "until I could appoint my people to a commission, and once they were appointed, they had no responsibility to anyone. They could tell me to go to hell—and sometimes did."

Another problem of the old system was its rural, antimetropolitan bias. The legislature had been reapportioned in the wake of the U.S. Supreme Court's "one man, one vote" edicts, but old-line Democratic governors had left control of most of the commissions in the hands of conservatives from the big rural area "south of the canal" (the Chesapeake and Delaware Canal), where only 30 percent of the state's people live. (The canal, significantly, is close to the Mason-Dixon line.)

Under the reorganization, all the old commissions (with one holdout, the board of higher education) were abolished. In their place, 10 cabinet-level departments were established, one of the "cleanest" reorganizations accomplished by any state in modern times. The result was a dramatic increase in accountability in state government. As soon as the cabinet form took effect, Peterson said, "my seat as governor got a hundred times hotter overnight. Now everyone knew the responsibility was with me and the cabinet secretaries I appointed and controlled."

Peterson claimed that a major reason for his eventual defeat was the irritation caused in southern Delaware "when it lost its preferred position" through demise of the old commissions that could decide everything from "whose mother got into a nursing home to whose creek got dredged." Other factors that hurt Peterson in the southern counties, he said, were his appointments of blacks to a number of state government jobs, signing an open housing law in the town of Camden in southern Delaware, and institution of a merit system that upset old patronage arrangements.

Probably more than any of these events, however, the real reason for Peterson's political demise was the same thing that has been the undoing of so many other governors: taxes. On taking office, Peterson had been forced to back a tax hike, and he unwisely promised that that would be his last tax increase. Two years later, after overly optimistic revenue projections, Peterson had to eat his words, and 12 different kinds of taxes were raised. Taken together with his prison reform and coastal zone policies, this made Peterson anathema to conservative Republicans, and he barely survived a primary challenge in 1972; thus weakened, he lost the general election that year to conservative Democrat Sherman Tribbett. A longtime veteran of Delaware politics, a man who has sponsored bills to reduce the impact of taxes on the du Ponts, Tribbett did manage to push a wetlands conservation bill of some merit. But many of his appointments were of under- or totally unqualified persons. A state lottery, begun in spring 1975, was so totally botched through maladministration that it closed down temporarily a few weeks after its start. One could say that where Peterson had put his own distinguished impression on governance of the state, Tribbett mostly bumbled. In 1976 he was opposed by U.S. Rep. Pierre S. (Pete) du Pont, a highly popular Republican votegetter, and went down to resounding defeat. Du Pont charged the Tribbett administration with corruption, political cronyism and government by crisis, and a hefty majority of the state's people seemed to agree. With du Pont as governor, there seemed a good chance Delaware would again receive the quality leadership it had enjoyed during the Peterson years.

Partisan Politics in the Diamond State

It would be a hardy prognosticator who would attempt to predict the result of a Delaware election; in this state where no more than 229,000 people have ever voted for a Senator, elections are inclined to be close. Pierre du Pont's 1976 election was an exception to the rule: he won with more than 33,000 votes to spare. Over the years, however, the partisan competition has generally been tight and ticket splitting rampant.* A reflection of the state's sensitivity to national trends, however, is that it has voted for the winner in every presidential election of this century except 1932 and 1948. Peterson calls Delaware a "microcosm of America," complete with its own industrial North, rural South, affluent suburbs, heavily black center city,

* Some examples: In 1948 the state voted Republican for President and the U.S. House, but Democratic for Senator and governor. In 1972 the vote went Republican for President and the U.S. House, but Democratic for governor and Senator. In 1976 it was just the reverse: Democratic for President but Republican for governor and Senator. The votes in 1960 and 1964 were equally split.

agriculture, and advanced industries. Some national polling organizations have used the state as a reflection of the entire country.

Predictably, the du Ponts have always been a factor in Delaware politics. But historically there have been both Democratic and Republican du Ponts

Perhaps the most interesting figure of Delaware politics in the mid-1970s was a figure of distinctly non-du Pont, non-establishment credentials: U.S. Sen. Joseph R. Biden, Jr. In 1972, just short of his 30th birthday, Biden made his first bid for statewide office and surprisingly upset veteran Republican Sen. J. Caleb Boggs. As a one term member of the New Castle County Council, he had made friends in all three counties of the state, and was considered a strong candidate for governor; he ran for the Senate instead. His campaign manager was his sister, and his wife, brothers, and parents all played key roles in the campaign. With a relatively small campaign chest, Biden had to depend on volunteers—and he attracted enough to have pieces of literature hand-delivered to every door in the state on the same day. Biden was shrewd enough not to attack the well-liked Boggs directly. And by making a virtue of his openness he managed to avert the abrasive effects of his own brash personality. He won, as Richard Nixon was easily carrying the state, by 3,162 votes. Then, a few weeks later, tragedy struck; the Senator-elect's wife and infant daughter were killed in a car crash near Wilmington. At the urging of Senate Majority Leader Mike Mansfield, Biden decided to carry on in the Senate, returning to Delaware every night for dinner with his young sons. There are those who think he might run for President some day. In 1975, Biden broke rank with the liberals by introducing and shepherding through the Senate a measure opposing forced school busing. Busing, Biden said, "is a counterproductive concept" and violates "the cardinal rule of common sense."

Senator Roth cuts a quieter figure in Washington. He is a moderate-to-conservative Republican who has worked to change some of the hoarier traditions of the Senate, including secret committee sessions. Roth also became a chief co-sponsor with Maine's Sen. Edmund S. Muskie, of "sunset" legislation to put all federal programs on a five-year life cycle, requiring specific congressional renewal if they are to continue after that period of time.

Our quick review of the Delaware congressional delegation should not omit Republican John Williams, whom Biden succeeded. Elected in the famous Republican class of '47 (along with men like John W. Bricker of Ohio, Henry Cabot Lodge Jr. of Massachusetts, Joseph R. McCarthy of Wisconsin, and William E. Jenner of Indiana), Williams outlasted them all to become third ranking Republican in the Senate. More importantly, he became "the conscience of the Senate," an indefatigable seeker of official wrongdoing who exposed a huge tax-fixing ring in the Internal Revenue Service, questionable defense contracts, excessive grain storage payments by the Commodity Credit Corporation, and the suspicious dealings of later-to-be-convicted Billie Sol Estes and Bobby Baker. A shy man, ill-equipped for public speaking, Williams won wide respect for his dogged investigations. After his retirement, there was a move to name a board of health building in Dover after him. But Williams demurred and suggested instead that the building be named after the recently deceased, previously anonymous tax expert who had given him the vital first tip in cracking Internal Revenue Service wrongdoing in 1951. The structure stands there today, "The Jesse S. Cooper Memorial Building." Cooper, it turned out, had been the Democratic state treasurer of Delaware. Williams' comment, after the dedication ceremony: "Corruption in government is not a partisan matter."

The Central City, the Chateau Country, and the Chicken Farms: A Quick Tour through a Tiny State

Wilmington owes its existence as a city to the du Ponts; before Éleuthère Irénée set up his powder mill on Brandywine Creek, it was just a tiny village, overshadowed by the town of New Castle. Now it is New Castle which exists, a grimy industrial village, in the wash of Wilmington's suburbs.* At the center of Wilmington—and it is really the center of all Delaware, too—is Rodney Square, a pleasant block-wide park. Across the street on one side is the du Pont Building (referred to locally as "the Building"), which with its neighbors the Nemours and Brandywine Buildings houses most of the company's chief executives. The Hotel du Pont (referred to locally as "the Hotel"), Wilmington's finest, is lodged in part of the du Pont Building; another portion houses the Playhouse, Delaware's only legitimate theater, which is also owned by the du Ponts. Also facing the square are the headquarters of the state's leading banks and most of Delaware's major law firms; within a block or two are the city and county governments and the Delmarva Power Company. About the only thing lacking to make this the focus of all power in Delaware is the state capitol. (For that one must visit the placid little colonial era city of Dover—population 17,488—several miles to the south.)

No one could resist noting the contrast between the neat but scarcely gaudy prosperity of Rodney Square and the condition of most of the rest of Wilmington: sad to say, much of the state's only large city is an undistinguished slum. Wilmington's problems are not much different from those of so many of the nation's central cities: tightly confined within city limits established years ago, Wilmington, only 15 square miles in size, has been losing population, especially affluent population, to the suburbs beyond. In 1970 Wilmington had 80,386 citizens, 15 percent of Delaware's population; by way of comparison, in 1940, the city had a population of 112,540, 42 percent of the state's total.

Thirty years ago, Wilmington's population was a fairly representative cross-section of society, from poor blacks and whites in low-lying row houses near the big factories to du Ponts living along Pennsylvania Avenue, a mile or so from Rodney Square. Today just about half of Wilmington's citizens are

* To be fair, we should point out that New Castle (1970 population, 4,814) does have a section of colonial and federal period homes and public buildings little changed from the early 19th century.

black (as are more than 80 percent of its public school pupils), most are poor, a disproportionate number are the very young or very old, and the bulk of the metropolitan area's population is firmly planted in the suburbs.

Wilmington made at least the fine print of the national press in April 1968, with the riots that broke out after the murder of Martin Luther King, Jr. But the riots remained a living presence because the governor, conservative Democrat Charles Terry, refused to order the National Guard troops back out of the city after the crisis was over, despite the pleas of the mayor. Wilmington literally lived under the gun for eight months until Terry left office. That same year, the city elected a Republican mayor, Harry Haskell, Jr., an extremely wealthy man whose fortune came out of his father's association with the 1920s Pierre du Pont. Haskell pushed some innovative programs, built public housing, and reduced property taxes (by imposing a wages tax). Respected nationally, he was a significant force behind the enactment of federal revenue sharing.* But none of this was enough to reelect him in 1972. The winner was councilman Thomas C. Maloney, just 30 years old, who was soon to make a name for himself by inaugurating what became the nation's first urban homestead act in 1973.

Under the homestead act, people may take possession of dilapidated houses abandoned for back taxes and, if they bring them up to housing code standards in 18 months and live in them for three years, receive title. The program made a splash in the national media; it has helped to rejuvenate a few Wilmington streets; but after three years in operation, only 23 houses in the city had actually been awarded to "homesteaders"—and five of those had been turned back because the new owners could not follow through on their plans.

It remains to be seen whether this law will do for center-city Wilmington what the original homestead law did for Nebraska, but Maloney and Wilmington were at least flattered by the passage of a National Homesteading Act, which allows the Department of Housing and Urban Development to turn over houses repossessed by federal housing programs to cities for homesteading. There are an estimated half million abandoned, boarded-up houses in America that could probably be rehabilitated. But even supporters of the program have emphasized that it is only one way to rejuvenate the cities and the work and expense involved make it a program not for poor people unless massive subsidies are attached.

Once the homesteading program was underway, Maloney turned to other ingredients in his prescription to revive his city. He successfully tackled a crucial problem of all U.S. cities in our time: increasing the productivity of government services by slashing into patronage-heavy city bureaucracies. Maloney discovered that the city's five-man trash crews were finishing their weekly routes in as little as 17 hours; a study showed a three-man crew

* Haskell was not a man without a sense of humor. At an Atlanta luncheon (safely distant from Wilmington, he no doubt thought), he said in 1971: "Being a mayor is something like a bitch in heat: If you run, you'll be chased; if you stand still, you'll get screwed."

could do the job in 28 hours. By attrition and transfers, the sanitation force was cut from 90 to 54 men. The move triggered a two-month slowdown strike and NAACP charges of race bias, since most of the collectors were black. But after a court suit, arbitration, and long debates, the cut stuck, saving the city an estimated $450,000 a year. Similarly, Maloney discovered through a Rand Corporation study of the fire department that two of the nine fire stations could be eliminated with response time cut no more than 5 to 10 seconds anywhere in Wilmington. The firefighters union objected heatedly and picketed to stop the plan; Maloney compromised by cutting out just one fire house. But still, 200 firefighters were dropped, mostly by retirement, and $250,000 saved in yearly operating costs. Similarly, the park department's rolls were cut back 27 percent, the city's urban renewal office by 25 percent.

The general consensus seemed to be that all the personnel cuts had not impaired the quality of Wilmington's city services. Compared to a doubling of the city budget in the prior four years, Maloney was able to hold the city budget increase to about 5 percent for two years running, averting a looming financial crisis and proving that politicians sometimes do keep their promises. In his campaign, he had promised to hold city budget increases down to 10 percent a year.

To maintain its economic base and generate new jobs, Wilmington enacted tax breaks for owners of new factories, office buildings, houses, and apartment buildings, and for owners who make substantial improvements in their property.

Maloney was attacked for using federal revenue sharing money to hold down taxes rather than for low-income housing. But he believes that if cities try, on their own, to improve poor people's standard of living, they'll just lose more job-providing businesses and tax-paying middle-class residents. The city's job, Maloney says, is to act as stimulator—"to do a little bit here to get a lot of people to do a lot more."

Being a forthright and tough mayor is not always the best politics, however. In 1976, when Maloney ran for the Senate, some leaders of organized labor proved lukewarm to his bid and he lost to Sen. Roth by a 56 to 44 percent margin.

Beyond Wilmington are its suburbs—stretching northeast toward the circular Pennsylvania border and southwest from the city toward the Maryland line and the town of Newark, where the University of Delaware is situated. They are not all that different from suburbs anywhere in the United States, some upper income, some lower income, many in between. Taken as a whole, suburban New Castle County, which surrounds Wilmington, is solidly prosperous, and with a population 305,470, it contains a clear majority of the state's people—and votes.

The most distinctive part of the suburban ring around Wilmington is the part which is least densely populated, the aptly named Chateau Country northwest of the city. One need only drive out a little past the city limits along Kennett Pike or Rockland Road, just to the Du Pont or Wilmington

Country Clubs, and the Chateau Country begins. One will find no traces of the petrochemical vapors of lower Wilmington here, just the rolling green hills, the manicured pasturelands, and the giant homes of the du Ponts and some of their wealthy friends. (Some are named after onetime du Pont estates in France, e.g., Bois des Fosses, hence the name Chateau.) Some of these are now museums, like Henry F. du Pont's 1,000-acre, 195-room Winterthur, which houses the world's largest collection of American antiques (some 40,000 items). Others are still lived in, like the $500,000 estate Lammont du Pont Copeland, Jr., managed to salvage despite his bankruptcy. The one time the Chateau Country sees traffic jams is on New Year's Day, when du Pont men traditionally call on du Pont women with gifts of candy and cheese and wine. As one close to the du Pont establishment told us, "It's one way to see all your cousins."

In a sense the du Ponts have created a kind of green belt around the urban sprawl of greater Wilmington—subsidized, it appears, by the scandalously low level of property taxes documented by Phelan and Pozen.

Most of the rest of Delaware, south of metropolitan Wilmington, bears little relation to either the central city or the Chateau Country. In the place of carefully tended forests, downstate Delaware tends to have billboards advertising scraple; instead of du Pont mansions, it has huge chicken coops. The latter are not just backyard affairs; they are part of a thriving industry, and broilers are the leading cash crop in the state.

Despite the invasion of industry (a du Pont plant at Seaford, light industry around tiny Dover), Delaware "south of the canal" remains predominantly rural and essentially Southern. It is more like the adjacent Eastern Shore counties of Maryland than like the bustle around Wilmington. The pace of life is slower, the accent thicker. To be sure, there are some areas of recent heavy growth, particularly around the pleasant seaside resort of Rehoboth Beach, which likes to call itself the nation's summer capital. Rehoboth received national publicity when Lynda Byrd Johnson spent a weekend there with her boyfriend, in the mid-'60s; it has some high-rises now but has avoided the stark and garish quality of nearby Ocean City. But for the most part Kent and Sussex Counties remain as they have for generations, peopled by the same families (including a good number of blacks), and growing the same crops. Downstate Delaware is one of those little cul-de-sacs off Megalopolis that one encounters from time to time in the Middle Atlantic states; but it is time now to move on to what is counted as the mainstream of the region.

PENNSYLVANIA

TWILIGHT TIME?

It's Twilight Time in Pennsylvania and the Bills Are Coming Due. That 1970 line in the *National Observer*, in the midst of one of Pennsylvania's bitter budget and tax crises, has a lot to say about public life in what a Harrisburg reporter friend of ours calls "this tired old state in a tax vise." This is a state of stagnant population. The growth rate during the 1960s was the least of any megastate—4.2 percent. (The national growth rate during the decade was 13.3 percent.) Between 1970 and 1975, the state gained a minuscule 0.2 percent in population, the nation's weakest showing except for New York and Rhode Island. Only an excess of births over deaths has saved Pennsylvania from absolute population loss in the 1970s. The state suffered a net outmigration of 182,000 persons in the first half of the decade. In the previous three decades, black immigration, chiefly from the South, had been large enough to offset outmigration by whites. Due to its standstill population levels, Pennsylvania has lost 13 U.S. House seats since 1910; its current apportionment of 25 seats is down two from the 1960s and five from the 1950s, with corresponding losses in national political power. A further loss after the 1980 Census is all but inevitable. Early in the '70s, the state slipped behind Texas in population to become the nation's fourth rather than third largest state.

Yet even in decline, Pennsylvania is not to be ignored. The 1975 population, according to Census estimate, was 11,827,000 persons. Any national politician or business planner ignores Pennsylvania at his peril. The state's Democratic primary of 1976 proved to be the crucial test for Jimmy Carter's presidential bid. The Georgian's sweep of 65 of Pennsylvania's 67 counties drove Henry Jackson from the race, left Morris Udall a distant third, and caused Hubert Humphrey to say farewell to presidential politics. That same autumn, Pennsylvania would prove a key factor in Carter's narrow electoral vote victory and the end of eight years of Republican rule in Washington.

Pennsylvania underwent an entire generation of depression, starting in 1928–29 and ending in 1965. During that whole period, its rate of unemployment was second highest in America—better only than West Virginia's. The reasons are fairly clear. It had been the banner industrial state of the 19th century, but its manufacturing plant had aged. Too much of the economy was geared to steel and coal and rails, even as those industries headed into a long decline in employment. There was too little investment in modern, intelligence-oriented industries. And even when the state's economy, along with that of the country, perked up in the 1960s, the rate of new capital expenditures by industries in Pennsylvania lagged behind the other major industrial states. Now, with the completion of big, technologically advanced steel plants in the Midwest, Gov. Milton Shapp predicts "a westward trek of production" that will cost Pennsylvania thousands of jobs in its most basic industry. Even the elements have been unkind. In June 1972 Hurricane Agnes swept into Pennsylvania and wreaked the worst destruction in the state's history. The most severe damage was in the chronically depressed Wyoming Valley around Wilkes-Barre, where the Susquehanna River, swollen by the hurricane's rains, rose 40 feet above its normal level and breached restraining dikes. Only three people were killed, but 25,000 homes were damaged or destroyed, 100,000 people were left homeless, and 30,000 jobs were eliminated—in an area which had been in serious economic decline since the 1920s. The federal government stepped in with aid, but many families complained that it was too little and too slow in coming and that they found themselves paying rent to the government for the mobile homes in which they lived while still paying off old mortgages on homes that had been destroyed or had disappeared.

But it is too soon to write off the old commonwealth as an economic disaster area. True to its old nickname of Keystone State, Pennsylvania is still dead astride the great transportation routes that connect the Great Lakes and the Midwest with the major markets and seaports of the East. Its rail service is suffering badly today, but at the same time a network of east-west

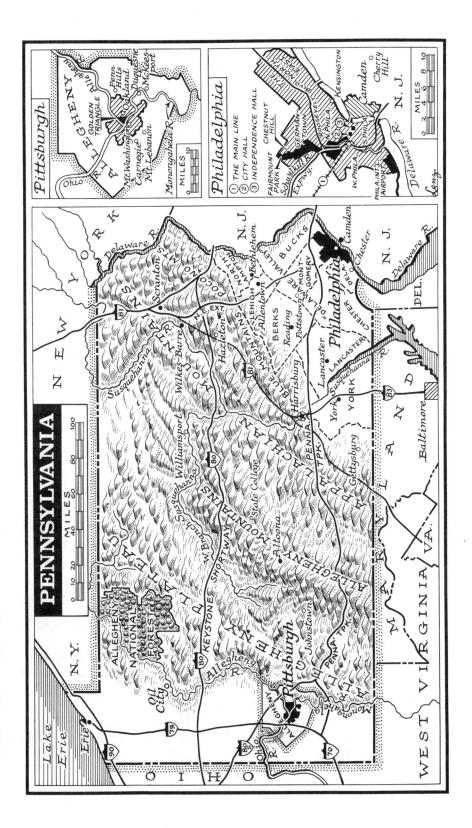

PENNSYLVANIA

MILES
0 10 20 40 60 80 100

Pittsburgh

MILES
0 10

Philadelphia

① THE MAIN LINE
② CITY HALL
③ INDEPENDENCE HALL

MILES
0 2 4 6 8 10

Lenz.

and north-south interstate roads has opened up previously inaccessible parts of Pennsylvania and put most of the state within quick, easy trucking range of both the East Coast and Greak Lakes megalopolises. Pennsylvania leads the country in television picture tubes, cigars, shoes, plastic materials, transformers, flat glass, and several other product lines. There are still close to 60,000 Pennsylvania farms, sending produce worth close to $1 billion to market each year. Some kinds of payrolls (especially retailing, services, real estate, and banking) have increased dramatically in recent years, all evidence of a more diversified economy.

The bright spots in the economic situation are not altogether accidental. In the late 1950s, a concerted effort was begun in industrial recruitment through the Pennsylvania Industrial Development Authority (PIDA), the first of its kind in the country. PIDA arranges low-cost loans for new and expanding industries. Part of its success has been in low-paying industries, especially apparel plants, which hire mostly women at rather low average wages. By 1969, apparel plants accounted for 182,000 jobs and were second only to steel as an employer in the state. But PIDA loans have gone to increasingly sophisticated industries in the last few years, and even some of Pennsylvania's giants (RCA, PPG Industries, etc.) have taken advantage of its financing. Under the state's Revenue Bond and Mortgage Program, initiated in 1967, local development agencies arrange low cost, tax exempt financing through participating banks. Investments under the program totaled $5 billion by the mid-'70s and were credited with creating or "protecting" 500,000 jobs.

The fruits of the various revival efforts can be seen in the growth of electronics firms (especially in the Philadelphia orbit), a heavy inflow of food and other distribution facilities, industrial parks sprouting up along the major arteries. In the 1958–61 recession, unemployment in Pennsylvania had zipped up to a catastrophic 9.4 percent, a third greater than the national average; in the later recession year of 1970, Pennsylvania's unemployment was only 4.0 percent, almost a whole percentage point *less* than the national average. And in 1975, in the midst of the worst recession since the 1930s, the unemployment rate was 8.3 percent, only slightly better than the national average, but over a full point less than any of the other northeastern states.

Former Governor William Scranton believes that the slow postwar growth may have a silver lining. With the exception of some areas in southeastern Pennsylvania, the state failed to get the huge suburban influxes that gobbled up the land in a reckless way in places like Southern California, northern New Jersey, or Long Island. "We do not have the problems of reckless suburban growth, and due to our conservation and public land policies, which are almost unique in the East, we have a chance to keep a good deal of the state for recreational purposes, and also to do a much better planning job for better living conditions around towns and cities," Scranton said in an interview.

Pennsylvanians are prone to grouse about their skyrocketing state taxes, which are now *five times* greater than they were at the start of the '60s. The state has a sky-high sales tax (6 percent) and the nation's highest cigarette tax (18¢ a pack). Asked in a 1970 poll to name the single most important problem facing the state, 50 percent of the people named taxes and budget problems, seven times as many as named the second-ranking category (crime and gang wars).

In 1971 the state adopted its first tax on personal income. The tax costs the people almost $1 billion a year and places Pennsylvania among the high tax states of the Union. By 1973, Pennsylvanians were paying a larger share of their personal income (11.6%) into state and local tax coffers than the citizens of 38 other states.

But for all its tax obligations, Pennsylvania has some hope for a better future. Under the administrations of three governors—Scranton, Raymond P. Shafer, and Milton J. Shapp—the state finally abandoned its derelict ways in the field of higher education and began to spend heavily for state-supported universities and technical schools. So there is hope that in the next decades Pennsylvania will have a much better-trained work force and be able to compete more effectively with California, Texas, *et al.* for sophisticated industries.

In national politics, it has long been fashionable to belittle Pennsylvania's contribution and point out that its first and last President was James Buchanan. Part of the reason for the paucity of great leaders emanating from Pennsylvania was the oppressive century-long control of its politics by narrow-minded business interests which were allied with often corrupt Republican bosses like Boies Penrose and Joseph Grundy. In the first years after World War II, Scranton told me, "Pennsylvania remained stagnant in its politics just as its economy remained stagnant. The Republican party was owned and operated by business, especially big business—the railroads, steel, and the like. The Democratic party was owned by the AFL-CIO. And there was little in between." But in the 1960s, the conservative big business clique was reduced to near impotency in Republican circles, and the Democratic bosses were challenged successfully in their own bailiwicks. We will return to those stories later, but the essential point is that the upper echelon of Pennsylvania officeholders no longer need be the marionettes of political bosses or vested interests.

Aside from prostituting the political process, Pennsylvania's old industrial barons did their state a second disservice: for private profit, they raped the natural landscape of Penn's Woods and spawned scabrous slum housing for their workers. Today, much of the blight endures: the anthracite fields of northeastern Pennsylvania, where fires and cave-ins of the earth go on for decades after abandonment of mine sites and monstrous smoking culm dumps mar the countryside; the soft-coal fields of the west, with thousands of acres churned up by reckless strip mining; the wretched little mill towns in the river valleys. Add that to the decay of many of the urban cores, and Pennsylvania seems to be in a sorry state indeed.

Yet here again, the picture is changing. Reclamation efforts are underway in the coal fields. Many of the mill towns seem beyond hope, and so do some of the slums of the two great Pennsylvania cities, Philadelphia and Pittsburgh. But the downtown areas of those two cities have experienced exciting physical renewal since World War II, in both instances the work of high-minded politicians and financiers. Now the alliances that effected the great urban renaissances (beginning more than 20 years ago) have fallen to pieces and the cities seem engulfed in self-doubt, racial tension, and bitter struggles for power. But new and creative forces are at work, too, even in the seething ghettos. Some of America's most promising black self-help projects are emanating from Philadelphia. Pittsburgh entered a trough of uncertainty following the death of its great billionaire mentor, Richard King Mellon, but then began to show a heartening capacity to pare its municipal payrolls and accommodate to an era of shrinking population.

Finally, Pennsylvanians are rediscovering the charm and beauty of the Pennsylvania countryside. Great mountain chains, lakes and meadows, forests and quiet farmland still cover most of the state, and they are there for Pennsylvanians and the other people of the crowded Eastern Seaboard to enjoy. Then there are the man-made reminders of Pennsylvania's early history: Independence Hall and the other colonial landmarks of Philadelphia, Valley Forge, the battlefield at Gettysburg, the Pennsylvania Dutch country, the great meeting place of the rivers at Pittsburgh. All of this has spawned a great wave of tourism, stimulating the sluggish Pennsylvania economy by some $5 billion a year (a fivefold increase in a decade). But the importance is ultimately not economic, but of the spirit. Urban people need quiet and solace in nature; Pennsylvania now provides it to millions each year, in the heart of Megalopolis. All Americans need to know more of their magnificent revolutionary era history and Pennsylvania, "cradle of a nation," offers that, and with scarcely a touch of tinseled Disneyism. Past the era of industrial pillage and cruel political bossism, still aching with problems, Pennsylvania is probably closer now than it has been for a century (and certainly closer than in 1890, when he wrote it) to the romantic vision of Rudyard Kipling:

> The things that truly last, when men and time have passed.
> They are all in Pennsylvania this morning.

Noble Beginnings

An extraordinary spirit of thoughtfulness, tolerance, and care runs through all the writings of William Penn, that remarkable Quaker who founded Pennsylvania and proved to be the noblest of the colonial proprietors. The Great Law which he worked out with his colonists, starting with his arrival in America in 1682, was so progressive as to be radical in its time. It included broad guarantees of religious freedom and of suffrage to males who could meet modest property requirements, an assurance of education for all young children, and stipulation that all laws would be made "with the Consent and Approbation of the Freemen in General Assembly met." "This clear mandate for a permissive, popular government," writer Ezra Bowen has noted, "was one of the pillars upon which, in time, the U. S. Constitution would rest."

Penn later regretted his loss of power, and it should be remembered that real power in colonial Pennsylvania rested with an oligarchy of Quaker leaders, not a broad popular mass. But Penn's promises of religious and political freedom were enough to draw great numbers of colonists. Welsh Quakers came first, then Scottish-Irish Presbyterians, Lutherans, Pietist Germans, Swedes, French Huguenots, and others. The Germans were most noticeable in inland counties such as Lancaster, where they concentrated in large numbers. They have left an important mark on this region in politics, economics, and mores. Indeed, the name Pennsylvania Dutch is derived from these Germans (Deutsch).

With a Quaker's penchant for wise business, Penn located Philadelphia at the tidewater confluence of two great rivers—the Delaware and the Schuylkill. Along their banks, back into the interior, lay tens of millions of acres of forest with a seemingly endless supply of prime white oak. And in the river openings, and under the forests lay prime farmland, which would make Pennsylvania the foremost food producer among the colonies.

By the time of the Revolution, Pennsylvania was the third largest colony with 275,000 people, and Philadelphia had forged ahead of Boston to become the metropolis of colonial America and in many respects its culturally most prominent city. The colony's most illustrious citizen was Boston-born Benjamin Franklin, that author, publisher, scientist, politician, diplomat, and inventor of world repute. While Boston was an earlier scene of revolutionary agitation, it was in Philadelphia that the first two Continental Congresses met and adopted the Declaration of Independence, chose George Washington as commander in chief, and first unfurled the American flag. In the Revolutionary War, Pennsylvania was a major scene of action, including the battles of Brandywine, Paoli, and Germantown. It was at Valley Forge that Washington and his troops spent the cruel winter of 1777–78. In the war, Pennsylvania's fledgling ironworks turned out weapons and its rich farmlands supplied grain, fodder, cattle, sheep, and hogs to feed the army. And it was a decade later, in 1787, that the Constitutional Convention met—again, in Philadelphia. Pennsylvania sent the largest delegation, which fought hard for a strong national government. Then Philadelphia became, for 10 years, the first capital of the United States.

The Age of Steel and Coal, and Its Decline

In the six decades stretching from the end of the Civil War and the advent of the Gilded Age through to the Great Depression, the life of Pennsylvania was characterized not by high idealism but rather by an incredible forward surge of great industry. Pennsylvania was amply endowed with the raw materials for industrial greatness. Western Pennsylvania was underlaid with vast fields of bituminous coal, low in sulphur content and thus easy to convert into coke for steel production. (By one estimate, there were 200 billion tons in and around Pittsburgh alone.) Iron ore was also present in substantial quantity, and later could be imported easily across the Great Lakes from locations such as the Mesabi Range in Minnesota. Limestone was plenteous. So were the tycoons who would build the great empires of iron and steel: Henry Clay Frick, who became the largest producer of coal and coke in the world; Andrew Carnegie, who arrived in Pittsburgh at age 13 to start work for $1.20 a week, brought the Bessemer steelmaking process to America, and eventually became the world's richest man by selling out his massive steelworks for $492 million; J. P. Morgan, the great financier who dared to create U. S. Steel (that gigantic corporation that had 149 plants, capitalization of more than $1.4 billion, and 65 percent of U. S. steelmaking potential the day of its birth in 1901); and Charles M. Schwab, sometimes called "the world's greatest salesman," who was midwife in the negotiations between Morgan and Carnegie that led to creation of U. S. Steel, served as its first president, and then went off to build the rival Bethlehem Steel Company into a giant producer of steel and ships.

Then there were the remarkable Mellons—Thomas, son of a poor Scottish-Irish farming family who arrived in Pittsburgh at the age of five, later became that city's greatest financier and real-estate dealer, and set the foundations of the great banking and coal combine that would prosper under his sons, Andrew and Richard B., and his grandson, Richard King Mellon.

Pennsylvania had oil; in fact the world's first spouting oil well was driven in 1859 near Titusville in the western part of the state. For a half century, oil contributed to Pennsylvania's prosperity, giving birth to the Standard Oil trust and eventually to the Gulf, Sun, and Atlantic oil companies. While the state's petroleum reserves were eventually eclipsed by those of the Southwest, Pennsylvania's Joseph N. Pew did build Sun Oil into one of the largest producers and refiners of oil.

But as varied as Pennsylvania industries might be, the big muscle remained with big steel, and after 1901, with U. S. Steel—The Corporation, as it was familiarly called. Closely allied were, of course, the coal-mining interests, and also the railroads, which themselves ran on steel rails with great steel locomotives and earned much of their money by carrying supplies for the mills and finished steel as freight. In the 1920s, The Corporation controlled as much as 46 percent of all U. S. steel production and had a work force averaging 240,000 men—larger than the U. S. Army. To assure itself of an adequate supply of bituminous coal, The Corporation was probably the largest U. S. coal operator—in an era when three-quarters of a million men worked in the mines. As for the railroads, there was none greater than the Philadelphia-based Pennsylvania Railroad, which employed more than 250,000 men and whose trackage carried an eighth of all passengers in the U.S.A.

Starting around 1890, reformist elements began an outcry about the power of big steel and the big rail interests, but to little avail. In much the same way that strategically placed Texans have been able to defend oil tax privileges in recent decades, strategically placed Pennsylvanians in the late 19th and early 20th centuries stopped antitrust, freight regulation, or child labor legislation which might harm The Corporation and its friends. The year U. S. Steel was formed, the Attorney General of the U. S. was Philander C. Knox, a close friend of Frick and Mellon. Elihu Root, a member of both the McKinley and Theodore Roosevelt cabinets, had been an attorney for the old Carnegie Steel Company. The list is a long one and perhaps is best capped off with the ultimate example: Andrew Mellon's position as Secretary of the Treasury during the Harding, Coolidge, and Hoover administrations. The massive mergers in the birth of The Corporation somehow got the approval of government antitrust lawyers. Obvious price-fixing agreements among the big steel producers went unpunished, nor did government do anything to curb the steel and coal companies' inhumane labor practices.

In historic perspective, it is clear enough that World War I marked the apogee of Pennsylvania's role as America's great energy and metals producer. The succeeding years have been a half century of steady decline, one of catastrophic proportions in the Depression, artificially relieved by World War II and to some degree by the Korean and Vietnam wars, but nevertheless of deterioration throughout.

The problems and terrors of Pennsylvania industry can be catalogued easily. Both big steel and big coal, in a frantic race to meet any demand of any peak year, built production facilities far beyond the needs of normal times and failed to diversify their operations so that they could withstand the shock of economic reverses. The prime steel customer of all time—the railroads—reached the full extent of their routes in the 1920s; after that, steel rails were no longer in great demand, and the need for rolling stock declined sharply. At that same moment in time, the Pennsylvania financiers made the fundamental error of failing to get in on the ground floor of the great *new* industry of 20th-century America—automobile and truck production. That business went to Michigan instead, and Midwestern steel mills supplied most of the automakers' needs. For decades, Pennsylvania was the only major state without an automobile assembly plant. This was finally corrected in 1976 when Volkswagen decided to take over a facility in New Stanton which Chrysler had started and then abandoned. But VW agreed to move to the Pennsylvania location only after the state offered concessions so great that critics said they amounted to a subsidy.

The steadily increasing national demand for steel in the past two decades (from 75 million tons in 1950 to 132 million in 1970) has kept many Pennsylvania mills busy. But the state is still producing only 50 percent more steel (about 30 million tons a year) than it did in 1918—hardly an impressive growth rate in a rapidly expanding national economy. A half century ago, about half of America's steel production came from Pennsylvania mills; in 1970, the figure was only 22.9 percent. Pennsylvania employed less people in its primary metals industry (253,000 in 1969) than it did 20 years before. The decline, slowed a bit by the Vietnam war, continued in the 1970s and was likely to get worse.

The steel industry has faced mounting criticism from citizens groups, government, and occasionally the unions over the issue of pollution. The production facilities of the major companies are in large part dated and many are quickly approaching obsolescence. These plants spew forth more than choking, blinding mountains of smoke; they emit literally deadly combinations of gases and vapors which pose danger to the health of both the workers and the residents of the localities in which the plants operate.

The American steel industry has been making its primary new plant investments in the Midwest in recent years, and sophisticated new factories that require only a fraction of the labor force needed in Pennsylvania mills have recently gone on line in Hennepin, Illinois (Jones & Laughlin), and Burns Harbor, Indiana (Bethlehem). A high percentage of Pennsylvania's mills are technologically old and may soon be obsolete. The average age of steelworkers in the state is over 50 years; the younger people are now being hired in the Midwest.

Topping it all off is the ailing condition of the entire U.S. steel industry. In the early '70s, American steelmakers faced difficult times with low profits and bruising competition from foreign producers, who seized 17 percent of the U.S. market. Projections indicated that the demand for steel in the rest of the 20th century would increase only 2.5 percent a year—far below the expected rise in gross national product. Steel producers were reduced to asking the government for protectionist measures. As the decade went on, the situation became less dire. Inflation abroad was driving up foreign steel wages and prices faster than they were rising in the U.S. Even so, steel profits were not particularly high, and the long-range prospects of the industry remained clouded at best.

Related to the woes of big steel are those of the railroads, traditionally the lifeline of commerce in Pennsylvania. Freight service—not to mention passenger service—has been declining in terms of area serviced and reliability over most of the postwar period, making it commensurately more difficult to maintain profitable industry in the state. In 1968, when the mighty Pennsylvania Railroad merged with the New York Central to form Penn Central, the number of lines was cut back, plus many service connection points for smaller railways. Pennsylvania was also hurt because the merged line began to upgrade its water level route over the former New York Central tracks, which is cheaper to ship over than the mountainous route of the Penn Central through Pennsylvania. This undercut the competitive position of the Port of Philadelphia and cost railway jobs in the Keystone state.

The great financial crash of the Penn Central in 1970 was the biggest commercial bankruptcy in American history, a blow to the pride and prosperity of Philadelphia, and an evil omen for the 50,000 Pennsylvanians still working on the railroads. (Back in 1947, there had still been more than 150,-000 railroad jobs in the state.) What was it that led the Penn Central to the abyss? To the railroad's customers, it seemed like the outgrowth of years of deferred maintenance, deteriorated roadbeds, outmoded equipment, chronic jam-ups at terminals and connecting points with other railways, misdirected freight cars, and archaic work practices forced by the unions. What was even more shocking than poor management was the revelation some months after the bankruptcy that some directors and key officers had neglected the railroad and saved themselves thousands of dollars by dumping personal stock before the Penn Central's troubles became public knowledge. The railroad kept on paying dividends on its stock even when its cash position had become desperate, and deceptive bookkeeping was used to hide the true state of affairs. And according to congressional staff reports and the suits of aggrieved stockholders, the company had been bled dry by a series of questionable acquisitions in nonrailroad businesses throughout the 1960s. A private investor's club made up of Pennsylvania Railroad officers, directors, friends, and relatives had been set up in 1962 and invested heavily in companies that the railroad later either invested in or acquired control of; in several cases the stock value of the companies soared when they were acquired and the investors could sell out at big profits to themselves. The Associated Press reported in January 1971 that even as the Penn Central was rolling toward bankruptcy court, its directors voted to buy a $10 million Lloyd's of London insurance policy to protect themselves, the company, and key officers financially against charges of wrongdoing. The three-year policy carried a $305,000 price tag and the full cost was placed on the teetering Penn Central, rather than on the officers themselves, by a timely new state law actually written by a Philadelphia lawyer whose firm represented the railroad. It was a move worthy of the most rapacious policies of the earlier Robber Barons.

Herculean efforts by appointed trustees and top management to revamp operating procedures and upgrade the Penn Central's equipment failed to return the railroad to solvency, and in 1976 the line became part of ConRail, a quasi-government corporation consisting of the Penn Central and six other bankrupt railroads in the Northeast and Midwest. Congress authorized $2.1 billion in federal government loans to start ConRail. Yet federal officials had to seek court action to try to prevent the railroads from selling real estate and easements for the benefit of stockholders and creditors before the turnover to ConRail. The goal of the legislation and ConRail was to make a profit and start repaying the federal government by 1980, but many political figures and financial analysts agreed that billions more will be required to make good on the government's resolve to keep the trains running. Gov. Shapp in particular became a bitter critic of ConRail, alleging in 1976: "Make no mistake. ConRail is merely Phase II of Penn Central, which will continue and accelerate the deterioration of the Northeast railroads. The ConRail concept was designed and developed by the Union

Pacific and other western and southern carriers to strip the Northeast of its vital rail service. Unless this trend is reversed within the next few years, we will not have an available rail system in this region."

Less than 29,000 men work in the coal mines of Pennsylvania today—a catastrophic decline from the 210,000 who worked there in 1940, and the 387,000 in 1910. Production in the great anthracite fields of northeastern Pennsylvania has declined to a mere trickle. The story is different in the western Pennsylvania fields, where there are still many deep-pit mines. They are almost exclusively the captives of the big steel companies—U. S. Steel, Bethlehem, Jones & Laughlin, and Republic—who continue to prize low-sulphur, metallurgical-quality bituminous for making coke in the steel process. But on the eastern edge of the bituminous field, around Johnstown and Altoona, there are beds of medium-sulphur coal and some huge mine-mouth electric generating plants where the coal comes up on a conveyor belt and is immediately fed into the power station. The expanding part of the western Pennsylvania coal industry is in strip mining, where it is now possible with huge earth-moving and coal-cutting machinery to get at deep seams of coal that previously seemed inaccessible or too costly to recover. And the entire Pennsylvania coal industry may prosper in the next decades as eastern industry converts from oil to coal because of expensive prices and uncertain supplies of petroleum, and as more efficient methods of coal gasification are developed.

The human costs of the dramatic reduction in coal-mining jobs can still be seen in Pennsylvania's old mining towns, where unemployed miners, unprepared for any other profession, live out their sad and unfulfilled lives. The problem is not a new one—it has been there since the 1920s. Life in the mines, especially the deep-pit ones, is still a dangerous affair for miners lucky enough to have work. Pennsylvania has had its share of hair-raising mine disasters. Underground miners still live in constant danger of being crushed, gassed, burned, or electrocuted and must reckon with the clear possibility of getting "black lung" disease from the coal dust they inhale through a lifetime.

If there is a bright spot in the modern-day coal story in Pennsylvania, it must be in the good efforts being made to reclaim the natural landscape when the strip miners are through. Our friend Ben Franklin of the New York *Times*, who has made a specialty of coal problems, says the Pennsylvania strip-mining law, first passed under the Scranton administration, is the best in the U. S. by far. One unique provision requires that after contour mining, the high wall—referring to the sheer rock face, sometimes as high as 120 feet, that's left after a bench has been cut to dig out coal from the side of a mountain—must be blasted away and filled in, so that no slope greater than 45° results. Another provision obliges strip-mining firms to post a very high bond which is not released by the state until the area is not only graded, but seeded, *and* the vegetation has begun to grow. (Other states generally release most or all of the bond when the seed is put down. But often the ground is "hot"—chemically toxic—so that nothing grows.) But as Franklin points out, the word *reclaimed* is something of a travesty as it is generally used. To get a strip-mined area back to its essential prior condition, with full vegetation and humus and a nitrogen base in its soil, is a century-long proposition. It also takes that long for rocks churned up in the earth-moving process to break down by freezing and thawing so that the land can be plowed again for crops.

Labor in Pennsylvania

The century preceding World War I witnessed the great "peopling" of Pennsylvania. The population rose from 810,091 (1810) to 7,665,111 (1910). Attracted by Pennsylvania's job opportunities, many settlers came from New York and New England. From the South came the first Negroes, attracted by Pennsylvania's strong abolitionist views. Starting in 1840, Ireland's potato famine brought a flood of immigrants from that country. As the wave of industrialization gathered steam after the Civil War, vast numbers of Germans, Irish, Italians, Poles, and other Slavs poured in, and then there were Jews from Eastern Europe and Russia. As recently as 1960, 22 percent of Pennsylvania's people were immigrants or the sons and daughters of immigrants —half a million Italians and large numbers of Germans, Austrians, Poles, British, Irish, Czechs, and Russians; if the count had included the third and fourth generations, it would doubtless have been well over 50 percent. The religious heritage of the immigration is revealed in modern-day figures showing that 32 percent of Pennsylvania's people are Roman Catholic and 4 percent Jewish, above the national averages.

The conditions in the early factory towns are one of the darkest chapters in American history. Men were obliged to work 12 hours a day, seven days a week, for wages as small as $350 a year—and often that pittance came in company-issued scrip which could only be spent at inflated prices in the company store or for rent of the shacks or tiny wooden frame houses owned by the company. In the coal fields, child labor was used extensively; only in 1909, in fact, did the state adopt a law against the practice. Tiny boys, sometimes only eight years of age, were put to work separating slate from coal and at other tasks deep in the mine shafts, at wages of 25 cents a day. The toll in miners' lives was appalling: 43,000 Pennsylvania miners lost their lives between 1880 and 1936. Thousands died in the steel mills, too; there, one of the greatest dangers was white-hot metal gushing out of giant ladles that frequently slipped off overhead cranes.

In the Pennsylvania mill and mining villages, Ezra Bowen recounts, living conditions—especially for the new immigrants—were sordid and disease-ridden. Backyards were often a filthy jumble of privies, open sewage ditches, and rubbish, and in one ward of Homestead occupied primarily by recent immigrants, one child out of two died before reaching two years of age.

The social ethos of the time allowed for little criticism of all this; indeed a prevailing feeling seemed to be that the poor were poor because they were lazy and needed only apply themselves to achieve affluence.

Labor unions pressed for higher wages and safety precautions for workers and were fought ferociously by the same owners who championed the sacred rights of property and the ideal of survival of the fittest. Indeed, the struggle of the workers for a more decent life was every bit as bitter, intense—and violent—as that of the modern American black. The universal reaction to strikes was to beat them down with troops and bullets, and the owners would not even consider talking to a union representative. In 1877, in Pittsburgh, a great general strike broke out after the Pennsylvania Railroad cut back weekly paychecks by 10 percent and 650 militiamen moved into the city to battle with mobs which surged through the city streets and rail yards, looting and wrecking railroad equipment, for two days. Finally federal troops had to be called in to restore order and the final toll was 26 dead, $5 million in damage, and bitter class hatred such as America had never known before.

Slowly, tentatively, with many setbacks, labor unions began to form—the American Federation of Labor (succeeding the old Knights of Labor) in 1881, the United Mine Workers in 1890, the Amalgamated Association of Iron, Steel and Tin Workers in 1878, and finally the Congress of Industrial Organizations in 1935 and the United Steelworkers that same year. The steel industry proved the most obdurate of all, its workers thoroughly cowed by experiences like the strike at Carnegie's Homestead Works in 1892 over the issue of the 12-hour day, seven-day week, low pay, and manager Henry Clay Frick's cold refusal to recognize any kind of union. For five months the workers stayed off their jobs and at one point engaged in a bloody fight with 300 Pinkertons dispatched by the company, a struggle marked by the use of cannon and pistol fire, dynamite and burning oil and gas. Finally the obliging governor acceded to Frick's request to send in 8,000 militia, who took over the plants, arrested many strike leaders, and started up the furnaces with scab labor. Their strike totally broken, the crestfallen workers went back to work without a single concession from management.

Part of the steelworkers' problem was that their union, the Amalgamated Association of Iron, Steel and Tin Workers, recruited only skilled workers and spoke only for their aims. The coal miners, by contrast, had by necessity learned teamwork in their dangerous underground work and showed much more solidarity. The United Mine Workers also developed shrewd, able leaders like ex-miner John Mitchell, who led successful strikes in 1900 and 1902 which led to an eight-to-nine-hour working day and a 10 percent pay increase. By the 1920s, the powerful and often dictatorial figure of John L. Lewis was leading the UMW. He scored some early successes, saw his union decimated by the aftermath of the 1929 crash, but came into his own with the arrival of the New Deal and passage of the National Industrial Recovery Act in 1933. That law guaranteed workers the right to organize and bargain collectively through "representatives of their own choosing"—a provision Lewis was instrumental in getting into the act, and which he proudly called Labor's Magna Charta. Soon 300,000 workers were signed up with the UMW and the major coal operators agreed to recognition of the union, a seven-hour day with time and a half for overtime.

Still, there were coal companies that resisted, and they might have succeeded in bucking the union if there had not been a new state administration at Harrisburg, headed by an illustrious liberal, Republican Gifford Pinchot. He pledged that the National Guard would be impartial to all citizens and revoked the commissions of all the private company police. By 1942, every commercial coal mine in America was operating as a closed union shop under the United Mine Workers' banner.

In the meantime, Lewis had broadened his sights to great industries like autos and steel and in 1935 broke with the AFL to form the CIO, putting his old friend Phillip Murray in charge of organizing the steelworkers. A great strategic victory was won with General Motors' capitulation to the CIO in Detroit in 1937. Soon after that, The Corporation (U. S. Steel) quietly succumbed to union organization.

The years since World War II have been sunny ones for the Steelworkers but grim ones for the UMW—the result in large part of the general health of the steel industry and declining days for coal, but also of the strikingly different ways in which the two unions have been run. Thriving under basically sound leadership and democratic operating procedures, the Steelworkers have expanded until they now represent 1.4 million workers in the U.S. In total size, the Steelworkers are about even with the United Auto Workers; they are easily the largest single union in the AFL-CIO.

Founder Phil Murray headed the Steelworkers until his death in 1952 and still shines in the memory of most union members as the finest leader they ever had. He was succeeded by David J. McDonald, the union's original secretary-treasurer, but in 1965 McDonald was ousted in unionwide balloting by I. W. Abel, the union's president until 1977. Abel, who began life as a blacksmith's son in Magnolia, Ohio, was able to capitalize on McDonald's loss of contact with his district directors and the notion that McDonald had become too popular as a golfing and nightclub companion of the steel executives he was supposed to fight.

There was a marked change in the Steelworkers' method of operating under Abel. Formerly, the union's top officers decided before any negotiations on a clear-cut set of demands and bargaining strategy and took it to the union's wage-policy committee where it would usually be accepted without major change; the wage-policy committee then had full authority to make or reject agreements and to order strikes. Under Abel, the wage-policy committee was retained but individual industry committees—for basic steel, aluminum, nonferrous metals, cans, and others—were set up and given authority and responsibility to implement the wage-policy program and modify it to the needs of their respective industries, and also to make agreements and recommend strike action. "Thus we have a broader base—much greater participation," Abel told us.

But Abel's most noteworthy—and innovative—program did not affect the internal workings of the union so much as its relationships with its longtime adversaries, the major steel companies. In the wake of the generous (and inflationary) 1971 contract with the major producers, Abel joined with management in setting up programs to improve workers' productivity —an unusual move in an industry where union leaders normally worked to stop speed-ups and piecework pay. And in 1974, the Steelworkers and the big companies set up an Experimental Negotiating Agreement, by which they agreed to settle their differences without a strike or lockout, and with major contract terms being settled, if necessary, through arbitration.

The next year, the USW and the majors reached agreement a full three months before their contract expired, and Abel's statesmanship was hailed by editorialists across the nation. He had avoided the economic dislocation of a strike, and the ENA policy recognized the interest the steelworkers themselves have in the health of what appeared to be a pretty sick industry. Indeed, the union and the companies agreed to use the ENA procedure again when their contracts expire in 1977.

But there was some dissent. Grumblings were heard in the ranks that Abel had given up the union's strongest weapon, the strike, and that he was becoming as inaccessible as McDonald had been. And—though ENA itself was not an issue there—Abel was certainly surprised when 36-year-old Edward Sadlowski was elected leader of the Steelworkers' Chicago-Gary district, the largest in the entire union, by a 2–1 margin over Abel's handpicked choice. Abel himself was not eligible for reelection in 1977, and it was possible that the steelworkers would elect Sadlowski as president, a man fundamentally at odds with Abel's programs.

Working in steel mills has always been a particularly hazardous occupation, with men exposed to great extremes of temperature and—especially in older mills—high levels of air pollution. The younger and more militant union members are pressing aggressively on the safety issue. They are less willing to accept union or company discipline than the older workers, many of whom are immigrants. In a recent survey of working conditions in industry, the New York *Times* quoted Ronald Koontz, a 22-year-old steelworker at the Bethlehem plant in Johnstown, as saying that younger workers were often refusing to do hazardous jobs like sealing the coke ovens. "You wear two to three shirts a day it's so hot," he said. "There's lots of gas, smoke, dirt. Some guys just tell the foreman 'No' and then rely on the union to protect their jobs."

By appearances, the political activity of the Steelworkers is more limited, and they are much less willing to take an advanced stand on social issues, than the United Auto Workers. In 1968 and 1972, Steelworkers worked hard, especially in Indiana, Ohio, and Pennsylvania, to defend Hubert Humphrey's interests over Eugene McCarthy and George McGovern.

Abel told us his union would continue its centrist Democratic course. But in 1972 Abel refused to back McGovern after he won the nomination, and the Steelworkers were not an important factor in the Democrats' midterm convention in Kansas City in 1974. More and more, the USW seemed isolated from what one would suppose are its natural allies in the Democratic party.* In 1976, most Steelworkers leaders endorsed Henry Jackson in the Presidential primary, but their members went for Jimmy Carter.

Whatever the problems of the Steelworkers may be, they are minor compared to those of the United Mine Workers. John L. Lewis began the postwar era with walkouts in violation of injunctions barring strikes, bringing down heavy fines on the union and himself. But the turbulence ended quickly in the late 1940s. Coal at that point found itself in an unfavorably competitive market as the railroads switched to diesel engines and homes to oil and gas heating. Coal's only real hope seemed to lie in large-scale automation that could hold coal prices down and make it the principal source of fuel for rapidly growing power-generating plants. Lewis agreed to the automation —despite the fact that it would throw thousands of miners out of work. But for the remaining miners, Lewis got a major concession: agreement by owners to finance, by means of a royalty on each ton of coal produced (originally 40 cents per ton and boosted to $1.60 by 1977), a welfare and retirement fund that made UMW workers among the first in American industry eligible for job pensions and free medical care. At the same time, wages advanced handsomely. The perennial conflicts between the UMW and the mine owners ceased, and peace seemed to reign in the coal fields for the first time in decades.†

Lewis retired in 1960 and soon afterward the presidency of the UMW was taken over by W. A. (Tony) Boyle, Lewis' hand-picked, $50,000-a-year successor. "Boyle carefully patterned his image after the master," writer Ward Sinclair has noted. "The self-righteousness, the roll of the tongue, the combative rejection of outsiders, the thundering responses to criticism all are pages from the Lewis book." Boyle also continued to run the UMW as a personal fiefdom, as Lewis had done. Years before, Lewis had placed 19 of the UMW's 23 districts under trusteeship (alleging that the districts were in financial straits, or that some "irregularities" had taken place). This permitted Lewis, and then Boyle, to appoint all the district presidents, secretary-treasurers, and members of the UMW executive board—in effect, a self-perpetuating oligarchy. The Landrum-Griffin Act, passed in 1959, limited all trusteeships to 18 months, but for years the government did nothing to clean up the practice in the UMW. Boyle's own concern with the fate of the ordinary miner was next to impossible to discern; in fact, as time

---

* Abel claimed the Steelworkers were major political factors in Pennsylvania, Illinois, Indiana, New York, and several other states. In Illinois, he said, "our fellows have always worked well with Daley." Potentially, the Steelworkers could be a major factor in U. S. politics. They have one of the largest staffs of any union in the U. S., concentrated in the big, electorally pivotal states.

† There was no peace, though, for independent mine owners and nonunion operators who felt they could not afford to pay royalties to the pension fund. Union organizers used terroristic methods to make them join up.

wore on and the UMW benefited from every ton of coal dug, the relationship with the mine operators seemed to get cozier and cozier. Until the Farmington, West Virginia, disaster of 1968, the UMW failed to support a single piece of mine safety legislation. The union failed to defend members of local safety committees from reprisals by mine owners. Boyle in 1969 said the UMW "will not abridge the rights of mine operators in running the mines. We follow the judgment of the coal operators, right or wrong."

In 1969, Boyle had to stand for reelection as president and suddenly an opponent emerged—Joseph A. (Jock) Yablonski, former president of District 5 in the Pittsburgh area and supposedly a stalwart of the Boyle regime. For years, Yablonski had silently balked at what he considered misrule of the union and neglect of rank-and-file miners. A key figure in persuading him to run for the presidency was Ralph Nader, and a key part of the package was Nader's assurance that Joseph Rauh, a liberal Washington attorney and Democratic leader, would be his campaign adviser and legal brains.

The Yablonski campaign had an electrifying effect on thousands of miners who had never thought anyone would have the courage to oppose Boyle's iron regime. Yablonski was a volatile, colorful personality who relished his rebel's role. He was for union democracy, for tough safety legislation, for a fair pension system (many miners had been denied pension or disability rights on flimsy technicalities), and for an end to "sweetheart ties" between the UMW and the coal industry.

The Yablonski-Boyle campaign was marked by appalling bribery, intimidation, fraud—and violence. At a campaign appearance in Illinois, Yablonski was knocked unconscious by a karate chop to the neck. He regarded the incident as a calculated attempt on his life. Rauh lodged repeated complaints with the U. S. Labor Department—which discounted them all and said, in a tortured interpretation of the Landrum-Griffin Act, that it had a policy of never investigating a union election until it was all over and the result certified. The result of that, Rauh and Yablonski said, would be to give Boyle and his cohorts three to four months to cover up before any investigation—time to destroy records, including those of the hundreds of thousands of dollars of union money allegedly misappropriated to finance Boyle's campaign. Early in the campaign, Boyle had himself appointed to the welfare and retirement fund's trustee board to replace Lewis, who died that year. Within a day, Boyle raised pensions from $115 a month to $150 a month for 70,000 retirees—thus garnering nearly 90 percent of the retiree vote (which is eligible in union elections). Boyle got just a bare majority of the reported active miners' vote in that December 1969 election. Yablonski immediately challenged the result, charging a stolen election. Twenty-two days later, the bodies of Yablonski, his wife, and his young daughter were found in his Clarksville, Pennsylvania home—each shot to death. Only then did the Labor Department prepare to enter the case.

In death, Yablonski became a near-legendary figure to rebels within the UMW. He had never been the world's most saintly man, but now he was lionized. A movement called Miners for Democracy sprang up in western Pennsylvania; its official head was Mike Trbovich, a flamboyant, uneducated miner from Clarksville (given to arm-waving, purple shirts, and yellow ties); another was Arnold Miller, a taciturn former miner from West Virginia who had to leave the pits because of black lung disease. Miners for Democracy filed a suit which ousted Boyle from the board of trustees of the welfare and retirement fund.

Meanwhile, the Labor Department was finally persuaded to bring suit to overturn Boyle's election on the grounds of fraud, intimidation, and irregularity. A federal judge set aside the election in 1972, and in the rematch Arnold Miller beat Boyle handily. Miller, Trbovich, and their associates cleaned out most of the Boyle *apparat,* and for the first time in years, the UMW had honest leadership, dedicated to the members' welfare.

Trouble still plagued the UMW, however. Reform movements, once begun, are often difficult to stop, as the new administration was quick to learn. Opposition to the Miller-Trbovich administration developed in the coal fields and in the Washington headquarters from a variety of elements, including miners who charged that the new administration failed to move far enough with reforms, from allies in the election who now charged that the new leadership was going *too* far, from men still loyal to Boyle, and from the continuing conflict between the Miller and Trbovich groups who remained skeptical and sometimes openly hostile to each other. An early result of this was the failure of Miller to win approval from the union's bargaining board for representatives for the first contract he negotiated, and later his inability to control the spreading wildcat strikes which swept the coal fields in the early 1970s and which closed down nearly every union mine in the late summer of 1975. By 1976, Miller and Trbovich had split and the future of the leadership was uncertain.

In the meantime, Boyle was convicted by a federal grand jury of embezzlement, conspiracy, and illegal use of union money for political purposes. The government charged the UMW with spending almost $11 million in 1967–69 in violation of Landrum-Griffin reporting requirements. But the worst for Boyle was yet to come. In 1971 the government began prosecuting some local union officials for Yablonski's murder. The driving force behind the prosecution was Richard Sprague, the chief assistant district attorney in Philadelphia, who served as a special prosecutor in this and the trials that followed. For, one after another, the small fry who were convicted implicated people higher up on the ladder. Finally, in 1974, Tony Boyle himself —a broken man, who had made a feeble attempt at suicide—was convicted of murder. In 1975, sentence was delivered: Boyle was given three life terms of imprisonment for the murder of Joseph Yablonski, his wife, and daughter.

But in January 1977 the Pennsylvania supreme court ordered a new trial for Boyle, saying the trial judge had improperly refused to admit evidence showing the local union officials in the chain of murder commands might have been motivated by Yablonski's threats to investigate their local union.

Keystone Politics

The Republican party got a hammer lock on Pennsylvania's body politic in the Civil War years and was not forced to let go until the New Deal came on the scene 70 years later. One reason was the protective tariff, which helped turn the state for Lincoln in 1860. Pennsylvania was the Union's preeminent manufacturing, rather than commercial or trading, state; thus the tariff, together with other policies to benefit big business, made the Grand Old Party the natural ally of steel, coal, oil, and textile interests—interests which in turn repaid the favor with ample campaign financing. Secondly, there was the memory of the Civil War. Pennsylvania *had* been invaded, Gettysburg had given the people a great fright, and the bloody shirt could be waved for a generation afterward. Third, no ethnic grouping rose up to fight the ruling classes as the Irish did in Boston. Protestant, Catholic, Jewish, German, Irish, Negro—everyone was Republican. Finally, a succession of Republican bosses, men of shrewdness and power rarely seen in America, sprang from Pennsylvania soil. They ruled over an Organization whose power extended from the sooty mill towns to the dogwooded suburbs of Philadelphia and Pittsburgh, from the ward clubhouse to the U. S. Senate—and was rarely thwarted. The Republicans scored an astounding chain of Presidential victories, unbroken from 1860 through 1932, except for 1912, when the state voted for Progressive party candidate Teddy Roosevelt. In the same seven decades, Pennsylvania elected 15 Republican governors and only two Democrats, though one of those Republican governors—Gifford Pinchot—was the renowned conservationist and progressive and an implacable enemy of the Organization.

Nathaniel Burt in *The Perennial Philadelphians* has given a colorful account of the trilogy of great Republican bosses—Simon Cameron (1865–87), Matthew S. Quay (1887–1904), and Boies Penrose (1904–21). Cameron was a somewhat unsavory character from western Pennsylvania who began his career by defrauding the Winnebago Indians of their lands and moneys and landed in Lincoln's cabinet as Secretary of War through a political deal. He used that position to benefit himself and his contracting friends and the only way Lincoln could get rid of him was to appoint him minister to faraway Russia. In 1867 the Republican legislature made him U. S. Senator and he continued as absolute boss of the state until his retirement a decade later.

Quay, the Latin-reading son of a clergyman, is depicted by Burt as "a sinister personage whom Kipling considered the best-read man in America, and who kept a file, known as 'Quay's Coffin,' which furnished him with items for blackmail, at need, on anyone of political consequence in Pennsylvania." He became the Republican state and national chairman and a U. S. Senator.

About Penrose, whom Gunther described in *Inside U. S. A.* as a man "who ate himself to death," Burt offers fine detail:

He was an Old Philadelphian of the most unquestionable sort; but there was also no question about the ungentlemanliness of his politics. . . . As absolute ruler of Pennsylvania after the death of Quay in 1904, and therefore dominant figure in the Republican party nationally, Penrose was in the early years of the 20th century one of the most powerful men in the country. . . . It was he who by choosing T.R. as V.P. "kicked him upstairs." [He] collected and distributed all major contributions to the party, dominated all important Senate committees and hence all legislation, and kept the Pennsylvania Organization he inherited from the Camerons and Quay in prosperous and working order. . . .

He disdained the People, the democratic process and other politicians. . . . He respected only power and force and the clever use of force to maintain power. . . . Graft disgusted him. No money scandals ever dented his own hide. [But] he had clients and he served them well [including] Frick and Carnegie, lords of Pittsburgh and steel, for whom he supported tariffs and emasculated antitrust and labor laws. . . . He was the Old Philadelphia figure of the Iron Age in politics. . . .

He swore, he drank, he whored and he didn't care who knew it. . . . He was a giant in size and strength, six feet four and powerful. . . . He grew immensely fat, almost 300 pounds, but till the very end never lost his dignity, presence or appetite. . . . There are awed accounts of his breakfasts—a dozen fried eggs, a half-inch slice of ham, a dozen rolls, a quart of coffee. . . .

Penrose could absorb immense quantities of liquor without showing it, but made no pretense of hiding either his occasional drunkenness or continued lecheries. "I do what I damn please," said Big Grizzly. "The masses like that."

One of Penrose's last acts, according to legend, was to order the nomination of Warren Harding for President from his deathbed in 1920. In the years that followed, the GOP splintered and a powerful right-wing faction rallied around Joseph P. Grundy, president of the Pennsylvania Manufacturers' Association and a perfect symbol of old-style exploitative capitalism. Grundy continued as president of the PMA, a pervasive influence in the legislative halls at Harrisburg, and was a factor in state politics until he died in 1961, at 98 years of age.

The Democrats' anemia through the 1920s was illustrated by the vote for their Presidential candidate in 1924—a skimpy 19 percent of the statewide vote. But the Depression changed all that. The Republicans were still able to carry the state for Hoover in 1932, but in 1934 the first Democratic governor and U. S. Senator of the 20th century, George E. Earle and Joseph F. Guffey, were elected to office.

With the waning of New Deal fervor, the Republicans returned to power in 1938, due in part to John L. Lewis' attempt to name the Democratic candidate that year. FDR carried Pennsylvania in 1936, 1940, and 1944, however, and even though the Republicans reestablished the legislature control they had lost in the mid-1930s and held the governorship and both the state senate and house from 1943 to 1955, politics were fought on much more even terms than in the earlier times. In 1948, Pennsylvania gave Dewey the biggest plurality he received in any state, and it was predictably for

Eisenhower in both his races; in 1960, however, John F. Kennedy rode to a narrow Pennsylvania victory (116,326-vote plurality) due in part to the gigantic margin (331,544 votes) he received in Philadelphia. In 1968 Humphrey carried Pennsylvania by 169,388 votes, the Philadelphia margin (271,-615 votes) again accounting for his entire plurality. The same pattern appeared in 1976: Carter won Philadelphia by more than 250,000 votes, about twice his statewide plurality of 128,456 votes.

Other Republican strongholds are Dauphin County (Harrisburg), Lancaster and York Counties in the prosperous Pennsylvania Dutch country of southeastern Pennsylvania, the Allentown and Williamsport areas, and virtually all the rural counties along the northern tier. The Democrats' base, outside of Philadelphia and Pittsburgh, has been in the depressed northeastern coal counties like Lackawanna (Scranton) and Luzerne (Wilkes-Barre) Northampton (Bethlehem and Easton), and virtually all of western Pennsylvania, from Erie down to the southwestern corner of the state (territory that includes all the tired steel and coal counties around Pittsburgh).

The Republican party might have slipped into perennial minority status in the postwar years if it had not been for a succession of moderate-liberals who took on the conservative Old Guard faction allied with the Pennsylvania Manufacturers' Association. The first of these was the late James H. Duff—a charming, practical political operator who made his start as a Theodore Roosevelt Progressive Republican in 1912. In 1943, Gov. Edward Martin brought "Big Red" Jim Duff in from Carnegie to be his attorney general. All Republican factions, including the PMA, then anointed Duff for governor in 1946, and he won handily. Once in office, however, Duff decided that business wasn't paying its fair share of taxes and broke decisively with the PMA faction headed by Grundy.

Duff turned out to be a remarkably progressive governor, putting across a tougher clean streams law, cleaning up the Schuylkill River to provide water for Philadelphia and Reading (so that it was no longer necessary, as Gunther reported, for Philadelphia to "drink its own sewage"), and passing an effective "tax anything" law that let hard-pressed local governments and school boards tax anything, including wages, not taxed by the state. In 1950, Duff won a decisive victory over the PMA faction—the "high-buttoned-shoes reactionaries," as he called them—by putting over his candidate for governor, John S. Fine, and winning election himself to the U. S. Senate. In the following two years, he won national stature by the part he played in persuading Gen. Dwight D. Eisenhower to seek the Republican Presidential nomination and helping to manage his primary campaign.

Duff and his allies gradually lost power and influence and Duff found himself less suited to life in the Senate than as a hard-hitting administrator in Harrisburg. In 1956, cut by many GOP stalwarts who resented his independence, he was defeated for reelection by the reform mayor of Philadelphia, Democrat Joseph S. Clark. But the PMA was never again to elect a governor. The Democrats, in fact, were able to elect their first two governors in succession since the 1850s—George M. Leader, a remarkably aggressive campaigner from rural York County who was only 37 at the time of his election in 1954, and David Lawrence from Pittsburgh, who became Pennsylvania's first Roman Catholic governor at the mellow age of 73. (Latent anti-Catholicism almost beat Lawrence, despite the strong Democratic tide in 1958. In office, as *Time* later reported, he was "one of those rare bosses capable of combining a strong party organization with a progressive, relatively scandal-free administration.") But Lawrence made no contribution to state government comparable to what he had done earlier in the postwar revival of Pittsburgh; it can safely be said he came to the office too late in life.

The 1958 election also saw the first election to the Senate of Hugh Scott, bucking the Democratic tide to defeat George Leader. The Old Guard had hoped to run Congressman James Van Zandt, a tried and trusted "regular" from Altoona, but Scott simply outmaneuvered the conservatives to win the nomination. It turned out to be a costly loss for the conservatives because Scott, reelected in 1964 and 1970, would turn out to be the most enduring and effective leader of the party's progressive faction. Scott's most brilliant maneuver came in 1962, when the PMA and the party's conservative legislative wing wanted to run a colorless old party wheelhorse, Judge Robert Woodside, for governor. Scott feared a conservative turn in the Pennsylvania GOP that would make his own reelection chances in 1964 practically nil. Scott went to visit retired President Eisenhower at his Gettysburg farm and emerged quoting Ike as saying the proposed slate of Woodside for governor and Van Zandt for U.S. Senator (to oppose Clark) would be a "miserable" ticket. Scott even threatened to run for governor himself. The man Scott really wanted, however, was the liberal young Congressman from Scranton and squire of that community, William W. Scranton. Scranton coolly insisted he would not run unless all the party factions backed him. Finally, a compromise was reached with Scranton slated for governor and Van Zandt for the Senate. That autumn, Van Zandt was beaten but Scranton scored a smashing 486,291-vote victory (55.4 percent) over Democrat Richardson Dilworth. (For all of Scott's coolness in the nomination maneuvering, "he literally turned white when he thought he might really have to run for governor," Scranton recalls.)

Scranton's fight against Goldwater for the Republican Presidential nomination put Pennsylvania into the Presidential sweepstakes, however briefly, for the first time in living memory. And in dealing with legislators and politicians at home, he demonstrated an extraordinary charm and an ability to get people to work with him and to move programs forward. But the Scranton meteor was a brief one: ineligible under state law to run to succeed himself as governor, under pressure from wife and family to abjure elective office, he said: "I am not going to run, ever again, for any office, under any circumstances." He has remained active in public life, however: as leading spirit of a convention which drafted a new Pennsylvania state constitution, as president of the National Municipal League, and in 1970 as chairman of the President's Commission on Campus Unrest, which was set up in the wake of the Kent State and Jackson State killings. The report criticized excesses among some student groups and law enforcement officers. And it also criticized President Nixon himself (to the administration's chagrin and anger) for failing to exercise stronger and more unifying national leadership. When Nixon resigned the presidency in 1974, Scranton was one of the men Gerald Ford called in to help him with the transition, and later as United Nations Ambassador.

To succeed Scranton as governor, the Republicans picked then Lt. Gov. Raymond P. Shafer, a craggy-jawed, plodding, well-intentioned former state senator from western Pennsylvania with important backing from the Mellon interests in Pittsburgh. Shafer won election with ease, but after his inauguration proceeded to press for the right things in such a maladroit way that his relations with the legislature and his public image declined disastrously. (History will probably be kinder to Shafer than immediate political commentary. He did give higher education a strong push forward, obtain meaningful constitutional reform, and had the courage to speak up for the state income tax which his successor, Milton Shapp, quickly enacted into law.)

By 1970, it seemed that the verve and direction of the progressive Republican era begun by Scott had been badly blunted. The gubernatorial nomination went to Raymond J. Broderick, who turned out to be the most abysmal candidate to get a major party nomination in the state in many years. Under pressure from Philadelphia GOP boss William Meehan, he came out openly against the income tax backed by Shafer, claiming that economies could balance the spiraling state budget—a notion shared by hardly anyone with a rudimentary knowledge of Pennsylvania's near-bankrupt condition.

Scott himself lost any claim to the progressive label by spending most of the Nixon years as an apologist for the administration, up to the very moment when he and his old antagonist Barry Goldwater went to the White House and told Nixon that his support on the Hill had vanished. Amid charges that he had accepted payments from a lobbyist for Gulf Oil, Scott announced in 1976, at the age of 75, that he would not seek reelection, which he surely would have lost. We asked many Pennsylvania Republicans—without hearing a single convincing answer—who will be the leader of the moderate Republicans. Pennsylvania's other Republican Senator, Richard Schweiker, is personally attractive and hard-working; and his 100 percent labor record earned him the endorsement of the AFL-CIO—an unheard of thing in Pennsylvania—when he ran for reelection in 1974. But Schweiker's comparatively easy victory was due less to this endorsement or Republican efforts than to the fact that his opponent, Pittsburgh Mayor Peter Flaherty, never bothered to conduct a real compaign. Schweiker's brief 1976 fling with a potential nomination for Vice President, when he agreed to be Ronald Reagan's prospective running mate, lost him many close allies without winning him any new friends. H. John Heinz III, the young Republican who succeeded Scott in the Senate in 1977, owed his seat more to his 57 varieties fortune (he spent more than $2 million on his campaign), coupled with his home town backing (Pittsburgh had not had a Senator since Duff lost in 1956) than he did to any close ties with the Republican organization. Before election to the Senate, Heinz had served in the U.S. House from a Pittsburgh area district.

Pennsylvania's Democrats have been split into two groupings in recent years. On the one side, there has been the camp of regular organization politicians who rose to the top through the precincts and wards—men like David Lawrence, Joseph Barr (who succeeded Lawrence as mayor of Pittsburgh and Democratic national committeeman), the late Congressman and city Democratic boss William J. Green, Jr., of Philadelphia, and James Tate (mayor of Philadelphia from 1962 through 1971). The other camp, consisting of insurgent reformers, began with the two men who upset the encrusted Republican machine in Philadelphia two decades ago—Richardson Dilworth and Joseph S. Clark. Their modern-day successors are few and far between—but include, significantly, Governor Shapp and Pittsburgh Mayor Peter Flaherty.

Relative peace reigned between the Democratic factions until the early 1960s, due in large measure to the immense personal power of Lawrence in the Pittsburgh area and Green in Philadelphia. (Both men also wielded national power and played key roles in getting the 1960 Presidential nomination for John F. Kennedy.) Lawrence and Green dominated the organizational slate-making sessions in which the Democratic statewide ticket was selected. In several elections, the slatemakers—sometimes to avoid a bloody open primary fight—gave major nominations to Clark and Dilworth. Dilworth was nominated for governor in 1950 and 1962, but lost both times; Clark ran for the Senate in 1956, 1962 and 1968, winning the first two times. But the Democrats' cozy method of operating was disrupted finally by a very nonconventional figure, Milton J. Shapp, who challenged and defeated the organization choice for governor, Robert P. Casey, in 1966 and 1970.*

Shapp was just the kind of candidate organization regulars abhor. First of all, he was openly contemptuous of old-line party structures and alliances. Second, he was initially a risky choice as a candidate because he is Jewish and Pennsylvania had never before elected a Jew as its chief executive. And third, Shapp has money and brains beyond the organization's own resources. A self-made millionaire businessman who had founded the first cable television company in the U. S. in 1958, he was worth, by his own estimation, $12 million by 1965. He immersed himself in study of state government, believing, as he said, that "state government is where an executive can make a contribution." Through his privately financed foundation, Shapp made in-depth analyses of Pennsylvania's economy, governmental structure, and trans-

* It would not be fair to limit our description of Casey to that of a twice-defeated organization candidate for governor. A former state senator, he served from 1969 to 1977 as the state's auditor general. The Philadelphia *Inquirer* reported that he turned his office from a haven for patronage drones into a professional force for reform of government spending.

portation problems—documents of outstanding quality, and all going far beyond any other privately commissioned studies of state government we are aware of, with the possible exception of those which the Rockefeller brothers have initiated from time to time.

Shapp's 1966 campaign was an early test of whether unlimited campaign funds, saturation television, and the accompanying services of a professional, outside campaign-management firm can take a state by storm. Shapp hired Joseph Napolitan and gave him authority over most phases of media and campaign organization. Shapp's name was made a household word through heavy mailings and a skillful mixture of convincing 30-minute documentaries on Shapp the man, followed up by saturation short commercials in the final stretch. The technique worked in the primary (to the regulars' dismay), but it backfired in the general election when there was much talk of Shapp "buying" the election. His overall campaign expenses were $4 million.

Instead of disappearing from the scene after his defeat by Shafer, Shapp remained active, speaking out frequently on Pennsylvania issues. In 1970, he openly scorned the Democratic slate-making process, and instead of rehiring Napolitan, virtually ran his own campaign. With his name already well known, he could order much less television time and concentrate on strategically timed announcements, letting the press do some of his campaigning for him. This time, he spent only $3 million. He beat Casey again for the nomination and then proceeded to swamp Broderick in a campaign in which he minced no words about the probable need for an income tax.

Even though Shapp's coattails swept Democrats to control of both houses of the legislature in the 1970 election, little love developed between the party troops and their new governor. In fact, Shapp had been governor less than four hours when the Democratic majority in the state senate rejected all 10 of his cabinet appointments. The reason? Because he had ignored the job recommendations of county chairmen—and even refused to listen to their suggestions, the senators said. The action was soon rescinded, but friction between Shapp and the regulars continued into his second term. (Thanks to a change in the state constitution, Shapp was the first Pennsylvania governor eligible to succeed himself; by a comfortable, but not overwhelming margin, he beat a young, wealthy Republican named Drew Lewis in 1974.)

In the summer of 1975, a year after his re-election as governor, Milton Shapp announced that he, too, was joining the already crowded field of contenders for the Democratic Party's presidential nomination. His almost invisible candidacy was one of several launched by governors from the megastates as they sought to break the grip maintained on Presidential nominations by U.S. Senators. Shapp's effort, financed mostly by his supporters and allies from Pennsylvania, was short-lived; he withdrew before the Pennsylvania primary in April.

Shapp's early press conferences as a presidential candidate were dominated by questions about the no less than 15 separate investigations by federal, state and local authorities under way into his administration. His 1970 campaign manager and a member of his cabinet were convicted of extortion. In 1976 Shapp fired a special prosecutor he had hired to ferret out political corruption in Philadephia after the prosecutor pursued corruption cases against Shapp's cronies. The special prosecutor was replaced with a man who had spent 78 hours of his 37 years in Philadelphia before his appointment.

Since the old masters like Lawrence and William Green the Elder passed from the scene, the Democrats' city machines have fallen into disrepair. Now an upstart reformer named Peter Flaherty presides at City Hall in Pittsburgh, and the Philadelphia organization has atrophied under row house politicians and law-and-order politicos. The Democratic city pluralities have declined, not precipitously but still enough to cause concern for the party. A governor like Shapp does little to provide the sustenance in patronage that once nourished the party, and old-style politicking is proving more and more repugnant to younger Democrats and blacks.

The Democratic split emerged most forcefully at the 1968 Democratic national convention, when the old-line regulars went solidly for Humphrey and employed the most autocratic methods to suppress dissent in the delegation—even though Eugene McCarthy had won the state's Presidential preference primary. Shapp, who of course was not yet governor, endorsed McCarthy and marched in the streets with delegates protesting the tactics of the police and Mayor Richard J. Daley in handling the convention. But once in office, Shapp found some use for the bosses he had previously scorned. When he needed votes for the state income tax, he called on Philadelphia Democratic chairman Peter Camiel. And in 1972, Shapp joined Camiel in endorsing the presidential candidacy of Edmund Muskie—who finished fourth in the state's primary, behind Humphrey, Wallace, and McGovern. The lesson was that even when the reformers and the bosses get together, the Pennsylvania voter can no longer be taken for granted.

Another case in point: In Philadelphia, the then very popular Democratic Mayor Frank Rizzo endorsed Richard Nixon in 1972, calling him "the greatest President in American history." Philadelphia was the only one of Pennsylvania's 67 counties to go for McGovern. But surely the most cynical maneuver did not occur until 1976, when Governor Shapp and Mayor Rizzo —longtime political enemies—joined together to support Shapp's brief Presidential candidacy and the senatorial race of Congressman William Green. This was the same Bill Green who had run a bitter race against Rizzo in 1971 and whom Rizzo—through a surrogate—had nearly beaten for the House a year later.

The 1976 election year also promised to be long remembered as the occasion of a humiliating defeat for the established Democratic leaders including Rizzo, and their close allies in organized labor. All lined up like a phalanx for Sen. Henry M. Jackson of Washington in the Democratic primary, only to see Jackson go down to defeat before Jimmy Carter. (Carter ended up with 507,000 votes, or 37 percent of the total, compared to Jackson's

337,000 or 25 percent. Even more astoundingly, Carter garnered 66 delegates to just 20 for Jackson.) By winning in a Northern state like brawny, industrial Pennsylvania, Carter performed a feat his opponents said the Georgia peanut farmer was incapable of. It seemed likely that future political histories would list the 1976 Pennsylvania primary on a par with West Virginia's 1960 contest, in which John Kennedy overcame his huge obstacle —winning as a Roman Catholic in a heavily Protestant state.

Pennsylvanians' vocabulary contains a peculiar word for which the reader will search in vain in his dictionary—*macing*. Broadly, it refers to shakedowns of government employees for political contributions, and despite a law prohibiting it, macing continues unabated to this day. Not only are there suspect dinner "invitations," but government workers who fail to give a percentage of salary must fear for their jobs. In 1970, the Harrisburg area Republican party went about it quite systematically, asking state employees for .5 percent of their salary for the primary election and 1 percent for the general election. Perhaps 100,000 public employees in the state of Pennsylvania are subject to such pressures. But macing seems to be in its death throes as a result of the threat to the old patronage system that has been posed by a public employees' bargaining law passed in 1970—a story to which we will turn later.

Pennsylvania Democrats have been much more systematic about macing than the Republicans. But particularly when they are in office, the Democrats turn up their share of substantial gifts from businessmen. They do receive a goodly share of liberal "conscience" money. And they have the great crutch of organized labor, which has in most elections been a working partner of the Democratic party. Pennsylvania has been lacking in recent years, however, in socially conscious, aggressive unions. The liberal, independent-minded Democratic candidate who hopes for important labor support may find himself out in the cold.

Business interests remain the mainstay of GOP financing, but the most overt supergifts designed to undermine politicians' independence have been declining. The most massive political givers of the right-wing variety have been the Philadelphia Pews, who control 42 percent of the Sun Oil Company and have a collective family fortune estimated at almost $1 billion. The Pews have given millions to favored political candidates since the turn of the century.

One great Republican contributor throughout his life was Pittsburgh's Richard King Mellon. We were told by Arthur B. Van Buskirk, Mellon's attorney, confidant, and chief agent in political campaigns, that Mellon "liked warm-hearted and honest people" and "Ike was his all-time favorite." When Eisenhower asked Mellon to open his checkbook for a candidate, in fact, Mellon invariably responded. In 1960, the Mellon family contributed an officially reported $40,000 to Republican causes, and in 1968 $118,000. In fact, Mellon contributions are usually much larger; in 1972 Richard Mellon Scaife gave Richard Nixon's campaign a cool $1 million.

Pennsylvanians on the Potomac

The circumscribed role of Pennsylvania in national circles is illustrated by the fact that Hugh Scott, by winning election as Republican leader of the Senate in 1969, became the first man from his state to hold a major leadership role in Congress since Frederick Augustus Muhlenberg was Speaker of the House in the First and Third Congresses. Joseph S. Clark, serving in the Senate from 1957 to 1969, gained distinction as a battler for liberal social causes and congressional reform but often seemed like a Don Quixote charging the seniority system, the filibuster, and other impregnable bastions of senatorial privilege. As *Philadelphia Magazine* wrote of Clark after his defeat for reelection in 1968, "His lofty conception of the role of the United States Senate and his persistent championing of high standards of personal ethics for members of the Congress established a moral tone which in our judgment easily compensated for whatever shortcomings he may have demonstrated as a political diplomat."

After Scott and Clark, one looks long and hard for Pennsylvanians who have made an important contribution in Washington in our time. Rep. Thomas E. Morgan, a country doctor from rural Fredericktown in western Pennsylvania, became chairman of the House Foreign Affairs Committee in 1959. But he failed (until some reforms were instituted in 1971) to advance that body far beyond the status of a detail-checker of the foreign policies espoused by the executive branch. Morgan retired in 1976. On the Republican side, John P. Saylor of Johnstown was ranking Republican on the Interior Committee and a strong backer of conservationist causes until his death in 1973.

Despite the bitter taste left by the Gulf Oil scandals when he retired, Scott did play a constructive role in national politics and legislation. For several years, he was the only really effective political operator among Republican moderates in the Senate. Scott's old friend but political antagonist, former Senator Clark, said of him: "His ear is closer to the ground than the ear of any other politician I know. . . . . He knows where all the bodies are buried, and he can cut your throat with the most charming smile. He wants to know what the people of Pennsylvania want him to do, and then he does it." *

Yet it would be a mistake to think that Scott is exclusively a political animal. The visitor to his office was quickly impressed by the exquisite pieces of ancient Chinese art standing about, and Scott was quick to tell of the interest in collecting 1,000-year-old pieces, which he and his wife Marian had been engaged in for more than 35 years. In fact, Scott was accomplished

---

* While Clark was still in the Senate, he and Scott had a unique weekly television show, aired across the state, in which they argued public policy between themselves and with guests with gusto and humor.

enough in Chinese art to have written a book during the 1960s—*The Golden Age of Chinese Art: The Lively T'ang Dynasty.* The story is told of the day Kentucky's Sen. Marlow Cook came to discuss a touchy issue with Scott. As Scott developed an argument trying to win Cook over, the visitor picked up a beautifully shaped white T'ang bowl from the coffee table and swung it between his fingers. After he had won Cook over, Scott relaxed and said as Cook was about to leave: "I just want to let you know, Marlow, that breaking a bowl like that would be the equivalent of pushing a Cadillac over a cliff."

Scorecard on State Government

Seldom an innovator among the states, Pennsylvania government by the '60s and early '70s was rushing to catch up with the times, rapidly expanding its services, trying some unique approaches, and suffering some severe fiscal headaches. Some salient items:

BUDGET. Pennsylvania's general fund budget was $990 million in 1961–62; by 1975–76 it had zoomed to $7.4 billion. Oddly enough, the last governor to hold expenditures fairly well in line was the Democrat David Lawrence. Then came the Scranton and Shafer administrations, determined to pull Pennsylvania out of its slough of unemployment and stagnation. They picked education as the key to progress, and now Pennsylvania spends $2.5 billion a year for education, more than three times the size of its entire budget during the Lawrence years. But other, less welcome items have escalated the budget as well. A prime example is welfare, $220 million a decade ago, recently over $630 million a year.

TAXES. As noted earlier, Pennsylvanians so abhorred the income tax that they permitted their sales tax to become what was then the nation's highest—6 percent—before they accepted the income tax. When Shapp took office in 1971, the state faced an immediate deficit of hundreds of millions of dollars and payless paydays for government workers. Even then, it took weeks of cajoling and arm-twisting of his own Democratic-controlled legislature to get an income tax passed. Then the state supreme court struck down the new tax because it granted exemptions to low-income families, which the jurists (mostly conservative Republicans) interpreted as violating the state constitution's prohibition against a graduated tax. (Nelson Rockefeller, then governor of New York, scornfully told us this indicated Shapp's "inexperience.") After more protracted negotiations, the legislature finally approved a flat-rate 2.3 percent income tax.

Pennsylvania has one of the highest corporate income taxes in the U.S.A. and business, through various levies, pays about $1.2 billion a year in taxes to the state—of the $5.5 billion total. Many big corporations think they are taxed far beyond reasonable rates by the state.

CONSTITUTIONAL REFORM. The anachronistic state constitution of 1874 was substantially revised by amendments in the 1960s and a state constitutional convention that met in 1967–68. Although the legislature restricted the scope of the convention and tailored the delegate-election mechanics to provide for partisan elections, some important changes emerged. A splendid local government article was written, and lines of responsibility among the three branches of the state government were made substantially clearer. The convention also worked out a major reorganization of the judiciary, with all state courts placed under the state supreme court in a unified administration.

Scranton, a leader of the convention, says it was a landmark in reducing the hyperpartisanship of Pennsylvania politics. Though Republicans had won a slight majority in the delegate elections, he and others staged a successful first-day fight to have it organized on a nonpartisan basis with a Republican president, Democratic vice president, cochairmen of both parties, and equally balanced party memberships on each committee. Scranton acknowledges that Pennsylvania is still one of the country's most partisan states. *Every* public officer—from governor and judges down to mayors and school boards —is elected on a partisan basis. Rarely will a member of the opposition party vote for a governor's budget. But men like Scranton, who was the first Republican governor to appoint a Democrat to his cabinet, have been pressing with some success for less partisanship, and gradually the idea is catching on.

PATRONAGE. Despite an expansion of civil service under Scranton, 45,000 of Pennsylvania's state workers were still appointed through a political patronage system—easily the highest percentage of any state of the Union. "Your only qualification," said Duke Kaminski, then of the Philadelphia *Bulletin's* Harrisburg bureau, "is endorsement by the party chairman, or the current administration, the blessing of the governor or a ranking staff member."

The days of the patronage system are numbered, however. In 1970, Pennsylvania suddenly took an innovative step by enacting a public employees' collective-bargaining act which actually guarantees to all government workers—state, county, and municipal—the right to strike. Pennsylvania was second only to Hawaii in enacting legislation of this type. Provisions are established for unions to win certification as bargaining agents. Strikes may then be called if (1) they are preceded by mediation and a report from a fact-finding panel, and (2) they do not imperil the "public health and safety" —a definition that was left to the courts to interpret. The practical effects are that workers can only be dismissed with cause and that workers need only turn to their unions for protection when a new administration comes to power and tries to dislodge them. The parties' only chance to designate workers is in high positions where union organizing will not reach, or when normal attrition creates vacancies.

The politicians are not, in fact, as sad about the end of wide-scale patronage as one might expect. Except for the 10 to 15 percent of jobs which pay good money, most are sought after only in hard times when unemployment is high. And the politicians' experience is that they may lose a couple of votes for every one they gain in handing out the desirable jobs.

The right-to-strike of Pennsylvania state workers has not gone unused. In July of 1975, 50,000 state employees, most of whom were members of the American Federation of State, County, and Municipal Employees, and a smaller number with the local unions composed of Pennsylvania social workers and unemployment service employees, struck in rejection of a proffered 3.5 percent wage increase. Numerically, it was the biggest strike of state or local workers in U.S. history. The unions originally demanded a 30 percent increase, then scaled that down to 10 percent, and finally had to settle for an increase only 1.25 percent more than the state's offer. Reasons for the union setback: tough bargaining by Governor Shapp, who said any larger increase would force the financially strapped state to raise taxes, and a spate of court orders sending workers with jobs of "critical importance" back to work.

Consumer Protection. Pennsylvania's regulatory commissions—especially the public utility commission (PUC), which regulates electric, gas, and water rates and franchises intrastate truckers, and the milk marketing board, which sets milk prices—are frequently accused by critics (including Governor Shapp) of protecting the vested interests of those they are to regulate, rather than the public. A favorite *bête noire* of such critics in the past was PUC Chairman George Bloom, one time Republican state party chairman. Bloom was appointed to the PUC by Governor Scranton for a 10-year term in 1965 and became a campaign issue in Milton Shapp's reelection effort in 1974. Shapp, pledging to support the interests of the Pennsylvania consumer, promised not to reappoint Bloom when the chairman's term expired in 1975.

But upon reelection Shapp discovered that it was easier to get Bloom off the PUC than it was to appoint someone else. To Bloom's seat he appointed the former chief counsel of the PUC, Philip Klodner, and to a second vacancy, he nominated the nationally known consumer advocate and former Pennsylvania insurance commissioner, Herbert Denenberg. The state senate rejected the nomination of Klodner, but under pressure from consumer groups within the state, the governor renominated him that same year. It quickly became apparent that the senate was about to reject the nomination again, and Klodner requested that the governor withdraw his name from consideration. The Denenberg case was equally unsuccessful, although more dramatic and the center of national attention because of Denenberg's stature among consumer advocates around the country.

Denenberg is an open and outspoken individual, with a quick mind and a comprehensive knowledge of consumer affairs. He is also brash and far less than politic. He was well known during his tenure as state insurance commissioner for making sharply derogatory comments concerning the state legislature, often questioning the members' general intelligence and their commitment to the welfare of their constituents. Additionally, he made enemies of many powerful groups, particularly in the insurance industry and with various professional organizations, including the state's doctors and lawyers. This came back to haunt him when his name was placed before the legislature. The AFL-CIO, considered by some the largest and most powerful lobby group for consumer interests in Harrisburg, did little for Denenberg. And there was the lack of support from the Shapp administration. Many observers believed Shapp had grown weary of Denenberg for what the governor believed to be the commissioner's grandstanding, for the constant turmoil in which Denenberg involved the administration, and for his feuding with the legislature. The best that consumer groups could do was to collect 80,000 names on a petition to Shapp calling for the reappointment of Denenberg to an interim position on the commission. Shapp refused—at which point Denenberg called a press conference and denounced the legislature *and* the governor.

Early in his administration, Shapp announced support for a plan which would have combined all of the major regulatory agencies in the state, including the PUC, the milk marketing board, and the insurance and banking departments into one super agency which would then be staffed with men and women committed to the protection and furtherence of consumer interests, not "special interests." After several years as governor, having learned to deal with the political forces in the state, including the legislature, the lobby groups, various pressure groups, and certainly not least of all the bureaucracy, Shapp quietly killed his plan. He refocused his efforts on an attempt to name a special counsel to each existing state regulatory agency, to represent the general public interest before the boards and commissions.

ENVIRONMENT. As an old industrial state with many outmoded sewage systems and ancient factories, Pennsylvania is extremely vulnerable to environmental dangers. Occasionally ecological disasters occur. At Donora, a steel-mill town of 12,000 people south of Pittsburgh, a heavy mixture of smoke and fog settled during the last days of October 1948 as a result of a temperature inversion. People's lungs became clogged with smoke from locomotives and factories, auto exhausts and floating solid particles. Five women and 17 men met their death as a result. Rivers are constantly threatened by acid mine water from abandoned coal mines. In summer 1970, a flow of up to five million gallons a day of acid water high in iron oxides and mineral salts was released from a mine in Cambria County into the Susquehanna River, killing all aquatic life for miles downstream.

In 1973, the federal Environmental Protection Agency cited the nation's largest steel mills, U.S. Steel's Clairton Works on the Monongahela River south of Pittsburgh, for 63 violations of air pollution standards. The Clairton case illustrates the problems pollution-fighters face in Pennsylvania. The Clairton Works were built in 1919, at a time when it was considered perfectly acceptable to dump coal and coke waste products into the water. Some 20 years later, U.S. Steel stopped doing that, and instead used the polluted water to quench the red-hot coke coming from its ovens. The result: polluted water was replaced by polluted air. By the early '70s, a local group called GASP (the Group Against Smog and Pollution) and United Steelworkers Local 1557 president Dan Hannan were attacking Big Steel and demanding an end to the contamination. The company replied that there was no way to reduce the pollution to acceptable levels—and hinted that continued demands for a clean-up might produce instead a layoff of workers. Eventually, U.S. Steel and the Allegheny County pollution authorities reached an agreement, with a clause granting the company a 10-year immunity from environmental prosecution. But EPA had a policy against such immunity, and stepped into the case itself. Clairton shows how difficult it is to achieve acceptable environmental standards in places like industrial Pennsylvania where the economy is based on huge capital facilities which were built with no concern for the pollution they would cause.

The most one can say of all this is that now, late in time, a serious anti-pollution effort does seem underway in state government. In the last year of the Shafer administration, a new state department of environmental resources was set up to assume the duties of 14 existing and often competing and ill-coordinated agencies. Dr. Maurice K. Goddard, a respected former professor of forestry at Penn State who had been secretary of forests and waters for 16 years, was appointed to head the new agency. About the same time, Shafer created—and Shapp later continued—an extraordinary strike force of six young attorneys (most from Philadelphia law firms, the oldest man 31 years old) to stop pollution in its tracks by heavy use of injunctions rather than going the route of criminal prosecutions and fines.

It will doubtless be a long time until Pennsylvania's air and water are really clean. When we discussed the subject with the *Bulletin*'s Duke Kaminski, he said:

I'm looking out the Capitol window here and I can see three smoke stacks belching out poisonous gases—two of them belong to Pennsylvania Power and Light Co. Down the road at Bethlehem there's one of the worst oxygen furnaces you ever saw in your life. The poisonous pink cloud is something to behold.
Shapp's best estimate is that unless you want to wipe out current industry, it might take 15 years to get it under control. My reply to that was: "Fifteen years?! Why, I'll be dead!"

UNIVERSITIES. Pennsylvania is just now emerging from the Dark Ages in respect to public support of higher education. Its investment in public colleges and universities is now six times greater, in relation to per capita income, than was the case in the early 1950s, but the combined state and local government's contribution to higher education ranks last among all the states.

For more than a century, Pennsylvania has had a public land-grant university—Penn State, located at remote State College (now called University Park) in the Allegheny Mountains some distance north of Harrisburg. By 1955, Penn State already had 14,000 students; today the figure at the central campus and 20 satellite campuses is over 50,000. But Pennsylvanians have never thought of Penn State as *their* college in the way that people from the South, Midwest, and West view their state university. Penn State's main feature has been a very good football team, plus good agricultural and engineering departments. These days its chief innovation is broad-scale use of television to let one professor cover many classrooms.

The great expansion in higher education started with Scranton, who more than doubled appropriations for higher education (to $134 million), and continued at a fast clip under Shafer to a total $509 million in his last budget. A whole new string of community colleges has come into existence in the past decade. But perhaps the most interesting innovation was the marriage of convenience between the state and the previously private University of Pittsburgh and Temple University. The state needed to increase its enrollment capacity to match the needs of its population; Pittsburgh and Temple were in a desperate way for money. So in return for an adjustment of their tuition fees and some minor changes on their boards of trustees, Pittsburgh and Temple suddenly became "state-related" institutions. The aid is not minimal: about $130 million a year between them at last count (covering about half their basic budgets). The University of Pennsylvania, on the other hand, continues as a "state-aided" school, which means the state pays less than a quarter of its budget. In addition, Pennsylvania youngsters from families with less than $16,000-a-year income are eligible for scholarships to study wherever they please, a program now costing over $68 million a year. A decade ago, the only comparable state-financed activity was a quite limited competitive scholarship program. It cost only $\frac{1}{325}$ as much.

In the meantime, state aid to public schools has gone from under $400 million to almost $2 billion a year in a 15-year span. Just before World War II, the state aid figure had been an incredibly low $21 a year; by 1975–76, it was $881 a year.

A particularly thorny issue has been state assistance to private (principally parochial) schools. A 1968 law permitted state assistance to the private schools for the "actual cost" of teachers' salaries, textbooks, and teaching aids in secular fields. Opponents of the law, saying it constituted a breach of the First Amendment-mandated separation of church and state, took the matter into the federal courts and in 1971 the U.S. Supreme Court declared it unconstitutional. In May of 1975, the U.S. Supreme Court reviewed the state's revised program of assistance to nonpublic schools and found that it, too, was unconstitutional. The only portion which the high court allowed was one providing for the loan of secular textbooks.

"The House of Ill Repute" Mends Its Ways

It may be a little rough to call Pennsylvania's legislature "The House of Ill Repute" as *Philadelphia Magazine* did in a 1974 review of shenanigans in the ornate halls of the Italian Renaissance–style capitol building at Harrisburg. The quality of legislative work, the ethics, and also the qualifications of legislators today are certainly a dramatic improvement over the days when Penrose and Grundy, working in tandem with the special interests, manipulated representatives and senators at will. Things are even a cut above a decade ago when the leader of the Philadelphia Democratic organization used to sit on the floor with a phone at his ear waiting for Bill Green's machine to flash the word on how he and his colleagues should vote.

One problem of the Pennsylvania legislature is the inordinately large size of its house—203 members. This leads to vast confusion during sessions, difficulties in organizing majorities to move legislation, and a distinct lack of decorum. (A number of proposals to reduce the house size were made at the 1967–68 constitutional convention, but all were voted down. Republicans from thinly populated rural areas join ranks with big-city Democrats, who want to retain every nuance of urban minority strength, to prevent a sensible reduction.) A second problem is the lack of staff professionalism; the legislature hires over 600 people, but the number includes sergeants at arms, messengers, secretaries, and janitors in addition to a limited number of professionals, and an estimated 5 to 10 percent "phantom" employees, who are on somebody's patronage and never show up for work. Without expert staffs, legislators more easily fall prey to lobbyist enticements on complex and/or innocuous-appearing bills that favor private groups at the public's expense.

The number of professional staff has, however, been increasing in recent years, and the legislature—while still far short of the professionalism of a California or New York—has been making real efforts to improve its decision-making capacity and oversight of the state bureaucracy. In a landmark effort, the legislature in 1976 moved to specifically appropriate all federal funds flowing to the state government, triggering a court showdown with the governor that could have national implications. The number of standing committees was substantially reduced, committee meetings were opened to the public, and an innovative new scheduling system introduced.

Before the courts forced one-man reapportionment in the mid-1960s, rural (generally meaning Republican) and big-business control of the legislature usually coincided neatly. For several years, it was said that the late Harry Davis, Sun Oil's lobbyist, and William A. Reiter (the Pennsylvania Railroad's and then Penn Central's man) were the 51st and 52nd senators respectively. It was their responsibility to see to it that the senate always had one more Republican than Democratic vote, and the appropriate dollars were invested to make sure that happy condition continued. In 1970, the senate fell to the Democrats for the first time in many years. "It was no accident," one Pennsylvania observer said, "that the senate fell to the Democrats in the year that the Penn Central Railroad went bankrupt."

Today there are still important business lobbies in Harrisburg—the steel companies, oil firms, public utilities—but a lot of the power has shifted to service-type industry lobbies (retailers and the like), who see things differently from the old industrial moguls. And for sheer power, one must look to entirely different types of lobbies—the Pennsylvania State Teachers Association (now considered by some the single most influential lobby), the Pennsylvania branch of the national Welfare Rights Organization, and the AFL-CIO (though labor usually involves itself only with labor legislation). A 1974 survey conducted by the Philadelphia *Evening Bulletin* among members of the legislature reported that the legislators ranked the seven most influential lobby groups in this order: (1) labor, particularly the state's school teachers, the state AFL-CIO, and the quickly expanding American Federation of State, County, and Municipal Employees, (2) the Pennsylvania Bankers Association, (3) the executive branch of the state government, (4) the state's Catholic Conference, (5) the large state universities, especially Penn State and Pitt, (6) the Pennsylvania Builders Association, and finally, (7) the state's highway contractors.

The *Bulletin* investigation found that most of the more senior members of the legislature believe that the control or dominance once demonstrated by lobbyists over legislation has vanished. Lobby groups now are more often found to be skilled advocates and negotiators, men and women who supply persuasive data more frequently than their predecessors did and less inclined or able to employ the traditional tactics of arm twisting or subtle corruption.

Philadelphia: Renewal and Decay

The city of Philadelphia, as its social historian, Nathaniel Burt, has written, is "a fine vintage, warm, rich, flavorful; but there's a drop of bitterness in the bottom of the glass." It has had three great flowerings, each followed by an era of decay. The first flowering was its birth as William Penn's City of Brotherly Love, building for a century to the crescendo of the Golden Age of Revolution, the Age of Franklin, when in government, finance, commerce, and letters, Philadelphia was the preeminent city of the New World. Then, early in the 19th century, the federal government went to Washington, the state government was transferred to Harrisburg, supremacy in commerce went to the great deep-water port of New York, and financial power—the *coup de grâce* administered by President Jackson's abolition of the National Bank—was transferred to New York, too. Cultural dominance shifted to Gotham as well, and Philadelphia has lived ever since in the shadow of the great world city to its north. It became (and largely remains) a private city, a place for living.

A second flowering, industrial in nature, rose through the Civil War and was signaled by the Centennial Exposition of 1876, attended by 10 million visitors and one of the grandest shows of technology the world had ever seen. The peak of the boom came in the 10 years before 1900. Burt writes: "Then boomed Iron and Railroads and Coal, Cramp and Baldwin. The fox hunting and . . . Cricket and coach-and-four flourished together. Then began the Orchestra and the Curtis Publishing Company."

For the prosperity of its Iron Age, Philadelphia had to pay the same kind of price all of Pennsylvania was paying: ugly political corruption (this was the era of the sinister bosses, culminating in Penrose) and physical blight. The almighty Pennsylvania Railroad decided it needed a station at the city's very heart, opposite city hall, and put up a great brick castle called Broad Street Station. To connect with its main lines, the railroad erected a massive stone causeway out to West Philadelphia, a block wide (so it could hold 16 parallel tracks) and appropriately called the Chinese Wall. It was penetrated only by gloomy dripping tunnels for cross streets and effectively blighted development in a large part of the city's heart. Simultaneously, the railroad built up sumptuous suburbs—which would become some of the most beautiful in all America—along its commuting routes, one westward along the Main Line, another northwesterly to Germantown and Chestnut Hill. Thus began the process of suburbanization of Philadelphia's aristocracy which would ruin center city.

Down from the Gilded Age, straight through the New Deal and World War II, Philadelphia's politics were unflinchingly Republican, in the grip of one of the most corrupt and unsavory political machines the country has ever known.

Since the 1880s, there had been sporadic reform efforts by good government types, but the Organization had quickly beaten them all back. But in 1939, the so-called "Young Turks"—a group of bright young Depression-era graduates of Ivy League colleges who had been inspired by the New Deal and La Guardia's achievements in New York—formed to work for charter revision and, later, physical renewal of the city and political change. By the start of the postwar era, the elements of a broad-based reform coalition had begun to coalesce—the Young Turks, Old Philadelphians, ideological liberals in the Americans for Democratic Action, ethnic minority leaders like Jack Kelly and Matthew McCloskey, and Democratic ward heelers.

But the whole reform movement might have collapsed, like so many in the past, had it not been for two bright, aggressive Democratic attorneys from old Republican families who emerged to assume leadership. The first was Richardson Dilworth, a colorful trial lawyer, who ran for mayor in 1947 citing chapter and verse on the pervasive municipal corruption he had learned about as lawyer for the Philadelphia Transit Company. He lost to the mediocre old GOP war-horse, Mayor Bernard Samuels, by about 90,000 votes. But revelations of wholesale corruption followed in the next two years, and in 1949 Dilworth was elected city treasurer and in 1951 his close associate in the reform movement, Joseph S. Clark, won election as mayor. The Augean stables at City Hall were cleansed and Philadelphia embarked upon a decade of remarkable physical and political renaissance. Dilworth, in turn, became mayor in 1956, finally leaving office to run for governor in 1962. Despite its shortcomings, the Clark-Dilworth era must be called Philadelphia's modern Golden Age.

Clark and Dilworth were not obliged to start the city's renewal from ground zero because the reform elements which elected them had already begun. A citizens' committee in 1947 had staged a spectacular "Better Philadelphia Exhibit" to show citizens, quite graphically, what good planning and renewal could do to revive their decayed city. The exhibit, viewed by 400,000 at a downtown department store, was most Philadelphians' introduction to the exciting ideas that would transform the city's inner core in the following years: a park and a great mall around Independence Hall, bright new buildings where the Chinese Wall still stood, a promenade along the Delaware River as William Penn had originally planned. Not all the plans have been implemented as foreseen that day, but many have, and more may be in the next years. The Independence Hall and neighboring Society Hill renewal efforts are among the finest in the nation and have given the city a new sense of its history and urban elegance. The ugly old Broad Street Station was finally torn down in 1952, and where the Chinese Wall stood, there are now the massive buildings and walkways of the Penn Center, centerpiece of the downtown renewal put through under a skilled and strong-headed master of urban renewal, Edmund Bacon.

The Greater Philadelphia Movement was launched in 1948 on the model of Pittsburgh's Allegheny Conference, its board composed principally of "movers and shakers"—presidents of home-owned corporations who can make decisions for them—along with a share of minority-group and labor spokesmen. The GPM made reform of Philadelphia's outmoded form of government its first order of business, and a new charter strengthening the mayor's executive role, upgrading civil service, and putting city planning on a long-range basis, was approved by the voters in 1951 and went into effect as Clark became mayor.

As time went on, Philadelphia developed an inventive structure of public interest corporations close to, but independent of, the government and political structure, performing vital tasks for the city rapidly and effectively. In 1957, for instance, the Old Philadelphia Development Corporation was formed at Dilworth's request with its top priority the renewal of center-city Philadelphia, starting with the Independence Hall area. The OPDC's board includes government officials but is also heavy on presidents and board chairmen of major banks, insurance companies, utilities, department stores, and hotels and the senior partners of prestigious law firms—the kind of a group that can give investors confidence that they are working with a responsible and nonpolitical type of effort.

While the thrust of many of these groups was elitist and business-oriented, real efforts were made to obtain extensive participation of interested citizen groups. If there is one unique element in the Philadelphia story, it must be the broad and diverse assortment of organizations and individuals who contributed to rebuilding. Philadelphia not only has its prestige organizations, but a multitude of thriving civic groups in its neighborhoods, and the lines of communication have usually been kept open. In a sense, this had to be so, because the economic power of the city lies in so many hands; Philadelphia lacks the single, dominant economic power, capable of making almost unilateral decisions, which the Mellons at least until recently have been in Pittsburgh. Thus progress has sometimes been slower, but more firmly based on citizen consent, than in the companion city to the west. There has been another dividend in the Philadelphia system: many believe that the inter-locking network of community organizations, rather than the publicized tough tactics of the city police department, can be thanked for the fact that Philadelphia's ghettos did not explode in major riots in the 1960s.

The greatest contribution of Clark and Dilworth was the high sense of dedication and belief in Philadelphia's future which they brought to City Hall. Dilworth, the utterly courageous man, warm and extroverted, and Clark, more the thinker, reflective, idealistic—they brought a quality to city govern-ment that old Philadelphia had not experienced in a century, and they en-couraged a generation of bright and idealistic young leaders. But that old goblin, rawly partisan politics, still lurked in the shadows, ready to restore the old order. The regular organization types in the Democratic party did not take to it kindly when Clark started out by appointing young reformers and talented Old Philadelphians to key posts in his administration, spurning the clamor for Democratic patronage after the long famine of the Republican century. Clark lacked enough power to prevent replacement of his own re-form-minded city chairman by William Green, a cultivator of precinct- and patronage-based power of the old school. The conflict endured through the Clark-Dilworth era.

James H. J. Tate, the man who succeeded Dilworth in 1962, had made his way upward as a plodding member of the Democratic organization, demonstrating, as he would in the mayor's job, excellent instincts for po-litical survival. "His great strength," one local observer told me, "was that he was always interested in the exercise of power. He discovered everyone else was interested in money. He wasn't. This gave him great power over others." From the start of his term, Tate seemed to assume that the business elite of Philadelphia which supported Clark and Dilworth and the reform era were against him. Or perhaps it was the other way around—in any event, the re-lationship led to an emotional counterreaction in a very proud man. Tate actually kept many of Dilworth's best department heads in office and tried for a while to keep the reform era alive. After Bill Green's death in 1963, Tate fought tooth and nail against the old party hack Francis Smith, who succeeded Green as Democratic party chairman in the city. In 1967, when the Democratic city committee decided Tate could not be reelected and tried to defeat him in the primary, Tate appealed to the business leaders for help. They turned him down cold. Tate turned to his friends in organized labor—especially James J. O'Neill, the ruthless boss of Plumbers Local 690, then president of the powerful building and construction trades council in the city. O'Neill, one local trade unionist told us, "forced Tate down the throat of the labor movement." But the labor support was decisive in Tate's easy primary win and then general election victory by only 11,000 votes over the popular young Republican district attorney, Arlen Specter. (In turn, Tate gave labor in the city practically anything it wanted.)

Overall, the signals were not positive for Philadelphia as the 1970s began. During the Tate decade, the city's once-vaunted urban renewal effort had slowed down alarmingly. A grand jury, convened by Republican District Attorney Arlen Specter in 1969, uncovered reeking corruption in area after area of the housing-redevelopment program, resulting in scores of indictments including a number against high-ranking officials and civic leaders. City government itself was badly in need of administrative reform, but Tate made only scattered changes, and they were of the kind that fragmented responsibility rather than coordinating it.*

As the 1970s wore on, it became increasingly evident that Philadelphia was mired in an impossible tax bind. The reasons were apparent enough: a large low-income population, dilapidated physical plant, languidly increasing property taxes, the heavy financial burden for poverty, slums and crime (including a yearly housing abandonmant rate of some 3,000 units), rampant inflation, and wages for government workers that constantly outstripped those paid by private businesses in the city. Though a payroll tax helped to tap some of the earnings of suburbanites as well as Philadelphians employed in the city, poor assessment practices and the flight of industries to the suburbs were undermining the property tax. The Pennsylvania Economy League, while emphasizing that the magnitude of Philadelphia's fiscal burden was much less than that of New York City, traced developments in the city's fiscal practices—sharp increases in taxes and debt, for instance, and an average annual compound increase of 12.5 percent in combined city and school budgets over a decade—ominously similar to those of the virtually bankrupt city to the north. To that one could add a vast amount of unfunded pension liability and borrowing from capital funds to balance the budget over a period of several years. Without dramatic increases in the productivity of city services and tighter financial management, there was real fear that Philadelphia could eventually face a financial catastrophe of New York style.

Behind those city fiscal problems, of course, lies the problem of stagnant or declining employment rolls in the city. By contrast, the economy of southeastern Pennsylvania as a whole has been moving forward briskly, with an increasingly diversified "mix," in the postwar era. The area continues to have heavy manufacturing—some steel mills (including the huge Fairless Works built by U. S. Steel in Bucks County after the war), heavy equipment and electrical machinery manufacture by companies like GE and Westinghouse, and transportation equipment by Budd (railway cars) and Boeing Veritol division (helicopters). The apparel, chemical, publishing, and drug industries employ many thousands. The area also has the biggest concentration of oil refineries in the East and a port which ranks among the top in the world in total tonnage. (It does less well in general cargo, having failed to adapt early to containerization. *Philadelphia Magazine* charges that "neglect, sheer incompetence and political dealing have badly mauled Phila-

---

* As an example of zero coordination, no one in city government knew how much money was coming from the range of federal assistance programs, nor which sections of the government were receiving it.

delphia's port" in the last few years.) Service industries have grown rapidly in recent years and accounted for the lion's share of growth.

The conclusions seem inevitable: unless some means of income redistribution between wealthy suburb and poor city can be found, the center city—even in an area of renaissance like the one Clark and Dilworth brought—will continue in perennial financial crisis. We heard constant disappointment expressed in Philadelphia about the low level of interest and help for the inner city shown by its suburban-based elite. And regional cooperation—not to mention metropolitan government—is an area in which Pennsylvania, among all the big industrial states, is the most retrograde.

Ward Politics and the Story of Frank Rizzo

Philadelphia ward politics are strictly a page out of yesteryear. For the ward and precinct committeemen, the reward is usually patronage—a number of city jobs still available (though most jobs went under civil service during the Dilworth-Clark era) and an even juicier prize, the 2,500 to 3,000 jobs that a state administration can make available within Philadelphia for friends of the party in power.* And Philadelphia has the kind of archetypal political leaders who seem to have died out in most major cities. One example is not even a Democrat but rather the leader of the beleaguered Republicans, William A. Meehan. Meehan is one of the most thoroughly delightful city politicians we have met in America—a firm-jawed Irishman of compact build in his late forties with a sunny personality who long ago learned to roll with the punches. His father was Sheriff Austin Meehan, a bald, barrel-chested man who was Republican monarch in the city for two decades. Technically, Meehan is not the "boss." His title is general counsel to the party, and somebody else always fronts as chairman. But no one is fooled.

And then there was the matter of Frank Lazzaro Rizzo.

One of the ways Tate paved the way for his difficult 1967 reelection contest was to appoint that volatile, controversial career cop as police commissioner. The selection was doubly brilliant: Rizzo, whose immigrant father was a policeman before him, became the first police commissioner of Italian ancestry in Philadelphia's history—a plus for Irishman Tate with the Italian vote. Secondly, Rizzo had a reputation as a fearless and colorful policeman whose technique of knocking heads first and asking questions later had already endeared him to Philadelphia's fearful middle-class home owners.

Rizzo ran a highly efficient police department which claimed it brought 42 percent of its cases to solution, double the national average. He increased the number of police from 6,000 to 7,200, put dog patrols in the subways, expanded the narcotics squad, equipped his men with walkie-talkies, and expanded the police budget from $60 million to $92 million. Confidential

---

* Typical state patronage jobs are in the revenue and highway departments, plus the turnpike and bridge authorities. In a sharp break with precedent, Governor Shapp began filling these positions *without* prior consultation of the city Democratic committee.

dossiers were kept on thousands of political dissidents and black activists. Rizzo's tactics with Black Panthers and other dissenters were tough—and well publicized—in the extreme. All this delighted his natural constituency— the people he describes as the "guys with lunchboxes and the oil-stained shirts." It horrified liberals, of course. Police services became the largest item in the city budget, at the same time that city outlays for health, recreation, and sanitation services held constant or declined. Wherever trouble erupted in Philadelphia, the big, muscular form of Frank Rizzo (six feet, two inches, close to 240 pounds) would appear to direct police operations, once with a billy club stuck in his cummerbund when he was called away from a formal evening affair.

Barred by the city charter from seeking a third consecutive term as mayor, Tate decided on the man he wanted to succeed him: Frank Rizzo. The Philadelphia Democratic city committee and its new head, Peter Camiel, went along. Rizzo ran on his image and his record, making over and over again the point "He made Philadelphia the safest of the nation's 10 largest cities." (The statistic is based on the once-sacrosanct FBI crime statistics, which are the only comparative figures of their type available but whose accuracy is questionable because of uneven crime-reporting techniques.) When the votes were counted, Rizzo had just a shade less than a majority, but he ran nearly 50,000 votes ahead of his closest opponent, liberal reformist Congressman William Green and thus won the Democratic nomination.

The Republican choice was Thacher Longstreth, who had already run for mayor once, back in 1955, and lost to Richardson Dilworth. An urbane and elegant member of the Philadelphia establishment, Longstreth had served as executive vice president of the chamber of commerce and as a city councilman. But, as Republican Leader Meehan said, "this whole election is a referendum on Rizzo." Longstreth had the endorsements—and they were highly unusual ones for a Republican—of former Mayors Clark and Dilworth, of black legislator and former Rizzo opponent Hardy Williams and liberal councilman David Cohen, and of the *Inquirer* and *Bulletin*. But Tate saw to it that the unions and the Democratic machine stuck with Rizzo. Longstreth carried the black wards by better than 2–1, but Rizzo had far larger margins in heavily Italian South Philadelphia, and carried the city by a 53–47 percent margin.

Aside from his law-and-order pitch, Rizzo's philosophy was surprisingly stand-pat for a candidate who had aroused such enthusiastic support—and opposition. He promised not to raise taxes, and during his first months in office told one reporter, "What we have to do—and have the courage to do it—is to try to save what we have left. If we raise taxes any more, we are going to cause an exodus of people. We have to stabilize." But temperamentally, Rizzo was not the man to stabilize anything. "In his heart," said former mayor Dilworth, "he's a cop, and he can't believe that someone who disagrees with him is not a crook." As a policeman, Frank Rizzo had made his way upward by fighting crime (and seeing that he got good publicity for it). Once installed in the mayor's office, he never seemed able to break the fighting habit. One after another, he took on just about everyone with political clout in Philadelphia—and he seemed especially eager to tangle with people who had helped him get where he was. The history of many mayors' years in office are stories of new programs and buildings; the history of Frank Rizzo's years is the story of one brawl after another.

Rizzo had won the mayor's office with the help of Jim Tate, the former mayor. But these two soon fell out and Philadelphia was treated to the spectacle of the new mayor calling the old mayor, and his former patron, a pirate captain who had allowed his crew to plunder the city for a decade. In reply, Tate lashed out at Rizzo, calling him a bully, a traitor, and a Gestapo chief. Rizzo soon found an additional enemy in liberal-reform governor Milton Shapp, whom Rizzo assailed as an incompetent, and whose programs the mayor opposed in the state legislature.

By 1973, a showdown was developing between the mayor and Peter Camiel, party leader for Philadelphia. Camiel was a strong party Democrat, a liberal allied with Governor Shapp and a man who found almost everything concerning Rizzo distasteful. The conflict came to a head in 1973 as Rizzo and Camiel engaged in open warfare over the election of the Philadelphia district attorney.

But before the election, in August, the *Bulletin* and the *Inquirer* suddenly reported that Rizzo had ordered a 34-man police unit to investigate the mayor's political enemies—including Peter Camiel and council president Schwartz. (The mayor's response: he called *Bulletin* editor John Farmer and said he should check out a rumor "that John Farmer is a faggot.") Camiel then announced that Rizzo, in a February conference in a Bellevue-Stratford Hotel bathroom, had offered him control of city architectural and engineering contracts if Camiel would support Rizzo's man for D.A. The mayor immediately denied the charge, and when the spunky tabloid *Daily News* challenged him to a lie detector test, he promptly accepted. "I have great faith in the polygraph," Rizzo said. "If this machine says a man lied, he lied." The machine said that Rizzo did lie on six of ten questions, and that Camiel, who also submitted to a test, told the truth. The *Bulletin* said that a man-on-the-street poll showed that only 23 percent of the people questioned believed Rizzo told the truth; and the man Rizzo backed for D.A., Republican incumbent Specter, lost in November.

Such was the tone of public life during the first administration of the "toughest cop" in the City of Brotherly Love. Rizzo had talked of running for governor in 1974, but after the lie detector incident neither party wanted anything to do with him. He had lost the support of labor (through his handling of the school strike) and of the Democratic machine (because of the Camiel business); the Republicans had no use for him, and most of the major candidates he backed (Nixon, Specter) had lost Philadelphia.

His ambitions for state-wide office temporarily checked, Rizzo continued to win the support of Philadelphians against candidates backed by the Camiel organization. Using his leverage over jobs and contracts, and appealing to his fellow Italians, who responded overwhelmingly, Frank Rizzo won renomination for mayor by 30,000 votes over the regular party candidate, State Senator Louis Hill, in the Democratic 1975 primary election. Congressman Bill Green, who declined to run, probably would have won. Rizzo's re-election against two weak opponents in the general election was anticlimatic.

During Rizzo's first administration, the number of city employees rose from 35,203 to 39,295, an increase of more than a thousand a year, 84 percent of whom were patronage. During this same period, the number of school employees grew 19 percent while enrollment dropped about 6 percent. A survey by the Pennsylvania Economy League found that Philadelphia, compared with other major cities, is exceeded only by New York in expenditures per pupil and ratio of teachers to pupils.

During the 1975 election year, Rizzo submitted a budget which included $65 million in revenues with virtually no chance to materialize—additional personal property taxes from anticipated court actions and real-estate taxes from the bankrupt railroads. Just before the primary, he handed municipal employees a 12.8 percent wage increase and other benefits. Asked where he would get the $26 million to pay for it, the mayor said, "I don't know. We'll find it."

Finally, in the first months of Rizzo's second term, the piper had to be paid. Rizzo conveniently forgot his promise not to raise taxes and said that the budget for the year was actually $80 million in the red. State help was not forthcoming: indeed, when the state legislature was asked for emergency aid and new taxing authority, Rizzo arrogantly refused to appear before the relevant legislative committee. The city then had to shoulder the entire burden itself, including a sharp increase in the wage tax and real estate taxes— the biggest single tax hike in the city's history.

And the bullying continued. In March 1976 Rizzo became enraged by a caustic article scheduled for publication in the *Inquirer* and kept his police away from the scene when his allies, members of the Building and Construction Trades Council, attempted to halt the *Inquirer*'s publication by blocking the paper's entrances. Rizzo called the incident a "labor matter," even though the *Inquirer* had no contracts with the unions involved. To many concerned Philadelphians, it appeared that Philadelphia was edging toward a police state in the Bicentennial year.

Shortly after the incident at the *Inquirer*, a recall Rizzo drive was launched. The first person to sign the recall petitions was former Mayor and Senator Joseph Clark, who called Rizzo "Philadelphia's Mussolini . . . a rascal, a liar—a man who is ignorant, arrogant, and stupid." A citizen writing to the Philadelphia *Inquirer* used equally colorful language: "Rizzo wrestles with the delicate fabric of liberty and civility like a bed pan orderly trying to perform brain surgery with a nightstick."

The civil liberties questions alone would not have been enough to make the recall effort creditable; what gave it a real impetus, including support from many former Rizzo supporters, was the pervasive feeling of betrayal by a political leader who had boasted so much of his ability to hold taxes down and given no inkling in the election that a massive increase was around the corner.

Some 211,000 Philadelphians signed recall petitions against their mayor—a man who had boasted he would deal with opponents in a way to "make Attila the Hun look like a faggot." Shelly Yanoff, the civic leader who led the recall effort, said it took substantial courage for citizens to sign the petitions. "For every two people who signed the petitions, there were four who didn't," she said. "They told us, 'I'll vote with you but I can't sign: I have a family, I've got a business that I need to protect.'" The city charter, she noted, grants Philadelphia's mayor formidable powers, and many citizens feared that Rizzo still controlled the police department.

The number of signatures gathered was well above the minimum 145,448 required under the city charter. But Rizzo's ally, the city solicitor, set down a nitpicking list of requirements for valid signatures intentionally designed to thwart the whole recall effort. When the Rizzo-controlled city commissioners finally decided only 116,943 signatures were valid, a minority commissioner called the validating procedures "the greatest display of stonewalling, stalling and arrogant abuses of power since the Watergate episode."

A local judge reversed the commissioners and ordered that the recall take place. Yet when the case was taken on appeal to the Pennsylvania supreme court, the justices there threw out the recall on murky technical grounds. It is likely that if the vote had taken place, Rizzo would have been ousted. But arbitrary judges, choosing to ignore the groundswell of revulsion against Rizzo and the courage of those who had signed the recall petition, left Philadelphia to suffer on, until 1980, under the ugly rule of the nation's most vindictive local leader.

The Philadelphia Black Community

The first Negroes were brought to the banks of the Delaware as slaves of the Dutch even before Penn and the Quakers arrived in 1682, and they have been a significant factor in Philadelphia history ever since. As W. E. B. Du Bois, the great black sociologist, told the story in his 1899 book, *The Philadelphia Negro,** the first expression against the slave trade occurred in Philadelphia, as did the first abolitionist organization, the first legislation to end slavery, the first attempt at Negro education, and the first Negro convention. The Du Bois book, read even 70 years after its first publication, is a compelling social documentary on the burden of being black in Philadelphia. Two themes appeared early and have endured to the present day. The first in-

---

* This seminal work in the sociology of American Negroes, long out of print, was reprinted in 1967 (New York: Schocken Books) with an illuminating introduction by Prof. E. Digby Baltzell of the University of Pennsylvania.

volves Philadelphia's location as a natural gateway from the South; as each generation of Philadelphia Negroes has begun to establish itself socially and economically in the city, a new wave of less educated blacks has arrived from the South, causing social tensions and vicious new discrimination by the white community, not aimed just at the newcomers but at *all* Philadelphia blacks. The second recurrent theme has been the fierce and often losing competition for jobs that blacks have found themselves immersed in as successive waves of immigrants arrived from Europe.

In the 1890s, Negroes were scattered throughout the city, a high proportion working as domestic servants close to (if not in the homes of) their white employers. Today, the vast majority of blacks live in clearly defined ghettos. The day-to-day social interaction of whites and blacks that marked earlier times is greatly reduced. Another change is that Philadelphia's middle- and upper-income blacks—now a growing and prospering group—do not live in the ghetto; instead they have migrated to desirable communities like Germantown and Mt. Airy, or all the way out to the suburbs. Many wealthy blacks in the mid-city luxury high-rises pay $400 or more a month in rent. (A measure of the change of things is that 35 years ago, *no* Philadelphia black moved into a new home—only old houses abandoned by whites.) The absence of the black business and professional people in the ghettos means that underprivileged children growing up there have few success models they can look to.

The second dramatic change from Du Bois' day is simply in terms of numbers. In 1890, Philadelphia had 39,371 blacks (3.8 percent of the total city population). According to the 1970 Census, there were 653,791 blacks in Philadelphia—33.5 percent of the city total. The figure continues to rise, and the day of black majority may not be too distant.

Summing up the change of conditions for Philadelphia's Negroes between 1960 and 1970, the *Evening Bulletin* reported: "The poorest parts of the city are probably worse off now. . . . There is more vandalism, more narcotics, more gang fighting, more filth in the streets, more dangers of all kinds." Indeed, a series of facts and statistics can be rolled out to support the projection of a violent explosion in the city:

▪ For reasons unclear, Philadelphia is a gang-fight center of the U. S. A. From 1963 to 1973, there were 248 gang murders—including 39 in 1972 and 43 in 1971. Most of the victims were in their early or middle teens, and some were simply innocent bystanders. (By the mid-1970s, however, the gang problem had been somewhat alleviated.)

▪ There are as many as 15,000 heroin addicts in the city, and three times that number hooked on amphetamine drugs—according to the city's own health commissioner.

▪ The black unemployment rate is twice that of whites and unlikely to improve much as more and more heavy industries—the kind that can offer blacks the most numerous job opportunities—desert the high-tax, crime-plagued city for the suburbs.

■ Despite scores of ambitious projects, the amount of new housing for low-income blacks is but a drop in the bucket compared to need. There are 13,000 people on the waiting list for public housing—but only 12,000 units were added through all federally subsidized housing programs during the *entire decade* of the 1960s. The picture was somewhat brighter in terms of individual housing-unit rehabilitation in the slums, a program in which Tate took a special interest; nevertheless, so hopeless are conditions in the ghettos that slumlords have abandoned an estimated 20,000 buildings.

■ In Philadelphia's schools, which by mid-decade had a black enrollment of 62 percent, an estimated 40 percent (80 percent in some inner-city schools) perform below the "minimum functioning level." (Students so ranked may be able to read a little and do sums, but not well; they place below 85 percent of the pupils in the U.S.A. in their age groups.) Basic educational attainment does not seem to have improved despite a brilliant reform effort led by Richardson Dilworth as school-board president (until his retirement in 1971) and Dr. Mark R. Shedd as superintendent (until his firing a month after Frank Rizzo was elected mayor).

Every discouraging fact notwithstanding, there are those who see hope in the Philadelphia black man's situation—perhaps more hope than in any other great city of America. Home ownership among blacks is rising rapidly, and the white noose around the ghettos is beginning to loosen, if ever so slightly. Since World War II in Philadelphia, the proportion of blacks who have finished high school has tripled, the proportion of college graduates has tripled. Where an educated black might be reduced to waiting on table in Du Bois' day, or even the 1930s, today the problem is to find qualified black applicants for the jobs that are available. Where in the 1920s none of the great Philadelphia law firms had black attorneys on their staffs—and a black could not even rent professional office space downtown—today the big firms hire blacks enthusiastically and some blacks sit on the local bench. Black business opportunities have multiplied, and black men sit on the boards of some of the great financial institutions. Philadelphia's universities actively recruit blacks for their faculties. Job opportunities for blacks in local government have expanded dramatically, starting in the Clark-Dilworth era. The Philadelphia police force is about 18 percent black (a figure topped only by Washington, D.C., and Atlanta), and despite Rizzo's outside reputation, relations between blacks and whites on the force appear to be fairly good.

Then there is the question of real leaders in the black community. Philadelphia not only has them, but it has them in amazing numbers. A brief assortment:

■ William Coleman, nationally recognized attorney of consummate skills, was appointed Secretary of Transportation during the Ford Administration. Coleman, a graduate of the University of Pennsylvania and Harvard Law School, had served as clerk to Supreme Court Justice Felix Frankfurter for three years before joining the leading Philadelphia firm of Richardson Dilworth.

■ Federal Judge A. Leon Higgenbotham, Jr., who was named an assistant district attorney under Dilworth in the early 1950s and became the first black of that rank to argue cases before the supreme court. He became president of the local NAACP and was appointed to the federal bench by President Kennedy in 1962; he is also a trustee of Yale University.

■ Charles Bowser, a former deputy mayor, a product of the Philadelphia public schools, who has learned to deal on equal terms with the monied elite of Philadelphia and ran an $8-million-a-year program as head of the Philadelphia Urban Coalition. In 1975, Bowser ran unsuccessfully for mayor. He is considered a likely candidate for another attempt to capture City Hall when incumbent Frank Rizzo moves on.

■ Cecil Moore, the flamboyant criminal lawyer, brash former head of the Philadelphia NAACP who was "Mr. Civil Rights" in Philadelphia for a few years in the 1960s. Moore bombed out with a tiny percentage of the vote when he ran for mayor, but he left a lasting imprint by initiating and doggedly pursuing to victory a court case challenging the provision of Stephen Girard's will which restricted to white males only the right of admittance to Girard College, a private school and home for orphan boys in the midst of the North Philadelphia ghetto.

■ Walther Palmer, who runs street-corner colleges teaching black power and black pride and has been identified by the Philadelphia *Bulletin*'s black columnist, Claude Lewis, as "perhaps the most articulate spokesman" among Philadelphia blacks. Palmer is now studying law.

■ Mattie Humphrey, a highly articulate social agitator who has stimulated many other black women to action for their communities and is forever ready to pounce on any black leader who makes a male-chauvinist statement.

■ Roxanne Jones, formerly of the Welfare Rights Organization—one of those "social workers without portfolios" leading the welfare masses and confounding the budgetmakers in Harrisburg.

There are many others, both in and out of politics, but two—Leon Sullivan and Herman Wrice—require our special attention.

Sullivan was born in 1922 in a little, unpainted clapboard house in an unpaved slum alley of Charleston, West Virginia. For the past 22 years, he has been pastor of the Zion Baptist Church in the heart of North Philadelphia, a position which represents his sole source of support. He is also the founder and guiding spirit of the Industrial Opportunities Center and its many offshoots, an enterprise which employs 3,000 people and is the largest program, in dollar terms, ever organized by Afro-Americans in the history of the United States. Since spring 1971, he has been a member of the board of directors of General Motors, a breakthrough of historic proportions for blacks in the American business world.

Sullivan is an amazing and multifaceted man, propelled forward in life by the memory of a visit back home as a young man to the alley home in Charleston where his grandmother, the matriarch of the family, lay dying of consumption:

As I looked about her room that night, I saw the misery of poverty. I noticed the wallpaper that had been plastered up layer over layer, thick and ragged, torn and spotted and damp, I noticed the pictures on the wall that were covering holes, trying to decorate the place. I saw the room's one small table, antiquated and brown, a little tilted, with an empty Pepsi-Cola bottle on it, and an empty water glass, and all kinds of drugstore prescriptions lying about. The mattress of Mama's bed sagged in the middle beneath her weight. And as I sat there in the faint light of the oil lamp, amidst the dreariness and the smell of death, Mama looked up at me and said: "Leonie, help your people. And don't let this kind of thing happen to anybody else."

A few days later Sullivan decided to become "a minister of God, to work for Him, to help people who were poor—people who were in the kind of condition Mama was in." In 1943, he met Adam Clayton Powell and on his invitation went to New York, a gangling youth six feet, five inches tall, studied at Union Theological Seminary, and learned the arts of community organization from A. Phillip Randolph of the Brotherhood of Sleeping Car Porters. He advised Mayor La Guardia on Harlem, became an assistant pastor at Adam Clayton Powell's Abyssinian Baptist Church. Then in 1945, Sullivan decided he was "losing touch with God" and took a pastorate in South Orange, New Jersey, for five years.

In 1950, Sullivan moved to North Philadelphia, a fetid slum that "beat Harlem in housing decay." But his major interests turned to juvenile delinquency, and then to a youth employment service he began in his church. The job referral system, he discovered, was to be frustrated at every turn by the city's continuing wall of segregation against hiring blacks in any but menial work categories. Only a handful of blacks held jobs as bank tellers, clerks, or secretaries. The major soft drink companies, big sellers to the black community, had absolutely no black salesmen-drivers for their trucks. In a Sunday sermon to the 2,000 regular attendees at his church, Sullivan preached on the theme "The Walls of Jericho Must Come Down!" With that, he launched his "selective patronage" campaign—a polite term for economic boycott. It was organized through 400 Negro preachers in the city, who picked target firms based on the experience of black applicants and inside tips and then visited the companies with specific demands for increases in black employment. Where firms refused to make the requested hirings, a boycott would be called through that best communications line to the black community, the church pulpits.

Not for three years, and not until selective patronage had won agreement from two dozen companies and opened up some 2,000 jobs, did a single news story about the effort appear in Philadelphia's daily newspapers or its radio or television stations. The campaign was well known to the local media chiefs (indeed the *Bulletin* itself was boycotted), but they apparently concluded that any piece of publicity would simply spread the idea. It took an out-of-town newspaper, the New York *Times*, in a front-page story in June 1962, to bring the campaign to national attention. By then, selective patronage had already wrung concessions from giant firms like Gulf Oil, Sun Oil, Coca-

Cola, and Esso and spread to several other cities. Sullivan may also take credit for the much-publicized Operation Breadbasket of the Southern Christian Leadership Conference, an idea which took form only after he went to Atlanta in 1962 to explain the boycott idea to black ministers and lay leaders at the request of Martin Luther King, Jr.

Soon Sullivan discovered that he simply could not produce enough qualified black applicants for all the opening-up jobs "that the white man had always kept to himself"—stenographic and secretarial, sheet metal and machinist, computer keypunch, merchandising, teletype, and manufacturing jobs. A massive training program was needed, and thus the idea of Opportunities Industrialization Center (OIC) developed. An abandoned old jailhouse in North Philadelphia was rented from the city government and training began in January 1964—but only after Sullivan, in what would prove to be one of the great keys to his success, had lined up the support of the chamber of commerce plus firms like Bell Telephone, General Electric, Philco, the Budd Company, and IBM, and among the unions, the restaurant and garment workers. The companies donated training equipment and the courses covered everything from sheet-metal work to electronics assembly. Financing was short and tenuous, but a grant of $200,000 from the Ford Foundation, arranged by Paul Ylvisaker, helped at an early, critical point.

But even as OIC got off the ground, Sullivan and his associates encountered the now-familiar bugaboo of all manpower programs for ghetto people and other underprivileged: slovenly work habits (or no work habits at all) and frequent illiteracy. The solution was a "feeder program." In brightly painted rooms (as unlike ghetto schools and daily life as possible) students were taught "cleanliness—time—think—work—togetherness." The three R's were taught, and minority-group history (principally black history, but also that of European minorities, Jews, and Appalachian whites). The feeder program became a prerequisite for *anyone* planning to enter an OIC technical course. The approach had sure-fire appeal to businesses, foundations, and government, and soon huge amounts of support were flowing in.

The program began to spread to other cities, and Sullivan saw the necessity to involve industry on a national scale to provide the OIC centers with technical assistance on a continuing basis. By this point, Sullivan really had the gold chips on his side with an advisory board which the press in 1968 called "the most formidable and influential group of business leaders assembled in the recent history of Philadelphia, at one place at one time." But there was more to come. President Johnson flew into Philadelphia to view OIC operations at first hand, Richard Nixon visited during his 1968 campaign. For the black preacher born in the Charleston slum, it was quite an achievement.

Leon Sullivan likes to talk in superlatives, and when we interviewed him in 1971, he could point to quite a few. The OIC, he said, had spread to 100 U.S. cities, enrolling 40,000 people a year, thus becoming "the largest nonprofit manpower training program in the country." It had also expanded to Africa with the active assistance of Sen. Hubert Humphrey. (However, it proved to be far from a success there and was sharply criticized by the Agency for International Development and found to be lacking support in host countries.) "Something internationally important has emerged out of Philadelphia and a Philadelphia Afro program. And it's the first program that serves the total American community—blacks, poor whites, Chicanos, and Indians," he said. From other sources, however, we heard that the OIC programs in other locations have yet to equal the quality of the effort in Philadelphia, where remarkably high levels of enrollee attendance and subsequent retention of jobs have been attained.

More has emerged from Sullivan's Zion Church than OIC and the boycotts (now long-since discontinued). Starting with his parishioners in 1962, Sullivan organized a collective mutual fund in which each member contributes $10 a month for 36 months. The best-known result of this has been the Progress Plaza shopping center on North Broad Street, where all the stores are owned or managed by blacks. The collective mutual fund also financed some large housing developments and made it possible, with GE's help, for Sullivan to start Progress Aerospace Enterprises in 1968. Now that company has annual sales of $2 million.

Sullivan's personal stature seemed to reach a hard-to-repeat zenith in 1971 when General Motors board chairman James Roche traveled personally to Philadelphia to ask him to join the GM board.

The story of Leon Sullivan can be dismissed as a fluke of black penetration of white-establishment America that is unlikely to be duplicated. But Philadelphia has also produced Herman Wrice, a dynamic young black who has captivated the business elite with his work and may prove to be one of the most amazing personalities to rise out of the ghetto in our time.

Back in 1965, as Wrice tells his own story, he was enrolled at graduate school at the University of Pennsylvania but still living in the West Philadelphia black community of Mantua. "The gangs were completely out of hand then—I was a former gang member myself. I'd gotten married, and I was headed toward business, to be the good nigger, to get out of the ghetto soon with a good house and two cars, maybe even play golf some day with some white guys." But one night Wrice's wife went to the local grocery store and was almost hit by a shotgun blast as the gangs pursued one of their victims through the store. Wrice heard the police sirens wailing, went to investigate and found his wife there shaking and the boy shot by the gang bleeding on the floor. "I was so mad I said, 'I'm gonna kill those guys.' I went back to my apartment, stuck a little piece in my pocket, and went out to teach the little bastards a lesson." But when he found them, Wrice decided "they needed someone to help them, not kick them." Within a few days, he had adopted several gangs, mediated dangerous disputes, organized baseball games, gotten personal T-shirts and equipment for the gang teams, and become a hero in his community. But he was also broke.

"Then one day," Wrice recalls "a white kid suddenly showed up and wanted to play baseball with us. He did better than the gang members. The second day he showed up with 25 baseball gloves—said his father had sent them." The father, it turned out, was named Clayton Hewett, an Episcopal clergyman who had been given a freely defined "urban mission"—to roam the black community and see how he could be relevant and helpful. Hewett helped write up a $25,000 foundation grant proposal; with the money Wrice could buy baseball uniforms for dozens of gang members, get transportation to drive the teams out of the neighborhood, rent a storefront (where 100 gang members would show up every night), and thus begin serious organization. Hewett introduced Wrice to then-Episcopal Bishop Robert De Witt, the man who had dispatched Hewett on his urban ministry. DeWitt hired Wrice at $100 a week as an urban missioner, so that he could keep up his work. Wrice's organization became known as the Young Great Society, and the projects it undertook multiplied like OIC centers—recreation programs, counseling and employment referral for youths, hundreds of appearances in court for young people in trouble, a self-help clinic, two day-care centers, a narcotics rehabilitation office, its own schools, and an "urban university." Wrice also scrounged in dozens of imaginative ways to find money he could parlay into renovated slum housing—taking shells of buildings and redoing them completely inside, in the process developing training programs for carpenters and other craftsmen.

The extent of black leaders' optimism in the face of phenomena like Frank Rizzo is amazing to behold. Talk is even turning to the possibility of a black mayor by 1979, with several of the names we have mentioned here openly discussed.

The Establishment Now

Philadelphia, John Gunther observed in *Inside U. S. A.*, has "an oligarchy more compact and more complacently entrenched than any in the United States."

Is it still so today? In some ways, the answer is surely yes. An aristocracy born to wealth and position lives on, maintaining and fostering its customs and institutions. First, there are the clubs, very exclusive and central to all Philadelphia Society. The most famous are the Philadelphia (a men's city social club considered the *crème de la crème*), the Rittenhouse (almost as prestigious), the Union League, the Racquet (excellently appointed and a favorite of eligible young men), the Acorn (tops for women); fox hunting, cricket, lawn tennis, and barge clubs (Nathaniel Burt calls the latter, centered in their quaint Victorian clubhouses, "the Schuylkill Navy"); and even eating clubs—the Fish House and the Rabbit.

The families that have adhered to Old Philadelphian codes over time include Biddles, Ingersolls, Morrises, Cadwaladers, Robertses, Wisters, Scotts, Cassatts, Lippincotts, Woods, Peppers, Pews, and the like; one can find them all in the *Philadelphia Social Register,* a black-and-orange-bound annual book one might mistake for a Princeton course catalogue. The *Register* has become progressively less exclusive over time (up from 135 families in 1890 to 5,150 in 1940 and about 7,500 today), but still it includes only a minuscule percentage of the people of Philadelphia and its suburbs.

Old Philadelphia Society, of course, cannot put itself in a time capsule and resist every tide of social change. Its daughters are increasingly rejecting the formal debut, which was *de rigueur* just a few years ago, in favor of trips to Europe or other fun. Sons are less likely to accept the appointed university and career courses. And the ideas of Maintenance, and especially a code which excludes all but old-family White Anglo-Saxon Protestants (WASPs) from positions of Privilege, become more anachronistic with every passing year in these United States. But in large measure, Old Philadelphia Society has withdrawn from a central role in Philadelphia's life by its own decision. Old Philadelphians started to suburbanize themselves almost a century ago, and only a few hundred of them live in the center city today. This disengagement as a class is underscored by the cautious way that the aristocracy has invested its wealth. Its risks were dispersed, with much less of a financial stake in Philadelphia-related enterprises than one might expect—nothing even faintly resembling the Mellons' stake in Pittsburgh, for instance.

Yet another factor has been the rapid pace at which Philadelphia has been losing corporate headquarters and turning into a branch-office town. Between 1956 and 1965, according to a study by the Federal Reserve Bank of Philadelphia, the city lost major corporate headquarters at a faster rate than any of the nation's other large metropolitan areas. Philadelphia's problem has been its lack of dynamic growth-oriented business leadership—the kind of settled contentedness that Old Philadelphia Society itself embodies.

Banker John Bunting, who was later to become president of the First Pennsylvania Bank, put his finger on the problem in a 1964 book, *Hidden Face of Free Enterprise:*

> Philadelphia and New York were similarly endowed with natural blessings making for great cities. Neither had a real strategic advantage. After a while, however, Philadelphia society closed itself at the upper end. To receive full social acceptance family money had to be old and substantial, with emphasis on the "old." But in New York, if you had *enough* money, you didn't have to wait in line very long. As a consequence, ambitious, talented people gravitated toward New York and away from Philadelphia.

Amidst the constant grumbles of Philadelphia Establishmentarians, Bunting—who was 51 in 1976—had suddenly become the city's prime mover and shaker. He helped Governor Shapp get through the state's first income tax, hitting the Old Philadelphians where it hurts the most, and he stepped in to bolster support for the faltering 1976 Bicentennial plans. His antagonists, who consider him a publicity-seeker and distastefully on the make, frequently block his efforts. But the fact is that Philadelphia now has a remarkably aggressive young business leader in a position of power where he should be able to effect many changes over the years. The death or retirement of many of the prestigious older leaders in the past several years has helped to clear the track for him.

A special word should be said about Philadelphia's Jews, since they have played an important role in the city's life since colonial days when the then Quaker establishment welcomed them with open arms. That early generation was welcomed in the choicest Philadelphia clubs through the past century and tended to conform by becoming Episcopalian. Gradually their blood stream merged with Old Philadelphia's. It was a later wave of Jews, coming from Germany in the mid-19th century, which had more difficulty being accepted by the Christian community. In recent times, Philadelphia's Jews have really come into their own. For many years, the late Albert Greenfield was the largest and richest real estate operator in Philadelphia, and he was actually a member of the third—or East European wave. More recently his protegé, Gus Amsterdam, a member of the GPM board, acquired fantastic amounts of real estate in the city. The Philadelphia metropolitan area has 350,000 or more Jews now, second only to New York City. They have separated out into two distinct groups: the lower-middle class, consisting of shopkeepers, teachers, and the like, who live in the city and may vote for a Frank Rizzo; and an upper-middle class that lives in the suburbs and is very civil libertarian. The two groups have practically nothing to do with each other.

Quakers, Episcopalians, Roman Catholics

The Quakers settled Philadelphia as a place of refuge against religious oppression for themselves and others, and though their day of numerical dominance is now a matter of distant history, their character has set a mark on the city that endures to this day. "Caution and calm," Burt observed—and of course this was written of non-political, pre-Rizzo Philadelphia—are the Quakers' and Philadelphians' middle names. And even though many of the famous Quaker families long ago converted to Episcopalianism, he pointed out, "the façade that Philadelphia still presents to the world is a Quaker façade—subdued, careful, moderate, puritanical but never ascetic, honest but shrewd, modest but firm." But along with these virtues come their defects—"conformism, anti-intellectualism, materialism and lack of enthusiasm." Anyone who has ever attended Quaker meetings, as one of us once did for several years, remembers the amazing sense of community, the search for "the sense of the meeting." Questioning and going against the grain of the body is discordant, unwelcome behavior.

Philadelphia is still the national headquarters of the Society of Friends and of its very effective adjuncts, the American Friends Service Committee and National Friends Legislative Committee. And in their activities, the Quaker conscience, vivid to America since they became foes of slavery two centuries ago, lives on. One hears that though the Quakers have quietism and don't assert themselves, they are able to accomplish a great deal in their own low-key way. This is true in some city issues, but especially international ones. They consistently opposed the Vietnam war, as they had opposed all wars before it, and took such steps as sending ships to Hanoi with medical supplies, furnishing surgical equipment to both the North and South Vietnamese, and drawing up a novel Jewish-Arab peace plan in 1971.

Little contention arises within Quaker circles, perhaps because few members question the society's agreed-upon liberal aims. Not so with the Episcopalians. The Episcopal Church was founded in Philadelphia and the Philadelphia diocese is the oldest in the country. For generations its face to the world was that of the church of the Best People, a handmaiden of Privilege. That element remains strong within Philadelphia Episcopalianism. But the quiet-spoken New Englander chosen as the bishop in 1964, Robert L. DeWitt, shattered the old tranquillity. DeWitt ringed himself with articulate and controversial churchmen imported from all over the country. He started program after program to deal with ghetto conditions, brought activist youth into the powerful diocesan council, and began to explore the meaning of women's liberation for the church. ("I hope we solve the black problem in order to be able to solve the youth problem in order to be able to face the women's liberation problem," he said in an interview.) DeWitt's course prompted a fierce counterattack from traditionalists within his own diocese and a severe decline in the diocese's financial support. But he persevered, generating fierce loyalty (especially among young people) and making the diocese, in the opinion of many people we spoke with a vital cutting edge in the struggle for social change in Philadelphia. Following DeWitt's retirement, Bishop Lyman Ogilby directed the Diocese through a much more conventional and less aggressive period in the middle-1970s. The image of social activism, concentrating on civil-rights was quickly changing to one of introspection and more traditional activity.

The Roman Catholic Diocese of Philadelphia could hardly be more different. First of all, it has many times the communicants of the Episcopalians or any other denomination—1.3 million, with about 1,000 priests. It has the largest percentage of Catholic children attending parochial schools of any U. S. city, a program for which local Catholics give some $40 million a year. And the leadership exercised by its leader, John Cardinal Krol, qualifies as perhaps the most conservative and authoritarian of any Catholic diocese in the U. S. today.

Krol was born in Cleveland in 1910 as the fourth of eight children of Polish immigrant parents. He was a fairly obscure auxiliary bishop in 1959 when Pope John singled him out to help with organization of the Second Vatican Council and then to speed John's far-reaching reforms over conservative opposition on the council floor. Krol's skills, according to a church theologian quoted in the Philadelphia *Bulletin,* are those of "a good administrator and perhaps the most brilliant canon lawyer in the church, . . . [but] he is not a theologian and not a philosopher." He assumed direction of the

Philadelphia diocese in 1961 and seemed to exercise fairly noncontroversial leadership until 1965, the bright hopeful years of the Vatican Council. Since then, he has been in the position of resisting any steps toward reform or change which go beyond the letter of Vatican II documents. He rarely speaks out on problems of race relations.

Philadelphia Journalism: A Tumultuous Time

The last decade has been a tumultuous one for Philadelphia journalism. The Curtis Publishing Company floundered, permitting the venerable *Saturday Evening Post* to die after 148 years of publication that dated back to Benjamin Franklin. The Philadelphia *Inquirer,* which had degenerated into a vehicle for the personal whims and vendettas of owner Walter Annenberg, was sold in 1969 to the Knight Newspapers and is now enjoying an illustrious rebirth. The ever-prospering *Evening Bulletin,* cautious and provincial, reacted to the *Inquirer*'s renaissance by becoming a lot livelier itself. And a sleeper, *Philadelphia Magazine,* emerged from its cocoon as a "magazine for executives" to become a lively, fearless journal that outstrips the entire new breed of city monthlies in quality and profits.

Curtis Publishing once dominated magazine publishing in America the way its brick-and-marble headquarters (now sold) dominate Independence Square. In 1960, Curtis looked healthy enough to the outside world. It had revenues of $248 million, published the *Post* (circulation six million plus), *Ladies' Home Journal,* and *Holiday,* and owned several big paper mills. But over the course of the 1960s, Curtis suffered an operating loss of over $80 million.

In 1968, when the *Post* was on the ropes, a young conglomerate builder named Martin S. Ackerman took over Curtis, slashed the *Post*'s circulation back to three million in an effort to make it profitable, sold *Ladies' Home Journal,* engaged in refinancing, and when all else failed, killed the *Post* and was in turn purged himself.* Ackerman's record is easily faulted, but he was doubtless right when he later wrote: "Since the early '30s the company had been run according to an outmoded Main Line Philadelphia philosophy, with the president, directors, officers, and most of the top executives hailing from the old school of management." There would seem to be at least some parallels in that story to that of the Penn Central.

In 1971, the heirs of Cyrus Curtis—those who had been chiefly responsible for the company's problems—sold their debt-ridden property to an Indianapolis industrialist named Beurt SerVaas. SerVaas revived the *Post* as a quarterly, heavily laden with reprints of its golden past and devoid of all controversy.

---

* Ackerman has been immortalized as the man who said to his new employees: "I am Marty Ackerman, I am 36 years old, and I am very rich. I hope to make the Curtis Publishing Company rich again."

Moses Annenberg was a Jewish immigrant from East Europe who made a fortune through racing papers that supplied information to bettors, and through a string of wire services to illegal "horse parlors." In 1936, he acquired the *Inquirer.* Three years later, "Moe" Annenberg, his son Walter, and others were accused of massive income tax evasion. "Moe" pleaded guilty and agreed to pay $9.5 million in back taxes, fines, and interest, the largest income tax settlement ever recorded. He was also sent to jail but paroled shortly before his death in 1942. As part of the court settlement, the charges against Walter and nine lesser defendants had been dropped. Walter Annenberg proceeded to build a fantastically successful communications empire, including the *Inquirer, Seventeen,* radio and television stations, and *TV Guide,* with more circulation than any other weekly magazine in America. He struggled, with only partial success, for social acceptance in Philadelphia and gave tens of millions of dollars to various philanthropies. By 1969, Annenberg had a personal fortune of more than $150 million and happily accepted the offer of his friend President Nixon to become U. S. Ambassador to the Court of St. James. Even after his resignation, Nixon was still a welcome guest at Annenberg's mammoth Palm Springs estate.

Under Annenberg, according to Philadelphia attorney and reform leader Henry Sawyer, the *Inquirer* was "the greatest institutional force for evil in the city." Annenberg abused his position by ordering total blackouts on news about persons or institutions he disliked—Annenberg's "shit list," as it was called in the *Inquirer* newsroom. Those honored by placement on the list included such diverse figures as University of Pennsylvania president Gaylord Harnwell, Dinah Shore, Ralph Nader, the American Civil Liberties Union, and Philadelphia's professional basketball team, the 76ers. In 1966, the *Inquirer* campaigned savagely against Milton Shapp's gubernatorial candidacy.* But favored politicians could easily influence news coverage. Tate and Rizzo, for instance, never had any difficulty in calling Annenberg and getting him to kill stories not to their liking.

The spiritual sickness of the *Inquirer* came to light in 1967 when Gaeton Fonzi revealed in *Philadelphia Magazine* that Harry Karafin, the paper's star investigative reporter for almost 30 years and the best-known and most feared newspaperman in the city, had been engaged in wholesale blackmailing, shaking down shoddy characters and even prestigious corporations and banks to keep unfavorable stories about them out of the paper. His take from this illegal operation apparently went as high as $100,000 a year.

So it was that few tears were shed in Philadelphia when Annenberg in 1969 decided to sell the *Inquirer* and its afternoon tabloid companion, the *Daily News,* to the highly respected Knight chain. John McMullan, an aggressive newsman in his mid-forties who had been executive editor of the Knight-owned Miami *Herald,* took over the same position at the *Inquirer* and

---

* Shapp's campaign was geared to fighting the proposed Pennsylvania Railroad–New York Central merger. Five months after the election, Annenberg was elected a director of the Pennsy and revealed to be the owner of $8.5 million of the company's stock.

the change in the paper was soon apparent. There was a substantial house-cleaning at the reporting level that included replacement of the *entire* city hall bureau. The paper deemphasized routine news in favor of depth reports and analyses written by specialists in several fields. Political hatchet jobs, like the one practiced on Shapp in 1966, were eliminated, and the editorial page took on a moderate-to-liberal stance. In 1972 McMullan was replaced by Gene Roberts, former national editor of the New York *Times,* and the paper seemed to be aiming at national stature.

The *Evening Bulletin,* owned by the local McLean family, has always been a voice of moderation and decency in Philadelphia, but terribly non-combative. Until veteran political reporter John McCullough took it over in the mid-1960s, the editorial page was tops in the country for landing squarely on both sides of any crucial issue. There were exceptions to the run-of-the-mill news coverage, especially the investigative stories of 20 years ago that exposed scandals in the old GOP regime and paved the way for the Clark-Dilworth era. But rejuvenation was needed in the late 1960s, and even before the stiffer competition from the new *Inquirer* developed, first steps were underway. In 1969, managing editor William Dickinson picked as his successor George R. Packard 3rd, the son of a wealthy Main Line family who had earned a doctorate · and become chief diplomatic correspondent for *Newsweek.* Only 37 when he took over his job, Packard soon enlivened urban affairs coverage, made room for a local black columnist, and started several other new features. Packard repeatedly clashed with more tradition-ally oriented members of the news staff, however, and in the spring of 1975 was forced out in a dispute over unionization of the paper and other issues that brought him into direct conflict with the paper's owners. He left be-hind, however, a far more progressive and aggressive paper than the *Bulletin* had been in earlier years. (A few months later, though he had never before engaged in partisan political activity, Packard ran unsuccessfully for the Re-publican nomination for Hugh Scott's seat in the U.S. Senate.)

The blueprint for a successful city magazine was not written in 1948 when the chamber of commerce sold *Greater Philadelphia,* as it was then called, to Arthur Lipson. Under Lipson's son Herbert, who is now publisher, and Alan Halpern, editor since 1951, the way has been found by trial, error, and some fine investigative reporting. The real blossoming of the magazine came in the 1960s as it hired some top writers and let them cover controver-sial Philadelphia stories which the comfortable big dailies were ignoring. These included the exposé of Harry Karafin, a story discrediting the nation-ally prestigious Pearl S. Buck Foundation, stories on rat infestation and air, water, and trash pollution (long before they became national issues), the plight of unwed black mothers, the impact of black influx destroying an ethnic neighborhood, and the real life of the Black Panthers. It was hard to see an ideological line in the story choice or orientation, though in 1971 the maga-zine disappointed many of its sophisticated readers by slanting its stories in favor of Rizzo over Longstreth in the mayoralty election. (The *Inquirer* and

Bulletin both endorsed Longstreth.) But with a dash of sex thrown into its coverage, *Philadelphia* had a 1971 circulation of 85,000, enthusiastic advertisers, and a healthy profit margin. In a move Ben Franklin would have approved, *Philadelphia* also bought out *Boston* and began to introduce some of the same aggressive reporting and packaging on Massachusetts Bay.

Geographic Philadelphia

Philadelphia, home of just under two million people (with two million more in its Pennsylvania suburbs),* is geographically immense, a groaning, sprawling metropolis filled with acres of railroad yards and factories and oil tanks and grimy docks and endless miles of homes, homes, homes, most of them in less than inspiring row house style. But Philadelphia also has physical excitement. It is a human and personal city, a city with a vivid past and vibrant possibilities, a city eminently worth saving. Nancy Love of *Philadelphia Magazine*, assigned to write a guidebook of the city a few years ago, found that though she had lived there most of her life, she had been taken in by the bad press Philadelphia has always had. But as she trudged the city streets,

I uncovered another Philadelphia that I didn't know existed. . . . I became fonder of the old brick row houses with their grill work and lanterns, of the racy Italian pushcart market, the colossus of City Hall astride Penn Square, freighters and tankers inching up the Delaware River under the airy Walt Whitman Bridge, scullers at sunset skimming the calm Schuylkill River, the busy Pine Street warren of antique shops, the urbane stores and apartment houses of Rittenhouse Square, the outpouring of cherry blossoms in Fairmount Park, the old world culture palaces and gardens and the new highrise apartments of the Parkway, the breath-taking gorge of the Wissahickon, the excitement of a crowd at a polo game, the special sound of the Philadelphia Orchestra rising in the elegant Academy of Music. . . .

In short, Mrs. Love reported, "I found that Philadelphia is really a great town. I found it has its own peculiar charm. I dig it."

A geographic look at Philadelphia begins appropriately with the two-mile-long rectangle on the peninsula formed by the Delaware and Schuylkill Rivers where Penn's original city was begun 290 years ago. Two great thoroughfares—Market Street (running east-west) and Broad Street (north-south)—converge neatly at City Hall and provide handy points of reference.†

East of Broad to the Delaware, where the first Philadelphia buildings were erected, is in large part "non-U" Philadelphia—docks, loft buildings, printing and clothing industry plants, cheap rooming houses, Skid Row, sleazy bars and B-girl clip joints, along Locust Street. But here too are some

---

* The 1970 Census takers found 1,948,609 people in Philadelphia, 2.7 percent less than a decade before but still enough to make it America's fourth largest city (after New York, Chicago, and Los Angeles). The metropolitan area, including three New Jersey counties, totaled 4,817,914, up 10.9 percent since 1960.

† Much of the background for this section was drawn from *Man Made Philadelphia*, by Richard S. Wurman and John Andrew Gallery (Philadelphia Magazine-M.I.T. Press, 1971).

of the glories of America's past, and perhaps the most imaginative renewal on the continent. If any one building is to be called the birthplace of America, it is Independence Hall, remarkable in that both the Declaration of Independence and the Constitution were framed within its walls. Looking across Chestnut Street from the red brick Hall, with all its tranquility and grace, Gunther noted these buildings and signs a quarter century ago:

> Scottie's Restaurant—Pure Food—Coca Cola
> Krug's Parking
> Sandwiches Toasted Grilled Large Variety of Desserts
> Land Title Bank and Trust Co. Chartered March 10, 1812. Charter
> Perpetual.
> Ben Burk's. Sandwiches, Platters, Souvenirs.
> For Rooms, Read *Bulletin* Want Ads

For years, a few imaginative Philadelphians pressed to have the blight around Independence Hall cleared away. In 1949 their long fight was won when Congress authorized the National Park Service to make the Hall and the area about it into a national park. The government then acquired the squares stretching eastward from the Hall to the Delaware River, cleared them completely of buildings except historic structures like Carpenter's Hall (site of the First Continental Congress), the First and Second Banks of the United States, and Todd House (the home of Dolly Madison). The space between them was filled with lovely brick-walled gardens and fountains. Then the state government was prevailed upon to undertake a three-block clearance north of the Hall. With excitement, Philadelphians watched the blighted buildings fall and the historic homes and buildings reappear to view.

The Mall was the first step in the restoration of Old Philadelphia, soon to be followed by the renewal of an area a few blocks to the east named Society Hill (after the Free Society of Traders, a stock company organized by William Penn). This had once been the site of many fine mansions and the home of the President when Philadelphia was still capital of the United States. Eventually, as the prime residential areas moved westward, the area became clogged with unsightly warehouses and slums and was the location of a terribly unsanitary old produce and meat market at Dock Street. Support of the Greater Philadelphia Movement was enlisted to remove the wholesale food center to a completely new, multimillion-dollar Food Distribution Center three miles away in South Philadelphia. Then city planning director Edmund Bacon pushed forward a splendid plan to survey, identify, and save all the significant historic structures—the most extensive collection of 18th-century dwellings in America—and to demolish the rest. The old homes, which had degenerated into cheap rooming houses, bars, and shops, were sold to private people for accurate restoration. Some members of Old Philadelphia society, whose ancestors had lived there centuries ago, began to return, joined by many younger professional families.

Society Hill also received three high, dramatic high-rise apartment buildings (designs of I.M. Pei), modern town houses of generally high architectural quality, and charming tree-shaded greenways through the blocks, with small gardens and parks. Society Hill directly overlooks the Delaware River and the site of Penn's Landing, saved, thankfully, from a ground-level expressway through determined citizen action.

Market Street has been Philadelphia's main street since Penn's day and the section in the first blocks east of City Hall contains Philadelphia's great to not-so-great department stores—John Wanamaker's, Lit Brothers, Strawbridge & Clothier and the new downtown Gimbel's, the first major department store to be built in the city in nearly half a century. Many have been hit so hard by suburban competition in the past quarter century that their total downtown business has declined 35 percent and one store—Snellenberg's—went out of business. Wanamaker's, which is advantageously located right beside City Hall, has been the lucky exception with a 50 percent rise in business in the same period. In fact, the store is one of the city's great institutions, a place never to be missed at Christmastime. Poised in its Grand Court is a huge bronze eagle where Philadelphians love to meet.

The massive Penn Center business and government complex has now risen on the site of the old Broad Street Station and part of the demolished Chinese Wall. Penn Center fits in nicely with the city's City Hall, a craggy, ostentatious affair built a century ago in the midst of the Gilded Age and still—by unwritten law—the highest structure in the city (548 feet, if you count to the top of the hat of the 37-foot-high statue of Penn that tops it all). It can be seen for miles around. Old Broad Street Station was finally torn down in 1952, and Nathaniel Burt records that "as the last train pulled out, the Philadelphia Orchestra, crammed onto the observation platform, played 'Auld Lang Syne' and there was not a dry eye in the concourse."

The visitor looking for the symbols of "establishment" Philadelphia need only stroll south from City Hall for a block or two along Broad Street. There are the offices of virtually all the major law firms (and being a Philadelphia lawyer is still a great, honorable, and profitable profession); the big banks (one on each corner at Broad and Chestnut, though the heart of banking is now shifting to Penn Center); the doughty old Union League in its General Grant red-brick mansarded building (still a great and prestigious men's club, though Democrats need not apply)*; the Academy of Music; and the Locust and Shubert Theaters. Privilege, Quality, Continuity—they are all there on South Broad Street. Or perhaps we should say all *were* there. In 1976, after several guests were killed by a mysterious illness, the famed old Bellevue-Stratford Hotel, one of the nation's most historic and illustrious, was forced to close its doors forever.

* Until recently, the would-be Union League member not only had to affirm his Republicanism, but to attest that he had never voted for a Democrat in a state or local election. Only occasionally were exceptions made for past, but repentant, sinners. The Republicanism goes back to the Civil War, when the League was formed to "seize treason by the throat" by combating Copperhead Democrats opposed to Lincoln; this was accomplished both by a great wave of pamphleteering and by recruiting anl fielding no less than 10 union regiments. The Union League has fought off hardening of the arteries by appealing to young members in recent years. Even among Republicans, it is exclusionary enough; there are only a handful of Jews among 3,500 members, and fewer blacks (Secretary of Transportation William Coleman is the most notable black member).

Philadelphia's poshest shopping area, with many boutiques and specialty stores, is along Chestnut Street west of Broad. This southwest quadrant of the old center city also has Rittenhouse Square, center of the city's outstanding residential section in the past century and still a beautiful, vibrant, exciting place. Elegant Old Philadelphians, visiting dignitaries, nurses and maids, businessmen and chic secretaries, boy-girl, boy-boy, and girl-girl couples, folk singers and hippies—the human mix is the most diverse in the city. The old Victorian brownstones in the area have been converted frequently to apartment houses for singles, and in the nearby blocks are streets like Addison and Delancey, filled with jewel-like little old and restored houses.

Now completed on ten blocks of Chestnut Street is an innovative "transitway" which has turned the city's most fashionable shopping area into an attractive pedestrian mall. Only buses are allowed to travel through the area; private automobiles and other vehicles are prohibited.

The inner city's northwest quadrant is dominated by Philadelphia's grand urban gesture of the early 20th century—the Benjamin Franklin Parkway, designed as a diagonal vista that would relieve the monotony of Penn's grid plan. With the Champs Elysées in mind, Philadelpia hired a French landscape designer, Jacques Greber, to draw up the plan. It got the grand plan it had hoped for. A broad, tree-lined parkway was laid out, anchored at one end by City Hall and at the other by a hill called Fair Mount on which the massive, sandy-toned Philadelphia Museum of Art (with one of the finest collections on the continent) would rise like a great acropolis. Other cultural institutions, like the Benjamin Franklin Institute with its fine science museum and planetarium, were already on the line of the parkway. Greber proposed many more, but only a few, including the delightful Rodin Museum and Courtyard, were added, and for years it seemed as if development along the parkway might never go further. Then, in the postwar era, more public institutions were added and the parkway became a center for what Philadelphia had never had before—high apartment buildings. They have been constructed under strict design controls and add a pleasant new vertical element to the city and a desirable residential community for middle and upper income people.

One of the most exciting inner-city developments of modern times is scheduled to take shape in the late 1970s in what is now a nondescript 50-acre plot beginning three blocks northwest of City Hall and running several blocks parallel to the Franklin Parkway. Centered on a new, elegant boulevard, it will be called Franklin Town and will include a broad mix of offices and stores to accommodate 20,000 employees, hotels and convention facilities, and 4,000 residential units ranging from high rises to town houses. The plan is by the distinguished New York architect, Philip Johnson. What makes Franklin Town a realistic possibility is that it will be a *private*, not public undertaking, thus avoiding the years of urban renewal red tape. The developers, including Smith, Kline & French and Philadelphia Electric, already own 70 percent of the land, and will privately raise the $400 million needed for development. Progress has been hampered, however, as the recession of the Nixon-Ford years has made money very difficult to obtain for the developers. Additionally, there have been protests from some of the area's residents who fear that they will be displaced and left with no acceptable alternative housing.

Now our account of the geographic area of Penn's original city is ended and we can list seven major sections that round out the picture of Philadelphia as it is today:

■   South Philadelphia. Here we start ethnic Philadelphia in earnest, beginning with South Street, historically and to this day the southern limit of the old center city. "From the Delaware River to the Schuylkill," the *Bulletin*'s Peter Binzen has written. South Street is "a noisy, jostling, crowded commercial street teeming with life and movement and people, many of them living in abject poverty. It's a street of black rage and white despair, of rats and rotten housing, of gang warfare and hoodlum terrorism, of bad dreams and broken promises." The street is the center of a black band, but there are also Ukranians, Poles, Irish, Jews, and hippies—a veritable ethnic museum. On its streets you can sell blood and buy dope. It is loaded with bars and storefront churches and second hand stores and vacant stores and mere shells of buildings. Many people viewed it all as a cancer to be removed, and a huge crosstown expressway was scheduled to slice right through, obliterating South Street. The odds were all on the side of the expressway— the state highway department, the auto clubs, the Chamber of Commerce, the Delaware Valley Regional Planning Commission, and important people like Edmund Bacon. What looked like an anemic coalition stood up in opposition: black residents of the South Street corridor, whites living in the area, West Mt. Airy liberals. A decade before, the expressway juggernaut would have triumphed, but by the late 1960s the charge of "suburban freeways through black bedrooms" had become too emotion-packed. The experts suddenly changed their minds and decided the expressway would not be economically feasible after all, and would add to rather than relieve center city's traffic problems. The little people won and the expressway would not be. South Street staggered on into a still uncertain future.

One reason for the ill-fated expressway was to build a solid barrier between the teeming black section to the north and the community for which South Philadelphia is most famous: Little Italy.

South Philadelphia today is a world of modest, neat row houses that often give little hint of their sumptuous interiors . . . of the old Ninth Street sidewalk market where you can still buy snails, shrimp, octopi, lambs and rabbits hanging by their hooves unshorn, whole suckling pigs, and an incredible array of fruits and vegetables . . . of resplendent funeral homes because "death is respected as much as life is enjoyed" . . . of Philadelphia's best Italian restaurants and the only real nightclub (Palumbo's).

There is an intense community feeling to Little Italy, a small town atmosphere and gregariousness. And the Italians feel it is all threatened by the ever-encroaching blacks, taking over a street here, a block there, many of them crowded into socially explosive high-rise public housing, triggering a flight of Italian youngsters into the parochial schools (which themselves are in trouble), and the predictable racial clashes in the schools and on the streets. Not surprisingly, this is the home turf of Mayor Frank Rizzo. But let our tale not stop there. South Philly also gave to the world such assorted characters as Mario Lanza, Eddie Fisher, Chubby Checker, Toots Shor, William J. Foster (the onetime Communist Party chief), and Angelo Bruno (longtime alleged Mafia chief). And while the Italians have held sway for the better part of a century now, they were not the first. South Philadelphia was the city's black ghetto in the 1830s, and there were race riots before a single Son of Italy set foot there. Nor is South Philadelphia black history without luster, for this was the birthplace, too, of Marian Anderson.

Altogether some quarter million people live in South Philadelphia, two-thirds of them white; the black population is growing steadily, and no one knows when and if the racial shift will stop.

- West Philadelphia. The Schuylkill River officially divides this section from the old city, but the big regional facilities right across the Market Street Bridge—Penn Central's 30th Street Station (now the principal one in the city), the post office and Philadelphia *Bulletin* building—really seem like part of downtown.

Immediately after that, one is in an area now called University City, which contains not only the University of Pennsylvania but Drexel University, Philadelphia's major hospitals and the city's civic and convention center. The newest addition is the $118 million University City Science Center, a joint undertaking of Penn, Drexel, and 18 other local colleges and medical centers.

The University of Pennsylvania dates back to the 18th century and has a rich heritage; nevertheless, it has always been rather imageless to the country as a whole, and even within its city. Anyone who thought about it would likely say Penn was Ivy League but not *really*, a decent university but not—with the exception, perhaps, of superb graduate schools like those in law and medicine—a *great* one. The impression was probably correct, but the last few years have been golden ones for Penn. We heard it said that the university made more progress during the 17-year presidency of Gaylord Harnell, who retired in 1970, than it had in its entire previous history.* The Wharton School of Finance and Commerce, which is part of Penn, has overcome its reputation as a trade school which caters to not-too-bright sons of Ivy League businessmen; for the past decade, in fact, it has been a vigorous college of both social science and business fundamentals.

Surrounded by largely black neighborhoods, Penn faced the delicate problem of how it could expand physically without generating fierce local

---

* Both trustees and students were also enthused about the man picked to succeed him: Martin Meyerson, former Philadelphia City Planning Commission member, onetime UP professor of urban planning, and from 1966 to 1970 president of the State University of New York at Buffalo.

conflicts. Years before Columbia showed how bad things *can* become if proper planning is neglected, Penn in 1959 took the initiative in founding the West Philadelphia Corporation (WPC). Its goals were to coordinate land needs of educational and medical institutions in the area under one unified urban renewal plan, to create a pleasant community for scholars and manual workers alike, and to improve the local schools. The other local institutions cooperated. Although substantial chunks of land were taken under urban renewal powers, WPC did assuage hurt local feelings with careful community consultation and its beautification and school-improvement plans.

Most of West Philadelphia on the north side of Market is now a black ghetto, as depressing a slum as one might find. It was the last big black area to develop in the city, but already stretches on (with housing conditions better as one moves further out) to the city limit. An important exception is a community called Powelton Village, wedged between University City and the ghetto. Here magnificent old Victorian houses, many of them pleasantly restored, line tree-shaded streets. The population is a mix of university faculty, graduate students, and other professional people with liberal and avant-garde attitudes, some even gathered together in communes. Powelton Village is interested in working with its ghetto neighbors. There is no other community like it in Philadelphia.

The city's great playground—Fairmount Park—runs along both sides of the Schuylkill for several miles (the east side now used mostly by blacks from nearby North Philadelphia, the west side by both races). Wooded and hilly, with an adjunct along the banks of the Wissahickon, a tributary of the Schuylkill, the park is not only the largest city park in the world but one of the most beautiful. But now the bulky wall of the Schuylkill Expressway (vintage 1955) scars the park along the entire western bank. The road is actually the major regional auto access to Philadelphia (connecting to the Pennsylvania Turnpike on the west, New Jersey on the east), and is the only expressway serving center city; as a result it is often congested and hated most by those who must use it most. (They have nicknamed it the Sure-kill Crawlway.)

Just where Fairmount Park reaches its northerly extremity on the west side of the Schuylkill there is a major commercial street called City Line Avenue—not old-style commercial, but a postwar invention of posh stores, television stations, motels, apartments, and offices where travel by auto, not foot, is *de rigueur*. The north side of the City Line is actually in Montgomery County, and on that side one finds the biggest commercial investment—safely insulated from the Philadelphia tax collectors.

▪   North Philadelphia. One of America's largest black ghettos, North Philadelphia stretches on for mile after mile after mile from Spring Garden Street (northermost boundary of center city Philadelphia) to the North Philadelphia railway station. It is almost entirely filled with two- and three-story row houses, grimy reminders of the 18th and 19th centuries when they were built. Graffiti cover the walls, trash spills out onto the streets, toughs lounge in doorways, children play wherever they can. Thousands of houses are vacant, comparatively few renovated. Along commercial arteries like Columbia Avenue and Ridge Avenue, large numbers of stores are boarded up, most of them testimonials to the fright and despair of Jewish merchants who have fled in the face of black hooliganism, including some senseless murders associated with armed robbery. Columbia Avenue was the ignition point of the 1967 riots, the worst Philadelphia has yet seen, in which two persons were killed, 339 injured, and some $3 million in property damage inflicted (a much smaller toll, of course, than Newark, Detroit, and Watts).

Despite the sodden hopelessness that overlies most of North Philadelphia, there are islands of exception. The brightest is Yorktown, where the first urban renewal project in the U.S. was begun in 1947 with complete demolition of 25 blocks of bleak "nowhere North Philly." The tract now includes some quite attractive public housing and OIC's federally subsidized Zion Gardens. But the real jewel is the Yorktown settlement of 590 new row houses, brightly decorated with spacious windows, garages, and green space, a place where middle class blacks—schoolteachers, clerks, police officers, ministers—can live in pride but still in the inner city. Yorktown has no shops, but Leon Sullivan's Progress Plaza is only a block or two away.

Temple University, now a state-related institution with over 40,000 students (almost all of them commuters) is set incongruously in the midst of the North Philadelphia ghetto, maintaining what has been called a "castle and moat" relationship with its neighbors. Temple, next to Wayne State in Detroit, has the highest black enrollment of any predominantly white university in the U.S.

There was hope for a while in the late 1960s that the federal Model Cities program might begin to save North Philadelphia from its squalor. But the program did not turn out to be very viable in Philadelphia, and the big black ghetto continues on its familiar course: waiting for some distant day of redemption, and rotting.

■   Kensington is a grim factory enclave set between the Delaware River and the North Philadelphia ghetto, an island of beleaguered whites whose own condition is almost as desperate as that of the blacks they despise. Rarely is this type of lower-class white community reported in the press, or studied in academia. But Kensington was the chief subject of a fine book, *Whitetown, U.S.A.*,* by Peter Binzen of the *Philadelphia Bulletin*. He told the story quickly and grimly:

Kensington is 99.7 percent Caucasian. It is home for 100,000 proud, irascible, tough, narrow-minded, down-to-earth, old-fashioned, hostile, flag-waving, family-oriented ethnic Americans. There you find living, often in nationality enclaves, the first-, second-, and third-generation descendants of Irish, Polish, Ukranian, Italian, Hungarian, German, even Scottish and English immigrants. Fewer than four in 100 are college educated. Kensington's population is falling and its people are

* (New York: Random House, 1970)

aging. But it remains Philadelphia's last large stronghold of the low-income white man. . . .

Kensington's air is polluted, its streets and sidewalks are filthy, its juvenile crime rate is rising, its industry is languishing. No more than a handful of new houses have been built there in the last third of a century. Its schools are among the oldest in the city. . . . Its dropout rate is very high and its college-going rate is very low. . . . Its playgrounds—the few that it has—are overrun with young toughs. Industry is moving out. Social workers and clergymen often give up in despair. . . .

A few years ago, Binzen reported, Kensingtonians were intensely proud of their community and blithely overlooked its crowding, heavy industrial noise and air pollution. By the late 1960s, the old confidence had gone and he heard comments such as these: "This is nothing but a dump. It's dirty and a slum area." Or: "We are lost and forgotten here in Kensington. God only help us now." Kensingtonians were bitterly critical of city government for cheating them—and correct in their complaint, since the Philadelphia capital building program has rarely included any new parks, playgrounds, swimming pools, libraries, or health centers for Kensington, despite the community's desperate need for all of them. Yet politically, Kensington lacked clout at City Hall.

In Kensington, white makes right and no wise black will be seen after dark. In 1966, when a black family tried to move into the area, there were five nights of riots by singing, cursing, rock-throwing demonstrators who spurned the efforts of their own Catholic priests to disperse them. The black man is feared (especially as the North Philadelphia ghetto nips away one block of Kensington after another); he is also resented for what seems to be the unfair attention he gets from the government. As Binzen described it:

Kensington has no leaders of its own to admire, nobody speaking for it in the press. But almost every night the drinkers in the neighborhood taprooms [of which Kensington has one for every 472 residents] see black faces on the television news. This infuriates them. And it has helped convince them that there's a conspiracy afoot among the press, the politicians, the clergy, and other white liberals to elevate the blacks at the expense of the working-class whites.

■ The Northeast. Philadelphia's great, sprawling Northeast is primarily a phenomenon of the postwar-era, a great spilling out of middle-class Catholic and Jewish families from the crowded inner-city wards. Out they rushed to occupy endless acres of $12,000 row houses in a green, semi-suburban setting. The area was a developer's dream—few planning restrictions, acquiescent zoning, and fast profits. Real estate salesmen cooperated by effectively excluding blacks. Now hundreds of thousands of people live in the Northeast. The principal artery is tree-lined Roosevelt Boulevard (perhaps the most attractive feature of the entire area). To the east of the boulevard, one finds mostly Catholics; to the west, Jews. While Northeast's blacks are few in number, black families moving in are not greeted with the rock throwing and rioting that awaits them in Kensington.

But a "development' 'of a far different kind was scheduled to take place in the Far Northeast, at a site next to the Philadelphia State Hospital at Byberry: the 1976 Bicentennial Exposition, celebrating the 200th anniversary of the signing of the Declaration of Independence. The site was selected after Philadelphia was chosen over Boston and other contenders as the site of the exposition by President Nixon in 1970 in what seemed to be a cheap political ploy to help Hugh Scott get reelected to the Senate that year. But after the election of Mayor Frank Rizzo, the Byberry site was killed, and the Exposition slated for an odoriferous, trash-filled 600-acre wasteland between the airport and an oil refinery complex. In May 1972, the American Revolution Bicentennial Commission axed that plan, and Philadelphia was left with no exposition at all—a telling commentary on the decline of civic leadership since the days of Clark and Dilworth.

▪ Germantown. Philadelphia's growth as a city of villages is underscored by Germantown, which was sold by William Penn to Daniel Pastorius and a group of Dutch and German Quakers in 1683 and developed as a community with distinct language, customs, and even architecture. In the latter half of the last century the new suburban rail lines made it possible for Germantown to become, for a while, a leading residential suburb of the city. Today, Germantown is a step upward for blacks wanting to escape the North Philadelphia ghetto and is becoming a bit more black every year. Germantown has the advantages of varied landscape, thousands of mature trees, historic mansions, and good public transportation; likewise it is troubled by shabby housing in some areas, a deterioration of its shopping district along Germantown Avenue, and increasing crime with gangs and unpleasant racial incidents in its schools. But many professional people live in Germantown, determined to make it a liberal, tolerant, viable city community; there are many community organizations, forever trying to work out problems. Germantown includes the community of Mt. Airy, a good racial mix with some of the finest homes occupied by blacks anywhere in the city.

▪ Chestnut Hill is Establishment Philadelphia, spacious and heavily wooded, filled with fine homes and mansions, still heavily WASP-ish in complexion. The area was in large measure the personal creation of Henry Houston, president of the Pennsylvania Railroad, a great landowner who built almost 100 grand homes there, gave the land for the Philadelphia Cricket Club and Wissahickon Park, built a family church (St. Martins-in-the-Fields) and a summer hotel which is now Chestnut Hill Academy. Chestnut Hill, along with the Main Line, is the home ground of Philadelphia's High Society—and, ironically, a nouveau-riche named Frank Rizzo.

A word about mass transit. Philadelphia pioneered, starting under Dilworth, with public subsidies to keep commuter lines operating. The Southeastern Pennsylvania Transportation Authority (SEPTA) was set up in the early 1960s to take over most local transit operations; beset by strikes and poor service since its inception, it has been accused of being a quasi-public body unresponsive to the people. But, at least, no transit lines have died under its aegis.

Surprisingly enough, the nation's first really automated, electronic-controlled suburban commuter system now serves Philadelphia on a 14-mile run from Lindenwold, New Jersey. The system was opened by the Delaware River Port Authority with Budd-built cars on seamless welded rails and a crew of just one man on a train. The trains, which cross from Camden into Philadelphia over the Ben Franklin Bridge, draw more than 40 percent of their customers from people who used to drive to work. A clever way was found to finance the $94 million system—doubling of the tolls to 50¢ on the Ben Franklin and Walt Whitman Bridges between Philadelphia and Jersey. Thus those who insist on driving still not only have to fight the traffic jams, but are obliged to help finance the ride of the rail commuters.

Beyond Philadelphia

The growth of Pennsylvania has been well described by James Reichley as one of concentric arcs ranging outward from Philadelphia. In the first arc are four suburban counties, heavily populated with Philadelphia commuters. Except for some pockets of heavy industry and poor quality tract housing— and the Philadelphia suburbs have less of these than any other major East Coast city—this is still an area of rich, rolling countryside, endowed with both present charm and colonial history.

- Bucks County (1970 population 415,056). The gentle hills, early stone houses, and colorful barns of Bucks make it one of eastern America's most beautiful areas, and for years it has attracted prominent artists and writers including Pearl Buck, Oscar Hammerstein II, and Dorothy Parker. New Hope, on the river, is an artists' colony, the home of the Bucks County Playhouse and a magnet for young people these days. The beauties of Bucks are confined to its middle section, which is pleasant exurbia, and the upper part of the county, rural and farm in character. The lower end of the county (nearer Philadelphia) has ugly old Bristol (67,498), the mighty Fairless U.S. Steel Works that went on line in 1952, every steelworker's dream in the 2,200 little box houses thrown up at Fairless Hills, and Levittown, equally cheap but better designed and landscaped.

- Montgomery County (623,799) is Pennsylvania's wealthiest and most sophisticated county, suburban and especially rich close to Philadelphia, German farm territory farther out. During the 1960s, Montgomery's job growth was almost 60 percent, but its population increase only 21 percent, underscoring the county's success in getting the tax-paying industries Philadelphia had lost or would have liked to snag. (In most of the suburban counties, the level of tax effort is only half of Philadelphia's.)

- Delaware County (600,035) has two distinct faces, generally classified as east and west of Media. Media is the county seat of 6,444 souls which sprang to national prominence in 1971, when 1,000 documents were stolen from the FBI office there and dispatched to politicians and news organizations around the country. East of Media the county is overbuilt, low-income, close to Philadelphia's industrial underbelly and the site of grimy, unlovable Chester (56,331). Chester is the home of Sun Shipbuilding and plagued by race troubles and pollution; the heavy industry theme continues along the county's 20-mile flank on the Delaware River. West of Media, Delaware is more rural, open, and beautiful countryside; it also has a few miles of Main Line wealth in Bryn Mawr and Wayne, in its northeastern corner. The county is the home of the infamous Republican "War Board" political machine, the creation of the late boss John McClure which continued to flourish past his death in 1965. There was virtually no important decision in politics or government in the county not dictated by the War Board, one of the most powerful and ruthless political organizations in America. Even in the impoverished precincts of Chester, people followed its dictates for decades. However, the War Board suffered a major defeat in 1974, succumbing to the national Democratic landslide and witnessing the election of their arch-rival, Robert Edgar, to Congress. This was the climax to several years of erosion of power within the area. It remains to be seen whether the Delaware County GOP organization will be able to recover and dominate so absolutely the political life and fortunes of the region as it once did. Most local observers believe the War Board's day in the sun is over.

■   Chester County (278,311) is where the Main Line ends at Paoli. Here one finds Valley Forge and the Brandywine Battlefield, the ultra-ultra Radnor Hunt and Devon Horse Show, Longwood Gardens,* covered bridges, no large cities, and lots of rolling peaceful farm land. But even here, industry intrudes —General Electric at Valley Forge and Lukens Steel at Coatesville, for instance.

The second arc out from Philadelphia swings from fruit-growing Adams County and Gettysburg, near the Maryland border, to the industrial Lehigh Valley cities near the Delaware opposite New Jersey. This arc contains a high proportion of those remarkable people, the Pennsylvania Dutch, who with pride and simplicity have preserved their 17th-century culture clear into the cybernetic age. The greatest number are found still in Lancaster County, where their ancestors were lured by Penn's promises of religious freedom and limestone soil rich beyond compare. Lancaster is still one of the preeminent farm counties of America, and the good farmers get a phenomenally high yield from the land. (The average farm is only 60 acres, a paltry size on which most American farmers would quickly go broke.) Nothing is more fun for city people jaded by pre-packaged supermarket life than to go through the traditional farm markets in cities like Lancaster, York, and Allentown, where families that have kept the same stalls for generations offer their

---

* Co-author Peirce is constrained to note that Longwood Gardens has borne that name only since 1906, when it was purchased by Pierre Samuel du Pont of the famed Delaware family. The previous name had been Peirce's Park, after its founders—Quaker farmers Joshua and Samuel Peirce, who in 1789 began an unusual collection of trees and shrubs that was to become one of the most famous horticultural institutions of early America. The land had been deeded to Joshua and Samuel's great-grandfather, George Pearce, by William Penn's land commissioners in 1700. George Pearce (the spelling of our family name varied early in its history) had left Gloucestershire, England, to settle in Chester County in 1684.

marvelous array of fresh fruits and vegetables and specialties like scrapple and Lebanon bolognas, Schmierkase and Swiss cheese, apple butter and strained honey, pepper hash and potato salad, pastries and homemade bread, and the flowers of the rainbow. The only drawback for a visitor may be how many *other* visitors he will find crowding into the same markets. In 1974, some 4,015,000 tourists visited Lancaster County and spent more than $100 million. A Lancaster judge, who used to run the 242-year-old Central Market there, has suggested half seriously that there should be a balcony around the market for sightseers—"like the New York Stock Exchange." Another part of the tourist influx has been cheap motels and gaudy signs lining the roads and terribly cheap amusement parks like "Dutch Wonderland." The main profiteers from all this are not the Pennsylvania Dutch.

The largest Pennsylvania Dutch culture is one of Lutherans and Reformed people, sometimes called the Church People, who decorate their barns with gay hex signs and can be thanked for introducing Santa Claus and the Christmas tree to American culture. Next in numbers come the Moravians, who came to America in 1741 led by Count Zinzendorf, founded the city of Bethlehem, and enjoyed a full cultural life before many of the large seaboard colonial cities. Finally, there are the Plain People—Mennonites, Amish, Dunkards, and River Brethen—about a tenth of the whole. Of these, the most striking are the Amish, most of whom still use only horse and buggy transportation and spurn telephones, radios, television, and magazines. The modern world is slowly gaining a hold around the whitewashed stone or red brick houses of the Amish in their little towns like Gap, Fertility, Paradise, and Intercourse. Many farms have electricity, tractors appear on the farms, and even some automobiles (black autos, of course, with the chrome painted black too).

Overall, there are now thought to be 50,000 Amish in North and South America. There are some 10,000 in Lancaster County. The state of Ohio, with 20,000, has the most. With families averaging seven to eight children, they keep on growing. The communities are tied together by a weekly newspaper, *The Budget*, printed at Sugarcreek, Ohio. Many members of the sect never read another newspaper, but *The Budget* will tell them of visits, singings, sewings, frolics, illnesses, and deaths in 19 states and even Paraguay and British Honduras. Wherever the Amish may be, you can always recognize them: the men in their great broad-rimmed black hats with full beard and suspendered trousers, the women in black bonnets and homemade ankle-length dresses of purple, blue, green, or rose. They are the most enduring page of our past, the antithesis of our rootless present.

The commercialism troubling parts of Pennsylvania Dutch country is even more concentrated and troublesome at nearby Gettysburg, where profit-hungry entrepreneurs keep throwing up more motels and quick eateries to snag some of the four million people a year who come to see the spot where the contending armies in blue and gray met in the great and tragic battle of July 1863. The latest battle of Gettysburg revolved around a $1 million 300-foot tourist observation tower conceived and financed by Thomas R. Ottenstein, a wealthy Washington news dealer and real estate promoter; despite a legal challenge brought by Governor Shapp, Ottenstein's tower went up in 1974.

One reason for all the trouble, it would seem, is that Adams County has no zoning and virtually no planning controls. The whole question could have been avoided, of course, if Congress or the Pennsylvania legislature had moved at a proper time to widen the park boundaries and control the nature of local commercial development. "This hallowed ground" would seem to deserve no less.

Now, moving northeasterly, a view of the major settlements in the Gettysburg-to-Easton arc:

■   York (50,335) is set in pleasant rolling farmlands, a place rich in Revolutionary history, the place where the Continental Congress met in 1777–78, qualifying the city as a former capital of the United States. Surrounding York County has the state's most diversified industry, plus fruit growing. "Though York has grown and prospered in 200 years, it has managed to keep the charm of its colonial heritage," a chamber of commerce brochure proclaims. York can, however, claim quite another heritage, stemming from its location just 17 miles from the Mason-Dixon line. Southern attitudes, even accents, can be detected, and several dozen citizens, including some on the police force, have been reported to be Ku Klux Klan members in recent years. Mayor John L. Snyder, a very popular man, brought police dogs to York in 1962 and to the day he died in 1968 wore high-button shoes and called blacks "darkies." Though only 6,500 blacks live in York, the city developed into an area of high racial tension with rumbles between rival black and white gangs and attacks by police and their dogs on the black community in 1968 and 1969. A black woman and a white policeman were shot to death and the National Guard had to be called in. Not until 1970, when the local antipoverty agency staged a kind of civic group therapy for leaders and citizens of both races, called a *charrette*, did a semblance of peace seem to descend on the city.

Later that year, a colorful era in newspapering ended when Jess Gitt, aged 86, finally sold the *York Gazette and Daily* which he had run as an outpost of outspoken, untamable ultraliberalism ever since 1915. Declining revenues forced Gitt to ask his printers to take a temporary 10 percent pay cut, but the International Typographic Union refused and went on strike. Thus a paper which had fought vigorously for the rights of labor for more than half a century was killed by labor.

We might mention another unconventional Pennsylvania-based paper which still thrives in rural Pennsylvania. Its name is *Grit*, it is a weekly published in Williamsport, and it goes to 1.3 million readers, most of them residents of small towns, in all 50 states. *Grit*'s essential formula is to print only good news. "Let us do nothing that will encourage fear, worry, temptation, or other forms of weakness. Let us make every issue of *Grit* ring the joy bells of life." That was the admonition of Dietrick Lamade, the German immigrant who founded the paper in 1882, and his successors follow the tradition, shunning sex, sensation, and violence and filling *Grit's* pages with rewrites of innocent local news stories and a diet of serials, checker game problems, sermons, and recipes.

■   Harrisburg (68,061), set dramatically on the banks of the Susquehanna River (central Pennsylvania's main waterway), enjoys a peculiar love-hate relationship with the state government which it houses. Harrisburg civic leaders complain that being the state capital is a terrible economic disadvantage because of all the tax-exempt land and extra services and police protection they must finance; they were enraged in 1971 when a study was released showing the city was the great beneficiary of having the government there.

The Harrisburg employment picture has been stagnant in recent years and there were fears of a rapid tailspin when the big Olmsted Air Force Base, which had a payroll of 13,000, was shut down by the Pentagon. But instead of fighting the closure, business and civic leaders quickly made a virtue out of adversity. They made the air base the city's chief civilian airport, replacing an old municipal airport that couldn't handle large airliners. The new airfield was also developed to handle civilian cargo. Other uses for the base have included conversion of old administration and storage buildings into a new campus for Pennsylvania State University, with married students using much of the housing originally built for married military personnel.

Fourteen miles east is the chocolate town of Hershey (7,407) which Milton Hershey started building in a cornfield in 1903. The attractions include a grand old hotel (the scene of two National Governors' Conferences in recent years) and a popular amusement park (Hersheypark), which draws visitors from far and wide. But the town itself has a crowded, 1920s feel to it and a 1934-vintage report in *Fortune* could well be repeated: "On windless summer days the town of Hershey is permeated by what the Pennsylvania Dutch farmers of the neighborhood call 'da chockl shtink'—the sweetish, cloying smell of milk chocolate in the making." Hershey gave his fortune to the Milton Hershey school for orphan boys in the town, and in effect the school owns practically everything worth owning in town. For those 1,500 boys, Hershey bars are sold across the world—but no longer for a nickel. Inflation finally killed the nickel bar in 1969, and at this writing a Hershey bar costs 15 cents.

■   Lancaster (57,690) typifies the Pennsylvania pattern of a city overshadowed by its county. The city lost 5.5 percent in population in the 1960s, while the county as a whole added 14.8 percent, for a new total of 319,693 people. The county's rich farm output is a leading element in the $1 billion-a-year Pennsylvania farm income (chiefly from dairy products, cattle, eggs, and hogs—plus specialty crops like Lancaster's leaf tobacco). But industry is booming here too; in fact Lancaster County has outpaced the entire Northeast region's growth in virtually every branch of manufacturing. A lot of the new factories—RCA, Schick, mobile homes, boats, etc.—are in suburban, industrial-parklike settings. Armstrong Cork is the biggest and strongest company.

■   Reading (87,643) gained a measure of national notoriety in 1967 when the President's Commission on Law Enforcement and the Administration of Justice published a report called "Wincanton: The Politics of Corruption," authored by John A. Gardiner, a young political scientist. "Wincanton" was a cover name for Reading, and Gardiner explains that he went to great lengths to substitute fictional names for all the *dramatis personae*. But the cover did not last long; the day the report was published, the New York *Times* ran a parallel story on "Reading, Pa., Sin City." Since then, "Wincanton" has become a textbook case of how city officials can tolerate and personally profit from illegal gambling, prostitution, and other criminal activities.

The report chronicled how a onetime bootlegger named Irving Stern (his real name was Abraham Minker) set up a gambling empire that grossed millions of dollars a year, his payoffs and control of the police permitting him to run his rackets with impunity. His downfall and that of Mayor Robert Walasek (real name John C. Kubacki) finally came in the early 1960s when federal investigations led to Minker's conviction on income tax evasion charges and Kubacki's dual convictions on extortion charges. Reform administration broke the back of organized crime in Reading, though some minor corruption continued.

For the general public in Reading, the end of the old system eliminated the embarrassment of having their hometown known through the country for vice and corruption. But there were detriments, too. Gambling had enriched Reading's multiple churches, clubs, lodges, and associations—all the way from lotteries and bingo in the churches to slots and pinball machines that helped the clubs and lodges remain economically viable. When a reform mayor closed down the bingo parlors in 1964, "he was ending the standard form of evening recreation of literally thousands of elderly men and women." Big contributions to churches and hospitals from Minker and his cohorts suddenly terminated. Many a "mom and pop" grocery or candy store went under when the numbers racket dried up, and restaurants and bars in the downtown area suffered when there was no more "action" to draw people there.

So it was that when the city's people were polled about their attitudes, a majority indicated they were quite willing to see gambling and even some prostitution flourish in Reading. But they apparently failed to see the connection between these activities and payoffs and corruption of government officials, which they roundly condemned. "On balance," the Wincanton report said, it seems "likely to conclude that gambling and corruption will soon return to Wincanton (although possibly in less blatant forms)." In 1971, the Democratic mayoralty primary was won by one Joseph Kuzminski, who had never raised a voice of protest as a city council member during the days of the worst corruption. The Wincanton report, it seemed, might turn out to be as prophetic as it had been illuminating.

No one should think Wincanton is unique. Author Gardiner told me that people who had failed to see the publicity linking the report to Reading had plenty of other suggestions for what city might have been written about. These included three nearby Pennsylvania cities—Scranton, Wilkes-Barre, and Allentown; Youngstown, Ohio; Wheeling, West Virginia; Utica, New York; and several cities in New Jersey. Richard Thornburgh, while he was U.S. Attorney in Pittsburgh, said western Pennsylvania was infected with the same disease. "Some people are critical of the military-industrial complex. But in these cities," he said, "they have what I call the 'politico-racket complex.' "

On a brighter note, we might add that Reading is a famous city for quite other reasons to aficianados of the sport of flying. Each year Reading is host to one of the largest privately sponsored airshows in the United States. Thousands of pilots, would-be pilots, their families and friends descend on Reading to admire the latest in aircraft and avionics, to watch the demonstrations of stunt flying in everything from replicas of World War I biplanes to the sleek jets of the Air Force's Blue Angels.

■   Allentown (109,527), a few miles northeast of Reading, may have had its problems with corruption, but it is a lot more optimistic city. The downtown area has benefited from substantial, quality urban renewal and the city as a whole is quite handsome. The city has widely diversified manufacturing and is the major distribution center of the prospering Lehigh Valley.

■   Nearby Bethlehem (72,686), hometown of the Bethlehem Steel Corporation, suffers a share of pollution from the great steel works that extend 4.5 miles along the Lehigh River. It is substantially a one-industry town, with all the attendant problems. A big 23-story corporate headquarters building went up not long ago—fortunately for Bethlehem, because the company almost abandoned the project in the wake of a long steel haulers' strike in 1970. Downtown Bethlehem has been upgraded with a new civic center and efforts to preserve historic buildings—a tannery, waterworks, and Miller's House—built by the Moravian settlers in the 18th century. Bethlehem is home of Lehigh University, one of a string of excellent small private colleges spotted around Pennsylvania. Prominent in the group are Lafayette (at Easton), Swarthmore and Haverford (Quaker institutions in the Philadelphia suburbs), Villanova (Catholic and Philadelphia suburban) and some we will note in the Pittsburgh area.

Northeastern Pennsylvania and the "T-Zone"

The early Pennsylvania Dutch stopped their penetration of Pennsylvania where the farmlands give out—namely, at the Blue Mountains, the front of the Appalachian Highlands which run north from Maryland to the Susquehanna at Harrisburg and then northeast to the Delaware north of the Lehigh Valley. North of the Blue Mountains the first settlers found a densely wooded region of high open hills and mountains west of the Delaware and running up to the New York State border. Much of the region is still

sylvan and charming today. But at an early point, some of the world's greatest beds of anthracite coal were found, and thereby hung the area's damna-
tion. The big coal companies came in, importing thousands of sturdy Welsh,
Irish, Italian, and Slavic miners. There was a time when more than 100 million tons a year were mined. Today, the anthracite industry is dead, leaving
behind this bitter legacy (as described by John Fischer):

> The landscape looks spooky, like a TV science-fiction planet. Culm heaps—
> the mountainous dumps of slate and low-grade coal discarded from the mines—are
> still smoldering with internal hard-to-put-out fires. More smoke seeps out of fissures
> in the earth, marking underground fires in abandoned mines. . . . The surface
> above it is literally scorched earth, and it is liable at unpredictable moments to cave
> into the inferno.

Some of the worst damage may be seen at Scranton, a city that had
143,433 people in 1930 but only 103,564 in 1970. Coal breakers, dark and
empty of life, still stand around the fringes of the city, forlorn homes clustered around them like mourners at a grave. The Cedar Avenue district has a
bluff and 200-foot-deep ravine of burned and blackened rocks where the
local, state, and federal governments have spent millions of dollars to exca-
vate and put out fires in underground coal seams and to compensate owners of
homes and businesses which had to be leveled to avoid collapse through the
ground or contamination by toxic gases. A Bureau of Mines official told the
New York *Times* that one burning coal seam had been extinguished just in
time. "If we hadn't reached it in a week—maybe two weeks—it would have
reached a bed under the city of Scranton and the town would have gone,"
he said.

The Dantean flavor is not restricted to Scranton. Some 665 culm
dumps have been counted in northeastern Pennsylvania, shouldering virtually every road including the 15-mile stretch of interstate road between
Scranton and its sister city of Wilkes-Barre (1970 population 58,856). Close
to Wilkes-Barre are the Huber burning banks, two cones hundreds of feet
high in weird colors of yellow, red, and brown, made up of tailings that contained enough coal so that spontaneous combustion occurred and continued
to give off poisonous sulphur smoke for a half century. In recent years they
have been slowly demolished and removed.

The region must also cope with millions of gallons of water, tainted with
sulphuric acid, which seep out of abandoned mines, turning the sweet streams
and rivers a brownish-yellow and killing fish. Some 600 feet below Scranton,
water flowing into old mine shafts has created a lake of acid water nine miles
long and 200 to 600 feet deep.

Hundreds of millions of dollars—as much as $1 billion, according to one
report—will be needed to restore the northeastern landscape over the next
several years. Virtually all of it will have to be public money, since the companies that dug the mines and created havoc for the present generation are
for the most part out of existence. In the meantime, the region has had to
pick itself up by the bootstraps in an effort to develop replacement jobs for

those lost in mining. The first effort, beginning in the 1950s, grasped for any kind of job and netted many garment plants which could hire the wives, widows, and daughters of the unemployed miners at bargain-basement wages. More than that was needed to attract better-paying industries like electronics, chemicals, and plastics, however. So cities like Scranton and Wilkes-Barre bought large tracts of land on their outskirts, cleared away the culm dumps, brought in utilities, and offered 100 percent plant financing through their own industrial development funds and assistance from the Pennsylvania Industrial Development Authority. Soon many plants were moving in, including printing and warehousing for major national publishers. Within a decade, Scranton added 5,300 new manufacturing jobs and Wilkes-Barre did even better with a 12,500 increase (some of them, sadly, wiped out by tropical storm Agnes in 1972).

All of this, however, was not enough to stem a continuing outflow of the region's young people or assure continued economic health. A Northeastern Pennsylvania Development Council was formed to coordinate regional development and received added stature when it was designated to act as the operating arm of the Appalachian Regional Commission in the area. It drew up a comprehensive regional plan, touching on every local problem from improved schools to a better road network. An even more visionary concept, involving expenditure of $1 billion to restore the landscape, to build new towns, new lakes for recreation, and attract broadly diversified industry, was released by the Mitre Corporation in 1971. With its broad green belts, stable labor force, and advantageous geographical location so close to New York and Philadelphia, the report said, "the region has all the potential needed to play a national role in leading the way to a sound and more attractive development of the eastern United States."

One part of the northeast is already developing nicely: the Pocono Mountains, that group of pretty, not very lofty ridges close to the Delaware Water Gap. Dotted with lakes, waterfalls, and marshes, these hills were long summer vacation spots but after World War II developed into a year-round resort. Thousands go there for skiing each year (thanks in part to the snow-making machines), and the area has evolved into one of America's biggest places for honeymoons.* The clientele is not particularly megalopolitan; in fact, there are more reservations from the Midwest than Philadelphia and New York. Some of the accommodations are elegant, some woodsy, some "schlocky." Another big development in the Poconos is construction of second homes for vacation and retirement. The location is ideal, the Philadelphia Reserve Bank notes in very unbanklike style, because it is "so near to the megalopolis axis and yet far enough out to be lulled to sleep by choruses of katydids."

North of the anthracite region and then stretching far out to western

---

*There are some special inducements, especially modern-day versions of the Roman bath: sunken affairs, luxuriously tiled, large enough for and obviously intended for two, with carpeted approaches and mirrors.

Pennsylvania is the Appalachian "T-zone," a far-flung region of forests and streams and mountains, mountains, mountains. These mountains, Conrad Richter has written, are Pennsylvania's "ancient symbol of freedom . . . not a few isolated ranges, as in some states, but a whole province swarming with them, often one against the other with only narrow valleys in between." The top of the "T" covers the northern tiers of counties, almost 300 miles across, with their Lake Country, the Endless Mountains and the Black Forest, the Seneca Highlands, Buckland State Park, and the big Allegheny National Forest in the northwest. "This whole area," former Governor Scranton told us, "is completely undeveloped in regard to any postwar boom—there just wasn't any." With remarkable foresight, the Pennsylvania state government —its forests and waters, fish and game commissions—bought up vast amounts of land here. (The program began with Governor Lawrence's $70 million "Project 70" and continued with a $500 million land acquisition program passed under Scranton in 1965.) Scranton says a great tourist boom is about to start in these northern counties. One reason is ease of access. A brand new road, the Keystone Shortway (Interstate 80), runs from the New Jersey border near the Delaware Water Gap to the Ohio border near Youngstown. Opened in 1971, it parallels New York Route 17, along that state's southern tier, which Rockefeller poured a lot of money into rebuilding. "These two new limited access highways," Scranton said, "just about border the open range of Pennsylvania—one on the north, one on the south. With the opening of both of them, all of Eastern America is going to pour in."

The lower portion of the "T-zone" is the main body of the Appalachians between Harrisburg and Pittsburgh. This was the great barrier of the past —first for the wagon trains, then for the railroads, then for automobiles. The final conquest of it was completion of the Pennsylvania Turnpike in 1940. In a nostalgic 1971 article, the *Wall Street Journal*'s Bill Paul recalled the excitement when the turnpike opened, the first all-weather, limited access superhighway in the country (and a model of all that were to follow). In the first year, thousands of motorists flocked to Pennsylvania just to drive the turnpike and then go home and tell their friends of the new magic carpet without stopsigns, intersections, steep hills, or curves. Howard Johnson's, which had been a strictly New England affair before the turnpike, built 26 restaurants along it and was on its way to becoming a national company. As much as the old National Road or the Oregon Trail, the Pennsylvania Turnpike deserves a niche in American history. But its days of glory were numbered. Its narrow median strip, lack of gravel undersurface, short acceleration lanes at entrances, and single lanes through dingy tunnels in the high mountains make it an anachronism by later superhighway standards. And now it is riddled with potholes and losing business by virtue of the Keystone Shortway that parallels it to the north. Some believe its major function may one day be restricted to commuter access to Philadelphia and Pittsburgh.

Two cities sit astride the Appalachians in south central Pennsylvania— Altoona (62,900), which grew and then declined with the Pennsylvania Railroad, and Johnstown (42,476), a soft coal city which declined an alarming 21 percent in population just in the 1960s.

Pittsburgh: Alliance, Renaissance, Decay

Pittsburgh is one of just three places in America—New York and San Francisco are the other two—where geography demanded a city. Here, the Ohio River, America's historic water life line to the West, is born at the place that the Allegheny River, flowing southward from New York, meets the Monongahela, flowing northward from West Virginia. A 21-year-old major named George Washington observed the site in 1753 and described it as "extremely well situated for a Fort, as it has the absolute Command of both Rivers." In 1754 Virginian troops started fortifications but were quickly driven out by the French who constructed Fort Duquesne; the French, in turn, were vanquished by British troops in 1758 and Fort Pitt (named after William Pitt, the English prime minister) rose at the juncture of the rivers. Since then, some form of Anglo-Saxon occupation has been continuous.

Before we visited Pittsburgh, we had heard of a superb view of the city from the heights of Mount Washington, just to the south across the Monongahela. Our host, Robert Pease, executive director of the Allegheny Conference, was kind enough to drive us up to one of the restaurants there for a late evening drink, and we discovered one of the most stunning views of a city anywhere in America. Down in the valley, the city of Pittsburgh on its thin trowel of land lies sparkling with a million lights like a little Manhattan. Off to the left (or west) one can see the spot where the rivers meet, with the new Three Rivers Stadium, home of the Pittsburgh Pirates (1971 World Series winners) and Steelers football team (1975 Super Bowl Champions), glowing white on the Allegheny's far bank.

Then, at the tip of the "Golden Triangle," lies 36-acre Point State Park. A dreary mélange of warehouses and railroad tracks was cleared away there in the late 1940s, and finally in 1970 two old bridges at the apex were demolished to give Pittsburgh a grassy front lawn centered on the still-standing Fort Pitt blockhouse. Immediately east of the park stand the jewels of Pittsburgh's postwar renaissance, the Gateway Center with towering office and apartment high-rises, the Pittsburgh Hilton Hotel, and buildings of the state government, Bell Telephone, Westinghouse, and IBM. Further to the east, one sees a grouping of great canyonlike buildings where the corporate behemoths of Pittsburgh have their seats of power: U.S. Steel, Gulf Oil, Koppers, Alcoa, and others. Towering above them all is the new U.S. Steel Building completed in 1971, 64 stories high, rust-colored, and each floor an acre in size. Then there is the Chatham Center (an office-apartment-hotel complex completed under urban renewal in the 1950s), Pittsburgh's Civic Arena with its sliding domed roof; the black ghetto called the Hill District (there is also Polish Hill, which is white, depressed, and hopeless like Philadelphia's Kensington); the Oakland area which includes the University of Pittsburgh, Carnegie-Mellon University, and the city's medical center; the nearby Shadyside neighborhood, Pittsburgh's answer to Georgetown with an architectual style dubbed "Gilded Age High-Ceilinged"; the big Schenley and Frick parks; and Squirrel Hill and East End, the Jewish neighborhoods.

As World War II ended, Pittsburgh lived as it had for a century under a thick pall of coal smoke. John Gunther, visiting the city then, described it as "one of the most shockingly ugly and filthy in the world." If ever there was a great American city that represented the exploitive excesses of the industrial revolution, it was Pittsburgh. As Jeanne Lowe has written of the era from the Civil War to World War II: *

> The huge steel works sprawled along the flatlands of the river banks, pouring industrial sewage into their waters, slag into the green valleys and heavy coal smoke into the air. . . . Docile, unlettered blue-collar immigrants [from Eastern Europe] became the main body of Pittsburgh's and Allegheny County's population. Their lives were mean and drab. . . . The poverty and insecurity of their lives were intensified by the violent cyclical ups and downs of the heavy industry and mines. . . .
> No sooner had the 40 new "Carnegie millionaires" [created by the formation of U. S. Steel] turned their shares into convertible securities than most of them took themselves and their stocks away from the source of their wealth. They built showy palaces in New York and Newport, and flaunted in Europe and Florida the wealth they continued to siphon off from the region. . . .
> As it "prospered," Pittsburgh continued to grow without plan or community-mindedness. Its steep slopes were covered helter-skelter with cheap frame houses that were reachable only by a long climb up rickety wooden staircases from the streets below. Factories expanded into attractive residential neighborhoods and drove the residents to the suburbs. Choking coal smog was pervasive, and the decaying wreckage from the late railroad wars cluttered up the city's gateway at the Point.

By the early 1940s, it was clear to many Pittsburgh business and civic leaders that unless something was done to improve the city, it would gradually be abandoned. And in one of those odd quirks of history, two men came on the scene whose alliance to rebuild Pittsburgh would create the now-legendary postwar renaissance of the city.

The first was Richard King Mellon, a shy and retiring man who in 1934 became the active head of the celebrated family of bankers which had built its wealth by lending money to promising ventures and taking ownership interests in return. As governor and president of T. Mellon & Sons, he managed the interests that controlled Gulf Oil, Koppers, and Alcoa and had a major influence in a number of other major corporations including Westinghouse Air Brake, Pittsburgh Plate Glass, Pittsburgh Consolidation Coal, and the Pennsylvania Railroad. Under his direction, the First Boston Corporation and General Reinsurance Corporation were added to the group. In addition, the Mellons have a controlling interest of about $250 million in the Mellon National Bank and Trust, which in 1972 had $9.9 billion in

* In *Cities in a Race with Time* (New York: Random House, 1968).

assets and ranked as the largest bank in Pennsylvania and 16th largest in the U.S. The value of the Mellon interests was estimated in 1971 to be between $3 billion and $5 billion, an American family fortune second only to the du Ponts.

Mellon was deeply influenced by his father, Richard B., who counseled him to "live where you work, work where you live and stay behind your home town." * In 1941, Mellon went off to war, and like many Pittsburghers, when he returned home on leave, he found the city he had accepted before choked with smoke from the war-busy mills and unbelievably drab and depressing. Not long after, in June 1943, associates of Mellon took a leading role in organizing the Allegheny Conference on Post-War Community Planning (subsequently renamed Allegheny Conference on Community Development). It would be the moving force to mobilize Pittsburgh's business elite to back smoke abatement, downtown renewal, and virtually every other major civic program in the succeeding years. Other figures like the late city planner Wallace Richards and Arthur Van Buskirk, an attorney who was Mellon's close adviser and anchor man in civic activities, played crucial roles. But everyone knew the powerful, determinative influence was that of Richard King Mellon. Mellon could, for instance, commandeer the top official of almost any of Pittsburgh's leading 20 corporations—in half of which he had a controlling or large ownership—to do any job he wanted done within the Conference.

As the nascent Allegheny Conference began to lay its plans, it became clear that businessmen's wealth alone would not do the trick. Before the New Deal, local Republican bosses, tied in with the corporate-oriented statewide GOP, had run Pittsburgh. But the local Democrats were able to use the Mellons and the PMA as their whipping boys and seize complete control of the city and county government by 1936. They would be able to block the Allegheny Conference, made up almost entirely of Republicans, at any turn.

Enter now the second key figure of the Pittsburgh renaissance, David Lawrence. By delivering Pittsburgh and then Pennsylvania to the Democrats in the 1930s, Lawrence had become a major power broker in national Democratic politics. But he had always been a political manager, never a candidate. In 1945, the Democrats seemed headed for a divisive mayoralty primary, and Lawrence solved the problem by agreeing to run himself. And though he had grown in the "hate-Mellon" tradition, Lawrence astounded the city by pledging he would work with the Republican-dominated Conference to improve Pittsburgh. He took another political risk by announcing in his campaign that he would enforce a strong smoke abatement ordinance, passed by the city council in 1941, which had been shelved for the war.

* In a rare television interview, Mellon recalled his father driving him as a boy along Fifth Avenue and Riverside Drive in New York pointing out the biggest mansions. "He said: 'You know, Charlie Schwab came from Pittsburgh. Henry Frick came from Pittsburgh. Phipps came from Pittsburgh.' And when I got back to the Plaza Hotel, I said to my mother: 'All the big houses in New York are owned by Pittsburghers or former Pittsburghers.' And my father said: 'Yes, but they shouldn't have moved from Pittsburgh. They'd have been more content had they lived there.' Well, that made a very deep impression on me."

Lawrence was narrowly elected, and before long his remarkable alliance with Mellon began to take shape. For example, coal interests threatened to boycott Pittsburgh industry if the smoke ordinance went into effect; Mellon used his power as a director and substantial owner of Consolidation Coal to get the threat withdrawn. Then the problem arose of the railroads firing up their old coal-burning locomotives outside the city limits and still throwing quantities of coal smog into the air. A state law was needed to ban the practice but ran into strong opposition from the redoubtable barriers of the Pennsylvania Railroad in the state senate. Mellon, a director of the Pennsy, let its management know that if the line failed to comply with the ordinance or blocked the new law, he would have the companies he controlled switch their business to competing railroads. Thus the smoke law quickly passed the legislature, and the railroads' change to diesels played an important role in the rapid, almost miraculous cleansing of the Pittsburgh air in the late 1940s.*

The monuments of the Pittsburgh renaissance may be seen all over the city today. The $150 million Gateway Center, for which the government people cleared legal hurdles and the business contingent arranged financing from the Equitable Life Assurance Society, is the most dramatic but only part of the strong boom in office building for the city's many corporations. In the very center of downtown, Mellon Square, an exquisite oasis of stone deck, lush with fountains and shrubbery, has been built on top of a subterranean garage to replace a blighted block of old buildings and parking lots.† Point Park was built, and so was the civic auditorium, giving Pittsburgh a chance to get major conventions and also a place for open-air concerts of the Civil Light Opera by use of the retractable roof. The auditorium and surrounding civic center buildings went into the Lower Hill district, which had been a festering slum right beside downtown. Finally, much work was done on highway improvement in and around Pittsburgh, and dams were built to prevent a recurrence of floods like the disastrous one of 1936, which had inundated much of the city.

The renaissance had its limits, however. By the mid-1950s, it was obvious that the city faced an alarming shortage of decent lower- and middle-class housing to replace deteriorated units and those demolished for urban renewal. The Allegheny Conference tackled the job with an offshoot called ACTION-Housing that concentrated on new buildings, and starting in 1967 with "AHRCO" (Allegheny Housing Rehabilitation Corp.), an organization that rehabilitated old structures. The cumulative effort has been called the best-conceived and most comprehensive attack on slum housing in America,

---

* Even when it lost the title of "smoky city," Pittsburgh had air pollution. With emissions from coke ovens and power plants posing an increasingly serious problem, irate citizens in 1969 forced passage of a new ordinance regarded as a model for industrial cities. Enforcement was placed in the hands of a board of appeals and variances which can fine industries, imprison company officials, or even close down a plant entirely.

† Mellon got the idea for a city park atop a garage from San Francisco's Union Square, which he had seen while on duty with the army in California in World War II. To build Mellon Square, which has miraculously created a little bit of San Francisco's human warmth in the midst of old Pittsburgh, Mellon arranged a $4 million gift from his family-controlled foundations. Lawrence used the city's powers of eminent domain to acquire the land.

producing the positive result of almost 5,000 new or rehabilitated units. But the new low-income-housing supply is still only a fraction of what is needed. Of the roughly 190,000 housing units in Pittsburgh, 30 to 35 percent are substandard, many of them relics of the 1900–1910 era when the city's housing inventory was doubled by cheap frame houses along the rivers and the valleys. The city needs thousands of new units a year of subsidized housing, but red tape and the glacial pace of federal funding is holding actual starts to a fraction of that amount.

A second drawback to the renaissance was the problematic Pittsburgh economy, muscle-bound by its century-long dependence on coal and steel. While the national economy boomed in the 1950s and '60s, Pittsburgh and environs lost 13 percent of their steel industry jobs (the remaining total: 122,000). The area's boosters point to an increase of white-collar jobs as evidence of Pittsburgh's growth as a service and distribution center. But the number of Pittsburgh-headquartered corporations on *Fortune*'s top 500 list dropped from 23 in 1965 to 14 in 1974, a sobering fact for a city whose jewels are its big companies.* There was some movement of new and diversified industries into industrial parks in the area, together with a growth in scientific laboratories, but not nearly enough to offset the loss in basic metals. If the population figures are any indication, there is a distinct loss of faith in Pittsburgh's future, especially among younger people. One study in the late 1960s showed that more than 220,000 persons, most of them 20 to 24 years old, had left the area since the start of the decade, while only 110,000 had moved in. The population figures for the city of Pittsburgh proper show a decrease of 23 percent between 1950 and 1970 to a total of 520,117 (25th in rank among the country's cities). The Census Bureau estimated an additional 7.8 population drop between 1970 and 1973. And the 1970 Census report for the entire Pittsburgh metropolitan area (2,401,245 people) showed a 1 percent drop since 1960, a failure of suburban growth to compensate for core-city decline that made Pittsburgh uncomfortably unique among the 50 large population centers of America.

Why, one asks, should the Pittsburgh metropolitan area lose population? In a 1970 survey, the New York *Times*'s Douglas Kneeland identified four reasons: Pittsburgh's location off the route of the black migrations from the South; steel industry recessions; the topography of the region, with steep hills and narrow river valleys that limit development of vast suburban tracts or new industrial sites; and finally the lingering image of Pittsburgh as a grimy steel town, spitting fire and smoke.

Even at its height, the renaissance never did much to change Pittsburgh's picture as the ultimate company town. "What gives Pittsburgh its own unique

* The 14 remaining were Gulf Oil, Westinghouse Electric, Alcoa, National Steel, PPG Industries, H. J. Heinz, Koppers, Wheeling-Pittsburgh Steel, Allegheny Ludlum Industries, Rockwell Manufacturing, H. K. Porter, Joy Manufacturing, Cyclops, and H. H. Robertson. Some of these might leave were it not for the Mellons' ownership interests and influence. The list does not include U. S. Steel, which technically has its headquarters in New York but in fact has most of its executive and office staff in Pittsburgh.

juice and flavor is not how it plays but how it works," according to writer Jack Markowitz: "This is what underlies the joyless, grimy image people have of the place: all work and no play." Even "socially and physically," he observes, "business holds the dominant role in town—its massed skyscrapers resembling nothing so much as the superstructure of a vast ship plowing relentlessly forward." Within that milieu, the arts have not been strong, though there are glowing exceptions: the Pittsburgh Symphony, the Annual International Arts Show, and especially in the earlier postwar years, the Pittsburgh Playhouse's repertory company. Both newspapers—the evening *Press* and morning *Post-Gazette*—are rather provincial, though each has some fine writers. WQED sprang up in Pittsburgh as the nation's first educational television station and its provocative nightly "Newsroom" hour of news often outshone the papers and strong television competitors like Westinghouse's KDKA.

Pittsburgh's main attraction, however, is for those who treasure an industrial rather than a cultural climate. A successful Pittsburgh businessman can have a real feeling of *belonging*. His day, as Markowitz puts it, is "a progress of conferences that *do* reach decisions, of meetings in paneled rooms guarded by worshipful receptionists, . . . and of a noon-day ritual enjoyed by the top brass, the stately processions to the Duquesne Club, where chauffeured Cadillacs line up as they do after Friday afternoon concerts at Philadelphia's Academy of Music." (The Duquesne Club is a grim old fortress of blackened stone, sitting directly opposite two equally blackened old and prestigious churches, one Episcopalian and the other Presbyterian. Pleasantly decorated within, the club is literally packed with private meeting rooms where many a business deal and corporate merger have been effected. Ethnically, the membership holds few surprises, but present-day doers rather than grand old families are dominant. The cuisine is superb.)

The renaissance did help to elevate Pittsburgh's self-esteem in myriad ways. In earlier times, for instance, the city never had confidence in the quality of its universities. The elite went to Ivy League colleges (especially Princeton) and local businesses did not look to Pittsburgh universities for top talent. Now that has changed substantially, in part because of the Mellons' contributions to and interest in the local universities (an attitude other wealthy Pittsburghers have learned in turn). The institutions of higher learning in Pittsburgh are now tied together in a compact that permits a student at any one of them to enroll in courses at any other, receiving full academic credit. The benefits for the individual student with special interests may, of course, be immeasurable. The most famous of the city's universities is the University of Pittsburgh, which went through a fascinating period of trying to be a national institution with prestigious graduate programs. That bubble burst in the mid-1960s when Chancellor Edward Litchfield was ousted and it was discovered, much to the surprise of its own board of trustees, that the university was $30 million in debt. An appeal was then made to Harrisburg, which took over Pitt as a state-related institution. Now

Pitt is an institution of mass education, even though it retains some distinguished departments—most notably philosophy—and excellent schools of law and medicine. (The city has become a major medical center by virtue of the millions poured into medical research by the Mellons.)

The two most nationally oriented institutions are 102-year-old Chatham College for women, a small prestige college prospering with advanced, free-form courses of education; and Carnegie-Mellon University, a recent merger of the old Carnegie Institute of Technology and the Mellon Institute, a high-level research institute. Carnegie-Mellon has a terribly ugly campus but academic standards that make it a good substitute for Cal Tech or MIT for engineering students; its fine arts and drama departments are also outstanding.

Less happy is the story of Roman Catholic-supported Duquesne University, a multi-purpose downtown institution that serves society by turning out more than a thousand baccalaureates each year, running a big education program for teachers and nurses, and providing a good legal education. But Duquesne, almost a century old now, has fallen on bad times financially. Its fees have risen sharply and now it faces the indignity of competition for students with Allegheny Community College, an upstart which has grown by leaps and bounds since it first opened its doors in 1966.

Pittsburgh: New Politics?

In retrospect, it is clear that the Pittsburgh renaissance, for all its accomplishments, was an elitist phenomenon in which the wealthy business and strong government leaders made rather unilateral decisions on what would be best for Pittsburgh. If the planning was at the expense of the well-being and self-esteem of a lot of communities in Pittsburgh, that was simply the price that had to be paid. The renaissance shone in solving physical problems, and it flourished in the 1940s and '50s, before emergence of the human collision of disparate economic, race, and generation groups typical of the '60s and '70s.

The deceleration began in 1959, when Lawrence left to become governor of Pennsylvania. Joseph M. Barr, his successor as mayor, was a standard big-city liberal Democrat and organization man. As Van Buskirk puts it, "He did his best to be loyal to Lawrence's ideas and ideals. But he was no Dave Lawrence." For one thing, Lawrence had always maintained a complete separation between his coterie of Irish Catholic political workers from the wards and precincts and the bright young men he hired to work with the Allegheny Conference. Barr, who would remain in office until 1969, made the mistake of allowing confrontation between the two camps.

A measure of the change of Pittsburgh's mood and temper in the 1960s was provided by the unhappy fate of an ambitious "Great High Schools" plan unveiled in 1966 by the city's distinguished superintendent of schools,

Sidney P. Marland, Jr. (later U.S. Commissioner of Education). Marland noted the deterioration of the city's 17 obsolescent academic and vocational high schools, the last of which was built more than 40 years ago. At the same time, he was alarmed by the patterns of *de facto* segregation in the schools and increasing flight of white families to the suburbs. As an answer, he proposed building five super-high schools on 40-acre campuses, each to accommodate 5,000 to 6,000 students. The project never got off the ground, however, as the combination of cost (conservatively estimated at $120 million) and racial and ethnic distrust proved fatal to Marland's dreams. The school board, almost uniformly viewed as an elitist representation of the monied interests which dominated the city, had been outside the political life of the community for decades. As a result, it had nowhere to turn to rally support for its program of new, unified schools. Furthermore, the Great Schools program carried with it the image of busing, an idea anathema to much of the white working and middle class of the city. Marland left the school board in 1968, and with him gone, the Great Schools concept was abandoned.

But Pittsburgh was left with its problems—still largely unsolved—of building a new series of schools to replace its outmoded structures. Altogether, Pittsburgh has more than 100 public schools. Robert Pease, executive director of the Allegheny Conference, points out that "since a school becomes obsolete in 50 years, we'll have to build two new ones a year forever." No one knows where Pittsburgh will find the money for that kind of job.

If the city did not develop a plan for replacing its aging school buildings, perhaps it did learn something about itself, about the way in which decisions are made, and the forces that are involved in the decision-making process within the community. The Great High Schools demise was used by the Institute for Community Studies to underscore its basic conclusions about the effectiveness of the city's social planning machinery to solve education, wealth, and welfare problems. The Institute decided the fundamental new reality is that *"process is policy"*:

> This simple statement means that the manner in which we seek to reconcile people and groups in our cities now alienated from each other transcends in importance the solutions we arrive at from time to time on particular questions at issue. . . . We are impressed with the need for creating wholly new organizations to serve the social needs of Pittsburgh. . . . *The process adopted for bringing about change is crucial*. It is necessary to give all groups a place at the table.

No entrenched group is very interested in inviting others to a place at the table. But the reaction of the heirs of Lawrence and Mellon to the pressures for change in the past few years has been instructive. First, we may consider the Democratic organization. Lawrence, for all his fame as a city rebuilder, was no reformer when it came to the old clubhouse way of practicing politics. Richard Thornburgh, an ambitious young Republican who was U. S. Attorney in Pittsburgh until his promotion to head the Justice Department's Criminal Division in 1975, offered a rarely heard critique of Lawrence:

> The mystique of Lawrence as a Second Coming is just not true. He and Barr gave free reign to Mellon and the Allegheny Conference just as long as they were left free to hold on to their own political power, clout and patronage. Syndicate operators in Allegheny County established their foothold in the '40s and '50s through the cooperation of the Democratic administration here at the time. . . . Lawrence was very tight with the guys in the rackets in the city. He never put a nickel in his own pocket in the corrupt sense. But these guys [the criminal element] were financing the Democratic party all this time. And he was tolerant of police corruption. . . .
> Under Lawrence and Barr, the favored politicians held four or five jobs. They'd be the alderman, the police magistrate, the Democratic ward chairman and probably be on the city payroll. We have 32 wards in this city. The Dave Lawrence claque held sway there, tolerating illegal operations in every ward. No one can tell me Lawrence didn't know about it. That legacy is part of the problem we have today.

During the Barr era of the '60s, little was done to clean house within the Democratic organization. On the city council, Democrats were expected to go along with Barr—or else. When allegations were made of widespread corruption in the police department, Barr made no move to fire the police superintendent, James Slusser. The Democratic machine, however, suffered a dramatic loss in 1969 when the voters turned down its hand-picked man to succeed retiring Mayor Barr and elected instead a dashing 44-year-old embodiment of the "new politics," Peter F. Flaherty. A product of Pittsburgh's tattered North Side, Flaherty had been a docile ally of the Barr regime on the city council but then broke with the organization in 1969 to run as a "man against the machine." He promised to be a mayor without strong ties or debts to big business, big labor, or the old political alliances—"nobody's boy," as he repeatedly boasted. After trouncing the organization in the primary, he spurned its offer of general election help, saying, "My severance with the Democratic machine in Pittsburgh is not a separation, it is a divorce."

Once installed in office, Flaherty replaced Barr's division chiefs with his own cadre of politically untried lawyers, architects, engineers, and business experts, most of them younger than himself. Along with the hacks, he fired John T. Mauro, the city's skillful planning director and Barr's liaison man with the Mellon Patch. The planning staff was decimated, apparently part of Flaherty's effort to deemphasize big downtown projects and turn attention (in ways rather ill-defined) to neighborhood development. By refusing to go along on patronage-based appointments and the familiar cozy deals, Flaherty was immersed in almost continuous bickering with the city council. He fired hundreds of city employees hired by past administrations for make-work patronage jobs and broke a jurisdictional strike by the Teamsters-controlled city garbage collectors (whose average pay is $11,000). "Flaherty," Ralph Hallow of the Pittsburgh *Post-Gazette* wrote, "was left the undisputed champion of the people and slayer of the ancient dragon of labor-political bossism."

Flaherty has been doing what most mayors in America have been unwilling or unable to do—cut the rolls of government employment. As Pittsburgh's population declines as the result of migration by middle and upper income families to the suburbs, the revenues of the city also decline; the tax base is narrower, and in order to avoid fatal overextension, the city must cut its expenditures. Flaherty has reduced the city payroll, previously swollen by patronage appointments, from 7,190 in 1970 to 5,400 in 1975 (authorized employment levels were higher—5,696 in 1975—but the mayor refused to fill every authorized position). This is considered by the mayor's office to be almost as low as the city can go in trimming the employment figures without threatening basic services.

Early in his first term, Flaherty appointed Charles H. Cooper, a black and former star in the National Basketball Association, to head the parks and recreation department. Through that appointment Flaherty won immediate support among Pittsburgh's blacks (20 percent of the population). Not only blacks, but low-income Poles, Slovaks, Czechs, Italians, Germans, and Irish welcomed his populist move to reject the mayor's black Cadillac limousine in favor of a small blue Ford. In a reform helpful to people generally, Flaherty overturned a corrupt old magistrate system. Overall, the new mayor seemed to be uniting blacks and other poor people in a way few modern American mayors are able to do.

It was such support from his Pittsburgh area base that won Flaherty the Democratic primary for the Senate in 1974, and made him a strong contender against the politically savvy, labor-endorsed incumbent Richard Schweiker in November. But Flaherty's habit of going it alone—he had no semblance of an organized campaign—for once was not enough, and he fell considerably short of victory.

Flaherty's reforms were not standard "liberalism," nor were his critics limited to those who lost their place at the public trough. Faced with a budget deficit, he devoted much of his time to slashing expenses, thus averting a tax increase. While proceeding to decimate the old Democratic machine, member by member (by cutting off patronage), he also became distant from many of his own original supporters. Some business-supported social programs began to languish because of Flaherty's determination to stay independent of the Allegheny Conference crowd.

And if the old politics is out of style in Pittsburgh proper, it continues to prosper in the Allegheny County government where figures with connections to the rackets are in key positions. As early as 1971, Richard Thornburgh said he had a strong suspicion of kickbacks in county business and suspected that a major portion of money that went into county elections came from racketeering interests. By 1975, Thornburg said "the very things I suspected have come to pass. We've convicted two councilmen from the Law-rence-Barr era. One obstructed enforcement of state gambling laws and took payoffs. The other was convicted on two counts of extortion." Thornburgh also obtained indictments of 36 police officers and other local officials that led to 19 convictions. "But Allegheny County," he added, "is so fragmented and the county is so ineffective on a regional basis that it really doesn't matter much as far as government goes." (The county government, we should note, has been Democratic for years, and Thornburgh is a Republican. But his view is widely shared. The GOP's own organization is pathetically weak, and few Pittsburgh Republicans winced when I quoted the words of an eastern Pennsylvania Republican politician: "I wouldn't trade you one Philadelphia ward leader for the whole Allegheny County Republican organization.")

Meanwhile, back at the Mellon Patch, the Allegheny Conference in 1968 debated its future course and decided to turn its focus from physical to human problems. Two leaders spearheaded the Conference's shift toward social renewal. The first was Henry Hillman, a financier active in coal, mining equipment, and airlines, whose family wealth ranks second (albeit a distant second) to the Mellons. He became chairman of the Conference's board. And Robert B. Pease, the cream of the crop of young technocrats assembled to effect the Conference's renaissance-era programs, became its executive director. The Conference chartered an employment committee which worked with the Pittsburgh National Alliance of Businessmen, finding more than 9,000 jobs for the disadvantaged between 1967 and 1970. (The retention rate was reported at a high 58 percent.)* Black capitalists got a helping hand through a minority enterprise loan program coordinated by the Conference; by the end of 1970 local banks had lent $5.2 million. In the wake of Martin Luther King's assassination, discussions between black leaders and the Allegheny Conference leaders led to establishment of a broad, entirely black-directed social welfare fund ("Program to Aid Citizen Enterprise") which was continuing in 1971 with an annual budget of about $700,000. But could the renaissance really be recycled in the nonmaterial, social sense? "There is an emotional tithe to some very pressing problems, but not the total commitment that was present in the physical rebuilding of the '40s and '50s," one local observer told us.

In June 1970, Richard King Mellon died, and Pittsburgh wondered if any leader of his vision and his *power* would again emerge. Mellon left two adopted sons, both around 30 years of age. Richard Prosser Mellon began to concentrate on the Mellon family's charitable interests—which include three family foundations with assets of $975 million. (One of these, the Andrew W. Mellon Foundation, made grants of $29.9 million in 1970. Only the Ford and Rockefeller Foundations dispensed more.) The other son, Seward Prosser, took charge of the family's multibillion-dollar investments and later was suspected of involvement in the kidnapping of his two children from their mother from whom he was estranged. It was obvious that the

---

* There are some skeptics on this score. Wendell G. Freeland, a prominent local Negro attorney, told me regarding the NAB effort: "If I could believe all the statistics I read, every black guy in this town would have three jobs. Unemployment among blacks is still very high."

vitality and wisdom had been drained away with Richard King Mellon's demise. Leland Hazard, attorney, author, and one of the leaders of the renaissance, told us:

No one exists in Pittsburgh now with the convictions of Mellon and Lawrence. We have lost the faith. While Richard King Mellon lived, the conceptions generally, though not invariably, came to him, and then emerged in the Allegheny Conference. . . .

What we don't know is whether Mellon was so dominant no one else was brave enough to think for himself—or if in truth and fact the heads of the 20 other great corporations were not community conscious individuals. An ill wind blows, and we'll learn now . . . whether the yearnings and hopes and ambitions and unselfish aspirations of the community will show up from sources which during Mellon's lifetime did not make bold to speak.

In Pittsburgh, we now have a complete loss of that rapport and mutuality of understanding, that joint dedication of wealth and politics, which made the renaissance. Our community is disorganized, disrupted, unled, and the forces of anarchy are uninhibited. Our mayor is a reflection of this. It's a distemper. But it will pass.

Hazard, who has gained the reputation of a "Mr. Transit" in Pittsburgh, has campaigned assiduously for federal funding for an 11-mile skybus track running from South Hills to the city. That would cost more than $200 million, and an eventual 60-mile system serving the entire county would cost $1 billion or more. He acknowledges that transit was an "orphan" in the heyday of the Allegheny Conference, when repeated studies were made but killed by Mellon, who "was misled by close advisers." As a result, Hazard says, Pittsburgh has had to "wait to approach that universal traffic jam in which some prophets of doom say the 20th century will end." Hazard sees only two possible alternatives to mass transit—outlying shopping centers reached by automobile, or totally new cities:

I've rejected those alternatives out of hand. Why? The cities of the world are the centers of excellence. There's little excellence anywhere outside of cities. How are you going to put a Titian in every shopping center? The great architecture is in the city—the cathedrals, the churches, the spires, the domes, the towers— those beauties of architecture which lift men's souls out of the muck of dreary, drab, routine existence. They can't be in "new cities." Unless the United States is to become a cultural waste, unless suburbia is to become a cultural slum—and it *is* a cultural slum, full of the banal—then there must be mobility, then there must be access: frequent, cheap, and maybe free, from the periphery (however wide it spreads) to those centers of excellence. . . .

In selecting a technology, there are fundamentals which can't be compromised. Public transit must have its own right of way, with utter separation from all other traffic. (A bus is no faster than the flat-tired car in front of it and express lanes for buses are only temporary expedients because they depend on the internal combustion engine which is now as anachronistic as the caveman's club, and because they require men to drive them, and that is one thing technology cannot tolerate.) Mass transit vehicles must be unmanned, operating on a planned, computerized system like horizontal elevators. And we must avoid subways; they are a product of the iron, coal, and steel age when the humanistically insensitive engineer was in charge of our society. As a man moves, he should be able to look, smell, feel color. A modern transit system won't make a smell in the environment. It won't make a sound in the environment. It will be as quiet as an Indian path in Penn's woods.

Beyond Pittsburgh

Downtown Pittsburgh today is a viable place by virtue of some good renaissance-era decisions, the chief of which was to make the Triangle its focal point. East and west, the Civic Arena and Three Rivers Stadium to which we referred earlier provide natural terminal points. The compactness is enforced by the rivers north and south, and the result is that most important business is consummated in the Triangle, the downtown department stores have withstood suburban competition with amazing vitality, and now more bars and nightclubs are moving in.

But beyond the Triangle and some immediate adjuncts like Oakland, Shady Side, and the South Side's Mount Washington and Duquesne Heights (where incline railways left over from Victorian times go up to the classy restaurants), the Pittsburgh geography is simply one of hills, hills, hills, and community isolation. Three-quarters of the region's people live outside Pittsburgh proper, in three general types of communities. For the privileged, there is Ligonier (population 2,258); 40 miles to the east is Westmoreland County, where the Mellons and the top brass of their various companies live; or Sewickley Heights (797), to the west, where wooded lawns overlook the Ohio; or Fox Chapel (4,684), across the Allegheny to the north, which is zoned 100 percent residential. One step down is Mt. Lebanon (39,596), a place of middle executives south of the city. East of the city there are sprawling middle-class suburbs like Penn Hills (62,886) and Monroeville (29,011).

Finally starting in Allegheny County and then covering the whole face of southwestern Pennsylvania, there are the blue-shirted steel mill towns crowded into their narrow valleys. Along the Monongahela south of Pittsburgh, there is a practically unbroken chain of them—places like Homestead, Braddock, Duquesne, McKeesport, Clairton, and Donora. Ambridge and Aliquippa on the Ohio are in the same category. Here are the massive blast furnaces and coke ovens, rolling mills and coal breakers of Big Steel, belching out their fumes over the landscape. The story is much the same in outlying cities like Sharon, New Castle, Washington, and Jeannette. None of these cities has more people than McKeesport (37,977), and all are dying cities, losing population and business at a rapid clip. Most of them are in the grip of small-time racketeering tied closely to the political structure, McKeesport being perhaps the most notorious of all. For the families of the hardy ethnics who serve the steel mills—Poles, Irish, Italians, and others— the future could hardly be more bleak.

The *raison d'être* for these towns is that they lie atop the great bituminous coal fields off which the steel mills feed. And where there are no mills, the picture is the grimmest of all. In Indiana County, a few miles east of Pittsburgh, the worst kind of Appalachian poverty prevails. Except for Indiana Borough (16,100), the county seat, which is lucky enough to have a college and streets of pleasant homes, the entire county consists of old run-down mining patches where strip mining has brutally scarred the earth. There is now some back-filling on the stripped land, but it is useless for anything but growing Christmas trees. Several generations of people have lived here in chronic poverty, and they know nothing else.

There are a few, but only a few, hopeful signs for the economy of western Pennsylvania. To the south, just north of the tristate border point of Pennsylvania, West Virginia, and Maryland, tourism is growing in the Laurel Highlands, an excellent skiing area. In the northwest, the small oil industry—a remnant of the heady years after the Civil War, when Pennsylvania was America's oil boom state—continues to prosper around Oil City, selling an exceptionally high grade of lubricants (Quaker State Oil, etc.). Thanks to new interstate roads, Governor Shapp told us, "northwestern Pennsylvania has a modern transportation system for the first time in its history." A strong effort will be made there, he said, to attract small fabricating plants and warehouses which could service Chicago, Detroit, Toledo, and New York simultaneously with one-day shipping.

Our Keystone State saga ends with a place that hardly considers itself part of Pennsylvania at all—Erie, in the far northwest corner, a Great Lakes city of 129,231 people (third largest in the state). One reason for Erie's isolation from the rest of Pennsylvania is that it is much closer to Buffalo and Cleveland than to Pittsburgh or Harrisburg, and trade and travel have always tended to go up and down along Lake Erie. Another is that Erie has never developed any real strength in either party in the Pennsylvania legislature, remaining a perennial stepchild in terms of state programs. Finally, there has been little inducement for other Pennsylvanians to visit Erie, a place where a sunny winter day is a unique event and brutal, cold weather closes in from the end of October to the end of April. With the new interstate connections, Erie might draw some more Pennsylvania visitors—if it can persuade them that Lake Erie, where it touches Pennsylvania, is not polluted as it is around Buffalo and Cleveland.

Erie enjoys a good business climate, with large General Electric and Hammermill Paper payrolls and a lot of small industries in diversified fields like precision tools and plastics. But neither political party has developed strong leaders, and the quality of city government has been inferior, dominated by political bickering and lacking imagination and initiative. Nor is this shortcoming made up for by a strong business power structure; in fact no one seems very gung-ho about Erie. Its central business district is rundown, and while several urban renewal projects have been started, the progress has been slow and laborious. The city has problems with various forms of racketeering and its syndicate effort is reportedly run as a branch town operation by the big-time gangsters from Buffalo. It is a long way from Penn's Woods.

NEW JERSEY

IN THE SHADOWS OF MEGALOPOLIS

NEW JERSEY HAS A PROBLEM WITH ITS IMAGE. Suspended between the massive urban centers of New York and Philadelphia, it still has some of the attributes James Madison ascribed to it—a cask tapped at both ends. There are places in America, like Oakland and East St. Louis, that suffer from what is known as a "second city" syndrome; only New Jersey could be said to have a second (or perhaps third) *state* syndrome. Even though it is, next to California, the most urbanized state of America, New Jersey lacks a single city of distinction. To recite the names of New Jersey's cities is depressing enough; the reader can test himself on the list of places like Newark, Jersey City, Paterson, Camden, Trenton, Elizabeth, Bayonne, Hoboken, and the rest. All have decayed alarmingly in the postwar years and have become cauldrons of racial discord. New Jersey is the most suburban state of America, the suburban towns ranging from handsome to drab and ugly.* Jersey's once glittering resort town, Atlantic City has sunk into decrepitude—though casino gambling may give it a flashier, perhaps even affluent future.

---

   * The terms "suburban" and "urban," as used here, require some definition. "Suburban" refers to the percentage of the population which lives in metropolitan areas but outside of the central core cities of 50,000 or more population. It is in this category that New Jersey leads the nation. "Urban" may refer to the center core cities, in which category New Jersey ranks about midpoint among the states. But if one uses the Census Bureau's time-honored alternative definition of "urban," meaning any town or city of 2,500 population or more, then New Jersey, at 88.9 percent is first in the U. S. except for California (with 90.9 percent).

New Jersey has the greatest population density of all the 50 states (953 people per square mile), but it lacks communications media of statewide scope. There is not a single commercial television station in all of New Jersey—a plight that only Delaware, among the 50 states, shares. The result, in an era when a vast majority of the public gets almost all its news concerning public affairs from television, is little short of disastrous. "New Jerseyans," according to Daniel Gaby, a member of the state board of education, "are probably the most misinformed and uninformed citizens in the country on matters applying to their own state." A 1973 Harris poll found that only 32 percent of New Jersey residents could name one of their U.S. Senators and only 24 percent could name both. (Nationally, 59 percent of Americans could name one Senator, 39 percent could name both. Governors, faced by a legislature dominated by local political dukedoms, are unable to take their message over the heads of the special interests to the statewide citizenry as a whole. A New Jersey Coalition for Fair Broadcasting, composed of 18 civic groups and individual public officials, was set up in 1971 to persuade or compel New York and Philadelphia stations to give fuller coverage to Jersey news; a few improvements were made, but the situation remained highly unsatisfactory through the middle 1970s.

The press situation is only a little less serious. Somehow the New York *Times* and *Daily News* steal the thunder of the last remaining big Jersey paper, the Newark *Star-Ledger*. Philadelphia papers circulate heavily in southern New Jersey. On the other hand, there are strong local papers— among them the Bergen *Record*, Trenton *Times*, Camden *Courier-Post*, Asbury Park *Press*, and Passaic *Herald-News*—which have their individual territories so well in hand that papers of statewide scope cannot penetrate. A source of new vitality in Jersey journalism was the purchase in 1974 of the Trenton *Times* by the Washington Post Company.

A measure of low public consciousness in New Jersey is the fact that organized crime, here more than in any other state of the Union, has been able to take over whole city governments and even infiltrate to high levels in the state government. And as if this were not bad enough, the image most outsiders have of New Jersey is confined to the dreary view of belching factories, oil refineries, railroad sidings, and auto graveyards along the Philadelphia-New York transportation corridor (also known as "Pollution Alley"), the most heavily traveled highway and rail route in America. Life in the heart of megalopolis, it seems, has more than its share of drawbacks. Jersey's problems have been made no easier by an archaic tax structure, based mainly on the property tax, which has bankrupted its cities, and a lack of high-level talent in its public life.

But it is not enough to accentuate the negative, as true as all we have said may be. Jersey's Revolutionary-era cities are not likely to get a face-lifting for some time to come, but a series of brilliant federal prosecutors have done much to clean up the infestation of organized crime and corruption that degrade New Jersey's public life. And under court order to revamp the school financing system, New Jersey was finally forced, in 1976, to adopt the income tax it desperately needed to tap the immense wealth within the state and relieve—if only slightly—local property taxes that have forced homeowners and business alike out of the older urban areas, generating egregious suburban sprawl.

The fact is that New Jersey has vast economic and human resources on which to live. The per capita income, $5,759 in 1973, ranks third in the nation. The percentage of people in the working age bracket (21 to 64) is second highest in the U. S. The state is seventh among the 50 in the value of its manufactures and is getting increasingly into sophisticated research-type industries. With its superb central location on the East Coast and proximity to the centers of national wealth, the state should have an unlimited economic future. Long a parasite on its neighbors in higher education, it has stopped exporting so many young people out of state for their college educations and has undertaken a massive university-building program. There is already the skill and knowledge in New Jersey's educated elite to effect fundamental changes, especially as the long entrenched and often corrupt county and city political machines wither away and make room for more effective citizen politics.

Frederick H. Sontag, a public affairs and research consultant based in South Orange, sees a "major hope for development of a vigorous New Jersey in the emergence of some gutsy, young, experienced leader who can really inspire its people." The older generation of leaders in politics, labor, and business, he suggests, is retiring or dying, and there is a real opportunity for an imaginative new generation, perhaps mobilized by a well staffed and financed citizens movement, to look for solutions that "go beyond taxation and more spending." With an active statewide network of highly motivated citizens, he believes, "New Jersey could become a state to be respected and emulated and, at long last, one to be reckoned with."

The population figures attest to New Jersey's continuing viability. In 1970, the Census found 7,168,164 people in the state, 72 percent more than the 4,160,165 who were there in 1940. (The national population grew by 54 percent in the same 30-year period.) New Jersey's largest increase, both in actual numbers and percent, occurred in the 1950s, the biggest decade yet for filling up the suburbs. But the decade of the 1960s saw a growth of 18 percent, compared to a national growth of 13 percent. And in the 1970–74 period, while the Census estimated that New York was losing population and Pennsylvania barely gaining, New Jersey posted a 2.7 percent estimated increase in civilian population. Of New Jersey's 1.1 million increase in the 1960s, 645,000 was due to natural increase (births over deaths) and 488,000 to net migration (the excess of people moving into the state over the number choosing to leave it). The net migration figure was actually the highest for any state except California.

Physically, New Jersey is vest pocket size—only 7,532 square miles, 46th among the 50 states. But there is a lot more to New Jersey than the congested cityscape and industrial wastelands one sees from a car on the New

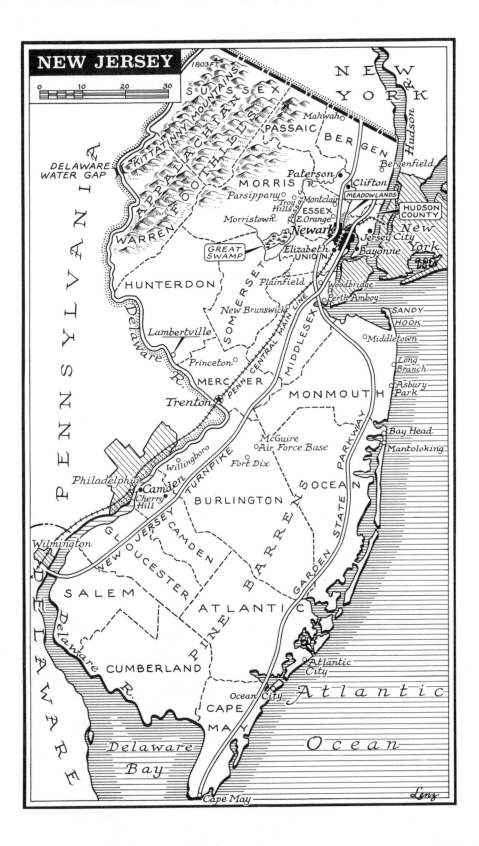

Jersey Turnpike, or from the window of a through train. Despite the constant inroads of suburbia, almost three-quarters of the land remains in forest, farms, and small towns, populated by a scant 11 percent of the state's people.

There are two broad areas of natural beauty in New Jersey—the Appalachian foothills in the northwestern part of the state, and the Atlantic Coast. The northwestern section, divided from Pennsylvania by the upper (and still relatively clean) waters of the Delaware River, is crossed by the Appalachian Trail and offers many cabin- and resort-lined lakes between forest-covered hills. The dramatic Delaware Water Gap, where the river has cut a 1,200-foot gorge through the Kittatinny Mountains, is a great tourist attraction. Although the region is threatened by an ever growing tide of summertime and retirement homes of refugees from the big cities, one still finds dairy farms in the valleys, as well as old settlements like Chester and Mendham, with a New England flavor to their village greens and church spires. Here, too, are lovely rural suburban areas and the homes of some of New Jersey's fabled old families like the Frelinghuysens and Forbeses, living a genteel life with their horses and estates in counties like Morris, Hunterdon, and Somerset. As the Delaware moves southward toward Trenton, still through countryside of quiet charm, it passes historic old places like Lambertville and Washington's Crossing where the Continental Army crossed the ice-choked river on Christmas night of 1776. A few miles to the east is Princeton, a university town of rare beauty.

The glistening white expanses of the Jersey Shore, stretching in more or less continuous form from Sandy Hook on New York's Lower Bay for 125 miles to Cape May at New Jersey's southernmost tip, offer the people of megalopolis some of the most magnificent natural beaches in America. Despite the affluence in old towns like Bay Head or Mantoloking, with their weather-silvered homes, the shore is not a chic resort area of modern America. But each spring winter's gray swells give way to a sunny blue Atlantic surf, and middle-class Jerseyites, Philadelphians, and New Yorkers pour in by the millions to claim their foot of beach. The shore communities have look-alike ways but differ greatly in character: honky-tonk Atlantic City and Asbury Park, puritanical Ocean City (a resort founded by Methodists in 1879 that still forbids public bars), sedate and quiet Cape May (where Lincoln and other Presidents vacationed in the last century, now a place of picturesque narrow streets, old shade trees, and historic homes). Only 12 miles from Atlantic City is the Brigantine Wildlife Refuge, where more than half a million birds gather during spring and autumn migrations. Surf fishermen and bird watchers predominate at Island Beach, a seven-mile-long state park. Sandy Hook, a government preserve for 200 years, has become part of the ambitious National Gateway Recreation Area shared with New York. And the southern parts of the shore include long stretches of beach where development is not yet heavy.

Just inland from the shore in South Jersey lie the Pine Barrens, 3,000 square miles of sandy soils, swamplands, pine stands, and blueberry and cranberry tracts, one of the largest ecologically undisturbed areas along the Boston-Washington urban corridor. The concentration of plant life in this vast botanical museum is unappreciated by the millions who speed by on the turnpikes.

An Economic Scorecard

New Jersey's difficult role as an economic hinterland of New York, but separated governmentally from the metropolis, dates from 1664 when the English took over the New York area from the Dutch. It was in that year that the Duke of York, given a vast tract of land on the eastern seaboard, unwisely severed the territory between the Hudson and Delaware Rivers from the natural capital in New York and assigned it to two of his court favorites. Unfortunately, the duke failed to inform Richard Nicolls, whom he had dispatched to New York to run the entire new province. Nicolls had already made land grants in Jersey conflicting with those of the new Lords Proprietors, and a century of court wrangles ensued. A few years later, William Penn gained control of West Jersey, making that territory the first Quaker settlement in America, and in 1682 he got control of East Jersey —and thus the entire present state of New Jersey—as well. But Penn presumably became discouraged with the interminable disputes over land ownership, dating from the Duke of York's original error, and petitioned Charles II for a patent to what is now Pennsylvania. Philadelphia, the great Quaker city, rose on the west bank of the Delaware River, instead of in New Jersey. Thus New Jersey was left between the two great cities and came to regard itself, as an 18th century pamphlet expressed it, as a "poor, slavish dependent" of its neighbors.

Due to its strategic location, New Jersey was the scene of nearly 100 battles and skirmishes in the Revolutionary War, a conflict which set neighbor against neighbor and brother against brother in the state. The future role of New Jersey began to appear in 1791 when Alexander Hamilton founded the Society for Establishing Useful Manufactures and chose the falls of the Passaic River as a site for the industrial town of Paterson. The 19th century witnessed rapid growth of canals and railways and of cities like Jersey City, Newark, Paterson, and Camden as manufacturing centers. Ownership either began in, or inevitably gravitated toward, New York or Philadelphia. Likewise, the chief market for Jersey's farm goods was in the big cities on its borders. Politics took on an unsavory color when the Camden and Amboy Railroad was granted an exclusive charter for the Philadelphia–New York run, and from the 1840s to the 1870s the railroads dominated economic and political life in the state. Liberal incorporation laws passed in the 1870s would lead to a charge by Lincoln Steffens that New Jersey was the traitor state that let the big corporations fleece the poor.

New Jersey has always been a melting pot of nationalities. Dutch, British, Finns, and Swedes were all there in ample numbers before the Revolution. In addition to the Quakers, there were Baptists from Long Island and New England who came in search of religious freedom. The 1800s brought vast numbers of Irish to dig the canals and build the railways. Germans immigrated in vast numbers, later to be joined by Poles and Hungarians who worked in the factories. Many Russian Jews arrived early in the 20th century, and today the state has about 400,000 Jews, or 5.5 percent of its population. Only New York state has a higher percentage. (Jersey's Jews, however, have shown fewer leadership qualities than their counterparts across the Hudson.) And then there are the Italians, who arrived in such huge numbers toward the end of the 19th century and early in the present one that they represent today, by some estimates, as much as 35 percent of the population. (The overall Roman Catholic share of the population, which would include most but not all the Italians, is 38.0 percent—the fourth highest Catholic population share among the 50 states).

The population of New Jersey is so polyglot, Professor Richard Mc-Cormick of Rutgers University has noted, that "the native, third-generation Jerseyman is a rarity." About a quarter of the people moving into New Jersey in recent years have been blacks, increasing the black share of the population from 5.5 percent in 1940 to 10.7 percent in the 1970 Census. Most have moved into the big cities, where they have been joined by growing numbers of Puerto Ricans and other Spanish-speaking peoples. But the new minorities' portion of Jersey's population is no greater than that of the U. S. as a whole, and it should be a manageable problem *if* more blacks and Latins can be channeled into the suburbs.

New Jersey's modern economy rests on several pillars: manufacturing, research, corporate headquarters, farming, commuting, and transportation. The $12 billion-plus output of the state's factories springs from a fantastic array of manufactures, perhaps the broadest of any state. Of the country's 75 largest industrial firms, 62 operate in the state; 90 percent of all types of manufacturing are represented. New Jersey is the national leader in chemical production, with big pharmaceutical, basic chemical, and paint plants. Among the states, it ranks third in apparel, sixth in food products, electrical machinery, and instruments, seventh in fabricated metal products, paper, printing, and publishing, eighth in petroleum, ninth in textiles.

New Jersey has long been a state of inventions, starting with Thomas Edison's electric light bulb and continuing with Lee De Forrest's basic vacuum tube, Allen Du Mont's cathode ray tube, Edwin Armstrong's development of FM radio, and the transistor for which scientists Walter H. Brattain, John Bardeen, and William Schockley received the Nobel Prize in 1956. The state is still a national leader in both pure and applied research and is said to have more scientists and engineers per capita than any other. There are more than 600 laboratories, including Bell Telephone at Murray Hill, Esso at Linden, and the James Forrestal Research Center at Princeton. Many of the laboratories are located in bucolic suburban or exurban locations, far away from the smoky industrial corridors.

Despite Jersey's heavy role in manufacturing, the white-collar share of the employment pool is higher than in all but six other states. A leader in the preferred office-job field is Prudential Life Insurance, located in Newark, the country's largest insurance company with $28 billion in assets. Insurance, real estate, retailing, service industries, and government all account for thousands of white-collar jobs, although government employment accounts for a significantly lower share of total jobs than the national average. Preeminently, New Jersey is a self-supporting state; its per capita grants-in-aid from the federal government rank only 49th among the 50 states. And in 1975, New Jersey residents and businesses paid $4.4 billion more in federal taxes than the federal government spent altogether in the state. New Jersey is the tenth biggest state in defense contracts (over $1 billion a year), but direct defense-generated employment accounts for only 3.1 percent of the labor force, less than the national average.

In the late 1960s, New Jersey revised its corporation laws to make them as liberal and flexible as any in the U. S., thus encouraging big firms to incorporate, and in some cases to actually set up headquarters staffs, in the state. Before that, the corporation laws, scandalously loose in earlier times, had become so encrusted that they actually discriminated against New Jersey-based corporations. The number of new industries coming into Jersey began to increase quite rapidly; among them were such giants as Corn Products (now CPC International), American Cyanamid, and Squibb Beech-Nut. The diversity of Jersey industry is illustrated by the names of the others on *Fortune*'s "top 500" list: Campbell Soup, Warner-Lambert Pharmaceutical, Johnson & Johnson, Walter Kidde, Merck, Union Camp, Curtiss-Wright, Fedders, Thomas J. Lipton, Jonathan Logan, General Instrument, Schering, Becton Dickinson, Interspace, Federal Pacific Electric, and Triangle Industries. Three Jersey-based retailers—Grand Union, Vornado, and Supermarkets General—are on the *Fortune* list of the biggest retailing firms. But significantly, not a single New Jersey bank is on the list of the 50 largest U. S. banks.

Despite the corporate growth, there was growing concern in Jersey by the mid-1970s that the state was taking on the characteristics of the stagnant, "mature" economy which has plagued New England in recent years. The state never recovered fully, in terms of employment, from the 1970 recession, and by early 1975 the total number of manufacturing jobs was down 110,000 from a peak of 900,000 in 1969. Many of the plants are old, and easily lured to the South or West where taxes and labor costs are lower. Even before the 1975 recession manufacturing employment was in clear decline—a serious blow to the economy of a state where fully one-quarter of the $55 billion gross state product comes from that sector. New Jersey was hit very heavily by the 1975 recession, and state economists feared it might never register a total recovery.

The Jersey business firm which has traditionally exercised the most influence in politics is Johnson & Johnson, first under the late General Robert

W. Johnson. Old General Johnson used to swing back and forth from left to right in politics. Johnson and Johnson pushes its employees into public life; of 38,000, more than 500 hold some sort of elective or appointive office, most of them in New Jersey.

Warner-Lambert Pharmaceuticals has had connections at the highest places through its honorary board chairman, Elmer Bobst, so long a friend and helper of Richard M. Nixon that he was known as "Uncle Elmer" at the White House. (Bobst is a rich uncle; he gave $110,000 to the 1972 Republican campaign.) Former Governor Driscoll was an ex-president and board chairman of Warner-Lambert. Other Jersey companies with a potentially great public role include Prudential Insurance, Campbell's Soup at Camden, and Becton Dickinson in Bergen County (a big instrument manufacturer). Among the individuals of unusual influence are W. Paul Stillman, president of the First National State Bank in Newark, Leon Hess of the Hess Oil Company, and Gene Mori, who operates the Garden State Race Track.

In the mid-1960s, the late Dr. V. D. Mattia, president of the pharmaceutical firm of Hoffmann-La Roche, helped a bright young slate of Essex County Republican reform candidates, headed by state senator James H. Wallwork, a former West Pointer, sweep to office. Dr. Mattia's own story—how he rose from the Newark Italian slums to the presidency of an internationally owned company—illustrated an upward mobility in Jersey that many states, especially in the eastern U. S., would not provide. Mattia was the same man who won some measure of national fame for refusing to cooperate with the Pharmaceutical Manufacturers Association's national advertising campaign to improve the industry's image and take the heat off customer complaints of high drug prices.

Tourism is a vitally important part of New Jersey's economy, bringing in some $2.7 billion a year from visitors to Jersey resorts, historic sites, and conventions. This business, plus heavy intra- and interstate commuting, helped to justify the vast superhighway net constructed within the state since World War II. New Jersey is fortunate it made the investment when it did, because even with the hundreds of miles of new roads, it still has the most densely traveled highways in the nation.

The New Jersey Turnpike, America's busiest toll road, now carries more than 90 million vehicles a year. When the turnpike opened in 1951, the projection had been for an eventual annual load of 30 million vehicles—in 1980! The turnpike stretches from the Delaware Memorial Bridge in the southern part of the state to the George Washington Bridge near New York, a distance of 118 miles, plus spurs to connect with the Pennsylvania Turnpike and Holland Tunnel. A multilane widening of the turnpike's "bread and butter" stretch from Newark to New Brunswick has been completed. And traffic has also soared beyond expectations on the 173-mile Garden State Parkway, opened in 1955, which runs along the entire length of the Jersey Coast and then through Newark to connect with the New York State Thruway.

The stories of gargantuan traffic tie-ups on the big toll roads, and especially the monster smash-ups when fog hits the New Jersey Turnpike, are almost legendary. Driving along their congested stretches can be among the more dehumanizing experiences of travel anywhere in America today. But the New Jersey highway authorities took one offbeat step when they commissioned a Garden State Arts Center, designed by Edward Durell Stone, on the parkway 30 miles south of Newark. The center, which opened in 1968, has botanical gardens, an art exhibition mall, nature trails, and a large amphitheater. The cost of the center, $10.5 million, was just a tiny fraction of the cost of the superhighways. But it *was* a first step toward humanizing the great macadam and concrete octopus.

New Jersey still has important agriculture—large dairy herds raised in the Appalachian valleys of the northwest, truck farming for vegetables on the rich soil of central and southwestern Jersey, peaches and apples on the sandy coastal plain, cranberries in the marshy bogs, and poultry in the Pine Barrens. Other crops of note include tomatoes, corn, asparagus, spinach, blueberries, and strawberries. In recent years about $250 million has been realized in annual farm income—the most per acre of any state, but a small overall figure compared to the country's major farm states. The land for farming seems to be shrinking at an alarming rate as suburban subdivisions, factories, highways, and shopping centers gobble up more and more fertile farm territory. Dairy herds are moving toward extinction. In 1960, there were 1.8 million acres in farms in New Jersey; in 1969, the figure had shrunk to one million and was still diminishing. The number of actual farms has declined even more precipitously: from 25,000 in 1930 to less than 8,500 by latest count. One can almost envision the day when only two farm occupations will survive: raising race horses for the sportsmen and race tracks, and growing ornamental shrubs for suburbia's million yards.

Politics: Prototype Suburbia and the History of Hague

New Jersey has always had close, competitive two-party politics. Now, like the prototype suburban state it is, Jersey is developing prototype suburban politics. Angelo Baglivo described it this way in a newspaper report in the early 1970s:

At this stage in New Jersey's political evolution, there is one dominant new force that is shattering traditional voting patterns. It is the independent voter who lives in his mortgaged home in the suburbs. On his middle-income salary, he frets about rising taxes—but demands more and better services from government.

He worries about the quality of education his children are receiving—but votes against increased school budgets and complains about teacher strikes and student activists.

He expresses sympathy with the plight of the disadvantaged in the city ghettos —but is frightened by black militancy and asks where it is all going to end.

When these voters lived by the thousands in the apartments and cold-water flats of Newark and Jersey City and Paterson, they formed the backbone of the Democratic machines. Jobs and favors from the local district leader were what politics and government were all about.

But they have migrated now to the sprawling housing developments of Manalapan Township in Monmouth and Madison Township in Middlesex and Jackson Township in Ocean County. They own homes, pay taxes and bills for utilities, have children in school and commute to work on congested roads and behind-schedule trains.

Government and the men who run it have direct impact now on the family budget and day-to-day life; there is a personal stake, an involvement in politics that was not there before. It has produced a voter who is neither Democrat, nor Republican; neither left-wing nor right-wing.

He seldom votes the straight party line. He votes his self-interest, or what he thinks it is. He can be attracted by the personal appeal of a candidate—that overworked word, "charisma." But most of all he is influenced by the times, the events of the day. . . . If there is any generalization that can be made about him in New Jersey, it is that he appears to prefer the middle ground of politics.

The elections of the past few years are dramatic proof of modern Jerseyans' scorn of party regularity. Compare, for example, the last three contests for the governorship. In 1965, Democratic incumbent Richard J. Hughes won reelection with a sweeping 363,572-vote plurality (57.4 percent), at that time the biggest vote lead of any governor in New Jersey history. On his coattails, Democrats won 2–1 majorities in both houses of the legislature, capturing the senate for the first time in half a century. Just two years later, in an astonishing reversal of political sentiment, the Republicans both dislodged the Democrats from control of both houses, and amassed 3–1 majorities themselves. In 1969, a year after Richard Nixon narrowly carried the state, Republican William Cahill won the governorship in a landslide even bigger than Hughes'. Cahill's huge margin of 500,902 votes (59.7 percent) helped keep Republicans in firm control of the legislature. But in the 1971 elections, the GOP lost most of its majority in the state senate and was on the verge of losing control of the assembly. Then in 1973—just a year after Richard Nixon carried New Jersey by a record margin—Democrat Brendan Byrne was elected governor with a plurality almost as large as Hughes' and Cahill's put together—some 721,378 votes (67.4 percent). And the Democrats won a 3–1 margin in the senate and an incredible 66–14 margin in the assembly.

Such wild gyrations in partisan preference are increasingly common around the nation, yet in few states are they as pronounced as in New Jersey. Certainly issues like taxes and corruption played a role in these turnarounds, as we shall see; governors of both parties have usually failed to get tax reform plans through the legislature and have too often appointed officials who proved unworthy of their—and the people's—trust. But beyond that, predominantly suburban New Jersey seems to respond to choices in a general election with something like unanimity. Bergen County in northern New Jersey, middle-to-upper income and the onetime banner Republican county in the state, actually went Democratic in the gubernatorial elections of 1965 and 1973—and by wide margins in each case. Indeed, in 1973 Democrat Byrne carried every county in the state but one, Cape May, the sparsely-populated home of his Republican opponent. Yet four years before, Republican Cahill had carried all 21 counties, including some that had once voted Democratic as surely as night follows day, such as Hudson (Jersey City) and Essex (Newark).

As we have seen, though, increasing suburbanization does not necessarily mean increasing Republicanism. In most elections, the suburbs are now much less Republican than they were 10 to 15 years ago. Two factors seem to be at work: the fact that a voter does not automatically shift to the GOP when he moves to the suburbs, and the weakening of the old-line Republican rural county organizations. While the Democrats labor under the shadow of now largely discredited machine politicians in many of the older counties, in some of the smaller and faster-growing counties that disadvantage belongs to the Republicans.

Though their days seem to be numbered, a word should be said about the county party bosses who made such an indelible mark on New Jersey. The entry into politics of the most illustrious Jerseyan of all time, Woodrow Wilson, was in fact sponsored by Democratic bosses such as James Smith, Jr., and James Nugent of Essex County and Robert Davis of Hudson County. (After Wilson's nomination for governor had been steamrollered by these worthies, who historians record "had auctioned off the state to the burgeoning railroads and utilities in return for juicy stock options and side deals," Wilson repudiated them, thus asserting his independence and beginning his climb to national fame.)

From 1917 to the late 1940s, the Democratic boss of Hudson County and mayor of Jersey City was Frank ("I Am The Law") Hague, a perfect example of his breed: born of immigrant parents and raised in the teeming Horseshoe slum of Jersey City, a devout and almost puritanical Roman Catholic who rose to power first on the issue of "reform," an intractable opponent whose enemies would often end up in jail—or the hospital—and an almost totally uneducated man with a taste for personal violence.* Yet Hague showed benevolence toward his constituents, who were rewarded for their support with Christmas food baskets, summertime boat rides and picnics, a great free medical center, and the highest city tax rates in America.

Hague himself earned only $7,500 a year as mayor, but by his own secret admission a few years before his death, he ended up worth at least $8 million. He said his wealth came from stocks and lucky investments; the more probable truth was that he got rich from the pound of flesh exacted from those who did business with Jersey City, and especially the gamblers who operated big off-track betting and numbers games there throughout his

---

* A major source for much of the account which follows is an article, "I Am The Law," by Thomas J. Fleming, himself the son of a Jersey City ward leader, which appeared in *American Heritage* for June 1969.

reign. (On the other hand, Hague drove out organized prostitution and was so intolerant of mobsters that his city detectives, disguised as bums, hung around the ferry slips and railroad stations, ready to ship any suspicious characters right back to New York.) Every Hudson County office-holder had to contribute 3 percent of his salary to Hague's organization, supposedly to finance election campaigns. "Jersey City Has Everything for Industry" was a slogan of those years, and a sweetheart contract was available for new factories since there was not a labor union in Hudson County which Hague had not reduced to docility.

Hague demanded extraordinary efficiency and breathtaking effort of his political machine. Not only did the Irish line up with him, but his ward and precinct captains found thousands of latter-day immigrants—Italians, Czechs, Poles, and Slovaks, many of them illiterates—who were cajoled into registering and then totally controlled. Republican poll watchers were bought out and made into "Hague Republicans." Thus it was that Hudson County could produce incredible pluralities, often in excess of 100,000 votes, at election time. Hague controlled the governorship for most of the 1920s and 1930s, since the Hudson County bloc vote was enough to control a Democratic primary and usually a general election. Hague delivered Hudson for the Democratic Presidential ticket by such huge margins in 1932, 1940, and 1944 that Republican pluralities in the rest of the state were overcome and Jersey turned to Franklin D. Roosevelt.* FDR openly embraced Hague in return, and Hague was chairman of both the Democratic Hudson County and New Jersey State Committees, as well as a member and vice chairman of the Democratic National Committee. He was one of the nation's great power brokers.

Hague's downfall came in the 1940s when he began to lose touch by spending inordinate amounts of time sojouring at the Plaza in New York or at his mansion on Biscayne Bay in Miami. A succession of Republican governors cut back on his power, and then rebellion arose within Jersey City itself, led by then ward boss John V. Kenny. In 1947, Hague resigned as mayor and had his nephew, Frank Hague Eggers, installed in his place; two years later, in a great wave of revulsion against Hagueism, the voters turned out Eggers in favor of Kenny.

The night of that election, Kenny's supporters snake-danced through the city streets and then stormed City Hall, hoping to find incriminating records. But the organization had known for hours that it was beaten, and nothing was found except charred paper in the furnace room. According to some witnesses, two suitcases full of money had been removed to a vault of the First National Bank earlier in the afternoon. Hague became a virtual exile from Jersey City, living in a Park Avenue apartment but fearing to enter Jersey because a subpoena was always waiting in connection with a

---

* Only in one FDR election—1936—did the rest of New Jersey register a plurality for Roosevelt. Those who now romanticize the Roosevelt era should not forget that an important part of his electoral strength rested on the likes of Frank Hague.

$15 million suit filed against him by the three percenters trying to regain their tribute money of the past decades. Thus the last half of Hague's oft repeated statement—"In the Horseshoe I was born, in the Horseshoe I will die"—was proven false. He died in New York on January 1, 1956, and only then was his body returned to Jersey City for burial. A sparse crowd of Jersey Cityites turned out to watch the funeral, one of them an elderly woman standing in the street holding an American flag and a hand-lettered sign. The sign read: "God have mercy on his sinful, greedy soul."

Hague's removal from the Jersey scene did not end bossism. John V. Kenny, as it turned out, remained the power upon or behind the throne in Hudson County into the early 1970s, presiding over a system rife with graft, vote-roll padding, nepotism in government, and outright thievery. There was scarcely a let-up, for instance, in the ancient 3 percent for the Democratic organization that all city hall employees felt obliged to pay. The tribute always had to be paid in cash—no checks accepted; the income reportedly amounted to millions of dollars that the organization could use secretly or to finance campaigns. The political kickbacks were augmented by a 3 percent kickback demand on all contracts done with the city or county. Kenny retired as mayor in 1953 to concentrate on running the organization, or as the United States Attorney later put it, to oversee the "plunder" of public money.

Late in 1970, Kenny and his satrap, Jersey City Mayor Thomas J. Whelan, were among nine persons indicted by a federal grand jury on counts of extortion, conspiracy, and falsifying income tax returns. Kenny's case was severed from the others because of illness, but the other eight defendants were convicted following a 1971 trial in which the government estimated they had netted $3.3 million in kickbacks. "Anyone who wanted to do business with Hudson County or Jersey City was required to pay tribute, to kick back," U.S. Attorney Herbert Stern said in his summation. He said the trial would last a year if every contractor forced to make kickbacks were to testify. (Kenny later pleaded guilty and was sentenced to 18 years' imprisonment.)

During the trial, one witness said that Bernard G. Murphy, the Jersey City purchasing agent and alleged "bag man" in the conspiracy, climbed aboard a private jet at Newark Airport to tell a contractor that a $3 million kickback in cash would be required if he wanted to be the successful bidder on a $40 million reservoir project. That particular offer was rejected, but other evidence indicated that Mayor Whelan and City Council President Thomas Flaherty, another defendant, had stashed away $1.2 million in cash and bonds in a Miami Beach bank.

The 1971 trial, revealing a depth of corruption almost unprecedented in American history, would most probably never have taken place if the opposition political party, the Republicans, had not held national power at the time. Old Frank Hague was protected from prosecution by a Democratic administration in Washington during his last years in power.

After his conviction, Whelan was removed from office and a special autumn 1971 election held to fill the remaining eighteen months of his term.

The Kenny organization at first decided to endorse no candidate for the seat, but then came out for a contender who ended up third in the balloting. The winner was a 30-year-old public health physician, Dr. Paul Jordan, candidate of the reformist Community Action Council. "Free at last!" Jordan exulted at a victory celebration. "We're free at last. Boss politics is dead in Jersey City, after 22 years of political corruption." And indeed, for the first time in living memory, Jersey City appeared to have elected a *truly* honest mayor. (Later on, some of the luster was taken away when Jordan became immersed in the seemingly inevitable political dealings of Hudson County. But he showed political courage in 1975 by dismissing 472 city employees, including a sizable number of the politically potent police and firemen, to meet a $20.4 million shortfall in the city's budget.)

Outside of Hudson County, the late Dennis F. Carey of Essex has probably been the most powerful Democratic boss of the last several years. Frank S. ("Hap") Farley was the best known equivalent on the Republican side. The power of the county chairman was ingrained in the basic structure of New Jersey government and politics. Down to the legislative reapportionment of 1967, for instance, virtually all public officials—senators, assemblymen (lower house members), freeholders, and sheriffs—were elected in each county at large. The county leader who controlled his party's machinery controlled the nominating process and thus the access to power. Inevitably, all patronage began to flow through his hands, and if his party controlled the governorship, it would be to the governor's interest to clear all local appointments with the county chairman first. Thus the state party organization was relatively weak, while the county chairmen operated like arrogant feudal barons.

Often a county chairman could tell the members of his county's legislative delegation to Trenton just how they should vote. When Democratic Governor Richard Hughes proposed a graduated state income tax in the mid-1960s, for instance, the bill was scuttled by the Hudson and Essex County Democratic leaders who forbade their delegations to vote for it. (When we asked a high-ranking Democratic official of that era why the leaders had bucked Hughes on the tax, a revenue idea which accords with general Democratic party philosophy and state platforms, he replied that they had done so to protect their "personal" incomes!) The state then had to turn to the general sales tax, which hits the masses of low- and middle-class people in counties like Hudson and Essex much harder than the affluent suburban population. Though Robert Meyner and Hughes, both highly regarded Democratic governors, presided over Jersey government from 1954 to 1970, it might almost be said that five big county Democratic leaders actually controlled New Jersey in that time. In 1961, for instance, scarcely anyone in New Jersey had ever heard of Richard J. Hughes until a small conference, dominated by the big county bosses, met and chose him as what they thought would be the sacrificial lamb for the gubernatorial race against the prestigious former U. S. Secretary of Labor, Republican James P. Mitchell. At the time, Hughes's sole distinction had been as a lower court judge. But as it turned out, the bosses had hit on a jewel—a warm, gregarious, and totally honorable man, who turned out to be the greatest New Jersey campaigner of modern times and in the autumn eked out a narrow victory over Mitchell.* But today in New Jersey even Hughes' closest friends will tell one that his major fault was in trusting people too much—especially the bosses. He went along with their recommendations of men to be county prosecutors, for instance, thus failing to avert the penetration of organized crime that would spring to view at the end of his term and badly tarnish his image.

Hughes himself became one of the first to warn his party to mend its ways through democratization—an end to the day of the closed, back-room direction by a handful of leaders—and finding a role for youth and people like the 1968 backers of McCarthy and Kennedy. In 1970, Hughes endorsed the controversial proposals of a Democratic party reform commission, headed by one of the state's most prominent congressmen, Frank Thompson, Jr. The Thompson committee proposed reapportioning of various party committees to eliminate vastly differing population bases of the members, and also direct election in primaries of county chairmen. Not surprisingly, the ideas encountered stiff resistance by party regulars, grown indolent and self-satisfied after 16 years of patronage support by Democratic governors. Hughes has gone so far as to call the Democrats a party "searching for its soul," the present status akin to "lying on our backs, clawing the air like a dying cockroach . . . but not quite that bad." (Hughes himself is out of politics now. In an unusual move, Gov. Cahill during his last months in office, appointed him chief justice of the state supreme court.)

Part of the Democrats' problem is the disorganization of the youthful and dissident members it might like to incorporate. The New Democratic Coalition, formed in the late 1960s to undertake that very task, fell apart in warring factions. New Jersey also lacks a strong, activist labor movement that could act as a catalyst of reform. The state AFL-CIO was long dominated by conservative building trade unions, which withhold support from outspokenly liberal Democrats and tend to be hung up on the race problem. Some of the old CIO unions broke away in 1964 to form a more aggressive and politically liberal state Industrial Union Council, which was headed initially by Joel Jacobson, the UAW's most prominent leader in New Jersey (later appointed by Governor Byrne to the public utility commission). The IUC and UAW (the latter with about 50,000 workers in Jersey) do the most of any unions to define issues, promote voter registration, and the like. New Jersey has 737,000 union members, who make up 31 percent of the work force, the 15th highest percentage in the U. S.; if unified, they could be a potent political voice in the state.

Another ticklish problem for the Democrats is how to retain the overwhelming support they have been receiving from blacks in the cities, es-

* Mitchell helped Hughes out by showing little sensitivity to New Jersey issues and then, after a few drinks one day, falling in a bathtub and breaking his leg, so that he couldn't campaign.

pecially as minorities gain in political sophistication and know-how and challenge the old white power structures in the urban counties—the process presently taking place, for instance, in Newark, which has twice elected a black mayor. The black population would justify a black congressman, but none has been elected to date. A number of aggressive younger black leaders claim they have been excluded from the important decision-making processes in the Democratic party.

Ethnic rivalries may also plague the Democrats. Many of their top leaders are now Irish in a state with many more Italians, who will be clamoring for a gubernatorial candidate of their own kind soon.

The Republicans' problems are both like and unlike the Democrats'. The party has had patronage-oriented county chairmen like Atlantic's Farley, but they have been neither as numerous or as powerful as their Democratic counterparts. The Republican governors—Alfred E. Driscoll in the immediate postwar years and Cahill recently—have been strong men intent on running their own shows, largely immune to county influence. However, there is a clear ideological split between the Republican moderate-liberals, including Cahill, Case, many of the congressmen and state legislative leaders, and the more conservative factions. The power of the GOP's conservative bloc was substantially undercut by reapportionment in the 1960s, which ended the old system in which each county had a single state senator, regardless of population. More recently, conservative Republicans have made major efforts to win the party's gubernatorial nomination. All of these fell slightly short of success until 1973, when Congressman Charles Sandman, who had run and lost twice before, upset Governor Cahill in the primary. Corruption was the issue which made the difference; some of Cahill's top appointees had been convicted or were facing criminal charges. Interestingly, this was the same Sandman who so loudly and sarcastically defended Richard Nixon at the House Judiciary Committee hearings a year later.

But the conservatives' triumph was short-lived. Despite the counsel of consultant F. Clifton White (who put together the Goldwater prenomination campaign in 1964 and planned the strategy that elected James Buckley Senator from New York in 1970), Sandman was snowed under in the Byrne landslide. That left the New Jersey Republican Party in a shambles. Sandman's hand-picked state chairman was soon gone, but the party was faced with the fact that its incumbent moderate governor and the conservative who had beaten him had both been repudiated by the voters. Moreover, federal investigations had taken a toll not only of the men around Cahill, but also of some of the party's once promising young leadership. A prime example is Nelson Gross, who delivered crucial votes to Richard Nixon at the 1968 Republican national convention and managed Cahill's campaign a year later. (Gross also ran unsuccessfully for the Senate in 1970, but his real forte was campaign management.) Sadly, Gross was convicted of income tax and fraud charges in 1974, and his political career, like those of so many figures in both parties in New Jersey, was over.

The story of how the corruption issue determined the outcome of the 1973 state election properly goes back to 1970, when under court order federal prosecutors made public tapes of wiretapped conversations of a local racketeer, Angelo "Gyp" DeCarlo. The tapes were full of references to major New Jersey politicians, most of whom, if the mobsters could be believed, were on the take. But one name stood out, that of judge and former Essex County prosecutor Brendan Byrne. DeCarlo (whose jail sentence was commuted by President Nixon a month after the 1972 election) was recorded as saying, "It's Byrne, we can't make him"—a way of saying Byrne could not be bribed. Another voice on the tape replied, "What's wrong with Byrne, doesn't he like money?"

Nevertheless, Byrne did not become a major political figure until well into the 1973 race. Just days before the filing deadline, he walked into Governor Cahill's office, resigned his judgeship, and in an outer chamber announced his candidacy for governor. He had already been promised the support of the new Hudson County organization, and two other candidates immediately dropped out of the race. Byrne won the fragmented primary easily, and ran even better in the general election. Some observers claimed that he lacked charisma and was a wooden speaker, but that didn't seem to matter to the voters. What was relevant was the Byrne slogan: "One honest man can make a difference." Byrne's margin might have been less if he had given the voters an inkling of what would become his stand on the thorny tax issue, since his Republican opponent, Sandman, was a firm opponent of any income tax.

Amid all these confusing cross-currents, New Jersey voters still like to reelect incumbents to most offices. The three governors before Cahill all won second terms with ease.* New Jersey political reporters have difficulty recalling the last time a sitting U.S. Senator was defeated for reelection (it was in 1942). Congressmen, once elected (and unless indicted), tend to win regardless of their districts' political balance. New Jersey has propelled few important leaders onto the national stage since the days of Woodrow Wilson (a born Virginian). The two Senators of recent years, Republican Clifford Case and Democrat Harrison A. Williams Jr., are able men but are not regarded as heavies on the Washington scene. Case's voice is one of quiet, responsible liberalism among Senate Republicans. He is a bit of a loner, a man of high intellectual ability and moral stature with strong commitment in the civil rights area but easily faulted as a press-release do-gooder. Williams, a liberal who became chairman of the Senate Labor Committee in 1971, undercut his own effectiveness for years by heavy drinking and partying ways until he finally went on the wagon around the end of 1968. (Earlier that year, the New Jersey chapter of the NAACP publicly censured Williams for behavior unbecoming a Senator after an appearance he made at the group's

---

* Governors are elected for four-year terms with elections in odd-numbered years, coinciding neither with Presidential nor congressional elections. Only three other states—Kentucky, Louisiana, and Mississippi—have an analogous pattern of "off-season" gubernatorial elections.

state convention.) Williams is best known for his work on pension reform, migrant worker and urban mass transit problems but remains largely unknown.

On the House side, Rep. Frank Thompson, Jr., of Trenton has built a record as one of the most articulate liberal Democrats and has a high-ranking slot on the Education and Labor Committee. Rep. William B. Widnall from Bergen County is the highly regarded ranking Republican on the House Banking and Currency Committee, where he has taken a leading position on housing legislation, and Rep. Peter H. B. Frelinghuysen of Morris County, scion of a family prominent in New Jersey public life for more than 200 years, was the ranking Republican on the House Foreign Affairs Committee at the time of his 1974 retirement. Frelinghuysen's outstanding successor was Millicent Fenwick, a vocal champion of consumer causes who had been director of the state division of consumer affairs under Cahill. In Congress, she quickly took aim at the Interstate Commerce Commission, alleging that its unnecessary regulations were costing consumers $16 billion a year.

But the most famous and probably most distinguished member of the New Jersey delegation is a man not very well known outside his native Newark until 1974. He is Peter W. Rodino, Jr., whose career until that year was mainly distinguished by advocacy of immigration law reform and the fact that he easily won renomination and reelection in a black-majority district in 1972. That victory, plus the defeat the same year of Emanuel Celler of New York, made Rodino chairman of the House Judiciary Committee, and that position, in turn, gave him critical power when, after the "Saturday Night Massacre" of 1973, the committee got down to serious consideration of the impeachment of President Nixon. Many observers considered Rodino a lightweight, and predicted that there would be massive leaks of testimony and deep partisan splits among the committee's members. But Rodino was able to enlist as Judiciary's chief counsel John Doar, a nominal Republican who was head of the civil rights division in the Kennedy Justice Department, and the committee, except for one week, became just about the most leak-proof body in Washington. Working slowly and deliberately, Rodino was able to satisfy the committee's eager pro-impeachment minority while at the same time retaining bipartisan cooperation on most issues. It was a performance few expected, but there were some clues in Rodino's past. In corruption-ridden Newark he had managed to maintain a clean record, according to no less an authority than former U.S. Attorney Herbert Stern. And in his youth this prosaic man had written both poetry and a couple of novels. It is a strength of the American system that effective leadership appears sometimes when it is needed and from quarters where no one expects to find it.

Among other Jersey congressmen who made a mark in the postwar years were Republican Fred Hartley, coauthor of the Taft-Hartley Labor Relations Act, and J. Parnell Thomas, who was at the center of the Alger Hiss controversy as chairman of the House Un-American Activities Committee in 1947–48 but later went to prison for padding his congressional payroll. *Life* magazine in 1968 accused Congressman Cornelius E. Gallagher from Hudson County of being associated with top Mafia racketeer Joseph Zicarelli; Gallagher was reelected that year and in 1970, but lost his seat after redistricting in 1972 and was eventually sentenced to jail on federal charges.

Only state legislators, more faceless and thus nameless to the general public, tend to get shunted in and out of office rapidly in Jersey. It may be that those fickle suburban voters, once they get the name of an officeholder in their heads, simply vote the familiar until some cataclysmic event propels them to change their habits.

In 1973, New Jersey passed a long-overdue reform of its campaign finance laws, requiring full disclosure of contributions and expenditures of $100 or more; the bill also set up an independent enforcement commission. Soon after its enactment, the law had an effect on the state elections when it was revealed that Governor Cahill and Congressman Sandman had received contributions from men who were indicted on federal charges or were linked to organized crime. Even with disclosure, however, election spending remains a special problem in New Jersey because of the very high costs of television ads on New York City and Philadelphia stations, which naturally charge candidates several times what the fair rate would be for reaching New Jersey alone. Partly for that reason, Governor Byrne pushed legislation for public financing of half the cost of state elections through the legislature in 1974; the law also sets a maximum of $600 on private contributions.

New Jersey has had a presidential primary since 1912, but the elected slates of delegates—at least until the Democratic reform era of the early '70s —were often just creations of the state party organizations. Thus few serious presidential candidates found it worthwhile to enter the nonbinding preference poll held the same day, and the state in effect left it to the professional politicians to decide on its role at national conventions. In 1976, an uncommitted slate favoring Hubert Humphrey and California Gov. Jerry Brown, and promoted by organization Democrats, won easily. Jimmy Carter's poor showing in New Jersey was all but obscured amid the endorsements from other states. As long as the Jersey primary is held on the same day as California's, however, its impact on the national consciousness will probably remain limited.

Under New Jersey law, it is almost ludicrously easy for minor-party candidates to qualify for the ballot. But the power of the major parties, and perhaps the lack of strong ideological movements, has suppressed third- and fourth-partyism on the model of neighboring New York. The last minor party which got any measure of public notice was the one-man effort of Henry Krajewski, a pig farmer from Secaucus. Krajewski ran for President in 1952, 1956, and 1960 on the Poor Man's Party and American Third Party tickets, trying to prove to the world that a poor man could become Chief Executive. George Thayer in *The Farther Shores of Politics* described Krajewski as a Runyonesque character from an earlier age, soft-hearted with a vivid wit. He spoke with a Jersey City accent, scorned the regular parties as "boids of a feather," and pulled stunts like taking a baby pig mascot with him when he filed for President. (The proceedings were disrupted somewhat when the little fellow defecated on some of the more vital documents.) Reporters had a field day covering Krajewski, one of the last men to mock the absurdities of American politics. He died in the 1960s, and Jersey is a poorer place for his departure.

Life Under a New Constitution and the Tax Dilemma

New Jersey state government deserves an "A" for its constitution and organizational simplicity. One can assign a "C" to the ill-staffed but still much-improved legislature. In 1976, the grading for Jersey's traditionally antediluvian tax structure could be raised from "F" to "C"—but by virtue of court pressure, not the wisdom of the legislature.

First the constitution. The state labored until 1947 under an incredibly outmoded constitution of 1844 vintage which gave the governor a three-year term with a prohibition on succeeding himself, let his veto be overridden by simple majorities in the legislature, provided one-year terms for assemblymen (facilitating county boss control of them), and in general fostered wasteful and inefficient government. For instance, the legislature created more than 100 independent or semi-independent agencies which the governor could not control. Some department heads were selected by the legislature, and the terms of officials the governor could pick generally did not coincide with his term, so that he might be stuck for the better part of his time in office with men not in sympathy with him. To top it all off, the court system was complex and cumbersome in the extreme.

Pressure for constitutional reform mounted rapidly in the 1930s, especially as government improvement groups recognized how the old document played into the hands of both Mayor Hague and the rural interests. After several false starts, an entirely new constitution was written in 1947 and approved by the voters the same year. It was practically the opposite of its predecessor. Instead of one of the weakest governors in America, New Jersey suddenly had the strongest. His term was extended to four years, and he could run a second time, he became the only official to be elected statewide, and he received sweeping powers of appointment—the normal "constitutional offices" like attorney general, treasurer, and secretary of state, the heads of all departments, some county administrative officials, members of policy-forming and advisory boards, commissions, agencies, and members of interstate and intrastate authorities. The legislature was given power to create departments, but they could not number more than 20, with no commissions, boards, or agencies independent of them. (Eventually 17 departments emerged, and there has been a proposal in later years to cut the number to six.) The new constitution also strengthened the governor's veto power and gave him authority to convene the legislature at will. In effect, he emerged with power in his state comparable to the President on the federal level.

At the same time, the new constitution took another leaf from the federal document by placing few specific restrictions on the power of the legislature to make laws for the welfare of the state. (One especially annoying provision was included, however: a requirement for voter approval of any state debt beyond a minuscule level. Governmental improvements, especially in the higher education field, have been seriously delayed by this provision.) The new charter extended assemblymen's terms to two years and set senate terms at four years. But it did not change the one-county, one-senator reapportionment rule—a change that only the federal courts were able to effect, two decades later. The 1947 constitution also decreed a simplified and more unified court system, under the clear control and direction of the chief justice of the state supreme court.

So admired was New Jersey's 1947 constitution that when Alaska joined the Union in 1959, the first new state in almost half a century, it copied its basic charter quite closely from the New Jersey model.

In large measure, the New Jersey constitution has lived up to its authors' fondest expectations. Alfred E. Driscoll, the man who was governor when it was passed, is thought by some to have been the finest chief executive in New Jersey's history. A true patrician and intellectual, he is given credit both for guiding the constitution to passage and for implementing it skillfully in the seven additional years he was governor. Indeed, for a man who once described himself as one of the world's worst politicians, Driscoll had a remarkable record of achievement. He was the father of the New Jersey Turnpike and the Garden State Parkway, won passage of early antidiscrimination statutes, obtained passage of a model option municipal charter law (as a result of which most of the larger Jersey cities and many smaller municipalities now operate under strong mayor or council-manager charters in place of the discredited old commission form of local government), and vigorously fought gambling and racketeering. After his retirement he backed state aid for hard-pressed urban areas and a state income tax, played a crucial role in establishment of the Gateway National Recreation Area, and served as vice chairman of the Advisory Commission on Intergovernmental Relations and as president of the National Municipal League. Among other things, he suggested the idea of federal revenue sharing years before its time. From 1970 to the time of his death in 1975, he was chairman of the New Jersey Turnpike Authority.

None of Driscoll's successors could quite match that record, but there were figures of real stature among them. Robert Meyner, amazingly prudent and frugal for a Democratic governor, was the man who brought his party back to respectability in the post-Hague era. Richard Hughes was a warmhearted liberal who made a manly effort to get Jersey to face up to its fiscal follies by enacting a broad-based tax. William Cahill, a tough Irishman, deserves credit for fighting for Jersey's interests in the New York Port Authority, holding budgets in line, and seeking, though unsuccessfully, a state income tax. Brendan Byrne, three quarters through his term at this writing, fought hard for the state income tax that could provide a key to a saner revenue system in the state. But politically, as we will note shortly, Byrne proved to be one of the most inept governors of any American state in recent times.

Unfortunately, even estimable New Jersey governors have not always made such estimable appointments. Hughes's secretary of state, Robert Burkhardt, and Cahill's secretary of state, Paul Sherwin, and state treasurer, Joseph McCrane, were all found guilty of federal crimes. In retrospect, Hughes seems to have been too willing to listen to the advice of Democratic county leaders, and Cahill erred in packing the State House with many of his South Jersey cronies.*

Even Byrne, the "Mr. Clean" swept into office on an anticorruption tide, soon had problems in the ethics area. His secretary of state, J. Edward Crabiel, a contracting firm executive apparently appointed to the post as a payoff for his support in the 1973 primary, was indicted for conspiracy to rig prices and fix prices on road construction contracts in the late 1960s. Crabiel was acquitted, the judge's decision revolving principally around expiration of the five-year statute of limitations in the case. Two other co-defendants in the case had previously pleaded guilty. Crabiel was permitted to return to his position in the Byrne administration.

In 1975 Byrne also let it to be known that he was considering recommending abolition of the New Jersey state commission of investigation (SCI), which had been set up six years before to fight organized crime and governmental corruption. The SCI had spearheaded some 20 major investigations that led to nearly 50 indictments. Byrne later backed down on abolishing the commission, making the remarkable comment that the negative reports on which he had based his position were "hearsay." The sponsor of the bill to do away with the commission, state senator Martin Greenberg, was a former law partner of the governor; the press made due note of the fact that one of the Greenberg's current law partners represented Tony "Bananas" Caponigro, an organized crime figure who had been called by the SCI for questioning. Few who knew Byrne believed he was deliberately trying to shield criminals, but the episode underscored, at a minimum, his political ineptitude.

The legislature was strengthened by the constitution but remained hung up for a number of years thereafter on the dual spikes of malapportionment and the caucus system. Equally populated districts were decreed for assemblymen, but senators were still elected on the old one-a-county basis, creating districts so grossly unequal that less than a fifth of the voters could elect a majority of the senate. Then the Republican caucus (sometimes just 11 of

* To be really "in" with Cahill, according to one of his protagonists in Trenton, "you got to be not only Irish, Catholic, Republican, and from South Jersey, but then you got to come from a triangle defined by the Garden State Racetrack, Mt. Holly, and Cherry Hill."

the 21 senators) would meet behind closed doors to scrutinize all bills and decide whether they should go to the senate floor for action. Thousands of meritorious bills—and probably some bad ones—met their death in the caucus. By tradition, the Republican senators voted en bloc, despite their personal positions, in support of any action taken by the caucus. Thus an old wheeler-dealer like Atlantic County's Hap Farley could control the entire senate by getting just five other senators (a majority of the Republican caucus) to vote with him.

For years, Democrats made a chief campaign plank out of the encrusted caucus system, which endured until the courts forced equally populated districts in the mid-1960s and the senate fell to the Democrats. When the Republicans returned to power in 1968, they reestablished their old caucus, but without malapportionment it seemed to lack its most Mephistophelean attributes. In the assembly, the caucus principle continues under the Democrats in the form of a Democratic "luncheon club." Overall it is probably necessary to have some mechanism to regulate the flow of bills and kill controversial measures. But one of the unhappy results of any caucus-type system is that it undermines the authority of the existing legislative committees, which sometimes lapse into nearly total inactivity. Only one or two of the committees have viable, full-time staffing, and the office of the legislative counsel, though expanded in recent years, is tremendously overworked. In short, the Jersey legislature is lacking in substantive work done by more than a select few legislators. Part of the problem is the weird scheduling practice, in which the legislature keeps meeting almost year-round, but only one or two days in each week. Members are expected to commute on chosen days (presently Monday and Thursday) from their homes to Trenton. When they arrive, they have no offices to work in, and they just mill around the assembly and senate chambers. Sometimes, before they have time for any serious debate or work, it is time to commute home again. The State House building is incredibly crowded, but although a new legislative building was authorized in the late 1960s, work has not gone forward; no recent governor has welcomed the prospect of a legislature with enough space and staff to be independent. All these impediments led the national Citizens Conference on State Legislatures, in its 1971 report evaluating legislative bodies across the country, to rank New Jersey only 32nd in terms of its decision-making capabilities.

These impediments notwithstanding, the Jersey legislature has produced some highly regarded leaders in the past few years, especially in its senate. The assembly, by contrast, is encumbered with an archaic rule limiting the presiding officer to a single two-year term. The assembly speaker chosen in 1974, in the wake of the big Democratic landslide the year before, was Howard Woodson, a black minister from Trenton. Woodson thus became the first black presiding officer in an American legislative body.

Such changes notwithstanding, events still transpire in Trenton that remind one of the days of Hap Farley's caucus. Consider the case of state senator Alene Ammond of Cherry Hill, who was expelled from the Democratic caucus by unanimous vote of her colleagues in 1975 after she openly accused several of her colleagues of blatant conflicts of interest and revealed secret caucus deliberations. A federal court quickly ordered her readmission to the caucus, on the grounds that her exclusion would have a "chilling effect" on her freedom of speech and deprive her constituents of equal protection of the laws. (Impartial observers suggested that Mrs. Ammond's charges about her colleagues, while exaggerated and lacking full evidence, often contained a germ of truth.)

When one talks with responsible Jersey legislative leaders, the claim is made that the quality of legislators, and their independence from the old county organizations, has risen dramatically in recent years. But the county rings have not lost all their power (particularly in Hudson, Essex, and Camden), and the public's perception is close to Mrs. Ammond's—that most legislators are in the business for financial gain. State senate president Frank Dodds told us: "I'm completing 10 years in the legislature. I'm discouraged and I'm embarrassed sometimes. Five years ago you could call yourself a politician with some pride and dignity. Today for excellent reasons, including the national impact of Watergate, the people just have no faith. . . . Do I leave because I'm embarrassed? I honestly don't know."

Beyond the ethics issue, the public mood in New Jersey by the mid-1970s had developed into a general aversion to government scarcely imaginable in earlier times in America. Gerald Ford's exploitation of the anti-tax theme, while stumping in Jersey, may have been responsible for his 2 percent margin of victory in the 1976 New Jersey presidential race. Ann Klein, Byrne's commissioner of institutions and agencies, described to Haynes Johnson of the Washington *Post* the reception she received when she went before a Bergen County citizens' meeting in 1975 to argue the need for an income tax in the face of the state's fiscal crisis:

> They practically turned the place into a riot. They were saying they don't want government, that government shouldn't be providing all these services, that it's socialism, that they don't want their pockets ripped off by the politicians. Every once in a while somebody would get up and say, "But my child's in a day care center and I wouldn't be able to work if I didn't have that"—and they would boo and hiss. I mean it was just an unbelievable meeting, and I've gone around campaigning for the legislature, for the governorship, for the last 20 years and I've never seen anything like this meeting. . . .
> It's strange, but the public really does hate government. It's like the total disintegration of a society.

Yet this same state government—for all its faults—has on occasion tried to be responsive to citizens' needs, to make government accessible to them. In 1974, Gov. Byrne pushed through the legislature the cabinet-level position of public advocate, to look into each and every agency in terms of services delivered to the public, their efficiency and dollar-effectiveness. The department has been described by a supporter as "the gadfly in government that stings the bureaucratic beast whenever it sits on the people."

Six major divisions were set up under the public advocate—a public defender insulated against political pressures through a fixed five-year term, inmate advocacy and parole revocation, defense, mental health advocacy, public interest advocacy, rate counsel, and citizen complaints and dispute settlement. In its first two years of operation, the department received more than 8,800 individual citizen complaints about how the state government was treating them. Apparently the service is well received by Jersey citizens. In a random survey of callers conducted by the Eagleton Institute of Rutgers University; 71 percent rated the service excellent or good; 90 percent said they would contact the office if they had a complaint in the future.

When it comes to state fiscal responsibility, New Jersey has reason to hang its head in shame. This is not because the state and local tax burden the average New Jerseyan pays is particularly low—the figure in 1975 was 11.2 percent of personal income, compared to the national average of 11.9 percent and the Mid-Atlantic average of 13.3 percent. The tax burden in 22 years, in fact, rose 68 percent in New Jersey, the fastest rate of growth of all but nine states. Where the real problem came was in the level of government which raised the money. Until 1976, state-level taxes in Jersey, related to income, were the lowest among the 50 states. But property taxes, raised almost entirely by local government, were so high that only one other state (New Hampshire) raised a greater percentage of its revenue from that source—so notorious for its regressivity and imbalance of public funds between affluent and poorer communities.

The excessive reliance on local taxation went back to the 18th century, when the primary wealth of Jersey was in land for agriculture and the colonial assembly delegated part of its taxing power to the counties, thus beginning a tradition of unfettered "home rule" which endures to this day. With its perennial inferiority complex vis-à-vis its neighbors, New Jersey seemed to feel through its history that (1) it lacked the financial resources for major universities or other facilities, and (2) in any case out-of-staters could be taxed to make up any shortage that property taxes failed to produce. In the 19th century, the Camden and Amboy Railroad, in return for the monopoly given it by the legislature, charged "transit duties" on all passengers and freight passing through (but not originating in) New Jersey. The yield was enough to finance the entire state government for many years, at the expense of citizens of other states. Along the same lines, a proposal was made in 1963 to float a $750 million bond issue for both current and capital needs. The bonds would have been amortized by toll receipts on the New Jersey Turnpike, again fleecing out-of-staters for Jersey's own expenses. Strangely, the voters turned down this idea, but in Trenton one still heard dark forebodings about the angry citizen reaction that would await any politician who raised taxes.

Only by the greatest wrench with instinct and tradition did the legislature bring itself to enact a sales tax in 1966. (Up to that year, Jersey had been one of only three states in the entire country without some form of broadbased tax, either on sales or income.) In 1970, the sales tax was increased from 3 to 5 percent to meet an impending budget crisis, but any-one with a rudimentary knowledge of state finances knew it was only a matter of time until Jersey joined its neighbors with an income tax. Local property taxes were raising about $2 billion a year, some $200,000 more than *all* other state and local taxes in New Jersey, including the sales tax. The property tax is an oppressive burden for everyone in the state, but has reached disaster proportions in big urban counties like Essex and Hudson, where low-income blacks have flooded into the center cities and the burdens of sharply increased public employee salaries and welfare are almost in-tolerable. Urban tax rates, in fact, are threatening the extinction of Jersey's cities as viable economic entities.

Still, New Jersey has tried to "gimmick" its way out of fundamental tax reform. A beautiful case in point was the state lottery that went into opera-tion in 1970 after an overwhelming referendum approval of the people. De-signed to outclass and outperform the fairly disappointing records of the state lotteries in operation at that time (New York and New Hampshire), the New Jersey version offered weekly drawings, less expensive tickets, and free availability of the tickets in supermarkets, drugstores, newsstands, and the like. Lottery proponents led New Jerseyans to believe that the lottery would be such a bonanza that the state's tax problems would be solved. In fact, the New Jersey lottery was much more successful than the earlier versions in other states had been. But in 1974 it was producing a mere four-tenths of one percent of total state and local government revenue in the state. In 1975 New Jersey tried to juice up its lottery revenue by going to a "pick-your-own-number" game, an attempt to compete with the illegal numbers games. State officials told us that no dramatic increase in revenues could be ex-pected, however.

But to face reality and accept an income tax—that leap into the un-known was taken by Jersey state legislators in 1976 only after the state supreme court closed the state's 2,500 public schools to force the legislature to modernize school finances. And even then New Jersey residents were treated to the spectacle of the legislature deadlocked for a week while the doors remained barred to 100,000 summer students and 4,000 teachers. The income tax measure had been passed, in one form or another, by the Assembly five times in the previous five years, but was always rejected by the Senate. Finally it squeaked through the upper chamber by one vote, and Gov. Byrne quickly signed it.

The state legislature had been on notice from the state supreme court since 1973 that it would have to effect a total revamping on the state's school financing system. The decision had been based on the court's finding that the existing system violated the section of the constitution which pro-vided that "the Legislature shall provide for the maintenance and support of a thorough and efficient system of free public schools for the instruction of all children in the state between the ages of 5 and 18 years." Under a state school aid formula, enacted in 1971, $220 million a year in state "equalization" funds were going to the poorest 30 percent of school districts. But a large additional sum was being handed out to all districts on a flat formula of $132 per pupil. As a result, gross disparities continued: in affluent Englewood Cliffs, for instance, $246,000 in assessed property value stood behind every schoolchild, so that the town could tax at only 99 cents per $100 of property and still afford $2,000 a year to educate each child; by contrast, in Camden only $18,000 in assessed value stood behind each child, so that with a tax rate of $1.94 and generous amounts of school aid, the per pupil expenditure was only $1,000.

The legislature had adopted a school finance act in 1975, but the appropriation for fiscal 1976—was $375 million short so the act—because too little money was appropriated—was ruled unconstitutional. Facing both fiscal crisis and an insistent court, the legislature finally agreed to a package which made New Jersey the 41st state in the country to adopt an income tax.*

The Jersey income tax structure, as passed in 1976, taxed the first $20,000 of a person's income at 2 percent and the amount above that at 2.5 percent. Thus it contained little of the equity found in income taxes of other states. The measure was expected to raise $775 million annually and increase state support for education from 28 percent to 40 percent, most of that money going to city schools, which would receive a $380 million increase in state aid. Local property taxes were reduced an average of $210 per home owner, with a greater break for the elderly and a tenants' share for the property tax break given to landlords.

The court order which finally compelled legislative action on the income tax struck at the heart of the inherent inequality of the distribution of wealth in modern New Jersey. The state, the court said, was responsible for seeing that there be as much money to educate a child in the slums of a Newark, Jersey City, or Camden, or in some of the poorer rural areas, as was available in the rich islands of Jersey's suburban prosperity.

Pure selfishness—the complacent suburbanite's determination to stay free of the burdens of the decaying older cities—lies at the heart of much opposition in New Jersey to school funding reform, income taxes, and the like. But the other side of the coin must be recognized as well—the gross inefficiency and waste and corruption in many of the impoverished areas that cry for state fiscal aid. The Newark school system, for instance, has paid astronomical salaries to middling management types in recent years, even while many of its graduates are functional illiterates. State senate president Dodd (himself an income tax supporter) said: "The problem in Newark is not money—it's in attitudes. If the parents and the children won't cooperate, where the hell are you going?"

Or let us quote from a letter we received from a politically astute member of an aspiring Jersey politician's family:

---

* Nine states are left without a personal income tax, including three with major population centers—Connecticut, Florida, and Texas.

The state needs an ironclad system of fiscal audits at every level of government. New Jersey does not have an audit system for county governments (where the political wheels are really greased), local governments or state government. That lack is one reason why citizens are so outraged by the threat of increased taxes. Almost every federal program in Newark, for example, has either been closed down or is under investigation because of misuse of funds.

Increased state aid, the letter writer suggested, might be an ineffective palliative against the backdrop of the social problems of the core cities with their large minority populations:

Population density is at the root of much urban decay and crime. No mother —however strong, loving, and virtuous—can adequately meet the physical and emotional needs of a huge brood, especially when she attempts to do so on a meager or welfare income. Large numbers of children make it difficult if not impossible for families "to get out from under economically." New Jersey has suffered from a failure at the highest levels of government to face up to the need for birth control. Hughes, as governor, would not permit a piece of paper with the Planned Parenthood insignia to cross his desk. Cahill exercised no leadership in this area either. Until a couple of years ago in some counties, it was against all regulations for a welfare caseworker to *even mention* that family planning information was available. Until birth control is made as available as bars are, urban blight and problems will remain unsolved.

Crime and vandalism have as much to do with urban blight as taxes. Business can write off taxes, but it can't cope with windows smashed each week, with secretaries mugged and the like. Every major business in Newark now has armed guards at elevators. Large companies have sealed off entrances to buildings. Small businesses operate with police dogs guarding the premises. Fear of assault is so widespread that it is difficult to find people who are willing to work in the city. These conditions reflect social problems, not tax structure.

Education, Transportation, and the Environment

New Jersey's per capita expenditures for public schools rank a quite respectable 15th among the 50 states, with one of the highest teacher salary scales in the country. But per capita outlays for higher education are quite a different story: 49th in the nation. The dismal record in higher education is a holdover from the days when New Jersey simply sloughed off its responsibilities in the field to private universities, with Princeton the centerpiece. The legislature designated Rutgers College at New Brunswick as the land-grant college for New Jersey in 1864 but did not favor the college with its first dollar of state aid for 38 more years. In 1945, still primarily a private college in character, Rutgers belatedly got the title of "state university," but it was more than a decade more until commensurate financial assistance appeared. "Meanwhile," Richard McCormick has written, "most of the children of New Jersey who sought higher education had to go to colleges out of state. And why not? If other state universities would accept and educate our children, why should we burden our own taxpayers with such costs?"

In the late 1960s, New Jersey was still the biggest "debtor" state in higher education in the U. S. The 1968 figures, for instance, showed Jersey was "exporting" 98,710 more students to out-of-state universities than it was accepting from other states. But starting under a master plan for education drawn up in the 1960s, plus much more generous state financing, major improvements have started and are progressing. Rutgers has been able to boost its enrollment to over 30,000 at 18 colleges and schools in five campus locations. The state moved from having no publicly supported medical schools to two by the late 1960s. Starting from ground zero, the state opened 13 community colleges with 35,000 students and anticipated three more within a few years.

In the aggregate, however, New Jersey has leagues to cover before it can even be mildly competitive with other states in higher education. But there are fields where it has been doing a lot better: court administration, social legislation, transportation planning, and protection of the environment.

Acting in 1948 under the new constitution, the Driscoll administration effected a reorganization of the courts that many considered a national model, and to this day impartial observers like the Institute of Judicial Administration in New York call the Jersey judiciary "one of the very best administered in the country." But this may be a case where the best is not good enough. After a 1970 survey, the New York *Times* reported that New Jersey courts had congested calendars, inadequate representation of the poor, erratic treatment of traffic and minor criminal cases. The reasons were familiar enough: too few judges, prosecutors, lawyers, and court personnel, a sharp increase in crime over the past several years, and the rulings of the U. S. Supreme Court which make possible a plethora of pretrial motions with great delaying effects. Former Chief Justice Joseph Weintraub suggested that criminals themselves are somewhat responsible for court delays. "Realistically," he says, "most of them are guilty, and they're in no hurry to go on trial."

New Jersey has taken some interesting steps in social legislation. In 1971, it passed one of the country's first divorce laws permitting "no-fault" decrees for couples living apart with no hope of reconciliation. The year before, it led the entire nation in passing a drug law which defined a "small amount" of marijuana, established reduced penalties for anyone caught with lesser amounts, but sharply increased penalties for convicted pushers of other drugs like barbiturates and amphetamines. There was real personal drama in the drug bill for Governor Cahill, whose 19-year-old son had been arrested twice on charges of possessing marijuana. And senator Fairleigh S. Dickinson, Jr., of Bergen County, a multimillionaire philanthropist and chief author of the legislation, had even more reason to be personally involved. His only son and heir, Fairleigh S. Dickinson, III, had died the year before at age 19 from an apparent overdose of opium in his room at Columbia College.

Another New Jersey innovation, enacted in 1972, was no-fault auto insurance; the bill passed by the legislature required a 15 percent reduction in insurance rates. Indeed, over the years New Jersey has been a leader in consumer protection, not so much because of actions by the legislature or the governors, but instead as a result of pioneering decisions by the state supreme court, led for many years by Chief Justice Weintraub.

But in programs that cost more money, New Jersey often falls down. One example, not unique to this state but still serious in the extreme: there is a need for 50,000 subsidized, low-cost housing units each year. But only a few are being built. In 1966, Hughes recommended and the legislature created a new state department of community affairs; to head it, Paul Ylvisaker, one of the nation's most brilliant urbanologists and a former Ford Foundation official, was selected. Ylvisaker's department handled federal poverty grants for New Jersey practically as a block grant, and administered low-income housing efforts. Ylvisaker demanded of Hughes and got the right to appoint his staff of about 85 professionals without regard to political connections; given that freedom, he picked a young, bushy-tailed group (average age: late 20s) with a sensitivity to race and urban problems. With its job ill defined, Ylvisaker's staff acted as a kind of mobile striking force. It moved into Newark during the 1967 riots to help in food distribution, bringing in medicine under fire and conducting peace-making missions. But the financing of the new department, while it was enough "to keep our bureuacrats occupied," as Ylvisaker put it, was not great enough to make a fundamental attack on urban problems as they exist in the state. He would have liked to inaugurate an experimental income maintenance (or "negative income tax") program for low income families, for instance, but never got the chance. Ylvisaker left the job after the 1969 Republican gubernatorial victory to take a seat on the faculty at Princeton, departing state government with a conviction that fundamental "flow changes" in the way public dollars are channeled would be necessary to a solution of the country's urban ills—putting all education costs on the state governments, for instance, and health and welfare expenditures on the federal government.

In transportation, New Jersey faces the excruciating problem of getting almost 300,000 workers across the Hudson into New York every day and back home at night with relative ease and comfort. Compared to this task, the building of the great New Jersey Turnpike and Garden State Freeway was a straight-forward, uncomplicated task. The *interstate* nature of the problem complicates it to begin with. New Jersey in 1921 joined in the Port of New York Authority with New York State but for years let the authority concentrate on New York City-oriented construction projects. A first break in Jersey's complacent attitude came in 1962 when it demanded that the authority take over, rehabilitate, and operate the old Hudson and Manhattan Railroad (the Hudson "tubes") as a *quid pro quo* for New Jersey's agreement to the authority's construction of the World Trade Center on Manhattan. Modernized and improved, the old tubes (now called PATH—Port Authority Trans-Hudson system) carry over 100,000 passengers a day, albeit with an annual deficit the authority must cover out of other revenues. In 1974, Governor Byrne pushed a long-sought repealer of the 1962 compact through the legislature. New Jersey, of course, would keep the PATH tubes, but at the same time the Port of New York Authority agreed to drop its ban on subsidizing other mass transit lines from the huge profits it reaps from airports (and may eventually from Manhattan's World Trade Center). With the New York legislature taking similar action, the only obstacle to such subsidy programs were lawsuits filed by Port Authority bondholders. Southwestern New Jersey also has its regional transportation agency, the Delaware River Port Authority, formed with Pennsylvania in 1951. It took over the major bridges across the Delaware River and also constructed a new high-speed transit line linking Philadelphia with the greater Camden area, one of the country's most successful rail mass transit experiments in decades.

These advances have only slowed the trend toward obsolescence and bankruptcy in the road, rail, and air transit systems of the heavily traveled New York-Jersey-Philadelphia corridor. Massive traffic jams and commuter-line breakdowns have become especially prevalent on the approaches to New York City, all the railroads have demanded subsidies to continue in operation, and New Jersey has feuded with the Port Authority over its effort to build a fourth New York area jetport somewhere in northern New Jersey. (Cahill became so frustrated with the Port Authority's nonessential undertakings that he issued an ultimatum saying he would henceforth exercise his veto power unless New Jersey got "dollar for dollar" parity on new construction projects.)

In 1966, at Hughes' instigation, a New Jersey department of transportation was created, starting overall planning in the transit area but often running afoul of the existing turnpike and highway authorities. The department issued a $2 billion, 10-year expansion program in 1968, which got underway with approval of a $640 million transportation bond issue that year (a third for rails, two-thirds for highways).* But Cahill, after one year in office, pronounced transportation the most difficult single problem he had to deal with and started to campaign for a fantastic array of programs, including the parallel roads and extensions to the New Jersey Turnpike and Garden State Parkway systems, a vastly expanded rapid-transit system radiating from Newark, big parking facilities beside the turnpikes and rail commuter lines of north Jersey, and consideration of ideas like mass transit lines along the turnpikes and restricted highway lanes for commuter buses. His get-tough stand with the Port Authority produced agreement—at least on paper—to build a $200 million rapid transit network linking Newark Airport with downtown Newark, Manhattan, and parts of Union County.

Environmental control is an area of special difficulty for New Jersey, but one in which it is making significant progress. Richard J. Sullivan, the young civil servant whom Cahill selected to head the department of environmental protection, stated the problem this way: "Bad things that happen to the environment happen in New Jersey first. We have more of the

---

* New Jersey is one of a small handful of states which finance their highways from general fund appropriations rather than earmarked or dedicated funds. One result is a climate much friendlier to mass transit alternatives than one finds in other states.

things per square mile that make the air and water dirty than any other state—we are the most densely populated, we have the most cars per square mile, and we have the biggest chemical industry. For decades, we've let the growth of New Jersey greatly outdistance the methods of waste disposal needed to accommodate that growth." Predictably, pollution problems are severest in the grimy industrial areas adjacent to New York and Philadelphia, but the problems spread throughout the state. New Jersey is practically an island, except for its 48-mile northern border with New York State, and makes intensive use of its waterways for water supply, industrial applica tions, seafood, recreation—and as effluent carriers. Obviously, the various uses conflict. Virtually all the major waterways are polluted, but the worst are the Passaic River in north Jersey * and the lower Delaware. As far as air pollution is concerned, one needs only to take a ride along the northern stretches of the New Jersey Turnpike, past putrid-smelling refineries and chemical plants, caught in an air pocket laden with the sulphur dioxide, carbon monoxide, and other noxious vehicle emissions, to know what the problem is all about.

Comparatively, Jersey has made its biggest strides fighting air pollution, and all in the limited period since 1967, when the legislature gave state authorities the strictest enforceable regulations of all the states. Since then, hundreds of cases have been taken to court, and the state has won every one. A celebrated battle was with the airlines to make them modify their jet engines to create less smoke while using Newark Airport; another was with the fuel and power industry on the sulphur content of coal and oil. New Jersey also became the first state to require inspection of all automobiles as sources of pollution.

Progress in water pollution control has been slower, because the most persistent offenders turn out to be municipalities and their inadequate sewage treatment plants. The local governments involved are often broke and can try to exert political pressure to avoid orders to upgrade their water treatment plants. (Jersey has about 750 sewage plants, which experts say is 500 too many. Larger plants can be manned full-time, have scientists and laboratory facilities, and can have sophisticated enough equipment to withstand a variety of wastes.) Since 1966, the state has had the power to disapprove any new plant that doesn't meet its plans. But the state still cannot *force* a certain local government to build a needed sewage plant. The state can crack down hard on industrial polluters, and does. In blossoming suburban Morris County, the state agency actually got a local court to forbid *all* further real estate development in nine towns until they could straighten out their waste disposal problems.

Under a strong 1970 bill, the state is also stepping in to protect some 300,000 acres of wetlands along the Jersey Coast—salt marshes, estuaries,

* In 1969, Murray Stein, assistant commissioner of the Federal Water Pollution Control Administration, called the Passaic a "disgrace to the United States, . . . a fetid, polluted stream that offends human sensibilities and is a danger to health and welfare." The river flows past Paterson, Clifton, Passaic, and Newark.

and inlet flats that are essential to the ecological life chain but endangered by uncontrolled growth. "We don't want to end up," Sullivan said, "with houses, marinas, lagoons, and waterfront restaurants lining our coast, elbow-to-elbow, from Sandy Hook to Cape May." Unsound sanitary and land-use methods are the worst danger. Some coastal communities have been poisoning themselves on their own waste, generally through a superfluity of septic systems which result in sewage rising in ground water on front lawns, spewing into bayside lagoons, and poisoning coastal tributaries. Under the 1970 legislation, the state is using its power to intervene in critical areas where it has the power to suspend all septic tank construction. New Jersey also passed a tough 1971 bill requiring that sewage sludges and industrial wastes be dumped 100 miles out in the Atlantic, or at least beyond the continental shelf, rather than the existing 12-mile limit. In signing the bill, Governor Cahill said: "Ocean dumping of sewage and polluted dredge-spoil a scant 12 miles from our coastline and beaches is a primitive, insensitive, and completely unacceptable method of waste disposal." It was hoped the new measure might save Jersey beaches from an annual "red tide" of tiny organisms that redden the sea, give swimmers rashes, and threaten the shore's ecology.

But in the area of solid waste disposal, Sullivan admitted, the state has "yet to move into a program we could dignify with the term management." It's not enough anymore, he says, to take garbage to the end of town and dump it—"because most of our towns don't have edges anymore."

But strong laws alone cannot do the job. As Cahill left office, Sullivan was eased out also by incoming Governor Byrne. The problem, apparently, was poor management; as Lark Wallwork wrote in *Newark!* magazine in 1974:

Last year, conditions in the New Jersey Department of Environmental Protection were in such a state of chaos that the federal government notified DEP that it was withholding all federal funds for water pollution control pending the department's complete reorganization. . . . DEP is understaffed and suffering from so much internal disarray that it has been rendered virtually ineffective in dealing with water pollution along the Passaic or anywhere else.

A Criminal Encounter

Up through the late 1960s, organized crime was able to bore within to take control of the city of Newark, infest other northern Jersey governments, and even influence New Jersey's state government to a degree never before documented and perhaps never achieved in one of the 50 states. Then the federal Justice Department stepped in with a concerted campaign to break the back of Jersey's Mafia. There followed a blizzard of indictments and convictions which, in the words of Fred J. Cook, author of *The Secret Rulers,* "outlined the most complete network of crime and official corruption that has yet to be brought to trial in an American courtroom. There has been nothing remotely comparable to this since the Murder, Inc., trials of 1940; and by comparison even Murder, Inc., was pallid stuff."

Not only are many of Jersey's hoodlums now behind bars, but so are literally dozens of former public and party officials—so many that to list them all, with their former titles, would take two pages of print. Among the best known of those convicted are: Hugh Addonizio (former mayor of Newark), Cornelius Gallagher (former Congressman), Paul Sherwin (secretary of state under Cahill), Robert Burkhart (secretary of state under Hughes and former Democratic state chairman), Joseph McCrane (secretary of state under Cahill), Thomas Whelan (former mayor of Jersey City), John V. Kenny (longtime Hudson County Democratic boss), Peter Moraites (former Speaker of the Assembly), Nelson Gross (former Republican state chairman and 1970 Senate candidate), and Louis Turco (former president of the Newark Council). Much of the rot centers in Newark and Hudson County (Jersey City), areas long controlled by Democrats. But it is worth noting that Jersey corruption is grandly bipartisan; of the men on our list, six are Democrats and four Republicans.

But why, one asks, did it all happen in New Jersey? There seem to be two answers: first, Jersey's peculiar governmental-political system, and secondly, the accident of geography. Voters turn out in such low numbers for primary elections that the county political bosses could hold almost unlimited power for decades. The governor technically appoints county prosecutors and judges, but the county political bosses in effect dictated the choices. Thus law enforcement officials became answerable to the county bosses, not Trenton. Under law, the county prosecutors had almost autonomous control over county law enforcement, and the state attorney general's office could do little to interfere.

New Jersey's strategic location was a major factor. Organized crime first took hold in the state during Prohibition. Newark's Abner ("Longie") Zwillman, a suave businessman of crime, organized a bootlegging ring that reaped some $50 million in profits between 1926 and 1931. The state's extensive, cove-dotted coastline offered a nearly endless supply of hiding places for the swift boats of the rumrunners, and it was thought that 40 percent of the nation's bootlegging operations took place there. Zwillman became the effective Democratic boss of Newark's Third Ward, and his money financed several Democratic gubernatorial and legislative campaigns.

During the 1930s, when Thomas E. Dewey made New York too uncomfortable a place for racketeers, many of them moved across the Hudson to New Jersey—tough practitioners of the art like Frank Erickson, Joe Adonis, Anthony ("Tony Bender") Strollo, Albert Anastasia, and Vito Genovese. Genovese was to head the New Jersey Mafia until he went to federal prison in 1960 on a narcotics charge and later died. His successor was said to be Gerardo ("Jerry") Catena, a man with a police record of eight convictions ranging from truck hijacking to bribery of a federal juror. Using the proceeds of his gambling, extortion, and loan-sharking rackets, Catena built up several legitimate businesses in trucking, restaurants, and vending machines and exercised heavy political influence in the Newark city government and, some said, in the state legislature. The New York *Times* reported that Catena's ties with Meyer Lansky and Zwillman helped strengthen the bonds between the Italian mob and their Jewish gangster associates.

Gradually the tentacles of organized crime spread across New Jersey. A police chief was bought here, a mayor there. Selectmen, sheriffs, and county political leaders were also cajoled, threatened, or greased. The money rolled in, from gambling, narcotics, loan-sharking, and labor racketeering. By the late 1960s, organized crime was estimated to gross up to $1 billion annually in northern New Jersey. Up to that time, the public only rarely got a glimpse of what was happening. A major exception came in the wake of the Kefauver Committee's investigation and tandem state probes in the early 1950s, which flushed out Mafia infiltration of the state Republican party, centered in Bergen County. There were indictments, trials, and convictions, which played a role in the 1953 Democratic takeover of state government.

Then came more years of silent prosperity for the Mafia. The range of activities was incredibly broad. Gambling, for instance, took the nickels and dimes of poor blacks playing the numbers and also the big bills of heavy gamblers who dealt with the syndicate bookmakers in betting on horse races and football and basketball pools. One of the biggest gambling operations was run out of Newark by Ruggiero ("Richie the Boot") Boiardo, a veteran mobster who had once been saved from death in an assassination attempt by Zwillman's boys when his $5,000 diamond belt buckle stopped a bullet. Zwillman and Boiardo later made peace and divided the Newark territory between them. Zwillman committed suicide in 1959, but Boiardo carried on until 1968 when, at age 78, he was convicted of running a numbers operation and packed off to jail. Boiardo's son Anthony ("Tony Boy") took over the gambling operation in his dad's place. (Back in 1950, when Tony Boy was married, more than 2,000 guests turned out for the wedding, including then Mayor Ralph Villani of Newark, then Congressman Addonizio, and Peter W. Rodino.)

The really big action, though, seemed reserved for Catena. He controlled Port Newark through minions who were officers of the International Longshoremen's Association, and it was reported that the syndicate was heisting tens of millions of dollars worth of goods each year at the docks. (More than two dozen New Jersey unions were said to be under mob influence, ranging from Teamsters to restaurant workers' locals, with many a sweetheart contract that lined the pockets of the gangsters but deprived workers of a fair wage or job security.)

The traditional wall of secrecy about Mafia activity and infiltration of government began to crumble in the wake of the 1967 Newark riots. The commission appointed by Governor Hughes to investigate the disorders reported that an important underlying cause was "a pervasive feeling of corruption" in Newark. The commission said several knowledgeable officials had used an identical phrase: "There is a price on everything at City Hall." In subsequent state legislative hearings, Professor Henry S. Ruth, who would later become Deputy Watergate Special Prosecutor under both Archibald Cox and Leon Jaworski, touched many a sensitive political nerve by saying: "Official corruption in New Jersey is so bad that organized crime can get almost anything it desires." (Apparently it had been that way for a long time. A former high official in the Meyner administration told me that a man one day walked into his office at the state house in Trenton asking to be a judge. In his hand, the visitor had a bag with $15,000 in cash—apparently the going price. In that case, the offer was rejected, but it is not hard to imagine that many similar offers were accepted.) In December 1968, William J. Brennan, III, a young state prosecutor and son of the Supreme Court Justice, caused a great uproar when he remarked that a number of legislators were "entirely too comfortable with members of organized crime." Initially, there was a strong effort to characterize Brennan's charges as groundless and irresponsible. But, in the end, he was vindicated. Two of the state legislators he named were censured and a third, Democratic assembly leader David J. Friedland, was found after a disciplinary hearing by the state supreme court to have improperly tried to have a criminal case dropped against a reputed Mafia loan shark. The court suspended Friedland from the practice of law.

Not long after the Newark report and Brennan's charges, a new Republican administration—unencumbered by political debts to Democratic-held New Jersey—took office in Washington. On the recommendation of Senator Clifford Case, Frederick Lacey, a highly successful 48-year-old lawyer and member of an old Essex County family, was appointed U. S. Attorney for New Jersey.* Lacey took the job only after winning Attorney General John Mitchell's assurance that he and his independently chosen staff would have a free hand to develop cases on their own, rather than simply waiting for leads from federal investigative agencies. Lacey had served as an assistant U.S. Attorney almost two decades before and got a conviction of Harold Adonis and Albert Anastasia on charges of paying $228,000 to a clerk in Governor Alfred Driscoll's office for protection. The experience convinced Lacey "that organized crime was taking us over," and he took office in 1969 determined to crack down hard on the still-prospering Jersey Mafia. Lacey had a straightforward view of organized crime: "First, it corrupts law enforcement and officeholders. Second, it corrupts unions and makes a mockery of the collective bargaining concept. Third, it corrupts the businessman. I flatly state that it will not even go into a municipality unless and until it has bought its protection against raids and arrests."

---

* Lacey, according to writer Fred Cook, was reluctant to give up his high-income law practice for a $29,000-a-year U.S. attorney's post. The turning point in his thinking came when William Sutherland, a 73-year-old lawyer, phoned him and said: "When you're my age and you look back on your life, your pride will not be the size of the estate you're going to leave, but what you have accomplished. I know that you have an extremly lucrative law practice, but when you get to this point the money you didn't make won't seem to matter so much. What you might have accomplished in a few years as U.S. Attorney could well be the one thing in your life you would be proud of." Ironically, Lacey's own father had been police chief in Newark during the 1950s when the rackets were obviously flourishing there. After making his mark in the U.S. Attorney's post, Lacey was rewarded with appointment to the federal bench. In 1974 he resigned the judgeship and returned to private practice.

To back up Lacey, Mitchell also ordered a Justice Department anticrime strike force into New Jersey. An invention of Mitchell's predecessor, Ramsey Clark, strike forces team up agents from various federal law-enforcement agencies, including the FBI, Internal Revenue Service, and Narcotics Bureau, thus effecting interagency cooperation often lacking in normal operations. Strike forces are also able to get testimony from nervous informants by offering them both immunity from prosecution and, in sensitive cases, relocation in different parts of the country under new names with new jobs, thus alleviating their fear of Mafia retaliation. The technique has been used especially effectively in northern Jersey, leading for example to the conviction on a numbers racket case of Sam ("the Plumber") De Cavalcante, the boss of a New Jersey Cosa Nostra family with operations in New York and Connecticut as well. Two one-time agents for De Cavalcante's rackets were the people who gave the crucial testimony against him, and have since been whisked off by the task force to new and secret lives elsewhere in the U.S.A.

In a little over two years, Lacey and the task force racked up a record virtually unprecedented in U. S. law enforcement: 37 indictments involving 179 defendants, and 53 convictions with many cases still pending. Law enforcement had moved into high gear, and the mob was in trouble. De Cavalcante and nine members of his Mafia "family" got substantial prison terms. Catena was jailed for the first time since 1934 and held indefinitely on civil contempt charges after refusing to testify before a state investigating committee. Addonizio and four other persons were convicted for taking part in a scheme to squeeze payoffs from contractors doing business with the Newark city government. Tony Boy Boiardo, who had been indicted with Addonizio, suffered a heart attack, but the government said it would try him if he recovered. Other indictments hit the Newark magistrate's court, IRS officials in Newark (some of whom were said to be bought off by the mob), and members of the Newark police department, accused of tolerating gambling in return for payoffs.

Some of the most revealing insights of Mafia activity came when Lacey chose to release the transcript of FBI wiretaps, made between 1961 and 1965, of conversations held at a Mafia meeting place in Mountainside, N.J. The tapes (which were hearsay and were not shown to the jury) were the ones released during the successful extortion conspiracy trial of Angelo "Gyp" De Carlo which mentioned Brendan Byrne, then Essex County Prosecutor, as unbuyable. References to other officials were not as flattering. On the take or otherwise cooperating with the mob were, according to the tapes, Newark Mayor Addonizio, then Newark police director Domininck Spina, former state police superintendent Dominick R. Capello, and Democratic county bosses John V. Kenny of Hudson and David Wilentz of Middlesex.

After Lacey's elevation to the bench, his work was carried on by Herbert Stern, his chief assistant. Stern had no Jersey political connections; indeed, at the time he was nominated for U.S. Attorney, he was not even a member of the New Jersey Bar. It was Stern who successfully prosecuted cases against key figures in the Hudson County Democratic machine and against high Republican politicians like Nelson Gross. After three dazzling years, Stern had indicted and convicted more than 50 New Jersey public officials, including some of the most powerful, and he, like Lacey, moved up to the federal bench. The depth of the corruption he faced was illustrated by a story recounted by Jerome Wilson in *New York* magazine. Stern had indicted the manager of the small government store in the Federal Building in Newark, just downstairs from the U.S. Attorney's office. Wilson asked Stern whether he would go after the shoeshine man next. "No," came the reply. "The I.R.S. got him."

Or consider another case. In August 1974, the *Wall Street Journal* broke the story of James Challender, a state police detective who had become convinced his higher-ups had been trying to cover up an investigation of campaign finances. Challender violated state regulations and brought his evidence to federal prosecutors, who as a result brought major indictments and obtained at least one important conviction. Soon Challender was transferred to service on the New Jersey Turnpike, where he was assigned to trace hubcaps and other lost items. One curious aspect of the whole affair: the target of Challender's original investigation had been the Cahill administration, but state officials had been exonerated of any wrongdoing in his case by Brendan Byrne's attorney general.

With so many of New Jersey's known Mafia leaders and high politicians behind bars, the question remains whether the state has developed a civic climate hostile to graft and corruption. The evidence is, at best, inconclusive. The Challender case, along with a bevy of mini- and not so mini-scandals affecting the Byrne administration, suggests that the voters' choice of Brendan Byrne on a platform of incorruptibility has not really made much difference. The U.S. Attorney's office, to be sure, remains in the hands of men who have taken a forthright, courageous stand against Jersey's endemic patterns of corruption. (From the early 1970s through 1975, the U.S. Attorney's office was bringing 700 to 800 "live cases" a year, roughly 150 of them either against government officials or contractors doing business with state or local government.) There are signs that the criminal justice division, within the state attorney general's office, has improved substantially, bringing indictments regardless of the party affiliations of its targets. Nevertheless, in 1976 a federal grand jury indicted Matthew Feldman, president of the New Jersey Senate and his son on charges of bribing a restaurant chain representative to obtain business for Mr. Feldman's liquor distribution company. And there were indications that other powerful figures in high echelons of New Jersey state government were not at all uncomfortable with the old, often-so-corrupt way of doing things in the Garden State. And if that is true, it means, inevitably, continuing headlines of scandal in New Jersey for years to come, and continuing debasement of the state's public life.

North Jersey: Sad Cities into Suburbia

Just over five million people, or 70 percent of the entire population of New Jersey, live in a ring of eight counties that extend 40 to 50 miles north, west, and south of Manhattan Island. They divide rather neatly into three groups.

First comes the part of New Jersey which is really part of the New York City core area—namely, that urban disaster at the other end of the Lincoln and Holland Tunnels which is called Hudson County. The population, as of the 1970 Census: 609,266, holding virtually steady since 1920.

Next comes an inner ring of counties generally suburban in character but also the site of aging industrial cities like Newark, Paterson, and Elizabeth. The inner ring cities blend into more purely bedroom communities in one vast urban-suburban complex where it is hard to know when one has left one municipality and entered the next. With some exceptions, like northern Bergen County, this is tired old suburbia. The big tracts of land were filled with houses years ago, and the process of the recent past has been to fill in empty strips with garden apartments and high-rise apartment buildings. Five counties are included: Bergen, Passaic, Essex, Union, and Middlesex. The total population in 1970 was 3,415,709, an increase of 12 percent since 1960 and 63 percent since 1950.

Finally there is the "exurban" territory of the outer ring, once the sole province of farmers and business moguls with their big estates, now fast developing with light industries and thousands of acres of colonial and ranch-style homes and even some garden apartments. The outer ring has three counties: Morris, Somerset, and Monmouth. In 1970, they had 1,041,205 people, up 41 percent since 1960 and 188 percent since 1950.

The "Core" County: Hudson

Hudson County is a relic of times past, the place that brought us Frank Hague and John V. Kenny and the most continuous stream of year-in, year-out political corruption that America has ever known. Leaf through the yellowed newspaper clippings of earlier decades and you come on story after story expressing hope that the latest wave of "reform" has really turned Hudson into a respectable community only to find reports a few years if not months later indicating that the corruption had returned to its old levels. Officials in Hudson County, newsman Peter Bridge has written, "have winked away more unexplainable situations in a year than most counties encounter in a decade." Shady dealings, vote-roll padding, nepotism in government, all are here in unprecedented quantity. Today, in the wake of the conviction of Hudson boss Kenny and former Jersey City Mayor Thomas

Whalen, it seems that reform may actually have taken hold here. A young public health physician, Paul Jordan, was elected mayor in the early 1970s, and even initiated a major renewal project featuring a new town on the Hudson River, new housing and parks in older residential areas, new downtown development and historic preservation. In view of Hudson's past, one might be inclined to be cynical about Jordan—but he has received the imprimatur of U.S. Attorney Herbert Stern, who nominated him as one of the U.S. Chamber of Commerce's Ten Outstanding Young Men of 1972. Jordan makes no bones about being a politician—"anybody who tries to run Hudson County and Jersey City without being political is naive," he told the *Wall Street Journal* in 1974, "because he'd end up with a political knife in his back."

In physical terms, the thought of Hudson County conjures up images of endless miles of low, dingy slums, crumbling waterfront, grime-caked bridges, oil tanks, and fetid marshlands. Practically alone among the urban counties of America, Hudson has virtually no sections one could call even faintly suburban. It is just one city after another: Jersey City, Hoboken, Union City, Bayonne, West New York—with the highest population densities in the United States except for Manhattan itself. The most significant residential construction of recent years has been a string of high-rise apartments along the Palisades, which attract some middle-income New Yorkers. As one of the cliff dwellers in West New York explained: "To live on the Palisades is to live in New York City without all the accompanying headaches. We have a spectacular view of Manhattan and the river to watch while cooking out on our porch, a park next door, a swimming pool and sauna bath and lower insurance rates and taxes. . . . We have an air-conditioned apartment with a rent that isn't prohibitive and a 15-minute air-conditioned bus ride to work versus 20 to 25 sweaty minutes on the subway when we lived in Manhattan."

Another contradiction of the prevailing griminess is found in no other place than the brawling old waterfront town of Hoboken, where massive rehabilitation of old tenements, apartment houses, and townhouses has been accomplished in the last several years through a fusion of private money and loan guarantees from the federal government. Now blue-collar Hoboken is even luring professionals from Manhattan.

The more significant population flow, however, is one of talented and educated young people, the children and grandchildren of the nationality groups that so faithfully supported Hague in days of yore, out to the suburban rings. Their place has been taken, to some degree, by blacks, though the black percentage in the county is still only 10 percent; and in the last few years there has been a heavy in-migration of Puerto Ricans, Cubans, and other Spanish-speaking people. In Union City, 30,000 Cubans—almost all refugee families—are in residence, more than half the city's official population figure of 58,537. Just as in Miami, the Cubans are actually helping to revive Union City's crumbling downtown through their hard-working entrepreneurial ways.

For the most part, however, those migrating outward are simply not being replaced at all, and Hudson County remains the ethnic stew it has been for decades. Consider this picture of Bayonne, the oil refining town on a key-shaped peninsula on the west side of New York Harbor, written by native son Steven V. Roberts:

> Wooden two-family houses fill narrow lots separated by narrow alleys. In front and back, each house has its little square of hard, barren dirt. [A total of 72,743] people squeeze into Bayonne's five square miles, and the land is so scarce that they are building houses in swamps and next to sewage plants. . . . It is a close-knit town, rather isolated and parochial, Eastern, ethnic, and industrial. . . . I think of the soot of Bayonne and its smell, an aromatic combination of barbecued garbage and smoldering inner tubes, with a dash of sulphur for tanginess.

Writer Roberts, it might be added, is one who escaped Hudson County, settling as far away as possible—first in Malibu, California, where he became, at age 26, the New York *Times'* outstanding California correspondent. He is only one example of many talented people who have come out of Hudson County—but virtually all of them have indeed come out, and made their names elsewhere.

But we heard another reaction from Paul Ylvisaker:

"Jersey City can no longer be isolated from the rest of society. Its kids are being exposed to the same influences as those everywhere else. And while ethnic, church, and political controls are being maintained, way past the 19th century, the kids are getting the message more and more.

"Watch the pluralism in Hudson County—more than the indictments. After Kenny goes [he is gone now], there will be a sudden pluralism among the ward chiefs. More diversity of leadership will emerge.

"And remember the great advantage of location that Hudson County enjoys. PATH goes down there, so that Jersey City is six minutes by subway from the World Trade Center. As soon as this county begins developing housing and new towns and gets income maintenance and the state income tax to relieve property taxes, you're going to see some dramatic flourishing of those places close to New York. They're a beautiful place for apartment buildings and offices."

A Special Case: The Meadowlands

Some 10 to 20 thousand years ago, a glacier carved out a valley between two long extrusions of igneous rock close to the place where the Hackensack River now reaches Newark Bay. The area was once a lake, and even today, at high tide, much of the land is flooded. This is the valley of the Hackensack Meadowlands, a giant swamp 18,000 acres in size, stretching 15 miles from Hackensack to Harrison. The area is actually larger than Manhattan, whose skyscrapers loom over the Palisades ridge and the strip of Hudson County cities to the east. For generations, Jerseyans have used the Meadowlands as a dumping ground—a process that continues at the rate of 42,000 tons a week. At midpoint in the valley stands a Romanesque building named the Joint Meeting Sewage Plant, surrounded by huge revolving fountains. So heavy is the load of human and industrial waste, programmed and unprogrammed, that the air and water have become contaminated, the Hackensack River turned opaque with pollution and virtually devoid of fish. The result of all the decay is the Meadowlands stench so familiar to travelers into Manhattan.

For 300 years there have been abortive attempts to develop the Meadows, which are presently thought to be worth more than $1 billion—the most expensive piece of undeveloped land in the world. In recent times, the hangup has been less technological than political—the rivalry of the 14 communities in Hudson and Bergen Counties in whose borders the Meadows fall. They succeeded in scuttling all development plans in their rivalry for ratables (tax-assessable property) and unwillingness to give up authority to any kind of regional body. But in 1968, largely as a result of imaginative Meadowlands planning by Paul Ylvisaker when he was Hughes' Commissioner of Community Affairs, the legislature finally agreed to formation of a unified, powerful Hackensack Meadowlands Commission. The intent, as Associated Press writer Campbell Gardett summed it up at the time, was to "make roads where there are now streams, make houses where now there are marshes, make industry where now there is only pollution—and most of all to make money." In a radical break with Jersey's home rule tradition, the commission was given authority to override the 14 townships in the Meadowlands. They were placated in part by an innovative intermunicipal tax-sharing account, giving all benefits from the tax yield of the new properties to be constructed.

Late in 1970, when the new commission unveiled its master plan, it was an exciting one indeed. If all the plans were to come to fruition, an urban complex with residences for 200,000 people and huge office buildings, shopping and cultural centers will rise above the Meadowlands. Most of the people would be housed in high-rise island apartment clusters to be erected on steel piles along the Hackensack River. Residents would be transported from their apartments to shopping centers and jobs by waterboats similar to Venice's. Rapid rail and bus connections to Manhattan and Newark were planned. More than 5,000 acres of the Meadowlands was to be set aside for conservation, parks, and recreation areas—a reflection of the good counsel of environmentalists, who have been looking for ways to preserve and restore the natural flora and fauna and eliminate the frightful pollution of the area. Incredibly, the commission had as its long-term goal making the Hackensack River safe for swimming! In practice, it did soon prove to be an extraordinarily aggressive policer of private and public polluters in the area.

An essential part of the plan is a massive 30-year flood control project to be carried out by the Army Corps of Engineers. Two-thirds of the $300 million cost will come from the federal treasury, making the Meadowlands the most expensive public reclamation project the U.S. government has ever undertaken east of the Mississippi River. (At last, one notes, there may be some equalization of the billions eastern taxpayers have paid for the huge federal projects in the West.) As for the actual Meadowlands construction, initial development capital will come from revenue bonds floated by the Meadowlands Commission, thus stimulating large-scale private investment.

At the moment, however, the Meadowlands project with the most momentum behind it is one which was initiated after the commission announced its master plan. In March 1971, Governor Cahill announced he had obtained a verbal agreement from the New York Giants football team to leave Yankee Stadium in the Bronx and play in a projected 75,000-seat stadium in the Meadowlands. Cahill's plans included not only the stadium, but a horse-racing track and indoor facilities for basketball, hockey, and conventions, plus a large hotel. New York's Mayor Lindsay, who had just announced a $24 million program to modernize Yankee Stadium, bristled at the Cahill announcement and said he was "confident" the Giants would remain. But the Giants moved to New Jersey in 1976 shortly after the stadium opened.

The Inner Ring

We begin the north Jersey inner ring of suburban counties, moving from north to south:

Bergen (population 898,012) grew by 241,116 people in the 1950s, but only 117,757 in the 1960s. It is getting filled up, but is still likely to pass Essex and thus become New Jersey's most heavily populated county by the 1980 Census. The southern parts of Bergen (bordering Hudson) are primarily blue-collar, middle-class, industrial—towns like Rutherford (20,802) and North Arlington (18,098) along the Meadowlands, and Hackensack (35,911), the county seat, just beyond. This area has a heavily ethnic flavor—especially Italian, Polish, and Slavic. But further north, Bergen blossoms into middle- and high-income suburbs, peopled by many professionals and some of New York City's most well-to-do commuters. Bedroom towns like Tenafly, Old Tappan, Haworth, and Alpine are among Jersey's handsomest communities.

The most noticeable growth in Bergen in recent years has not been out, but up—in the huge high-rise apartment developments that have begun to line the tops of the Palisades. The high-rises have brought much tax money, and some troubles, to the small cities and townships. One example is Fort Lee, where in 1974 two large contractors were charged with offering 31-year-old Mayor Burt Ross a $500,000 bribe. The stakes were big: the defendants were planning a $250 million shipping and entertainment complex —on land which was not yet zoned for such heavy development. Ross cooperated with the FBI to trap the bribers, who were subsequently convicted, but only after a chilling threat on Ross's life.

Bergen County provides one of the most dramatic illustrations in the

U.S.A. of how local governments use their zoning powers to bolster their own fiscal positions in a way that fosters racial and economic ghettos. In 1970, reporters Sharon Rosenhause and Edward Flynn of the *Hackensack Record* spent six months compiling a report on zoning in Bergen. Their chief findings on its effects:

■   All but the top 20 percent of wage earners, by national averages, are effectively priced out of the single-family housing market.

■   After decades of living in a community, retired residents and others on fixed incomes are being forced by spiraling local taxes to move from their homes and seek cheaper housing elsewhere.

■   Low wage earners and minority workers travel long hours daily to suburban jobs and then back to their core-city homes. They can't find nearby housing within their means.

■   Ironically, industry, courted by suburbia to pay the rising costs of local government, threatens to move out or delay expansion because of a limited labor supply.

■   Many municipalities—35 of them in Bergen—ban apartments. Others restrict construction to luxury high-rises. Some impose limits on the numbers of bedrooms—a practice referred to as architectural birth control—because they don't want more schoolchildren. . . . Some Bergen communities have increased minimum lot sizes from half to one or two acres.

One of the worst examples is found in the isolated Bergen County town of Mahwah, close by the New York state border. In 1955, the Ford Motor Company opened an assembly plant there, becoming the town's largest employer and taxpayer. But Mahwah has a one- and two-acre zoning requirement on its 7,000 acres of undeveloped land that serves to bar all but a few of the Ford workers—40 percent of whom are black or Spanish-speaking—from living in the town. Most nearby municipalities have similarly restrictive zoning. As a result, less than a quarter of the 5,000-man work force lives in Bergen County. Some 1,600 of them live in New York State and another 900 in New York City; many travel up to 60 or 70 miles a day to their jobs. As a result, the plant has an exceptionally high turnover and absentee rate.

But the ultimate example of zoning abuse in Bergen County and perhaps the nation is the town of Teterboro, which acted about 30 years ago to zone in an airport and space for several factories but exclude almost all people. Today the town has more than $75 million in assessed ratables but must provide services for a total population of only 14 people! Teterboro's tax rate, 68¢ per $100 of assessed valuation, compares to rates as high as $4.84 in other Bergen County townships (and the rate of over $9.00 in not-too-distant Newark).

Such zoning abuses, not peculiar to New Jersey but seemingly more widespread and outrageous in their social consequences than those in most American states, have finally come under successful attack in the courts. The state's supreme court in 1975 declared invalid all local zoning ordinances that exclude poor persons or families with low or moderate incomes. Every community, the court ruled, must share in the housing needs of its surrounding region. "This is the decision we have been waiting for," Paul Davidoff, executive director of the Suburban Action Institute, Inc., a group dedicated to opening up New York region suburbs for lower income families, declared. He called it the most significant court decision on the subject to date in the United States. The political implementation of the decision, however, required a comprehensive state land use plan—which affluent Jersey communities were sure to oppose in the legislature. The vestiges of Jersey's exclusionary zoning practices of the last several decades may last for centuries to come.

Passaic County (460,782) is a mixture of close-in, older cities like Paterson (144,824) and Passaic (55,124), dingy and polluted and wracked with the problems of sharply increasing black and Puerto Rican populations, and in the upcounty area burgeoning bedroom communities like Wayne township (49,141). Anomalously tucked into the Paterson-Passaic area is Clifton (82,437), a staid and stable old middle- to upper-class community with one of Jersey's lowest tax rates and highest rates of "clean" industrial growth.

Paterson has had racial disturbances, but the wonder is that they haven't been worse; it is a town long guided by its industrial elite and very conservative newspaper. The problems of the old north Jersey cities were well summed up in a film made by six students at the Passaic High School in 1968. Called *River City*, it showed abandoned stores, decrepit playgrounds, and the polluted Passaic River. The film ended with the young filmmakers, suitcases in hand, walking down the Erie-Lackawanna tracks—and away from their city. Yet in 1971, the New York Regional Plan Association suggested that Paterson be transformed into a major "metropolitan center" for northern New Jersey, second only to Newark in importance. The city has good highway and bus connections and could be developed as an alternative to suburban business sprawl.

Essex County (929,986) is split between its great and problem-ridden city of Newark (382,417), a story to which we will return later, and its suburban hinterland. The suburbs themselves are a very mixed bag. Some, like West Orange (43,715) and Maplewood (24,932), are upper-middle to high income with quite stable populations; two of the smaller towns, South Orange (16,971) and Essex Fells (2,541), are among the most beautiful residential places in the state. A step below in wealth are Bloomfield (52,029), Belleville (34,643), and Nutley (32,099), all with big Italian-American populations. A city like Irvington (59,734) brings one into the middle income, blue collar category with ethnic concentrations of Poles, Italians, and Germans; at about the same economic level are Orange (32,566), predominantly Italian with blacks now more than a third of the population, and finally East Orange (75,471), which was found to be 53.1 percent black in the 1970 census. *Time* in 1971 did a study on the American suburbs and picked East Orange as its prototype of the "low-income stagnant" group, reporting in part:

East Orange has many faces: the tree-lined streets of the well-heeled First Ward, the old rundown frame houses of the Fifth Ward, the modern apartment buildings that tower over both (and house many middle-income Jews). The citizens of East Orange lead parallel but unlinked lives. Black-white contacts are guarded; . . . the lines also divide the haves from the have-nots, the black middle-class from the black working class. . . .

For many of the blacks, East Orange has been the first step out from the city, from Newark or New York, a reach for a suburban hinterland of open space and green grass and fresh air. Once it was that for wealthy whites. . . .

For short periods, parts of the town were integrated, but in the long run, blocks with some black families almost invariably went entirely black. . . . The racial ratio of the schools changed quickly: 21 percent black in 1952, 49 percent in 1962, around 90 percent today. Most white children switched to private or parochial schools if their parents chose to stay in East Orange.

Union County (543,116) is a New Jersey bellwether in many elections and also runs the gamut in types of traditional cities and suburbs. On its eastern edge, astride the New Jersey Turnpike and Penn Central Railway tracks, lies Elizabeth (112,654), certainly one of the most rundown, bleak, depressing cities in America. Elizabeth is packed with oil refineries and chemical plants and is a prime air polluter. Ethnically, the city has big Italian and Polish elements, plus considerable Irish, Lithuanians, Ukrainians, Puerto Ricans, and blacks. Mayor Thomas G. Dunn is a tough, practical Irish politician with such conservative views that he refused to apply for a federal Model Cities program—some think because he wanted no federal investigators coming in to judge the way he runs the city government. The city's urban renewal programs are all in the doldrums. Nearby Linden (41,409) and Rahway (29,114) are aging industrial towns in the Elizabethan mold, but not quite as unattractive.

The western part of Union County, by contrast, is higher-class commuting territory and has a number of "clean" research-oriented industries, including Bell Laboratories. Best known is Plainfield (46,862), a comfortable old bedroom town with tree-lined streets and many handsome old houses. Plainfield's middle class was slow to catch on to the implications of black population growth in their city, which rose from a minimal level in 1950 to almost 40 percent in the late 1960s. That apparent indifference, coupled with local black militancy and incredibly poor police tactics, led in 1967 to some of the most severe disorders which any American city of comparable size has ever experienced. The town's power structure responded quite positively, appealing successfully for a federal Model Cities program and other grants under the leadership of Mayor Frank H. Blatz, Jr.

Middlesex County (585,813) has been growing by leaps and bounds and now has more than twice as many people as it did in the early 1950s. Many of them are migrants from old northern Jersey cities in Hudson or Essex Counties, and they have made of Middlesex a classic ethnic melting pot— Italians in Woodbridge, Slavs and Poles in South River, Hungarians in New Brunswick (the nation's largest concentration of Hungarian-Americans, in fact). There is also a sizable black community in New Brunswick and a Spanish-speaking area of Perth Amboy. Almost half the people in the county are Catholic, and another 10 percent are Jewish; only 10 percent are adherents of one of the Protestant denominations. The long-dominant local machine headed by David Wilentz has been slowly crumbling.

Middlesex has an old industrial heartland in the northern part of the county, around Perth Amboy (38,798) and Carteret (23,137). But the real economic strength is no longer in that region of giant smokestacks and oil tank farms, but in newly developed areas along the New Jersey Turnpike and Garden State Parkway, which have experienced an amazing influx of research centers, publishing houses, chemical firms, and assorted light industries. Suburban housing developments have boomed in towns like Woodbridge (98,944), Edison (67,120), Madison (48,715) and Piscataway (36,418).

One of the more interesting cities is New Brunswick (41,885), a Revolutionary-era town on the banks of the Raritan River that finds itself ringed by chemical, steel fabricating, auto assembly, and oil refining factories, many of which contribute to a nightly odor known locally as Raritan miasma. But New Brunswick also has Rutgers University and a large, liberally-oriented academic community in its environs, introducing both variety to the population and some fierce town and gown tensions. The town was fortunate in recent years to have a good, honest government headed by a woman mayor, Patricia Sheehan, a sensitive but no-nonsense leader who showed considerable skill in working with every element from the ethnics to the blacks and academics. In one of his first major appointments, Governor Byrne appointed Ms. Sheehan to his cabinet.

The Outer Ring

The outer ring counties have received a massive influx of people in the last quarter century, but nonetheless retain large strips of undeveloped, rural territory. Today they are a curious mixture of open fields, industrial parks, fast-growing tract housing—most of it in the middle-upper income range—and the remaining estates of the landed gentry.

The counties of Morris (383,454) and Somerset (198,372), west of the metropolitan core, evoke images of lush, rolling hills where the affluent ride to their hounds. In many communities, a house must occupy a third if not a half acre at a minimum; in the Somerset communities of Bedminster and Bernardsville the minimum is five acres, and in posh Far Hills, the minimum is 10 acres.

But the affluent-only pattern does not apply everywhere, even in Morris and Somerset. In sprawling Parsippany-Troy Hills (55,112) in Morris County, where the population more than doubled in the 1960s, many garden-style apartments have risen, and much of the development took place so rapidly that it was a *fait accompli* before adequate building codes and controls could be imposed. Nor have the outer ring counties learned much from the experience of the older inner-ring cities. Historic Morristown (17,662) has begun the process of decline. It has its own little ghetto and suburbs like surrounding Morris township trying to separate their school systems from the inner "city." Industries are going into the suburbs (Morristown itself has no physical space left), repeating the dreary story of separating the tax base from the area of real local need.

A great conservation victory was won in Morris County in 1965 when Jerseyans rallied to fight and defeat a proposal by the Port of New York Authority to drain the Great Swamp, a preserve of natural fauna and flora unmatched anywhere in the northeastern U.S., and build in its place a monstrous jetport big enough to accommodate supersonic planes. The Great Swamp is a true red maple swamp with large stretches of meadowlands and marsh, visited by dozens of species of birds, its woods thick with deer, red fox, raccoons, and other wildlife. Aroused conservationists raised $1.5 million to purchase 3,000 acres of the 13,500-acre swamp and contribute the land to the federal government for a wildlife preserve, which Congress duly created.

Less certain is the ecological fate of the Passaic River as it flows downstream from the Great Swamp. By the time it enters Newark Bay, the river has become one of America's dirtier bodies of water. The more pristine upper stretches have been threatened by a flood control plan pressed by the Army Corps of Engineers and Passaic County Congressman Robert Roe. In order to protect downstream communities which have built on the flood plain (most of which are in Roe's district) from periodic inundation, the plan would dam and flood the upper stretches—where the local communities have taken care to leave the flood plain undeveloped.

Finally, the outer ring includes the southern (but lightly populated) section of Middlesex County, and Monmouth County on the coast. The resort industry, centered in towns like Asbury Park (16,533) and Long Branch (31,744), has traditionally been the economically dominant force in Monmouth, but in recent years bedroom communities like Middletown (54,623), Hazlett (22,239) and Manalapan (14,049) townships have been filling up with people at an amazing rate. There are some very high-income communities, like Spring Lake and Deal, but basically Monmouth is middle-income, noticeably less wealthy than Morris or Somerset. Blacks represent 8.3 percent of the population and are a major factor in Asbury Park and Long Branch, both of which have experienced racial disturbances. Long Branch has some colorful history—President Garfield was brought there in the vain hope that the cooling sea breezes might restore his strength. More recently, Long Branch gained a touch of notoriety as an entertainment area for Jersey mobsters.

Newark's Plight

The name of Newark has become a generic term for the pauperized, ghetto-ridden American city, deserted by its upper and middle classes, filled with poorly educated blacks from the South, afflicted with horrendous crime rates, faced with social problems far beyond its own capacity to solve, on the verge of bankruptcy.

One tells the story with sadness, because of what Newark was, and what it might be. Settled in 1666, it postdates only Boston and New York among the major cities of America. The city's heart is still the "Four Corners" intersection selected by the first Connecticut Puritan settlers. Its ethnic history is a microcosm of America—from the time of the Yankee Protestants through German and Irish eras, times when Jews set the tone of public life, then Italian ascendancy, and now the black man's turn. An engaging and well-meaning man, Kenneth Gibson, now sits in City Hall as Newark's first black mayor.

There are good reasons why Newark should *not* be a dying city. It has always been, and remains today, New Jersey's most heavily populated city and its business and financial center. Newark banks have assets of $2.5 billion, and the city is second only to New York in life insurance sales. Newark is both a corporate headquarters and a factory town. Its port ranks among the largest in the U. S. A. (first in auto imports, with advanced containerization facilities) and has been expanded so greatly that it is now dominant in the New York area. Newark Airport, one of the nation's busiest and safest has also undergone major expansion. The Amtrak main route goes straight through town, and America's greatest superhighway (the Jersey Turnpike) goes by the front door. All told, the city must be considered a natural transportation point unmatched in eastern America. And then there is the fact of Newark's physical rebuilding: $1 billion worth of new construction since 1957, including a quota of gleaming downtown office buildings and the ambitious Gateway Plaza urban renewal area beside the Amtrack railroad terminal, over $100 million worth of private apartment houses, the fourth highest number of public housing and other federally assisted low-income housing units among all American cities, and the impressive new academic facilities—Rutgers' new $60 million Newark campus, a new medical and dental school on a $90 million campus, and a vast expansion of the Newark College of Engineering.

A driving tour of Newark reveals no garden city, but at least a much better looking place, on the whole, than most outsiders would expect. The city is divided into five wards. The most depressing, predictably, is the Central Ward, predominantly black, containing riot-scarred Springfield Avenue, which has been described as "a cobblestoned horror of abandoned, filthy buildings, derelicts, and palpable disrepair." The Central Ward has big, vertical, ghetto public housing projects and vast stretches of empty lots. But it also has the very attractive middle-income, integrated Collonades apartments.

The East Ward includes the downtown business district, which went through a great valley of doubt in the early 1950s when it was rumored that the big Mutual Benefit Life Insurance Company might leave. But then Mutual Benefit lit a flame by announcing it would stay and build a new home office facing Washington Park; since then Prudential and several other firms have put up impressive buildings. But now there are doubts again. In the daytime, downtown is still crowded with commuting workers, but after six, it is virtually deserted and the city has been losing amenities like good department stores. Prudential is increasing employment in suburban areas—leading to reports that it may pull out of its downtown skyscraper altogether, an event that would destroy the vitality of downtown Newark for years to come.

East of downtown, the East Ward includes the clanging industrial district known as the Ironbound, where factories are interspersed with blocks of very plain row houses that would quickly become slum were it not for the tidy ways of the area's multitudinous ethnic groups—Italians, Poles, Germans, Brazilians, Dominicans, Puerto Ricans, Ukrainians, and Portuguese. Nearby is the airport, the seaport, and the Newark Meadows.

The South Ward used to be the heart of Newark's Jewish community, but after 1960 underwent a traumatic change to almost all black, with the classic problems of a transitional neighborhood. There are sections of solid-looking semidetached public housing units, some handsome high-rise public housing for the elderly, but also stretches of empty urban renewal land.

The West Ward includes solid middle-class Italian and Irish neighborhoods, but now blacks are moving in in large numbers. Here one finds the Pabst Brewery, which draws on a big watershed (twice the size of the city) that gives Newark some of the best quality municipal water supply in the world. Finally, there is the Italian stronghold in the North Ward, which includes some handsome middle-class residential neighborhoods like Forest Hills and has succeeded better than any other Newark community—not always in the most delicate way—in keeping oncoming blacks at bay. The North Ward was the site of the Kawaida Towers imbroglio—a dispute over the building of a housing project by a group led by Imamu Baraka (the poet and political activist formerly known as Leroi Jones). For months the project was held up by pickets led not only by Anthony Imperiale, the gun-toting state senator who symbolizes North Ward resistance to integration, but also by more moderate neighborhood leaders like Steve Adubato.

One need not search far to discover that the city labors under a set of frightening disabilities. Mayor Gibson acknowledges that Newark "may be the most decayed and financially crippled city in the nation." The evidence is clear enough:

- Crowded land area (24 square miles) of which a full third (eight square miles) is occupied by Newark Airport (whose owner, the New York Port Authority, has refused to make payment in lieu of taxes). Fully two-thirds of the land is tax-exempt, occupied by various levels of government, the church and educational institutions—facilities which exist in large measure for the benefit of the city's suburbs.

- One of the highest crime rates in the United States.
- A population density of 16,273 persons per square mile, second only to New York City.
- The lowest percentage of college graduates (4.3 percent of the population) and the lowest percentage of high school graduates (37.5 percent) in the U.S.
- The least park and recreational acreage, relative to population, of any American city.
- The highest per capita incidence of venereal disease and infant mortality in the nation.
- Unemployment (in spring 1975) of 20 percent. Manufacturing, long the source of training for the unskilled, has declined almost 25 percent in the past two decades; while the expansion of bank and insurance company headquarters has added many new jobs, the vast bulk of them have gone to suburbanites, not ghetto dwellers. One out of every two residents of Newark interested in work cannot find adequate employment. Thirty percent of the un- or underemployed group consists of youths aged 16 to 22; among them unemployment runs at close to 35 percent, even in "good" years.
- A third of the entire population is on welfare. In 1966, the city's welfare bill was $42 million; by 1970, it had gone up by 107 percent, to $87 million.
- Real estate tax rate of $9.94 per $100 of assessed valuation, either the highest or close to the highest in the entire U. S. A. This means that the owner of a Newark house valued at $25,000 has to pay about $2,500 in taxes, $700 more than he would have to pay for a $50,000 house in the fashionable suburb of Short Hills. Gibson has one word for the Newark tax rate: confiscatory. It is an inducement, if not a compelling reason, for homeowners and businesses to leave the city.
- Grave fiscal problems. Standard & Poor's rates Newark's municipal bonds BBB, defined as "the lowest investment grade security rating." The city's finances might be in even worse shape than they are if state laws did not require a balanced budget and prohibit the type of deficit financing that brought New York City to its knees. Faced with a projected budget deficit of $35.7 million in 1975, the city was forced to lay off 900 workers, including 112 policemen, as well as some 900 persons from the city school staffs.
- Deteriorated housing. Only 20 percent of Newark's dwelling units are owner-occupied, compared to 66.8 percent in nearby Bergen County; the common pattern is for absentee slumlords, many traceable only by a post office box in the suburbs, to run their properties into the ground, and then abandon them. We have already alluded to Newark's huge numbers of abandoned buildings and the wide expanses of onetime slums that have been

cleared and then simply left vacant. Nearly 80 percent of the city's dwelling units are at least 40 years old, the vast majority of them wooden. One sees scarcely any mortar and brick construction. Thirty percent of the housing units are so dilapidated they are beyond hope of rehabilitation.

■   Deteriorated municipal facilities. Of Newark's 84 public schools, almost half predate the First World War; there is one all-black elementary school that was built in 1851. Mayor Hugh Addonizio ended a long quietus in school construction by starting 26 buildings in the 1960s, but an estimated $1 billion investment would be needed to bring the Newark school plant up to par. Underground, Newark is rotting too. There are miles of 125-year-old sewers; the cost of replacing them and repairing the pothole-studded streets could run to $2 billion. But Newark has reached the end of its bonding power.

■   A population (by 1975 estimates) 60 percent black, 10 percent Puerto Rican, 9 percent Cape Verdian Portuguese, 21 percent white (largely ethnic). The black population rise began with World War I but has taken on its incredibly rapid pace in the last two decades. Blacks represented 17 percent of Newark in 1950, 34 percent in 1960, 54.5 percent in 1970.* Newark could well become the first major all-black city of the U.S.A. And it will not be a socially diverse black city, but one composed almost exclusively of the economically disadvantaged. The black middle class has been moving out to suburban towns like East Orange and, from there, further into suburbia. "White flight is no concern of mine," Mayor Gibson said in 1975. "I am worried about black flight. We are losing black professionals, people of higher-income brackets."

These were precisely the social ingredients that led to the 1967 Newark riots, in which 23 persons—one white fireman, one white detective, and 21 blacks—lost their lives. Most of the fatalities were attributable to the inept reaction of white police and National Guard to the scattered rioting and looting led by young blacks; many of those killed were clearly innocent bystanders. One was a 73-year-old woman, and two were children. Property damage was about $10 million, three-quarters of which was stock loss from looting, the rest damage to buildings.

Two immediate causes are often cited for the Newark riot—the refusal of Mayor Hugh Addonizio, who had been elected by an Italian-black coalition in 1962, to appoint an able black contender to the post of secretary to the city board of education, and a dispute over the massive displacement of low-income black housing for the new state College of Medicine in the Central Ward. But another, largely unspoken factor was the feeling in the black community that the Addonizio administration and its police were "on the take" for illicit profits, a standard of official conduct hardly conducive to docile obedience among those who felt themselves oppressed.

---

* Whites have been leaving Newark faster than blacks replace them. Almost 100,000 whites left Newark in the 1950s, and a similar number in the 1960s. Even with black arrivals and a high black birth rate, the overall population slipped from 438,776 in 1950 to 405,220 in 1960 and 382,417 in 1970. A half-century ago, one out of every eight New Jerseyans came from Newark; today the figure is one in 20.

Three years later, Newark was treated to the unusual spectacle of its incumbent mayor spending his days in Trenton, where he was being tried before a federal court on charges of plotting with others to extort more than $1.4 million from contractors doing business with the city, and having succeeded in extorting $253,000 over a five-year period.† Then Addonizio would return in the evening to Newark and campaign for reelection until the early morning hours. "Hughie," one of his admiring supporters said, "is a wounded bull who simply won't go down." His career had all the earmarks of an American tragicomedy: born of Italian immigrant parents in 1914 on Newark's Bergen Street, World War II service in which he enlisted as a private and was discharged as a captain with a variety of medals for bravery in action, 14 years of service in Congress (1948–62) when he voted a straight liberal line. In 1962, when he announced for mayor, big, affable Hugh Addonizio had said: "I want to come home. I want my home to be in a decent city, a place my wife, my children, and myself can be proud of." Eight years later, when he stood accused in federal court, U. S. Attorney Lacey would accuse Addonizio of running for mayor "because, in his [Addonizio's] own words, there was no money in being a Congressman, whereas *you could make a million as mayor of the city of Newark.*" [Emphasis supplied.] Addonizio, as previously noted, was convicted along with two City Hall associates and two Mafia figures, and given a 10-year prison sentence.

In the 1970 mayoralty election, blacks were in a slight minority among the 133,502 registered voters. In the first voting (the election is nonpartisan), Kenneth Gibson outpolled Addonizio by a 2–1 margin but failed to get an absolute majority because of the vote received by four minor candidates—including 15 percent for Imperiale. In the runoff, Gibson combined solid support from blacks with a significant white minority vote—some of it from older Italians who deeply resented the dishonor Addonizio had brought on their ethnic group—to win election by a margin of 12,011 votes (56 percent).

Kenneth Gibson is a sturdy, seemingly imperturbable man of palpable good will. Born in Alabama, he grew up in Newark's Central Ward as the son of a hard-working butcher and an aggressive, Bible-teaching mother. He was a successful structural engineer before entering politics in the early 1960s. As mayor, he has helped restore confidence in Newark city government as an honest, albeit rather lethargic institution. Gibson makes no bones about the depth of Newark's problems; indeed his most noticeable achievement has been to convince both the national press and many prominent officials in Trenton and Washington that Newark's crisis is worse than that of any other American city—thus coaxing out some amount of extra state and federal funds for his city. His favorite saying is: "Wherever America's cities are going, Newark will get there first." (Fittingly enough, Gibson in 1976 was elected chairman of the U.S. Conference of Mayors.)

Gibson is not without faults. Some suggest that he fails to move with the vigor and dedication required to make a dent on Newark's ills—that his

† There are many in Newark today who believe that Addonizio's actual take may have approached $1 million a year.

style of leadership is overly cautious and unaggressive. A frequent criticism, one made by blacks as well as whites, is that Gibson spends too much time traveling around the country to appear before black groups—for whom he has become a kind of folk hero. But some dire predictions have not turned out to be accurate. In the 1970 campaign, Addonizio supporters had charged that Gibson was the puppet of Baraka, who indeed did play an important role in that campaign and in the early Gibson administration. Baraka also had great sway over the school board, which voted at one point to require the flying of the black liberation flag in all schools. But by the time of the 1974 election, Baraka had broken with Gibson. In spite of that break, Gibson swept the black wards in the 1974 election by margins exceeding 10 to 1. Imperiale, again his opponent, was deprived of the Baraka issue and actually made a pitch for black votes himself. But Gibson got almost 20 percent of the vote in Imperiale's own North Ward and won with 56 percent overall. He carried a city council dominated by his followers into office.

Less than three months after taking office, Gibson and his aides discovered that the government they had inherited was even more corrupt than they had imagined. Virtually every contract signed by the city in recent years, they found, had been inflated 10 percent to allow for kickbacks. Gibson said he could personally have received $31,000 "under the table" in exchange for appointing certain persons to four city posts, including police director and tax assessor.

Race-related problems continue to plague Newark, but they are changing in nature. In a crippling 11-week 1971 teacher strike, staged by a teachers' union with 70 percent white membership, the school board, with a black-Puerto Rican majority, rejected the teachers' demands, in effect backing up the claims of militant, separatist blacks like Baraka that the union was trying to frustrate community control of the schools, and that teachers were showing a "racist" disregard for black children. But by the mid-1970s, black dominance of government in Newark was almost complete, encompassing the city administration, school board, the police, poverty agencies, and the welfare, health, and employment programs of the city, state, and federal governments in the city. The remnant of white children in the schools were finding themselves obliged to learn black history and live in a world of the clenched fist of black liberation. Steve Adubato, the Italian-American who founded the North Ward Educational and Cultural Center—"a kind of white NAACP," as he described it—was quoted as saying: "We're the new niggers. By nigger I mean anyone who's in the wrong place at the wrong time."

Another much put-upon group emerged—the city's Hispanic citizens, who complained that the black city administration took little interest in them. In 1974 a Labor Day weekend festival at a city park turned into a full-scale riot by young Puerto Ricans; when it was finished two were dead, 54 injured, 57 arrested.

The fervor of the black movement was dissipated by the mid-1970s. "Today," one young black who was caught up in the 1967 conflagrations said, "the mood is despair, not anger." Late in 1974 Baraka even gave up his ideas of black nationalism, saying that movement had become too racist and ineffective, and it was time to regroup, with poor white allies, under the banner of Marxist-Leninist "scientific socialism."

Gibson never warmed to the idea of a "black nation" in Newark. "The real power through history," he said, "is economic power. . . . How can you have a black nation when you don't even control the economics of the city? There are no black banks in this city at all. This is the banking and financial capital of the state of New Jersey, and we [blacks] don't control any of that. We could have the mayor and nine city councilmen and all 7,000 city employees and still no real power. It's important for black people to go through the political process and get better government services, as all other ethnic groups have done—but not to assume that's utopia, or the real route to power."

The Philadelphia Orbit, Trenton, Atlantic City, Princeton

Close to a million more Jerseyans—exactly 952,104, according to the 1970 Census—live in the three-county ring of Camden, Burlington, and Gloucester across the Delaware from Philadelphia. All three counties are much poorer than the Jersey-wide average, and in fact it is difficult to think of a suburban grouping of such minimal distinction.

The core city is Camden (102,551), separated from Philadelphia by the 1.81 miles of the Benjamin Franklin Bridge. "But the body of disjunction might just as well be warped space, the path of union 1.81 light years, writer Barry Rosenberg of *Philadelphia Magazine* has observed. "A distinct provincial mentality exists in Camden. . . . Beyond large-scale administrative ineptitude, political improbity, police brutality, repression of minorities, traffic, pollution and wealth of social ills, all of which bear the big city stamp, the place has no metropolitan culture of its own." Alfred R. Pierce, mayor during the 1960s, upset an entrenched and corrupt old municipal machine, crushed the numbers racket, cleared vast acres of slums—and then waited for federal money for reconstruction. But the money never came and Pierce, tired and bitter, his dreams dashed, stepped down in 1969. In 1973, the city's Democratic boss, Angelo Errichetti, became mayor himself, and even managed to win the support of militant black and Puerto Rican community leaders. Errichetti was subsequently indicted by a state grand jury for conspiracy and misconduct in office when he was Camden's director of public works several years before; after trial, however, he was acquitted of all charges.

Camden is physically repulsive, an unordered *mélange* of ancient boxlike factories like those of RCA and Campbell Soup, dingy row houses (average value $8,300), a blighted waterfront, and barren, empty fields. Among Jersey cities, Camden is closest to Newark and in some respects worse, because it lacks Newark's big insurance industry or education complex. Race tensions are high, with both black and Puerto Rican contingents long at odds with the white establishment and its police.

The rest of Camden County (353,740 people outside Camden) is broken up into small boroughs and townships, one of which—Cherry Hill—may be New Jersey's fastest growing, having risen from virtually zero population in 1960 to 64,395 in 1970. To the south lies Gloucester County (172,681), which has a northern section filling up with standard suburbia and thus reducing the political clout of the conservative farm interests in the south (truck farms, apple and peach orchards). Gloucester's stretch along the Delaware River is a major industrial complex, with matching environmental problems.

North and east of Camden County is Burlington (323,132), an old rural Jersey pine belt county that is now "blessed" by mushrooming housing developments and new industry. It is also the home of two big military complexes, Fort Dix and McGuire Air Force Base, remembered with mixed emotions by those (including one of the writers) who ever endured basic training or shipped out for overseas from them. Politically, Burlington is marginal, with a concentration of rabid right-wingers, including a few Ku Klux Klan members, thrown in for spice. But in 1970, an enterprising reporter for the *Wall Street Journal* found that Willingboro (43,414)—it used to be one of the Levittowns, but changed back to its historic name—was one of the most peacefully and amicably integrated suburbs to be found anywhere.

New Jersey has a capital city. Its name is Trenton. Trenton has a grand Revolutionary era history, the State House, some gleaming new government buildings, and acres of dreary row houses and vacant land awaiting renewal. The population (104,638 in 1970) has been declining, off 18 percent in 20 years. In a competition for America's least attractive capital, Trenton would be a strong contender. It is a working class city, dominated by Italians and blacks; there have been some ugly racial incidents, but good poverty and Model Cities programs may relieve some animosities. The state government provides many jobs but doesn't make payments it ought to in lieu of taxes, so that Trenton, like so many other Jersey cities, is broke.

New Jersey also *had* a vibrant, exciting resort city. Its name was Atlantic City, the first sizable U. S. city devoted exclusively to amusement. It was the birthplace of the boardwalk, saltwater taffy, the rolling chair, and the picture postcard. Up to the early decades of this century, Philadelphia and New York aristocracy loved to check into the Byzantine hotels along the ocean front, and the memory of that era lingers on in grand old hostelries like Chalfonte-Haddon Hall, the Claridge, and the Marlborough-Blenheim. During the 1930s and '40s, the bluebloods began to lose interest and were replaced by the stolid middle class of the big Eastern cities. The course after that was steadily downhill. People with some money came to prefer the Caribbean or Florida or Europe, easily reached by air, and in hot weather it was easier to turn on the air conditioning at home than to drive down to Atlantic City.

By the start of the 1970s there was still a place called Atlantic City, complete with boardwalk, steel pier, big hotels, and all the rest. But in style, it was nothing like the old. The clientele was lower and lower middle-class: ethnic working families from megalopolis and the Appalachian coal regions, poor blacks coming in busloads from New York, Philadelphia, and Wilmington, millions of conventioneers each year (the likes of the Lions and Shriners —big income producers for Atlantic City), and old people (for whom it seemed too late in life to find a new place). Atlantic City had one of the blackest and oldest populations among American cities: 44 percent black (out of a city total of 47,859 permanent residents in 1970), and among the whites 45 percent 65 years of age or older, a geriatric quotient probably excelled only by Miami Beach. The old élan was gone: now one found constant gouging (starting with exorbitant parking fees), plenteous slums, brazenly visible prostitution, a crime rate that rivaled the big cities, and a deterioration of boardwalk stores into little more than souvenir and junk shops, second-class restaurants, and hot dog stands.

The old dowager by the sea did have some claims to vitality: an $11 million addition to an old convention hall (where the Democrats held their 1964 National Convention), four new boardwalk hotels in as many years, and an urban renewal program replacing 16 slum blocks with modern low-income housing.

In late 1976, it suddenly became possible that Atlantic City might have a lot more vitality—perhaps too much. The reason: introduction of casino gambling. New Jersey voters approved, by a 300,000-vote margin, a referendum to make Atlantic City the first place in the U.S. outside Nevada to offer casino gambling. Residents talked of a "rebirth," and the Committee to Rebuild Atlantic City, which had spent $1 million promoting the measure, envisioned lavish new hotels and six gambling casinos by 1980 and 10 by 1985. Opponents, including U.S. Attorney Jonathan L. Goldstein and Col. Clinton L. Pagano, Sr., the head of the State Police, warned that the casinos might attract organized crime, loan sharks, and more prostitutes. Critics also pointed out that state revenues from the casinos—estimated at $17.7 million in 1980—would provide less than 18 cents a year for each of the one million Jersey poor for whom the money was earmarked.

For almost 30 years, Atlantic County and the city were in the iron grasp of the old-style political machine of state senator Frank S. (Hap) Farley. Farley's predecessor, Enoch (Nucky) Johnson, went to jail for tax evasion. The ingrained corruption continued, a matter of public knowledge in the state. Finally, in 1971, U. S. Attorney Herbert Stern and Internal Revenue Service officers began a thorough investigation. In a stunning 1971 election upset, Farley was ousted from the state senate seat he had occupied for 31 years.

Nothing about Atlantic City has been more ossified than the Miss America Pageant, now more than half a century old and still glorifying the idea of sanitized, white, female postadolescence. The old rules still hold—that Miss America girls do not smoke, drink, date, or go around unchaperoned during the pageant. "Make-up," Judith Martin wrote for the *Washington Post* after a recent pageant, is still worn by the girls "to create the kewpie doll look of decades ago—bright red lipstick, blue eye shadow and hair teased into beehives with wiglets of curls added." The women's liberation movement protested the very idea of the pageant.

Finally, we conclude with New Jersey's preeminent university town: Princeton (25,962), which F. Scott Fitzgerald once described as "rising, a green Phoenix, out of the ugliest country in the world." (Princeton's superior attitude toward New Jersey continues to this day; in fact the university would be just as happy to be located in another state, and contributes not enough of its talent and brainpower to solving New Jersey's problems.) Princeton harbors not only the university, but the Institute for Advanced Study, a number of industrial plants (mostly research-oriented), and one of the most sophisticated groups of commuters in the world. Many of them are high-ranking officers of investment and publishing houses, advertising agencies, banks, and insurance companies, who ride the train to New York each day but then return to a town that is uniquely cosmopolitan and cultured. The affluence is easy to document. The median value of a home in Princeton in 1970 was $41,200—compared to $17,400 in surrounding Mercer County and $23,400 in the entire state of New Jersey. Princeton has its pockets of poor (mostly black people), who watch with some envy the good life of students and commuters. But overt racism is nil, a fact proven in 1970 when Princeton picked a black police lieutenant to be its new police chief and then selected a black mayor for a year's term.

Despite its relatively small size (about 5,000 students), Princeton remains one of America's finest universities in two respects: a faculty-student ratio which is exceptionally high among undergraduate schools, and a graduate school which ranks among the top five in the U. S. for 16 departments (including number one rank in philosophy and mathematics). Princeton's strength is that its faculty members, even men of national repute, are expected to teach both graduate and undergraduate courses in addition to their research activities. Because of its student body membership, Princeton was long known as "the northernmost Southern school," and it stayed loyal for 90 years to its exclusive eating club system with a careful pecking order of social acceptability. The "Bicker," or process by which the clubs picked members, was a convenient tool for snobbish exclusion; anyone who failed to get picked by a club, or even the club of his choice, could end up feeling like a social pariah. As more public schools and scholarship students entered Princeton, however, the clubs in the 1960s became an increasingly obsolete institution and began to decline. (As an undergraduate at Princeton a decade before, one of the writers had by odd circumstance ended up as president of one of the clubs, and still remembers sitting in the interclub council meetings wondering what could be done to sink the whole system.) The problem was solved when the university opened eating and unified dormitory facilties, with open admission policies. Ironically, once the eating clubs became less central to the Princeton experience, they began gaining popularity with the less ideologically charged college generation of the mid-1970s. Princeton also opened its doors to women undergraduates in 1969—a step taken, if we may interject a personal note, 20 years too late.

The town of Princeton is home of the Institute for Advanced Study, the nation's ultimate ivory tower, directed by J. Robert Oppenheimer for many years, and the place where Albert Einstein worked for the last years of his life. (The institute is not related to the university, but Einstein was a familiar figure on the campus, rambling along to some errand wearing an old sweater and knit woolen hat.) The institute's tradition is one of pure, unharried scholarship; in the words of one faculty member, former Ambassador George F. Kennan, it "fills the place of a monastery in the Middle Ages. It's a refuge for the highest order of scholarship."

The institute's scholarship remains of the highest order, but it has scarcely enjoyed the serenity of a monastery in recent years. The trouble began when Carl Kaysen, a former Harvard economist and adviser to President Kennedy, opened a new social sciences division. Kaysen, who some say is as close to a universal man as anyone in our time, apparently did not count on the adverse reaction to one of the first appointments in the division in 1973. Appointments traditionally had been approved by faculty vote, but when the faculty turned this one down Kaysen persuaded the board of trustees, which technically has the power, to approve the man in question anyway. The faculty rebelled, and for a full year was embroiled in the kind of acrid politicking that is found only when very bright men become very angry.

And so the serenity of the institute has been disturbed, just as the landscapes of Cherry Hill or Newark have been altered—not really for the better. New Jersey is a state with so many assets—so much brains, so much prosperity—that one thinks it surely should be in better shape than it is. But its politics are still laced with rottenness, its air and water with pollution, its roads with too many cars, and its once green lands with too many tacky subdivisions and high-priced zoning havens. The clues to what is wrong with America are all in New Jersey, and the clues to much of what is right. The question is whether the puzzle can be put together properly.

NEW YORK

STILL THE "SEAT OF EMPIRE"?

I. THE STATEWIDE SCENE

BEFITTING ITS SOBRIQUET OF EMPIRE STATE, New York is a place of many civilizations.

It is New York City, that perpetually fascinating, pain-plagued Colossus on the Hudson, one of the greatest cities on earth, our continent's center of finance, arts, crime, and municipal paralysis.

It is the state of bustling but obscure upstate cities—Buffalo, Rochester, Syracuse, Albany, Schenectady, *et al.*

It is a state of natural grandeur: the beautiful valley of the Hudson, Adirondack and Catskill mountains, of millions of acres of placid farmland, and woods and lakes.

It is the home of Westchester, America's senior suburb, and of Long Island, where a slapdash suburban civilization has been superimposed upon an ancient vacation retreat and farming-fishing economy.

It is a state which was ruled—and that word is not too strong—for 15 years by Nelson A. Rockefeller, a man who for all his false starts and foibles still left as indelible a mark on New York as any chief executive of a state in American history.

It is a state that has pioneered, in area after area, in innovative methods of government, a shining example of federalism in action.

It is a state that has spent and lived beyond its means.

It is the state where greed and selfishness of self-centered groups threaten to undermine the community of consent by which free peoples live.

It is a state now strangely in the shadows, doubted and mistrusted by the rest of the nation.

But still, it is the state of financial power and cultural distinction beyond all others.

Geography almost ordained that it would be so. Fifty million years ago the Hudson gnawed its way from the Great Lakes across the highlands of upper New York State to the sea. Forty million years later it carved a gigantic gorge and its waters cascaded for 36 miles down off the coastal plain into the great valley of the Atlantic basin. (From the air on a clear day, it is still possible to see that old gorge of the Hudson as the river streams out into the ocean and disappears, finally, into the depths off the Continental Shelf.) The ice came some 20,000 to 25,000 years ago, shaping and smoothing the hills of Manhattan, making it the island we know today. And the ice, as it melted, filled and flattened the land and the great gorge of the river. It made the Hudson an estuary, subject to tidal action, as far as Albany, 150 miles upstream. Man could hardly have planned a more superb harbor than the one at the Hudson's mouth. And as European explorers came on the scene, they found an excellent means of access to the hinterland along the Hudson Valley, on its line northward past Albany and into the Adirondacks, and the connection near Albany to the Mohawk River Valley and then the flatlands of the Lake Ontario Plain all the way out to Buffalo and Lake Erie—the chief natural highway into the interior of the continent. This incomparable "water level route" was exploited first by boat and barge, then by rail and highway connections, to capitalize on New York's unique status as the only American state that faces both the Atlantic Ocean and the Great Lakes.

From the time of Henry Hudson's first exploration in 1609, down through the development of the Dutch West India Company's Colony of New Netherland, Great Britain's arbitrary seizure in 1664 and up to the American Revolution more than a century later, New York developed slowly. But New York's strategic position made it an important battleground of the Revolutionary War, the scene of 92 of the 308 engagements in that conflict. In 1784, after a tour of the state's harbors, waterways, and fertile countryside, George Washington ventured the prediction that it would become the "seat of empire." Just at that time, changes were taking place to make his prediction come true. The back of Indian power was broken by a military campaign in 1779, making it possible to penetrate the wilderness in peace. Thousands

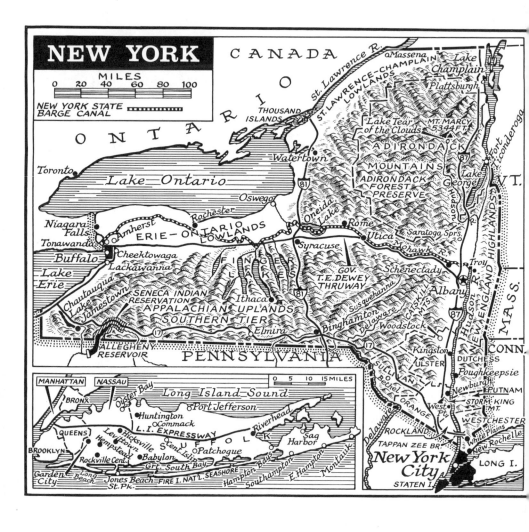

of sturdy farm folk, despairing of ever making a good living on the thin, rocky soil of New England, were pouring into New York. The manorial system of colonial times was beginning to crack with sale of land to the new immigrants. a process accelerated by state laws restricting rights of inheritance in family-held land. The Yankee influx also had a profound political impact, transforming New York, as writer Seymour Freegood has noted, from "the most aristocratic of states [into] a mercantile-agrarian democracy."

New York City began to boom in the wake of the Revolution. Before, it had always been held back by the sparse population of its hinterland, the conservative ways of the Dutch merchants, and restrictive English trade laws. (It had, though, grown rich through government contracts and privateering during the French and Indian Wars, and while it lacked the population, trade, or culture of Philadelphia, it was the gayest of the colonial cities, number one in taverns, bawdyhouses, and the incidence of crime—a seeming constant in all subsequent development.) The War of 1812 slowed down development, but afterward the British dumped a large stock of textiles on the American market through the port of New York, and aggressive Yankee merchants closed in to make New York what it has been ever since, the textile center of the United States.

To become truly dominant, however, New York needed inexpensive access to the farm products and raw materials of interior New York and the Great Lakes. The obvious answer was water transportation, but the Mohawk was a largely unnavigable river. For 15 years, Gov. De Witt Clinton struggled against loud opposition and public derision to have the Erie Canal built to make possible barge transportation from the Hudson River to Lake Erie. Major engineering innovations and a then unprecedented $7 million investment went into the building of the 363-mile canal, but in 1825 the feat was completed and Clinton boarded a barge in Buffalo and traveled all the way to New York City by water, emptying a barrel of fresh water from Lake Erie into the Atlantic Ocean in a symbolic joining of the waters. Instantly, the cost of shipping a ton of freight from Buffalo to Albany dropped from $100 to $10. Within a few years, the little villages along the canal's route—Buffalo, Rochester, Syracuse, Rome, and Utica—had become important cities. To this day, the population of New York State remains thickly clustered along the Hudson Valley up to Albany, and then the Mohawk Valley westward toward Buffalo. Railroads took to the same route, and in the present generation, when the decision was made to build the New York State Thruway (since renamed the Gov. Thomas E. Dewey Thruway) from New York City to Buffalo, touching the major population centers of the state, it was no accident that a route was chosen which in large part parallels the Erie Canal.*

---

* Many feeder canals were built along the Erie, linking it with the centers of farm and industrial production and assuring New York City's destiny as a great port. With the coming of the railways, part of the canal fell into disuse, but early in this century the Barge Canal, following generally the old Erie route, was constructed. There are 36 locks on the canal between Buffalo and Albany, a distance in which the water level drops a total of 546 feet.

The People Story

When the first Census was taken in 1790, New York had 340,120 people and occupied a humble fifth ranking among the 13 states—behind Virginia (which then led with 691,737), Pennsylvania, North Carolina, and Massachusetts. A decade later, New York's population had almost doubled and it was third largest; by 1810 the state had almost three times as many people as it had had in 1790 and was first. For a century and a half, the state remained unchallenged as the nation's most heavily populated state. By 1840, it had 2.4 million people; by 1900, 7.3 million; by the eve of Pearl Harbor, 13.5 million. Sometime late in 1963, according to Census estimates, California overtook New York in population. The 1970 Census found 18,241,266 people in New York State, well below California's 19,953,134. Reflecting a deep economic malaise, the state's population actually fell in the first half of the 1970s, by 121,000 persons. (Only beleaguered Rhode Island shared with New York the distinction of actually losing population in the 1970–75 period.) Still, no other state seems likely to dislodge New York from its second place in national population—not in this century, anyway.

The traditional way of looking at New York population (and politics) has been in terms of New York City versus upstate—the latter a conglomerate of everything north of the Westchester County line, plus Long Island. The first half of this century was clearly the era of New York City dominance by this test. From less than 30 percent in 1830, the city's share of the state population rose to 52 percent in 1910. It peaked at 55 percent in 1930. By 1970, the figure was down to 43 percent, and it seems likely to continue dropping as the city's population dwindles—or at most holds static. The political consequences are even greater, since New York has a lower voting turnout than upstate. In 1946, the city still cast 51.5 percent of the statewide vote; by 1974, its vote was only 33.2 percent of the state total.

The postwar years, however, have introduced the new factor of heavy population in the suburbs. If one counts its entire metropolitan area, New York still represents 62 percent of the statewide total. But it is the breakdown between city, suburb, upstate, and then between metropolitan areas and small city-rural areas upstate, that tells the difference:

	1950 Population	1975 Population	% Change
New York City (5 borough total)	7,891,957	7,567,100	−4.1
Suburbs (Nassau, Suffolk, Westchester, Rockland counties)	1,664,207	3,747,500	+125.2
Upstate Total	5,274,028	6,805,400	+29.0
State Total	14,830,192	18,120,000	+22.2

Up to 1820, most of New York's population was of English or Dutch extraction. Then commenced the great floods of European immigration, bringing five million immigrants into America, most of them by way of New York, between 1820 and 1860. The dominant groups were Irish, fleeing famine in their homeland, and Germans, seeking escape from political upheaval at home, or religious freedom, or both. A majority of the immigrants passed through, but many remained. Later in the century, the flood of Germans and Irish continued, complemented by many English, Scots, and Welsh. Millions of Italian peasants, uprooted from the land, joined the immigrant flow starting in the 1880s; by 1917, there were over 700,000 first- and second-generation Italian immigrants in New York City alone. Hundreds of thousands of Jews were driven out of Russia and Eastern Europe by persecution; collectively, they made New York the most Jewish state of the Union, which it remains today. (By one count in the mid-1970s, New York State had 2.5 million Jews, constituting 14 percent of the total population—several times the totals, both in raw numbers and percentages, of the runner-up states of California and New Jersey. New York was also one of the nation's most heavily Roman Catholic states, with 6.5 million Catholic residents—35 percent of the state population.)

The figures from the 1950 Census, when many of the turn-of-the-century immigrants were still living, provide a good measure of the modern-day foreign-stock composition of New York. Counting both foreign born and their children, the count was about 1.5 million from Italy, 800,000 from Russia, 700,000 from Germany, 650,000 each from Poland and Ireland, 400,-000 from Britain, and 35,000 from Austria. Altogether, New York then had 4.7 million first- and second-generation immigrants, and almost one in four of all foreign-born people in the United States. Upstate as well as in New York City, Italians continue to be the largest single foreign-stock group. The exception is Buffalo, where Poles are predominant.

Since 1940, there has been a net inmigration of blacks into New York State of 917,000.* In 1970, the Census takers found that New York City had 1.7 million blacks in all, New York State as a whole 2.2 million. No other city or state in America even approaches those totals. A major portion of the racial and economic problems of the South, and of the overpopulation and economic problems of Puerto Rico, have simply been transferred to the banks of the Hudson—without New York ever having asked for the favor.

State Government: The Grand Tradition

The state government of New York has so long set the pace for all other states, and has so frequently been the incubator of inventive ideas later adopted for the nation as a whole, that a writer on the subject approaches it

---

* The 1940–70 period also showed a net outmigration of 716,000 whites, almost 90 percent of the exodus occurring in the 1960s.

with something of the timidity he might feel in describing the development of the federal government.

The model was not so enviable in the decades of the Gilded Age following the Civil War. "In the state and its leading cities," David Ellis and his coauthors wrote in their *History of New York State*, "this was largely an era of boss domination, corruption, and favors for special interests." The infamous Tammany Hall leader in New York City, William Marcy Tweed, known to his contemporaries and history simply as "Boss Tweed," capitalized on the naiveté of the unlettered Irish to build an invincible political machine. The Tweed Ring pilfered as much as $75 million from the city government and with the help of blatant vote stealing even placed an ally in the governor's chair in Albany. It was smashed in the early 1870s by Samuel J. Tilden, who in turn became a respectable reform governor of the state. But neither Tilden nor Grover Cleveland, the other prominent Democratic governor of the late 19th century, undertook any fundamental changes in the weak and generally ineffective format of state government. Tammany Hall Democrats and Republican bosses like Roscoe Conkling and Thomas C. Platt remained powerful, often dominant, manipulating political office for private gain.

It was only in the Progressive Era, begun with Theodore Roosevelt's inauguration as governor in 1899 and climaxed in the administration of Charles Evans Hughes a few years later, that the tables were turned and New York government began to place public interest ahead of selfish private interests. The outstanding legislation of that era included laws to curb the excesses of utilities, regulate public service corporations, unify and improve the civil service system, guarantee certain basic rights to industrial workers, and create the nation's first workmen's compensation law. But still, state government was notoriously ill-organized and ill-equipped to guide the fortunes of a state that already had nine million inhabitants. A constitutional convention, held in 1915 and presided over by Elihu S. Root, recommended sweeping changes to make the governor chief executive in fact as well as in name. The amendments were opposed by various vested political interests and defeated in a popular referendum; nevertheless, in the succeeding years all the individual suggestions would be approved individually by the people.

In 1918, Alfred E. Smith, a native son of Manhattan's Lower East Side, a product of a close-knit Irish neighborhood, the Roman Catholic Church, and Tammany Hall, was elected governor of New York. Except for two brief interregnums (1921–23 and 1973–74), New York State has since been governed in a continuous stream, for a period now exceeding half a century, by men of the highest character and ability—a record no other American state has even begun to match:

Alfred E. Smith (Democrat)	1919–20; 1923–28
Franklin D. Roosevelt (Democrat)	1929–32
Herbert H. Lehman (Democrat)	1933–42

Thomas E. Dewey (Republican)	1943–54
Averell Harriman (Democrat)	1955–58
Nelson A. Rockefeller (Republican)	1959–73
Malcolm Wilson (Republican)	1973–74
Hugh L. Carey (Democrat)	1975–

The vicissitudes of national politics have barred all but one of these—Roosevelt—from becoming President of the United States. But three of the others—Smith, Dewey, and Harriman—were very serious presidential candidates; indeed, in every election from 1924 to 1968 at least one serious presidental contender was a resident of New York. Nelson Rockefeller eventually became the nation's Vice President.

Al Smith set the pattern for what was to follow. Through years of service in the state legislature, he had been molded into what the Republican New York *Herald Tribune* called "a true leader, a genuine compeller of men, a man of wit and force with an instinctive grasp of legislative practice." He was a leader of the constitutional convention of 1915. His political acumen was demonstrated by the fact that he never broke with Tammany Hall, but was able to demand and get increased independence from it. Yet as a good government reformer, he picked up backing from independent voters. His success in accommodating such disparate supporters, William Allen White once said, was due to the fact that he retained his old friends with his heart while winning new ones with his head. Smith's accomplishments as governor, David Ellis writes, "made New York a model for every other state in the Union."

In the administrative realm, Smith first got the legislature to approve and then the people to ratify the consolidation of 187 boards and commissions into 19 departments, the executive of each appointed by the governor and serving at his pleasure. Fifty years later, many states have still to take this fundamental step toward effective gubernatorial control. The second major reform was institution of the executive budget system, another step first recommended by the 1915 constitutional convention. The executive budget places on the governor responsibility for reviewing the needs of all branches of state government and then preparing an overall state budget, listing expenditures and tax sources, for submission to the legislature. The reform vastly increases the power of the governor, and reduces the legislature's power proportionately. The federal government adopted the system long ago, but amazingly, a majority of the states have yet to do so. Dr. T. Norman Hurd, New York's budget director for close to a quarter century under Dewey and Rockefeller, told us that the executive budget "was the start of responsible state government in New York. Since the 1920s, New York has not changed its constitutional language on the executive budget, and there have been only moderate changes in implementing legislation. There was not a week in the budget office when I didn't need to check back to those constitutional or legislative provisions."

Throughout Smith's regime of the 1920s, New York stood out as a liberal island in a conservative nation. Under goading from Smith, the legislature vastly increased state aid to local schools and through an accompanying equalization program, which is still considered the best in the nation, saw to it that poor districts got commensurately greater aid. Consolidation of rural school districts was begun, the 48-hour maximum work week adopted for labor, many park and other public works projects initiated, and an income tax approved that would eventually become the mainstay of state government financing. State income was shared with local governments, so that property taxes could be cut. Smith's theory was that people were willing to pay more taxes if they were convinced they were getting sound value in return. In New York, he proved the case, creating perhaps the most alert and progressive citizenry in the U.S.

In 1928, Al Smith went off to make his unsuccessful bid for the Presidency, unfortunately 30 years ahead of the time that the country was willing to accept a Roman Catholic as its leader. Franklin D. Roosevelt, scion of an aristocratic Dutch-descended family from Dutchess County, ran in his place and was elected. FDR was not as distinguished a governor as he would prove to be a President—perhaps because he viewed Albany chiefly as a stepping-stone to Washington, and was not forceful about taking stands on controversial issues. He proposed many reform measures, based on suggestions of gubernatorial commissions, which the legislature rejected. Reluctantly and belatedly, Roosevelt cracked down on the extraordinary corruption then being revealed in New York City. But as the Depression deepened, he moved decisively to prevent bankruptcy of municipalities and starvation among New Yorkers by providing imaginative measures for public relief, including establishment of a temporary emergency relief administration. Thus the formula was developed in New York for the New Deal programs that would effect America's recovery from the severest depression it had ever known.

Herbert Lehman, the son of an immigrant Jewish family from Germany and founder of the successful banking firm of Lehman Brothers, was favored both by Smith and FDR to become governor in 1932, and won despite initial opposition from Tammany Hall. He was totally lacking in the charisma of his political mentors, and let the headlines go to President Roosevelt and Mayor Fiorello La Guardia, who were in office at the same time. But his record as governor was astounding. Not only did he push forward myriad Depression relief measures, but he managed to convert an inherited budget deficit into a surplus. He was one of the greatest champions the civil service system ever had, and he single-handedly pushed to approval a series of labor laws more progressive than either the federal or any other state's at the time.

For sheer administrative talent, it is difficult to think of a 20th-century governor who has excelled Thomas E. Dewey. A native of the little city of Owosso, Michigan, he went to New York City in 1923 to study music and law, became the fabulously successful prosecutor of mobster Lucky Luciano and countless other racketeers in the trucking, restaurant, poultry, and bak-

ing businesses, and after a first unsuccessful try in 1938, was elected governor
in 1942 and served 12 years in the job. Dewey is the father of the tradition
of progressive Republicanism which has thrived in New York State as nowhere else. He did it through forward-looking programs and hard-headed
political maneuver. As Warren Moscow noted some 25 years ago in *Politics
in the Empire State,* Dewey as governor "assumed complete control of his
party. County leaders who opposed him were broken by cold, hard-bitten
use of the patronage powers of the governor's office. Legislators suffered a
similar fate. He brooked no interference."

Confident enough of his own abilities to surround himself with the best
men, Dewey professionalized the governor's staff, the civil service department, and state purchasing arm, and brought in more professionally qualified
department heads than any of his predecessors in Albany. Like his contemporary (and 1948 Vice Presidential running mate), Earl Warren in California,
he refused to lower tax rates while the state experienced wartime budget
surpluses. The result was a $450 million fund that could be expended for
delayed public works projects after the war. Hundreds of thousands of New
York youngsters owe him thanks for his leadership in creating a state university—which New York had lacked up to that time. A vigorous health department program virtually eradicated tuberculosis in New York, highway
building was pushed forward, and the state's mental hygiene program was
thoroughly reorganized. And in response to Dewey's initiative, the legislature
in 1945 passed a proclamation of economic emancipation for New York's
minority groups—the nation's first fair employment practices law. The legislation boldly stated that "the opportunity to obtain employment without discrimination because of race, creed, color or national origin is hereby recognized as and declared to be a civil right." A commission was established to
enforce the law. It would be another 19 years before the federal government
took the same step.

Fiscally, Dewey believed in "pay as you go" and could be called a straight-
forward Republican conservative; it was his political acumen that set him
apart. A typical Dewey technique was to let the Democrats arouse the public's interest in some new social legislation. But just when the Democrats felt
they had an appealing public issue, Dewey would step in with legislation,
tailored to suit his party's needs, and take credit for the accomplishment.
"This was a technique that had been perfected long ago by Britain's Tories,"
David Ellis notes, "but it was perennially new to New York's Democrats,
and they never learned to cope with it."

Dewey's loss of the 1944 Presidential campaign against FDR, a popular
wartime President, was no surprise or particular disappointment to him. His
1948 defeat at the hands of Harry Truman was another story. All that summer
and up to and including the early edition of the Chicago *Tribune,* Dewey
was elected President; sadly for him, his term ended late in the evening of
the actual election day, November 2, 1948. Dewey's reserved public manner
(belying real inner warmth), his somewhat platitudinous calls for national

unity, some say even his mustache, had something to do with the surprise defeat. But pocketbook issues were chiefly responsible, as pollster Sam Lubell reported: "People voted for Truman because they thought he would protect their bread and butter interests. Labor rolled up the traditional Democratic majorities; farmers worried by the 80th Congress' refusal to extend grain storage were seeking down to earth promises which they didn't find in Dewey speeches."

A man of lesser stature than Dewey might have taken to sulking and recriminations after the 1948 election, but instead he effected a graceful retreat from the front rank of national politics, winning a final term as governor in 1950 and then "retiring" to a Wall Street law practice in which he became a multimillionaire. It is difficult now to appreciate Dewey's youth when he first became a national figure. He was only in his mid-thirties when his racket-busting made his name nationally known, 40 when he was first elected governor, 46 when he lost the Presidency for the second time. Twenty years later, President Nixon offered to appoint him Chief Justice of the United States. But Dewey declined, saying it was too late for him. At last, he was too old for the job.*

In retrospect, Dewey's 1948 defeat may be viewed as a critical turning point in American postwar politics. Had Dewey been elected, he would in all probability have brought to the presidency the same qualities he brought to the New York governorship—and might have succeeded, as President Eisenhower never did, in impressing his stamp of moderate progressivism on the Republican Party. Instead, the Republicans in the 1960s moved sharply to the right, with Barry Goldwater in 1964 and the "law 'n order" Richard Nixon of 1968. Things might have been different for the Democrats, too. For with Dewey in the White House, Joe McCarthy and his ilk could not credibly have accused the party of the New Deal of "losing" China to the Communists in 1949. Democratic Presidents' fear of losing another Asian country to the Reds was a major cause of the Vietnam war of the 1960s. All this, of course, is speculation—but it is one of the more interesting might-have-beens of recent American history.

Dewey's influence, even behind the scenes, was not to be discounted. In 1952, he played a crucial role in getting Eisenhower the Republican nomination over Robert A. Taft. He helped Richard Nixon win the 1952 Vice Presidential nomination, and then keep his place on the ticket after the private-fund uproar that climaxed in the "Checkers" speech. Six years later, Dewey's circle of friends played an important role in getting Nelson Rockefeller his first gubernatorial nomination. Even in 1970, it was Dewey's law partner

---

* New York has been a breeding ground of great jurists, including the likes of Charles Evans Hughes, Benjamin Cardozo, Harlan Fiske Stone, John Marshall Harlan, Harold Medina, and Learned Hand. Dewey, with his logical mind, would probably have made a fine judge, too. But a man he appointed to the New York court of appeals 30 years ago, later that court's chief judge, Stanley Fuld, was one of the nation's most outstanding jurists. Fuld often had the pleasure of seeing his dissents on issues such as free speech, obscenity, and literacy tests become law through decisions of the U. S. Supreme Court.

and associate of 33 years, R. Burdell Bixby, who managed Rockefeller's fourth-term campaign for governor.

Dewey's successor, Averell Harriman, the only Democrat to have broken the solid 30-year wall of Republican control in Albany, was a real disappointment in the job—a man of great renown in foreign affairs, but unfortunately preoccupied with the possibility that he might run for President in 1960. He did set up the nation's first office of consumer affairs, headed by Dr. Persia Campbell, but was frequently blocked by the Republican-controlled legislature. Withal, Harriman would probably have been elected to a second term in 1958 without an opponent of Rockefeller's stature.

Nelson Rockefeller and His Works

Thomas Dewey gave New York State government its finishing gloss of professionalism; Nelson Rockefeller took the instrument, experimented with it and reshaped it, added on appendages (some of dubious constitutionality) to make the money available to accomplish what he willed,* and in the process built the most complex, fascinating, and socially advanced state government in U.S. history. To the job of being governor, Rockefeller brought (1) years of business-philanthropic-government experience; (2) the expansive world of knowledge, contacts, and staff support that comes with being a Rockefeller; and (3) the personality of an absolutely irrepressible builder-manager-operator. Despite his reputation as a liberal Republican, Rockefeller is essentially nonideologic, a *doer* rather than a *thinker*, a total pragmatist. Perhaps for that very reason (plus some lucky political breaks), he won four successive four-year terms in office, becoming the senior governor of the United States.

Nelson Aldrich Rockefeller was born in July 1908 in the fashionable summer resort of Bar Harbor, Maine. He was named for his maternal grandfather, Nelson Aldrich, a Senator from Rhode Island and a power in Republican politics. But the vital antecedent name was Rockefeller; Nelson was born, in fact, on the 69th birthday of his paternal grandfather, John D. Rockefeller, who in the best robber-baron tradition had manipulated his Standard Oil empire into monopolistic control of the U. S. oil industry—and then, just as industriously, began to give away part of his fortune. The story of the Rockefeller Foundation, Rockefeller University, and other philanthropies begun by Rockefeller with the encouragement of his son, John D., Jr., is beyond our scope here. But mention must be made of the remarkable generation of Rockefellers of whom Nelson is but one: John D., III, head of the Rockefeller Foundation and the Lincoln Center; Laurance, manager of the family's business interests and founder of the American Conservation Association;

---

* The Rockefeller techniques of circumventing state constitutional restrictions on deficit spending were adopted by New York City and pursued with even greater vigor there than in Albany. The result, according to most economic observers, was that these fiscal sleights of hand were chiefly responsible for the budgetary crisis facing both the city and the state during the 1970s.

Winthrop (now deceased), cattle breeder and twice Arkansas governor; and of David, president of the Chase Manhattan Bank, a leading promoter of the physical rebuilding of Manhattan, chairman of the board of Rockefeller University and of the Museum of Modern Art. With the exception of Winthrop, all were New York based, clearly the premier family of their city and state. Now a fourth generation of 23 members is standing on the threshold, ready to take over stewardship of one of the world's greatest fortunes. But the fourth generation is active in more varied professions, and lives further afield; the best known, to date, is John D. Rockefeller, IV, or "Jay" as he is popularly known, elected in 1976 as governor of West Virginia.

Nelson graduated from Dartmouth College, Phi Beta Kappa, in 1930, married a childhood friend, Mary Todhunter Clark, "apprenticed" for a period in the family-owned Chase Manhattan Bank, and in 1937 traveled through South America on family (oil) business, thus beginning a lifetime interest in Latin American affairs. In 1940, he helped formulate President Roosevelt's Good Neighbor Policy and was a major architect of U. S.-Latin American policy in the State Department through 1945.

President Eisenhower in 1953 appointed Rockefeller Undersecretary of of the new Department of Health, Education and Welfare, and later his Special Assistant for Foreign Affairs. At one point, Eisenhower was reportedly ready to make Rockefeller Undersecretary of Defense, with the plan of making him Secretary when Charles Wilson retired. But Treasury Secretary George Humphrey opposed the nomination, because Rockefeller was "a spender." That was the last straw impelling Rockefeller to go into elective politics, where he would have his own base. (It may also have been George Humphrey's most substantive contribution to American government.) In 1958, Rockefeller waged an astounding, high-impact campaign as the New York Republican gubernatorial candidate. He mingled with the masses, gulped down blintzes and bagels and pizza, kissed babies, and assailed Democratic "bossism." The public responded, and he beat a thoroughly outclassed Averell Harriman by more than half a million votes.

Rockefeller was hot news from 1958 onwards. There was, for instance, all the news coverage about his abortive bids for the 1960, 1964, and 1968 Republican Presidential nominations—presidential politics apparently being the one area in which the fabled Rockefeller expertise comes to naught. The whole country watched with fascination, sometimes with opprobrium, as he divorced his wife of 32 years and in 1963 married Mrs. Margaretta Fitler Murphy, the just-divorced mother of four. Early in Rockefeller's governorship, much public attention, and ridicule, surrounded his proposal that New York should prepare for nuclear war by installing a fallout shelter in every building, theater, school, and home. Appropriately, the press rode him hard for preaching frugal "pay-as-you-go" fiscal policies in his first years in office and later incurring fantastic debts through questionable bonding practices, and for promising "no new taxes" in his 1962 reelection campaign, and then promptly proceeding to enact them. The nation was surprised (New Yorkers somewhat less so) when he resigned the governorship in December 1973, after 15 years, purportedly to head the Rockefeller-money-backed Commission on Critical Choices; his real motivation, of course, was to seek the presidency once again, without the impediment of having to run (and risk losing) the governorship in 1974. It was not many months later when the Commission became less important to Rockefeller than public office, in this instance the vice presidency, to which he was appointed by Gerald Ford and, after some lengthy hearings, confirmed by Congress. The public, perhaps because it suspected the truth anyway, perhaps out of post-Watergate ennui, seemed not particularly interested in learning the details of Rockefeller's family fortune, nor even in discovering how he had had his brother Laurance finance a scurrilous book attacking his 1970 gubernatorial opponent, Democrat Arthur Goldberg, former Secretary of Labor, U.S. Supreme Court Justice, and Ambassador to the United Nations.

Eclipsed in this public debate were the vast programs of Nelson Rockefeller, the planner and doer, which have, in the words of one writer, "changed the physical face of New York more than any governor since DeWitt Clinton built the Erie Canal." Richard Dougherty, the delightful New York journalist whose service as George McGovern's press secretary in 1972 might be thought to have immunized him to Rockefeller's appeal, commented: "You can't go around New York State with Nelson, his slides and his twang, without being impressed." It is these programs, more than anything else, which are the legacy of Nelson Rockefeller's 15 years as governor —and are probably the best indication we have of what kind of president he might have been. In just about every case, Rockefeller succeeded in changing the way New Yorkers live. But in just about every case, the effects—or momentum—of the programs he began vastly diminished within a year or two after he left Albany. The programs are best viewed one by one:

UNIVERSITIES. When Rockefeller took office, the decade-old State University of New York had only 38,000 students and was, in the words of Ford Foundation president McGeorge Bundy, "an empty holding company." But projections by the state board of regents, and by a special commission which Rockefeller appointed, indicated that without vastly expanded facilities, thousands of qualified students would be denied a college education in New York State by 1975. With that, an expansion program of unique proportions ensued. "Others have built state universities over long periods of years. We did it over eight to ten years," Rockefeller said, adding (typically): "and we'll come out the largest." The State University's total full-time enrollment reached 263,000 in 1974, culminating years of rapid growth. The state of California has a more extensive system but it has separate boards of regents or trustees for the University of California, state colleges, and community colleges. In New York, a single board of trustees now supervises four university centers (at Albany, Binghamton, Buffalo, and Stony Brook) as well as the 12 four-year colleges of arts and sciences and 38 community colleges. The state's annual appropriations for higher education rose from $95 million in 1959–60 to $846 million in 1972–73, a rise of 791 percent.

All this growth would have been impossible, however, without an unprecedented program of capital construction costing upward of $1 *billion* since Rockefeller became governor, and eventually expected to reach $4 billion. The state constitution provides that approval of the people in a popular vote must be obtained to issue new bonds, but Rockefeller was anxious to begin construction on a broad scale, rapidly, and on a self-liquidating basis. He demanded that his legal counsel and budget office find a way around the barrier of submissions of a bond issue to the people (where there was always a risk of rejection). The idea that emerged and was then implemented was to set up a semi-independent agency, the State University Construction Fund, which could issue bonds without popular approval. The construction fund receives all tuition and other fees and income from the university, and uses that income to pay the debt service on the construction bonds. The real legal brain that perfected this system was that of John Mitchell, later Nixon's Attorney General and Watergate felon, who at the time was a senior partner in the Nixon law firm and one of the nation's leading experts in the municipal bond field. The "backdoor financing" bonding method has plenty of critics—as we will note later—but it has made possible a much more rapid expansion of state facilities than would otherwise have been possible.

Within a few years, the four university centers, offering both graduate and undergraduate degrees, have become not just diploma mills but distinguished centers of learning, actually luring (through high salaries and other devices) topnotch faculty from major institutions in other states. The State University at Buffalo has drawn the most national attention by its bold, pioneering educational patterns—and criticism for turbulence (which hit a peak in spring 1970). In 1960, Buffalo was a private university, primarily a streetcar college for the city. By 1970, it had doubled its enrollment to about 23,000 students, had an English department marvelously innovative and creative by national reputation, a school of pharmacology regarded as among the country's best, and pioneer graduate programs in fields like computer sciences and policy sciences. The State University at Albany has eight professional and graduate schools, offers undergraduates flexibility in their study patterns (including an opportunity to study abroad for a semester or a year), offers the country's first doctoral program in criminal justice, and is noted for its Atmospheric Sciences Research Center, one of the country's top centers for the study of pollution. The State University at Binghamton is especially well known for its programs in history, mathematics, and economics. The State University at Stony Brook, on Long Island, has already won recognition as a national leader in a number of scientific fields, including ecology and evolution, urban engineering, petrology, and marine sciences. In addition, enrollment has grown rapidly at medical schools in Syracuse, Brooklyn, Buffalo, and the new medical center at Stony Brook.

As Rockefeller poured ever greater amounts of money into the state university system, private groups—mainly Roman Catholic—muttered about the unfair competition. The answer was the so-called Scholar Incentive Program, under which the state supplements tuitions of students attending colleges in New York State by several hundred dollars. In effect, it is a subsidy to the colleges, which promptly raised their tuitions to match the amount paid by the state. By the late 1960s, some quarter million New York students were receiving some form of state financial assistance.

Yet as Rockefeller left Albany, the state's system of higher education was facing problems which seemed more serious than ever before. Just as enrollments were beginning to decline, costs seemed about to rise at least as precipitously as in the expansionary decade of the 1960s. The state has just about reached its goal of making available to every high school graduate with the necessary motivation and aptitude at least some form of post-secondary education. But with private colleges' costs rising rapidly, there were moves to increase fees at state-supported schools—especially at the City University of New York, where loyal alumni for years had blocked *any* tuition—which would of course make achievement of the long-term goal more difficult. The number of university and college students in the 1990s is expected to be no larger than that in 1972, and the question facing the state was whether the taxpayers would want to continue to foot the increasing bills for his enterprise, which in recent years has consumed 11 percent of the state budget.

HOUSING AND NEW TOWNS. New York had begun state-subsidized low-income housing projects before Rockefeller took office, but the total inventory of new units produced was not satisfactory. Rockefeller wanted a vehicle to stimulate low-income and medium-income housing and on John Mitchell's advice created the Housing Finance Agency, which is able through local-property-tax abatement and the mortgage bonds it issues to facilitate participation of limited dividend groups in moderate-income housing projects. Since the HFA's creation in 1960, it has made $1 billion available for new housing; presently there is $4 billion in the fund for mental-hygiene facilities, for nursing homes, day-care centers, hospitals, youth facilities, and senior-citizens centers, all of which the state is financing for local government and private groups through the device of self-liquidating bonds.

But as Rockefeller explained the problem, New York found that even with low-interest government money, housing projects, complicated by zoning and code regulations, soon became too difficult for all but a limited group of sponsors. Thus the decision was made in 1968 to create the Urban Development Corporation, which as a single entity would have the power to do whatever might be required—condemn property, raze old structures, override local zoning and building code requirements, and use mortgage loans or just about any other conceivable form of financing, and sell up to $2 billion worth of its own bonds, secured by a "moral obligation" (since the state constitution forbade such indebtedness being imposed on the state without approval of a popular referendum). It could develop entire projects either on its own or in conjunction with private enterprise, and then operate or sell or lease back properties when completed. To head the UDC,

Rockefeller selected Edward J. Logue, former redevelopment chief of New Haven and then Boston. Logue seemed happy to have the opportunity, claiming that the UDC represented "the most versatile and the most all-inclusive development legislation on the books in any of the 50 states." He brought an unusual sense of urgency and push to the new agency and then staffed it with a highly competent group of people from outside the civil service system. (The result was a much freer, less constrained staff, with those on a professional level—architects, lawyers, planners, and the like—showing much more initiative and energy than in a typical state department.)

The standard run of UDC projects was usually a chunk of city housing, anywhere from 100 to 2,000 units. The projects in New York City were usually high-rise, those in upstate mixed. But there are some dramatic exceptions. The most interesting effort is underway on Welfare Island (renamed Roosevelt Island for obvious reasons), a thin strip of mostly vacant land in the East River opposite midtown Manhattan. Mayor Lindsay set up a committee to study the island's future, and on the basis of its recommendations an exciting master plan for the island emerged, designed by Philip Johnson and John Burgee. The UDC then went to the city and offered to be the developer. A 99-year lease was agreed on (after long negotiations).

Unfortunately, it appears that the UDC's reach considerably exceeded its grasp. In February 1975, 14 months after Rockefeller's resignation as governor, the UDC went belly-up. It defaulted on $100 million of bond anticipation notes, admitting that it did not have the money to pay its obligations. Logue had already been fired by Governor Carey, but it was not clear if the responsibility was his. The main problem was that in January 1973 the Nixon administration stopped the federal housing subsidy program, on which UDC had depended for much of its income. The corporation had broken ground on 6,900 housing units in 1970, 11,300 in 1971, and 12,000 in 1972. Then disaster: 3,200 units in 1973, 761 in 1974. It seemed that those skeptics who had criticized Rockefeller's strategy of funding programs through independent agencies floating bonds finally gained vindication. Governor Carey and bipartisan majorities in the legislature scrambled to bail out the UDC and in the late spring of 1975 were able to put together a package which included some $410 million in support from the state government and an additional $140 million in loans from major New York lending institutions. The UDC's fall was doubly tragic—for New York State, which needed the housing units, and for states across the country, which saw a model of innovative state action discredited. The danger was that other states would "lose their nerve" in the area of housing projects, at the very time that it was becoming apparent that federally directed and financed housing projects were rapidly diminishing and/or hopelessly ensnarled in red tape. In late 1975 the UDC was continuing under new management with a sharply reduced budget, as its supporters awaited better days.

TRANSPORTATION. Rockefeller was an enthusiastic highway builder, and in fact capitalized on his record with a famed television commercial in his 1966 campaign, in which the viewer was taken down the central white strip of a seemingly endless highway as a voice pointed out that one can take all the roads Governor Rockefeller has built "and they'd stretch all the way to Hawaii—and back." Among the major projects were the Long Island Expressway, the Southern Tier (Route 17) Expressway, the Adirondack Northway, and the North-South Expressway (Interstate Route 81).

But lots of governors have built highways; Rockefeller's uniqueness was in the absolutely unprecedented way he inserted a state government into the field of urban mass transit. Again, Rockefeller turned to a special authority to do the job—developing a way to avoid the slow bureaucracy of old-time agencies, a technique pioneered by Al Smith. The story is best told in Rockefeller's own words:

> Our problem was that the Port of New York Authority didn't want to stretch out into mass transit. It just stuck to airports, bridges, tunnels, and seaport facilities, and did a good job on those. But the Port Authority has two weaknesses: it's bistate [with New Jersey], so that neither state really controls it, and it's too independent of elected officials. Also, its usefulness is restricted by its unwillingness to go into the money-losing proposition of buses and railroads.
>
> I started out trying to help the private companies stay in the field of mass transit by cutting their taxes in half, setting up a commuter-car construction fund to finance new equipment, and similar steps. But it didn't work. They started to go into bankruptcy. We took over control of the Long Island Railroad—if it had gone out of business, it would have meant $1.5 billion in new highways.
>
> Then we set up the Metropolitan Transportation Authority with very wide powers. And it has ended up taking over not only the Long Island Railroad, but all New York City subways, all New York City buses, the Triborough and other bridges, and now the New York share of the New Haven Railroad, and the Penn Central line running through Westchester.
>
> The system moves 7 to 8 million people a day. We're re-equipping facilities. We've already put 640 modern new cars on the Long Island.
>
> The MTA does a fantastic job. There are about 44,000 employees just in this one authority. The federal government talks about doing these things. But the state is doing it, as the *effective, active agent.*

The man Rockefeller chose to head the MTA system was William J. Ronan, so trusted a confidant that he had served eight years as the governor's executive secretary and had also been the appointee most blessed by the governor's largesse: Ronan was the recipient of $625,000 in loans, later forgiven, from his onetime boss. Ronan has been variously described as brilliant, cool, resilient, brusque, and arrogant, but no one has ever gainsaid that he represented the views and worked for the goals of Nelson Rockefeller. In turn, Ronan totally dominated the MTA's 11-man board; as Fred C. Shapiro reported, that "it's Ronan's board. So total is his control, in fact, that the MTA was often described as a 'Wholly Ronan Empire.'" The power was extraordinary for a man who, as dean of New York University Graduate School of Public Administration and Social Services a few years before, was known as a severe critic of authorities and advocate of decentralized government. Inevitably, Ronan and his board were a lightning rod for protest from all quarters about service, equipment, and ideology. Jack Newfield wrote in *New York* in 1970 that "the MTA includes no commuter, no poor person, no woman, no student, no black or Puerto Rican, no union representative. [A black was subsequently added.] It consists exclusively of affluent people who rarely use the dirty, unreliable, overcrowded, cold, dangerous New York City subways." New York City people point to the fare increase to 50 cents in 1975 as evidence of MTA's cold-heartedness, especially to young and old people for whom the high fares constitute a real hardship, and sometimes a terrible burden on an already strained family budget. (Until 1948, the fare was only five cents.) From Long Island, there have been heated complaints about higher fares and slow progress in making up for 70 years of neglect by the previous owners. State Controller Arthur Levitt has been upset about unconscionable concessions to the unionized workers of the Long Island Railroad, who have been aptly described as "some of the nation's highest-paid and least-burdened railroad workers." And the unions themselves complained bitterly about indignities inflicted on trainmen by passengers in retaliation for delayed, inefficient (and of course rude) service.

The complaints about the MTA, however well justified, should not obscure what it has been doing. It has begun a $2 billion modernization and expansion of a vast transportation system which had simply been allowed to depreciate, without any major improvements, since well before World War II. Not only has the Long Island Railroad gotten modern new equipment, but 800 high-acceleration, stainless-steel cars, 600 of them air-conditioned, were ordered for New York City's straphangers. Under the East River, a massive four-track tunnel had been under construction for use by Long Island Railroad trains and as the keystone of a 52-mile addition to the subway system with new lines in Manhattan, Queens, the Bronx, and Brooklyn. Even long-forgotten Staten Island's transit line has undergone a $25 million face lifting. Most of these improvements are financed under part of a $2.5 billion general transportation bond issue approved in 1965.

Ronan himself has since moved on to become chairman of the one agency with the resources to provide such subsidies—the Port of New York Authority. Not only does the Port Authority get revenue from the activities we have seen Rockefeller describe, it also owns the 10-million-square-foot World Trade Center in lower Manhattan. Critics have argued that the Port Authority should have poured some of its money into mass transit, rather than compete with private developers in the real estate market—but over the years the Port Authority has not listened much to critics. There may be a difference in the next few years, however, for even Ronan may have to pay attention to the two Democratic governors, Carey of New York and Byrne of New Jersey, who have ultimate control over the Port Authority —and who have frequently criticized the agency in the past.

THE ARTS. In 1960, Rockefeller acted to create the nation's first state-sponsored Council on the Arts. Its highly successful programs, based on suggestions by Senator Javits that even predated Rockefeller's interest, have centered on bringing symphony and theater into small cities that would never have been able to attract them otherwise.

NARCOTICS. Rockefeller acknowledged that narcotics control was the least successful effort of his administration. "We've spent over half a billion dollars so far and experimented with every possible approach and we still haven't found the answers," he told us in 1971. A state Narcotic Addiction Control Commission was started in 1966, after Rockefeller had made control of drugs an issue in the 1966 campaign. The commission, after some false starts, learned to make wise use of its power to commit addicts. (Before 1966, addicts who did not want treatment could refuse it, and most, out of hedonism, immaturity, narcissism, or a desire for short-range kicks, took that option.) The programs of the commission (later renamed the State Office of Drug Abuse Services) cover a wide range—from prison incarceration for addicts who are violent and dangerous to special treatment for the emotionally disturbed to the drug maintenance approach (methadone) for a large number of heroin addicts. In addition, the state subsidizes Daytop, which is a New York equivalent of California's Synanon, plus a whole host of private agencies, Odyssey houses, Exodus House, and Quaker rehabilitation programs. Millions of dollars are passed on to localities for narcotics guidance councils and similar programs.

Nevertheless, by 1971 only some 25,000 addicts had received direct state treatment—a small pass at the narcotics problem which some have called the "bubonic plague of the 1970s." Two years later, again with Rockefeller proclaiming that he was going to solve the problem, harsher measures were passed. Among the penalties: mandatory life sentences with no possibility of parole for possession or sale of drugs; an end to youthful offender treatment for late-teen pushers; a 100 percent tax on drug dealers to allow confiscation of their earnings and property; and a bounty to be paid informants whose information led to drug convictions.

Compulsory commitment was criticized initially by civil libertarians, but it soon became clear that the real problem with the program—at least as far as most New Yorkers were concerned—was that Rockefeller's draconian measures had little effect in choking off the supply of illegal narcotics. A federal government report showed there were "fewer dispositions, convictions, and prison sentences for drug offenses" between 1973 and 1975 than under the old laws. In those two years, 891 persons were sentenced to prison, but only 31 drew the maximum penalty of 15 years to life. The New York *Times* reported that more suspects sentenced to the severest terms appeared to be low-level dealers, not major traffickers in heroin or cocaine. The Rockefeller law didn't restrict plea bargaining or reduction of criminal charges as intended. "About 87 percent of those indicted for A-1 felonies are pleading to lower charges," according to state senator Ralph J. Marino, chairman of the New York State Senate Select Committee on Crime. "They'll do a year any time on one foot with the profits they can make." Yet even Rockefeller's harshest critics (and successors) failed to suggest any better solutions to the drug problem.

ALBANY MALL. Nelson Rockefeller once said, "I always wanted to be an architect," and his critics are fond of accusing him of having an "edifice complex." He has been building things for most of his adult life, having played a hand in Rockefeller Center, Colonial Williamsburg, the United Nations headquarters, Lincoln Center, the World Trade Center, and the building of 17 new university and college campuses in New York State. Where many a critic thinks he has really gone overboard is the grandiose Albany South Mall project, which Rockefeller conceived in 1959 to make the decaying old city of Albany into "the most spectacularly beautiful seat of government in the world." The idea was to return the center of state offices, which Dewey and other predecessors had permitted to go suburban, back into the center of Albany, thus creating a nucleus for the city's renewal.

William K. Harrison, a lifetime Rockefeller friend, coarchitect of Rockefeller Center, and designer of many other notable structures, was asked to do the overall Mall design. *Fortune*, which has done the definitive coverage on the Mall, describes the Rockefeller-Harrison concept this way:

What the two master builders dreamed up was a modern imperial enclave, rising on a hill overlooking the Hudson River. A half mile long and almost a quarter mile wide, the site lies between the executive mansion and the nineteenth-century capitol building, and by this connection creates one great government complex.

The Mall itself [contains] a forty-four-story office tower, four identical twenty-three-story agency buildings, a legislative building, a justice building, a headquarters for the motor-vehicles department, a cultural center (including museum and library), a meeting center, and a laboratory for the department of health. The heart of this complex of concrete and marble is a huge platform, 1,440 feet long and 600 feet wide, with a 500-foot reflecting pool flanked by two smaller pools as well as lawns, trees, fountains, and promenades.

One may dispute Rockefeller's assertion that the Mall "is going to turn out to be the greatest thing that has happened in this country in 100 years," but there is no questioning that it will be the most expensive project ever undertaken by a state government. Informal early estimates of the Mall's cost were $250 million, the first formal state estimate in 1964 was $400 million, and the final cost was more than one billion dollars. State Controller Levitt had maintained for some time that the construction cost will be at least $1 billion and that bond financing will cost another $500 million. The bonding arrangement, Levitt says, is "beyond the control or even the comprehension of the electorate." Under it, the county of Albany floats the bonds to build the Mall and then leases the whole to the state on a schedule designed to amortize the bonds by the year 2004. This idea was conceived by Albany Mayor Erastus Corning II, who told *Fortune* that Rockefeller went for the idea "like a trout for a fly," since it was commonly assumed the state's voters would never approve a bond issue for a big mall in Albany. But as Levitt pointed out in an interview with the writers, using the credit of Albany County (single-A) as against that of the State of New York (double-A) is a difference of a half percentage point in interest—"a helluvalot of money over 30 years."

What Rockefeller Left Behind

The South Mall has been completed, and Nelson Rockefeller has left Albany. (He never spent that much time in New York's capital, preferring to operate out of his privately owned office on Manhattan's West 55th Street; Carey, in contrast, made a point of moving his 12 children to Albany.) Rockefeller's achievements are there to see: the State University and its many campuses, roads and dams and buildings and even some new subway cars. But some of his accomplishments eroded away; the physical structures built will last, but the governmental structures, without the force of Rockefeller's personality (and money) behind them, have withered. The UDC case is instructive, for this is an agency which was wholly Rockefeller-created. Despite the clear social need for new housing, there was no other major constituency behind the UDC idea when Rockefeller advanced it in 1968, no other force pushing it in the legislature; Rockefeller, using his iron control over the Republican Party, jammed it through by main force. However lofty the social goals, this was as much a perversion of the legislative process as, on the national level, was Lyndon Johnson's insistence that Congress pass his Great Society legislation just as the executive branch mandarins had written it. The executive had grown too powerful and eventually the body politic had to pay.

During most of his tenure Rockefeller had not been subject to critical scrutiny in the legislature or anywhere else—except, perhaps, in the pages of the rather esoteric *National Review*, the Buckley-owned and run conservative magazine. But perhaps the best summation against Rockefeller's record, Jack Newfield's "The Case Against Nelson Rockefeller," was written as long ago as 1969.

It was the middle of January, and the subway fare had just been raised to 30 cents, and the sun was slanting through the window in silver shafts, and John Lindsay was sitting behind his desk, his glasses on top of his head.

"They tell me you're doing a piece on Nelson," the mayor said. "I'll give you a title for it. You should call it 'The Last Colonialist,' because that's what Nelson is all about.

"He just doesn't believe in local participation, in the common sense of ordinary people. He thinks he knows what's best for everyone. So he walks right in and builds things, big things. He's a colonialist."

Lindsay was right. He cut to the core of Nelson Rockefeller, to the central distinctive quality of the governor's sensibility. Perhaps *paternalist*, or *technocrat*, or *elitist* is a better word, but the idea is the same. It is a set of mind and character beyond the postures of politics. It is the sensibility behind Lincoln Center; the new billion-dollar Mall in Albany. . . . It is his indifference to the idea of community control or participation. . . . It is, in sum, his elitist social engineering, bereft of soul and blind to the consequences his manipulations led to.

One legacy which one might have expected Rockefeller to leave behind in New York, but which he did not, was sound financing of state government. Packed with good intentions (including the dramatic rise in aid to local governments), the New York budgets demonstrated the near-geometric growth rate that threw the state into what Rockefeller eventually acknowledged was a financial "maelstrom." These figures contrast the state budgets in Rockefeller's first and last years in office:

	Fiscal year 1959–60	Fiscal year 1973–74
	(figures in millions)	
Assistance to local school districts, community colleges, and private schools	$ 634	$2,400
Higher education, (University of New York, state colleges, City University of New York, scholarships)	95	1,110
Assistance to localities for public assistance (aid to the aged, blind, needy children, etc.) and state welfare activities	176	1,351
Total budget	$2,041	$8,881

The state began to retrench as early as 1971, when a rebellious Republican legislature cut $760 million out of Rockefeller's budget—and still had to pass the second highest tax increase in the history of New York. In that year welfare allowances were cut 10 percent, medicaid eligibility was reduced, and a state commitment to share revenue with local governments was trimmed back. In the wake of the legislature's budget-cutting spree, Rockefeller felt obliged to dismiss over 7,000 state employees. Soon the newspapers were running poignant stories about disheartened personnel and callous cutbacks in the schools and mental hospitals. For a state long dedicated to liberal big-government spending traditions, it was a dramatic reversal of form.

And there was another dramatic reversal of form in 1975, when Hugh Carey succeeded to the governorship, the first Democrat elected to that office in 20 years. Suddenly it was Carey, with a 14-year record of liberal votes in the U.S. House, calling for economy, frugality, and retrenchment. "All around us in this capital are symbols of splendor, monuments of glass and marble," said Carey in his inaugural speech, in the shadow of the nearly-finished Albany Mall: "They stand as living embodiments of an idea of government as an over-expanding institution, to be paid from the ever-expanding riches of tomorrow. To the citizens of New York I say: Tomorrow is here. We have learned that every resource of this earth is finite, so is the resource by which the government sustains itself: the earnings of the people."

When he took office, Carey quickly decided he didn't have any choice but to try to hold down the rise in spending and to raise taxes to cut the deficit caused by recession-shrunk revenues, inflation-spurred increases in ordinary state expenses, and new spending commitments from the Rockefeller years. It was, said Harry O'Donnell, a top aide to Rockefeller—and Carey—"a period of historic irony."

For almost all of 1975, Carey battled with New York City officials, bankers, and union leaders, the legislature, and Washington to resolve the city and state fiscal crisis. As soon as the legislature enacted, in special session, Governor Carey's three-year financial plan for the city, and President Ford agreed to federal aid, attention turned to New York State's financial crisis, which had worsened when the state tied its debt to that of the city earlier in the year. In late December, Carey, with backing from New York bankers, won from the legislature a $600 million package of new taxes on businesses and banks.

In his 1976 budget message, Carey did not call for new taxes. The Economic Development Board, a group established by Carey to protect the health of the private sector, had advised him that the state's economic decline and loss of jobs was its foremost, long-range problem. (Between 1970 and 1976, the state's labor force shrank by over 700,000 workers. Total employment in the state went down by more than a million, to 6.9 million, in that period.) Seeking to alleviate the problem, the legislature in 1976 approved a package of tax incentives for business expansion and delayed the date when industries must start producing environment impact statements for construction programs. But the impatient business community remained leery of the state's efforts to improve the business climate. (The sorest of points for business was the state's personal income tax, which is the most progressive in the United States and totals 15 percent of incomes in the executive bracket of $25,000 and upwards.) The Council on the Economy, which Carey created to spearhead the state's fight against economic stagnation, was reshaped into a consultative role after it publicly recommended sweeping tax reductions for business and the rich.

Carey proposed cuts in state payrolls, programs, and aid to local governments for education and welfare. He insisted he was not running out on his liberal past, calling his program "beneficent austerity" and citing his proposals for more spending on mental health, youth services, and correctional institutions.

The result tells us a lot about the way the political process has worked —and works—in New York. For one thing, the budget was "balanced" only by assuming that the state would be able to borrow $2.75 billion from private investors—a quite possibly shaky assumption. Second, the draconian cuts which Carey had said were so necessary had more or less disappeared in the legislative process. As the New York *Times* put it, Carey had

wanted to implement another $600 million worth of spending reductions—$370 million in revenue-sharing, school aid, welfare, and other local assistance programs; the rest on the state's own operations.

Most politicians in Albany had said they would be astonished if Mr. Carey were able to persuade the legislature to cut local aid in an election year. They need never have wondered. In an exercise one budget expert termed a "restoration comedy," Republicans and Democrats united to reinstate all the cuts—save those that reduced Medicaid reimbursement rates and other social welfare programs. . . . In effect, the cutbacks were the least visible ones, in that direct services to residents were saved.

The legislature overrode a governor's veto, for only the second time in New York's history and the first time in 104 years, to enact an education bill aimed at restoring heavy cutbacks in school spending in New York City. Both Carey and Mayor Beame opposed the measure; even some legislators admitted it was 'irresponsible" in light of the fiscal crisis. But they proved no match for teachers union lobbyists. (A State Supreme Court judge later declared the act unconstitutional.)

Carey supported the legislators in their passage of an historic court reform bill requiring the state to assume all costs of county and city courts on a gradual basis over the next four years, a boon to hard pressed localities that had been paying two-thirds of court costs. The bill also provided for appointment, rather than election, of judges to the Court of Appeals, centralized court administration and streamlined judicial discipline. But legislators questioned whether those sections would make it through future legislative tests.

Unlike most of his predecessors, Carey could not look back on his first two years in office to count programs passed to improve people's lives. The closest he had come to glory was avoiding fiscal disaster, and the problems of New York City kept popping up again and again. His personal choice for state Democratic chairman, Patrick Cunningham, had been indicted in the alleged sale of Bronx judgeships.

Carey did prove his leadership capabilities, however, in bringing together the governors of Connecticut, Massachusetts, New Jersey, Pennsylvania, Rhode Island, and Vermont to organize the Coalition of Northeastern Governors to work together on the economic problems of their region. At a historic conference in Saratoga Springs, N.Y., in November 1976, the governors focused on the fact that Northeastern states pay far more in taxes to Washington than they get back in expenditures.

Even with federal revenue sharing, New York State and City seem doomed to remain forever shortchanged in federal aid programs. Federal grants to various levels of New York government went well over $2 billion a year in the early 1970s, but the dollar figure was 47 percent below California's. As a share of state and local revenues, federal aid represented 14 percent in New York—compared to 19 percent in California and 18 percent in the country as a whole. New York ranks 47th among the 50 states in the percentage of its government budgets paid by Washington.

The major reason for New York's shortchanging is that federal aid formulas favor low-income and lightly populated states—a kind of residual congressional attitude, as Senator Javits has put it, "that the greatest virtues are the rural or small town virtues." Geographic formula discrimination harms New York on airport aid (despite the fantastic amount of national air travel that passes through the state), and waste treatment facilities and hospital construction are parceled out on a formula that favors states with low per capita incomes—of which New York is most definitely not one. (The per capita income of the state is 13 percent over the national average, but in the metropolitan New York area, the cost of living is almost that much above the country as a whole—not to mention the extra vacation budget New Yorkers deserve "to get away from it all.") None of the federal aid formulas seem to take into account the problems of population density and higher cost of land and services in congested urban areas.

To top it all off, New York finds itself penalized by virtue of the very pioneering nature of its governmental programs. In water pollution, air pollution, and freeway programs, for instance, New York was years ahead of the rest of the country, and its constant battle in Congress often focuses not so much on new programs as getting reimbursement for refinancing of what it has already done. The state has never been reimbursed for the Thomas E. Dewey Thruway, for instance. "It's a shocking thing," Javits says. "Every other state got a 90 percent ride. We've never been brought up to par on probably the greatest road in the United States."

This grim fiscal picture raised the legitimate question, at least a half decade before the dénouement of 1975, of whether New York was not simply living beyond its means. The state comptroller, Arthur Levitt, was expressing grave concern about the state's financial future years before the public perceived the problem. (Levitt was a man who could speak with some authority, since he antedated even Rockefeller in Albany, having won election to the first of six four-year terms in 1954. He built a popular reputation as a kind of fearless nonpartisan fiduciary—"the people's comptroller," he called himself.)

Levitt was especially critical of the method of bond financing adopted by Rockefeller on John Mitchell's recommendation—the use of quasi-independent sponsoring agencies, which can offer the state's "moral pledge" of repayment but not the "full faith and credit" of New York State which stands behind bonds that are approved by the people in popular refenda. Levitt's objection to "backdoor financing," as he calls it, is based on two grounds:

First, it circumvents a constitutional restraint which I believe is more needed today, because of inflation and high taxes, than ever before in the history of the state.

Also, it is much more costly than the constitutional method of borrowing. . . .

You have to remember that some of the bonds, like those for housing, run up to 50 years. I doubt if they will be able to maintain the debt service through rentals. Now the State Housing Agency is financing the State University, housing for the elderly, child day care centers and mental hygiene institutions—hardly things one would expect to make money, especially in light of the inflationary thrust of our economy. . . .

The only reason Rockefeller failed to go to the people for financing of the new bonds, Levitt told us in 1971, was that the people would have rejected many of them:

What we really need now is to take stock of where we are and decide on priorities. What this state (like others) has done is to proceed on the assumption it can do everything it wants—that it can take the aggregate of public wants and satisfy them right away. . . . What the people have to decide now is what comes first—What is so compelling, so vital, that it needs to be done right now. The people are the best judges of that.

The bonded indebtedness of New York State, Levitt said, was several times over what it was 10 years before. Direct debt, to which the state has pledged its full faith and credit by popular vote, reached $3 billion in spring 1971, triple the amount of a decade before. Indirect debt (like the Albany Mall) reached $2.4 billion in 1971, up from $24 million a decade before. Contingent debt—based on a "moral guarantee" of the state, and issued through special authorities—rose to $1.6 billion, where there had been none at all a decade before. "By any measurement," Levitt contended, "the state of New York is mortgaging its future to a point which approaches the capacity of public burden."

Levitt was obviously vindicated when the Urban Development Corporation defaulted on $100 million of bond anticipation notes and the state—despite its "moral obligation"—hesitated before moving to pay them off. Indeed, by 1976 the state's indirect debt had reached $3.1 billion and contingent debt—including Big Mac bonds—was a staggering $9.1 billion.) Including full faith and credit bonds, the total indebtedness of New York State was $16.3 billion.

Another serious problem New York faces is the need for greater productivity in the public sector. New York State, and New York City in particular, have been the breeding grounds in the last few years of a new militancy among public employees. It began with school teachers, has spread to numerous other categories of government workers, and is already beginning to move across the country. As Dean Alan K. Campbell of the Maxwell Graduate School of Citizenship and Public Affairs at Syracuse University pointed out, "This has great implications for public sector costs, because we haven't figured out how you get—simultaneously—increases in productivity to match wage increases. In some areas, public employee salaries are now 20 percent ahead of private sector salaries for similar work." In New York City, the high government wages are inducing workers to desert taxpaying private industry jobs, and forcing some companies to flee the city. Municipal workers in the city presently put in a 35-hour work week, and if one counts "sick leave" and holidays, they get 45 days vacation in their first year—a privilege unheard of in private industry. Unions move into an actual management role by such devices as teachers' contracts specifying pupil-teacher ratios and specifying that teachers can't stay overtime. In the summertime, the much-put-upon bureaucrats also get to go home at 4 P.M.—a privilege granted by Mayor Wagner, which no one has had the temerity to repeal. Mayor Abe Beame in 1975 finally ordered a halt to the practice, but was overruled by the courts.

Even more than basic pay or work privileges, the controversial element in public sector employment is now pensions. The problem is centered in New

York City, but applies statewide, and it is not new; for years, mayors have been negotiating higher and higher pension benefits with unions, often as a substitute for some immediate wage gains. Such settlements often let a mayor off the hook politically on the short run, but the long-term effect on city budgets—as New York City has been discovering—can be disastrous. By 1975, the time of New York City's greatest financial crisis since the Great Depression of the 1930s, the city government found itself obligated to pension support for municipal workers in the amount of more than $1 billion annually. All pension agreements have to be approved by the state legislature, and in fact the public employee unions have been exceptionally influential there. Once approved, the agreements are irreversible because under the state constitution, membership in a public pension system is a contractual right that may not be diminished or impaired. But in 1971, the legislature finally balked when New York City negotiated a pension agreement with the 90,000-member District 37 Council of the American Federation of State, County, and Municipal Employees that gave the workers half pay after 20 years of service and full pay after 40 years service. One leader said that the agreement meant, in effect, that a man could retire after 40 years at 190 *percent* of his last pay, because he would also be receiving Social Security (not considered a part of New York's pension agreements), a total tax exemption from the state and city income tax, and an exemption from federal income tax until he gets back as much as he paid into the pension fund. In protest against the legislature's refusal to approve their pact with the Lindsay administration, the workers called a wildcat strike that tied up the drawbridges coming into the city and caused the most monstrous traffic jam in New York City's history. In 1976, the legislature—with belated endorsement from Carey and the Democrats—moved to test a consolidation of eight separate state and New York City public pension groups into a single uniform system, a reform proposed by a pensions commission established by Rockefeller. New State employees were required to contribute 3 percent of their salaries, and supporters of the plan claimed it could save the state up to $1.5 billion over the next 10 years.

The political potential in this issue is not hard to divine, since the taxpayers are not only being inconvenienced by public-be-damned strikes, but must sooner or later get the message that they are being asked to pay for pensions far beyond those they get themselves. (In fact, private industry pension plans in the U. S. are something of a scandal, since workers' rights are generally terminated when they shift jobs, and plans often fail to pay anticipated dividends by all varieties of actuarial legerdemain.) Dean Campbell suggested in 1971 that New York might soon witness the unusual sight of "politicians instead of running with appeals to the public sector employee, running against him." But there is the problem, he added, that "the public sector is now so large, if you take each employee and his family members, that if you take them on you have a helluva political fight on your hands."

New York has had more than its share of public employee strikes, and they became more and more frequent prior to 1975. The history goes back to the immediate postwar era, when school teachers at Buffalo struck and the legislature responded with the very tough Condon-Wadlin Law outlawing all strikes, requiring immediate discharge of all strikers—with permission to rehire them on a probationary basis for five years but without a penny additional compensation for three years after a worker was engaged in a job action. The law kept labor peace in New York for many years, but was inherently unfair because it had no provision for negotiated settlements. But when Lindsay became mayor of New York City in 1966, he was hit immediately by a transit strike. Lindsay at first stood up to the union—striking a fine pose—but then he caved in and made an immensely expensive settlement and triggered a series of leapfrogging demands by municipal unions that have brought the city immense fiscal woes. As part of the transit workers' settlement, Lindsay agreed to ask the legislature to provide amnesty for the strikers, thus spelling the beginning of the end of the Condon-Wadlin Law.

In 1967, the legislature passed the so-called Taylor Law, allowing public employees to organize and engage in collective negotiation but still forbidding strikes. The law has a provision permitting heads of unions who strike to be fined and sent to jail. It has effectively averted strikes by state employees. But it has not been well enforced in New York City. There was a possibility by the mid-1970s that the law might be altered in a restrictive way because localities could no longer afford what critics said were high settlements made under the law.

At the upper rungs of government, both the state and city have some exceptionally able executives. Comparing the state government with other states, Dean Campbell says only California, and to some degree Michigan, can compare to the quality of men at the upper and middle levels of the bureaucracy. Improved salaries under Rockefeller, he says helped in this area, and New York State can now compete effectively with the federal government, and in many areas the private sector, in the pay scales offered for junior executive entering jobs. Over the years, this could make a tremendous difference in the quality of state government.

Government and People

New Yorkers are constantly affected by their activist state government. In welfare, for instance, the rolls shot up from 420,000 recipients in 1955 to 1.7 million in 1971, triggering controversial cutbacks in aid levels. The state welfare load by mid-decade was leveling off at 1.44 million with an additional 400,000 covered under various programs for the aged and disabled. New York City had reached the one million figure and passed it by the summer of 1975 and foresaw the possibility of topping 1.25 million before the end of the 1970s.

For almost a decade, New York State's $3 billion medicaid program—the largest, most comprehensive and most expensive in the nation—served as the cornerstone of what the state legislature called "its long proud history of providing generously for people in need." But the state's fiscal crisis and rising medicaid costs forced New York for fiscal 1977 to cut back on medicaid benefits, tighten eligibility requirements, and reduce reimbursements to hospitals, physicians, and nursing homes.

The state's mental health hospitals now contain a third less people than they did in 1960, a result of better community facilities; of the hospitals that remain, one national expert told us, "They're probably the best in the country—and that's bad enough." One exceedingly restrictive statute went off the books in 1966—the 179-year-old law that had forbidden divorce on any grounds except adultery. The law had forced thousands of New Yorkers to stage scenes in which a private detective would find one of the partners in intimate association with a third party; no other state had a law so regressive or foolish. Now several other grounds are permissible for divorce in the state.

One of the most fascinating modern stories surrounded the effort, finally successful in 1970, to repeal an 1830-vintage statute that forbade all abortions in New York, except to save a woman's life. The new law, most liberal in the nation, permitted any woman to have an abortion, on her doctor's counsel, up to the 24th week of pregnancy (and after that to save her life). Nor were there the restrictions of new abortion laws in some other states: Hawaii's 90-day residence requirement, for instance; or Maryland's insistence that all abortions be performed in an accredited hospital. In New York, abortions could be (and were) performed in clinics, and there was a big out-of-state business from women whose states are more conservative. (More than half the 70,000 abortions performed in New York City in the first year were for out-of-state women.)

What made abortion reform possible in New York? The New York *Times*'s Bill Kovach put it this way: "Population pressures, limited resources, illegal abortion butchery and the demand of women for more control of their own lives demanded change." In the end, only the Roman Catholic Church fought the new law, and in legislative debate there was much talk of the "murder" of unborn fetuses. The senate Republican leader, Earl W. Brydges of Niagara Falls, played a key role in letting the bill come to a vote, though he had blocked it in the past; yet as the legislation was approved, Brydges, a Roman Catholic, wept openly. In the assembly, the bill was a single vote shy of the required minimum of 76 "yeas" when an obscure upstate Democrat, George M. Michaels of Auburn, rose to stop the voting. His hands trembling and tears welling in his eyes, he said: "I realize, Mr. Speaker, that I am terminating my political career, but I cannot in good conscience sit here and allow my vote to be the one that defeats this bill—I ask that my vote be changed to 'yes.'" (Michaels was, indeed, defeated in his own party's primary in the next election.) Even after final passage, Terence Cardinal

Cooke, speaking for the state's Roman Catholic bishops, appealed to Governor Rockefeller to veto the bill. But the governor signed it. The outcome marked a nadir in Catholic influence on modern state government—in large part, because so many laymen refused to support their own Church's position. (The abortion issue was later settled on a national basis, of course, by the decision of the U.S. Supreme Court setting basic standards—the same decision which prompted the right-to-life forces to start a campaign for a constitutional amendment.)

In the troublesome area of penology, New York has a reasonably progressive history, going back to 1876 when the Elmira Reformatory was opened in order to separate young first offenders from hardened criminals. In the early years of this century, wardens at Sing Sing—the legendary "big house" up the Hudson 30 miles from New York—introduced a new degree of understanding into the treatment of convicts.* Over the years, more and more constructive vocational training programs were introduced into the prisons, and in 1965 the legislature abolished the death penalty, except for murders of policemen and peace officers. But the general attitude of prison officials has been that security comes before rehabilitation, a position opposed only by small numbers of psychiatrists, counselors, and chaplains. Starting in the late 1960s, the base of protest widened, among both civil rights organizations and the prisoners themselves. The objections were against the worst abuses of solitary confinement, the "strip cells" in which prisoners are forced to remain naked in empty cells, and the arbitrary rights of prison officials to cancel "good time" which convicts try to build up so that they can win early release.

As black and other minority prisoners became increasingly politicized, seeing themselves as political prisoners of the state, trouble began to mount around 1970. A serious sign of trouble was the major disturbances that hit New York City's detention houses in summer 1970. Later that year, a one-day riot occurred at the Auburn Correctional Facility, touched off by a black solidarity day sitdown. Six months later the press carried harrowing reports of 72 black and Puerto Rican inmates at Auburn still kept in special disciplinary areas. The isolated men smuggled out letters (some written in blood) telling of repeated beatings, gassings, and allegedly unprovoked assaults by guards.

Several of the most defiant prisoners at Auburn were quietly transferred to the Attica Correctional Facility (about 30 miles east of Buffalo), thereby laying the groundwork for the bloodiest prison uprising in American history in September 1971. The all-white guard force at Attica was already ill-equipped to deal sensitively with a prison population 70 percent black and about 15 percent Puerto Rican, and even less prepared to cope with the radical, desperate prisoners it received from Auburn. (Of this new breed of prisoner, then New York State Corrections Commissioner Russell Oswald said:

---

* Sing Sing, the place where the electric chair was introduced in 1891 (and took 614 lives until it was last used in 1963), celebrated its 145th birthday in 1970 by being converted into an adult reception center for transfer of prisoners to other and more modern penal facilities around the state. The costs of renovating Sing Sing, and its vulnerability to escape, were the basic reasons for the change in status.

"They have the idea that they are victims of a racist society, repressed by racist pigs and racist institutions.") In the uprising at Attica, 32 guards were taken as hostages and the convicts then issued a long list of demands— more religious freedom, the right to communicate with anyone at their own expense, "realistic rehabilitation," less pork (which Black Muslims do not eat), more fresh fruit, "competent" doctors, and the like. The state agreed to meet all these demands but refused to grant amnesty to all participants in the uprising (in which a guard had been killed), or to guarantee the prisoners "free passage" to a "nonimperialistic country."

The stalemate between the rebellious prisoners and state authorities lasted four days, and finally state police and National Guard troops stormed the prison. When the smoke had cleared, 32 prisoners and nine hostage guards were dead from the bullets of the attackers. Rockefeller, who had refused the prisoners' request that he come personally to Attica to negotiate with them, was subsequently blamed by some for precipitous action that cost so many lives. (Activist civil rights lawyer William M. Kunstler called him a "murderer.") Rockefeller, in turn, took full responsibility for the decision to storm the prison (a decision he said was the toughest of his career as governor), but insisted he had had no alternative. At a meeting with Commissioner Oswald, Rockefeller said, the rebellious convicts "just lined up eight of the prisoners [hostages], bound, blindfolded, with an executioner with a knife at his throat. At that point the decision was made. There was no alternative but to go in."

An official New York state investigation into the uprising concluded that Rockefeller should have visited the scene before ordering the armed assault. The report, prepared by the McKay Commission, also criticized police actions during the assault, charging that the attack was characterized by mass chaos with no communication between police commanders and those leading the assault and no way for squadron leaders to tell men to stop firing. By and large, the commission found that the inmates' grievances were legitimate and that they had tried unsuccessfully to work within the system to correct them. The report said: "That the explosion occurred first at Attica was probably chance. But the elements for replication are all around us. Attica is every prison, and every prison is Attica."

Five years later, Attica and other state prisons had new gyms, grievance committees, and fewer strip searches. But the fundamental shortcomings persisted: overcrowding, racial tension, inadequate rehabilitation programs, and small staffs. A State Commission of Correction team found in 1976 that the conditions at Attica were "just as bad, perhaps worse" than in 1971. "If the right circumstances came along, yes, we could have another 1971-type uprising," said a prison official.

Legislators and Lobbyists

On the level of technical competence and depth of resources, the New York legislature ranks high among the states. The Citizens Conference on State Legislatures ranked it second only to California, and listed these strengths:

Annual unlimited sessions; control over its own resources; time, staff and funds, and the ability to set legislative salaries by statute; a wide range of staff services, including fiscal research, committee staffing, leadership staffing and a full array of technical support; uniform, published rules of committee procedure, the jurisdiction of committees spelled out in the rules, and committee roll-call votes regularly taken, recorded and published.

The Citizens Conference faulted New York on only a few points—long night sessions, crowded calendars, "the circus atmosphere which attends the ending of annual sessions," passage of many bills without extensive public hearings, and a lack of rules barring legislators from practicing before state regulatory agencies.

Within the New York system, the elected leaders—the senate temporary president and assembly speaker—wield vast power. They name the committee chairmen and memberships, control a legislative budget of more than $22 million, appoint all legislative employees, and largely determine which key bills can go to the floor, and when. Today those leaders are Stanley Steingut and Warren M. Anderson.

Two more different types can scarcely be imagined, symbolizing the rift between upstate New York and the City which has characterized New York legislatures for at least 70 years. Senate majority leader Warren M. Anderson is a colorless, austere Republican from the small upstate city of Binghamton. It might be said that his Republicanism is more akin to the Midwestern Taft variety than to the New York Dewey-Rockefeller tradition, and indeed places like Binghamton are closer physically and spiritually to parts of the Midwest than they are to New York City. Leaders like Anderson, one observer said, "are able to view the big city only as a constant thorn in the side of their tidy upstate world—not as the heart and soul of the Empire State." Yet that judgment—like many assessments of politicians, before their hour of trial—was to be proven incorrect in 1975, when Anderson worked closely and tirelessly with Carey and others, even using his best offices in Washington, D.C., to help New York City avoid bankruptcy.

Stanley Steingut, the Democratic Speaker from Brooklyn, is from an entirely different background: the world of the regular Democratic clubhouse, the interlocking directorates of lawyers, judges, insurance companies, appraisers, and banks, all referring business to one another, that makes a career as a regular Brooklyn politician something other than a hair-shirt occupation. In 1975, Steingut finally achieved his lifelong ambition of following in his father's footsteps and becoming Speaker; his father had served in that post in 1937, after one of the few other times the Democrats controlled the assembly. (Republican gerrymandering kept the Democrats out until 1964; and they had lost the assembly later, despite one-man-one-vote districting, largely because of their own lassitude.) The charge was constantly made that Steingut and the regulars he led were more comfortable in their minority status, the recipient of occasional largesse from Rockefeller and holder of the extra salaries and patronage that the minority leadership can give. Steingut's supporters reply that he has always strongly backed progressive legislation.

The budget and powers of New York State government are so colossal that Albany draws lobbyists as flowers attract bees. The lobbyists are now a highly sophisticated group, representing virtually every interest in the state, and a far cry from the old stereotype of the cigar-chomping, vote-buying influence peddler.

By general consensus, the education lobby is the biggest, and many believe the most powerful, on the Albany scene. Numerous organizations are included, not the least of which is the state board of regents, which has vast powers over the $2 billion-plus in aid to schools which the legislature doles out each year. The more direct pressure for teachers' salaries is exerted by the New York State United Teachers, a merger of the old NEA affiliate and the American Federation of Teachers; the whole organization is headed by Albert Shanker, the New York City teachers' union boss, whose power extends to the top reaches of Democratic politics and the AFL-CIO. The teachers' union pension fund is also one of the major buyers of city bonds which helped the city avoid bankruptcy—and gave Shanker leverage he has not failed to use.

Practically all the major universities, public and private, lobby in Albany. Industry is also very powerful, especially on the "little bills" that no one notices. Some major companies hire lobbyists to represent them during legislative sessions, but there are also umbrella groups like the Associated Industries of New York and the Empire State Chamber of Commerce. Banks are quite likely to send their own representatives to Albany, but they hardly need to: according to one report in 1971, nine of the 22 members of the Senate Banks Committee and five of the 22 members of the same committee on the assembly side were shareholders, officers, or directors of banks or savings and loan associations. However, there is a running feud between the savings and commercial banks.

While business interests swing the most weight with upstate Republicans, organized labor is especially influential with New York City Democrats. The AFL-CIO carries the burden for most labor lobbying, but the Teamsters have their own man in Albany too. Other important lobbies represent organized medicine and the Roman Catholic Church, although the Church's power, as we have noted, has recently been on the decline.

Not to be overlooked is the very active New York City lobby. It has a large staff which does hundreds of favors for legislators, and in turn hopes to get a favorable ear from them on the multitudinous bills of each session that relate to the city. Most of the city bills get handled on their merits in the legislature, except for the controversial city aid measures that are perennially mired in the tug-of-war between the city, governor, and legislative leadership. (New York City—and also New York State—maintain their own lobby operations in Washington, too.)

"Good government" interests are represented by groups like the Citizens Union and League of Women Voters. But Stephen J. Solarz, elected at 28 to the Assembly and in 1974 to Congress, suggests that there are "significant interests in the society that go underrepresented"—including "the poor, the consumer, the non-union wage-earner, and the young."

Politics I: The GOP

As the weight of population and power in America has shifted westward, New York has lost its unique status as *the* preeminent source of Presidential candidates. In the course of American history, five Presidents have come from New York (Van Buren, Fillmore, Cleveland, both Roosevelts) and a sixth man (Tilden) won in the popular vote but lost in the electoral college. Between 1900 and 1948, 11 of the 26 Republican and Democratic party nominations for President went to New Yorkers. But in the five Presidential elections since 1952, only one New Yorker—William E. Miller, Goldwater's running mate—has appeared on a national ticket, and even his candidacy was taken seriously by few people (least of all himself). From this count one may exclude Eisenhower and Nixon, who though they had resided in New York for a few years just before their Presidential nominations, belonged spiritually to the open plains and Southern California respectively.

More than demographic change has reduced New York's Presidential role. With the exception of Robert Kennedy, who became a legal resident of the state to run for the Senate, not a single New York Democrat has mounted a major Presidential campaign in recent years—simply because the New York Republicans have monopolized virtually all the major offices in the state. And while local Republicans have been winning statewide elections in New York, their brand of Republicanism has been too liberal for national GOP tastes. In fact, it might be said that for countless Republicans who live south of the Mason-Dixon Line and west of the Appalachians, New York Republicans have been pariahs ever since 1952 when Dewey and the New York GOP got Eisenhower nominated over Taft. (New York-based communications media—especially *Time*—were used to publicize the alleged "steal" of delegates by Taft forces.) An essential part of the Goldwater movement was an emotional reaction against the monied Eastern liberal "establishment" within the GOP.

From the 1890s to the start of the New Deal, New York was strongly

Republican in its presidential voting. Then it turned Democratic with the ascension of its own Democratic Roosevelt and has usually voted with the Democratic nominee in subsequent elections. The exceptions to this have been the candidacy of native son and sitting Governor Thomas Dewey in 1948, the nonpolitical General Eisenhower in 1952 and 1956, and the Mc-Govern debacle in 1972. In 1960, John Kennedy captured the hearts and votes of New Yorkers over Ike's Vice President and Dewey protegé, Richard Nixon, who was also to lose to Hubert Humphrey in 1968. Lyndon Johnson simply overwhelmed Barry Goldwater in 1964 by reaping nearly 70 percent of the vote cast. It was much closer in 1976, but Jimmy Carter's 52 percent in New York was enough to give him its electoral votes—and the election.

One could cite many reasons for New York's liberal-Democratic orientation in presidential campaigns, starting with its heavy urban-minorities population. Perhaps the most convincing explanation is the activist-progressive model of executive which New York has had since the days of Al Smith, reinforced by the state's strong civil rights tradition.

For 10 of 11 successive gubernatorial elections, from 1918 through 1938, New Yorkers chose Democratic governors, and in almost every election the Democrats won by piling up huge New York City pluralities that overwhelmed the normal GOP upstate majorities. In those days, one old hand in New York campaigns told us, "the Republican party was a patsy for the Democratic governors—Smith, Roosevelt, and Lehman." The governors made a whipping boy out of the almost constantly Republican legislature, suggesting that the GOP was a regressive force controlled by Old Guard upstate utility interests and banks. Each succeeding Republican gubernatorial candidate would get tarred and feathered with the same brush, and go down to defeat.

It took a city man, Tom Dewey, to turn the personalities and historical pattern upside down. Dewey had an aura of glamor and courage from his success in driving the racketeers out of the city, and he exploited his advantage to get the votes of upstaters (always suspicious of the city's venality) *and* New York City people (who considered him one of their own). When Dewey took office, he quickly exercised his patronage powers to change the Republican party from a group of provincial baronies into a coordinated instrument under his own direction. By the same methods, he dominated the legislature, so that it began to lose its reactionary reputation. And he preempted the strong executive image of his Democratic predecessors and backed progressive programs that sometimes shocked the old GOP chieftains, but had wide voter appeal.

Under Dewey, the Democratic majorities in New York City (which had averaged well over 500,000 in the 1920s and '30s) were cut down to less than 200,000—though it was all done, as his longtime confidant, R. Burdell Bixby put it, by personal appeal rather than any strong grass-roots Republican organizing drive in the city. At the same time, the upstate Republican majorities almost doubled, from a prior average of about 400,000 votes to a new average close to 800,000. Under Rockefeller, essentially the same pattern was continued. There was some slackening in Republican majorities in the upstate cities, but it was offset by the rapidly growing Republican suburban vote, and even more importantly, by Rockefeller's improved position in New York City. In 1958, Rockefeller lost the city by 309,814 votes, but in each succeeding election he narrowed the margin until in his fourth-term race in 1970, he was behind in the city by a minuscule 16,541 votes. In that election, Rockefeller carried upstate by 746,547 votes and emerged with a statewide plurality of 730,006, a margin then unmatched by any gubernatorial candidate since Lehman in the depths of the Depression.

A lot of the credit for Rockefeller's amazing four-term winning streak goes to the dull, awkward campaigns of his Democratic opponents. Averell Harriman (1958) and Arthur Goldberg (1970) were men of national renown, but seemed more interested in debating international than state issues. Robert Morgenthau (1962), picked because of his famous family name and because he was Jewish, was a totally colorless candidate (but later turned out to be a superb U.S. attorney in New York City and in 1974 was elected District Attorney, succeeding the eminent Frank Hogan and his predecessor, Thomas E. Dewey.) The other opponent, Frank O'Connor, (1966) bore the marks of a big-city machine candidate and was a weaker choice than any of several candidates rejected by the party leaders. Rockefeller also won because people thought he was sincere and tried hard. Finally, and some say foremost, there were the lavish, incredibly sophisticated Rockefeller campaigns. No state candidate in American history has ever mounted a comparable effort.

In 1966, the Republican organization reported spending $5.2 million to reelect Rockefeller, while the O'Connor campaign cost one-eighth as much ($576,000). By 1970, the Rockefeller outlay was up to $6.8 million, of which $4.4 million came from Rockefeller and his family. But the reporting laws under which the sums were disclosed were filled with loopholes, and a more reasonable estimate of the total cost, according to Fred Powledge in *New York*, would be $12 to $15 million. The Goldberg campaign reported spending $1.7 million. The unpaid organizational help of some labor unions (principally the municipal workers and International Ladies Garment Workers Union) doubtless added considerable value to the Goldberg effort. But Rockefeller, too, had labor support, and in fact on an unprecedented scale for a Republican candidate. Victor Borella, Rockefeller's Dartmouth classmate and longtime associate, successfully nurtured union support for the governor over many years. In 1970, he was instrumental in getting Rockefeller endorsements from unions representing over one million members, including 400,000 members of the Building Trades Unions ("the cornerstone of Rockefeller's labor support," Borella says), the Teamsters, and in a disputed but unambiguous vote at its state convention, the New York State AFL-CIO. Aside from personal cultivation of leaders, labor seemed to like Rockefeller because of

New York's $1.85-an-hour minimum wage (highest in the country) and a remembrance of how well Rockefeller treated unions that endorsed him. In 1963, just after he won reelection with first-time support from the Patrolmen's Benevolent Association and Uniformed Firefighters Association of New York City, Rockefeller asked the legislature to pass a bill establishing the principle that firemen's and patrolmen's pensions after 20 years on the job would be computed on the basis of the individual's salary during his last year. The legislation was passed in 1967 and the principle later spread to transit police, sanitationmen, housing police, and correction officers. Rockefeller's action, the New York *Daily News* reported, was "the principal spur behind the rocketing costs of pensions" in the city. Rockefeller never sought repeal of New York's law granting unemployment compensation to strikers when they have been off the job seven weeks. (Only one other state, Rhode Island, has similar legislation.) The building trades, of course, had reason to be delighted with Rockefeller's vast construction programs, which caused labor shortages and drove up wages across the state.*

Like so many dominant figures, Rockefeller left no direct political heirs in New York. His lieutenant governor for 15 years, Malcolm Wilson, succeeded to his office but not his power. Wilson had come into the succession in gratitude for his efforts in introducing Rockefeller to upstate and suburban Republicans in 1958 ; his continued renomination was a sop to conservatives in the party. But Wilson's polysyllabic oratory and careful inaction did not inspire many New Yorkers in his 12½ months as governor, and he was easily beaten by Hugh Carey in November 1974.

The question now is where does the Republican Party go? Candidates of the Rockefeller stripe are hard to find these days in New York. Neither Rockefeller (born in 1908) nor Javits (born in 1904) is likely to head a statewide ticket again, and younger progressive Republicans—like John Lindsay and former Congressman Ogden Reid—now seem quite comfortable in the Democratic Party. Indeed, any Republican with a reputation for liberalism would probably have a hard time winning a Republican primary in the state. The reason candidates like Rockefeller and Javits were nominated was that they never had to face the voters until election day; New York didn't have statewide primaries for years, and on more than one occasion, Nelson Rockefeller vetoed primary legislation. Indeed, so lock-step are New York's organization Republicans that even with the current law whereby candidates can challenge the party convention's choice, until 1976 there had yet to be a Republican primary in New York.

Overall, the party will probably continue its turn to the right which began even under Rockefeller. But the conservatives, like the liberals, lack viable candidates. Wilson, after 20 years in the assembly, 15 as lieutenant governor and one as governor, has retired. Senator James Buckley lost in

* The building trades, with their intransigence on letting in blacks—on the Albany Mall job, workers were brought in from Canada while local blacks tried in vain to get construction jobs—are *enfants terribles* in the eyes of New York liberals. New York *Post* columnist Murray Kempton once said of the building trades leadership: "They would build gas ovens if it was steady work."

1976. The most energetic Republican on the state scene today is former Speaker and now minority leader Perry Duryea. But he has a problem: a 1973 indictment on charges of illicitly aiding Liberal Party candidates. The charges were dismissed almost immediately, and Duryea stalwarts consider them a Rockefeller plot to ease Wilson's nomination for a full term—but it hardly seems possible that a politician with an indictment on his record could be elected governor.

Perhaps someone will come along to carry the Republican torch, as Rockefeller himself did four years after Dewey retired, or—to use a more conservative, and probably more apt, analogy—as Ronald Reagan arose to lead the California GOP to victory in 1966. But it still says something about Rockefeller and the men around them that they did not leave behind political figures with the apparent potential to follow in their footsteps.

Politics II: The Democrats . . .

New York's Democrats have always been as quarrelsome a group as one can find in American politics, though they had an era of relative unity during the "Golden Age" of Smith, Roosevelt, and Lehman. In the early 1940s, as Lehman left the governorship, the Democratic coalition forged by the governors—a coalition essentially analagous to the national New Deal coalition, for which it was the prototype—began to break up. Ethnic rivalries were boiling to the top, and in 1949 the Italians, led by Carmine De Sapio of New York City, finally wrested control of Tammany Hall (the regular Democratic Manhattan organization) from the Irish. De Sapio looked mildly reformist when he came to power, and succeeded in electing Robert Wagner mayor in 1953, Harriman in 1954, and getting himself appointed secretary of state in the Harriman administration. Only time would tell how totally power doth corrupt. (In 1968, De Sapio was indicted for conspiring to bribe Lindsay's water commissioner, James L. Marcus, and for extorting contracts from the Consolidated Edison Company. He was convicted and went to prison.)

In 1949, the first glimmerings of the modern reform movement in New York Democratic politics emerged on Manhattan Island. Suspicious of the old Tammany way of doing things, the reformers responded naturally to a leader like Adlai Stevenson; in fact, his race for President in 1952 drew many of them into politics for the first time. Numerous reform clubs came into being during the 1950s, peopled by young professionals, especially from the publishing and communications industries. The movement made a quantum leap forward in strength after the 1958 Democratic state convention in Buffalo where De Sapio crudely dictated, in public view, the nomination of New York District Attorney Frank Hogan for the U. S. Senate. Hogan was an honorable and able man, but Harriman and many other delegates had wanted a "more liberal" candidate. Republicans promptly raised a cry of "bossism" and Harriman and Hogan went down to defeat the following

November—while Democrats were sweeping elections in most other states.

The debacle at Buffalo gave the reformers the *cause célèbre* they needed to attract thousands of new supporters. An umbrella reform organization, the Committee for Democratic Voters, was established in 1959, and three prestigious Democrats—Mrs. Eleanor Roosevelt, Herbert Lehman, and Thomas Finletter—headed up a powerful drive to change the operation of the party, especially in New York City. Mayor Wagner, who had been De Sapio's candidate in his first two runs for office, decided that support was now more detriment than help and ran in 1961 as an "antiboss" candidate, trouncing De Sapio's candidate in the primary.

The reform element built strength steadily through the 1960s. One reformer, William Fitts Ryan, had been elected to Congress in 1960 from West Side Manhattan (a center of reform strength); that victory was followed up by two congressional victories in the Bronx in 1964, one of them the immensely symbolic defeat of one of the toughest old-line bosses, Charles A. Buckley, by reformer Jonathan B. Bingham. De Sapio was ousted from control of Tammany Hall in 1961. In 1965, Wagner and Robert Kennedy effected the election of John Burns, a man basically friendly to the reform cause, as state chairman. The Kennedy and McCarthy Presidential campaigns of 1968 invigorated the reform movement, and that was the year Paul O'Dwyer, an irascible liberal and one of the reform movement's founders, won nomination to the U.S. Senate in the first statewide primary after the old convention system had been abolished. The contrast between 1958, when De Sapio forced Hogan down the throat of the party, and 1968, when O'Dwyer was nominated, could scarcely have been more striking.

In 1967, the reformers achieved a long-term goal with repeal of New York's noisy convention system of nominating statewide candidates. Conventions, they charged, were prone to boss control and essentially undemocratic. The campaign for a direct primary system also had strong backing from good government groups like the Citizens Union and League of Women Voters, and important newspaper support. But instead of shifting to a simple primary, New York opted for a hybrid system patterned after recommendations of the National Municipal League and American Political Science Association and actually used, in varying forms, by Colorado, Massachusetts, Connecticut, Utah, and Rhode Island. Under the New York version, the state committee of each party meets in the spring and designates its preferred candidate for each office. His name automatically goes onto the primary ballot. A losing candidate for the state committee endorsement, providing he has received 25 percent of the committee vote, can also get on the ballot without petitions. And other candidates can get on the primary ballot by collecting 10,000 signatures of party members, with at least 50 signatures from each of 47 of the state's 62 counties. The nomination is then finally decided in the primary. A like system had actually been in effect in New York a half century earlier, from 1913 to 1921, championed by Charles Evans Hughes who said the preprimary conference was a feasible way to curb the arbitrary powers of party organizations while leaving them a significant voice in the selection of candidates.

On paper, this hybrid committee-primary system seems a suitable compromise, sure to please those political scientists who want to see "the party" have a major voice in the nomination process. But in practice, it has proved to be a fiasco. The first time it was employed, in 1970, it seemed to be tailor-made to the Republicans' campaign needs—which was probably just what Rockefeller and the legislature wanted.

Thus the candidate who is nominated by the Democrats' convention inevitably becomes—regardless of past eminence or personal integrity—"the bosses' hand-picked candidate." This is an absolutely unavoidable outcome, since the majority of the votes in the convention—like the majority of Democratic voters in the state—are from Brooklyn, Queens, Manhattan, and the Bronx, and the convention delegates, according to most New York editorialists and all Republican campaign orators, are just a shade removed from Boss Tweed. And any candidate who challenges the convention's nominee is obviously the Democratic insurgent, who is splitting the party, which will not be able to get together again before November.

Thus the Republicans have two lines, one or the other of which they can employ after the Democratic primary. Each has the advantage of having been used, before the primary, over and over again by certified Democrats and presumably objective editorial writers. Thus in 1970, former Supreme Court Justice Arthur Goldberg was the bosses' hand-picked candidate, and Rockefeller could pretend that electing him was handing over the keys to the state treasury to Boss Tweed. If Goldberg had lost to Howard Samuels in the primary that year, as he almost did, then Samuels would have been the candidate who couldn't keep the party together and was antagonizing regular Democrats.

Four years later, having won the convention's nod, Samuels was set up himself to be the candidate of the bosses. But, unfortunately for the Republicans and Malcolm Wilson, who had been governor some months by then, Hugh Carey won the primary. Carey was a hard man to tag as a party-splitter or a left-winger who would turn off regular Democrats. A six-term Congressman from a conservative, middle-class part of Brooklyn; a Roman Catholic and a widower with 12 surviving children; a beefy Irishman who looked a lot like a cop—Carey was not a man who could plausibly be attacked in such terms. Wilson and the legislature had jimmied the primary date from June to September, to give the Democrats less time to reconcile; instead, it was the Republicans who had no time to stop the Carey momentum, and Malcolm Wilson lost the governorship by the biggest margin in the 20th century. The committee-primary system, which had been intended to and had beaten the Democrats, now had beaten the Republicans too. There seems to be no reason why it should not be changed to a more sensible straight primary system, which has served the vast majority of the states well for many years.

The Democrats will still face the problem, however, of the particularly strong voice which Jewish voters play in their primaries. Voting far out of proportion to their numbers, they can swing key primaries. In the 1976 Democratic presidential primary, they were instrumental in giving their friend on the Israel issue, Washington State's Henry M. Jackson, a clear plurality in New York. But it was a narrow-constituency type win Jackson was unable to repeat in later state primaries in which the Jewish vote was not nearly as important.

And what has happened to the old Democratic "bosses"? There are still a few around, notably Patrick Cunningham, the Bronx party leader and state Democratic chairman, and Meade Esposito, the Brooklyn leader. But none has a fraction of the power De Sapio exercised: there is relatively little patronage, and the regulars are notoriously unable to turn out a sizable vote on election days. The "machine's" mainstay these days is probably judicial patronage. Judges in New York City are nominated by county party conventions, which the oldtimers still control (though not in Manhattan). The judges so nominated never have to face a Democratic primary, and they are routinely elected in November; a Democratic candidate for such a nondescript office (there are literally hundreds of elected judges in New York City) never loses. The judges in turn appoint law secretaries (the post held by many Brooklyn Democratic pols); they appoint appraisers and executors and administrators and trustees; naturally, most of these appointments go to the people who helped them get their nominations—and can get them renominated. The biggest boodle is in the Manhattan Surrogate's Court, through which some $2 billion per year worth of wills are probated. In 1965, a coalition of reformers and Robert Kennedy managed to get a distinguished lawyer elected as one of Manhattan's two Surrogates; he dispensed patronage with little regard for politics. But the work was so dull he got bored and went back to law practice; only hacks, it would appear, want the job.

Aside from that, the machine Democrats do very little, except get quoted by reporters who assume they possess a commodity called power. The regulars played little role in electing Hugh Carey: they endorsed Howard Samuels in the primary, and in the general election turnout in their areas was far below normal.

The present-day umbrella group of the reform organizations is the New Democratic Coalition, which seems to model its political action on the example of the regulars. (There are reformers, for example, who concentrate on getting themselves nominated for a judgeship.) NDC reached an acme of apparent influence in 1974, with approximately one-third of the votes at the Democratic state convention. The organization was courted by everyone who even thought of running for governor; eventually, like the regulars, it supported Howard Samuels. They all lost.

All of which illustrates just how important this business of state conventions and delegate support is: not very. The Carey nomination is the best case in point. Samuels had everything coming out of the convention: its endorsement, support by regulars and reformers, strong and generally favorable name identification, plenty of money, an opponent who was not very well known. But the outcome made clear that none of those supposed advantages—except perhaps the money—was worth much. Carey, as it turned out, had money, too, more than $1 million either contributed or "loaned" by his brother Edward, president of an independent family-owned oil company. Carey used the money to hire David Garth, the TV film specialist who had helped John Lindsay win a second term in 1969, among other feats. Garth insisted that Carey lose 20 pounds, dye his hair black (it was graying), and started filming.

So while the political reporters were plowing through Carnarsie or Cayuga to find out who the local district leader was really for, Carey was winning the primary on television. He could run as the candidate against the bosses—after all, they had come out for Samuels—and at the same time appeal, because of his very nature and background, to the kind of middle-income Roman Catholic voters who formed the putative machine constituency and who had been voting Republican (or Conservative) increasingly often in recent elections. While the leaders and reporters were predicting a photo finish, Carey beat Samuels by a solid 60–40 margin.

Off the momentum of that victory, Hugh Carey coasted to an easy win in November. (One problem was how to juggle Edward's loans and gifts to stay within the law and still pay the campaign's creditors.) The question the Democrats faced was whether Carey's victory was replicable.

The 1976 election of Daniel Patrick Moynihan to the U.S. Senate suggested that it was. Moynihan's chief sponsor was former Democratic state chairman Joseph Crangle, who cleverly engineered votes at the convention so that three of the "left"—Ramsey Clark, Paul O'Dwyer, and Rep. Bella Abzug—all qualified in addition to Moynihan for primary ballot spots. The strategy worked: though Abzug gave Moynihan a close race on primary day, the liberal vote was sufficiently split to let him triumph. Moynihan was the composite candidate Crangle wanted: a contender who could appeal to blue collar, Catholic, Jewish, and liberal voters. An Irish wit who was born in Oklahoma and raised in New York City's Hell's Kitchen, Moynihan had little connection with the state in later years except as the quotable U.S. Ambassador to the United Nations—a role in which he eloquently defended U.S. and Israeli policies for the Ford Administration.* During the campaign against Sen. James Buckley, Moynihan did not object to being described as both a "decent liberal" and a "neo-conservative." Moynihan said the two designations meant roughly the same thing: that concern for the poor is tempered by the realization that capitalism, rather than socialism, may be a more efficient way to create wealth for all and that government programs to correct inequities must undergo a sterner test than good intentions. But Moynihan also defended Franklin Roosevelt's New Deal and fondly recalled the sense

* A member of the Harvard faculty, Moynihan dutifully repaired to Cambridge each week—even in the heat of the Senatorial campaign—to fulfill his lecturing responsibilities.

of community and hope in the New York City of his youth. New Yorkers followed the plea of their "center Democrat" candidate, as he called himself, to reject "the radicalism of the right" and Sen. Buckley, who had advocated bankruptcy for New York City. The vote was 3,422,594 (54.6 percent) for Moynihan and 2,836,633 (45.4 percent) for Buckley.

. . . and a Note on Congress

For years the New York City delegation was packed with unimaginative machine stalwarts who generally viewed election to Congress as a way station to that juiciest of all patronage rewards, a judgeship. They refused to move their families to Washington, belonging instead to a "Tuesday to Thursday" club of commuting Congressmen who spent the majority of their time back home. Then-Republican John Lindsay was the first New York City Congressman to move his family to Washington, believing he became a better Congressman, husband, and father by so doing. Others followed suit, and by the early 1970s more than half the New York delegation had Washington residences.

Indeed, by 1977, there was precious little of the old guard left in the New York ranks, the most notable exception being James J. Delaney of Long Island City, Queens. Technically the most senior Democrat in the delegation, Delaney was seriously out of step with the rest: "a superhawk and stalwart of the status quo" in the words of the Boston *Globe*'s Martin Nolan, one of the most sensitive observers of New York politics there is. By 1970, Delaney had got into a slugging match with Bert Podell of Brooklyn and was refusing to speak with Ben Rosenthal, of the next door district in Queens. That same year he endorsed James Buckley for the Senate. But just a few years later, thanks to the good offices of then Congressman Hugh Carey, things were patched up: Delaney, a senior member of Rules, was helping other New Yorkers' pet projects on that committee; in return, he was elected chairman of the state's Democratic delegation; everybody was talking to everybody.

The peacemaker in that episode, Hugh Carey, was probably the most accomplished legislator in the delegation; he was especially instrumental in pushing revenue sharing through the House Ways and Means Committee on which he served. Traditionally, liberal New Yorkers have had trouble operating effectively on Capitol Hill. Their ideas were just too far out, and a talented reformer like William F. Ryan of Manhattan's Upper West Side often was just a voice crying out in the wilderness. But the Hill has changed since 1960, when Ryan was first elected, and by the time of his premature death, in 1972, he and other New Yorkers were getting things done.

By 1977, the most accomplished liberal New York legislators included: Ben Rosenthal of Queens (consumer protection agency, Turkish aid cutoff); Elizabeth Holtzman of Brooklyn (impeachment, federal court rules changes);

Shirley Chisholm of Brooklyn (the headlines she got were for her 1972 presidential race, but she also secured a minimum wage law for domestic workers); Edward Koch of Manhattan (tax exemptions for single people); Charles Rangel of Manhattan (impeachment); Jonathan Bingham of the Bronx (who introduced the motion in the Democratic steering committee that resulted in the ouster of three senior committee chairmen). Yet for all its advances over yesteryear, this New York City group proved singularly ineffective—and sometimes an object of colleagues' derision—when it tried to push in 1975 for federal legislation to save the city from imminent bankruptcy. Congress did not act on the issue until President Ford finally agreed to a limited program of short-term loans for the city.

Two other New York State Democratic Congressmen deserve mention, Sam Stratton of Schenectady and Otis Pike of eastern Long Island. Both have seniority on the House and Armed Services Committee; both were first elected in 1958 and have won easily since then because of personal, not party popularity (the Republicans gave up on Stratton, and provided him with a safe Democratic district around Albany). In the summer of 1975, Pike was selected to head the House's Special Intelligence Committee which was then investigating the actions of the CIA, the FBI, and other secret or intelligence gathering agencies within the executive branch of the federal government.

Despite the Republicans' assiduous gerrymandering efforts, Democrats have controlled the New York delegation since 1958, and in their 1974 landslide increased their advantage to 27–12. For the most part, the Republican delegation has not been distinguished, and in the early 1970s most of its more senior members retired (or, in Ogden Reid's case, turned Democrat). The deans of the GOP delegation at this writing were upstate liberal Frank Horton and Long Island conservative John Wydler; its best-known member is Hamilton Fish, because of his exposure on the Judiciary Committee impeachment hearings (he voted against Nixon, though his father, a 24-year Congressman himself and lifelong enemy of his Dutchess County neighbor FDR, was heading up a pro-Nixon publicity campaign).

In terms of sheer ability, the most outstanding upstate Republican is probably Barber Conable of the Rochester area. A skilled legislator, Conable concentrates on tax and fiscal matters and also chairs the House Republican Policy Committee.

Even before Rockefeller, a leading exemplar of liberal Republicanism was Senator Jacob K. Javits, the son of immigrant parents on New York's Lower East Side who has been in the upper house since an initial victory over Mayor Wagner in 1956. (Two years before that, Javits had been elected state attorney general over Franklin D. Roosevelt, Jr.) Javits was voted the brightest senator in a poll of legislative aides, and as ranking Republican on the Labor and Public Welfare Committee he has made real contributions on legislation. Among the important bills for which he can take a major share of the credit are the student college loan program, major civil rights laws between 1957 and 1965, the medicare law, all major housing in the past two decades, the Pension Reform Act of 1973, and the War Powers Act. Javits has a reputation as a phenomenal vote-getter, which he certainly was when he beat Wagner and Roosevelt in successive elections. More recently, which is to say since 1956, he has been blessed with unexceptional opposition. In 1974, when he was 70 years old, he finished way ahead of Democrat Ramsey Clark and Conservative Barbara Keating in actual number of votes, but neither had been expected to be a formidable challenger, and Javits's 45 percent of the votes looked pretty weak for a man who had been running statewide for 20 years. The fact is that Javits's support has often been broad but never deep; liberal Democrats and conservative Republicans have found him acceptable, but he has never been their preferred choice. Javits faces the same problem in the Senate, where he is doubtless serving his last term; in 1975, he was beaten for chairman of the Republican conference by Nebraska's lightweight Carl Curtis. His fellow Republicans respect him, and perhaps agree with him more than they might have expected to, but they do not love him, and so his influence depends solely on his brilliance, his excellent staff, and hard work.

As these lines were written, Patrick Moynihan was just taking office as U.S. Senator. There did seem real hope that he could become a major spokesman for New York State and the entire Northeast on two fronts—reversing federal policies which favor the sunbelt over the older industrial states, and instituting a simplified, uniform national welfare system. Moynihan had made much of the former issue in his campaign, and had just the verve and color needed to dramatize it on the national stage. And in his earlier incarnation as a special adviser to President Nixon, he had been the chief author and salesman of the administration's innovative—though eventually defeated—family assistance plan to replace the nation's discredited existing welfare programs.

Politics III: Liberals and Conservatives

New York State has a history of significant "third" (and later fourth) parties that goes all the way back to 1829, when disgruntled laborers in New York City formed their own Working Men's party and upset the powers-that-were by electing several candidates to office. The minor-party tradition has been carried a lot further in this century, aided and abetted by New York laws which permit a candidate to run on the ticket of more than one party. This has opened the way for highly ideological minor parties that sometimes endorse major-party candidates, sometimes run their own, and frequently succeed in whipsawing the big parties into compliance with their policies.

In 1936, the American Labor party was founded in New York by a group of socialist-type union leaders, including David Dubinsky of the International Ladies Garment Workers Union and Sidney Hillman of the Amalgamated Clothing Workers. Initially, they had only one important purpose: to give

New Deal supporters, who were unwilling to vote Democratic because of their opposition to Tammany Hall, a line on the ballot on which they could vote for Franklin D. Roosevelt. They did produce more than 275,000 votes for FDR that year, and in 1937 they stayed in business to provide the margin of victory for La Guardia as mayor and Dewey as district attorney.

The ALP eventually fell under Communist domination, and in 1944 Dubinsky and Alex Rose, chief of the United Hatters, Cap and Millinery Workers, broke away to form the Liberal party.* One of its important goals was to keep the Democratic party in the city and state left of center. The organizational core of the Liberals were first-generation central European Jews who worked in the needle trades and belonged to the sponsoring unions. But on election day, the Liberal party line was a favorite haven of independent voters who were Democratic at heart but fervently anti-Tammany. The Liberal vote was the margin of victory for Lehman when he ran for the Senate in 1950, for Harriman for governor in 1954, for Kennedy for President in 1960, and for Lindsay for mayor in 1965. Four years later, when Lindsay lost the Republican primary, the Liberal party represented the only organized support for his reelection. Nelson Rockefeller may well have owed his 1966 reelection to the Liberals, because they decided that year to boycott Frank O'Connor, the regular Democratic nominee, and nominate Franklin D. Roosevelt, Jr. The Roosevelt vote was more than Rockefeller's winning plurality.

The Liberal party is criticized by some who say that instead of being a lofty, crusading force, it is really an encrusted organization of elderly Jews, almost totally subservient to leader Alex Rose (now in his early 70s), a prime example of a wheeling-and-dealing political machine. Under Rose, for instance, the Liberals have shown scarcely more sympathy for reform Democrats than they have for Tammany regulars. Rose claims the party has no interest in patronage, but many of its leaders were awarded prominent posts in the Lindsay administration, and the mayor frequently turned to Rose for counsel. One hesitates to repeat the premature funeral rites for the Liberal party which political writers have been making over the years, but the fact is that without youth, with leadership both aged and tied to the dying garment industry, its future is not bright.

In March 1962, the New York *Times*'s late and great political reporter, Leo Egan, wrote some prophetic lines:

The emergence of a militant conservative movement in New York State is raising serious political problems for Governor Rockefeller and other Republican leaders. Depending on how these problems are resolved, they could have a major impact on elections and government in the state for many years to come.

Egan was writing just after formal announcement of the creation of the New York Conservative party—an idea hatched one day at lunch by two young

* The ALP gave up the ghost in 1952.

Manhattan lawyers who happened to be brothers-in-law—Kieran O'Doherty and J. Daniel Mahoney. The Conservative party was founded to shift the spectrum of New York politics to the right by providing a pressure on the Republicans to balance the pressure of the Liberals on the Democrats. With some variations, the tactic has been essentially that of the Liberals—whose operations the Conservatives studied carefully before they got underway. The effort has been a smashing success. From 141,877 votes in the 1962 governorship campaign, the Conservatives advanced to 510,023 in 1966, even though their 1966 nominee, Paul L. Adams, was an obscure college professor. "That was the first and best tip-off," as Jack Germond of the Wastington *Star* puts it, "that it was a movement and not a candidate." The 1966 election also shattered the simplistic old idea of "liberal" New York City and "conservative" upstate. Roosevelt, the Liberal party nominee, ran ahead of Adams in upstate New York. But Adams outpolled FDR Jr. by such a substantial margin in New York City that the statewide Conservative vote total was higher than the Liberal. (Adams ran especially strong in Queens and Staten Island, places packed with white, Catholic, middle-class homeowners worried about taxes and school integration—the very constituency the regular parties had been ignoring.) By edging the Liberals in 1966, the Conservatives got the coveted third line on the New York voting machines. In 1970, their gubernatorial vote was off slightly (but still ahead of the Liberal), but by then, they had already forced Rockefeller a few degrees to the right, thus achieving one of their fundamental objectives. And 1970 was the year that the Conservative party nominee, James L. Buckley, was elected to the U.S. Senate over Democrat Richard Ottinger, and (still sweeter for the hard-hitting Conservatives), over Charles Goodell, the Republican-Liberal nominee. The vote was 2,288,190 (37.2 percent) for Buckley; 2,171,232 (35.3 percent) for Ottinger; and 1,434,472 (23.3 percent) for Goodell—an amazing feat for a minor party in America.

Buckley's 1976 defeat at the hands of Patrick Moynihan suggested strongly that his earlier victory had been a fluke, and that a candidate that far to the right normally would have little chance in a statewide race. But in the primary, Buckley had been able to defeat a moderate Republican challenger, and the Conservative influence on the Republican party seemed likely to persist for several years into the future. It was solidly established that the Conservative party had become a more potent force than the Liberals. The 1976 returns, for instance, showed Buckley receiving 302,000 votes on the Conservative line, compared to the 184,000 Liberal party votes for Moynihan. In the Presidential race, Ford received 275,000 Conservative party line votes, Carter only 144,000 as the Liberal party nominee.

A fatal development for the minor parties would be legislation prohibiting the familiar pattern of dual endorsements of candidates. The idea, of course, is to isolate Conservatives and Liberals *by law* in the state. The idea comes up periodically, but both Republicans and Democrats shy away from leading the fight for such legislation, fearing reprisals if it fails to win passage. If the step were taken, however, and the Conservatives and Liberals lost their principal weapon of bargaining for their endorsements, then these minor parties would begin to wither away. Their major premise, particularly in the case of the Liberals, is clearly no longer true; for people will vote for candidate X—or not—if they want to, regardless of which party line or lines the candidate appears on.

Geographic New York

New York's land area is the greatest of any northeastern state. It is a Great Lakes and Canadian border state along its northern reaches, a New England state on the east, a Pennsylvania-Appalachian state along its Southern Tier, an Atlantic state around New York Harbor and out along Long Island. Through our discussion the reader should bear in mind the historic and present-day belt of heavy population. It starts in the southeast with Long Island and New York City, stretches northward along the Hudson River Valley to Albany, then extends west along the Mohawk River Valley and the Lake Ontario Plain to Buffalo. The belt averages only 25 miles in width, but about 85 percent of the state's people live within it. Only one of New York's seven metropolitan areas (Binghamton) is excluded. Outside the belt are the life-sustaining watersheds in the great mass of forested mountain or upland country that covers two-thirds of the state's land area—the broad Adirondack Uplands, filling the land mass of northern New York State between the St. Lawrence Valley on the west and Lake Champlain on the east; the smaller Catskill Mountain group closer to New York City; and the Appalachian Uplands, which extend from the Catskills practically all the way to Lake Erie in the west.

Any geographic division of the state raises some conceptual problems, but if the reader will keep his eye on the map, he may be able to keep his bearings as we move around the state in a clockwise direction, starting with the Catskills and leaving for last the New York City metropolitan region.

The Catskills and the Southern Tier

THE CATSKILLS. These gently rounded hills emerge from the Hudson's wooded west banks where Rip Van Winkle once slept and include the famous borscht belt in Sullivan and Ulster counties, where New Yorkers have headed for a bucolic interlude and sometimes gaudy entertainment since the turn of the century. The pacesetting hotels are Grossinger's and the Concord, which can feed, pamper, and entertain 1,200 and 3,000 guests respectively. They still specialize in Kosher food, though there is now more of an effort to attract gentile guests. There are still 250 hotels and 1,000 bungalow colonies in the Catskills, providing permanent employment for some 45,000 local residents. But more than 100 hotels and homes have burned to the ground in the last 30 years, symbolizing the decline of the Catskills as a resort area. Behind the fires is arson, emanating from the owners of hotels no longer grand, from the rural young without enough to do—and, some say, even from volunteer firefighters who have become fascinated with flames.

The Catskill town of Woodstock, long a haven for painters, musicians, sculptors, writers, and craftsmen, acquired a not-altogether-welcome notoriety when some of its residents promoted the gigantic Woodstock rock festival in 1969. The affair was actually held, though, at Max Tasgur's farm in another Catskill town, Bethel, 50 miles away. For three days, hundreds of thousands of 14- to 24-year-olds created a commune large enough to be New York's third largest city, an Event of their generation immortalized in the movie *Woodstock.*

THE SOUTHERN TIER. This section of deeply wooded hills and valleys, part of the Appalachian Highlands shared with Pennsylvania, runs along two thirds of the state's width and is cut by strong rivers like the Delaware, the Susquehanna, and the Allegheny. It is sparsely populated by eastern standards, the only cities of appreciable size being Binghamton (64,123), Elmira (39,945), Jamestown (39,795), and Ithaca (26,226).* All have been losing population in recent years. One of Governor Rockefeller's pet projects was making a four-lane, limited-access road out of Route 17, the east-west connector along the Southern Tier. As noted in our Pennsylvania chapter, Route 17 parallels the newly completed Keystone Shortway some distance to the south, and the two roads encompass an immense, still unspoiled section of remote wildlands close to the eastern megalopolis.

Binghamton has suffered from the loss of many jobs in the tanning and shoe manufacturing business, its historic main support, but the principal plant of International Business Machines is in adjacent Endicott, providing thousands of well-paid jobs. IBM, begun as a small tabulating-machine enterprise, later became, under the leadership of Thomas J. Watson, a great national and international corporation. Its computers and electric typewriters dominate their fields, and sales in 1975 totaled $14.4 billion. IBM's corporate headquarters are presently at Armonk, in Westchester County, and the Binghamton plant has only a small percentage of the company's total employment.

The Southern Tier also has some oil wells and refineries, famous factories for furniture and voting machines at Jamestown, and the Corning Glass Company, which produces the world-famous Steuben glassware and gigantic telescope mirrors. Both tourism and agriculture are mainstays of the local economy, and one finds here one of the nation's leading grape-producing areas. A big Indian reservation is home for the last of the proud Senecas. Near Lake Erie is Chautauqua Lake, center of the famed Chautauqua Circuit that once brought culture, with a small "c" and a loud voice, to crossroads and hamlets of the nation. William Jennings Bryan was one of its great orators.

---

* All population figures are based on the 1970 census.

Now it is a musical and philosophical center on a lake lined with superb summer homes and the delightful old Victorian-era Hotel Athenaeum, replete with high-ceilinged rooms and porches and galleries and immense fireplaces in a remembrance of the leisure of a time gone by.

THE FINGER LAKES. Set between the Southern and Northern Tiers are the slender Finger Lakes, cradled in long, narrow basins cut out by the Ice Age. Now these lovely streaks of blue water—Lakes Canandaigua, Keuka, Seneca, Cayuga, Owasco, and Skaneateles—are a favorite summertime refuge for New Yorkers. Between and around them lies fertile agricultural country.

The social tensions of our time have not left the placid rural stretches of western New York untouched. A prime example is Cornell University, situated "high above Cayuga's waters" at Ithaca, where tension between black students and a university community not without vestiges of white racism led in spring 1969 to the shocking picture of protesting black students brandishing shotguns and rifles.

The Upstate Urban Corridor

Now our focus shifts to the urban corridor that stretches along the Great Lakes coastal plains, and then the Mohawk Valley, from Buffalo to Albany.

BUFFALO (462,768) AND ITS METROPOLITAN AREA (1,349,211). This is New York's second largest city—a place, as John Gunther noted, perennially "overshadowed by Manhattan, though the latter is 398 miles away." Buffalo is a troubled city, a classic example of Northeast suffering as companies close up old inefficient plants and move to the sunbelt. This city has a superb location—the eastern terminus of the Great Lakes shipping lanes, the western terminus of New York's low-level water route from the east. Millard Browne of the Buffalo *Evening News* writes: "It is where the lakes meet the rails, where Dakota grains are milled into flour for eastern markets; where the water-borne ore from Minnesota and Labrador meets coal from Ohio and Pennsylvania to form steel for New York and New England." The building of the Erie Canal opened up Buffalo, then the railroads made it second only to Chicago as a railhead. It is a sinewy city, a place a labor leader once called a "toll-gate town with a toll-gate mentality." Great grain elevators along the lake front remind one that this city mills more grain into flour than any other city in the world; to the south, one sees the smoke billowing out of the great Lackawanna plant of Bethlehem Steel, third largest steel factory in America. The city has big foundries, too, a Westinghouse plant, and Chevrolet and Ford plants inside and outside the city boundaries. Many of the early auto companies first started operations in Buffalo, but in time those that survived switched their base of operations to Detroit, leaving Buffalo, as it is in most of its enterprises, a branch town. The same thing happened with aircraft, and today that industry is all but gone (except for the Bell Aerospace Division of Textron).

Downtown Buffalo and its industrial suburbs are grim, gray, and outmoded. A grandiose street plan with radial avenues, laid out in the early 19th century, has been faithfully retained, but most downtown streets are either seedy or strangely deserted. At night, Buffalo is like a ghost town. New center city buildings have been few and far between for a city of Buffalo's size. But now there is some action, including the 40-story Marine-Bank building, set audaciously astride Main Street. In 1976, Buffalo won partial federal funding for a 6.4-mile light rail line to connect downtown Buffalo with the campus of the State University of New York at Buffalo. To obtain the grant, Buffalo construction contractors and unions signed a written no-strike agreement.

Overall, the condition and appearance of Buffalo has deteriorated since World War II. Total assessed valuation actually declined during the inflationary era of the 1960s.

Buffalo has a celebrated inferiority complex. George Wyatt, a spirited young city budget officer who really seemed to love his city, complained:

Our national image since the days of the completion of the Erie Canal has been a bawdy, raffish, frontier town without class. And as a kid, I recall we only made the national newsreels when there was a big snow or windstorm. Ask people what they know about Buffalo and they'll reply, "a snow-covered Pittsburgh." But we're no dirtier than other cities, and cleaner than many. The unfair treatment we get from the national press reinforces the old dirty image. Some outside reporters come to town with their stories already written. People outside are unaware of many very beautiful parts of this city—the big stretches of pleasant middle-class frame dwellings, and the clean neighborhoods.

But after talking with Wyatt, we went to have lunch with his friend, Ray Herman of the Buffalo *Courier-Express*, who said there was a "germ of truth" in a *Sports Illustrated* article that talked of Buffalo as the "armpit of the East." Buffalo gets its basic character from steel and milling, Herman said, and so "people are more attuned to sports than the arts." They give gung-ho backing to their teams—major league in football, hockey, and basketball. One of the most vivid civic disputes of recent years has been over the location and design of a new sports stadium.

Winter comes early and stays late in Buffalo; on April 30, one is still able to see ice still clogging the harbor. Wind and snow storms sweep in from Lake Erie, where there is nothing to stop them for 240 miles until they hit Buffalo and other parts of the New York shore. After a fierce 1977 snow and wind storm, sure to be remembered in Buffalo for years to come, President Carter designated the city and its environs a major national disaster area.

Except for high mountain areas, there are no sections of America that get a heavier annual snowfall than upstate New York, Northern New England and the Upper Midwest—an annual average of about 100 inches. Midwinter news reports, like this one from the New York *Times*, are not unusual:

An intense winter storm . . . isolated 7,000 square miles of northwestern New York State yesterday. Driven by winds up to 70 miles an hour, a foot-deep snowfall drifted into eight-foot banks, closing all roads in 11 counties.

Rochester and Buffalo, as well as many smaller communities, were virtually snowbound. . . . Thousands of motorists were stranded. A 260-mile stretch of the Gov. Thomas E. Dewey Thruway was closed. . . .

New York City received only a light dusting of snow.

Oftentimes, however, the city of Buffalo escapes the worst of the snow; instead, it warms the air passing over it so that the snow falls a way inland. In summer, the cool winds off Lake Erie keep Buffalo air conditioned to a pleasant 68° average.

Buffalo is a premier American town for raw, muscular ethnic politics. The city divides into rather homogeneous nationality pockets: Italians on the West Side; Poles, Hungarians, and Czechs on the northwest; Irish in south Buffalo; blacks on the Near East Side, and Poles on the Far East Side; Jews and Wasps in the northern and northeastern sections; a last cluster of Germans in the farthest northeast; American Indians on the Lower West Side; a Puerto Rican community that rings the black community and comes up into the Lower West Side. The Poles, who came to work in the steel mills, are the largest single group, about 25 percent of the city's population—in fact, only Chicago has more Poles; Italians are about 20 percent; Irish 10 percent. The last two mayors, Frank Sedita and Stanley Makowski, reflect the Italian and Polish strength respectively. But the real political power is a youngish Irishman, county Democratic chairman Joseph Crangle, who also served for several years as chairman of the state party.

Buffalo the city is forever Democratic; Erie County is generally so in state and national elections, although it has elected a Republican county executive since 1960. The area became upset with Rockefeller's early tax programs and turned out a majority against him in each of his three reelection races.

For a century now, the center city has been rigidly contained within its boundaries. Many of the factories are actually in the suburbs, and as George Wyatt put it, this anomalous situation has developed: "The lower group of income earners go outside the city to work in factories and then come back to the city to spend their meager earnings. The big earners—the white collar people and professionals—come into the city from the suburbs to work in the office center, and then they get on the expressways to get out of the city and spend their money somewhere else."

Buffalo was long able to escape the ultimate fiscal crisis of New York City because the Erie County government had been transforming itself into a kind of metropolitan-area government, taking over one basic function after another from the city—welfare, hospitals and psychiatric facilities, sewer districts, and air- and water-pollution control. The decision to adopt a "strong executive" charter in 1960 was crucial to the county's expanded role. But metropolitan area government cannot save an entire metropolitan area that is suffering, which is Erie County's case. In 1976, the county's welfare budget ran out, and the county refused to make welfare payments until the state won a court fight over the issue. And New York state audited the county's books amid rumors it would default.

Talking to people in Buffalo, one would think that organized crime is a negligible phenomenon there. The crime rate (the way the FBI estimates it, anyway) is quite low for a city of Buffalo's size, and we heard flat denials of any Mafia influence in political life. *But* officials of the Justice Department's criminal division consider Buffalo an important smaller pocket of organized crime in the U.S.; eight Buffalo mobsters were at the famous Appalachian meeting in 1967; and from officers of the General Services Administration, one hears that it took nine extra months to put up a new federal building in Buffalo because of harassment by mob-connected unions against an outside construction firm which was the successful bidder for the job.

Buffalo's most famous suburb is Niagara Falls (85,615), where the world-famous cataract draws some three million visitors a year to a sight that hasn't changed much since Father Louis Hennepin first saw the falls in 1678. (Erosion on the American side of the falls has caused increasing concern since massive rock falls in 1931 and 1954, however.) In 1969, the Army Engineers diverted the flow of the American side to the Canadian side for several months while they examined the 1,100-foot American brink and made test borings and other tests to determine what long-term steps could be taken to slow the eroding process. The "dewatering" exposed to view a bed of rock called lockport dolomite that is fascinatingly reminiscent of the moon's surface, pockmarked and grayish in color.

In a half hour from Buffalo, one can follow the Thruway down the Niagara River, across the Grand Island and then along the American rapids by the new Robert Moses Parkway. The use of hydroelectric power on the American continent was pioneered here, and the new Niagara Falls power development, constructed by the New York State Power Authority, is the largest hydroelectric power source in the free world. The city of Niagara Falls, physically so dreary in comparison to its Canadian twin, makes everything from carborundum, carbide, electrolytic and other chemicals to paper products and aerospace equipment (Bell Aerosystems).

We end our visit to Buffalo with a glimpse of the new State University at Buffalo. For more than a century, the old University of Buffalo existed quietly as a peaceful streetcar college to turn out the local doctors and dentists and judges. Then came 1962 and the designation to become the primary center of graduate education of the state university system. Martin Meyerson, former acting chancellor at Berkeley, was brought in to head the startling new program, and did a highly creditable job until he left in September 1969. The quality of students escalated unbelievably; by the end of the decade the university actually found it necessary to reject some holders of Regents scholarships (the top 6 percent of high school graduates in New York State). But a tremendously impersonal institution evolved and it came to the point that when some students wanted recommendations, they couldn't find a professor who knew their name. Spring 1970 brought convulsions rarely seen on an American campus. Millard Browne told us:

A lot of people think that if Buffalo can get through the growing pains of a major new university, it will be redeemed. There is a sense of pioneering at the State University—that's why the good faculty and students come—to be in on the floor of a good thing. Already, there are many prominent new faculty. But the whole development has attracted a lot of frontier-radical-type faculty. Setting all of this down in an ethnic, blue-collar town has dangerous potential. Lots of our kids from New York City ooze contempt for Buffalo from every pore—a bad scene!

But we must shepherd it through to the stature of a Berkeley or a Madison.

ROCHESTER (296,233) AND ITS METROPOLITAN AREA (882,667). Writer Seymour Freedgood, in *The Gateway States*, quotes a Rochester citizen who depicts his city's image as "quiet, conservative, contented and Kodak." The city was an old flour-milling town that grew and flourished with the opening of the Erie Canal. The first breakthroughs toward a modern scientific economy came in the 1850s when Joseph Bausch opened the optical business that would eventually become the world-famous Bausch & Lomb Co. Thirty years later, a young bank clerk named George Eastman became interested in photography and effected a major breakthrough by developing a practical and economic "dry plate" photographic process in place of the incredibly cumbersome "wet plate" method in use until then. He opened a factory, discovered the economic uses of nitrocellulose film, and evolved his great invention, the Kodak camera. An important factor in his success was that other Rochester firms, like Bausch & Lomb, had made the city into a center for advanced work in optics and other precision instrumentation. In 1912, the Kodak Research Laboratories were organized and became world-famous in photography and the varied uses of chemistry and physics related to photography.

In those years around the turn of the century, Jane Jacobs suggested, it seemed "that Rochester was destined to become one of the country's most economically creative and important cities. But George Eastman . . . put an end to that. . . . Once he had developed Kodak into a strong company, . . . Eastman fought breakaways from his company with every means at his command; and he was successful."

Today, of course, Eastman Kodak is a great national corporation (30th largest in the U.S.), dominating the amateur photography market (with nervous glances over its shoulder at Polaroid) and providing photographic devices that give it a stake in such glamor industries as education, medicine, and dentistry. Kodak is a leader in microfilming technology and does half a billion dollars a year in its chemicals, fibers, and plastics operations. In 1975, total sales were $4.9 billion, and the company had 116,000 employees. Bausch & Lomb lopes along comfortably with annual sales of $333 million; it was also the first firm to go to market with "soft" contact lenses.

In the three quarters of a century since Eastman made Rochester a company town, only one new company of importance has emerged. Its name used to be Haloid and it managed to exist "in the shadow of Eastman" by turning out photo supplies—tolerated, perhaps, because it was formed before Eastman Kodak became so dominant. Right after World War II, Haloid began to buy up the rights, held by other companies, to photocopying techniques. The Xerox 914 Copier went on the market in 1960; pushed by a well-trained and aggressive sales force, it (and successor models) rapidly gained entry to corporate, bank, publishing, law, school, and university offices. The company (itself renamed Xerox) grew at a spectacular rate, becoming the country's 39th largest industrial corporation with sales of $4.1 billion in 1975. (Earnings per share rose in the decade of the '60s from 5¢ to $2.40; greatest growth of any on *Fortune's* top 500 list.) In the mid-1960s, Xerox plunged into the educational field, buying out established firms like University Microfilms, R. R. Bowker, and Ginn & Co., but also developing its own information and educational materials and prudently emphasizing such "software" first, biding its time on using its proven "hardware" skills. Where other firms failed in the educational field, Xerox prospered. In 1970, the company's total payroll was 60,000 (12,000 of them in Rochester). But, as Jane Jacobs noted, even "Xerox's success, great as it has been, has not transformed Rochester into a vigorous, developing city."

Xerox shifted its corporate headquarters to Stamford, Connecticut, in 1969, apparently in hopes of wheeling and dealing better from the New York City area (or as Kenneth Patton, Lindsay's economic development administrator, put it, "How do you run an international enterprise with Mohawk Airlines as your lifeline?"). But only a small number of executives and support personnel made the move. The heart of Xerox is still in Rochester, and manufacturing operations continue to expand there.

Rochester has been described as an orderly town with methodical, hardworking citizens—natural products of a technological work milieu. Important ethnic groups, outside of native Wasp stock, have been German, Italian, and Polish. In the late 1940s, a significant number of poorly educated Southern blacks began to arrive. It frequently turned out they were unqualified for the better jobs in the highly technical local job market—at the same time that firms were importing skilled labor from outside. Summer 1964 brought a nasty riot—a major urban disturbance for its time. This prompted local clergy to bring in Saul Alinsky on a two-year, $100,000 contract to organize the poor. Under Alinsky's tutelage, a group named FIGHT (acronym for Freedom-Independence-God-Honor-Today) was formed, and a powerful community organizer, the Reverend Franklin Florence, took over its leadership. The FIGHT group picked Eastman Kodak—"the plantation," they called it—as their principal target in the demand for more jobs for blacks. The riots and the FIGHT program came as a profound shock to Rochester's leaders, including Kodak, and much serious soul-searching ensued. Many new jobs and programs for the minority community have resulted, and Rochester is also one of the few cities today making provision for low-income housing, open to minorities, in its suburbs.

In the 1960s, when the Republicans controlled both the Rochester city and Monroe County governments, a large number of municipal functions were transferred to the county in one of the country's more interesting cases of "creeping metropolitanization." Function consolidation has continued in the '70s, despite Democratic control of the city, though the city took back at least one function—central purchasing—on the grounds that the county government wasn't able to handle it efficiently.

Elisha Friedman, the exceptionally able Rochester city manager who took office in 1974, waxes eloquent on two subjects: home rule and public labor relations. On the former, he complains that New York State grants entirely too little flexibility to local governments: "Why the hell should the state legislature, at this time in the history of New York State, when it's going down the (fiscal) tubes, be fooling around with thousands of local bills that can be handled by any council or mayor or manager at the local level? Why don't they clean the slate and deal with a truly state agenda?"

On labor relations, Friedman asserts that when he took office, "the unions were in control" of the city government "because there was no such thing as 'management.' " His first move, Friedman said, was to hire a professional labor negotiator to handle collective bargaining and grievances. "Now," he claimed, "we're getting it clear to our own people what it means to control your own city."

The Rochester *Times-Union* and the *Democrat and Chronicle* are flagships of the Gannett Newspaper chain, which controls newspapers in six other upstate cities as well as those in Westchester County. The Gannett papers provide continuous, high-grade Albany coverage and their influence is second only to the New York *Times* in the state. The editorial voice of the Rochester papers is one of moderate conservatism; many of the papers in the chain follow Rochester's editorial lead, although all have local autonomy and some (like the excellent Binghamton *Press*) are very independent. A quick review of the upstate press should also include the Buffalo *News* (full news staffs, comprehensive coverage, distinctly Republican but less so in news columns than it once was); the Buffalo *Courier-Express*; the Syracuse *Herald-Journal* and *Post-Standard* (both Newhouse papers, tough and hard-core conservative in their views); the Albany *Times-Union* and *Knickerbocker-News* (Hearst-owned, good coverage of state government); and the Watertown *Times* (a power in the Northern Tier).

SYRACUSE (197,208) AND ITS METROPOLITAN AREA (635,946). Politically, Syracuse and its environs are regarded as the real capital of upstate conservatism, a phenomenon for which the Syracuse newspapers are given major credit. A few years ago, when a prominent Republican legislative leader from Syracuse backed Rockefeller's tax proposals in Albany, he was damned and literally hounded out of office by the *Herald-Journal* and *Post-Standard*.

But Syracuse is not a closed, narrow-minded community. Local observers say one finds a real sense of community in the city, a feeling on the people's part that they have some control over their environment and institutions, that they can get a hearing at City Hall regardless of which party (it has usually been the Republican) is in power. There have, however, been eruptions in the black community and blacks are underrepresented in government and on the police force.

One can point to several factors that make Syracuse an "open city." It has always been a crossroads: first, Indian trails passed through from every compass point; then came the Erie Canal, the Barge Canal, and the railroads; and today, two great superroads—the Thomas E. Dewey Thruway and the North-South Expressway (Interstate 81)—pass through. (The city has 80 truck terminals and massive rail-marshaling yards.) Syracuse makes everything from soda ash to electrical goods, from special steel to pharmaceuticals, in some 500 manufacturing plants. No single industry dominates, as Eastman Kodak does in Rochester; people need not be concerned that the gut decisions are all made in the back rooms of some corporation.

Ethnic diversity is another factor. Syracuse has quantities of Yankees, Irish, Germans, Italians, Poles, East European Jews, blacks, and Puerto Ricans, all living in clearly defined neighborhoods. But no ethnic group has disproportionate strength; in fact, market research firms like to use the city to test new products, just because of its broad mix (One ethnic vignette: the city's Tipperary Hill district is one of the last enclaves of militant Irish in the state, except for a few Queens bistros. It is the only area where the green traffic signal is on top, a concession the city made years ago when the red was broken nightly.)

Finally, there is the influence of Syracuse University, one of the country's largest private universities (19,356 students). Local people still speak of the university as something of a place set apart—"the university and the *host* community"—but the fact is that it is the largest single employer in the city, its faculty participates in local politics on all sides of the political fence, and its contacts with Washington help keep Syracuse in touch with the world. The university is especially well known for its excellent departments of geography and electrical engineering, for the outstanding forestry school it runs in conjunction with the State University of New York, and its Maxwell Graduate School of Citizenship and Public Affairs.

Local government is honest and competent, though sometimes indifferent to the city's poor people. The current mayor, Lee Alexander, is, surprisingly, a Democrat, and has shown more social concern than his Republican predecessors; he looked less impressive as the Democratic designee for U.S. Senate in 1974, trailing far behind Ramsey Clark in the primary. Inner-city poverty and decay continue to plague Syracuse as they do so many cities, in sharp contrast to the economic vigor seen in the outlying areas.

What is Syracuse's chief drawback? It may be the snow—an average of 108 inches a year, more than any other major American city. Not-so-old-timers remember with little fondness the blizzard of '66—January 1966, that is—when 42 inches fell in three days, accompanied by winds of up to 40 mph that created drifts as high as 20 feet.

THE MOHAWK VALLEY. We now pass into mountainous territory, cut by the handsome, historic Mohawk Valley. All the significant settlement is crammed into the rather narrow river valley; the two principal cities are Utica (91,611) and Rome (50,148). Industrially, this is tired, aged territory with little dynamism; not only did the cities lose population in the 1960s, but the entire metropolitan region (340,477) barely averted a net loss.

Utica's ethnic mix is heavily Italian, Irish, and Polish, but it also has the distinction of supporting the only Welsh-language newspaper in the U.S., *U Drych*, founded in 1851. Rome is big in various kinds of metal manufacture and is suffering from cuts in the payroll of nearby Griffiss Air Force Base. The proximity of Syracuse has prevented full growth of trade and services in the Mohawk Valley.

In Utica, one finds a splendid center of community cultural life, the Munson-Williams-Proctor Institute. Philip Johnson's design for the building had made it, in the opinion of some, the most elegant structure in the entire upstate area. A few miles to the south is picturesque Cooperstown, where baseball was supposedly invented in 1839 and where the Baseball Hall of Fame now stands.

Normally, the politics of the area are true-blue Republican, but a new and exciting dimension was added in 1973 with the election of Ed Hanna, a son of Lebanese immigrants, as mayor of staid, declining, and stodgy Utica. Hanna, a former state parks commissioner under Governor Harriman and member of the state legislature during the 1960s (until the Republicans gerrymandered him out of office), campaigned as an independent against both the nominees of the Republican and Democratic parties and against the Utica "Establishment." Hanna charged that the business, labor, and political leaders had arranged a convenient and cozy alliance for control of the city to the detriment of the citizenry. Hanna promised never to separate himself from the people. And, true to his word, one of his first acts upon becoming mayor was to rip his office door down from its hinges. Even a symbolic separation would not be allowed by the man who answers his own phone in City Hall with the greeting, "Hello. People's government, Ed Hanna speaking."

Hanna and the traditional leaders of the city exchanged epithets almost daily, with Hanna usually giving better than he got, calling his opponents fakers, bluebloods, flunkies, and worse. But the early results of his administration were impressive: the first property tax reductions in a quarter of a century, a budget surplus while expanding city services to minorities and creating temporary employment, the planning of a dramatic and drastically needed revitalization of the decaying and almost abandoned downtown core of the city, an end to 200 patronage jobs which carried with them little or no obligation to work, the consolidation of several departments within the office of the mayor, and perhaps most importantly, restoring a sense of hope, of optimism, and of expectation in a tired and all but defeated city.

THE CAPITAL DISTRICT. The 1970 Census counted 720,786 residents in the Albany-Schenectady-Troy metropolitan area. The area is heavy with state offices, federal regional offices, and factories; if one's interest runs to history, the story is of Indian massacres, Dutch patroons, and colonial and Revolutionary War heroes and governors waiting for a chance to become President.

Albany (114,873) was once described as "one of the most resolutely backward communities in the state," a reputation it tries to live up to. The city is old and decayed, and aside from the fantastic rush of state-government building—the South Mall, discussed earlier, and the strikingly beautiful new State University of New York at Albany—the city per se shows little life. City taxes are low, but so is the level of services; as an embittered out-of-town reporter noted a couple of years ago, "the snow and ice are still taken away by the same methods the city fathers used in centuries past— solar heat."

Another thing about Albany that never seems to change is the political boss in charge. It has been the same *for half a century* now—Daniel P. O'Connell, 90 years old, who runs a smooth organization that has sustained remarkably few losses since it came to power in 1921. The O'Connell machine has been investigated repeatedly for corruption and tax favoritism to the boss's cronies, but even Governor Dewey, after a highly publicized investigation, could not lay a hand on "Uncle Dan." Albany is heavily Irish and overwhelmingly Catholic, but O'Connell has preference for mayoralty candidates from well-born Protestant families. The incumbent mayor, Erastus Corning II, is the epitome of the established upstate gentry and has been in office since 1942. Uncle Dan, reputed to have a personal worth of some $500,000, is rarely seen these days. In fact, Governor Rockefeller never cast eyes on him, and when John Kennedy came through Albany campaigning for President in 1960, he had to be satisfied with a telephone call.

Rockefeller's mall has attracted a new class of urban settlers to Center Square, the city's enclave of pretty row houses and quiet streets. An attempt by McDonald's to build its golden arch in the neighborhood mobilized community preservers in Albany into one of the most sophisticated neighborhood associations in the country. They have blocked plans for a highway through the middle of the area and obtained federal money to pay a third of rehabilitation costs of the privately owned, middle class houses.

Schenectady (77,859), a grimy industrial city on the Mohawk, is home of General Electric's original and oldest plant, which turns out heavy electrical equipment and provides jobs for 12,500 workers. Close by on the Hudson lies Troy (62,918), the town where Uncle Sam was reputedly "born," a city really behind the times with an economy still tied primarily to the textile and apparel industries.

The illustrious old resort town of Saratoga Springs (18,845), just north of the capital district, leads a double life. During most of the year, it is like most other upstate towns, quiet and uncrowded under its old shade trees. But when summer comes, the Saratoga Performing Arts Center begins its season in its sylvan-set modern theater (the New York City Ballet, the Philadelphia Orchestra), and the social elite, millionaires, and gamblers descend on the town for the races at America's most beautiful thoroughbred track. The crowds along the brick sidewalks are terribly reminiscent of the 19th century, when Saratoga was called the "Queen of the Spas." The mineral baths are still there, and in recent years winter activity has picked up with skiing in the nearby hills.

The North Country and the Hudson River

THE NORTH COUNTRY AND THE ADIRONDACK MOUNTAINS. Here is distant and truly "uncivilized" New York State, known to comparatively few Americans. In the northwest is Lake Ontario and the region of the Thousand Islands (there are actually some 1,700) and then a long stretch of the St. Lawrence River. At Massena (14,042) one finds the third largest electricity generating complex on the continent, and the largest one on the St. Lawrence Seaway. Yet as remote as the location is, one can still watch the commerce of the world on its way through the great locks, moving to or from the Great Lakes and the Midwest. Then, on the state's northernmost extremity, are 60 miles of border with Quebec. On the east, one comes upon the beautiful Champlain Valley, centered on 107-mile-long Lake Champlain (across from Vermont), which connects with Lake George to form the great north-south waterway that was the path of empire through several wars.

Making a living is an acute problem for the sturdy, independent people of this region; aside from some dairy farming, the chief industries are tourism, mining for iron ores, lead, and zinc, lumbering, and paper mills—all characterized by seasonal job opportunities. Thousands of families live in abject poverty in tarpaper houses, their plight unrecognized until welfare and services of the federal antipoverty program became available to them in the last few years.

The Adirondack Mountains fill the great land bulk of the North Country; for mile after mile, the uplands and mountains roll on, their slopes shaded by thick evergreens, bordering literally thousands of lakes and ponds and miles of streams and rivers. The terrain is too rough for much farming and too distant to attract industry. The Adirondack Park, decreed by the New York legislature in 1892, covers most of this territory. Within the park are more than two million acres of the New York Forest Preserve, guaranteed by an 1895 amendment to the state constitution to be "forever kept as wild forest lands." But 3.7 million acres of land in the park are in the hands of towns, businesses, and individuals, and now there is fear that the region's untamed character may be imperiled by uncontrolled summer-home and recreation-facilities growth. Less than 10 percent of the territory is zoned, and as the New York *Times* reported in 1971:

Together, the private and public lands are now a jumble of small towns, wild rivers, motels, alpine peaks, gas stations, housing developments, lakes, advertising signs, open-pit mines, marshes, logging industries, deer trails, restaurants, ski areas, campsites, river gorges, golf courses, marinas, and riding stables—all elbow to elbow with no plan for achieving compatability in the future.

Laurance Rockefeller, the governor's brother, suggested in 1967 that a national park be carved out of a section of the state park as a way to preserve the wild forest character of eastern America's largest wild forest area. But state officials were critical of the land-expropriation procedures and prohibition of hunting and logging, and the governor set up a temporary commission on the future of the Adirondacks. Its report, released in 1971, suggested an Adirondack Park Agency to control the future growth of the area, and a $120 million bond issue to acquire scenic easements, purchase land, and construct facilities.

Saving the North Country, however, will not be an easy job. A half million visitors pour in every year, leaving 100 tons of litter on the high peak trails, converting remote campsites into unsightly tent cities, posing severe problems in sewage disposal, and introducing the noisy pollution of motorboats, seaplanes, and snowmobiles into the mountain and lake stillness. Lake George Village, at the southern tip of lovely (and still pure) Lake George, is a garish strip development of motels, gas stations, and stores with huge and unsightly signs. (By contrast, one of the lakeside lodge owners, William C. Busch, headed a movement that got passage of an ordinance requiring smaller and tasteful signs, approved by an artist-civic leader-businessman committee, for all the land within Lake George State Park. The park covers a mile-wide collar of land all around the lake.) On the industrial front, only the last half-decade has seen real progress to cut down on the pollution of pulp and paper mills. Yet even when corrective action is taken, the sins of the past haunt the present. At Ticonderoga, on Lake Champlain at the foot of the Adirondacks, the International Paper Company in 1971 closed down a 94-year-old mill that had contaminated the air and water for generations. The company moved into a new $76 million mill, that included $5 million in pollution controls. The lake suddenly stopped smelling like rotten eggs— yet under its surface lay a 300-acre mound of sludge left from paper mill and other industrial operations of the past two centuries. Gas bubbles and bits of decaying matter kept floating to the surface. Many people were demanding that International Paper—or *somebody*—spend the millions of dollars needed to clean up the mess.

THE HUDSON RIVER. Among the great rivers of America, the Hudson is one of the shortest. From its point of birth—jewel-like Lake Tear of the Clouds, a two-acre pond below the summit of Mt. Marcy in the high Adirondacks—it flows only 315 miles until it enters the Atlantic at New York Harbor. Yet its role in the story of New York State—geologic, economic, aesthetic, ecologic—is a major one.

Three hundred years ago, Dutch explorers rhapsodized about the handsome forests and mountains that line the Hudson's banks, the abundance of game, and the fish teeming in its waters. In time, roads and railways crowded into the valley and old colonial settlements turned into dirty industrial towns. Now, a great suspense story of the late 20th century is whether the state and federal pure-waters programs will be sufficient to restore the Hudson to something approaching its cleanliness of times past, thus fulfilling the river's rightful role as a thing of beauty and a place of recreation for millions.

The upper Hudson is a fast-flowing trout stream, in springtime wild and often turbulent as it cuts down through the Adirondacks past such famous spots as Blue Ledge, where Winslow Homer did some of his finest paintings. But after the Adirondack Forest Preserve, paper company and other wastes intrude. The Mohawk, joining the Hudson near Troy, adds volume but not cleanliness. The accumulated municipal sewage and industrial wastes (acids, oil, dyes, and chemicals) of the capital district are so great that sanitary engineers speak of "the Albany Pool"—or sometimes "the Albany Cesspool." Massive fish kills have been recorded there in recent years.

About 25 miles south of Albany, the natural cleansing action of the river reduces the pollution to less egregious levels, and the river will be relatively clean until it reaches New York. After it has passed the Catskills and the cities of Kingston, Poughkeepsie, and Newburgh, the Hudson suddenly enters a narrow gorge. Naturalist Robert Boyle writes:

> The Hudson Highlands is perhaps the most magnificent stretch of the river. For 15 miles, forested mountain ramparts rise along both shores from Newburgh south to Peekskill, and there is vista after vista of incredible beauty. They have a common theme—a sort of fairybook magic that lingers in the mind from childhood, the notion that this is the way the world is supposed to look.

Storm King is where New York City's Consolidated Edison Company has been seeking for several years to build a massive pumped-storage hydroelectric project that would provide two million kilowatts of electricity for peak or emergency periods.

After Peekskill, the Hudson widens abruptly to its broadest areas—Haverstraw Bay and Tappan Zee, more than three miles across. This is the location of Indian Point, where Con Ed has operated a nuclear power plant since 1962, and has several other nuclear plants in the process of construction. The conservationists have been highly critical of these installations on the basis of the immense fish kills already caused by thermal pollution, but the work has proceeded without interruption.

The Hudson narrows again a few miles north of New York City, flowing past the dramatic 500-foot banks of the New Jersey Palisades on its west bank. Civilization thickens, the majestic sweep of the George Washington Bridge comes into view, and Manhattan's towers. Centuries ago, the world's greatest oyster beds were in New York Harbor and up the Hudson for several miles. Boyle writes:

> Today, the oyster grounds are no more, and the Hudson is a mess as it flows into New York Harbor. Every day, without cease, the West Side of Manhattan alone empties 175 million gallons of absolutely raw sewage into the river. The sewage emanates from every variety of human activity and habitation. It pours down pipes from skyscrapers, gushes from apartment houses, issues from hospitals, gas stations, restaurants, laboratories, theaters, public rest rooms, tenements, factories, stores, and the streets themselves. All this washes down the

drains that gird the streets and vomits directly into the river, where the tides rock it back and forth.

There are similar contributions from the New Jersey shore, and it is the considered opinion of one marine biologist that if Manhattan were not surrounded by salt water, which is inhibiting to pathogenic bacteria, the island would be a ghost town.

THE MID-HUDSON AND ITS ENVIRONS. The mid-Hudson Valley—from the capital district southward to the Westchester County line—is still relatively undeveloped. The biggest population concentrations are in the ramshackle, rundown river towns, but even the two largest of these, Poughkeepsie and Newburgh, have populations of only 32,029 and 26,219 respectively. There is only one really large employer—IBM—and it skims off the best of the local labor pool. Yet it takes little imagination to see that the population wave from New York City will continue to press inexorably northward in the next years. A major task of state and local planners is to find ways to cluster the housing developments and leave broad expanses of open space—so that, as Stephen Lefkowitz of the Urban Development Corporation said, "it doesn't all come out looking like Queens when it's finished."

The U. S. Military Academy at West Point has long added luster to the mid-Hudson region, incidentally adding a stimulus to the local economy. Recent years have not been kind to the Point. The Academy has been under attack for its martinet-like rules and rigid curriculum and, most notoriously, for its Honor Code—which literally dozens of cadets admitted violating.

Agriculture—especially apple-growing and dairy-farming—is strong in the mid-Hudson area. (Overall, New York farms produce goods valued at about $1 billion a year, three-quarters of the total from livestock, poultry, and their products.) Lovely Dutchess County remains a leading dairy county and has a special niche in American history as the location of Hyde Park, FDR's ancestral home and the site of his Presidential library. The growth of light industries and population expansion from the metropolis were clear in the 1970 Census figures, which showed Dutchess County population up 26 percent in a decade (to 222,295), Orange County up 20 percent (to 220,558), and little Putnam County up 79 percent (to 56,696).

In sheer numbers, however, no growth compares to that of Rockland County. It encompasses 173 square miles of flatlands and rolling hills opposite Westchester County on the widest part of the Hudson, flanked by New Jersey's Bergen County on the south. Rockland had 89,276 people in 1950; 229,903 in 1970; and is projected to have 350,000 by 1985. The New York State Thruway and the Tappan Zee Bridge were the keys to opening up the country. Today bulldozers rip up the earth to build even more housing developments, shopping centers, schools, and offices where all was quiet and rural a few years past. And so now we come on the suburbs of New York City, in themselves a civilization of more people, more prosperity, and certainly more growth than the mother city herself.

Classic Suburbia: Westchester and Long Island

WESTCHESTER COUNTY (891,409). "Westchester County," the New York *Times* commented in 1971, "is the ultimate suburban myth":

The myth is Scarsdale, symbol of a nation of self-satisfied suburban affluence. Surely all Westchester must be one big Scarsdale, the myth goes, one chain of fine Colonial homes and Tudor-style grocery stores stretching from the Hudson to [Long Island] Sound. . . .
Westchester is no more one big Scarsdale than Manhattan is one big Fifth Avenue, or one big Times Square. . . .

In reality, Westchester is many worlds. It does have some of the choicest suburbs of the continent—clipped, groomed, and lovely places like Larchmont, Rye, Bronxville, Mount Kisco, Pound Ridge, Bedford, Irvington, and Scarsdale itself. Within their confines one finds America's greatest concentration of highly paid corporation executives. But Westchester also has tens of thousands of people on the welfare rolls. It is not lily white; in fact 85,020 or 9.5 percent of the county's people are blacks, and there are a few thousand Puerto Ricans too. In northern Westchester, the scene is still an idyllic one of rolling farmland, lush forests, and pristine villages; by contrast, the city of Yonkers (204,370) is really just an extension of the Bronx.

Until a century ago, Westchester was a prime farm area of eastern America, supplying wheat and oats and corn; then the estates and golf courses began to gobble up the farmlands, and railroads provided easy commuting to the city. By the turn of the century, 184,000 people already lived there, and by 1940, there were 574,000, making Westchester a relatively completed suburban area when the Long Island counties had only a small fraction of the population they have now.

An important change of the postwar era has been the decision of several major corporations to abandon Manhattan and set up headquarters in parklike settings in Westchester—IBM in Armonk, General Foods in White Plains, Pepsico in Purchase, and others. Many smaller industries began or expanded operations in the county, so that by latest count, there were almost as many people commuting *into* Westchester as out to jobs in New York City and elsewhere.

The county seat of White Plains (50,220) used to be a quiet little town of neighborhood stores where one parked his car in front of his home or office, but blight struck in the late 1950s and early 1960s. Urban renewal arrived, with acres of brick-strewn sites awaiting new construction. Now the demolition era is beginning to end as high-rise parking garages and new office towers go up. Mount Vernon (72,778) got its share of underworld activity, including a police commissioner who ran a bookie joint in the middle of town. New Rochelle (75,386), a classic bedroom suburb, has a rapidly growing black community (14 percent in 1970) that runs the gamut from low-income people to substantial middle-class commuters.

But for all its difficulties, there is much to say for Westchester as a model for evolving suburbs. Back in the late 1930s, it went to a county-executive form of government—a model still followed by less than two dozen American suburbs. The county government has suffered from a lack of imagination or ability to impose its will in zoning or other matters on the fiercely independent towns and municipalities. Westchester, because it had already functioning communities with zoning and planning regulations, was able to avert some of the worst effects of rapid postwar suburban growth noted in counties like Nassau. Nor is Westchester all affluence or all poverty. Ex-Congressman Ogden Reid has pointed that "industry is bringing in a lot of creative young people who are aware of the issues. This is really a national district, with a real cross section of points of view."

LONG ISLAND. If Nassau and Suffolk counties were a city rather than a melange of townships, villages, and unincorporated areas on New York State's Long Island, they would rank fourth among the cities of the U.S.A., trailing only New York City, Chicago, and Los Angeles. Nassau alone, with 1,428,080 people in the latest Census, would be America's sixth largest city, and Suffolk, with 1,124,950, would be the seventh largest. The history of European man's civilization on the island dates back to the 17th century, but 76 percent of the population growth there has occurred in the brief three decades since Pearl Harbor. It is a story of a fantastic, largely unordered boom in people, houses, and industrial plants that only modern California can match. Many, indeed, are the parallels to California's growth and problems, and fittingly enough Long Island has experienced a slump in aerospace to match California's, while its premier newspaper, *Newsday*, founded by the late Harry F. Guggenheim in 1940, has been sold to the Los Angeles *Times*.

In 1940 Long Island was still a series of quiet little villages, each with a Main Street, some shops, a movie house, and a soda parlor, with the land of the farmer at the back doorstep. Commuting in those days was almost entirely by the Long Island Railroad, and most workers headed daily for the city. The aviation industry had opened up plants on the island before the crash of 1929, however, and after Pearl Harbor the factories suddenly received multimillion-dollar government contracts and a great job boom ensued. After the war, New York's returning GI's were desperate for new housing and in 1947 entrepreneur-builder William Levitt and his brother began building the first of thousands of inexpensive Cape Cod-style homes on a potato field in the center of Nassau County. The result was the first Levittown—17,544 homes in all. There were many predictions that the Levitts' basementless houses, with their inexpensive construction, would be the "slums of the future." It did not prove to be so. The homes were kept up, expanded, and improved upon, vegetation improved their stark early appearance, and by 1970 they sold for an average price of $35,000, compared to their original selling price of $6,990. But Long Island's Levittown set the pattern for postwar suburbia: look-alike houses, row upon row, mile after mile.

For shopping, Levittowners turned to an arterial road called Hempstead Turnpike, an ugly strip of stores, shops, pizza parlors, and gas stations, all with varying setbacks and gaudy signs. Human scale was lost; Hempstead Turnpike is six lanes of fast-moving traffic that blasts off from every stoplight, and let the pedestrian (there usually are none) beware. There are versions of Hempstead Turnpike all over Long Island, yet it need not have been so, as the village of Garden City proved by imposing tight controls and getting stores that blended with the area. As the postwar development proceeded, the separation between the towns of yore disappeared; now unless you watch for signs, there is no way to know when you have left one town and entered the next. Sometimes the greatest landmarks are the squat shopping centers—which do, however, include branches of the finest New York stores.

"For all intents and purposes," our friend Stan Hinden, formerly of *Newsday*, says, "you could hang a 'no vacancy' sign on the door of Nassau County." The farms that provided land for development are all gone. Some big estates are left on the north shore, but even when they are sold off, restrictive one- and two-acre zoning keeps down the number of new homes. The pressure is on for high-rise buildings, but the local, home-rule-minded Republicans are adamantly opposed, continuing their fight of many years to stop New York City from invading Nassau. As Nassau County filled up, the population pressure shifted to Suffolk County, and one need only check the latest home-builders' ads in the newspapers to see how far east the movement has progressed at any moment in time.

Geographically, Long Island has the shape of a fish. It actually includes the New York boroughs of Queens and Brooklyn on its western end, but even from the city line, it is 100 miles out to the island's eastern tip at the lobstering and resort village of Montauk. Much of the scenery, according to writer Jay Nelson Tuck, is reminiscent:

> The miles of sand dunes along the southern, Atlantic Ocean borders of the island recall Cape Cod or Cape Hatteras, while the steep, narrow, and tree-shaded village streets of the green and hilly North Shore, facing Long Island Sound, and on the rocky cliffs that swoop down to the pebble beaches, remind one of Maine. A Midwesterner driving over the flat farmlands in the [western part of the island] would have no difficulty developing a nostalgic feeling.

The settlement pattern of the island has been that the wealthy people have come out of the city and bought expensive lots and built expensive homes along the shores, while the middle classes have been obliged to head for cheaper homes in the interior. The Long Island Railroad, organized in 1834, has always been the great connecting link to New York City. But as early as 1924, Robert Moses, the master planner-builder, began developing plans for a great series of freeways on Long Island and new bridges to facilitate access to the city. Several freeway stretches and the Triboro and Bronx Whitestone Bridges and Queens Midtown Tunnel were finished just before World War II, and the postwar era brought more roads, including the Long

Island Expressway, a six-lane monster choked with autos and trucks and obsolete even in its youth. Commuters' new alternative of easy highway access to New York City cut deeply into the business of the Long Island Railroad in the early postwar years, plunging the line into the sea of red ink and maintenance problems that have plagued it ever since.

Long Island is no longer preeminently a bedroom area for New York City. A study in the late 1960s showed that only 30 percent of the Nassau-Suffolk work force actually commuted to jobs in New York City—some 90,000 by the Long Island Railroad, and 100,000 in their own automobiles (generally with no one else in the car). The auto commuters often head for jobs in the outer New York boroughs, but 25,000 of them—in what must surely be the grimmest commuting routine of the megalopolis—insist on driving their autos all the way into Manhattan, there to pay an exorbitant parking fee, each working day. In return, New York City sends about 100,000 commuters a day to jobs in Nassau and Suffolk Counties.

The 70 percent of the Nassau-Suffolk labor pool that now works on the island depends first and foremost on the military-industrial complex. The biggest contractor is Grumman Aircraft, which employed 37,100 workers in 1969 (but only 24,000 by 1974, as a result of the aerospace depression). Service industries are major employers, and the construction industry is a huge one on the island. Agriculture is still a vital factor in Suffolk County. The three big crops are potatoes, cauliflower, and ducks, in that order. Farm income was $67 million in the late 1960s, the most of any county in New York State. But farming's days on Long Island may be numbered. Rising real-estate taxes, low prices on farm goods, and difficulties in recruiting migrant farm workers from the South are encouraging more farmers to quit each year. The county has, however, instituted a program of outright purchase of farmland and development rights, in a promising effort to retain what it can of the last vestiges of Suffolk's agricultural heritage.

Tourism is also vital to Long Island, and increasingly so as more and more New Yorkers come out not just for the hottest summer weeks, but often for the whole season from May through October. Vacation resorts are scattered all about the island's shores, with some of the most beautiful near the tip of Suffolk, including the illustrious Hamptons (South-, East-, and West-) so popular with high society. For the masses, there is Jones Beach on the south shore, where 2,500 acres of beaches and woods can accommodate 100,000 bathers and, of course, their cars (23,000 at a time).

Jones Beach was the work of Robert Moses back in 1929, when he held the position of Long Island State Park Commissioner among his many other posts. In the early 1960s, Moses still directed park development and carved out a 1,000-acre state park at the western end of Fire Island, a beautiful and unspoiled barrier beach that stretches on for mile after mile off the south coast. The bridge to the state park was the first road connection to Fire Island; before then access had been by ferries that carried no autos. Then Moses proposed constructing a motor highway down the whole length of

Fire Island. Devotees of the island envisaged destruction of the lovely dunes—and inundation by thousands of motorists. The friends of Fire Island raised a great public uproar and enlisted on their side Otis Pike (whose district then included Fire Island), John V. Lindsay (then a Manhattan Congressman with many summertime Fire Islanders among his constituents), and Interior Secretary Stewart Udall. The outcome was that the 31-mile stretch of Fire Island east of the park was made into a National Seashore, with all its shore-front in the public domain. The enabling legislation expressly prohibited a road—and now even dune buggies, once unrestricted on the island, are strictly limited.*

There is a temptation to identify Long Island's conservative brand of politics with Orange County, California, both places of scientific-age workers mostly anxious to protect their own turf against outsiders. But for all its conservatism, Long Island sometimes pulls surprises. Even if it was for just a single term, Nassau County voters did elect Allard Lowenstein to Congress, a man who related to and expressed youth's questioning of American values on war and economic policy. In 1968, George Wallace could pick up only 4.8 percent of the vote in Nassau, 8.4 percent in Suffolk. And for three successive three-year terms in the 1960s, Nassau elected a Democratic county executive, Eugene Nickerson, who established the county's first human rights commission, its first governmental code of ethics (badly needed in the developer-wheeler-dealer-zoning-variance atmosphere of modern-day Long Island), the first narcotics commission, job development center, and departments of labor and commerce. Nickerson was a man who made no bones about Nassau's problems in areas like drug abuse and pollution of the air and water, which he said were "reaching disaster proportions."

In 1975, the voters of Nassau County surprised many observers and defeated a proposal that would have created a county-wide legislative body. Low voter turn-out (a mere 9 percent) perhaps demonstrated that there was less than a raging public debate among the citizens, but the issue was of vital importance to local political leaders. The present system in the county allows great power to rest in the offices of existing municipal chiefs and the Republican Party, which dominate much of the county's politics through the local city halls. Indeed Joseph Margiotta's Republican organization is a much more effective and well financed "machine" than the Democratic organizations in the city which are more often tarred with that label.

The black population of both Nassau and Suffolk is about 5 percent, but it is heavily ghettoized. Further movement of blacks onto Long Island is now impeded by zoning practices that exclude low-income people; thereby hangs one of the crucial social and political issues of the times. The National Association for the Advancement of Colored People selected the township

* The Fire Island defeat was a bitter one for Moses, but apparently only one factor in his 1962 resignation from the state park commission and the bulk of his other state development jobs. (Rockefeller was anxious to have Moses replaced and he was beyond the maximum age of 70 for several of his posts.) Querulous, forceful, visionary, and bull-headed, Moses left behind a fantastic legacy of public works from Long Island to the St. Lawrence River. The incredible hold he gained over public officials and public opinion is chronicled in Robert A. Caro's *The Power Broker* (1974).

of Oyster Bay in Nassau County for a major class action. Of Oyster Bay's 329,142 residents, only 2 percent are black; Grumman Aircraft actually employs 1,248 minority group members at its big plant in the township, but only 50 of them have been able to find housing locally. Yet the same township, anxious to improve its local tax base, has been wooing "clean" industries with special zoning variances and offers of 100 percent site and plant financing.

Even outside its relatively small black communities, Long Island has many people living in poverty or close to it. By the mid 1970s, the combination of skyrocketing welfare costs and inflation resulted in a financial squeeze for wealthy Nassau and Suffolk counties. And there are social problems aplenty. As Stan Hinden writes:

One of the key things about suburbia is mood. It's deceptive. The tree-shaded streets and neat houses with their trimmed lawns and bushes look peaceful and serene enough. They don't look like the places you'd find drug addicts or alcoholics, car thieves and embezzlers, people who can't afford shoes for their kids or three squares a day, welfare cases and school dropouts, and race antagonisms, if not actual warfare.

You're not surprised to find all this in the slums—it's just bad environment. But when you find it in the green grass atmosphere of suburbia, what is it then?

Perhaps people take with them the problems of their time, no matter where they live. Perhaps it is as shattering to a man's well-being to have to come up with a big mortgage payment to the bank each month and to get caught in a rising tax squeeze as it is for him to live in a crummy city apartment house where he can hear the mice rattling in the walls.

Perhaps, too, in the homogeneous society, there are no city and county lines to problems, to social ills. Suburbia is in many ways a grand illusion. For many people in Nassau and Suffolk, the facts of life (soaring taxes, high crime rates, inadequate transportation) have helped shatter the illusion about suburbia.

But still they come. Of all the possible worlds, suburbia still seems to be the best one available.

II: THE CITY: NEW YORK, NEW YORK

ON THE DAY OF Thomas Dewey's funeral in 1971, President Nixon flew into New York City for the services, accompanied by New York's Senator Javits. As the two looked down, viewing the soaring towers of Manhattan and the rest of that premier city of America, where almost eight million people make their home, Javits turned to the President and said: "It's fantastic. It could all go by the boards."

Nixon's response is unrecorded (and one would be surprised if he cared much), but there is an element of pathos in Javits' afterthoughts:

> The city is in such trouble. It's a terrible thing for me, because I was born there and lived there all my life, and I adore the city. But it needs massive assistance—a lot from without, *but a lot more from within.*

Certainly the interior resources are there, if they could be mobilized. For all its pains and sorrows, New York is the world's most brilliant and creative city. Name practically any human endeavor outside of government, and New York is the capital of America. What happens within it, in terms of finance, communications, art, theater, fashion, or intellect, sets the pace for the nation and sways the world. California is beginning to offer serious competition in several fields, and now seems to lead in that amorphous area known as lifestyles. But the *power* is still New York's. It is not as dominant as it was in past times, because the nation is so much larger and more diverse. But a society, no matter how immense, has its controlling and creative center, and New York remains—in large measure, despite its reversals—that center. Javits offers an observation on this score:

> Notice how anyone who's running for President beats a path immediately to New York to raise a little dough. It's not just because there's money in New York—there's money in Dallas, too. It's because New York is an open market for

ideas, and courageous enough to back new things. And this has been its role for a century or more.

If New York were to "die," one suspects, we would quickly recreate it.

Yet for all its eminence, New York is an easy place to be frightened of. Across the country, in hundreds of interviews, we found confirmed what Richard Reeves, then the metropolitan correspondent of the New York *Times*, had told us: "The people of America are scared of New York City. They see it as a big, tough, vicious place."

It is true that turmoil, brashness, and a feeling of loneliness amid the millions have always marked life in the city. Walk down the streets and look into people's eyes, and you see the emptiness, the shell of desperate self-defense built up around each cell of the urban organism. The wellsprings of hostility are forever close to the surface, even if ameliorated a bit by a feeling of "pulling together" in the face of the fiscal crisis. Pushy subway riders, predatory motorists, abusive cab drivers, arrogant city workers, surly sales clerks and waiters, argumentative customers—they all fairly crackle with hostility. Philip G. Zimbardo, a Stanford psychologist but longtime New Yorker, said (in a New York *Times* interview) that the city's uncivil behavior stems from a feeling of anonymity, or as he puts it, deindividualism. "If no one knows who I am, what difference does it make what I do?" In the present day, as the city's traditional homogeneous ethnic neighborhoods begin to break up, no one is known as a person any more, so that the incivility (and, incidentally, the crime rate) seems to get steadily worse.

The same phenomenon exists in politics and government. Everybody has to have his piece *now*. Confrontation, not compromise and reconciliation, was the prevailing model, at least until the mid-'70s. "John hates the word *demand*," Mayor Lindsay's wife Mary noted in an interview. We asked Lindsay about it and he reacted philosophically: "You learn to roll with those things. Legitimate pressures are often involved." Perhaps so, but it must be nerve-wracking. Lindsay's deputy mayor, Richard Aurelio, noted: "You make a decision at 9 A.M., and they're out picketing at 11."

One reason New Yorkers are so uptight is the roster of afflictions in everyday life. These are just a few of them:

▪ A daily barrage of ear-shattering noise from air compressors, pneumatic drills, emergency sirens, garbage trucks, jet aircraft, commuter railroads, motorcycles, and honking traffic that must exceed any other place on the continent.

▪ Traffic jams of such horrendous proportions that there are recurring proposals to ban all private autos from the streets of Manhattan, or charge high bounties. In 1907, the average speed of horse-drawn vehicles on the city's streets was 11.5 miles per hour; in the 1960s, motor vehicles in the central business district averaged only 8.5 miles an hour (and less during the noontime crushes).

- The subways, described by John Burby in *The Great American Motion Sickness* as "236 miles of gloomy, grimy, gamy caves filled with steel beasts that scream and scrape around curves in mechanical agony." They do move as many as 61,000 people an hour per line of track during rush hour, 40 times the number that can travel a lane of highway by auto. But the system is plagued by breakdowns, delayed trains, begrimed stations, the most ornate graffiti in the world, bands of hyperkinetic youths roving the cars after school, robberies, and molestations. The ranks of armed subway patrolmen have been tripled in recent years to deter felonies against passengers and station attendants, and still scores of incidents take place each month.

- Streets left filthy from belching incinerators and the careless litter of an indifferent populace. A "small' but significant item: some 500,000 New Yorkers insist on having pet dogs. Each day the canines leave behind a reminder of their presence—110,000 pounds of excrement on New York's sidewalks, streets, and parks (not to mention 2,000 gallons of urine).

- One of the highest air-pollution rates in the whole world (although Consolidated Edison has reduced the rate in the last several years through the burning of low-sulphur fuels). On Thanksgiving Day 1966, an inversion layer settled on the city, trapping fumes laden with sulphur dioxide and other gases; 168 people died. (Similar inversions in 1953 and 1963 killed 220 and 300 respectively.) In July 1970, a thick blanket of smog again settled on the city, combined with a 90° heat wave, power brownouts, subway slowdowns, wrecks, and fires.

- A high crime rate which, though statistically far below cities like Detroit and Atlanta, is enough to keep many frightened people off the streets, especially at night.

- A housing shortage of near disaster proportions.

- Crowded, inefficient hospitals (although New York has the most extensive free public health system in the country).

- Schools of declining quality.

- The nation's most breakdown-prone telephone system. (In 1975 the telephone system all but collapsed for several days following a series of mysterious fires and equipment failures.)

- Fear of a repetition of the 1966 drought when there were grave fears about the future of the city's water supply.*

Then there is the rash of strikes, which were most frequent during the early years of the Lindsay regime, but still go on from time to time. Among the most famous were the 1966 transit strike that immobilized the city just after Lindsay took office; the 1968 sanitation strike which resulted in the undying Lindsay-Rockefeller feud; the 1968 teachers strike over the Ford Foundation-funded experimental school district in Ocean Hill-Brownsville; and the 1971 municipal workers strike, in which union members immo-

---

* New York actually has a splendid water reservoir system, constructed in Putnam County on the Hudson's east bank and in the Catskill Mountains on the other side, connected to New York by a tunnel underneath the polluted river.

bilized 27 of the city's 29 drawbridges. There have been, and continue to be, scores of other work stoppages, including firemen, policemen, postmen, taxi drivers, janitors, plumbers, construction workers, parking-lot attendants, and various categories of municipal and service industry workers. New York is so interdependent that practically any small group can plunge the whole metropolis into chaos. And just about every organized group, to obtain its own specific goals, has felt free to do just that.

Two decades ago, the famed *New Yorker* essayist E. B. White wrote:

By rights, New York should have destroyed itself long ago, from panic or fire or rioting or failure of some vital supply line of its circulatory system or from some deep labyrinthine short circuit. Long ago the city should have experienced an insoluble traffic snarl at some impossible bottleneck.

It should have perished of hunger when food lines failed for a few days. It should have been wiped out by a plague starting in its slums or carried in by ships' rats. It should have been overwhelmed by the sea that licks at it on every side. The workers in its myriad cells should have succumbed to nerves, from the fearful pall of smoke-fog that drifts over every few days from Jersey, blotting out all light at noon and leaving the high offices suspended, men groping and depressed, and the sense of world's end.

Yet somehow, the magnificent city has survived. And indeed, if one looks backward in time, the trials and tribulations of the present age seem more like a natural continuum than a sudden descent. So let us look backward in time a moment.

An Historic Perspective

From its earliest times, New York was a place of remarkable ethnic, cultural, and racial differences. Most of the colonial population was Dutch, but there were many Englishmen as well as Brazilians, French, Finns, Portuguese, and Swedes. There were blacks, most of them from Brazil, and there were slaves. There were Protestants, and then came Catholics and Jews. Quakers were persecuted, tortured, and banished.

In 1712, 23 black slaves rebelled and killed nine white householders. The rebels were cornered; one slave was suspended alive in chains without food or water until he died several days later. Two (one owned by a Roosevelt) were burned alive. In all, 21 were executed by various ghastly devices. In 1741, authorities arrested more than 150 blacks on a series of wildly false charges. By summer's end, 14 blacks had been burned alive, 18 hanged, and 71 banished to the West Indies. Four whites were also executed. Edward R. Ellis, in his *Epic of New York City*, called this the "ugliest orgy of Negro persecutions occurring anywhere in America during the colonial period."

In the early 19th century, as New York made its rise to prominence, displacing Philadelphia as the population center of America and Boston as the cultural center, immigrants began to pour in from Europe. Ethnic hatreds were pronounced and men gathered into gangs to protect themselves, their neighborhoods, and their property from other gangs. The Irish were particularly despised, except by Tammany Hall, by then an arm of the Democratic party. The working classes lived in squalor while the wealthy languished in comfort.

During the Civil War, the draft was deeply resented, and in July 1863 riots broke out on a scale that make 20th century disturbances seem pale by comparison. Between 50,000 and 70,000 Irish Catholics, who blamed blacks for the war and the draft, rampaged through the city and left a wake of death and destruction. They tortured and hanged blacks and burned and looted houses. Before order was restored, at least 1,000 people had been killed, hundreds of buildings burned, and millions of dollars of damage done. By contrast, in the worst racial disturbances of recent years, there was a week of rioting in July 1964 in Harlem and the Bedford-Stuyvesant section of Brooklyn. Some 140 persons were injured, but only one killed.

In the half century following the Civil War, New York was the fulcrum of fantastic growth generated by freewheeling capital and the industrial revolution. Lords of finance like Cornelius Vanderbilt, Jay Gould, John D. Rockefeller, and J. P. Morgan masterminded the building of great empires of rail, steel, and oil and built their gaudy mansions along Fifth Avenue. The first Madison Square Garden and the dedication of St. Patrick's Cathedral occurred in 1879; the Metropolitan Museum of Art opened the following year; the first mass use of electric lights took place in 1882; the Brooklyn Bridge (regarded as the greatest engineering triumph since the Erie Canal) opened in 1883, and the Metropolitan Opera House the same year; in 1886 there was the deeply moving dedication of the Statue of Liberty; the first Waldorf-Astoria Hotel opened its doors in 1897; New York's first skyscraper, the 13-story Tower Building, was completed in 1889; the first service was held in 1899 in the unfinished Episcopal Cathedral of St. John the Divine, the largest cathedral in the world.

Yet in this same era politics was dominated first by the infamous Tweed Ring, and then by a succession of lesser Tammany Hall thieves. In 1898, a new city charter effected the consolidation of Manhattan with Brooklyn, Queens, the Bronx, and Staten Island, making a city of 3.3 million people, covering 320 square miles of territory. But as this vast metropolis entered the 20th century, it was crowded with the great waves of immigration (especially Jews and Italians) who had been pouring in in ever increasing numbers since 1880. Working conditions for the average man and woman were abysmal, more than a third of the populace was foreign born, thousands were illiterate or unable to speak English; ethnic and racial intolerance was rampant. Some 1.5 million poor people were jammed into hovels and rat-infested buildings on the lower East Side; Ellis contends that they "lived under worse conditions and paid more rent than the inhabitants of any other big city on earth."

As is often the case, great disasters precipitated reform. The excursion ship *General Slocum* burned on the Hudson River, taking the lives of 1,031 people, after which there was a tightening of regulations and inspections. A tragic fire in the Triangle Shirtwaist Company lofts in 1911 brought about a rewriting of the state labor code and the beginnings of unionism in the city. Some 141 persons, including 125 girls, died in that fire as they fled from their sewing machines in the crowded, dingy sweatshops, piling up at the locked doors in the stairwells or jumping to their death from the eighth floor while firemen helplessly maneuvered their six-story-high ladders.

As the U. S. entered World War I, New York—though it was a city with a huge German population—was torn by anti-German sentiment. Germanic sculpture was chipped off public buildings, names of foods changed, German operas canceled at the Met. After the war, New York was torn by the infamous campaign of U. S. Attorney General A. Mitchell Palmer against anything and anyone he could label Red or Bolshevik. There was the bombing of Wall Street in 1920, when 35 persons were killed, 130 injured, and the House of Morgan seriously damaged. The Weathermen's depredations of recent years never came close to that destruction.

New York was a hyperactive, swinging town in the 1920s as its investment bankers increasingly took over world financing. The Stock Exchange boomed, the entertainment world blossomed with 60 theaters on or off Broadway, and thousands of speakeasies flourished. It all came to a roaring end on October 24, 1929, when the stock market crashed. The Depression saw New Yorkers by the thousands standing in bread lines or queuing up at the soup kitchens. Professional men slept in subways or on park benches. The city government almost went bankrupt, amassing a public debt nearly equal to that of the 48 states combined. Despite "recovery," 23 percent of the city's population was still on relief in 1934. And the blacks, as writer Seymour Freedgood notes, were "scarcely better off than they had been during the Civil War." It really took World War II to revive New York again, but no sooner had peace come than the flight of the stable middle-class citizenry to the suburbs began.

In our time, it is fashionable to say that New York is dying. In a fiscal sense, that may be right. But every prophet of doom should recall what the city has faced in the past and has surmounted. And for all of today's problems, life is better than it once was. Fires no longer ravage great stretches of the urban landscape. The muddy streets and the worst municipal thievery are gone. Street urchins no longer starve or freeze to death. Poor women no longer die in childbirth without medical attention. Racial murders are a pale shadow of what they were in the past. Everyone gets a chance to have an education (however mediocre). Why, then, has New York seemed to be in such dire straits—even before the specter of municipal bankruptcy arose in 1975? Roger Starr, later to become administrator of the city's housing and development administration, put his finger on it in the early 1970s: "The city of New York," he said, "is in trouble because it has set itself standards it's unwilling to pay for. It's like a person living beyond his moral means."

Mayors and Their Problems

New York is so huge, so complex, so diverse that it became vogue in the 1960s to speak of it as simply "ungovernable." If the city were Manhattan alone, one might stretch his imagination and see a way to control the mass. But Manhattan contains only 19 percent of New York's population. "You move through the teeming areas of the Bronx and Brooklyn," Senator Javits notes, "and it's just beyond belief as to the problems and the seeming inability to solve them."

New York City's budget is larger than that of New York State or any government except the federal. In 1965–66, it was $3.5 billion a year; in 1975–76, it had shot up to $11.1 billion. By the early 1970s, the city had 415,-000 workers, also a record among all governments save the federal. There were 65,000 school teachers, 12,000 sanitationmen, 25,00 welfare caseworkers, and the ranks of the New York police had swollen to 32,000, more than the standing army of Australia. No other big city required workers in like proportions in any of these categories. Overall, New York had 49 public employees per 1,000 population, compared to 35 in Los Angeles and only 30 in Chicago. Why did New York need so many more? Edward K. Hamilton, then city budget director, explained it this way to the New York *Daily News*:

> Because it is so big, because it is so dense, because it has a tradition of high levels of public service along with high expectations, because it has rigidities in its laws governing work load and work rules, and because it has unions, which tend to push very hard, much harder than unions in other cities.

A complementary explanation was offered by Edward N. Costikyan, a former Tammany leader. He claimed that in the process of insulating its departments from political influence, the city had in effect succeded in leaving all the major institutions of government—police protection, education, health and hospitals, sanitation, housing, and welfare—free of any significant exterior political or executive control. Who then ruled? The bureaucrats, Costikyan suggested. And what is their primary interest? High pay, security, and building their own administrative empires. What is the result? Bloated, mediocre government.

Radical change—including a virtual takeover by the state of the city's ultimate financial decisions—was to come in the wake of the 1975 fiscal disaster. Perhaps being mayor of New York will never be what it once was—the ultimate prize a political figure could win in Municipal Politics, U.S.A. Whoever won the office was the biggest man in the biggest town, surrounded by trappings of power: a beautiful City Hall from which to reign, an historic private residence (Gracie Mansion), a high salary, private limousine always available with chauffeurs, aides, and police bodyguards. He was the representative of urban America, sought out by the great from America and abroad—

though the quality of men elected rarely matched the governors of New York State. Some of the mayors remembered from earlier years are:

JIMMY WALKER (1926–32). A symbol of old Tammanyism but also a man of immense charm and wit. Walker neglected city business outrageously and brought back fraud and favor reminiscent of the Boss Tweed days. He kept a rather steady string of mistresses, to the distress of the Catholic hierarchy. The first citywide sanitation system, the first hospitals department, and tunnels for many subways came during the Walker regime, but the corruption in the city eventually got so bad that Governor Roosevelt appointed a commission, headed by anti-Tammany Democrat Samuel Seabury, to inquire into city government. Walker wisecracked his way through the sordid disclosures of the probe, but one step ahead of removal from office by FDR, he resigned in autumn 1932. The next day he sailed for Europe and oblivion.

FIORELLO H. LA GUARDIA (1934–45). La Guardia is still widely regarded as the best mayor New York ever had. Taking office in the depths of the Depression, he gave New York honest and effective government, instilled its citizens with a sense of hope, and added humor and personal charm to City Hall. (What hired PR man would ever have thought up an idea like reading the comics to children over the radio on Sunday mornings?) La Guardia ran for office at various times as a Republican, a Socialist, and a Progressive, and it was with independent Democratic backing, plus the official Republican nomination, that he first won election as mayor—thus inventing the "Fusion" model Lindsay would use 30 years later.

La Guardia made superb appointments to office, cracked down on crime and police corruption, brought in Robert Moses to rebuild the parks and start bridges, got new housing started, brought aviation to the city, obtained a new city charter, and reformed civil service. In 1947, only two years after leaving office, he died of cancer at 65.

WILLIAM O'DWYER (1946–50). A Tammany Hall regular who appointed some good men to high posts and rushed postwar school- and housing-construction programs. But O'Dwyer was reputed to have underworld connections even before his election. In 1949, after the *Brooklyn Eagle* ran a series on how bookmakers were buying police protection, President Truman was prevailed upon to appoint O'Dwyer ambassador to Mexico. (O'Dwyer later returned home, just to prove, it seemed, that he was not afraid of being indicted. He never was.)

ROBERT F. WAGNER, JR. (1954–65). Son of the distinguished New Deal era Senator who authored the Wagner Labor Relations Act in the 1930s. Wagner, Warren Moscow has written, inherited from his father a social consciousness, a keen ability to negotiate conflicting interests, and a tendency to delay decisions. The result was a bad press image, although when Wagner stepped in to settle a long newspaper strike in the winter of 1962–63, publishers were amazed at his capacity, sagacity, and endurance. Wagner was as honest in money affairs as La Guardia had been, and went much further in fields like education, housing, hospitals, health, traffic, and civil rights. His middle-income housing program, Moscow says, was the nation's best, but he let two obscure state legislators take credit for it. Wagner ended up covering city deficits through bonding, a practice that would pave the way for financial disaster in the following decade.

Lindsay and Beame

They faced each other in 1965: the one tall, with a chiseled face and wavy hair, tailor-made for television; the other, not much over five feet, with a rather squeaky voice. In that election, Lindsay, the Republican-Liberal, beat Beame, the Democrat, 45 to 42 percent, with some unintended assistance from Conservative William Buckley, whose third party candidacy hurt Beame, especially in conservative Catholic areas. For more than 10 years, these two men have been the only mayors New York has had; they have been not only in charge of the vast city government, but also, in New York more than in most cities, they have set the tone for the city as a whole.

There is no doubt of the tone Lindsay wanted to set. "He is fresh and everyone else is tired," wrote Murray Kempton when Lindsay, then a Republican Congressman from the Upper East Side, was campaigning in 1965. Educated at St. Paul's, Yale, and Yale Law, Lindsay wanted to give the city a style and verve it did not seem to have under prosaic Bob Wagner. One of his favorite innovations was closing Central Park to car traffic and opening it to bicycling on Sundays; the mayor and his photogenic wife riding their own bikes were a natural shot for Monday's papers. Lindsay also made a major point of his concern for the most down-and-out people in the city. As the great ghettos seethed with racial tension in the 1960s, Lindsay personally strode the streets, bringing by his very presence a message of concern and respect unknown before. New York might well have experienced a holocaust if Lindsay's sympathetic figure had not been there, moving among the mourners in the black neighborhoods.

But if Lindsay was successful in convincing rich Manhattan whites and poor blacks and Puerto Ricans that he really cared about them, his most conspicuous failure was with the great white middle class—the traditional backbone of the city. In the flurry of Lindsay's brief 1972 presidential campaign, it was forgotten that he won only 45 percent of the total vote for mayor in 1965, and only 42 percent in 1969—hardly demonstrations of massive voting power. In fact, if one excludes the results from Manhattan—scarcely a typical constituency—Lindsay was outpolled by his opponents both times. And that understates the hatred with which he was regarded in Archie Bunker-type neighborhoods in Queens, Brooklyn, the Bronx, and Staten Island.

When we asked Lindsay what he considered his most important accomplishment as mayor, he named the reshaping and modernization of city government. Lindsay created 10 "superagencies" or umbrella agencies, replacing 50 old city departments, and, in a fascinating administrative balancing act, tried simultaneously to decentralize power to the city's multitudinous small communities. The "superagencies" did make it possible to rationalize and coordinate many city functions as well as for Lindsay to recruit some of the finest young executives in America to head them. (Lindsay pointed with pride to "the caliber of the cabinet I could attract—they'll be heard from again, in business and political administration in the country." Many knowledgeable observers agreed with him.) The superagencies were faulted, however, for just adding a new level of bureaucracy, contributing to a surge of thousands of new municipal jobs noted during Lindsay's term in office (including a trebling of public relations costs, to $3.6 million a year). The city administration remained snarled in red tape; for the Model Cities program, for instance, five agencies had to process pieces of paper through 56 steps before a person could be hired.

In his effort to change city government, Lindsay faced a merit system that was once a noble improvement over the spoils system but is now bogged down by outdated, rigid, and regressive rules and regulations. Most entry positions of the New York Civil Service System are filled on the basis of written examination when there is no scientifically supportable evidence that these examinations are related to on-the-job performance. After an employee has spent six months on the job, he is virtually guaranteed the job for life; promotions and salary increases are completely unrelated to job performance. Supervisors sometimes belong to the same union as employees, and the unions have enough political power to influence the appointment of top level managers.

According to Sigmund G. Ginsburg, and E. S. Savas, both assistant city administrators under Lindsay, "the system prohibits good management, frustrates able employees, inhibits productivity, lacks the confidence of the city's taxpayers, and fails to respond to the needs of citizens."

Like Rockefeller, Lindsay left no obvious political heir, and the city he led for so long ended up in quite different hands after his retirement. The frontrunners in the 1973 race were Congressman Mario Biaggi, a former policeman and law and order candidate; City Controller Abraham Beame, Lindsay's 1965 opponent; Herman Badillo of the Bronx, the first Puerto Rican borough president (1965–69) and Congressman; and Assemblyman Albert Blumenthal, a reformer from Manhattan's Upper West Side. Biaggi, whom neither Lindsay nor Rockefeller wanted, was an early scratch as it was revealed he had lied about invoking the Fifth Amendment. Blumenthal got the Liberal nomination, but faltered as Badillo won the NDC endorsement. Beame seemed lackluster, but his only real problems were at the beginning of the race, when former Mayor Wagner beguiled reporters for about 10 days by hinting that he might run (he didn't). Beame barely led Badillo in the first primary, and for the first time in New York history there was a runoff under a new law, because no candidate had received 40 percent. The winner this time, by a wide margin, was Beame; there was a flood of voters from the white, middle class parts of the city, apparently not eager for a Puerto Rican mayor or at least for anything that looked like a continuation of the Lindsay policies.

Beame seemed to be the kind of mayor who would give the city a breather after the hectic pace of life under Lindsay. He was on the white homeowners' and renters' side, without being a racist; he was an expert on the city's budget, without being an Ivy League pedant; and he was—and this is the part that is hard to believe—the first Jewish mayor of New York City, which contains some 20 percent of all the Jews in the world.

If New Yorkers in 1973 had elected Abe Beame mayor in hopes of a period of tranquillity, they were rudely shocked. Before his term was half over, the great New York City fiscal crisis of 1975 and beyond had left Beame's reputation—in matters both financial and political—in tatters. Both as comptroller and as mayor, Beame had told his constituents that the budget was balanced when it wasn't, borrowed money at high interest rates rather than cut the budget, and falsely certified to investors that city revenues matched expenditures. Despite the odds, Beame geared up to run for reelection in 1977, perhaps hoping that his early support for Jimmy Carter would result in a federal miracle to alleviate the city's woes.

The shock of the Urban Development Corporation's default forced underwriters to turn a sharp eye toward New York City fiscal practices. Bankers and investors began to realize that for many years the city had been spending beyond its means, paying its employees the highest municipal wages in the world to provide an unmatched array of social services to a population that could no longer pay for so many luxuries—if indeed it ever could. We shall not attempt a blow-by-blow account of that crisis here. But it is important to note the factors which converged in something very close to financial *Götterdammerung*:

■ Fiscal gimmickry and complexity. Mayor Robert Wagner began, in 1965, his last year in office, to borrow against tax revenues on the grounds that it was better to borrow now and pay later to work on the war on crime, narcotics addiction, and slum disease. John Lindsay faced this budget gap, denied by Wagner, and was confronted by sharp union demands literally on his first day in office, Jan. 1, 1966. At first "tough" with the unions, he soon capitulated and for much of his time in office bought off the unions with concessions that startled even union leaders themselves. In 1965, the short-term debt was $526 million. In spite of a sharp decline in the early Lindsay years, by 1975 it was $5.7 billion.

Since the city's charter forbids the adoption of an unbalanced budget, Wagner also resorted to budget gimmicks like collecting the same taxes twice in one fiscal year by changing the due date. He and Lindsay learned to play intricate games with the budget, placing various types of spending in inappropriate categories, counting anticipated revenues from the state and federal government in one fiscal year while actually receiving them in later years, dramatically overestimating anticipated revenues while clearly under-estimating expenses (predicting a decline in the welfare rolls was a favorite maneuver).

Through the years, the city's financial system grew incredibly compli-cated. Hundreds of separate funds were established. "To try to cut through it at any one point and figure out where you are, what you owe, what you're spending and what you can afford to do is incredibly complex," said Don-ald Kummerfeld, the city budget director brought in by an embattled Mayor Beame looking for a top fiscal expert untarred by New York's past fiscal sins.

"I would say, having worked eight years on the federal budget, that the New York City budget is easily ten times as complex and difficult to under-stand and grasp," Kummerfeld added.

The result of this gimmickry and complexity was that the city was pay-ing for an expanded set of services with what was at its core a regressive tax system, supplementing it with high yield bonds (held mostly by native New York institutions and individuals and exempt from city, state, or federal tax-ation) and then borrowing to repay the money originally borrowed. Eventu-ally this fiscal madness overtook the city.

■ State's responsibility. From 1964 onward, the state legislature and Gover-nor Rockefeller, who had to pass on every city budget, allowed the city to use the capital budget to borrow money for current expenses and indeed often initiated the use of the capital budget for programs that should have been in the expense budget, simply not done, or cut back. "State super-vision could have called a halt to such practices and more closely monitored the growing tendency of the city to issue short term debt. In fact, the record indicates that no political leader wanted to or was in a position to demand fiscal prudence," according to Enid Beaumont, formerly of New York Uni-versity's Graduate School of Public Administration.

■ Departure of private industry. Fifty years ago, New York was a beehive of small manufacturing concerns, lodged in cramped brownstone and cast iron buildings. With unionization, wages rose and so did virtually all other costs; small manufacturers gave way to their bigger competitors. About 1950, the bigger manufacturing concerns began pulling out of New York at a stead-ily increasing rate; during 1973 and 1974 alone, New York City lost fully 7 percent of its manufacturing jobs. During the 1960s, New York could ignore this loss of manufacturing jobs because of a building boom and an increase in "service jobs." But these "service jobs" were financed mostly by govern-ment, which became the city's largest growth industry. Taxes had to be in-creased even more to pay for them, further depressing the economy and driving away private business.

And on top of all that came the fearsome inflation of the first half of the 1970s, which constantly eroded the purchasing power of the beleaguered city government.

■ Population shift and the federal government's role. Since World War II, two million primarily white middle-income residents have departed from

New York City and have been replaced by two million largely poor and more dependent citizens. This lowered tax base finally proved insufficient to provide for the growing dependent population.

Federal government policies have both encouraged the departure of middle class residents and upped the expectations of what government will do for poor people. Federal housing mortgage programs and highways made it attractive to move to the suburbs. And throughout the 1960s, Washington was offering one new social aid program after another, almost always with a city matching fund requirement. Lindsay, determined to prevent major social unrest, quickly adopted each program as it became available. Then, as the programs disappeared or declined in funding under the Republican administrations of Richard Nixon and Gerald Ford, New York was left holding the bag. As John Keith, head of the New York Regional Plan Association commented, "The 'feds' made us pregnant and then they abandoned us."

Many of the programs, however, were of New York City's own choosing —drug clinics, ever-expanded health and welfare benefits, the tuition-free City University of New York, and countless others. When proposals were rejected at the federal level, New York City tended to accept them in the hope that federal dollars would be forthcoming some day.

- Welfare responsibilities. As New York's racial and ethnic composition changed, the "welfare problem" emerged. The recessions of 1969–70 and 1974–75 added to the difficulties. Unemployment went up, and the public assistance rolls came close to tripling in 15 years. By the mid-1970s they included nearly one million New Yorkers (or, since most of the recipients were children, some 250,000 families). About 85 percent of them were black or Hispanic. The increased problem came with federal medicaid in 1965 and with the New York State medicaid Law passed in 1966. In 1967–68, the local cost for welfare was $267.2 million; by 1975–76, the city share of welfare and medicaid has multiplied to more than $1 billion.

- Unique burdens. New York City has been a leader in providing a wide range of services to its populace, including 19 public hospitals, the most extensive fire protection service of any urban area in the nation, low transit fares, public housing, and municipal radio and television stations.

"New York has always been a big spender in a very liberal society," Kummerfeld noted. For years, he added, the city was constantly "identifying needs and then restructuring programs to meet those needs." Each program, once authorized, was quickly viewed as a "right."

While other cities concentrated on aiding the poor, New York subsidized the middle class as well. The policy of a free tuition city university (until finally abandoned in 1976) cost the city $175 million in potential revenue each year. The city cooperated with the state in financing middle class housing projects, and its rent control policies have cost several hundred million dollars a year in tax revenue and contributed substantially to tax delinquency and abandonment of buildings by distraught investors.

In addition, the state has assigned, or allowed New York City to perform, functions that in most cities are performed directly by state government: public assistance (which such cities as Boston, Chicago, and Baltimore have been able to transfer to the states), care for long-term prisoners, and a high proportion of the state court system costs. State aid, while high, does not fully compensate for the local imbalance in the division of operating responsibilities.

New York claims to bear the burden of being the country's port of entry. It pays the cost of police for the United Nations and provides social workers to help diplomats settle in the city. Critics say these costs are recovered by revenues received from activity generated by these services. But New York officials can also claim that the recent wave of illegal aliens, predominantly from South and Central America, adds to the drain on municipal services and depresses the wage scale. (Others, incidentally, view the aliens as ripe for exploitation, unskilled workers receiving less than the prevailing wage. "Far from being a burden to the city, they may well be playing a crucial role in keeping alive large sectors of the city's economy," James Ring Adams wrote in *Commentary*.)

▪ Unions and management deficiency. New York City, in 1958, was one of the first cities to grant collective bargaining rights to city employees. The city is basically pro-union, without a private sector force to counter the role of the union in enhancing the interests and benefits of city-paid workers. A decision by Governor Rockefeller in 1960 to allow an increase of 5 percent in the state's contribution to the state employees' pension signaled the beginning of a contest between city and state to reward civil servants. In the 1960s, New York City's package of wages, fringe benefits, and work rules became considerably more beneficial than counterparts in other cities and well ahead of the private sector in New York. The number of city employees grew at a rapid pace, and no politician dared buck the combined voting place power of those workers, their friends and relatives.

New York's city government lacks any tradition of a professional managerial group with the ability to manage resources and people. The city promotes from within to high managerial levels. "Compared with the federal government, agency heads don't think like managers. They don't think in terms of being responsible for (a) living within their budget and (b) producing services. They think more in terms of surviving the political hazards of the job," Kummerfeld noted.

When the state and city leaders finally absorbed the fact that *this time* the combination of spending, inflation, and changed economic base could not be ignored, the state took control of city finances, programs were cut and city taxes raised. Eventually the federal government provided limited assistance.

▪ New financial controls. As part of the financial package supplied to the city by Carey and the legislature, a new superagency was created, the Municipal Assistance Corporation, or Big Mac, as it came to be known popularly. This agency was charged with supervising the city's budgetary process and aiding in the generation of new working capital. It was to advise the mayor on how to cut spending while raising more money to meet the city's ever growing deficit. The powers of Big Mac were far greater than those of an impotent blue ribbon panel, however, since the governor and the state legislature were relying on the recommendations and approval of Mac in granting further state aid to the city.

The Big Mac device failed to work fully, because of the rapid decay of investor confidence. In the fall of 1975 Carey signed a bill creating the Emergency Financial Control Board, which would run the city's budget and approve all spending. The city thus lost control of its budget to a new state-dominated board including the governor, mayor, state controller, and three appointees of the governor. The board began to take all city revenues into its own accounts and to disperse money in accordance with a mandated financial plan approved by the board. Felix Rohatyn, a senior partner in the global investment banking company of Lazard Freres and director of five corporations, including ITT, was named chairman of Big Mac and a member of the Emergency Financial Control Board. Rohatyn soon emerged as the financial wizard of New York finances. New Yorkers praised him for his bold businesslike approach to the federal government, and labor condemned him for insensitivity. When Big Mac's debts were "stretched out," Rohatyn suggested that the money saved be used to finance a new convention center, rather than rehire city workers. "We don't want to see this money simply thrown away," he said. But it was just this kind of talk that appealed to prospective customers for New York bonds.

■   Layoffs and economies. Years of midnight solutions to annual budget crises made it very difficult for administrators to realize that New York was out of money. People came into Budget Director Kummerfeld's office, saying, "Well, I know the city's got problems. But you can't possibly close that school, that tropical disease center, that addiction services center. How can you possibly eliminate the youth council?" Yet by 1976, cuts amounting to 19 percent were made in the areas that could be cut: police, fire, sanitation, education, health and welfare. The workforce dropped from 294,522 on Jan. 1, 1975 to 238,627 on Oct. 1, 1976. With the possible exception of the darkest years of the Great Depression, no large American city had ever been obliged to make budget reductions of such immense magnitude. Multibillion-dollar construction was halted, even though in some cases most of the money was already spent, and only a little more was needed. Some 44,000 city employees were laid off, including a disproportionate number of blacks and Puerto Ricans, since they tend to have less seniority than others. Three quarters of the blue collar and clerical workers laid off in 1975 found their way back onto the city payroll by early 1976. Many with seniority regained jobs in a lower pay category by bumping less senior workers, and a quarter of the firemen were taken back under the federal Comprehensive Employment and Training Act program. Most municipal unions initially protested the depletion of their ranks and loss of pay increases, but proved remarkably cooperative in working with city officials to achieve a workable relationship. An exception was the Patrolmen's Benevolent Association. Hundreds of off-duty police officers blew whistles and blocked traffic near Yankee Stadium and encouraged roving bands of youth in unsuccessful efforts to crash the gates to the 1976 Muhammad Ali-Ken Norton heavyweight championship fight. Some uniformed police cheered on their colleagues and joined them in whistle-blowing—an example of police rowdyism that galvanized public sentiment against the police union and its refusal to accept the austerity conditions under which other public workers, and indeed the entire city were obliged to live.

▪   Additional city taxes. Seeking desperately to show how serious it took its own financial plight, and to win federal aid, the city in late 1975 was obliged to accept a $205 million laundry list of new taxes weighing heavily on the citizens of New York. The tax package, approved by the state legislature, boosted bank taxes from 11.8 to 12.8 percent, cigarette taxes from three and four cents a pack to eight cents, and the minimum corporation tax from $35 to $125. Most onerous of all, personal income taxes, already far above similar levies in other large cities, were increased by an average of 25 percent. The dark question for the future was whether the increased tax burden would simply accelerate middle class and business flight from the city, dooming any chance of sound economic recovery.

▪   Federal role in bailout. For many months in 1975, national debate centered on whether the federal government should "bail out" beleaguered New York—through flat grants, through loan guarantees, or direct loans of some type. The initial national reaction was hostile—a feeling that the profligate, once-haughty great city should live within its means. The anti-New York sentiment abroad nationally was symbolized by President Ford's hardnosed attitude toward any type of assistance, characterized by the *Daily News* headline "Ford to City: Drop Dead"—a sentiment that city voters apparently returned, giving big margins to Jimmy Carter in 1976.

Gradually the national mood shifted, however—particularly in the wake of the state's takeover of the city's finances, major layoffs, and announced economies. Fear spread that actual default by the city might trigger a general collapse in the huge national municipal bond market. Bankers and foreign leaders warned that default could jeopardize the United States' entire position in world money markets. President Ford eventually capitulated—in a limited way. He agreed to sign legislation providing high-interest federal loans not to exceed $2.3 billion at any given time. The money was to be doled out month by month on a program set to end June 30, 1978, when the city would theoretically have reached the point of a balanced budget and be able to reenter the municipal securities market. By spring of 1976, however, it had become abundantly clear that the city's three-year plan of fiscal recovery was far too optimistic, and that other, perhaps massive, federal aid programs would be necessary to avert eventual bankruptcy. When the Court of Appeals late in 1976 ruled invalid a state-imposed moratorium on $1 billion in notes, politicians, municipal union leaders in charge of pension funds and the banks began to look more intensely toward Washington for help.

■   Outcome. As these pages were written in late 1976, New York's financial situation was still far from smooth. Donna Shalala, a tax and government expert on the board of Big Mac, was optimistic. "There will be ten years of agony," she predicted, "but the city can be saved. It will have to carefully reduce the things it does by balancing its budget, and it will have to do things to keep the middle class here, such as improving education, and it will have to beef up the port facilities and the tourist-entertainment area."

What, though, where the immediate effects of the austerity budget on New York residents? By the end of 1976, halfway through its timetable to achieve a balanced budget, the city had shown a surprising capacity to provide essential services. City officials calculated that many operations were working more efficiently—but at a sharply reduced total output. Physically the city was deteriorating. Only 815,000 potholes were filled in 1976, compared with 916,800 in 1975, and repaving of entire streets seemed to have become a thing of the past. Frequency of garbage collection was down. The number of children in day care slumped 21 percent in a year. The total of school teachers had dropped to the levels of the early 1960s. The total of police arrests declined a startling 34 percent in two years (though one city official said: "They're concentrating on quality arrests now." The big drop-off occurred in arrests for public morals violations; mass sweeps in prostitution cases, for instance, were terminated.)

Kummerfeld likened the immediate situation to a giant poker game with four players—the city government, its unions, the state, and the federal government. Each player had certain cards in his hands; the game was when they would play them and when they would bluff.

The city had just one card—to go bankrupt—"which terrifies all of the other players."

The unions had two cards. The most obvious was to strike. But, Kummerfeld added, "the unions are also our bankers," because they controlled the huge pension funds that had promised $2.5 billion to tide the city over its borrowing problems until 1978. Thus, when the city bargained with its workers, he said, it also bargained with its bankers. "It's very easy to see that we have no leverage. We must in the end do whatever our workers want us to do, because they can refuse to give us the money for us to survive."

The third player, the state government, controlled the Emergency Fiscal Control Board, which by law sets the city's spending limits and must approve all city contracts over $100,000.

Finally, there's the federal government, a reluctant player, which could withdraw the short-term loans to which it agreed. Also, Kummerfeld noted, Washington "owns the printing press and can change the laws to reduce the city's burdens, particularly in welfare and medicaid, if it wants to."

As the game is played out, he added, "it's in the interest of each player to bluff—to threaten to play his ultimate card, even though he's not going to.

In the end, all four parties have to cooperate, or New York City will go into bankruptcy and decline rapidly in a hopeless downward spiral."

Edward N. Costikyan, who for several years compiled the list of "The Ten Men Who Run New York City" for *New York* magazine, saw the fiscal crisis as the final blow to the establishment that had run New York City for the 30 years following World War II—municipal unions, Ivy League good government groups, various special interest groups and their media enthusiasts. The crisis, he said, was proving the catalyst for basic changes in New Yorkers' attitudes, goals, and expectations. Several myths had been destroyed, Costikyan wrote in *Empire State Report*, including the beliefs that forward-looking public servants were solving city problems and that any fiscal problems were due to short-changing by the state and the callousness of the federal government. In 1970 Costikyan had given up his list of powerful New Yorkers because "no one was running New York City; it was going to hell." By 1976, he saw the city in the midst of "an unfinished revolution. . . . The legacy of the past is still running New York. The real test will come as new power groups seek to fill the vacuum, and as new values are translated into public policy."

What Makes New York Tick

New York appeared in the decades following World War II to have achieved its historic destiny as a global nerve center. As Robert Alden wrote:

> Its office towers are magnificent and can be counted among the greatest achievements of man. They are more than a miraculous kaleidoscope of massive shapes and soaring spires and myriad lights. They provide the interplay and excitement that breeds invention and inspiration.
> New York has become the cockpit of cultural and commercial interchange. It is a glorious vehicle for the exchange of ideas, for the cross-fertilization of minds, for the propagation of ideas, for the inspiration that drives man to achieve.

Several major "industries" make New York what it is (and are part of the reason it is in so much trouble).

CORPORATE HEADQUARTERS TOWN. In the late 1960s, New York was at a zenith, with the headquarters offices of 140 of the nation's 500 largest industrial corporations. By 1976, when Union Carbide decided to move from Park Avenue to Danbury, Connecticut, the city was down to 95 of the top 500—and falling fast. The reasons for the concentration (and it still is great) are obvious: because the others are there, so that big executives can finance each others' projects, exchange ideas, steal personnel. But these are often no longer enough to overcome executives' desire to leave. One problem: a company like Union Carbide could not persuade its middle managers from other areas to move to New York, with its long commutes, high taxes, often poor schools, and high cost of living.

CENTER OF FINANCE. Six of the seven largest commercial banks of the nation—First National City Bank, Chase Manhattan Bank, Manufacturers Hanover Trust, Morgan Guaranty Trust, Chemical Bank, and Bankers Trust —are located in the city. Among them, they have assets of $150 *billion* dollars. The New York Stock Exchange and its junior partner, the American Stock Exchange, are in the city. The New York Stock Exchange alone handles about 70 percent of the shares traded in the United States; though in dollar terms it now does a majority of its business with such big institutions as mutual funds, insurance firms, and banks, the number of owners of corporate stocks has ballooned since the 1950s. New York is the insurance capital of America, accommodating three of the five largest life insurance companies of the nation—Metropolitan Life, Equitable Life, and New York Life. Together with Prudential in nearby Newark, this remains a fantastic source of financing. The city is also the chief bond market of the nation, whose decisions can make or break thousands of governments and school districts in search of long-term capital financing.

Not all the city's great financial institutions, however, are in the best of shape. The Chase has had management problems, and even Citibank has some problems; the Stock Exchange has complained because many of its functions are being performed by other traders, who can as easily be in Chicago or Denver as New York.

COMMODITY EXCHANGES. Again, one finds a concentration unparalleled elsewhere: the Produce Exchange (wheat and other grains), Cotton Exchange (cotton and wool), Coffee and Sugar Exchange, Commodity Exchange (hides, silk, rubber, metals), Cocoa Exchange, and Mercantile Exchange (butter, eggs, and many other farm products). Each of the exchanges is a world unto itself, composed of men who know their particular markets in minutest detail; their face-to-face communication on the floors of the exchanges reaches an almost psychic level—the phenomenon of personal interaction which is New York's secret but perhaps greatest asset.

RETAILING. Ten of the 50 largest retailing companies of America have their headquarters in New York, led by such multibillion-dollar giants as J. C. Penney, W. T. Grant, and F. W. Woolworth. The nation's most illustrious group of department stores is in New York City—Macy's, Gimbel's, Lord & Taylor, Bloomingdale's, Abraham & Straus, Saks, Bergdorf Goodman, and others. In all the world, there is no shopping town like New York. There are thousands of smaller stores of every imaginable variety; New York, as John Gunther noted, is the town where "you can buy anything from Malabar spices to Shakespeare folios."

SERVICES. Every conceivable type of service industry, from the mundane to the incredibly sophisticated, is located in New York. Firms specializing in market research, advertising, public relations, management consultation, engineering, custom brokerage—the biggest and best are all in New York. They are a major inducement to great corporations to make their headquarters in the city. The same, of course, is true of New York's multitudinous law firms, packed with experts on taxes, corporate law, bonds, or virtually any other specialty.

WHOLESALING. New York State accounts for about a fifth of the nation's wholesale trade, and five sixths of that total is in New York City. The wholesaling is national and international in scope, but also intensely local because the New York-Connecticut-New Jersey urbanized area, with 16.2 million people, is the largest market area of the hemisphere. Second-place Los Angeles, with 8.3 million people, is barely half as large.

PORT. The port that made New York still sustains it. The harbor is the best in North America and one of the largest and best in the world. It is virtually fog and ice free; it is calm and protected; its shores are easily accessible. The port has an astounding 833 miles of direct water frontage, 578 of which are in New York City, the remainder in New Jersey. There are 400 berths for ocean-going vessels, the world's greatest docking capacity, and each year some 26,000 ships come and go. The dollar volume of goods handled is about one quarter that of all the ports of the nation. Kennedy International Airport handles more than half the country's overseas air travel and is the largest import-export air-cargo center of the nation.

MANUFACTURING AND CONSTRUCTION. New York State leads the nation in value added by manufacture—$30.78 billion in 1972—and New York City accounts for almost half the employment and half the value of goods. The city's greatest employers are the garment trade and allied textile products, accounting for about a quarter of a million jobs. Printing and publishing come second with 125,000 jobs. Food products account for 60,000 jobs; one finds the workers in hundreds of bakeries, breweries, distilleries, cold-storage warehouses, packing houses, and confectionaries. Tens of thousands of people work in factories turning out fabricated metals, machinery, paper products, chemicals, leather goods, and furniture. The construction industry, up to the '70s, employed over 100,000—and with good reason; in 20 years, Manhattan alone added twice as much office space as the next nine cities combined.

The problems of big corporations in doing business in New York are probably milder than those of retailers, distributors, and others doing business directly "on the street" in the city. For them, the problems of crimes against persons, burglary, high taxation, and arbitrary urban-renewal decisions are likely to be much more immediate. There are countless stories of the smaller companies, even those who have done business in New York for years and years, being forced out of the city.

Thousands of new low- and middle-income jobs will be needed in the future to offset the loss in manufacturing jobs the city had suffered in recent years. The most troublesome story is that of the garment trade. One would not expect it to be so, since New York remains the undisputed center of fashion in America, home of the most creative designers, the trend-setting place where the buyers from across the country congregate, the receiving port for the choicest hides and skins, and the home of America's best fashion libraries and textile and costume collections. The garment district on the Lower West Side has much the aura of decades past, with boys pushing racks loaded with dresses through incredibly snarled traffic in the narrow side streets. But actual production of standard-type garments has been drifting away from Manhattan since the 1920s; manufacturers figure, with good reason, that designs originating in New York can as well be executed in abandoned old New England textile plants or cheap new buildings put up in rural Pennsylvania or the South—especially since labor is often cheaper there. Garment industry employment, within the city, is now down below 175,000, a loss of more than 100,000 since the early 1960s.

Sad to say, the garment industry may not "belong" in New York at all. Some of the skilled pressers and cutters earn more than $12,000 a year, but unskilled employees like cleaners, pushboys, and shipping clerks usually make $6,000—much less than a living wage in the city today. The venerable old ILGWU (International Ladies Garment Workers Union), which organized early in the century to drive the sweatshops out of the city and now has 460,000 members across the U. S. A., has been faulted by some for fighting for high pay for its older, Jewish craftsmen, while letting much lower wages prevail for the unskilled, black, and Puerto Rican workers.

The port of New York presents a wholly different set of problems. The modern-day move to big prepacked containers caught the city asleep as it continued to put its port investments into obsolete piers on the Hudson River, even while the Port of New York Authority was building special containership piers at Newark and Elizabeth. The Manhattan waterfront lacks enough backup space for containership freight, but it can and should be developed for cruise-ship piers. (Jet aircraft finally swept the last American ships out of the North Atlantic run in 1969, but the cruise business is still a healthy one.) The city now hopes to get Brooklyn, and later Staten Island, converted to containership piers. The whole process is complicated by burgeoning dockside and airport pilferage (sometimes whole truckfuls of goods), the relationship among the feuding longshoremen's unions (Irish locals in Manhattan, Italian locals in Brooklyn), and the guaranteed wage which the shippers granted the longshoremen in return for being able to shift to containerization. The men get paid, in effect, whether they work or not. There have been a great many workless days in Brooklyn, despite the big work force of skilled longshoremen there, and the city has now dedicated all the landfill from its new subways to produce the technical equivalent of Port Newark in Brooklyn—with a much better disciplined and experienced work force than Newark's.

Communications and Culture

New York television, radio, newspapers, magazines, books, and fashions mold and influence American thought year-in, year-out, as no other force in the land. Sometimes the country reacts *with* New York, sometimes *against* it, but always *to* New York. The major networks (CBS, NBC, ABC) all have their headquarters in the city and determine the news and entertainment diet of a nation. The evening network news programs have replaced the daily newspaper for a formidable proportion of the American people and have played a major role in the history of our times (i.e., bringing the horrors of the Vietnam war into the nation's living rooms, making race riots and student demonstrations an almost personal experience for millions of Americans, and making household faces and names of many once-obscure politicians and public figures). An almost equally powerful role is played within New York City by the local evening news programs of the network's wholly owned subsidiaries in the city, plus Metromedia. In all, New York has 46 television and radio stations, including the country's only municipal broadcasting system, which operates a UHF television station and broadcasts on AM and FM radio.

The New York *Times,* despite growing competition from the Washington *Post* and Los Angeles *Times,* is the country's only national newspaper, in that it is read by government, business, and other opinion leaders from one coast to the other and influences millions of other readers through syndication of its news service. In quality and comprehensiveness, the *Times* may be the finest newspaper in the world today. The tabloid New York *Daily News,* a property of the Chicago *Tribune,* speaks with a more conservative voice and caters to the less sophisticated and affluent New Yorkers. It is far ahead of the *Times* in circulation—1,941,917 to the *Times's* 806,495 on weekdays, and 2,790,760 to the *Times's* 1,415,515 on Sundays. But it is little read outside the city. The *Wall Street Journal* and *Women's Wear Daily* are the national opinion leaders in business and fashion respectively, though the *Journal* (circulation 1,406,192, in several regional editions) also provides excellent feature coverage on almost any subject under the sun. The New York *Herald Tribune* was an important voice of liberal Republicanism until its demise in the labor and price-squeeze wars of the 1960s, one of the saddest occurrences in modern American journalism.* The evening *Post* stands alone in the P.M. market. Longtime liberal publisher Dorothy Schiff sold the paper in 1976 to Australian newspaper lord Rupert Murdoch, who pledged not to turn the *Post* into the skin and sadism journals he was noted for.

The two leading national news weeklies—*Time* and *Newsweek*—emanate from the city, as does *Sports Illustrated; McCall's* and *Ladies' Home Journal* for the distaff side; *Fortune, Forbes,* and *Business Week* for executives; *Vogue* for the fashion consumer; *New Yorker* for the literary and

---

* Big trouble for New York's newspapers was presaged by the union-forced collapse of the *Brooklyn Eagle* in 1955. In 1962–63, there was a disastrous strike that resulted in all the city's big dailies being closed down for 114 days. Rising costs and fear of another long strike prompted the *World Telegram and Sun* and *Journal American* to merge with the *Herald Tribune* in 1966, but the combined paper was immediately hit by a disastrous strike by the printer's union demanding security for its workers. The newspaper published for a few months but then expired, causing *all* the workers to lose their jobs and irreparable loss to the city.

cultured; and *Harper's Magazine* for the literati and politically sophisticated alike. There are several magazines of quite differing tastes and approaches for the book world—*Saturday Review* (which also takes a lively interest in environment), *Rolling Stone* (which actually moved to Gotham from San Francisco, the *New York Review of Books, Publisher's Weekly*, and *Printer's Ink*. Scores of specialized trade publications emanate from the city. In a hostile era for new magazines, an amazingly successful one was launched in 1968 —*New York*, a spunky weekly that focused on the city's foibles and glories and included lively political coverage—on every level from city to nation— by fine personal journalists. After a shaky start, *New York's* circulation reached robust levels—though no one was quite sure what would happen after the aggrandizing Rupert Murdoch gained control in 1977, triggering resignation of several key writers. Another addition of recent years, *Ms.*, is directed primarily toward the liberal and assertive woman who is emerging in the wake of the women's liberation movement.

Finally, we should note that New York remains, as it has been since the early 19th century, the book publishing center of America.

Foundations and charities abound on the island of Manhattan, making it the center of America's "Philanthropic Industrial Complex." National and international philanthropies there raise well over $1 billion each year, not to mention the distribution of grants from the multimillion- and multibillion-dollar foundations. Among the best known of these are Ford (far and away the largest*), Carnegie, Guggenheim, Mellon, Rockefeller, Twentieth Century, Field, Stern, Clark, and Vera. The city even has a Council on Foundations, set up to aid community foundations like those in Cleveland and Kansas City.

Some of the inventiveness and daring of the country's foundations was doubtless sapped by the Tax Reform Act of 1969, which circumscribed their activities. (Part of the impetus for the act was real abuse by foundations of their tax-exempt status; part was also due to opposition in Congress to some daring social projects, especially Ford's.) The foundations flock to New York for many of the same reasons corporations do—for communication among themselves and rapid access to the financial and intellectual communities. New York is also filled with nonprofit institutions of every stripe, from the businessmen's Committee for Economic Development to the National Association for the Advancement of Colored People, from the Council on Foreign Relations to the Urban League.

In the performing arts, New York seems ever to have been the premier city of the land. Despite the growth of a strong regional theater in America since World War II, no play is considered a true success until it has undergone baptism by fire of the critics and audiences of Manhattan. A classical concert artist may receive warm receptions in Los Angeles or Cleveland, but

---

* The Ford Foundation's headquarters building on Manhattan's East Side is a sight to behold: a stunning 12-story gallery of offices that surrounds a giant roofed courtyard with great plants, and birds flying about.

not be counted a full success until New York joins in the accolades. New York remains the cultural center of the nation because it has the huge, sophisticated audiences concentrated in one great metropolitan center, and because the required money—lots of it—is there to launch productions.

New York's overall number of legitimate theaters—35 or 36 in the last few years—has held fairly steady, but there have been low seasons like 1969–70, when at one point half of Broadway's legitimate theaters were "dark"—without plays. Due in large part to extremely high labor costs (and no small amounts of featherbedding), the costs of launching a new play, not to mention a musical comedy can be staggering. One result is that Off-Broadway theater, which was conceived as an opportunity for actors to make their mark, has taken on many of the characteristics of its parent—frequent money-losing plays and ticket prices that are seemingly astronomical. There is also Off-Off-Broadway, which critic Clive Barnes describes as "a kind of inspired amateur theater of professional standards," but one where "the actors are not paid nor is anyone else."

By the mid-1960s, expansion of the midtown office area had reached the heart of the traditional "great White Way" and legitimate theaters were threatened. Mayor Lindsay created a consultative group known as the Urban Design Group which pressed hard for a new zoning regulation covering a specified Theater District from 40th Street to 57th, and from Eighth Avenue to the Avenue of the Americas. Within it, developers of new office buildings may increase the size of their structures by 20 percent if they will include a theater in their new structure. As a result of this so-called "incentive zoning," substantial new theater construction has occurred.

Until World War II, the symphony, opera, and ballet in New York were frequented almost exclusively by society elite. Since then, these serious forms of culture, both in live performances and through records and tapes, have become the province of millions. The physical embodiment of this is New York's massive Lincoln Center for the Performing Arts, which covers no less than 14 acres, a block to the west of Central Park between 62nd and 66th streets. The concept was born in the mid-1950s when the Metropolitan Opera decided it would have to abandon its romantic but decrepit old quarters and the New York Philharmonic feared that Carnegie Hall might be torn down. The idea of a federation of cultural institutions emerged; the Juilliard School of Music, the Music Theatre, the New York City Ballet, and the New York City Opera decided to join in; and a gap was filled by creation of the Lincoln Center Repertory Company. The construction funds —over $160 million—were raised from foundations, wealthy individuals, the city and state governments.

The Lincoln Center building complex has become one of the city's prime tourist attractions; behind the monumental walls of the New Metropolitan Opera House, Philharmonic Hall, New York State Theater, and the other structures, the nation's greatest concentration of the lively arts thrives—albeit with grim financial crises like those that plague so much high culture in America today. Some of the constituent parts of the Lincoln Center might find their match in other American cities, but not so the New York City Ballet or the Metropolitan Opera. The gala opening of the new opera house in 1966 was one of the most glittering events in New York's history.

New York is also the art nexus of the continent, and one of global importance; as American artists operating largely out of New York made their mark internationally in the years after World War II, the English critic Lawrence Alloway said that "New York is to mid-century what Paris was to the early 20th Century: it is the center of Western art." The abstract expressionism of our time, photography, sculpture, applied graphic arts—they are all centered in the city. There are hundreds of distinguished private galleries, and then the great public museums: the Metropolitan Museum of Art (largest museum of the Western Hemisphere), the Museum of Modern Art (founded in 1929 by Mrs. John D. Rockefeller); the striking Whitney and Guggenheim museums opened in the postwar era; the Cloisters; the Brooklyn, Riverside, and Jewish museums; the Frick Collection; the Museum of Primitive Art—and more.

Crime in Fun City

Of the monstrous problems facing New York, none is more frightening than crime. New Yorkers—rich, poor, white, black—are preoccupied by it. Fear of crime molds election campaigns, shapes judgments at government and business levels, dictates the life style of a city's people. A fortresslike mentality develops in which people resort to incredibly complex locks and security alarm devices, are afraid to walk the streets at night, and close their stores earlier every year.

And with good reason. In 1973, according to the Uniform Crime Reports issued by the FBI, there were 5.4 crimes per 100 population in the New York SMSA. For the nearly 10 million persons living in the New York metropolitan area, there were more than 540,000 crimes of a serious nature witnessed by, or reported to, the police. This includes 1,741 murders, 90,090 automobile thefts, and 3,871 forcible rapes. Department of Justice officials estimate that 80 percent of the organized crime in the U.S. is centered in New York City and neighboring northern New Jersey. The city is the heroin and numbers-racket capital of America. And then there is the problem of corruption within the huge New York police department. In a major exposé printed in 1970, the New York *Times* reported:

Narcotics dealers, gamblers and businessmen make illicit payments of millions of dollars a year to the policemen of New York, according to policemen, law enforcement experts and New Yorkers who make such payments themselves.

Despite such widespread corruption, officials in both the Lindsay administration and the Police Department have failed to investigate a number of cases of corruption brought to their attention.

Catching wind of that upcoming exposé by reporter David Burnham, Lindsay had appointed a blue-ribbon citizens' commission to investigate police corruption, headed by Wall Street lawyer Whitman Knapp. The commission did not, as defenders of the police expected, turn up a picture of a few bad apples in a basically honest and effective police department. Instead, it reported in 1971 that the whole barrel had become so rotten that corruption had become the rule rather than the exception. For example, members of the narcotics squad were found to be engaged in extortion and bribery and some even in the sale of hard drugs themselves. Police officers were being paid off regularly, it was reported, by gamblers, pimps, illegal liquor distributors, construction bosses, and restaurants.

Up to the 1960s, the police department functioned as a semiautonomous duchy, effectively isolated from control of mayors from the early Tammany times up to Wagner's era. Lindsay tried to change that, refuting in his inaugural address the idea that the department could be a law unto itself. But his first move, to create a civilian review board to hear complaints of police brutality, backfired badly when the powerful Patrolmen's Benevolent Association (PBA) led a successful campaign to have the board abolished in a 1966 popular referendum. Howard R. Leary, whom Lindsay recruited from Philadelphia to be police commissioner, instituted a number of promising innovations, including the country's first emergency dialing number, a computerized dispatch and control system which keeps track of all men on the street at any moment, neighborhood patrols of black and Puerto Rican policemen who live in communities like Harlem and can speak the ghetto language, and recruitment of college graduates to be members of the force. But in 1970, as revelations of police corruption were aired, Leary resigned.

The police commissioner picked to succeed Leary was Patrick Murphy, former police chief of Syracuse, a certified member of the New York Irish ascendancy that has dominated the department for almost 100 years.

Organized crime is so extensive and deeply ingrained in the city that the New York *Times* occasionally prints stories on the five leading Mafia "families" as detailed as its reportage on political organizations and major industrial concerns. The coordinated federal attack on the Mafia, made possible by new legislation in recent years, is taking its toll among top syndicate leaders, however. Murphy began with a sweeping shake-up of the police department, the most thoroughgoing in 20 years, and sternly made precinct commanders accountable for any corruption found in their areas. But in less than two years Murphy was out, succeeded by men more comfortable with the system as it has been.

Every conceivable problem seems to land in the hands of New York's cops, from keeping peace in the seething ghettos to protecting United Nations personnel from terrorist groups to restraining the surge of blatant prostitution and pornography houses that have infested Manhattan. Vast quantities of heroin flow into the New York syndicate-controlled heroin factories, by ship, car, and plane. Anyone at a city high school, one of the universities, or in the slum neighborhoods knows where to pick up his "smack," pot, or pills. Heroin begets still more crimes, and the police have yet to show they can deal with the problem.

Directly related to New York's police dilemma is the shocking condition of its clogged courts and antiquated, overcrowded prisons. Mayors have been criticized in some quarters for responding to citizen complaints about crime by increasing the number of men on the police force while failing to follow the advice of penologists who say more police will never cut crime, that the courts must be improved and massive rehabilitational services provided for inmates. But the problems of the correctional system go back over decades, and are not easily corrected. The criminal court of the city of New York is a fractured, uncoordinated complex of 96 judges and six courthouses, which open their doors every morning to some 15,000 shackled prisoners, victims, witnesses, and police and detectives diverted from street duty. The courts begin each year with a backlog of hundreds of thousands of cases; and even if no new arrests were made, it would take the judges two and a half years to clear the calendars. Despite the staggering backlog of work facing them, many judges fail to work a full day. Corruption has always attended the selection of judges in the city, and to this day payoffs of one or two years' salary must be made to appropriate party leaders to get a place on the bench, according to Martin and Susan Tolchin.*

For the prisoners languishing in New York's jails, it must often seem that justice is unobtainable. (Convictions are hard to get, too; if you commit a felony in New York City, the chances of your being arrested, indicted, found guilty, and sent to prison are less than one in 200.) The prisons have an official capacity of 8,000, but many weeks there are almost double that number of men and women locked into crowded cells. About half of them have never been convicted, but they may wait almost a year for their first court appearance.†

Even better courts and jails and an honest police department would not be enough to purge New York of its rising tide of lawlessness. Eventually, the tap roots of organized crime in the city must be attacked. And many believe illegal gambling is central to the whole system.

The numbers racket began in Harlem as a money-sucking wrinkle invented by a beer baron named Arthur Flegenheimer (Dutch Schultz). He ran the numbers racket so well it developed into crime's major money producer after Prohibition ended. It was so good that it was taken over (in a hail of bullets and blood) by Charles ("Lucky") Luciano. That empire eventually broke into smaller duchies, but the numbers racket has since continued to be the financial foundation from which the organized mob has invaded

---

* The Tolchins quote an anonymous state judge describing how he got his judgeship: "The county leader told me to pay the district leaders in cash . . . untraceable."

† An imaginative program to free some suspects without bail pending trial, initiated by the Vera Institute of Justice, a private foundation, has helped some, but the magnitude of the problem is beyond easy solution.

other enterprises—loansharking, bookmaking, labor racketeering, narcotics, industrial extortion, and corruption of government.*

Here is how the regressive cycle of growing horror operates today. From desperate people in Bedford-Stuyvesant, Harlem, and the South Bronx, the numbers racket takes about $105 million a year (perhaps as much as $250 million citywide). The money is used to finance the importation of heroin, which is sold retail for about $180 million in a year. The narcotics addicts have to maraud in the communities in order to get money to buy the heroin. Since from resale they get on the average only 20 percent of the value of the property they steal, the average amount of money that must be stolen is over $1 billion a year. The organized mob takes its percentage out every step of the way. According to the New York State Joint Legislative Committee on Crime: "At the same time that this lecherous cartel is siphoning off millions of dollars from the ghetto as a result of its policy, loansharking and other illicit operations, it is spewing back into the same ghetto a reign of misery and death in the form of traffic in Heroin!"

These days, the mob princes do not come even close to the street action. From lofty positions they "cream" wealth out of the ghettos through the percentage they get from the numbers racket. They still control (through the capital they provide) the importation of heroin, even while they allow increasing control of the wholesale drug market by black and Spanish-speaking manpower that they have developed or tolerated—and to which they may be obliged to cede a large part of their operations in the next few years.

The numbers game has become such an integral part of ghetto life that in the opinion of black leaders like Basil Patterson, Charles Rangel, and Hulan Jack, it could not be routed even if the U. S. Army came in to help and placed men with fixed bayonets at every corner. The obvious solution would be for government to step in and take over the numbers, and that is precisely what New York City's new Off-Track Betting Corporation (OTB) would like to do. OTB officials estimate that they could run the system at a 10 percent overhead; even if they turned in 15 percent of the take to the local and state governments, they could still return to the people of the community 75 percent of every dollar bet. That would compare to the meager substantially lower 25 to 50 percent which is reportedly returned to the public under the present illegal numbers games.

The OTB sprang into being in 1970 after the state legislature voted to let cities with 125,000 or more people have off-track betting to raise revenues for local government. (The city had been asking the authority for some 20 years, but had been rebuffed by leaders like Governor Dewey, who called the idea "shocking, immoral and indecent," saying that "corruption and poverty" followed gambling wherever it had been legalized.) The legislature's purpose in approving off-track betting was to give some relief to the city's financial

---

* A typical form of the numbers game in New York is the "Brooklyn" number, in which the player picks any number he likes from 000 to 999; the winning "number" will then be the last three digits of the total mutuel handle for the day at one of the local race tracks (Belmont or Aqueduct) or Saratoga during the month of August.

squeeze, but Howard ("Howie the Horse") Samuels, whom Lindsay appointed to head up the OTB, said his primary purpose was a social one—to undercut organized crime. Samuels also used OTB's resources to run hard for governor, a race he eventually lost by an unexpectedly large number of lengths to Hugh Carey in the Democratic primary.

The Housing Mess

The gangrenous growth of slum housing, Congressman Herman Badillo told us, is the most alarming single social trend facing New York City today. "All else is irrelevant," Badillo said. "Once an area becomes a slum, it takes 50 to 100 years to recapture it. This damage is irreparable—although it may have been, in large measure, inevitable."

The grim facts about housing are these:

- By conservative estimates, 400,000, or 14 percent of the city's 2.9 million housing units are substandard (other estimates run as high as 800,000). Hundreds of thousands more are on the brink of disintegration. The entire population of Arizona could fit into New York's substandard housing. Yet in most cases, the abandoned buildings are structurally sound; their problem is tenant abuse and landlord desertion.

- The private housing market is at a virtual standstill. Large quantities of luxury apartments were constructed in the city from the 1950s through the mid-1960s. But then inflation and a tight money market hit, halting all new construction except a trickle of ultra-ultra-posh apartments. Construction and mortgage-loan interest rates have soared to near-prohibitive levels. And mortgages are not available at all in huge swaths of the city where deterioration is advanced, or even threatened—most of the Bronx, much of Brooklyn, parts of Manhattan and Queens.

- Hundreds of thousands of apartments and houses have been abandoned in New York City in recent years. Landlords face the quandary of high repair costs, expensive fuel oil, high real estate taxes, high mortgage interest costs, and tenants slow in paying rent. Many are in real financial straits—yet tenants still harbor unmitigated hostility toward them, seeing the landlords as rank exploiters, ready and anxious to collect rent but never available when repairs are needed to rotting walls, broken windows, or leaking pipes. In an hostility-packed city, the landlord-tenant hostility may be the deepest and most enduring. Robert Alden of the New York *Times* tells the story of a small entrepreneur who bought an apartment house 20 to 25 years ago as a hedge against inflation:

Now his age of decline has arrived and he stands on a littered Bronx street before the rundown six-story apartment house, once his dream, now his nightmare. From some open window above, an angry, derisive call is heard: "The Jew landlord is here to collect his bloody money!"

Sooner or later, as such a man's costs run beyond his rental incomes, he will look for a buyer—and probably find none. The next logical step is simply to abandon the property.* Then the electricity is turned off, there is no heating, tenants begin to flee, derelicts and dope addicts break in, garbage piles up, rats begin to infest the property, and the cancer begins to spread up and down the street and may soon engulf a whole community.

Many housing experts believe this discouraging downward spiral cannot be reversed as long as such huge sociological and attitudinal differences exist between landlords and tenants. In an atmosphere of all-out warfare between the two sides, the prospect for satisfactory housing is almost nonexistent. So more must be done to foster new forms of ownership, often cooperatives, in which tenants have a real stake in keeping their apartment houses in good condition. That happens frequently in better-off Manhattan neighborhoods, but extremely rarely in the deteriorating communities that need it most.

The need for some kind of a radical breakthrough in the city's housing quandary can hardly be overstated. The citywide rental vacancy rate is under 1 percent, less than a fourth of the national rate. Poor and middle-income people alike are affected. The waiting list for public housing is well over 100,000, a family at the bottom of the list could wait half a century to get in. Many poor families break into condemned buildings just to have a roof over their heads.

On the upper end of the income scale, the prices demanded and received for apartments in Manhattan are beyond belief. In a desirable neighborhood like the East 70s, small, cramped one-bedroom apartments may cost $600 a month, and a commodious three bedroom apartment near Fifth and Park Avenues as much as $1,500 to $2,000 a month. Some of the highest prices are paid for cooperative apartments, which do provide buyers (if they can afford the price) with security, equity, and pride of ownership. But 85 percent of available co-ops sell for over $60,000, with monthly maintenance fees of hundreds if not thousands of dollars.

So it is that quality housing soars beyond the price range of even the upper-middle class. Robert Alden notes: "People are driven to the suburbs and, as land values increase, to the far suburbs. The breadwinner finds himself spending more and more of his life aboard crowded, uncomfortable, tardy commuter trains [or] backed up bumper to bumper each day on the West Side Drive, the Long Island Expressway or the approaches to the Lincoln Tunnel." And corporations encounter increasing reluctance of middle management executives to transfer to New York and bear the city's hardships.

There are, of course, hundreds of thousands of apartment units in the city with more reasonable sounding rental levels. About 1.3 million of the 2.1 million apartment units are under rent control, which New York (alone among major U. S. cities) has clung to since World War II. In many cases,

---

* A black leader in the city offered us a more cynical interpretation: "Guys buy tenements, put them in dummy corporations, and when they get too bad, the owner just runs away."

it has been the artificially low payments for rental apartments that has forced owners to abandon their properties. In 1971, the state legislature directed that when rent-control apartments changed hands in the future, they could seek their own open market price. The immediate result was an approximate doubling of rents in those apartments leased by new tenants.

The housing story is doubly tragic because no city in America has tried so hard over the years to fill the housing needs of its people. New York got a huge infusion of postwar public housing, enough to hold more than half a million people. Designed with barrackslike monotony, the projects dot the horizon in several boroughs. And the effort was not only federal; since the days of Al Smith, New York has made a strong effort in city- and state-sponsored low-income housing, and has more housing put up with that kind of backing than the rest of the country put together.

But in the 1960s, federally assisted public housing came to a dead stand-still because Washington objected to the high unit costs of construction in the city. The flow of federally assisted housing opened again around 1969–70, but ended again with the Federal cutoff of January 1973. Several big state-assisted projects (including Roosevelt Island) are underway, but not on the massive citywide scale needed to really save the situation.

There might be more new housing in New York, both public and private, if it were not for the modern-day sensitivity of government and private developers to community objections about proposed development sites. Some vocal residents will almost invariably have an objection to building new housing in *their* community. Always, they say developments should go else-where. So high-income projects get blocked, middle- and low-income proj-ects stymied, new public facilities are stopped in their tracks, and the entire city of New York suffers.

One gargantuan state-aided project, begun in the mid 1960s, has now opened its doors. Its name is Co-op City, it is located in the northeast Bronx between some parkways on 300 acres of land, and it is the world's largest housing cooperative and the nation's largest single apartment complex. Sponsored by the United Housing Foundation and financed primarily by a $261 million mortgage loan from the New York State Housing Finance Agency, Co-op City has 35 high-rise apartment buildings that range between 24 and 33 stories. It houses more than 50,000 people—enough to make it, if it were built outside an already existing city, a metropolitan area on its own right. The population of Co-op City is roughly 75 percent Jewish, 15 percent black and Puerto Rican, and 5 to 10 percent Irish and Italian. No one can doubt the excruciating need New York has for projects on the massive scale of Co-op City, and the people who live there are delighted with the oppor-tunity. But the sight of that army of massive buildings, rising to the sky at such a height that each man's apartment looks like a fly speck on the face of a vast and monolithic structure, is one of the most frightening we have seen on the American continent. If this is how the multimillions of the future must be housed, one fears for the spirit of man.

The Worlds of New York

And now for a view of the fantastic city in its constituent parts, though we will be obliged, for reasons of space, to omit many interesting communities. The raw statistics are these:

Boroughs	Population (1970)	% Population Shift (1960–70)	Black Percent	People Per Square Mile
Manhattan	1,539,233	−10.2	24.9	66,923
Brooklyn	2,602,012	− 1.0	25.2	37,172
Queens	1,986,473	+ 9.1	13.1	18,393
Bronx	1,471,701	+ 3.3	24.3	35,895
Richmond (Staten Island)	295,443	+33.1	5.3	5,094
Total	7,894,862		21.2	26,316

During the first half of the 1970s, the citywide population declined fairly sharply, to an estimated 7,567,800, 4.2 percent less than the start of the decade. Only in 1974–75 did the hemorrhaging appear to abate somewhat, as Manhattan and Queens actually gained slightly and the large declines in Brooklyn and the Bronx trailed off to a trickle.

MANHATTAN

Everyone knows the story of how the crafty Dutch managed to buy Manhattan Island from the Manhattoes Indians in 1626 for $24 worth of doodads. The Indians did not realize what a fine deal they had. Sidney Homer of Salomon Bros., author of The History of Interest Rates, has calculated that if the Indians had taken a boat to Holland, invested the $24 in Dutch securities returning 6 percent a year and kept the money invested at 6 percent, they would now have $13 billion. That would be enough to buy back all the land on the island, and still have $4 billion left for trinkets.

What kind of a place is Manhattan today? Along with all its woes, it is a romantic vision unequaled on earth and one seen best, like a beautiful woman, at night. As Le Corbusier wrote:

Beneath the immaculate office on the 57th floor the vast nocturnal festival of New York spreads out. No one can imagine it who has not seen it. It is a titanic mineral display, prismatic stratification shot through with an infinite number of lights, from top to bottom, in depth, in a violent silhouette like a fever chart beside a sick bed. A diamond, incalculable diamonds.

Is the load of people and activity on Manhattan simply too much? The New York City Planning Commission, in a Lindsay-era report, argued that it is not:

Concentration is the genius of the city, its reason for being, the source of its vitality and its excitement. We believe the center should be strengthened, not weakened, and we are not afraid of the bogey of high density.

Growth, status quo, and decay, we view in some of Manhattan's chief districts and neighborhoods, moving south to north:

LOWER MANHATTAN. Here is Battery Park, and within a handful of blocks north and west of the park, the greatest concentration of financial power in the world: the canyons of Wall Street, the Stock Exchange, great banks and insurance combines, offices of such colossal firms as American Telephone & Telegraph, and the huge law firms.

In the summer of 1970, Anthony Lewis, the New York *Times*' London bureau chief, returned by ship on home leave. As his vessel steamed into New York Harbor one morning, Lewis expected to glimpse first the Statue of Liberty. But instead, his eye was caught by

twin massive towers, the tallest building in the world, rectangular blocks, thrusting gracelessly into the sky, dark and hulking, beyond human scale. It was a sight that cried out: money! power! technology! It spoke of the America that has relentlessly sought profit, and "progress," at the expense of human values. It seemed to me a brutal symbol of what has gone wrong in our society.

A lot of New Yorkers agree with Lewis' assessment of the World Trade Center, the 110-story, 1,350-foot towers put up by the Port of New York Authority with tax-exempt dollars. The Center contains 10 million square feet of floor space—seven times that of the Empire State Building and 80 more acres of office space than the Pentagon. At 2:15 P.M., October 19, 1970, the north tower rose above the height of the Empire State Building, ending that illustrious structure's 40-year reign as the world's tallest. But work was already underway in Chicago on a building that soon topped the World Trade Center.

Each day, 50,000 workers crowd into the World Trade Center, adding to the already unbelievable congestion of downtown Manhattan. Scores of other great buildings have risen in Lower Manhattan since World War II, several over 50 stories, the square footage of office space numbering in the tens of millions.

In 1971, construction began on Battery Park City, a $1 billion self-contained community of apartments, offices, schools, shops, and parks located off a one-mile section of previously decaying waterfront. City officials see a bright future for Lower Manhattan, its development anchored by the World Trade Center on its west flank and the new Stock Exchange building on the east and Battery Park City adding the first residences of this century.

■ CIVIC CENTER TO THE LOWER EAST SIDE. As Broadway starts boldly up the middle of Manhattan north of the financial district, it passes the Civic Center—elegant, old City Hall surrounded by government office buildings and the courts, city, state, and federal. Chinatown, an eight-block area along Mott Street, is still a cultural center for Chinese-Americans and has traditionally fine restaurants and shops—together with the same problems of cruel overcrowding, a growing crime rate, and rebellion against the entrenched community powers that the San Francisco Chinatown is now experiencing. Just to the north is a Little Italy, still the most important Italian neighborhood in Manhattan, though most young Italians have left for other parts of the city or the suburbs.

New York still has its legendary Lower East Side of bustling streets filled with shops and street vendors and fruit carts, the port of entry of multitudinous ethnic groups (Irish, Italians, and Jews especially), the boyhood neighborhood of men like Al Smith and Jacob Javits. The Lower East Side was always poor; today it is desperate. Conditions are perhaps half tolerable in the huge public housing developments along F. D. Roosevelt Drive (Baruch Houses, Alfred E. Smith Houses, etc.), but consider the staid New York *Times'* description of the rest: "A grimy string of tenements, murky storefronts and nondescript industrial establishments" that is populated by "motorcycle gangs, hippies, drug users and thieves," a world where "rape, assault, gang warfare and even murder are almost commonplace."

A study commissioned for the City Planning Commission declared that the neighborhood had some 35,000 apartments which "are not fit to live in" and should be torn down, and that a program of social and economic help was sorely needed for the growing population of impoverished Puerto Rican families, who represent some 37 percent of the area's population of 190,000. The contingents of Jews, Italians, and East Europeans have now dropped to less than half of the population, many of them older people left behind in the exodus of their children to the suburbs.

Yet some of the best shopping bargains of America can still be found in Lower East Side stores; the difference is that the merchants will pull and draw the metal grates and escape to safer places before nightfall.

▪   THE VILLAGES. Chic, bohemian Greenwich Village is the home of artsy millionaires, musicians, entertainers, hipsters, students, and dope fiends. It is probably the most individualistic neighborhood on Manhattan, possibly because it is still a stronghold of small homeowners and has maintained its traditions and look. The population remains overwhelmingly white.

There is the West Village, a quiet neighborhood of residences. There is the East Village, recently a East Coast hangout for hippies and runaways. There is Washington Square, at the foot of Fifth Avenue, one of the more urbane places in New York, where New York University students lounge illegally on the grass and old men play chess on summer afternoons.

Greenwich Village's traditional *laissez-faire* attitude toward deviationist life styles is now being put to the test as crime rises alarmingly. Villagers are demanding more police protection, are helping police catch dope peddlers (hard drugs seems to have lost their chic), and are cooperating to blunt an onrush of robberies.

The Bowery, traditional hangout of drunks and derelicts on the east edge of Greenwich Village, remains the mixture of commercial activity and human squalor it has been for a century. But an interesting sociological phenomenon is taking place; the Bowery is being depopulated as its older denizens die off, and younger men (perhaps due to the relative prosperity of our times) fail to replace them. The population was 14,000 in 1949, but fell below 5,000 in the late 1960s and continues to decline by about 5 percent a year. The Depression produced as many as one million of the rootless Skid Row dropouts, who abjured marrying, voting, or close friendship for a drifting life, seeking only hermetic shelter. Now there are probably no more than 100,000 in all the U.S.A.

■   MIDTOWN—WEST. This is the highly variegated area along the Hudson River from 14th Street north to 59th, mixed industrial-residential, the distinctive communities of Chelsea and Clinton, the garment district, the West Side Highway and Lincoln Tunnel, Port Authority Bus Terminal and Penn Station. It is an area in transition from slow decline to potential redevelopment.

Chelsea, just north of Greenwich Village, went to slums and slaughterhouses early in this century but is now undergoing rehabilitation as a living area as many rooming houses filled with Puerto Ricans and single old men are converted to or torn down for luxury housing. The famed Chelsea Hotel is there, once the home of countless authors from Mark Twain and O. Henry to Thomas Wolfe and Dylan Thomas, who were drawn by the publishing houses centered in the area. The hotel still jumps with high-velocity culture. Chelsea is the location of the General Theological Seminary, and, on the other hand, the belly dancing center of the Western Hemisphere.

Clinton—the modern name for old Hell's Kitchen—is packed with tenements, auto body repair shops, factories, and warehouses, mostly east of 10th Avenue. Eventually, it may all be gobbled up by the expanding Midtown business district. The garment district (32nd to 34th Streets, Fifth to Ninth Avenues) faces an uncertain future because of its incredibly crowded conditions and dispersion of clothing manufactures to other boroughs and out across the country.

Illustrious old Pennsylvania Station came crashing down in a sea of rubble during the 1960s to make way for a new Madison Square Garden. The railroad station is still there, underground; on top of it is a 20,000-seat "garden," a 1,000-seat Felt Forum, named after the entrepreneur who built it, a 500-seat movie house, a 48-lane bowling center, and a 29-story office building. A neat example, one might say, of maximum use of space. Across the street is one of the new office building behemoths: One Penn Plaza, 57 stories, 2.4 million square feet of office space, surrounded by a landscaped plaza, connected underground to Penn Station and the Long Island Rail Road terminal.

■   MIDTOWN—EAST. We skip past, temporarily, the vortex of human activity in mid-Midtown Manhattan and take a look at the long strip of the island on the East River from 14th to 59th Streets.

The area is anchored on the south by what used to be the old Gashouse

District, a notorious slum as early as the 1840s that took its name from four large, leaky gas tanks that overshadowed it. It was a Tammany stronghold —first Irish, later German, Jewish, and other East Europeans. Right after World War II, the gas tanks and the worst slums were demolished to make a place for Metropolitan Life's Stuyvesant Town and Peter Cooper Village—a group of massive, deadening brick high-rises for middle income people. Metropolitan Life came under heavy fire in the late 1960s for the minuscule number of black and Puerto Rican families it had let into these developments.

Just to the west is Union Square, a traditional meeting place of speakers and hecklers, of radicals and agitators, and Gramercy Park, a private place restricted to the tenants who live there. One of America's largest clusters of medical institutions is concentrated along First Avenue from 23rd to 34th Street, including Bellevue, a teaching hospital for the NYU School of Medicine, the largest and most famous municipal hospital in the city. Next to this vast complex of medical buildings is Kip's Bay, a grouping of 21-story slab apartment buildings so placed and set back that the living density is extraordinarily low. One resident, Brooks Atkinson, called Kip's Bay "civilized and hospitable. . . . The Kip's Bay tenants represent all races and all parts of the world. Although they do not live together cordially, they are courteous and tolerant. They represent a degree of democracy that works."

In 1946, six city blocks of slaughterhouses along the East River were razed to make way for the United Nations headquarters. The city agreed to plow First Avenue underground, John D. Rockefeller donated $8.5 million for acquiring the site, and an international team of architects designed the structures. The 544-foot-high slab of the Secretariat dominates the group, with a library to the south and the striking General Assembly building to the north. The U. N. is a major national tourist attraction (10,000 visitors a day). This whole area of the city, known as Turtle Bay, has been rejuvenated. A number of swank apartment complexes now surround the U.N., including Sutton Place South and the United Nations Plaza. The latter, with twin 32-story towers, is perhaps *the* ultimate apartment house of the world, filled with corporate and society leaders beyond compare. There are 27,000 U.N. personnel in New York, including families of delegates and 5,000 staff members. Their consulates add an exotic touch, underscoring New York's status as *the* world city.

▪ MIDTOWN. Here is the glittering heart of Manhattan, 234 square blocks throbbing with people, packed with soaring skyscrapers. Midtown has experienced the most extensive growth of its history in the past 25 years; more than ever it deserves to be called the business-entertainment center of the nation and the world. The street and place names alone are evocative: Fifth Avenue, Park Avenue, Madison Avenue, Broadway, 42nd Street, Grand Central, Times Square, Empire State Building, Rockefeller Center.

No "economic development" plan is needed here, but some controls are to assure that Midtown does not become a monolith of steel and glass slabs that repels people. That fate has already overtaken the upper stretches of the Avenue of the Americas (Sixth Avenue) and has been threatening Fifth Avenue, the nation's choicest and most exciting shopping street.

Fifth Avenue retains most of its famous stores like Saks, Bonwit Teller, and Tiffany's, but high rents have driven many stores a block east to Madison where the last few years have seen an opening of boutiques, art galleries, design shops, and the like, complementing the older Madison institutions such as Brooks Brothers and Abercrombie and Fitch. Madison Avenue, as part of the American lexicon, means the center of the advertising industry, but many of the large firms have always been located elsewhere in the city.

Fifth and Madison Avenues are fun to shop along if one's wallet is full; where the masses go, however, is the Herald Square area around the Sixth Avenue-Broadway-34th Street intersection, where the volume monarchs of retailing are located: Macy's ("the world's largest department store,") Gimbel's, Korvettes (a relative newcomer), and of course scores of smaller stores.

Finally, two touches of prewar Manhattan that live on. Carnegie Hall, that famous and excellent concert hall, was saved by the concern of New Yorkers and music lovers from all over the country when it seemed doomed for demolition in the 1950s. Then, at the point where Midtown comes to an end on the southern border of Central Park, stand a row of splendid old hotels including the Plaza, St. Moritz, and Essex House. The Plaza faces Grand Army Plaza, one of Manhattan's most pleasant open spaces, where horse-drawn hacks line up to offer tourists a ride through the park. The city has established a special zoning district that forbids anything but residential and hotel construction on Central Park South.

Times Square, at 42nd Street and Broadway, continues to jump 24 hours a day, but these days the jumping may be to avoid a marauding prostitute. (The brazen hookers, run by what must be small armies of pimps, seem to survive every big clean-up the city orders.) Amidst the porno shops and dirty movies, Times Square still has numbers of top-flight movie houses, legitimate theaters, actors' hangouts like the Lambs Club and Sardi's, and the national New Year's Eve celebration every year.

So much is concentrated in Midtown that a mere cataloguing could take pages. The major television networks are centered here, the splendid New York Public Library, airline and travel bureaus beyond count, the art gallery concentrate near 57th Street, the nation's jewelry center (with almost 2,000 people working on diamonds alone), hotels swank and not so swank (51,000 rooms within a mile's radius of Times Square), and restaurants without peer on the continent. Just on the Avenue of the Americas, more than 25 million square feet of office space were under construction in the late 1960s; the avenue has received such giants as the CBS and Sperry-Rand headquarters, and the New York Hilton and Americana Hotels. Rockefeller Center, begun in 1931, remains the largest and by far the most successful effort at urban-office-building clustering in the city and its Christmas tree competes with the one on the Ellipse in Washington as the nation's favorite.

The power and elegance of New York is at its most complete in the one-mile stretch of Park Avenue north of Grand Central—the stunning new glass buildings of giant corporations and banks, the elegant apartment houses of the socially prominent. Some of the distinguished buildings are Lever House (built in 1952 as the first glass-walled building in the city), the Seagram Building (with its formal plaza of granite, trees, and pools, and wonderfully luxurious Four Seasons Restaurant), and the Union Carbide Building (53 stories of stainless steel and gray glass). Unfortunately, there are also many unimaginative office towers where greed for maximum allowable floor space dictated every design decision. But good or bad, note again, the postwar development is the determinative.

■ CENTRAL PARK. Now, and one hopes forever, this is one of America's grandest municipal parks, 840 sylvan acres, filled with sunken roads (revolutionary when the park was laid out in the 1850s), miles of paths, bridges, gates, lakes, lawns, statues, the zoo, and skating rinks. The parks programs have made the park a safer place to be, although dangers remain; in 1971, for instance, there was a wave of attacks on unsuspecting bicyclists, who fell victim to knife- and bottle-wielding assailants who lurked along bike paths waiting to knock riders off their cycles and steal their bikes.

WEST SIDE. From the Lincoln Square and Columbus Circle area all the way up to the Upper West Side, this portion of land between Central Park and the Hudson River has been improving rapidly from the condition of deteriorated slumhood that characterized it at the end of World War II. The congested tenements around Lincoln Square have been replaced by the impressive travertine marble Lincoln Center complex and two middle- and upper-income housing developments. New boutiques and theaters are springing up, and the rents are going up, too. In the 70s, 80s and 90s, young people are moving into and remodeling brownstones and paying for private guards to watch their streets—with a substantial reduction in crime rate. The massive West Side Urban Renewal Plan created thousands of new units of low- and middle-income housing.

The Upper West Side has undergone many ethnic changes, from wealthy Protestants around the Civil War to Irish in the 1870s and heavily Jewish after the turn of the century. Blacks and Puerto Ricans began to move in in heavy quantities in the late 1940s and the district became one of the most densely populated on Manhattan Island. But instead of growing and growing, the black-Puerto Rican population share has dropped to about 30 percent and the area is a relatively harmonious mix of whites (Irish, Jewish), Orientals (Chinese, Japanese, a few Koreans), blacks, Puerto Ricans, and even some Haitians and Dominicans.

In the amenities department, the West Side is not limited to Lincoln Center and Central Park. At 77th Street, there is the illustrious American Museum of Natural History and attendant Hayden Planetarium; along the Hudson runs Riverside Park, a green relief from the apartment jungles.

■ UPPER EAST SIDE. This choicest of all areas in the city begins at the southern end of Central Park and extends up the East River to the border with East Harlem. It has New York's greatest concentration of wealth, culture, and treasures. This is the New York of elegant apartment houses, exclusive clubs of the rich, art galleries, museums, cultural and scientific academies, expensive cafes and restaurants, town houses, and great hospitals. The affluence runs up Fifth and Park Avenues and their side streets, and in a narrow strip right along the East River (East End Avenue—where John Gunther lived—Sutton Place, et al.). Only as one approaches East Harlem does the scene shift to old and decaying brownstones, kids hanging out on the street corners, and stores with wire grills over the windows to fend off burglars.

But along Fifth and Park, it is luxury living. Here one finds the long rows of ornate old apartment buildings which house the families of ancestral wealth and nouveau riche alike. The uniformed doormen open the doors of the Cadillacs and Rolls Royces and Mercedes as the residents leave or arrive home, some of them now-generation jet-setters, others tottering old dowagers with canes. Jackie Kennedy Onassis has had an apartment in one of these buildings for a number of years.

The great art museums of New York (Metropolitan, Whitney, Frick, Guggenheim) are in this district, but also art galleries and shops and stores of international repute, U.N. missions, expensive cafes and restaurants, and clubs for the U people: the Union Club (New York's oldest), the Brook, Harmonie Club (the nation's oldest and most prestigious Jewish club), the Metropolitan Club, Knickerbocker Club, Lotus Club, Colony Club (more for grandes dames), Cosmopolitan Club (more for rich young lady activists) Junior League of the City of New York (in the former Vincent Astor House) and the Colonial Dames of America (in the former Abigail Adams Smith House). Only a handful of leading clubs are outside the Upper East Side, notably the Century Association (7 West 43rd, for "authors, artists, and amateurs of the letters and fine arts"), and the Union League (38 East 37th, almost as Republican as its Philadelphia counterpart). There are the past and present town houses of families like Whitney, Mellon, Root, Roosevelt, Day, Lowe, and Bronk. Hospitals and centers of medical research abound, including Mt. Sinai Hospital, Cornell University Medical College, the Sloan-Kettering Cancer Center, and Rockefeller University (Rockefeller Institute for Medical Research). The mayor of New York lives on the Upper East Side, in historic old Gracie Mansion, located in Carl Schurz Park on the East River at 88th Street.

Also along the East River is Franklin D. Roosevelt Drive, a swirling, crowded jam of automobiles most of the day and night, fighting their way up and down the island's rim. A block back from the river is York Avenue, tucked into a bulge in Manhattan's waistline, a pleasant mixture of shops and restaurants and stores, with a growing sprinkling of new-culture bars.

The northern part of the Upper East Side is known as Yorkville. It is also called "the richest suburb" in the world because of the growth in recent years of high-rise luxury apartment buildings, office buildings among the small shops and deteriorating brownstones that are remnants of the German community that thrived here at the turn of the century. In the late 1960s, Gimbel Brothers, Inc., opened a new branch store in Yorkville, and city planners expect it to become a major shopping district in Manhattan. The signs of the old German community are rapidly disappearing. Along East 86th Street it is still possible to buy German periodicals and newspapers and to find a restaurant with cloth napkins and checkered tablecloths, waiters who carry handfuls of beer steins and a menu featuring Ochsenmaul, Bratwurst, Knockwurst, or Weisswurst. But the *echten Deutschen* who made this community are fewer in number now. After 40 years, the German Brauhaus on East 86th Street came down in 1968, making way for a new luxury apartment building.

HARLEM. Harlem dominates Manhattan above Central Park (116th Street). The image is one generated by the flamboyant politicians such as Marcus Garvey early in this century and Adam Clayton Powell, Jr, in later years, by the great black nightspots now gone by (the Sugar Cane, the Savoy, the Cotton Club), and by modern-day riots and crime.

Reality differs from that image in that Harlem really is many places and large parts of it are now undergoing substantial change. At the northwest corner of Central Park, for example, at 110th Street and Eighth Avenue, is one of the bleakest sections in New York, row after row of dilapidated but inhabited walkups, garbage-strewn streets and sidewalks, broken windows, and burned-out apartments, people lounging around on the stoops and street corners (almost half of Harlem's 240,000 people are on welfare). Harlem also has Lenox Terrace, which boasts 25 doormen, four gardeners, carpeted halls, and occupants who are making it big—judges, entertainers, politicians (including Manhattan Borough President Percy E. Sutton). A small but growing number of black middle class families have begun to buy brownstones on Convent Avenue. Harlem is an area with numerous churches, including the Abyssinian Baptist Church where Powell was pastor, the largest (12,000) Protestant congregation in the country, and St. Phillip's Protestant Episcopal Church, once reputedly the wealthiest black congregation in the nation. There are other churches, some huge and modernistic and some tiny and makeshift. One block is said to contain 11 churches.

An uneasy neighbor in the Harlem community is Morningside Heights, along the Hudson River, the site of Columbia University, a great academic institution whose land-aggrandizing policies caused major tensions, especially in the 1960s.

■ WASHINGTON HEIGHTS. This northern tip of Manhattan is one of the most densely populated in the city, not because it is—yet—a slum but because it has long been a haven for people escaping tenement life, who have moved into its many apartment buildings. The Irish came first, followed by Greeks and Armenians, and in the 1930s and '40s, many European Jews fleeing the Hitler regime. Blacks have been moving in from nearby Harlem since World War II, joined in the last few years by Puerto Ricans, Dominicans, Haitians, and Cubans. The population of some 190,000 is about 75 percent white, 10 percent black, and 15 percent Spanish-speaking. A general shabbiness lies over much of the area today, and there is some concern about its future.

The important landmarks of this "land's end" of Manhattan are the George Washington Bridge (one of the world's greatest, in both engineering and esthetics), Yeshiva University, the great Columbia-Presbyterian Medical Center, and the Cloisters, a gift from the Rockefellers.

THE BRONX

Despite its new status as the first majority nonwhite borough in New York City's history, the Bronx, in greater or lesser degree, has the same general groups that appear in almost every borough:

- AFFLUENT AND ALMOST AFFLUENT NEW YORK. An echo of the East Side. The Bronx has precious little of this, but the community of Riverdale, just above Manhattan, is an example: a white suburbia within the city, people living in gracious colonial, Tudor, and Georgian homes in rustic elegance. Many public, political, and professional people live in Riverdale, including well-known names like Robert Morgenthau, Theodore Kheel, and Louis Harris. Sociologically, there is not much difference between these people and younger professionals like those restoring brownstones in Brooklyn today. Politics: reform Democrat.
- MIDDLE-CLASS NEW YORK. Heavily Irish, German, Italian, and Jewish, these people live in quite stable neighborhoods and are preoccupied with keeping their neighborhoods the way they are. They are office workers, teachers, minor bureaucrats, and the elite of the blue-collar class. In the Bronx, you will find them living north of the Cross Bronx Expressway (the safe, or Westchester side). Politics: regular Democrat, and many (especially the Irish and Italian) showing Republican tendencies in recent years.
- LOWER-MIDDLE-CLASS NEW YORK. Again, an Irish-Italian-German-Jewish polyglot, but older and poorer. In the Bronx, they are heavily Jewish and may be discovered along the Grand Concourse, living on small pensions or Social Security, their income stagnant and decreasing in buying power. Their children have often gone to college, becoming accountants and attorneys, and have moved to better parts of the city or to Nassau, Suffolk, Westchester, or New Jersey. But the old folks are stuck where they started. Politics: a mixture of regular and reform Democrat.
- POOR NEW YORK. With limited exceptions, this means simply black and Puerto Rican. In the Bronx, it means the South Bronx, a seething ghetto. The South Bronx is part of a black-Hispanic poverty belt of the city which runs from New York Bay up the west sides of Brooklyn and Queens to the Bronx, with counterparts on Manhattan's Lower East Side and Harlem. Today 40 percent of the Bronx population and two thirds of the school enrollment is black or Puerto Rican. Politics: the few who vote here go Democratic.

Roughly speaking, 33 percent of New York City is black and Puerto Rican now. Another 15 percent consists of the older lower-middle class. Thus well over 45 percent of the city is poor, and that percentage increases steadily. Thereby hangs the city's problem.

The Bronx has lots of heavy industry, especially along its southern flanks, and it is a place of many neighborhoods, not all as simple as our income-ethnic groupings may suggest. In the north section of the borough, for instance, is Baychester—a community of middle-class whites (two thirds) and blacks (one third) who have both risen above their childhood circumstances and now share the pressure of mortgage payments, rising property taxes, and fear of slipping back into tenement life.

Along the Harlem River facing Manhattan's Washington Heights is the community of Highbridge, determined not to become a slum. The community is integrated, even to the same block of brownstones or the same apartment building. The population is one-third black, one-third Puerto Rican, and one-third white (Irish, Italian, Jewish).

The Bronx has its extremes, however. Consider the South Bronx. Photo-journalist Herb Goro spent one year getting to know the people and rooftops and back alleys of a block on 174th Street near Washington Avenue in the South Bronx. He wrote a book about what he found there—the indifferent landlords, the broken buildings with their broken windows and doors and broken plumbing, the rats, the garbage-strewn alleys used as playgrounds, the cold, the job discrimination, the filth and noise of the El, the drugs. This is one of the most densely inhabited areas of the nation; it has some 50,000 people living in a 55-block area, 48 percent black, 48 percent Puerto Rican, and 4 percent elderly white. So decayed and hopeless is this area that serious suggestions have been made that the city ought to abandon it altogether.

The Grand Concourse is still the major connecting link of the southern and northern parts of the Bronx. Once it was the scene of bustling stores and entertainment, but now it is in painful change. Black and Puerto Rican families, looking for lower-cost housing, have been streaming in for the past few years. Many whites live in near-panic—fearing muggings and robberies and talking of wholesale departure. Apathy and panic may combine with lack of local leadership to allow the Concourse section to slip further into decay.

As one moves further north, the land begins to rise and the air to cool, the streets are quieter and there are large parks and university campuses and museums. A typical neighborhood here is Belmont, largely Italian, which is trying somewhat desperately to hold on to its Roman Catholic parochial school system, its customary shopping areas, its way of living. The kids play stickball in the streets and talk easily with cops, many of whom come from this area. When the Tremont antipoverty program was being developed, Belmont's 30,000 people chose to keep out of it, determined to go it alone.

The Bronx is not without its landmarks. It has Yankee Stadium, newly renovated at a cost of $50 million to the city, Jesuit-run Fordham University, swank schools like Horace Mann and Riverdale County School for Girls,

Manhattan College, Wave Hill (a castle that has been the home of Mark Twain, Theodore Roosevelt, and Arturo Toscanini, among others), Poe Cottage (where Edgar Allen Poe lived with his ailing young wife and wrote poems like *Annabel Lee*), and the Jerome Park Reservoir (which can hold 773 million gallons and has next to it a second basin, almost twice as large, that was never completed and now contains a college, a park, an armory, two subway yards, three high schools, and a housing development). The Bronx is the home of gargantuan Co-op City, the Botanical Gardens, and the magnificent Bronx Zoo, America's largest and famed the world over.

Perhaps the most interesting political fact about the Bronx is not that it has gone reform (good-bye Charles Buckley and the Edward J. Flynn tradition), but that it has become the first seedbed of political growth by New York's Puerto Ricans. New York today has about one million Puerto Ricans (more than San Juan). There have been Puerto Ricans in the city since early in the century, but in significant numbers only since 1940. The influx went first to East Harlem, then shifted to the South Bronx, and later to Brooklyn (the borough with the most Puerto Ricans today). But only in the Bronx have the Puerto Ricans taken hold politically, starting with Herman Badillo's 1965 election as borough president.

The Puerto Rican crisis—in the homeland, and in major American cities —is one most Americans know little of, but one that will force increasing national attention in the future. The island's population density of 546 persons per square mile is one of the world's highest, the unemployment rate over 12 percent, per-capita income only half of Mississippi's. At the same time that agricultural mechanization has reduced farm-labor needs on the island, a combination of better health care and Roman Catholicism has caused a population explosion of awesome proportions. The safety valve has been immigration to the U. S. mainland, which is unlimited due to Puerto Rico's commonwealth status. The immigrants are only the poor and desperate people of the island. Once they arrive in the U. S., they cannot hope for much more than menial, low-paying jobs in factories and restaurants. Compared to blacks, Puerto Ricans have a higher unemployment rate, a lower median income, a greater percentage of school dropouts, and are four times as likely to be on welfare.

Most alarming of all, only the young and the poor Puerto Ricans remain in the U.S. Those with initiative, who save up money or manage to get a good education or technical training, almost invariably return to their native island where their skills will permit them to live better than they can in the U.S. How does one build stability and leadership in this revolving-door community? It is a tough job, Badillo responds, and made no easier by the fact that the median age of the Puerto Ricans in the U. S. is only 19 years.

The Southeast Bronx today illustrates the worst side of the Puerto Rican problem: thousands of kids on each block, open narcotics trade, derelict cars, shootings on the street, conflicts with the police, and the language barrier most cops face in trying to deal with the young Puerto Ricans.

QUEENS

Queens is the most well-to-do of New York's four major boroughs, and also the whitest and most spacious. Compared to population losses elsewhere in the city, Queens has grown, or at least remained static. It hopes to become a significant office center to complement its present mix of factories and homes, homes, homes. It is a borough of distinct communities; instead of saying they are from 'Queens," people say they are from "Flushing," "Jamaica," or "Astoria," reflecting often intense community pride. The borough has an astounding 16,397 acres of parks, almost as much as the other four boroughs combined. Until 25 years ago, there were endless jokes about Queens being "the borough of cemeteries," and, indeed, those prime wasters of space still form the bulk of the borough's open urban areas. But the jokes vanished in the wake of a postwar apartment-house explosion that terminated Queens' rurality and brought with it the familiar suburban headaches of sewers, schools, and even urban renewal. Often, Queens feels slighted and neglected by the city government.

Highway congestion and inadequate public transportation are key problems. The borough lies between Nassau County and Manhattan, feeds 40 percent of its own work force into Manhattan every day, and has to accommodate the vast flow of people to and from the New York City airports—La Guardia and John F. Kennedy—both of which lie within its borders.

Quiet stability characterizes many parts of Queens. In towns like Flushing, the scene is often one of two- and three-story white clapboard Victorian houses on tree-lined streets. In Hollis Hills, a Jewish and Catholic community near the Nassau border, the only break from single-family homes and garden apartments are a few high-rise apartment houses, and they are for the wealthy. All of northeast Queens is filled with stable communities, including many that are heavily Irish. Some of the better areas have a nautical air about them, reminders that Queens is on Long Island. Along Long Island Sound and the broadest parts of the East River are prime areas like College Point, Whitestone, and Beechurst, filled with spacious single-family homes close by beach and yacht clubs. The neighboring Bayside-Douglaston area, around Little Neck Bay, is more in flux as people put up houses on the hilly crests overlooking the bay, and where some developers have thrown up new houses so close together that they resemble a scrunched up Levittown. A massive Korvette's has gone into this area, and hundreds of sailboats crowd the waters on warm days. Racially, this area is as white as the most pristine suburbs.

A lot of Queens is undistinctive in the extreme, starting with its main artery, Queens Boulevard, which provides a link with the Queensboro Bridge and Manhattan. The boulevard is lined with dense apartment conglomerations void of any creative plan or design. Over toward the East River, facing Manhattan, are older places like Long Island City, Astoria, Hunter's Point, and Steinway (after the piano company founder), a melange of factories and housing for low- to medium-income families. More blacks and Puerto Ricans are moving in, and one big public housing area at Ravenswood is virtually all black, though the preponderance is Italian, Irish, and German. Astoria, once heavily Italian, has received a great wave of immigrants from Greece since the 1965 immigration law.

Queens has formidable numbers of blacks—more than a quarter of a million, in fact. The largest concentrations are in southwest and southeast Queens. There are middle-class black enclaves where the biggest problem is sewers; but also places like South Jamaica, a massive slum where the shanties on South Street are reminiscent of Tobacco Road.

The Rockaways, an 11-mile-long peninsula that encloses Jamaica Bay, began as an exclusive summer resort in the last century and still have many posh sections, and of course the magnificent beaches. But one section, filled with flimsy summer bungalows, was taken over by blacks as year-round residences; the city demolished many of these tinderboxes.

Finally, we should note the new Gateway National Recreation Area (at the extremity of the Rockaways), including Breezy Point, Jamaica Bay, and Sandy Hook (across the mouth of the Hudson in New Jersey). With 10 miles of ocean beach and 23,000 acres of land and water preserve, the area is becoming a close-in recreation point for the millions of the metropolitan area.

BROOKLYN

Brooklyn is first of all a massive fact: 2.6 million people, enough to make it, if it were independent, the fourth largest city in the United States. At the start of the 1970s, it had 225,000 manufacturing or wholesale jobs with an annual payroll of $2.8 billion. The downtown Brooklyn retail district attracts 200,000 visitors on a typical day. The Brooklyn waterfront receives half the general cargo coming into the port of New York. The borough has great cultural and educational institutions: the Brooklyn Museum, the Academy of Music, the Botanic Garden, Brooklyn College, Pratt Institute, Long Island University.

Second, Brooklyn is a legend. Do you remember when the Dodgers came from Brooklyn; when Coney Island, massed throngs and all, still stood for summertime fun; and when all America thought warmly of *A Tree Grows in Brooklyn?* Why, the place even had its own patois and a fierce local nationalism practically no other American community could match.

Third, Brooklyn is a place in trouble—deep trouble. It harbors two of the largest, worst ghettos in the world—Brownsville and Bedford-Stuyvesant. Writer Peter Hamill sums up Brownsville as a "bombed-out shell of a community"; when Boston's Mayor Kevin White made a 1971 tour of Brownsville, he saw it as "the first tangible sign of the collapse of our civilization." *

---

* In 1950, Brooklyn was 90 percent white; today it is about 60 percent white, 25 percent Black, 15 percent Puerto Rican. Brownsville was predominantly Jewish at the end of World War II; now it is more than 90 percent black and Puerto Rican. Bedford-Stuyvesant was 50 percent black in 1950, 90 percent by the late '60s.

Fourth, Brooklyn has islands of growth and renewal. The most vivid examples are Brooklyn Heights (directly opposite Lower Manhattan) and nearby Park Slope, both of which began as suburbs of Manhattan's well-to-do in the past century, declined during the Depression years, but then were revived after the war by young adults who restored or remodeled old homes and created one of New York City's most pleasant and desirable neighborhoods. In addition, there are stable, attractive middle-income communities in Brooklyn, of which Bay Ridge (across from Staten Island) is perhaps the most distinguished example.

The great bulk of Brooklyn, however, is a case study of what happens when a city begins to decay, its more stable citizens leave and only the old and weak and poor are left. Most of the broad belt of northern Brooklyn, running from the East River to Jamaica Bay, is like that. So are parts of southern Brooklyn, including Coney Island.

Consider the problems: neighbors who speak different languages and have differing religious customs; communities bitterly divided over whether land should be used for housing or schools; absentee landlords and a steady downward slide in services; real-estate blockbusters playing on the fears of homeowners; and, overriding all other considerations, racial conflict.

The people who hold neighborhoods together leave. A typical case is a bus driver or postal clerk who earns $10,000 or $12,000 a year and has two children he wants to send to college (he made it through high school). He pays $300 a month rent for a four-room apartment in Brooklyn, but now he can't find the landlord and the neighborhood is getting rough. He moves out to a new apartment he probably cannot afford, and the old house begins to deteriorate. The landlord may have got his money out of the building and no longer cares about the property. Or the case might involve an Italian baker who had made a good living serving an Italian clientele in his neighborhood. But now the young people are leaving and he does not know his customers personally the way he used to. He doesn't dare stay open at night, so the length of his sales day is reduced. He fears holdups even in daylight. He still needs the Italian clientele, so he doesn't want to leave the neighborhood. But he sees his life's work dwindling away in front of him. The same is true of the kosher butcher or of the pharmacist who now fears holdups by heroin addicts day and night.

Consider the blighted area at the Brooklyn end of the Williamsburg Bridge. (It seems that the shaded areas under bridges and elevated railroads everywhere in New York are blighted.) Here, in the Williamsburg section, there are few community services, no community center; streets deadend at the Brooklyn-Queens Expressway; buildings are boarded up. This section is entirely Puerto Rican.

Moving to the east, out to Nostrand Avenue, the neighborhoods of Williamsburg change abruptly from Puerto Rican to ultraorthodox Jewish. A large group of Jews, the Chassidim, are led by a Grand Rabbi and observe the traditional customs: the men wear long sideburns and long black coats;

the women shave their heads and wear wigs. On Friday night and Saturday, everything in these neighborhoods shuts down. Custom prohibits the Jews from operating anything, such as a car or an elevator. Less orthodox Jews can use an elevator if they don't punch the floor button. Thus, in city housing for these people, there are elevators programmed to stop at every floor on Friday night and Saturday—they are known as "Sabbath elevators." The Jews speak Yiddish and the Puerto Ricans speak Spanish, and the two groups cannot even talk with each other, much less resolve differences. The deep recession of the 1970s has hit these people particularly hard. Dependent upon support and employment from other Jews during normal times, they now find that traditional sources of employment are closed to them as the economic decline strikes New York's garment industry. The Chassidim are largely without the contacts necessary to establish themselves on an equal basis of competition for employment in other areas of the region.

Farther east, one comes on the six square miles of Bedford-Stuyvesant, the second largest black ghetto (after Southside Chicago) in America. The population is between 400,000 and 450,000. There are really two communities in one. On tree-shaded streets of sturdy brownstones, many freshly restored, live members of a settled old West Indian community. Many are leaders in law, medicine, government, and politics, and they include Congresswoman Shirley Chisholm, Bed-Stuy's most prominent political figure today. The rest of Bed-Stuy is the fruit of recent years' immigration from the South. It is of these people and their world that Jack Newfield wrote when he described his boyhood community in the early '70s:

Diseased debris rotting under a halo of mosquitoes in a vacant lot. Teen-age girls ducking and punching with the fluent fury of grown men. Rorschach tests of vomit staining the gutter. Burned-out houses with families living behind the boarded-up windows. . . .

There is the sour stench of urine that pollutes the Myrtle-Willoughby IND subway station. . . . The visor of suffocated hatred that comes down across every black youth before his 13th birthday. . . .

Then, the statistics: Eighty percent of the teen-agers high school dropouts. Thirty-six percent of the families headed by women. Twenty-seven percent with annual incomes under $3,000. The highest infant mortality rate in the country. One of the highest homicide rates in the country. And no one has ever counted the rats.

And if one is to take the word of the New York University Graduate School of Social Work, "Bedford-Stuyvesant is more depressed and impaired than Harlem—*i.e.*, fewer unified families, more unemployment, lower incomes, less job history. . . . Furthermore, the Bedford-Stuyvesant youths have a vastly lower degree of self-esteem than does Harlem youth." Yet it was from Harlem, in a sense, that Bed-Stuy was born. In 1936, a new subway line linked Brooklyn and Harlem and the route was celebrated in a Duke Ellington song, "Take the A Train," inviting whites to take the subway as the fastest way to Harlem nightlife. As it turned out, the mass traffic was in the other direction—desperate Harlemites following the A train to what were then the relative amenities of Bedford-Stuyvesant.

On a February day of 1966, the late Sen. Robert Kennedy made a walking tour of Bedford-Stuyvesant; several months later he announced a comprehensive rehabilitation plan, which still functions largely as he envisaged it. There are two corporations. One is black, community-based, and highly visible. It was named the Bedford-Stuyvesant Restoration Corporation, and Franklin A. Thomas, a black former police commissioner and lifetime Brooklyn resident, became its president. The second corporation was named Development and Services Corporation; it is primarily white and works behind the scenes to attract private finance. Its choice as president was John Doar, former head of the Justice Department's civil rights division and later chief counsel of the House Judiciary Committee during the Nixon impeachment hearings.

There have been concrete results from the effort Kennedy inspired. The Superblock, a new recreational area, was completed early in the game. Some 1,800 brownstones have had at least their exteriors renovated. IBM opened a plant with more then 400 employees—though no major corporations followed it into the area. The Restoration Corporation has channeled loans to several dozen small businessmen. And a community center was created in an abandoned dairy, using mostly indigenous workers.

At the same time, the Bed-Stuy community has learned to press more effectively for the things it wants. In July 1971, we watched Mayor Lindsay and Congresswoman Chisholm dedicate a handsome swimming-pool complex that covers an entire block (the main pool large enough to hold 1,000 kids at once!). The community had not only been consulted on every planning phase of the pool, but there was general agreement that without the community's insistence, the pool would never have materialized.

Brownsville has only a quarter of Bed-Stuy's population, but it is a more hopeless place, and always has been. In recent years, there has been the hopeful experiment with the Ocean Hill-Brownsville school district, but also outcroppings of nihilist black and Puerto Rican militancy. In 1971, when the state legislature cut back on the programs that provide practically the only significant income for Brownsville—Aid for Dependent Children, Medicaid, drug-addiction centers, and school aid—hundreds of Brownsville teenagers, along with derelicts and addicts, staged a medium-level riot in which dozens of stores were looted and 15 major fires started. The Associated Press released a frightening photograph of three teenagers lounging contentedly along a mesh wire fence while flames licked from every window of the tenement building in front of them.

The New York City Planning Commission reports that $70 million was spent on public housing in a small section of Brownsville following 1948, but that the projects were planned without provision for new schools, adequate recreational space, health facilities, or job training. "They helped institutionalize poverty, and the ghetto. Whites, and those blacks who could, fled in the wake of the new construction." At the same time, the Commission noted:

> Brownsville's vacant apartments became the dumping ground for many of the city's poor, including welfare clients, dislocated by redevelopment in other areas. The process fed on itself. Panic spread. Tenements emptied out as though hit by plague. Landlords simply walked away, abandoning their buildings.
>
> Today, along streets bordering the public housing tract are broken glass, rusting cars, garbage and debris. Block fronts look as if they had been shelled by heavy artillery. . . .
>
> Four of every five families receive some form of public assistance. Unemployment is more than double the citywide average; many of those with jobs do not make a living wage. Other indices of poverty—juvenile delinquency, venereal disease, infant mortality, malnutrition—are from two to four times the city's norm. Resident merchants, businessmen and professionals who could help provide an economic base for the community are almost totally absent from its population.

Moving south and east from Brownsville, one finds East Flatbush, a section of Jews and Italians who are in constant friction. But these also are homeowners who feel a sense of investment in their neighborhood. The old Italians still make wine in the backyard. There is some vandalism, but police consider the section relatively peaceful.

Flatbush itself is changing. The famous high school, Erasmus, long a leading producer of athletes and scholars, is trying to cope with all the problems attendant in a student body that becomes increasingly black and Puerto Rican. Young white families are moving out. Black and Puerto families are moving in. The old white people, who have no place go, stay—in fear.

Coney Island is a serious problem. At the tip end that juts into Gravesend Bay and the mouth of the Hudson, is Sea Gate, a private community of whites who have barriers across the roads and guards who permit only residents, their guests, and service vehicles to pass. On the other side of those barriers is a grim ghetto of blacks and Puerto Ricans, perhaps the most utterly forgotten people in New York City. The ghetto stretches from Sea Gate to the Boardwalk. The city has built high-rise apartments for the elderly; these excellent buildings and apartments have a fine view of the ocean. But the waiting lists are long.

People fear and hate Coney Island now, once the fun center of the city. Blacks and Puerto Ricans go there on the subway for a little relaxation, but the whites largely keep away. Nobody dares go there at night. The place and the beaches are dirty and depressing. The boardwalk needs new boards. The water is so polluted that it may not be swimmable much longer.

STATEN ISLAND

Staten Island (the borough of Richmond) is the most un-New Yorkish of the five city boroughs. It is only now emerging from a leisurely, rural history. Its hills still offer splendid vistas of the city and the ocean; it still has a few dirt roads and marvelous old buildings; it still has beaches with room to walk and sunbathe and—water pollution levels permitting—to swim. The borough has 20 percent of New York City's land area but only 3.8 percent of its population (295,433 in 1970).

A rush of land speculation and building came to Staten Island, however, with completion of the lovely, soaring Verrazano Bridge in 1964. The bridge provides easy vehicular access to Brooklyn, and thence to Manhattan; previously the only bridges had been to New Jersey. The developers are coming in with their blueprints and bulldozers, and the future is assured only in terms of numbers of people—by estimate of the New York City Planning Commission, 550,000 by 1985. What exists now is a rather untidy assemblage of two-story houses, crowded row upon row onto treeless 40 by 100-foot lots, interspersed with lovely old mansions that recall the island's days as a fashionable summer retreat for wealthy New Yorkers.

The new Verrazano Narrows Bridge is not the most pleasant way to get to Staten Island. Since 1712, there has been some form of ferry service from Manhattan, and you can still take the famed Staten Island Ferry, one of the great short water voyages of the world. The price was a wonderfully low five cents from 1898 until 1975 (and the near collapse of the city's finances).

The view of New York Harbor is stupendous, but two sights are food for thought: the Statue of Liberty and Ellis Island. In a way, they speak to a time past—when the floodgates of immigration were open and Ellis Island accepted 20 million new Americans, when America really meant what Emma Lazarus wrote for the statue's pedestal, those romantic lines: "Give me your tired your poor, / Your huddled masses yearning to breathe free . . . / Send these, the homeless, tempest-tost, to me, / I lift my lamp beside the golden door!" The closing of Ellis Island to immigrants in 1954 (in 1976 it was reopened as an historic relic) underscored the end of all that. But did it? The great city continues, really, to be the port of entry and point of sojourn for the tired and poor. The only difference is that they come now from the American Southland and Puerto Rico instead of Europe. New York never had an easy time with its immigrants, and does not today. But as the city's former economic development administrator, Kenneth Patton, told us:

Urban economies are the only places that do what America is supposed to care about—the resurrection of people who've been left out, and newcomers who have yet to get in, and are not admitted to other places. Cities are successful in their ability to take people from some point of entry and elevate them to some higher level in the economic order of things. Suburbs look successful, but they are not. They just preserve and contain a certain measure of achieved success. They are not creative. Cities look unsuccessful, but by definition they are not. . . . It's an outrage that the country looks at New York and other cities as down and out. They are the only thing that holds the country together.

PERSONS INTERVIEWED

The following persons kindly agreed to interviews with the authors in the preparation of this book. Affiliations shown are as of the time of the interview.

ABEL, I. W., President, United Steelworkers of America, Pittsburgh, Pa.

ABRAMS, Herbert W., Director of Public Affairs, Chase Manhattan Bank, New York City

ALEXANDER, Clifford, Jr., Attorney, Arnold and Porter, Washington, D.C.

AURELIO, Richard, Deputy Mayor, New York City

BACON, Edmund N., Former Executive Director, Philadelphia Planning Commission, Philadelphia, Pa.

BADILLO, Herman, U. S. Representative from New York

BAGLIVO, Angelo, Political Writer, Newark News, Newark, N.J.

BALTZELL, Professor E. Digby, University of Pennsylvania, Philadelphia, Pa.

BATEMAN, Raymond H., State Senate President, Trenton, N.J.

BEAUMONT, Enid, Director, Public Administration Program, New York University Graduate School of Public Administration

BIXBY, R. Burdell, Attorney and Republican Campaign Manager, New York City

BLACK, Creed, Editor, Philadelphia Inquirer, Philadelphia, Pa.

BOND, Richard C., President of the Board of Trustees, John Wanamaker Department Store, Philadelphia, Pa.

BOOKER, James E., James E. Booker Associates, Inc., New York City

BORELLA, Victor, Special Adviser to Governor Rockefeller on Labor Affairs, New York City

BOWSER, Charles, Executive Director, Urban Coalition of Philadelphia, Philadelphia, Pa.

BRIDGE, Peter, Correspondent, Newark Evening News, Newark, N.J.

BRISCOE, John Hanson, Speaker, Maryland House of Delegates, Baltimore, Md.

BROWN, C. Harold, Director, Division of Urban Affairs, University of Delaware, Newark, Del.

BROWNE, Millard C., Editorial Page Editor, Buffalo Evening News, Buffalo, N.Y.

BROWNE, Stanhope S., Attorney and Civic Leader, Philadelphia, Pa.

BUCCI, John, Public Opinion Analyst, Swarthmore Pa.

BURKHARDT, Robert J., Former Secretary of State and Democratic State Chairman, Trenton, N.J.

BURNS, John, Chairman, Democratic State Committee, New York City

BURT, Nathaniel, Author, Princeton, N.J.

BUTTON, H. Warren, Professor, State University of Buffalo, Buffalo, N.Y.

BYRNE, Michael, Former Deputy Mayor, Philadelphia, Pa.

CAMPBELL, Allen B., Dean, Maxwell Graduate School of Citizenship and Public Affairs, Syracuse University, New York

CARTER, Peter, Chief, Trenton Bureau, Newark News

CITRINO, Robert, Vice-Chairman, N.J. Turnpike Authority, Nutley, N.J.

CLARK, Joseph S., Former U. S. Senator from Pennsylvania and Mayor of Philadelphia

CLARK, Timothy, Editor and Publisher, Empire State Report, Albany, N.Y.

CONMY, Jack, Press Secretary, Office of Sen. Richard Schweiker (Pa.)

COWAN, Eugene, Assistant to the President, Washington, D.C.

CRAIG, John G., Jr., Editorial Director, Wilmington News & Journal, Wilmington, Del.

CRANGLE, Joseph F., Democratic State Chairman, Buffalo, New York

DARLING, Charles, Research Director, National Industrial Conference Board, New York City

DeFILIPPO, Frank, Press Secretary to Gov. Marvin Mandel, Annapolis, Md.

DERRICKSON, J. Eugene, Plastics & Fibre Workers, Wilmington, Del.

DeWITT, The Right Reverend Robert L., Bishop of Pennsylvania, Philadelphia, Pa.

DILTS, James, Urban Affairs Reporter, Baltimore Sun, Baltimore, Md.

DODD, Frank, President, New Jersey Senate, Trenton, N.J.

DOUGHERTY, Richard, New York Correspondent, Los Angeles Times, New York City

EASTBURN, David, President, Federal Reserve Bank, Philadelphia, Pa.

EDDY, Edward D., President, Chatham College, Pittsburgh, Pa.

EMBRY, Robert, Commissioner, Baltimore Department of Housing and Community Development, Baltimore, Md.

EPPS, Richard, Economist, The Federal Reserve Bank, Philadelphia, Pa.

FARRAR, Eleanor, Metropolitan Applied Research Center, Washington, D.C.

FITZPATRICK, Robert, Dean of Students, Johns Hopkins University, Baltimore, Md.

FRANK, William P., Wilmington *News & Journal,* Wilmington, Del.

FREE, Lloyd, Public Opinion Analyst for Nelson Rockefeller, Chevy Chase, Md.

FREELAND, Wendell G., Attorney and Republican Leader, Pittsburgh, Pa.

FRIEDMAN, Elisha, City Manager, Rochester, N.Y.

FRIEDMAN, Eugene, Reading *Times,* Reading, Pa.

GALLERY, John Andrew, Acting Director, Philadelphia 1976 Bicentennial Commission, Philadelphia, Pa.

GARDINER, John A., Law Enforcement Assistance Administration, Washington, D.C.

GERMOND, Jack W., Correspondent, Gannett Newspapers, Washington, D.C.

GIBSON, Kenneth, Mayor of Newark, N.J.

GIRARD, Karen, Economic Consultant on Urban Affairs, Chase Manhattan Bank, New York City

GLASGOW, Jesse, Financial Editor, Baltimore *Sun,* Baltimore, Md.

GLEASON, Jack, Director, Division of Citizen Complaints, Department of Public Advocate, Trenton, N.J.

HAGUE, Howard, Former Vice President, United Steelworkers of America, Pittsburgh, Pa.

HALPERN, Alan, Editor, *Philadelphia Magazine,* Philadelphia, Pa.

HANSON, Royce, Chairman, Montgomery County (Md.) Planning Board

HARRIS, Roger, Correspondent, Newark *Star-Ledger,* Newark, N.J.

HARVEY, Gregory, Attorney and Civic Leader, Philadelphia, Pa.

HAZARD, Leland, Civic Leader and Author, Pittsburgh, Pa.

HELLSTERN, Richard, First Assistant U.S. Attorney, Newark, N.J.

HERMANN, Ray, Correspondent, Buffalo *Courier-Express,* Buffalo, N.Y.

HINDEN, Stan, Washington Correspondent, *Newsday,* and Editor, Washington *Post District Weekly,* Washington, D.C.

HURD, T. Norman, Director of State Operations, State of New York, Albany, N.Y.

JACKSON, Kay Gauss, Critic, New York City

JACOBSON, Hugh N. B., Architect, Washington, D.C.

JACOBSON, Joel, Director, Community Relations, Region 9, United Auto Workers, Cranford, N.J.

JAMES, William S., President, Maryland State Senate and Chairman, State Democratic Party, Bel Air, Md.

JAVITS, Jacob K., U. S. Senator from New York

JAY, Peter, Columnist, Baltimore *Sun,* Baltimore, Md.

KALODNER, Philip, Attorney and Civic Leader, Philadelphia, Pa.

KAMINSKI, Duke, Harrisburg Bureau Chief, Philadelphia *Evening Bulletin*

KEENAN, Francis, Administrative Assistant, Office of Rep. Florence Dwyer (N.J.)

KENDALL, William, Administrative Assistant, Office of Rep. Peter Frelinghuysen (N.J.)

KUMMERFELD, Donald, Budget Director, New York City

KURZMAN, Peter, New York City

LANIGAN, Charles T., Republican State Chairman, New York City

LARSON, Peter A., Executive Vice-President, Greater Wilmington Development Council, Wilmington, Del.

LEFKOWITZ, Stephen, New York State Urban Development Corporation, New York City

LEO, John, Press Relations, Environmental Protection Administration, New York City

LEVITT, Arthur, Comptroller, State of New York

LINDSAY, John V., Mayor of New York City

LINDSAY, Mrs. Mary Anne, New York, N.Y.

LOVENHEIM, David, Administrative Assistant, Office of Rep. Frank Horton (N.Y.)

LYNN, Frank, Political Correspondent, New York *Times*

MALONE, Larry, American Institute of Planners, Washington, D.C.

MALONEY, Thomas, Mayor of Wilmington, Del.

MANDEL, Marvin, Governor of Maryland, Annapolis, Md.

MATHIAS, Charles McC., Jr., U.S. Senator from Maryland

McCABE, Michael, Former Aide to Sen. Joseph Biden (Del.)

McCULLOUGH, Jerry, Political Writer, Philadelphia *Evening Bulletin,* Philadelphia, Pa.

McCULLOUGH, John, Editorial Page Editor, Philadelphia *Evening Bulletin,* Philadelphia, Pa.

MEDSGER, Betty, Religion Reporter, The Washington *Post,* Washington, D.C.

MEEHAN, William A., General Counsel, Republican City Committee, Philadelphia, Pa.

MIKULSKI, Barbara, City Councilwoman, Baltimore, Md.

MORGAN, Thomas B., Press Secretary for Mayor John V. Lindsay, New York City

MORROW, Hugh, Director of Communications, Staff of Governor Nelson A. Rockefeller (N.Y.)

NEVIUS, John, President, City Council, Washington, D.C.

O'BRIEN, Emmet N., Bureau Chief, Gannett News Service, Albany, N.Y.

O'DONNELL, Harry, Deputy Commissioner, N.Y. State Department of Commerce, Albany, N.Y.

ORRICK, Bentley, Political Writer, Baltimore *Sun,* Baltimore, Md.

PACKARD, George, Managing Editor, Philadelphia *Evening Bulletin,* Philadelphia, Pa.

PALMER, Bruce, President, National Industrial Conference Board, New York City

PASNICK, Raymond W., Director of Public Relations, United Steelworkers of America, Pittsburgh, Pa.

PATTON, D. Kenneth, Economic Development Administrator, New York City

PEASE, Robert B., Executive Director, Allegheny Conference on Community Development, Pittsburgh, Pa.

PERROTTA, Fioravante G., New York City Coordinator, New York Committee for the Re-election of the President (1972), New York City

PERRY, Christopher, Administrative Assistant to Governor Peterson (Del.)

PETERSON, Russell, Governor of Delaware, Dover, Del.

PIKE, Otis, U.S. Representative from New York

RAFSKY, William, Executive Director, Greater Philadelphia Movement, Philadelphia, Pa.

REEVES, Richard, Correspondent, New York *Times,* New York City

REICHLEY, James, Writer, *Fortune,* New York City

RICHARDS, Peter, Director of Administration, New York City Planning Commission

ROBB, Rick, Administrative Assistant, Office of Rep. Albert Johnson (Pa.)

ROCKEFELLER, Nelson A., Governor of New York

ROSENFELD, Harry, Assistant Managing Editor, Washington *Post,* Washington, D.C.

ROUSE, James, Developer, Columbia, Md.

RUSSO, Louis J., Director of the Budget, Erie County, New York

RYAN, Thomas P., Mayor of Rochester, N.Y.

SAMPSON, Arthur, Commissioner of Public Building Service, General Services Administration, Washington, D.C.

SAMUELS, Howard, President, New York City Off-Track Betting Corporation

SANGER, Richard P., Executive Editor, Wilmington *News & Journal,* Wilmington, Del.

SCHEIBER, Walter A., Executive Director, Metropolitan Washington Council of Governments, Washington, D.C.

SCHNEIDER, Pauline, Metropolitan Applied Research Center, Washington, D.C.

SCOTT, Dwight, Director of Public Affairs, National Biscuit Co., New York City

SCOTT, Hugh, Superintendent, District of Columbia Public Schools, Washington, D.C.

SCOTT, Robert, Peirce-Phelps, Inc., Philadelphia, Pa.

SCRANTON, William W., Former Governor of Pennsylvania

SENNETT, William, Former Attorney General of Pennsylvania, Erie, Pa.

SENSENING, Jack, Director, Washington Office, Commonwealth of Pennsylvania

SHAPP, Milton, Governor of Pennsylvania

SHEA, John, Chairman, Reform Caucus, N.Y. State Democratic Committee, New York City

SHEA, Nancy, Office of Governor Nelson A. Rockefeller, New York City

SHIDLER, Atlee, President, Washington Center for Metropolitan Studies, Washington, D.C.

SIMON, Ed, Assistant to Governor Milton Shapp (Pa.)

SKLOOT, Ed, Office of Mayor John V. Lindsay, New York City

SMITH, Dr. Albert F., E.I. du Pont de Nemours & Co., Wilmington, Del.

SONTAG, Frederick H., Public Affairs Consultant, South Orange, N.J.

SPOFFORD, William, Attorney, Trustee of Temple University, Philadelphia, Pa. (deceased)

STEVENS, R.W., Professor of Urban Sociology, George Washington University, Washington, D.C.

SULLIVAN, The Reverend Dr. Leon H., Chairman of the Board, Opportunities Industrialization Center, Inc., Philadelphia, Pa.

SULLIVAN, Richard J., Commissioner, Department of Environmental Protection, Trenton, N.J.

THEMAL, Harry, Wilmington *News & Journal,* Wilmington, Del.

THOMAS, Evan, Vice President and Editor, W.W. Norton & Co., New York City

THORNBURGH, Richard, U.S. Attorney, Pittsburgh, Pa.

TRENT, Peter, C.B.W.L.-Hayden Stone Inc., New York City

TUNNELL, James M., Jr., Attorney & Chairman of the Board of Trustees, University of Delaware

TURCO, Louis, President, Newark City Council, Newark, N.J.

UHL, Sherley, Correspondent, *Pittsburgh Press,* Pittsburgh, Pa.

VAN BUSKIRK, Arthur B., Former Attorney for T. Mellon Sons, Pittsburgh, Pa. (deceased)

VAN NESS, Stanley, Public Advocate, State of New Jersey, Trenton, N.J.

WAGNER, Robert F., Former Mayor of New York City

WALLWORK, James, State Senator, Essex County, N.J.

WASHINGTON, The Rev. Paul, Rector, Church of the Advocate, Philadelphia, Pa.

WEINGARTEN, Victor, Director, Institute for Public Affairs, New York City

WEISMAN, Dan, Bureau Chief, Newark *Star-Ledger,* Trenton, N.J.

WHITE, F. Clifton, Public Affairs Consultant, New York City

WILCOX, William, Secretary of Community Affairs, Commonwealth of Pennsylvania

WILSON, Malcolm, Lieutenant Governor of New York

WISHART, Alfred W., Jr., Director, The Pittsburgh Foundation, Pittsburgh, Pa.

WRICE, Herman, The Young Great Society, Philadelphia, Pa.

WYATT, George E., Budget Division, City of Buffalo, Buffalo, N.Y.

YANOFF, Shelly, Coordinator, Citizens' Committee to Recall Rizzo, Philadelphia, Pa.

YLVISAKER, Paul, Professor, Princeton University, Former Director, N.J. Department of Community Affairs

YOUNG, W. W., President, Retail Clerks Union Local #1357, Philadelphia, Pa.

BIBLIOGRAPHY

I<small>N</small> <small>ADDITION TO THE EXTENSIVE INTERVIEWS</small> for these books, reference was made to books and articles on the individual states and cities, their history and present-day condition. To the authors whose works we have drawn upon, our sincerest thanks.

NATIONAL BOOKS

Barone, Michael, Ujifusa, Grant, and Matthews, Douglas, *The Almanac of American Politics—1972, 1974, and 1976.* Boston: Gambit Publishing Co., published biennially.

Birmingham, Stephen. *The Right People—A Portrait of the American Social Establishment.* Boston: Little, Brown, 1968.

Book of the States. The Council of State Governments. Published biennially, Lexingon, Ky.

Brownson, Charles B. *Congressional Saff Directory.* Published annually, Washington, D.C.

1969 Census of Agriculture, Bureau of the Census, Washington, D.C.

1970 Census of Population, Bureau of the Census, Washington. D.C.

Churches and Church Membership in the United States—An Enumeration by Region, State and County, by Douglas W. Johnson, Paul R. Picard, and Bernard Quinn. Washington, D.C.: Glenmary Research Center, 1974.

Citizens Conference on State Legislatures. Various studies including *The Sometime Governments: A Critical Study of the 50 American Legislatures,* by John Burns. New York: Bantam Books, 1971.

Congress and the Nation, 1945–64, Vol. II, *1965–68,* and Vol. III, *1969–72.* Congressional Quarterly Service, Washington, D.C., 1967, 1969, and 1973.

David, Paul T., *Party Strength in the United States, 1872–1970.* Charlottesville: University Press of Virginia, 1972.

Editor and Publisher International Year Book. New York: Editor and Publisher. Published annually.

Employment and Earnings—States and Areas, 1939–71. U.S. Department of Labor, Bureau of Labor Statistics, Washington, D.C., 1972.

Encyclopedia Americana. Annual editions. New York: Americana Corporation. (Includes excellent state and city review articles.)

Facts and Figures on Government Finance. Published annually by the Tax Foundation, Inc., New York.

Farb, Peter. *Face of North America—The Natural History of a Continent.* New York: Harper & Row, 1963.

Federal-State-Local Finances—Significant Features of Fiscal Federalism. Published periodically by the Advisory Commission on Intergovernmental Relations, Washington, D.C.

Guide to U.S. Elections (Washington: Congressional Quarterly, 1975).

Gunther, John. *Inside U.S.A.* New York: Harper & Row, 1947 and 1951.

Jacob, Herbert, and Vines, Kenneth N. *Politics in the American States: A Comparative Analysis* Boston: Little, Brown, 1971.

Life Pictorial Atlas of the World. Editors of *Life* and Rand McNally. New York: Time, Inc., 1961.

The National Atlas of the United States of America. Geological Survey, U.S. Department of the Interior, Washington, D.C., 1970.

Phillips, Kevin H. *The Emerging Republican Majority.* New Rochelle, N.Y.: Arlington House 1969.

The Quality of Life in the United States: 1970, Index, Rating and Statistics, by Ben-Chieh Liu with Robert Gustafson and Bruce Marcy. Kansas City, Mo.: Midwest Research Institute, 1973.

Rankings of the States. Published annually by the Research Division, National Education Assn., Washington, D.C.

Saloma, John S. III, and Sontag, Frederick H. *Parties: The Real Opportunity for Effective Citizen Politics.* New York: Knopf, 1972.

Sanford, Terry. *Storm Over the States.* New York: McGraw: Hill, 1967.,

Scammon, Richard M., ed. *America Votes—A Handbook of Contemporary American Election Statistics.* Published biennially by the Government Affairs Institute, through Congressional Quarterly, Washington, D.C.

Sharkansky, Ira. *The Maligned States: Policy Accomplishments, Problems, and Opportunities.* New York: McGraw Hill, 1972.

State Government Finances. Published annually by The U.S. Department of Commerce, Bureau of the Census, Washington, D.C.

Statistical Abstract of the United States. Published annually by the U.S. Department of Commerce, Bureau of the Census, Washington, D.C.

Survey of Current Business. U.S. Department of Commerce, Bureau of Economic Analysis, Washington, D.C., monthly. April and August editions contain full reports on geographic trends in personal income and per capita income.

These United States—Our Nation's Geography, History and People. Reader's Digest Assn., Pleasantville, N.Y., 1968.

Uniform Crime Reports for the United States. Published annually by the U.S. Department of Justice, Federal Bureau of Investigation, Washington, D.C.

Who's Who in American Politics (New York: R. R. Bowker Co., published biennially).

The World Almanac and Book of Facts. Published annually by Newspaper Enterprise Assn., Inc., New York and Cleveland.

REGIONAL BOOKS AND SOURCES

Among the more helpful books in understanding megalopolis are *The City in the Seventies,* by Robert K. Yin (Itasca: F.E. Peacock Publishers, 1972); *On the City's Rim: Politics and Policy in Suburbia,* by Frederick M. Wirt, Benjamin Walter, Francine R. Rabinovitz, and Deborah R. Hensler (Lexington: D.C. Heath, 1972); The American Way of Graft, by George Amick (Princeton, N.J.: Center for Analysis of Public Issues, 1976); and *The American People: The Findings of the 1970 Census,* by E.J. Kahn, Jr. (New York: Weybright and Talley, 1973). Helpful articles include "Mapping Megalopolis U.S.A.," *National Geographic,* August 1962, and "U.S.: Northeast: Edge of Center?" by Richard A. Nenneman, *Christian Science Monitor,* June 13, 1970; "Where the Funds Flow," by Joel Havemann, Neal R. Peirce, and Rochelle L. Stanfield, *National Journal,* June 26, 1976; "Northeast Governors Map Battle Plan for Fight Over Federal Funds Flows," by Neal R. Peirce, *National Journal,* Nov. 27, 1976; "The Frostbelt Fights for a New Future," by Timothy B. Clark, *Empire State Report,* October-November 1976.

DISTRICT OF COLUMBIA

The outstanding books on Washington history are Constance McLaughlin Greene's *Washington: Village and Capital, 1800–1878,* and *Washington: Capital City 1879–1950 (Princeton University Press,* 1962 and 1963). *Other helpful sources were Washington Journal: The Events of 1973–74,* by Elizabeth Drew (New York: Random House, 1974); "Significant Trends in Growth and Change in Greater Washington in the 1970s" by Atlee E. Shidler (Washington: Metropolitan Council of Governments, 1973); "Washington Region '74" (Washington: Center for Metropolitan Studies, 1975); and an unpublished manuscript by Barbara Dubivsky.

The Chapter draws on regular coverage of the Washington *Post,* Washington *Star,* and *The Washingtonian.*

GOVERNMENT AND POLITICS "Washington's Way: From Integration to a Black System," by Lawrence Feinberg, Washington *Post,* May 12, 1974; "Is Our Mayor Too Nice?" by Robert F. Levy, Washington *Post,* July 12, 1970; "The Man Who Wants to Be Wanted," by Susan Truitt, *The Washingtonian,* June 1974; "Washington's Black Leadership," by Walterine Swanston, *The Washingtonian,* January 1972. "GAO Backs Eagleton on D.C. Audit," by Helen Dewar, Washington *Post,* Nov. 29, 1975; "Fauntroy Tapped New Constituency," by Bart Barnes, Washington *Post,* Jan. 14, 1971; "Jr. Village: Dumping Ground," by Aaron Latham, Washington *Post,* Jan. 17, 1971. "Report on D.C. Cites Millions in Lost Funds," by Lawrence Meyer and "Mayor 'Not Going to Bicker' About Report's Findings," by LaBarbara Bowman and Stephen J. Lynton, Washington *Post,* June 10, 1976; "10 Areas Listed to Ease Problems of City's Poor," Washington *Post,* July 1, 1976; "94th Congress Blew Hot and Cold on District Legislation," by Karlyn Baker, Washington *Post,* Oct. 4, 1976; "Mayor Signs District's Gun Law," by Jacqueline Bolder, Washington *Star,* July 24, 1976.

ECONOMY "Civil Service: Poor No More," *Newsweek,* June 28, 1971; "R&D in Washington," by John Carmody, Washington *Post, Potomac,* Dec. 29, 1968; "Lobbyists Shifting Quarters to Capital," by Richard D. Lyons, New York *Times,* June 8, 1975.

CRIME "Wilson to Quit Police," by Martin Weil, Washington *Post,* April 2, 1974; "VIPs Learn about Street Crime," by Carl Bernstein, Washington *Post,* Feb. 1, 1969; "Behind the President's Crime Plan: 2 More Bank Holdups, Fatal Knifing, 2 Arrests in Robbery," Washington *Post,* Feb. 1, 1969; "D.C. Safer than Most Big Cities, New Crime Study Shows," by Orr Kelly, Washington *Star,* Aug. 1, 1975.

METROPOLITAN AREA "Population Change Overtakes Growth as Key to Future for Washington Metropolitan Area," *Metropolitan Bulletin,* June-July 1973; "COG Planners Oppose I-66 Leg," by Jack Eisen, Washington *Post,* Feb. 21, 1974; "Congressman Backs Tax on Commuters," by William Taffe, Washington *Star,* Sept. 19, 1975; "Survey Finds Decline in Black Population in Capital with a Sharp Rise in Suburbs," by Ernest Holsendolph, Washington *Post,* May 20, 1975; "A Beltway Is Creating New Patterns which Increase the Independence of the Suburbs from Their Parent," by George Brier, *City,* January-February 1971; "Beltway Emerges as 'Main Street' of Metro Area as Some Suburban Densities Increase to Urban Levels," *Metropolitan Bulletin,* March 1972.

EDUCATION "More Negroes Turn to Private Schooling," by Lawrence Feinberg, Washington *Post,* Jan. 25, 1970; "Clark Plan Dies, Children Victims," by William Rasberry, Washington *Post,* Jan. 20, 1971; "Black Excellence: A History of Dunbar High," by Thomas Sewell, Washington *Post,* April 28, 1974. "D.C. Has 22 New Schools, A Declining Enrollment," by Lawrence Feinberg, Washington *Post,* Oct. 16, 1976.   ,

GENERAL "Arena Stage: Full Speed Ahead," by Henry Hewes, *Saturday Review,* March 27, 1971; "Kennedy Center Busy Despite Early Fear of Failure," by Barbara Gamarekian, New York *Times,* Dec. 26, 1974; *"Star-News* Control Bought by Texan," by Benjamin Bradlee, Washington *Post,* April 10, 1974; "Washington: A Capital at Last," by Henry Fairlie, Washington *Post,* March 14, 1976; "The Washington Tourists Don't See," by Juan Cameron, *Fortune,* March 1975; "Metro May Prove World's Costliest Ride," by Jack Eisen, Washington *Post,* Sept. 1, 1975.
    "DC Height Ceiling Traced to 1910," by

1973; "City's Core Still In Ruins," by Thomas W. Lippman, Washington *Post,* April 4, 1974; "Neighbors-Inc., No Longer Cares What Color the Neighbors Are," by Barbara Raskin, Washington *Post, Potomac,* Dec. 6, 1970; "Capitol Hill, in Throes of Restoration, Is Rivaling Georgetown for Elegance," New York *Times,* May 30, 1973; "15 Big Firms Bid to Build City Housing," by Thomas W. Lippman, Washington *Post,* April 5, 1974; "In the 1970s, More People Are Moving Out of the Metropolitan Area Than Are Moving In," by Lawrence Feinberg, Washington *Post,* April 29, 1976; "Renewal Gets Under Way in Riot Corridor," by Charles A. Krause, Washington *Post,* Oct. 16, 1976; "The Renovation of Shaw," by LaBarbara Bowman, Washington *Post,* Dec. 6, 1976; "Canal Barge Goes Back Into Operation," by Paul Hodge, Washington *Post,* Sept. 30, 1976. James M. O'Leary, Washington *Post,* July 21,

MARYLAND

Two books were helpful in preparing the chapter on Maryland: *The Story of Maryland Politics* by Frank Richardson Kent (Hartboro: Tradition Press, 1968) and Jules Witcover and Richard Cohen's book on Spiro Agnew, *A Heartbeat Away* (New York: Viking, 1974). Other sources: Regular coverage of the Baltimore *Sun,* Washington *Post,* and Washington *Star.*
    BALTIMORE " 'The Block,' Seat of Old Baltimore's Libido, Awaits Bulldozers," by J. Anthony Lukas, New York *Times,* April 13, 1970; "Baltimore's Bright Prospects," by James J. Kilpatrick, Washington *Star,* June 6, 1974; "Who Runs Baltimore?" by Frank DeFilippo, Baltimore *News-American,* Dec. 17, 1967; "City Fairgoers Jam Harbor," by William Ward, Baltimore *News-American,* Sept. 2, 1974; "Mikulski Sheds Roly-Poly Image," by Bill Peterson, Washington *Post,* April 9, 1976; "Split in Black Vote Seen in Baltimore," by Lawrence Meyer, Washington *Post,* Sept. 12, 1971.
    MARYLAND POLITICS "The Fall of Mr. Law and Order," *Newsweek,* Oct. 22, 1973; "Agnew: A Look at His Governorship," by James B. Rowland, Washington *Star,* Jan. 5, 1969; "When Agnew Was Young and Moderate," by Jules Witcover, *The Progressive,* April 1972; "The Biggest Baltimore Loser of All Time," by Russell Baker, *New York Times Magazine,* Oct. 21, 1973; "Md. Democrats, GOP Shell Out 'Walking Around Money,' " by Richard M. Cohen, Washington *Post,* Oct. 31, 1972; "Corruption in High Places in Maryland," by Wes Barthelmes, Washington *Post,* Aug. 22, 1975; "On 'Corruption' in Annapolis," by Donald B. Robertson, Washington *Post,* Sept. 16, 1975; "Mandel and Patrons: Power in Maryland" and "Mandel Sees 'Class' Enmity," by Fred Barbash, Washington *Post,* June 1 and 2, 1975; "Political Scandal Is a Maryland Tradition," by Peter Jay and John Hannahan, Washington *Post,* Oct. 14, 1973.
    "Gore Drive Begins to Woo Democrats," by Barry C. Rascovar, Baltimore *Sun,* Sept. 15, 1974; "Skill, Gall Make 'Softshoes' a Power," by Richard M. Cohen, Washington *Post,* Feb. 26, 1973; "What's Right and Wrong with the General Assembly," by William S. James and Julian L. Lapides, Baltimore *Sun,* April 28, 1973; "Mathias: Following His Thread of Responsibility," by

Michael Kernan, Washington *Post,* June 2, 1974; "Sarbanes: Private Man in Public Career," by Helen Dewar, Washington *Post,* May 5, 1976; "Gov McKeldin: Supported Civil Rights," by Douglas Watson, Washington *Post,* Aug. 11, 1974; "William L. Hodges, 66, Maryland State Senator," by Fred Barbash, Washington *Post,* Aug. 13, 1974; "Eastern Shore's Talbot: 'What U.S. Used to Be,' " by Peter A. Jay, Washington *Post,* Oct. 20, 1969; "Suburban Democrat Polls Rise," by Richard M. Cohen, Washington *Post,* August 19, 1970; "Cambridge: the Older Order Changes," by Douglas Watson, Washington *Post,* Nov. 11, 1973; "Gov. Mandel, 5 Others Indicted on Fraud, Corruption Charges," by Edward Walsh, Washington *Post,* Nov. 25, 1975; "Mistrial Is Declared in Mandel Case," by Donald P. Baker and Felicity Barringer, Washington *Post,* Dec. 8, 1976; "Mandel Trial: Morality of Md. Politics on the Stand," by Jerry Oppenheimer, Washington *Star,* Sept. 5, 1976; "The Ivy League Ethnic," by Harold J. Logan, Washington *Post,* Oct. 6, 1976; "Beall Defeat Seen Ending Political Era," by Bill Peterson and "Democratic Sweep Leaves Maryland GOP in Crisis," by Harold J. Logan, Washington *Post,* Nov. 4, 1976.
    COLUMBIA "Why No New Columbias?" by William H. Jones, Washington *Post,* March 3, 1974; "Columbia, Planned City, Finds It Shares Woes Facing Unplanned Cities," by Monroe Karmin, *Wall Street Journal,* July 14, 1971.
    CHESAPEAKE BAY "The Old Breed,' by Lee Flor, Washington *Star,* April 27, 1972; "Ocean City Here We Come," by Vicki Olian, *The Washingtonian,* July 1970; "Discover Annapolis," by J. Timberlake Gibson, *The Washingtonian,* November 1970; "Ecologists, Officials See Damage to Chesapeake," by Douglas Watson, Washington *Post,* Nov. 2, 1975; "The Dump," *Newsweek,* July 22, 1974; "Safeguarding the Bay," Washington *Star-News,* June 8, 1974.
    WASHINGTON, D.C. SUBURBS "Sewer Power: The Engineers of Suburban Sprawl," by John Fialka, Washington *Star,* Nov. 16, 1970; "The Outer City: Growth Turning into a Menace," by Linda Greenhouse, New York *Times,* June 3, 1971; "Maryland's Rural Area Growth Up," by Lawrence Feinberg, Washington *Post,* July 6, 1976.

DELAWARE

Among the books most helpful in preparing the chapter were *The Delaware Citizen,* by Cy Liberman, James M. Rosbrow, and Harvey B. Rubenstein (New York: Taplinger, 1967); *The du Ponts of Delaware: A Fantastic Dynasty,* by William H. A. Carr (New York: Dodd, Mead, 1964); and *Delaware: A Guide to the First State,* compiled by writers of the writers' program of the WPA (New York: Viking, American Guide Series, 1938).

GOVERNMENT, POLITICS "Executive Reorganization in Delaware," by James L. Cox, *State Government,* Summer 1970; "A du Pont Looks to Washington," by Theo Lippman, Jr., Baltimore *Sun,* Oct. 12, 1970; "Fiscal Advisers Cost Peterson His Seat," by Robert Schwabach, Philadelphia *Inquirer,* Nov. 9, 1972; "The Battle Is Close and Bitter for Delaware's Governorship," by Robert P. Schwabach, Philadelphia *Inquirer,* Nov. 5, 1972; "Departing Conscience [Sen. John Williams]," by Alan L. Otten, *Wall Street Journal,* June 11, 1970; "No. 4 Republican [John Williams]," by Sam A. Hanna, Wilmington *Journal,* Jan. 3, 1966; "Peterson and His Party," Wilmington *Journal* editorial, May 8, 1972; "Governor from du Pont," New York *Times,* Jan. 22, 1969.

ECONOMY *The Company State: Ralph Nader's Study Group Report on Delaware,* by James Phelan and Robert Pozen (Washington: Grossman, 1972); "Delaware's Reign Seems Fading," by Kristin Goff, July 21, 1974; "Du Pont to Abandon Dynamite Production for Safer Explosive, Marking End of Era," by Jerry E. Bishop, *Wall Street Journal,* Jan. 25, 1974; "Du Pont Wins SEC Approval to Absorb Christiana, as Family's Control Wanes," *Wall Street Journal,* Dec. 16, 1974; "Boss-to-Be at Du Pont Is an Immigrant's Son Who Climbed Hard Way," by Thomas J. Bray, *Wall Street Journal,* Dec. 14, 1971; "Lammot du Pont Copeland Jr. Is Surviving Nicely in Wake of Stunning Financial Collapse," by Thomas J. Bray, *Wall Street Journal,* May 8, 1974; "Du Pont Co. Planners Stake Future Growth on Current Changes," by John E. Cooney, *Wall Street Journal,* Jan. 20, 1972; "Du Pont Scion's Woes Spotlight the Influence of Family in Delaware," by Thomas J. Bray, *Wall Street Journal,* Dec. 4, 1970; "How a du Pont Scion with Millions Ended in Bankruptcy Court," by Thomas J. Bray, *Wall Street Journal,* Nov. 11, 1970; "Anti-du Pont Talk: Predictable, but Sometimes Relevant," by John G. Craig, Jr., Wilmington *News,* July 4, 1969; "A Management Leapfrog at Du Pont," *Business Week,* Dec. 15, 1973.

ENVIRONMENT "Delaware Bars Heavy Industry from Coasts to Curb Pollution," by Donald Janson, New York *Times,* June 29, 1971; "Oil Crisis Aids War on Delaware Law," by George C. Wilson, Washington *Post,* Feb. 5, 1974; "1971 Coastal Law Delaware Issue," New York *Times,* Feb. 17, 1974; "A Debate Over Delaware's Tough Coastal-Use Law," *Business Week,* March 2, 1974; "Delaware Law Halting Development on Coast, Seen as Ecological Milestone, Is Threatened," by Harry B. Anderson, *Wall Street Journal,* March 15, 1974.

PRESS "Du Pont Newspapers in Delaware Shaken by News-Control Dispute," by Martin Arnold, New York *Times,* Jan. 6, 1975; "2 Editors Quit, 2 Fired in Dispute at Wilmington, Del., Newspaper," by Andrew Wallace, Washington *Post,* Jan. 3, 1975; "Norman Isaacs Is Named Head of 2 Newspapers in Wilmington," by Martin Arnold, New York *Times,* Jan. 21, 1975; "News-Journal Denies Issue Was 'Control'," by Andrew Wallace, Washington *Post,* Jan. 4, 1975; "The Second Battle of Wilmington," by Philip M. Boffey, *Columbia Journalism Review,* March/April 1975; "A Behind-the-Scene Account of the Wilmington Crisis," by Carla Marie Rupp, *Editor & Publisher,* Feb. 8, 1975.

WILMINGTON "Wilmington: Under Guard," *Newsweek,* Oct. 14, 1968; "Renewal Hits Business Most," by Cy Liberman, Wilmington *Journal,* May 6, 1969; "On the House," by Art Spikol, *Philadelphia Magazine,* March 1974; "Wilmington Does with Less and Manages to Pay Its Bills," by Seth S. King, New York *Times,* June 15, 1975; "Cut Costs and Keep Up Services? Some Cities Know How," by Harry Toland, Philadelphia *Bulletin,* March 30, 1975; "What's Doing Around Wilmington," by Donald Janson, New York *Times,* April 27, 1975; "Urban Homesteading," by Dee Wedemeyer, *Nation's Cities,* January 1975.

OTHER "Educational TV Dies in Delaware; Critic Says It Avoided Mathematics," by James R. Conant, *National Observer,* Aug. 3, 1970; "Du Pont and Delaware: Academic Life Behind the Nylon Curtain," by Philip M. Boffey, *Science,* May 10, 1968; "The 'Chateau Country' of Delaware Is Hard to Beat for Affluence," by Thomas J. Bray, *Wall Street Journal,* March 21, 1973; "Rehoboth Beach Is Sprucing up for Influx of Washingtonians," by James T. Wooten, New York *Times,* April 27, 1974; "Winterthur: Elegance in Early America," by James Daniel, *Reader's Digest,* August 1973.

PENNSYLVANIA

Considering its size and importance, Pennsylvania has been the subject of remarkably few modern-day books. Among the works to which primary reference was made on the statewide scene were: *The Middle Atlantic States,* by Ezra Bowen (New York: Time-Life Library of America, 1968); *Pennsylvania Politics,* revised edition, by Edward F. Cooke and Edward G. Janosik (New York: Holt, Rinehart & Winston, 1965); *Discover the New Pennsylvania* (Harrisburg: Pennsylvania Department of Commerce, 1967); *Poverty in Pennsylvania* (Harrisburg: Community Services of Pennsylvania, 1968); "Pennsylvania," by Conrad Richter, chapter in *American Panorama* (Garden City, N.Y.: Doubleday, 1960); *Pennsylvania—A Guide to the Keystone State,* compiled by the Writers' Program of the WPA (New York: Oxford, 1940); *New Growth . . . New Jobs for Pennsylvania,* by Milton J. Shapp and Ernest H. Jurkat (Philadelphia: Shapp Foundation, 1962);

"Pennsylvania: Business As Usual," chapter in *States in Crisis*, by James Reichley (Chapel Hill: University of North Carolina Press, 1964); *Pennsylvania: Birthplace of a Nation*, by Sylvester Kirby Stevens (New York: Random House, 1964).

Other Sources: Regular coverage of the Philadelphia *Evening Bulletin*, Philadelphia *Inquirer*, Pittsburgh *Press*, and *Philadelphia Magazine*, as well as the following articles:

STATE GOVERNMENT "It's Twilight in Pennsylvania and the Bills Are Coming Due," by James M. Perry, *National Observer*, Dec. 14, 1970; "Income Tax Voted in Pennsylvania," New York *Times*, March 5, 1971; "Shafer Signs Public Employee Strike Bill," by Sanford R. Starobin, Washington *Post*, July 26, 1970; "Some Health Care Industry Reform," by Judith Randal, Washington *Star*, March 22, 1971; "Has Constitutional Reform Ruined Ray Shafer?" *Ripon Forum*, June 1968.

LEGISLATURE "The House of Ill Repute," by Bernard McCormick, *Philadelphia Magazine*, November 1969; "Pennsylvania Legislature Not in the Top 20," by Rem Rieder, Philadelphia *Bulletin*, Feb. 3, 1971; "New Lawmakers?" by Robert Heath and Joseph H. Melrose, Jr., *National Civic Review*, October 1969; "The Electronic Age and the Pennsylvania Legislature," by R. D. Steighner, *State Government*, Spring 1968; "A State Legislature Is Not Always a Model of Ideal Government," by Jack H. Morris, *Wall Street Journal*, July 28, 1971.

EDUCATION "Students Lobby in Pennsylvania," by Donald Janson, New York *Times*, Feb. 16, 1970; "Saving Parochial Schools," *Time*, Dec. 19, 1969.

ENVIRONMENT "Our Stinking Schuylkill," series of articles by Gary Brooten, Philadelphia *Bulletin*, Sept. 29, 30, Oct. 1, 1970; "Waste Lagoons in State Likened to 'Time Bomb,'" by Gary Brooten, Philadelphia *Bulletin*, Nov. 17, 1970; "The Battle to Save the Susquehanna," by Fred Jones, *Pittsburgh Press*, Oct. 1, 1970; "Donora, Pennsylvania," by Croswell Bowen, *Atlantic Monthly*, November 1970; "Legal Watchdogs Fight Pollution," *Saturday Review*, April 3, 1971.

POLITICS "Jim Duff Died As He Lived—Making His Own Way," Pittsburgh *Press*, Dec. 21, 1969; "Rating the Legislators," by Dan Rottenberg and Alexandra Sandler, *Philadelphia Magazine*, October 1974; "Getting Something for the Money," by Rose DeWolf, *The Nation*, Nov. 1, 1971; "Insurance Regulator in Pennsylvania Stirs Disputes and Headlines," by Thomas J. Bray, *Wall Street Journal*, Feb. 1, 1972; "Gulf, Goodyear Disclose Gifts to Nixon Fund," by William Chapman, Washington *Post*, Aug. 11, 1973; "Defying Predictions, Shapp Proves Re-Electable," by Stephen Isaacs, Washington *Post*, May 19, 1974; "But How Can He Get To Be a 'Serious' Candidate," by Jack W. Germond, Washington *Star*, June 11, 1975; "There's An Issue in the Penna. Auditor's Race," by Paul Critchlow, Philadelphia *Inquirer*, March 28, 1976.

CONGRESS "The Politician Starring Hugh Scott," by Julius Duscha, *Washingtonian Magazine*, October 1970; "Whips in the Senate," by Roy Reed, New York *Times*, Jan. 4, 1969; "Pepper Pot—Recessional," *Philadelphia Magazine*, December 1968; "Pennsylvania—Case History of Decay," *Time*, Oct. 18, 1968.

STEEL, THE STEELWORKERS "Trying to Avoid an Unwanted Strike," *Time*, May 24, 1971; "A New U.S. Campaign," *Newsweek*, March 1, 1971; "Foreign Threats to a Basic Industry—Interview with Edwin H. Gott, Chairman of U.S.

Steel Corporation," *U.S. News and World Report*, Oct. 26, 1970; "Young Workers Raising Voices for Factory and Union Changes," by Agis Salpukas, New York *Times*, June 1, 1970; "The Steelworkers' Militant Mood Deepens," *Business Week*, April 3, 1971; "Abel of Steelworkers," by Robert Walker, New York *Times*, Oct. 25, 1970; "New Steel-Mill Rules Open Good Jobs to Blacks," by Ed Townsend, *Christian Science Monitor*, June 2, 1973.

COAL, THE UMW "Anarchy Threatens the Kingdom of Coal," by Thomas O'Hanlon, *Fortune*, January 1971; "Coal Mining," by A. Britton Hume, *Atlantic Monthly*, November 1969; "UMW Money Maze," by George Lardner, Jr., Washington *Post*, Feb. 28, 1971; "Rough, Tough Yablonski Accepted Death Risk," by Fred Barnes, Washington *Star*, Jan. 6, 1970; "A Coal Town: Boom Times Have Returned, but for How Long?" by Earl D. Caldwell, New York *Times*, Dec. 30, 1973; "Anthracite Industry Barely Survives in U.S.; Costs Up, Demand Off," by Bob Harwood, *Wall Street Journal*, June 2, 1972.

RAILROADS "The Penn Central," by Rush Loving, Jr., *Fortune*, August 1970; "Penn Central Officials in Investment Club Used Insider Information, Patman Charges," *Wall Street Journal*, Feb. 16, 1971; "How Decaying Service, Bickering Officials Led to Penn Central Crisis," *Wall Street Journal*, June 12, 1970; "Pennsy Officials Bought 'Wrongdoing' Insurance," by H. L. Schwartz III, *Associated Press Dispatch*, Jan. 25, 1971.

GEOGRAPHY "Wincanton: The Politics of Corruption," by John A. Gardiner, (Washington: Government Printing Office, 1967); "The Disaster that Won't Go Away," by Robert Douglas Mead, *Philadelphia Magazine*, May 1973.

PHILADELPHIA—GENERAL *The Perennial Philadelphians*, by Nathaniel Burt (Boston: Little, Brown, 1963); *Philadelphia Gentlemen*, by E. Digby Baltzell (Glencoe, Ill.: The Free Press, 1968); "Survival Through Planning—Philadelphia's Style," chapter in *Cities in a Race with Time*, by Jeanne R. Lowe (New York: Vintage Books, Random House, 1958); *Philadelphia Magazine Guide*, by Nancy Love (Philadelphia: Philadelphia Magazine, 1965); "Philadelphia, a Triumph over Time," by John Keats, *Holiday*, April 1971; "Philadelphia," by George Sessions Perry, *Saturday Evening Post*, Sept. 14, 1946; "The Champ's Town," by David Butwin, *Saturday Review*, April 3, 1971.

PHILADELPHIA—GOVERNMENT AND POLITICS "Urban Renewal Beset by Delay and Scandal in Fourth Biggest City," by Stephen J. Sanswet, *Wall Street Journal*, March 17, 1970; "Richardson Dilworth: My Dream for Philadelphia," Philadelphia *Bulletin Magazine*, Oct. 3, 1965.

"Why the Democrats Sing Chorus of Big-City Blues," by James R. Dickenson, *National Observer*, Dec. 22, 1969; "Plumber's Friend," by Gaeton Fonzi and Greg Walter, *Philadelphia Magazine*, October 1967; "Jim Does the Job but Civic Types Leave Him Cold," by Joseph R. Daughen, Philadelphia *Bulletin*, July 29, 1968; "Supercop," *Newsweek*, March 15, 1971; "Philadelphia Nominee," by Donald Janson, New York *Times*, May 20, 1971; "Philadelphia Boomerang," by James Higgins, *The Nation*, Oct. 12, 1970; "It's Hard to Be Neutral about Super Cop," by Fred Hamilton and Jon Katz, Philadelphia *Daily News*, Feb. 3, 1971; "Right Now, Rizzo Faces Long Odds," by Paul Critchlow, Philadelphia *Inquirer*, Sept. 19, 1976; "Mr. Rizzo Declares War on the Public's Trust," editorial in Philadelphia *Inquirer*,

June 17, 1976; "Phila. Fiscal Prospects Dim," *Journal of Commerce*, Oct. 14, 1976; "A Financial Tale of Two Cities: It is a Scary Story," by George Wilson, Philadelphia *Inquirer*, Oct. 15, 1976.

"The Union League Club of Philadelphia Clings to Conservative Ways," by Glynn Mapes, *Wall Street Journal*, Sept. 23, 1968; "The Pews of Philadelphia," by Michael C. Jensen, New York *Times*, Oct. 10, 1971.

"Philadelphia Teachers Out Despite Court Injunction," by Jo Ann Levine, *Christian Science Monitor*, Jan. 13, 1973; "End of a Strike," *Time*, March 12, 1973; "Politics of Compassion," by Roderick MacLeish, *Christian Science Monitor*, Feb. 1, 1974. "Rizzo Plays an Old Political Game with City Payroll," by Creed Black, Philadelphia *Inquirer*, Aug. 10, 1975; "In West Philadelphia, Gang Wars Are a Way of Death," by Wayne King, June 11, 1976.

PHILADELPHIA—ECONOMY "Headquarters Have Human Problems," by Elizabeth P. Deutermann, *Business Review*, February 1970; "Penn Central Debacle Creates Repercussions in Much of Philadelphia," by Jack H. Morris, *Wall Street Journal*, Aug. 10, 1970; "Jack Bunting, the All-American Boy Banker," by Willard S. Randall, *Philadelphia Magazine*, February 1971; "Bunting's Bet," *Time*, June 28, 1971; "Suburban Shift Problem to Philadelphia's Blacks," New York *Times*, Nov. 16, 1969; "Easy Ride on a Philadelphia Transit Line," by Robert Lindsey, New York *Times*, Feb. 16, 1970.

PHILADELPHIA—RELIGION "Bishop De-Witt Awakens Diocese to Issues Long Kept under Wraps," by Willard S. Randall, Philadelphia *Bulletin*, Sept. 2, 1969; "The Changing Catholic Church," by Willard S. Randall, series in Philadelphia *Bulletin*, May 24–31, 1970.

PHILADELPHIA—PUBLISHING "The Saturday Evening Post's Resurrection Is Planned by Curtis," *Wall Street Journal*, Nov. 6, 1970; "Post Mortem," by Charles MacNamara, *Philadelphia Magazine*, September 1970; *Decline and Fall*, by Otto Friedrich (New York: Harper & Row, 1970); *The Curtis Affair*, by Martin S. Ackerman (Los Angeles: Nash Publishing, 1970); "Return of the Post," *Time*, June 14, 1971; "Review of *Annenberg*," by Edward W. Barrett, *Columbia Journalism Review*, Spring 1970; "The Knights Invade Philadelphia," by Eugene L. Meyer, *Columbia Journalism Review*, May/June 1971; "Newspapers Vie in Philadelphia," by Donald Janson, New York *Times*, Dec. 6, 1970; "Getting the Old Lady off Her Duff," by Bernard McCormick, *Philadelphia Magazine*, October 1969; "The Name of This Game Is *Philadelphia Magazine*," by Robert W. Ankerson, *Pennsylvania Gazette*, March 1970.

"The *Bulletin* Cranks Up for Battle," by Dan Rottenberg, *Philadelphia Magazine*, August 1973; "Action in the Afternoon," by Bill Mandel, *Philadelphia Magazine*, June 1975.

PHILADELPHIA—GEOGRAPHY *Man Made Philadelphia*, by Richard S. Wurman and John Andrew Gallery (Cambridge, Mass.: Philadelphia Magazine—MIT Press, 1971); "Tales of Little Italy," by Jim Riggio, *Philadelphia Magazine*, March 1971; "There's Plenty of Love in That Small Town Called South Phila.," by Peter H. Binzen, Philadelphia *Bulletin*, Dec. 7, 1969.

PHILADELPHIA—BLACKS *The Philadelphia Negro*—A Social Study, by W. E. B. Du Bois, with an introduction by E. Digby Baltzell (New York: Schocken Books, 1967); "The Blacks of Philadelphia," by Joseph R. Daughen, Philadelphia *Bulletin*, Dec. 6, 1970; "Right On!" by Maury Levy, *Philadelphia Magazine*, June 1970; "Black Mayor for Philadelphia in the '70s?" by Sandy Grady, Philadelphia *Bulletin*, June 21, 1970; *Housing in Philadelphia* and *Criminal Justice in Philadelphia* (Information Papers issued by the Greater Philadelphia Movement, March 1971); *Build Brother Build*, by Leon H. Sullivan (Philadelphia: Macrae Smith, 1969); "A Black Director Pushes Reforms at GM," *Business Week*, April 10, 1971.

PITTSBURGH "The New Coalition—Pittsburgh's Action Formula Saves a City," chapter of *Cities in a Race with Time*, by Jeanne Lowe (New York: Vintage Books, Random House, 1968); *Pittsburgh—The Story of an American City*, by Stefan Lorant (Garden City, N.Y.: Doubleday, 1964); *Reports of the Allegheny Conference on Community Development* for 1968, 1969, 1970; *Social Planning in Pittsburgh—A Preliminary Appraisal* (Kansas City, Mo.: Institute for Community Studies, 1969—Homer C. Wadsworth, project director); "Pittsburgh—Is It Pennsylvania's Second City . . . or Its First?" by Jack Markowitz, *Philadelphia Magazine*, September 1969; "See How Pittsburgh Got Itself Cleaned Up," by John Koenig, Jr., Washington *Post*, Nov. 15, 1970; "Pittsburgh: A Brawny City Puts on a Silk Shirt," by Douglas E. Kneeland, New York *Times*, Oct. 3, 1970; "Nobody's Boy in Pittsburgh," by Donald Janson, *The Progressive*, June 1970; "Pittsburgh Renewal Plan Completes Major Phase," by Donald Janson, New York *Times*, Nov. 29, 1969; "An Old Fortune Moves On," by Michael C. Jensen, New York *Times*, May 2, 1971; Pittsburgh Cracks Down on Polluters," *Business Week*, Dec. 27, 1969.

"Lochinvar of the West," by Stuart Brown, *Philadelphia Magazine*, January 1971; "Pittsburgh's Flaherty: Nobody's Boy," by James P. Gannon, *Wall Street Journal*, Jan. 22, 1971; "The View from Mellon," by Alvin Rosensweet, New York *Times*, Sept. 29, 1974.

NEW JERSEY

The best general history of New Jersey is John T. Cunningham's *New Jersey—America's Main Road* (Garden City, N.Y.: Doubleday, 1966); the same author has also written an interesting account, *Newark* (Newark: New Jersey Historical Society, 1966). The New Jersey League of Women Voters published in 1969 an excellent examination of state policy and programs, *New Jersey—Spotlight on Government*, ed. Elizabeth Brody with an introduction by Richard P. McCormick (League of Women Voters, Montclair). Other helpful sources included: *The Gateway States*, by Seymour Freedgood (New York: Time-Life Library of America, 1967); "New Jersey," by Carl L. Biemiller, chapter in *American Panorama* (Garden City, N.Y.: Doubleday, 1960); and *Six Cities Forward*, by John T. Cunningham (a promotional folder published by Public Service Electric and Gas Co., Newark, about 1970).

Other sources: Regular coverage of New Jersey events in the Newark *Evening News*, the New York *Times* and Philadelphia *Evening Bulletin*, and the following articles:

POLITICS "I Am The Law," by Thomas J. Fleming, *American Heritage,* June 1969; "Ten From New Jersey—A Report on the State's Ten Most Influential People," by John T. McGowan, Newark *Sunday News,* May 31, 1970; *Financing Campaigns for Governor: New Jersey, 1965,* by Herbert E. Alexander and Kevin L. McKeough (Princeton: Citizens Research Foundation, 1969).

"Critics Call Gov. Byrne a calamity for Jersey; Feud, Vacancies Cited," by William M. Carley, *Wall Street Journal,* Sept. 8, 1975; "Bill Is Passed in Jersey to Alter Primary Voting," by Ronald Sullivan, New York *Times,* Nov. 25, 1975; "Campaign Disclosure Law Nearly Nullified in Jersey," by Joseph Sullivan, New York *Times,* Aug. 16, 1975; "A Byrned Out Case," by Tony Green, *Philadelphia Magazine,* July 1975; "A Blueblood with a Social Conscience," by Louise Sweeney, *Christian Science Monitor,* June 25, 1975; "New Jersey Is a Wasteland (No Major TV Station)," by Les Brown, New York *Times,* Jan. 26, 1975; "The 15 Most Powerful People in New Jersey," New York *Times,* Jan. 11, 1975.

"Impeachment Unit's Head Wears His Status Uneasily," by Martin Tolchin, New York *Times,* January 17, 1974; "Peter W. Rodino, Jr.: Little Known New Jersey Congressman Finds Himself in Rare Spotlight," by Richard L. Lyons, Washington *Post,* Nov. 15, 1973.

STATE GOVERNMENT "Praise for N.J. a Welcome Rarity," by William May, Newark *News,* Sept. 27, 1970; "Jersey Justice Has Prestige, but Problems, Too," by Lesley Oelsner, New York *Times,* Sept. 17, 1970; "Youth's Death Changed N.J. Drug Laws," by Leon Zimmerman, Atlanta *Journal and Constitution,* Jan. 17, 1971; "Cahill's Plan to Reduce Drug Penalties Enacted," by Ronald Sullivan, New York *Times,* Oct. 9, 1970; "New Jersey Master-Zoning Fight Looms," by Peter Bridge, *Christian Science Monitor,* Aug. 15, 1970; "N.J.'s Lottery: Hope Sells for 50 Cents," by Rose De Wolf, Philadelphia *Bulletin,* Dec. 18, 1970; *Direction for Urban Progress* (interim report of the New Jersey Select Legislative Committee on Civil Disorders in Urban Affairs), State Senator James H. Wallwork, chairman, January 1969; "Ex-Gov. Hughes Is Named as Chief Justice by Cahill," by Ronald Sullivan, New York *Times,* Nov. 8, 1973; "Black To Be Sworn In as N. J. Speaker," by Neil Lewis, Washington *Post,* January 8, 1974; "Plan Snagged by Tax Needs," by Martin Gansberg, New York *Times;* "Jersey Town's Zoning Is Voided: Court Orders Housing for Poor," by Ronald Sullivan, New York *Times,* May 3, 1972; "Court to Shut Schools If Aid Law Isn't Funded," by Robert Cohen, Newark *Star Ledger,* May 14, 1976; "Income Tax Bill Passed in Jersey by Both Houses," by Alfonso A. Narvaez, New York *Times,* July 9, 1976.

"New Jersey Acts on Transportation," by David J. Goldberg, *State Government,* Autumn 1968; "The New Jersey Department of Community Affairs," by Paul N. Ylvisaker, *The Urban Lawyer,* Winter 1971; "The Workings of Urban Politics, Problems, and Alleged Payoffs Within Paul Ylvisaker's New Jersey," by Louise Campbell, *City,* April–August 1969; "Public Advocate Coming of Age," by Bradley Graham, Trenton *Evening Times,* Nov. 19, 1975.

ENVIRONMENT "Jersey Cites Shore Area Water Pollution Crisis," and "Jersey Extends Ban on Dumping," by Ronald Sullivan, New York *Times,* May 9 and June 2, 1971; "The Pine Barrens," *Princeton Alumni Weekly,* April 20, 1971; "Cancer-on-the-Job, Hazard in N.J.," *Newsday,* Feb. 8, 1976.

EDUCATION "A Rating of Graduate Schools," by John M. Fenton, *Princeton Alumni Weekly,* Jan. 26, 1971; "Changing Times Beset Princeton Clubs," New York *Times,* May 18, 1970; "The Institute Advances," *Newsweek,* April 6, 1970; "New Jersey Fails to Enact School Funding Plan," *National Civic Review,* February 1975; "New Jersey's Need Is New Math to Pay for Schools," by Edward B. Fiske, New York *Times,* Dec. 22, 1974.

ECONOMY "A Pill-Giving Maverick," by Judy Gurovitz, *Life,* February 1969; "N. J. Laws Now Lure Industry," AP Dispatch, New York *Times,* May 25, 1969; "Jersey's Economic Illness Called Chronic by Analysts," by Lee Dembart, New York *Times,* March 10, 1975; "Will Jersey City Replace Wall St.?" by Richard Phalon, New York *Times,* Oct. 12, 1975.

CRIME "The Mob's Grip on New Jersey," by William Schulz, *Reader's Digest,* February 1971; "Jersey Legislature Approves Stiff Anticrime Bills," by Ronald Sullivan, New York *Times,* May 8, 1970; "The Mafia in Jersey: Nervous and No Longer Above the Law," by Ronald Sullivan, New York *Times,* March 16, 1970; "How 'Mama' and 'Andy' Helped to Break up a Mafia Organization," by Monroe W. Karmin, *Wall Street Journal,* April 27, 1971; "Why New Jersey?" by Richard Reeves, New York *Times,* Dec. 16, 1969; "The Cosa Nostra Finally Is Put on the Defensive," by Patrick Young, *National Observer,* Dec. 22, 1969; "Jersey I.R.S. Men Backed, But New Indictments Loom," by Ronald Sullivan, New York *Times,* Dec. 17, 1969; "A Jersey Legislator Cited on Bar Ethics; 2nd Guilty in U.S. Suit," by Ronald Sullivan, New York *Times* Feb. 24 1971; "An Overseer of Mafia," by Charles Grutzner, New York *Times,* Dec. 19, 1968; "FBI Tapes Underworld Talk," UPI Dispatch, Washington *Star,* Jan. 7, 1970; "Jersey Leaders Deny Mafia Ties Implied on Tapes," by Douglas Robinson, New York *Times,* Jan. 7, 1970; "In Jersey They Are Calling It a 'Pogrom'," by Sidney E. Zion, New York *Times,* Dec. 21, 1969; "Jersey Investigation," New York *Times,* Dec. 18, 1968; "Corruption by Consent," *Time,* Dec. 26, 1969; "The Mob: New Jersey's Second Government," by William Federici and David Hardy, New York *Daily News,* Jan. 23, 1969; "Can the Garden State Weed Out Organized Crime?" by William Federici and David Hardy, New York *Daily News,* Jan. 24, 1969; "Knowlton, Burkhardt Indicted in Building Firm Shakedowns," by Robert Rudolph, Newark *Star-Ledger,* Aug. 12, 1971; "N. J. Politico Indicted in 2.4 M Fraud," by Alex Michelini, New York *Daily News,* Aug. 26, 1971; "Foot Patrolman Decries Politics" by Alfonso A. Narvaez New York *Times,* Nov. 30, 1975.

"The Clean-up Of New Jersey," by Fred J. Cook, *The Nation,* July 16, 1973; "Young Crime Buster Seeks New Scalps," by Peter Bridge, *National Observer,* Nov. 20, 1971; "He Threw the Rascals Out," by Jerome Wilson, *New York,* Oct. 2, 1972; "Who Was Who in New Jersey," by Jerome Wilson, *New York,* July 16, 1973; "Battle On Corruption Carries Jersey Crusader To Bench," by Stephen Issacs, Washington *Post,* Dec. 10, 1973; "NJ Republican Leader Indicted in Funds Case," by Stephen Issacs, Washington *Post,* May 23, 1973; "Sherwin and 2 Are Guilty of Conspiracy in Road Bid," by Joseph F. Sullivan, New York *Times,* Oct. 27, 1972; "Representative Gallagher Pleads Guilty to '66 Income Tax Evasion," Washington *Star News,* Dec. 22, 1972; "Mayor of Camden Indicted in Bid-Rigging Conspiracy," by Ronald Sullivan, New York *Times,* December 14, 1973; "Jersey Senate President Indicted With 2 Others in Liquor

Bribery," by Joseph F. Sullivan, New York *Times*, Oct. 13, 1976.

HUDSON COUNTY "Where the Ward Politicians Still Call the Shots," by Martin Arnold, New York *Times*, Nov. 22, 1970; "Crime Gaze Hits New Jersey County," by Peter J. Bridge, *Christian Science Monitor*, Aug. 3, 1970; "Jersey Mayor Indicted with 3 Alleged Mafiosi," by Ronald Sullivan, New York *Times*, May 7, 1970; "John J. Kenny, Ousted Hudson County Leader, Is Indicted for Extortion," by Ronald Sullivan, New York *Times*, Sept. 16, 1970; "Jersey City Mayor, Aides Are Indicted," Washington *Post*, Nov. 17, 1970; "Reversal of Kenny Organization's Mayoral Strategy Beclouds Race in Jersey City," by Ronald Sullivan, New York *Times*, Oct. 7, 1971; "Dr. Jordan Breaks Grip of Jersey City Machine," by Roger Harris and Lawrence H. Hall, Newark *Star-Ledger*, Nov. 3, 1971.

PHILADELPHIA ORBIT "Fasten Your Seatbelts. You Are Now Entering Camden," by Barry Rosenberg, *Philadelphia Magazine*, October 1968; "The Trouble Maker," by Barry Rosenberg, *Philadelphia Magazine*, September 1970; "Forgotten Camden Faces Uncertain Future," by Leroy F. Aarons Washington *Post*, April 6, 1969; "Trenton's Watergate," *Passaic Herald News* March 4, 1975.

ATLANTIC CITY "A Dowager's Decline," *Newsweek*, June 8, 1970; "No Tears for Atlantic City," by Anthony M. Rey (letters to the editor), *Newsweek*, June 22, 1970; "Bust-Out Town," by Gaeton Fonzi and Bernard McCormick, *Philadelphia Magazine*, August 1970; "Atlantic County Under Scrutiny," by Joseph Carragher, Newark *Star-Ledger*, Aug. 14, 1971.

NEWARK—GENERAL "Newark Held an Angry and Anguished City," by Fox Butterfield, New York *Times*, April 12, 1971; "The First Nine Months" by Peter J. Bridge, Newark *Sunday News*, March 21, 1971; "Gibson Finds Graft Worse than Expected" by David K. Shipler, New York *Times*, Sept. 20, 1970; "The City Politic," by Frank Borsky, *New York*, Feb 9, 1970; "Is Newark Where the Death Throes of Cities Are Starting?" by Theo Lippman, Jr., Baltimore *Sun*, June 8, 1969; *Testimony before the Joint Economic Committee of the 92nd Congress*, by Mayor Kenneth A. Gibson, January 22, 1971; "Gibson Is Widely Regarded As Successful in Restoring Integrity to City Hall," by Fox Butterworth, New York *Times*, Oct. 3. 1971; "Gibson's Rx for Newark's Ills: Large Doses of Federal Funds," by Thomas A. Johnson, New York *Times*, Feb. 23, 1976; "Elizabeth is a Small City with Problems All Its Own," by Gary Hoenig, New York *Times*, Oct. 12, 1975.

NEWARK—RACE "Police Brutality Seen Rising under Gibson in Newark," by Larry Jackson, Washington *Post*, May 8, 1971; *Report of the National Advisory Committee on Civil Disorders* (Washington, 1968); "Autopsy in Newark," *Newsweek*, Feb. 19, 1968; "What Are the Problems of Health Care Delivery in Newark?" by Paul N. Ylvisaker, reprint from *Medicine in the Ghetto* (New York: Meredith, 1969); "Gibson Called a 'Puppet' by Baraka in Open Split," by Joseph Sullivan, New York *Times*, Aug. 18, 1973; "Baraka Constructing a Spiritual and Political Base for a Worldwide Nation of Blacks," by Rudy Johnson, New York *Times*, Feb. 4, 1974.

NEWARK—POLITICS AND GOVERNMENT "Hugh Joseph Addonizio," by Robert D. McFadden, New York *Times*, June 16, 1970; "Riches Cited as Motive of Addonizio," by George Lardner, Jr., Washington *Post*, June 6, 1970; "Addonizio, 4 Others Are Found Guilty," AP Dispatch, Washington *Star*, July 23, 1970; "Savage Strike in Newark," *Time*, April 19, 1971; "Newark at the Brink," *Newsweek*, April 26, 1971; "Baraka Abandons 'Racism' as Ineffective and Shifts to 'Scientific Socialism' of Marx," by Joseph F. Sullivan, New York *Times*, Dec. 27, 1974; "Newark's Worry: 'Black Flight,' " by Luis Overbea, *Christian Science Monitor*, July 11, 1975.

NEW YORK

For an overview of New York's development, no book is finer than *A History of New York State*, by David M. Ellis, James A. Frost, Harold C. Syrett, and Harry J. Carman (Ithaca, New York: Cornell University Press, 1967). Other books that provided valuable background: *The Gateway States*, by Seymour Freedgood (New York: Time-Life Library of America, 1967); *New York State Statistical Yearbook*, by Theresa M. Speciale (Albany, New York: New York State Division of the Budget, Office of Statistical Coordination, 1970); *New York: A Guide to the Empire State*, compiled by writers of the Writers' Project Administration of the WPA, American Guide Series (New York: Oxford University Press, 1940); *Politics in the Empire State*, by Warren Moscow (New York: Knopf, 1948); *Profile of a City* by Economics Department, First National City Bank (New York: McGraw Hill, 1972).

Other sources: Regular coverage of the New York *Times*, New York *Daily News*, *New York* magazine, *Newsday*, the Gannett newspapers, *Empire State Report*, and the following articles:

STATE GOVERNMENT "Anti-Racial Bill Signed by Dewey," by Leo Egan, New York *Times*, March 13, 1945; "1948 Revisited: A Political Lesson," by Henry Owen, Washington *Post*, April 7, 1971; "Elder Statesman: Thomas E. Dewey," *Newsweek*, March 29, 1971.

"The Public Record of Nelson A. Rockefeller," *Congressional Quarterly Weekly Report*, July 21, 1967; "The Case against Nelson Rockefeller," by Jack Newfield, *New York*, March 9, 1970.

"New York's Mr. Urban Renewal," by Richard Schickel, New York *Times Magazine*, March 1, 1970; "Notes from the Underground" by John Fischer, *Harper's Magazine*, February 1970; "The Wholly Ronan Empire," by Fred C. Shapiro, New York *Times Magazine*, May 17, 1970.

"Rising Protests and Lawsuits Shake Routine in State Prisons," by Michael T. Kaufman, New York *Times*, Nov. 15, 1970; "Troubles Persist in Prison at Auburn," by Michael T. Kaufman, New York *Times*, May 17, 1971; "Once a Community Blight, Sing Sing Prison Now Mourned by Neighbors," by Owen Moritz, *National Observer*, April 6, 1970; "Governor Defends Order to Quell Attica Uprising," by William E. Farrell, New York *Times*, Sept. 16, 1971; " 'New Breed' Sparked Attica Uprising," by Philip D. Carter and Stephen Isaacs, Washington *Post*, Sept. 15, 1971; "Prison Paradox: Life for Many Inmates Improves, but Chances of More Atticas Rise," *Wall Street Journal*, Sept. 16, 1971; "Abortion Reform after Long Fight," by Bill Kovach. New York *Times*, April 12, 1970; "State Crisis: The Same Only Different" by Linda Greenhouse, New York *Times*,

Dec. 12, 1975; "Can Carey Keep His Pledge to Businessmen," by Amy Plumer, *Empire State Report*, January/February, 1976; "To Survive in Adversity, Region Must Pull Together," by John B. Keither New York *Times*, April 4, 1976; "A View of N.Y. in Economic Pinch," by Jim Klurfeld, Feb. 13, 1976; "Experts: Balance State Budget Fast," *Newsweek*, Feb. 13, 1976; "Has Carey Kept His Promise to Business?," by Frank Comes, *Empire State Report*, September 1976; "The Second First Carey Administration," by Steven R. Weisman, New York *Times*, Oct. 3, 1976; "Sound Rule on Stavisky," editorial in New York *Times*, Aug. 25, 1976; "Attica Is Termed as Bad as Before 1971 Rebellion," by Fred Ferretti, New York *Times*, July 21, 1976; "The Prisons As Always, Are Short on Real Reform," by Rinker Buck, New York *Times*, Aug. 29, 1976; "Impact of Stiff Drug Law Is in Dispute After 2 Years," by Selwyn Raab, New York *Times*, March 29, 1976; "U.S. Study Backs Critics of New York's Drug Law," New York *Times*, Sept. 5, 1976; "State Takeover of Court Costs Voted in Albany," by Linda Greenhouse, New York *Times*, Aug. 5, 1976.

LEGISLATURE "Lobbyists Play Big Role in Albany Lawmaking," by David K. Shipler, New York *Times*, Feb. 1, 1970; "Banking 'Conflict' in Legislature Charged," by Charles Grutzner, New York *Times*, March 12, 1971; "Brown, Mayor's Man in Albany, Serves Legislators in Serving City," by Martin Tolchin, New York *Times*, May 26, 1971; "Legislative Swing to Right Clips Governor's Power," by Frank Lynn, New York *Times*, June 9, 1971.

POLITICS "The Marketing of Nelson Rockefeller," by Fred Powledge, *New York*, Nov. 30, 1970; "Rockefeller Funds Key Factor in Race" by Richard Phalon, New York *Times*, Oct. 25, 1970; "Well-Oiled Political Organization," by Richard Reeves, New York *Times*, Oct. 12, 1970; "The End of Liberalism," by Paul Hoffman, *The Nation*, April 12, 1971; "The Great Rockefeller Power Machine," by Edward Jay Epstein, *New York*, Nov. 24, 1975.

"The New York Primary: Return of Pre-Primary Designating Conferences," by Robert L. Tienken, *Harvard Journal on Legislation*, January 1969; "These Two Parties Could Make All the Difference," by Richard Reeves, New York *Times*, Nov. 6, 1970; "The Beginning of the End of the State's Minor Parties," by Gus Tyler, *New York*, May 3, 1971; "The Public Record of Jacob K. Javits." *Congressional Quarterly Weekly Report*, Aug. 18, 1967; "Cash and Carey," by Alan L. Otten, *Wall Street Journal*, Feb. 12, 1976; "For the Senate: The Main Event East . . . ," by Tom Buckley, New York *Times Magazine*, Oct. 31, 1976.

UPSTATE CITIES "Buffalo, N.Y.," article by Millard C. Browne in *Encyclopedia Americana;* "Snow Doesn't Bother Syracuse," by Clarence D. Bassett, Washington *Post*, March 8, 1970; "Syracuse Split by Racial Views," by Thomas A. Johnson, New York *Times*, Aug. 11, 1971.

"Rocky's Monumental Error or the Billion-Dollar Misunderstanding," by Wolf Von Eckardt, *New York*, April 20, 1970; "Rockefeller, 'Edifice Rex,' Builds a Monument in Albany," by James M. Perry, *National Observer*, Sept. 28, 1970; "The O'Connell Machine in Albany," by Charles Van Devander, *American Mercury*, Oct. 1, 1944.

"Buffalo: A City Beset on Many Sides," by Steven Rattner, New York *Times*, May 14, 1976; "Erie County, Facing a Possible Note Default, to Be Audited by State," by Linda Greenhouse, New York *Times*, Oct. 9, 1976; "Neighborhood: Center Square Reviving," by Iver Peterson, New York *Times*, May 3, 1976.

REGIONS "Beauty of Upstate County Hides Poverty of Its Residents," New York *Times*, March 24, 1971. "The Hudson River Lives," by Robert H. Boyle, *Audubon*, March 1971; "The Tainted Image of West Point," by Robert B. Johnson, Jr., *The Progressive*, February 1971; "The Roar of Bulldozers Echoes through Once-Rural Rockland County as Rapid Growth Continues" by Ralph Blumenthal, New York *Times*, March 25, 1968. "Rash of Fires in Catskills Points Up Growing Decline," by Richard Severo, New York *Times*, July 27, 1976.

WESTCHESTER "Westchester Disproves Suburban Myth," New York *Times*, May 31, 1971; "Blacks Take Pride in New Rochelle Role," by C. Gerald Fraser, New York *Times*, Dec. 6, 1970; "Westchester Government Needs Modernization, Ottinger and Reid Agree," by Linda Greenhouse, New York *Times*, Feb. 22, 1970.

LONG ISLAND "Politics in the Suburbs," by Stanley J. Hinden, chapter in *Practical Politics in the United States*, ed. Cornelius P. Cotter (Boston: Allyn & Bacon, 1969); "Silver Anniversary Edition," *Newsday*, Sept. 10, 1965; "Levittown: 25 Years Later," *Newsday*, July 9, 1971.

"Nickerson Sets Nassau Goals," by Roy R. Silver, New York *Times*, Jan. 5, 1970; "Zoning Suit Threatens Oyster Bay," by Peter Braestrup, Washington *Post*, May 9, 1971; "NAACP Sues to Tear Down Oyster Bay Zoning Barrier," by Owen Moritz, New York *Daily News*, March 26, 1971.

NEW YORK CITY—GENERAL *The Epic of New York City*, by Edward Robb Ellis (New York: Coward-McCann, 1966); *To the Victor . . . Political Patronage from the Clubhouse to the White House*, by Martin and Susan Tolchin (New York: Random House, 1971); *Governing New York City*, by Wallace S. Sayre and Herbert Kaufman (New York: W. W. Norton and Co., 1965); *New York, N.Y.* by David G. Lowe (New York: American Heritage, 1968); *AIA Guide to New York City*, by Norval White and Elliot Willensky (New York: Macmillan, 1967); *When the Cathedrals Were White*, by Le Corbusier (West Caldwell, N.J.: William Morrow, 1947); *What Have You Done for Me Lately?—The Ins and Outs of New York City Politics*, by Warren Moscow (Englewood Cliffs, N.J.: Prentice-Hall, 1967); *The Great American Motion Sickness—Or Why You Can't Get There from Here*, by John Burby (Boston: Little, Brown & Co., 1971).

NEW YORK CITY—POLITICS "Feud," by Richard Reeves, *Life*, June 25, 1971; "Is Statehood for New York City Really the Answer?" by Michael Harrington, *New York*, Aug. 23, 1971; "The Civil Service: A Meritless System," by E.S. Savas and Sigmund G. Ginsberg, *Good Government*, Winter, 1974; "The Ultimate Schutzpa—Beame Is Running Again," by Ken Auletta, *New York*, July 19, 1976; "New York City's Bicentennial Revolution," by Edward N. Costikyam, *Empire State Report*, August 1976.

NEW YORK CITY—HOUSING "Co-op City, Home to 40,000, Is Given Tempered Praise," by James F. Clarity, New York *Times*. May 27, 1971; "Vast Co-op City Is Dedicated in Bronx," by William E. Farrell, New York *Times*, Nov. 25, 1968.

NEW YORK CITY—THE ECONOMY "Why Companies Are Fleeing the Cities," *Time*, April 26, 1971; "Far from the Madding Crowd," *Forbes*, Jan. 15, 1971; "The Future of Corporate Geography," *Corporate Financing*, November/December 1970.

NEW YORK CITY—COMMUNICATIONS

AND CULTURE "TV: Is the Bloom Off the Old Rose?" *Forbes*, Oct. 15, 1970; "New Life in New Places for the American Theater," *U. S. News & World Report*, May 4, 1970; "Off-Broadway: Economic Tragedy in Rehearsal," by Clive Barnes, New York *Times*, Jan. 10, 1971.

NEW YORK CITY—CRIME AND JUSTICE "Graft Paid to Police Here Said to Run into Millions," by David Burnham, New York *Times*, April 25, 1970; "NYPD: Nightmare for a 'Dream Cop'," by Karl E. Meyer, Washington *Post*, Sept. 28, 1970; "Leary Assails Articles in *Times* on Police Corruption as Unfair," by William E. Farrell, New York *Times*, April 29, 1970.

"Memorandum" by Robert Sullivan, New York City Off-Track Betting Corp., regarding operation of the numbers game and its relationship to drug traffic (dated Jan. 28, 1971); "Memorandum" by Rich Tapia, New York City Off-Track Betting Corp., regarding forms of numbers-game operations in the city (dated Oct. 12, 1970).

NEW YORK CITY—GEOGRAPHY One of the most fascinating public planning documents ever published is the profusely illustrated *Plan for New York City—A Proposal*, with separate volumes: *Critical Issues, The Bronx, Brooklyn, Manhattan, Queens, Staten Island* (New York: New York City Planning Commission, 1969).

NEW YORK CITY—FISCAL CRISIS Series of articles in the New York *Daily News* entitled "Spend City," 1971; City Avoids Default by Hours as Teachers Relent, Buy Bonds; Financial Markets Disrupted," by Steven R. Weisman, New York *Times*, Oct. 18, 1975; "N.Y.C. Fiscal Woes Linger Despite U.S. Rescue Plan," by Jack Egan and William Claiborne, Washington *Post*, Feb. 4, 1976; "Beame Proposes New Budget Cuts Ending 8,000 Jobs," by Francis X. Clines, New York *Times*, March 26, 1976; "Doubt Expressed on City Finances," by Martin Tolchin, New York *Times*, April 3, 1976; "States Cutting Back on Medicaid Spending," by John Taft, *National Journal*, May 1, 1976; "Why New York Went Broke," by James Ring Adams, *Commentary*, May 1976; " 'Friend in Washington' ", editorial in New York *Times*, Nov. 5, 1976; "Police Flout Writ by Blocking Traffic At Ali-Norton Fight," by Pranay Gupte, New York *Times*, Sept. 29, 1976; "Many Laid Off Found Back on New York City Payroll," by Glenn Fowler, New York *Times*, July 3, 1976; "The Unaccountable Elitist: Rohatyn Is Our New Robert Moses," by Jack Newfield, *Village Voice*, Aug. 2, 1976; "Evidences of Deterioration Abound in New York Crisis," by Steven R. Weisman, New York *Times*, Dec. 5, 1976.

NEW YORK CITY—MANHATTAN "Notes on the New York Skyline . . . ," by Anthony Lewis, *Atlantic*, June 1971; "Violence Common in Nether World of Lower East Side," by Sylvan Fox, New York *Times*, March 20, 1959; "Law and Order Gains Where Least Likely—Greenwich Village," by Roger Ricklefs, *Wall Street Journal*, July 9, 1971.

"Slaughter on Sixth Avenue," by Peter Blake, *New York*, April 12, 1971; "Touches of Sidewalk Splendor Planned for Midtown," by Murray Schumach, New York *Times*, Aug. 6, 1971; "The West Side: A Polyglot of Races, Creeds and Cultures," by Richard F. Shepard, New York *Times*, Oct. 25, 1968; "A Day in Harlem," by David Butwin, *Saturday Review*, July 25, 1970; "Neighborhoods: The Home of Harlem's Affluent," by C. Gerald Fraser, New York *Times*, June 29, 1970; "Homage to Adam Clayton Powell," *The Black Politician*, July 1971 (reprinted from the New York *Times*); "Middle Class Blacks Return to Harlem," by Lena Williams, Aug. 21, 1976.

NEW YORK CITY—THE BRONX *The Block*, by Herb Goro (New York: Random House, 1970); "Neighborhoods: A Bit of Italy in Bronx," by Murray Schumach, New York *Times*, March 27, 1970; "Neighborhoods: Baychester Racially Tense Beneath a Calm Veneer," by Joseph Lelyveld, New York *Times*, Aug. 15, 1969; "Uptight in Riverdale," by Fred Ferretti, *New York*, Oct. 6, 1969; "The Puerto Ricans," *Newsweek*, June 15, 1970.

NEW YORK CITY—QUEENS "Queens Striving to Keep Balance," by Murray Schumach, New York *Times*, March 1, 1970; "Rediscovering Queens in Its Time of Quiet Racial Transformation," by Thomas A. Johnson, New York *Times*, Aug. 22, 1976.

NEW YORK CITY—BROOKLYN "Let's Break Up the City . . . Starting with Brooklyn," by Pete Hamill, *New York*, June 21, 1971; "Robert Kennedy's Bedford-Stuyvesant Legacy," by Jack Newfield, *New York*, Dec. 16, 1968; "A 90-Cent Riot," *Newsweek*, May 17, 1971; "Neighborhoods: West Indies Flavor Bedford-Stuyvesant," by C. Gerald Fraser, New York *Times*, Oct. 28, 1970; "Good News from Bed-Stuy," by John J. Goldman, *New York*, Sept. 7, 1970; "Superblock in Bed-Stuy: Just a Million Dollar Slum," by Mark Zussman, *Village Voice*, Dec. 11, 1969.

NEW YORK CITY—STATEN ISLAND June 15, 1970; "Neighborhoods: Staten Island Continues to Be Isolated," by Linda Greenhouse, New York *Times*, Jan. 8, 1970; "The Urbanization of Staten Island," by Fred Powledge, *New York*, May 24, 1971.

INDEX

Page references in **boldface** type indicate inclusive or major entries.

Scale of Miles

0   100   200   300   400   500

C A N A

WASH.
Seattle
Olympia   Spokane
MONT.   N.D.
Portland   Farg
Salem   ORE.   Helena   Bismarck
Eugene   IDAHO   Butte   S.D.
                                        Billings   Aberdeen
                    Boise   WYO.   Pierre
                                YELLOWSTONE
                                NATIONAL
                                PARK
CALIF.   NEV.   Pocatello   Casper   NEB.
                    Great   Ogden
                    Salt Lake
        Reno   Salt Lake City   Cheyenne   C
Oakland   Carson City   UTAH   COLO.   KAN.
Sacramento   Denver
San Francisco   YOSEMITE   Colorado
                NAT'L. PARK   Springs
                Mt. Whitney   GRAND   Wichita
        Santa   Las Vegas   CANYON
        Barbara   NAT'L. PARK   Farmington   Oklaho
                                                Santa Fe   City
            Los Angeles   ARIZ.   Amarillo
Pacific   San Diego   Albuquerque
                        Phoenix   N.M.   Wichita
Ocean   Lubbock   Falls
                    Tucson   Fort Worth
                                    El Paso
                                                TEXAS

                                                Austin
U.S.S.R.   San
                                                Antonio
            Kotzebue
            ALASKA
U.S.S.R.   Nome   Fairbanks   CANADA
U.S.

Bering   Anchorage   Juneau   MEXICO
Sea

                    MILES
            0   200   400   600